NEW HAMPSHIRE PLANNING AND LAND USE REGULATION

2007-2008 EDITION

Issued by
New Hampshire Office of Energy and Planning
Concord, New Hampshire

Reprinted from LEXIS New Hampshire Revised Statutes
Annotated and 2007 Cumulative Supplement

QUESTIONS ABOUT THIS PUBLICATION?

For CUSTOMER SERVICE ASSISTANCE concerning replacement pages, shipments, billing, reprint permission, or other matters,

please call Customer Service Department at 800-833-9844
email *customer.support@lexisnexis.com*
or visit our interactive customer service website at *www.lexisnexis.com/printcdsc*

For EDITORIAL **content questions** concerning this publication,

please call 800-446-3410 ext. 7447
or email: *LLP.CLP@lexisnexis.com*

For **information on other LEXISNEXIS MATTHEW BENDER publications,**

please call us at 800-223-1940
or visit our online bookstore at *www.lexisnexis.com/bookstore*

ISBN: 978-1-4224-3736-0

 LexisNexis®

Matthew Bender & Company, Inc.
Editorial Offices
P.O. Box 7587
Charlottesville, VA 22906-7587
800-446-3410
www.lexisnexis.com

Product Number 2882123 (with CD-Rom)
2882816 (without CD-Rom)

(Pub. 28821)

Preface

This publication is designed to provide a compilation of statutes relating to the performance of planning and land use regulation by municipalities in New Hampshire. It includes the full text of the statutes most frequently employed by local officials, including Title LXIV, "Planning and Zoning", accompanied by statutory notes and annotations, and an appendix listing and summarizing the content of other statutes relating to planning and land use regulation, and an Index. We have included a convenient listing of "Sections Affected by 2007 Legislation."

The statutes included in this publication include new legislation and amendments enacted through chapter 382 of the 2007 Session of the General Court.

This publication contains annotations taken from decisions of the New Hampshire Supreme Court, and from decisions of the appropriate federal courts posted on *lexis.com* with decisions dates up through August 17, 2007. These cases will be printed in the following reports:

> New Hampshire Reports
> Atlantic Reporter, 2nd Series
> Federal Supplement, 2nd Series
> Bankruptcy Reporter
> Federal Rules Decisions
> Federal Reporter, 3rd Series
> United States Supreme Court Reports, Lawyers'
> Edition, 2nd Series

Additionally, annotations have been taken from the following sources:

> Opinions of the Attorney General
> New Hampshire Bar Journal
> American Law Reports, 6th

Public officials and private citizens having questions regarding the material included in this publication are invited to contact either the publisher or the Office of Energy and Planning, 57 Regional Drive, Suite 3, Concord, New Hampshire 03301. The publisher wishes to thank the New Hampshire Office of Energy and Planning for their support and assistance in producing this publication.

December 2007

Table of Contents

v

TABLE OF CONTENTS

Sections Affected by 2007 Legislation

NOTE: In addition to the sections listed below, users of this edition should be aware that additional section and case note annotations have also been appropriately incorporated throughout this publication. The sections with new and/or revised annotations do *not* appear in this listing.

RSA	Effect	Bill No.	Act No.	Act Sec.
4-C:1*II(i)	Amended	HB 2	263	173
4-C:24	Enacted	SB 217	348	1
4-C:25	Enacted	SB 217	348	1
4-C:26	Enacted	SB 217	348	1
4-C:27	Enacted	SB 217	348	1
4-C:28	Enacted	SB 217	348	1
4-C:29	Enacted	SB 217	348	1
4-C:30	Enacted	SB 217	348	1
21:34-a	Amended	HB 56	157	1
31:39*I(o)	Amended	HB 609	43	1
40:13*V-a	Amended	SB 58	305	2
47:17*XIV-b	Amended	HB 609	43	2
79-E:11	Amended	HB 198	42	3
91-A:2*II	Amended	HB 152	59	2
155-A:1*I	Amended	SB 81	187	1
155-A:1*IV	Amended	SB 81	187	2
155-A:1*VI	Amended	SB 81	187	3
155-A:10*I(h)	Amended	HB 155	11	1
155-A:10*II	Amended	HB 155	11	2
162-C:8*I-III	Amended	HB 813	151	1
162-N:1	Amended	HB 2	263	120
162-N:2	Amended	HB 2	263	120
162-N:3	Amended	HB 2	263	120
162-N:4	Amended	HB 2	263	120
162-N:5	Amended	HB 2	263	120
162-N:6	Amended	HB 2	263	120
162-N:7	Amended	HB 2	263	120
162-N:8	Amended	HB 2	263	120
162-N:9	Amended	HB 2	263	120
236:73-a	Enacted	HB 418	87	1
483:3	Amended	HB 722	285	1
483:4*XV	Amended	HB 722	285	10
483:8*I(b)	Amended	HB 722	285	2
483:8*I(k)	Amended	HB 722	285	3
483:8*II	Amended	HB 722	285	4
483:8-a*III(a)	Amended	HB 722	285	5
483:9*VI(a)-(b)	Amended	SB 71	308	1
483:9-a*VII	Amended	SB 71	308	2
483:10*III	Amended	HB 722	285	6

SECTIONS AFFECTED BY 2007 LEGISLATION

RSA	Effect	Bill No.	Act No.	Act Sec.
483:10-a	Amended	HB 722	285	7
483:12-a	Amended	HB 722	285	8
483:15*XV	Amended	HB 61	66	1
483-B:4*VII-a	Amended	HB 383	267	1
483-B:4*X-a	Amended	HB 383	267	2
483-B:4*XI-a-XI-c	Amended	HB 383	267	3
483-B:4*XVI(c)	Amended	HB 383	267	4
483-B:4*XXIV-a	Amended	HB 383	267	5
483-B:4*XXVI	Amended	HB 383	267	6
483-B:5-a	Enacted	HB 663	269	1
483-B:5-a*I(b)	Amended	HB 663	269	1
483-B:5-a*III	Amended	HB 663	269	1
483-B:5-a*V	Amended	HB 383	267	12
483-B:6	Amended	HB 383	267	7
483-B:9*IV-b	Amended	HB 383	267	8
483-B:9*V	Amended	HB 383	267	9
483-B:11	Amended	HB 383	267	10
483-B:17*III-X	Amended	HB 383	267	11
483-B:17*XI	Amended	HB 663	269	2
483-B:19	Repealed	HB 383	267	14
483-B:20	Repealed	HB 383	267	14
485:3-b*I	Amended	HB 472	219	9
485:3-c	Amended	HB 472	219	10
673:1*II	Amended	HB 293	266	2
673:4-b	Enacted	HB 293	266	3
673:7*II(c)	Amended	HB 293	266	4
673:10*I	Amended	HB 293	266	5
673:14*I	Amended	HB 293	266	6
673:18	Amended	HB 293	266	7
673:20	Amended	HB 293	266	8
673:21	Amended	HB 293	266	9
674:2*III(h)	Amended	HB 42	40	1
674:44-e	Enacted	HB 293	266	1
674:44-f	Enacted	HB 293	266	1
674:44-g	Enacted	HB 293	266	1
674:54*I-II	Amended	SB 82	361	32
674:54*II-b	Amended	HB 98	29	1

NEW HAMPSHIRE PLANNING AND LAND USE REGULATION 2007-2008 EDITION

TITLE I

THE STATE AND ITS GOVERNMENT

CHAPTER 4-C

OFFICE OF ENERGY AND PLANNING

Amendments
—**2004.** 2004, 257:44, eff. July 1, 2004, substituted "office of energy and planning" for "office of state planning and energy programs" in the chapter heading.

—**2003.** 2003, 319:8, eff. July 1, 2003, added "and energy programs" following "planning" in the chapter heading.

Cross References.
Council on resources and development, see RSA 162-C.

Interstate Regional Planning Compact, see RSA 36-B.

Lakes management and protection program, see RSA 483-A.

Planning and zoning generally, see RSA 672 et seq.

Rivers management and protection program, see RSA 483.

4-C:1. Establishment; General Duties and Responsibilities.

I. There is established the office of energy and planning within the office of the governor. The office of energy and planning shall be under the supervision and direction of the governor or the governor's designee. The governor's designee shall be known as the director of the office of state planning and energy programs.

II. The office of energy and planning shall:

(a) Plan for the orderly development of the state and the wise management of the state's resources.

(b) Compile, analyze, and disseminate data, information, and research services as necessary to advance the welfare of the state.

(c) Encourage and assist planning, growth management, and development activities of cities and towns and groups of cities and towns with the purpose of encouraging smart growth.

(d) Encourage the coordination and correlation of state planning by agencies of state government.

(e) Participate in interstate, regional, and national planning efforts.

(f) Administer federal and state grant-in-aid programs assigned to the office by statute or executive order.

(g) Participate and advise in matters of land use planning regarding lakes and rivers management programs.

(h) Take a leadership role in encouraging smart growth and preserving farmland, open space land, and traditional village centers.

(i) Administer the following programs: the statewide comprehensive outdoor recreation plan, the national flood insurance program, the land conservation investment program, the scenic and cultural byways system, fuel assistance contracts, and weatherization contracts. The office shall employ necessary personnel to administer these programs. In administering fuel assistance and weatherization contracts, the office shall ensure that when an individual applies for fuel assistance or weatherization, the individual shall be provided with application forms and information about the Link-Up New Hampshire and Lifeline Telephone Assistance programs, and shall be provided assistance in applying for these programs.

(j) Perform such other duties as the governor may assign.

Source.

1987, 283:3. 1989, 263:10. 1990, 118:1, eff. June 18, 1990. 1996, 251:4, eff. Aug. 9, 1996. 2000, 292:1, 2, eff. Aug. 20, 2000. 2003, 319:10, eff. July 1, 2003. 2004, 257:44, eff. July 1, 2004. 2005, 20:3, eff. May 10, 2005. 2007, 263:173, eff. July 1, 2007.

Amendments
—**2007.** Paragraph II(i): Added the third sentence.

—**2005.** Paragraph II(i): Deleted "the coastal zone management program, the New Hampshire estuaries project, the saltmarsh restorability program, the southeast New Hampshire groundwater sustainability program" preceding "the statewide comprehensive".

—**2004.** Substituted "office of energy and planning" for "office of state planning and energy programs" in par. I and in the introductory paragraph of par. II.

—**2003.** Rewritten to the extent that a detailed comparison would be impracticable.

—**2000.** Paragraph II: Added "with the purpose of encouraging smart growth" following "groups of cities and towns" in subpar. (c), added a new subpar. (j) and redesignated former subpar. (j) as present subpar. (i).

—**1996.** Paragraph II(h): Deleted "under RSA 149-M:13-a, II" following "towns".

—**1990.** Paragraph II: Added a new subpar. (i) and redesignated former subpar. (i) as subpar. (j).

—**1989.** Paragraph II: Added new subpars. (g) and (h) and redesignated former subpar. (g) as subpar. (i).

Transfer of Estuaries Project From Department of Environmental Services to University of New Hampshire.
2005, 20:1, eff. May 10, 2005, provides:
"I. Notwithstanding any provision of law to the contrary, all of the functions, powers, duties, and responsibilities of the department of environmental services relating to the New Hampshire estuaries project shall be transferred to the university of New Hampshire. The

transfer provided for in this section shall include, but not be limited to, the following personnel from the estuaries project: position numbers 9T003, 9T005, and 8Temp. The transfer provided in this section shall include all of the equipment, books, papers, records, unexpended appropriations, and other available funds in any account or subdivision of an account of the department of environmental services related to the above function and authorized for use by the department of environmental services for said project.
"II. All existing rules, statutory responsibilities, regulations, and procedures in effect, in operation, or adopted in or by the New Hampshire estuaries project are transferred to the university of New Hampshire, and are declared in effect and shall continue in effect until rescinded, revised, or amended in accordance with applicable law."

Cross References.
Administrative attachment of Connecticut River Valley resource commission to office, see RSA 227-E:3.

4-C:2. State Development Plan.

I. The office of energy and planning, under the direction of the governor, shall:

(a) Assist the governor in preparing, publishing, and revising the comprehensive development plan required under RSA 9-A.

(b) Develop and maintain a technical data base of information to support statewide policy development and planning.

(c) Coordinate and monitor the planning efforts of various state agencies and departments to ensure that program plans published by such agencies are consistent with the policies and priorities established in the comprehensive development plan.

(d) Coordinate and monitor the planning efforts of the regional planning commissions to ensure that the plans published by the commissions are consistent, to the extent practical, with the policies and priorities established in the state development plan.

II. In preparing the state development plan, the office of energy and planning shall consult with the chief executive officers of the various departments and agencies of state government. The office shall also consult with officials of regional planning commissions and regional and local planning and development agencies, local officials, representatives of the business and environmental community, and the general public.

III. All state agencies and departments shall provide the office of energy and planning with information and assistance as required by the office to fulfill its responsibilities under RSA 4-C:2, I. The office shall maintain the confidentiality of any information which is protected by law.

Source.

1987, 283:3, eff. May 25, 1987. 2002, 229:2, 3, eff. July 1, 2002. 2003, 319:9, eff. July 1, 2003. 2004, 257:44, eff. July 1, 2004.

Amendments

—2004. Substituted "office of energy and planning" for "office of state planning and energy programs" wherever it appeared throughout the section.

—2003. Substituted "office of state planning and energy programs" for "office of state planning" in the introductory paragraph of par. I, and in pars. II and III.

—2002. Paragraph I(d): Added.

Paragraph II: Deleted "with responsibilities which are relevant to economic development" following "state government" in the first sentence, and substituted "shall" for "may" following "office", and "local officials, representatives of the business and environmental community, and the general public" for "and representatives of business and industry" in the second sentence.

Cross References.

Coordination of state resources and development activities, see RSA 4-C:6.

4-C:3. Data and Information Services.

The office of energy and planning shall:

I. Gather, tabulate, and periodically publish information on the location and pace of development throughout the state, including, but not limited to, population, housing, and building permit data.

II. Initiate data coordination procedures as the state agency responsible for coordinating data collection and dissemination among the state, the private sector, and the various political subdivisions.

III. Gather information for storage in a data bank concerning the data which is currently available within all state agencies. This data shall be used to provide information which is useful in measuring growth and its impact and for statewide planning purposes in general. The data available for dissemination shall include, but shall not be limited to, information for determining future demands for state services and demographic and economic statistics. Any other state agency or department which initiates a data collection program shall inform the office of energy and planning of its efforts so that the office may utilize that information for planning purposes in its dissemination program.

IV. Cooperate with the department of environmental services in identifying potential sites for hazardous waste facilities.

V. Develop and maintain a computerized geographic information system in support of state, regional, or local planning and management activities.

VI. Cooperate with the Bureau of the Census and other federal agencies with the objective of improving access to the statistical products, data, and information of the federal government.

VII. Annually estimate the resident population for all cities and towns of the state pursuant to RSA 78-A:25.

Source.

1987, 283:3, eff. May 25, 1987. 1996, 228:108, eff. July 1, 1996. 2003, 319:9, eff. July 1, 2003. 2004, 257:44, eff. July 1, 2004.

Amendments
—**2004.** Substituted "office of energy and planning" for "office of state planning and energy programs" in the introductory paragraph and in par. III.

—**2003.** Substituted "office of state planning and energy programs" for "office of state planning" in the introductory paragraph and in paragraph III.

—**1996.** Paragraph IV: Substituted "department of environmental services" for "division of waste management".

Cross References.
Hazardous waste facility review generally, see RSA 147-C.

4-C:4. Coordinator of Federal Funds.

I. It is the intent of the general court that the position of coordinator of federal funds be created in the office of energy and planning to inventory, coordinate and monitor the availability and use of federal funds in New Hampshire. The general court intends that the executive and legislative branches of state government shall be aware of all federal funds received and used in New Hampshire.

II. There is established in the office of energy and planning a position to be known as coordinator of federal funds. The duties of the coordinator shall include, but not be limited to, the following:

(a) To seek out federal programs and funds which may be available to New Hampshire, notify the appropriate state department, municipality or other agency and coordinate the application process. The coordinator shall give priority to federal programs related to economic development and credit.

(b) To monitor the efforts of state departments, municipalities, and other agencies to apply for and secure federal funds.

(c) To advise state departments, municipalities, and other agencies within the state of the availability of federal surplus equipment. The coordinator is authorized to contract for services to procure federal surplus equipment on behalf of New Hampshire departments, municipalities and other agencies within the state.

(d) To maintain a data base, to which the general court shall have access, concerning all federal funds available to all state departments, municipalities, and other agencies within the state.

(e) To report on all such federal funds coming into the state of New Hampshire, whether to public or private agencies, to the director of the office of energy and planning who shall annually issue such report to the public.

Source.
1987, 283:3. 1992, 242:5, eff. July 12, 1992. 2003, 319:9, eff. July 1, 2003. 2004, 257:44, eff. July 1, 2004.

Amendments
—**2004.** Substituted "office of energy and planning" for "office of state planning and energy programs" in par. I, in the introductory paragraph of par. II and in par. II(e).

—**2003.** Substituted "office of state planning and energy programs" for "office of state planning" in pars. I, II and II(e).

—**1992.** Rewritten to the extent that a detailed comparison would be impracticable.

4-C:5. Rulemaking Authority.

The director of the office of energy and planning shall adopt rules, under RSA 541-A:

I. Establishing procedures for grant programs administered by the office. These rules shall be adopted for all federal or state grant programs administered by the office in which the office has authority to establish requirements or procedures or interpret federal requirements and state statutes. These rules shall include, as appropriate:

(a) Application or grant distribution procedures.

(b) Criteria and procedures for evaluating applications.

(c) Procedures for administration of funds by grantees.

(d) Monitoring and report procedures.

(e) Appeal procedures for parties dissatisfied with grant decisions.

II. As provided by RSA 4-C:16, I(a).

Source.

1987, 283:3, eff. May 25, 1987. 2003, 319:9, eff. July 1, 2003. 2004, 257:44, eff. July 1, 2004.

Amendments

—2004.   Substituted "office of energy and

planning" for "office of state planning and energy programs" in the introductory paragraph.

—2003.   Substituted "office of state planning and energy programs" for "office of state planning" in the introductory paragraph.

4-C:6. Coordination.

I. The office of energy and planning shall formulate policies and plans for consideration by the governor which serve to integrate and coordinate resource and development activities affecting more than one state agency, level of government, or governmental function. Nothing in this paragraph shall be construed to grant the governor any additional authority to implement such plans beyond that which has been granted to him under the constitution and other laws of this state. Such activities may include, but shall not be limited to, the following subject areas:

(a) Water resources.

(b) Transportation.

(c) Recreation and natural resources.

(d) Solid waste and hazardous waste management.

(e) Off-shore, coastal, and estuarine resources.

(f) Housing.

(g) Economic development.

(h) Energy.

(i) Shoreland protection.

(j) Smart growth.

II. The director of the office of energy and planning or his designee shall promote coordination of state agency planning and management activities through participation in the deliberations of the following statutory bodies:

(a) Council on resources and development as established in RSA 162-C:1;

(b) Water council as established in RSA 21-O:7;

(c) Wetlands council as established in RSA 21-O:5-a;

(d) Site evaluation committee as established in RSA 162-H:3;

(e) Energy facility evaluation committee as established in RSA 162-H:3;

(f) Agricultural lands preservation committee as established in RSA 432:19.

Source.
1987, 283:3. 1989, 339:3. 1991, 303:2, eff. July 1, 1994. 1996, 228:2, eff. July 1, 1996; 296:2, eff. Aug. 9, 1996. 1998, 264:5, eff. June 26, 1998. 2000, 292:3, eff. Aug. 20, 2000. 2003, 319:9, eff. July 1, 2003. 2004, 257:44, eff. July 1, 2004.

Amendments
—2004. Paragraphs I and II: Substituted "office of energy and planning" for "office of state planning and energy programs" in the introductory paragraphs.

—2003. Substituted "office of state planning and energy programs" for "office of state planning" in pars. I and II.

—2000. Paragraph I(j): Added.

—1998. Paragraph II: Deleted "Bulk power supply facility" preceding "Site" and substituted "162-H:3" for "162-F:3".

—1996. Paragraph II(b): Chapter 228 deleted "supply and pollution control" following "water".

Paragraph II(c): Chapter 296 substituted "council" for "board" following "wetlands" and "RSA 21-O:5-a" for "RSA 482-A:5".

—1991. Paragraph I(i): Added.

—1989. Paragraph II(c): Substituted "RSA 482-A:5" for "RSA 483-A: 1-c".

Effective date of amendments
—1991. 1991, 303:10, I, as amended by 1994, 383:25, eff. July 1, 1994, provided that the amendment to this section by 1991, 303:2, shall take effect on July 1, 1994.

Reports on Economic Development Loans and Grants

4-C:6-a. Reports on Economic Development Program Loans and Grants.

I. The office of energy and planning shall include, as part of its annual report or as a separate report published and made available to the public annually on or before September 1, beginning September 1, 1997, the following information regarding each economic development program for which state grants and loans have been awarded:

(a) Information regarding the number of jobs to be created or saved as a result of the award, and the related wages and benefits levels.

(b) The growth potential of the program.

(c) The environmental impact and smart growth impact of the program.

(d) The amount of the loan, grant, loan guarantee, bond guarantee, or tax incentives awarded.

II. The annual report shall also include information regarding the criteria for the awarding of economic development assistance and the means by which the office tracks the progress which each awardee makes in meeting the job, wage, and benefit projections included in its application for assistance.

Source.
1996, 189:1, eff. Aug. 2, 1996. 2000, 292:4, eff. Aug. 20, 2000. 2003, 319:9, eff. July 1, 2003. 2004, 257:44, eff. July 1, 2004.

Amendments
—**2004.** Paragraph I: Substituted "office of energy and planning" for "office of state planning and energy programs" in the introductory paragraph.

—**2003.** Paragraph I: Substituted "office of state planning and energy programs" for "office of state planning" in the introductory paragraph.

—**2000.** Paragraph I(c): Inserted "and smart growth impact".

Regional and Municipal Assistance

Cross References.
Planning and zoning generally, see RSA 672 et seq.

Regional planning commissions, see RSA 36:45 et seq.

4-C:7. Program Established.

The director shall establish a program of regional and municipal assistance within the office of energy and planning. This program shall coordinate state, regional, and local planning efforts with the goal of assuring delivery of efficient and effective assistance to local governments in areas related to growth management and resource protection.

Source.
1987, 283:3, eff. May 25, 1987. 2003, 319:9, eff. July 1, 2003. 2004, 257:44, eff. July 1, 2004.

Amendments
—**2004.** Substituted "office of energy and planning" for "office of state planning and energy programs" in the first sentence.

—**2003.** Substituted "office of state planning and energy programs" for "office of state planning".

4-C:8. Responsibilities for Assistance.

The office of energy and planning shall:

I. Provide technical assistance and, within the limits of biennial legislative appropriations, financial grants to regional planning commissions established under RSA 36:45-36:53 in support of:

(a) Planning assistance to local units of government.

(b) Preparation of regional plans.

(c) Contributions to and coordination with statewide planning and management activities, including the formulation and updating of the comprehensive state development plan prepared pursuant to RSA 4-C:2.

II. As requested and in cooperation with regional planning commissions, provide technical assistance and information in support of the planning and growth management efforts of local units of government, including training requested under RSA 673:3-a. The office shall encourage municipalities to first seek assistance from established regional planning commissions.

III. Provide computer interface capability among and between each regional planning commission, the office of energy and planning, and state data collection and storage sources. The computer interface capability shall be used by regional planning commissions to respond to municipal requests for assistance in the preparation and amending of master plans and in the evaluation of municipal infrastructure needs. The computer interface capability shall also be used by regional planning commissions to develop and update regional master plans, as provided in RSA 36:47. The computer equipment used for the purposes of this paragraph shall be compatible and able to interface with the office of energy and planning's geographic information system, as well as with other similar state computerized data collection and storage sources.

IV. Provide technical assistance and information to municipalities with the cooperation of other state and regional planning agencies in the following areas:

(a) Use and application of geographic data available in the state's geographic information system (GIS) for local planning and growth management purposes.

(b) Recommending standard procedures for the establishment of accurate, large-scale base mapping to support municipal administrative functions such as tax assessment, public facility management and engineering.

Source.
1987, 283:3. 1988, 102:1. 1989, 366:2, eff. July 1, 1989. 2003, 319:11, eff. July 1, 2003. 2004, 257:44, 45, eff. July 1, 2004.

Amendments
—2004. Substituted "office of energy and planning" for "office of state planning and energy programs" in the introductory paragraph.

Paragraph III: Substituted "office of energy and planning" for "office of state planning and energy programs" in the first sentence and "office of energy and planning's" for "office of state planning and energy program's" in the fourth sentence.

—2003. Inserted "and energy programs" following "planning" in the introductory paragraph; substituted "RSA 36:45-36:53" for "RSA 36:45 et seq." in the introductory paragraph of par. I, "statewide" for "state-wide" in par. I(c); inserted "and energy programs" following "planning" in the first sentence and substituted "planning and energy program's" for "planning's" in the fourth sentence of par. III.

—1989. Paragraph IV: Added.

—1988. Paragraph III: Added.

4-C:9. Coordination at State Level.

The office of energy and planning shall coordinate efforts by state agencies to provide technical assistance to municipal governments in areas related to growth management and resource protection.

Source.
1987, 283:3, eff. May 25, 1987. 2003, 319:9, eff. July 1, 2003. 2004, 257:44, eff. July 1, 2004.

Amendments
—2004. Substituted "office of energy and planning" for "office of state planning and energy programs".

—2003. Substituted "office of state planning and energy programs" for "office of state planning".

4-C:9-a. Revolving Funds.

In order to enhance its ability to provide education and training assistance to municipalities and regional agencies, the following nonlapsing revolving funds, which shall not exceed $20,000 on June 30 of each year, shall be established in the office of energy and planning:

I. A revolving fund known as the publications revolving fund.

(a) The moneys in this fund shall be used for the purposes of printing materials for distribution. A reasonable charge shall be established for each copy of a document. This charge shall be only in the amount necessary to pay the cost of producing such document.

(b) The amount in the nonlapsing publications revolving fund shall not exceed $20,000, on June 30 of each year and any amounts in excess of $20,000 on June 30 of each year shall be deposited in the general fund as unrestricted revenue.

II. A revolving fund known as the municipal and regional training fund.

(a) The moneys in this fund shall be used for the purpose of providing training to local and regional officials. A reasonable charge shall be established for such training. This charge shall be fixed to reflect the cost of payments to experts to provide the training, the cost of written training material, rental of facilities, advertising and other associated costs. Such training shall be conducted in a geographically dispersed manner and scheduled with the convenience of part-time officials in mind.

(b) The amount in the nonlapsing municipal and regional training revolving fund shall not exceed $20,000 on June 30 of each year and any amounts in excess of $20,000 on June 30 of each year shall be deposited in the general fund as unrestricted revenue.

Source.
1989, 245:1, eff. July 25, 1989. 2003, 319:9, eff. July 1, 2003. 2004, 257:44, eff. July 1, 2004.

Amendments
—**2004.** Substituted "office of energy and planning" for "office of state planning and energy programs" in the introductory paragraph.

—**2003.** Substituted "office of state planning and energy programs" for "office of state planning" in the introductory paragraph.

4-C:10. Contact Point.

The office of energy and planning shall serve as the state's point of contact for local and regional officials seeking assistance from the state on growth management and resource protection matters.

Source.
1987, 283:3, eff. May 25, 1987. 2003, 319:9, eff. July 1, 2003. 2004, 257:44, eff. July 1, 2004.

Amendments
—**2004.** Substituted "office of energy and planning" for "office of state planning and energy programs".

—**2003.** Substituted "office of state planning and energy programs" for "office of state planning".

Community Development Block Grants

4-C:11–4-C:18.
[Repealed 2003, 319:15, eff. July 1, 2003.]

Former section(s).
Former RSA 4-C:11–4-C:18, which were derived from 1987, 283:3, related to the community block grant program.

Transfer of the community block grant program
2003, 319:14, eff. July 1, 2003, provided:
"I. All of the functions, powers, duties, and

responsibilities of the office of state planning relative to administration of the community development block grant program are hereby transferred to the community development finance authority. The transfer provided for in this section shall include all of the personnel, books, papers, records, equipment, unexpended appropriations, or other available funds, property, or obligations of any kind of the office of state planning for administration of the community development block grant program.

"II. All existing effective rules adopted by the office of state planning under the former RSA 4-C:16 relative to the community development block grant program shall continue in full force and effect until such rules, in accordance with RSA 541-A, expire, or are amended or repealed by the community development finance authority pursuant to RSA 162-L:16."

Water Protection Assistance Program

Cross References.
Groundwater Protection Act, see RSA 485-C.
Future supplies of water for domestic use, see RSA 485:49 et seq.
Safe Drinking Water Act, see RSA 485.

Water pollution control generally, see RSA 485, 485-A.
Waters and water resources generally, see RSA 481 et seq.

RESEARCH REFERENCES

ALR.
Validity and construction of anti-water pollution statutes or ordinances. 32 A.L.R.3d 215.

4-C:19. Establishment and Purpose.

There is established within the office of energy and planning, hereafter referred to as the office, the water protection assistance program. The purpose of the program is to encourage and assist municipalities individually and, where appropriate, collectively to evaluate their water resources and to develop local and regional measures for the protection of both ground and surface water. The program shall recognize the interdependency of municipalities which lie within a common watershed and shall facilitate cooperative planning for the management and protection of common water resources. By providing a range of technical assistance, the program shall help municipalities to exercise powers within their jurisdictions, including, but not limited to, land use regulation, to enhance water protection measures, and to ensure the continued availability of this resource.

Source.
1987, 283:3, eff. May 25, 1987. 2003, 319:9, eff. July 1, 2003. 2004, 257:44, eff. July 1, 2004.

Amendments
—2004. Substituted "office of energy and planning" for "office of state planning and energy programs" in the first sentence.

—2003. Substituted "office of state planning and energy programs" for "office of state planning" in the first sentence.

4-C:20. Program Administration.

I. The office shall prepare guidance materials for use by municipalities in the development of local water resources management and protection plans as provided in RSA 674:2, III(d), and other appropriate protection measures. If the written guidance materials discuss any requirements which exist under state or federal law and which the office believes may be applicable to the municipalities' plans, the materials shall identify the source of such requirements.

II. The program shall be implemented by the office primarily through the established regional planning agencies. Other technical services and advice may also be utilized. The program shall be coordinated with plans and programs of other state agencies, especially those of the department of environmental services, and regional planning agencies, and with activities of the county conservation districts. The office may authorize regional planning agencies to perform specific phases of the administration of this subdivision, especially the collaboration with municipalities.

Source.
1987, 283:3. 1989, 346:1, eff. Aug. 1, 1989. 1997, 196:1, eff. Aug. 17, 1997. 2002, 178:5, eff. July 14, 2002.

Amendments
—**2002.** Paragraph I: Substituted "RSA 674:2, III(d)" for "RSA 674:2, VIII" in the first sentence.

—**1997.** Paragraph I: Substituted "prepare guidance materials for use by" for "adopt rules under RSA 541-A to serve as a guide to" pre-

ceding "municipalities" in the first sentence and added the second sentence.

—**1989.** Paragraph I: Substituted "to serve as a guide to" for "relative to criteria for water protection and suggested model language to guide" following "RSA 541-A" in the first sentence and deleted the second sentence.

Paragraph II: Deleted "including that available from the university system of New Hampshire" following "advice" in the second sentence and rewrote the third sentence.

4-C:21. Technical Assistance.

I. The office may employ necessary personnel to coordinate the municipal technical assistance program with state and regional planning agencies. The technical assistance program shall rely to a significant extent on the regional planning agencies, which shall work directly with all municipalities within their jurisdiction to accomplish the objectives of this subdivision.

II. The office, using guidance materials and programs developed under RSA 4-C:20, shall meet with and provide technical assistance to the regional planning agencies. These agencies shall then work with local municipalities to enable the municipalities to incorporate appropriate water protection measures in their master plans and municipal codes. The regional planning agencies shall provide progress reports as required by the office.

Source.
1987, 283:3, eff. May 25, 1987. 1997, 196:2, eff. Aug. 17, 1997.

Amendments
—**1997.** Paragraph II: Substituted "guid-

ance materials" for "criteria" and "technical assistance" for "guidance" in the first sentence.

4-C:22. Local Water Resources Management and Protection Plans.

I. A municipality may include in its master plan a local water resource management and protection plan, hereafter referred to as the local water plan.

Once the local water plan has been adopted, it shall be placed on file with the office in accordance with RSA 675:9. The plan shall be made available to the public upon reasonable request and payment for any costs incurred in the duplication of the report.

II. Implementation of local water plans shall be through the adoption and enforcement of municipal ordinances consistent with the plan and through such other measures as are appropriate and legally available to municipal government as tools to further the water protection objectives set forth in the plan. Assistance shall be available through the water protection assistance program established in RSA 4-C:19 and programs of the department of environmental services as provided in RSA 21-O:3, IX, to advise municipalities on appropriate implementation measures.

III. If a municipality determines there is an immediate need to develop or amend subdivision or site plan review regulations in the manner provided by RSA 675:6 or to prevent deterioration of a critical water resource through a zoning ordinance or amendment in the manner provided by RSA 674:23, II, it may adopt such temporary measures for protection of water resources. Such measures shall be valid as provided in RSA 674:23, III.

Source.
1987, 283:3. 1989, 346:2, 3, eff. Aug. 1, 1989. 1997, 196:3, eff. Aug. 17, 1997.

Amendments
—1997. Paragraph I: Rewritten to the extent that a detailed comparison would be impracticable.

—1989. Paragraph I: Rewritten to the extent that a detailed comparison would be impracticable.

Paragraph II: Rewritten to the extent that a detailed comparison would be impracticable.

RESEARCH REFERENCES

New Hampshire Practice.
15 N.H.P. Land Use Planning and Zoning § 3.04.

4-C:23. Regional Water Resources Management and Protection Plans.

Municipalities are hereby authorized and encouraged to enter into agreements with other municipalities for the purpose of developing and implementing regional water plans and ordinances to enhance the effectiveness of their local water plans where water protection needs to extend beyond municipal boundaries. Appropriate action of the municipalities by ordinance, resolution or other action shall be necessary before any such agreement may enter into force, and the agreement shall be adopted pursuant to RSA 53-A. Municipalities are encouraged to seek the assistance of their regional planning commission in the development and implementation of their regional water plan, and shall coordinate these plans with the regional water resource planning efforts of their commission.

Source.
1989, 105:1, eff. June 30, 1989. 1997, 196:4,
eff. Aug. 17, 1997.

Amendments
—**1997.** Deleted the former third sentence
and made minor stylistic changes.

Housing and Conservation Planning Program.

4-C:24. Definitions.

In this subdivision:

I. "Eligible applicant" means a single municipality or 2 or more municipalities applying together.

II. "Growth and development strategy" means a plan by a single municipality or 2 or more municipalities to guide community growth in a way that creates a balanced housing supply, including higher density and workforce housing opportunities, while preserving valuable natural resources and the community's quality of life through efficient and compact development.

III. "Program" means the housing and conservation planning program.

IV. "Stage" means one of the 4 specific stages of developing and implementing a growth and development strategy to be funded through the housing and conservation planning program.

Source.
2007, 348:1, eff. July 1, 2007.

4-C:25. Housing and Conservation Planning Program Established.

There is hereby established the housing and conservation planning program, which shall be administered by the office of energy and planning. The program shall provide technical assistance matching grants to municipalities to plan for growth and development in a manner that permits a balanced housing stock, including higher density and workforce housing opportunities, and promotes, whenever possible the reuse of existing buildings, including historic properties, while protecting communities' natural resources through more efficient and compact development. Participation in the program is voluntary.

Source.
2007, 348:1, eff. July 1, 2007.

4-C:26. Program Administration; Eligible Applicants; Use of Program Funds.

I. Eligible applicants shall include:

(a) Municipalities; or

(b) A group of municipalities applying together to plan on a regional basis.

II. Awards of program funds may be used to purchase technical assistance from third-party technical assistance providers, including but not limited to regional planning commissions, to achieve the purposes of the program.

Source.
2007, 348:1, eff. July 1, 2007.

4-C:27. Program Administration; Eligible Technical Assistance.

I. The program shall award matching grants to fund technical assistance activities in the development and implementation of a growth and development strategy. The 4 specific stages of activities are as follows:

(a) Stage 1: Natural and Historic Resource and Housing Data Gathering and Analysis. This stage includes:

(1) Understanding and mapping housing, income, and demographic data, including housing market costs, housing units needed to meet future expected growth in a municipality and the region, and the affordability of a municipality's housing for all income ranges.

(2) Mapping land use values, including conservation, soils, wetlands, working forests, farmlands, and other natural resources.

(3) Developing a build-out analysis of growth and development impacts on housing availability and natural resources.

(4) Mapping historic structures and buildings within communities.

(b) Stage 2: Development of the Growth and Development Strategy. This stage includes:

(1) Drafting and endorsing a growth and development strategy to guide future growth, including using land more efficiently and encouraging compact development and reuse of suitable historic and existing structures. The growth and development strategy would also identify specific areas to be conserved and to be developed.

(2) Engaging in a public process to develop the growth and development strategy.

(c) Stage 3: Integration of Growth and Development Strategy into the Master Plan. This stage includes:

(1) Auditing the existing master plan to identify portions that conflict with or pose a barrier to achieving the growth and development strategy.

(2) Rewriting or amending the master plan so that it can realistically implement the growth and development strategy.

(3) Adopting the revised master plan.

(d) Stage 4: Implementation into Regulatory Framework. This stage includes:

(1) Auditing existing municipal ordinances, including zoning, site-plan, and subdivision regulations, to identify conflicts with the growth and development strategy and the revised master plan.

(2) Rewriting and amending municipal ordinances, including zoning, site-plan, and subdivision regulations, to allow for the realistic implementation of growth and development strategy and the new master plan.

(3) Drafting and adopting new articles that incorporate new tools to accomplish the growth and development strategy, including transfer of development rights, density bonuses, cluster development, and inclusionary zoning.

(4) Adopting the needed amendments to municipal ordinances.

II. Each stage shall require that:

(a) Municipalities address housing and conservation together in an integrated manner.

(b) Municipalities engage in a communication and education process that will promote informed decision-making and communicate with and educate citizens regarding the work being undertaken in each stage of the process.

III. Municipalities may be awarded technical assistance for only one stage at a time but may apply and obtain funding for each successive stage. Funding for future stages shall require a demonstration that the previous stage was accomplished in a manner consistent with the principles of the program. Such a showing shall also result in a priority for additional funding.

IV. Municipalities' initial applications for funding need not start with the first stage in the process. However, to begin with a later stage, an initial application shall demonstrate prior completion of the previous stage's work in a manner consistent with the program principles.

Source.
2007, 348:1, eff. July 1, 2007.

4-C:28. Rulemaking Authority.

The office of energy and planning shall adopt rules, pursuant to RSA 541-A, relative to operation of the housing and conservation planning program, including:

I. The application process.

II. The amount of matching funds required and permissible sources for matching funds.

III. Reporting requirements by municipalities.

IV. Scoring criteria for awarding grants that provide a priority for applications that address growth and development on a regional basis and provide opportunities for municipalities without professional planning staff to access the program.

Source.
2007, 348:1, eff. July 1, 2007.

4-C:29. Housing and Conservation Planning Program Advisory Board Established.

I. There is hereby established the housing and conservation planning program advisory board.

II. The advisory board shall review and comment on proposed rules and scoring criteria used by the office of energy and planning to evaluate applications for matching grants.

III. The advisory board shall consist of:

(a) Two members of the house of representatives, appointed by the speaker of the house of representatives.

(b) One member of the senate, appointed by the senate president.

(c) One member appointed by each of the following entities:

(1) The New Hampshire Housing Finance Authority.

(2) The New Hampshire Municipal Association.

(3) The New Hampshire Association of Regional Planning Commission Executives.

(4) The Business and Industry Association of New Hampshire.

(5) The New Hampshire Community Loan Fund.

(6) The Home Builders and Remodelers Association of New Hampshire.

(7) The Land and Community Heritage Commission.

(8) The New Hampshire Preservation Alliance.

(9) The New Hampshire Main Street Program.

(10) The Society for the Protection of New Hampshire Forests.

(11) The Audubon Society of New Hampshire.

(12) The Jordan Institute.

IV. Members of the advisory board shall serve without compensation, except that legislative members of the board shall receive mileage at the legislative rate when attending to the duties of the board.

Source.
2007, 348:1, eff. July 1, 2007.

4-C:30. Program Principles.

The program shall be guided by the following principles. Awards of technical assistance funding shall be based on consistency with these principles:

I. Consistency with smart growth principles in RSA 9-B:3.

II. Development of a comprehensive growth and development strategy through which a municipality integrates housing and conservation planning.

III. Identification of and planning for the full range of current and future housing needs for families of all income levels, as encouraged in RSA 672:1, III-e.

IV. Identification of natural and historic resource values and planning for their protection, as encouraged in RSA 36-A:2, including the preservation of working forests and farmlands as provided in RSA 672:1, III-b and III-c, and critical or sensitive natural areas and resources, including water resources as provided for in RSA 674:2, III(d).

V. Evaluating these conservation and housing issues on a community-wide, site-by-site, and regional basis.

VI. Understanding the interrelationship between natural resources and housing development in a municipality and the impact each has on the other.

VII. Encouragement of higher density, compact development and allowing for the infrastructure needed to support such development.

VIII. Encouragement of reuse of existing properties, especially historic structures.

IX. Integration of the growth and development strategy into the municipality's master plan and implementation into regulatory structure.

X. Encouragement of community input and education of citizens about the growth and development strategy and the need to plan for future conservation and housing growth.

Source.
   2007, 348:1, eff. July 1, 2007.

CHAPTER 9-A

STATE DEVELOPMENT PLAN

Rescinded 1987 amendments.

1987, 76:1, eff. July 1, 1987, provided for amendment of this chapter by the addition of a subdivision, entitled "Regional and Municipal Assistance," and comprised of RSA 9-A:5-9-A:8. However, under the terms of 1987, 283:14, eff. May 25, 1987, the provisions of 1987, 76:1 did not take effect. Provisions similar to those which appeared in 1987, 76:1, were included in RSA 4-C, as added by 1987, 283:3, See RSA 4-C:7-4-C:10.

Cross References.

Council on resources and developement, see RSA 162-C.

Office of state planning, see RSA 4-C.

RESEARCH REFERENCES

ALR.

Amount of appropriation as limitation on damages for breach of contract recoverable by one contracting with government agency. 40 ALR4th 998.

9-A:1. Comprehensive Plan.

I. There shall be a comprehensive state development plan which establishes state policy on development related issues and proposes new or expanded programs to implement such policies. The plan shall provide a basis for identifying critical issues facing the state, determining state priorities, allocating limited state resources, and taking into account the plans of various state, regional, and local governmental units.

II. The comprehensive development plan shall establish policies in areas related to the orderly physical, social, and economic growth and development of the state.

III. The comprehensive development plan shall include:

(a) State policies to provide for the orderly growth and development of the state and to maximize smart growth.

(b) Goals and policies which are relevant to the topical areas included in the plan, including but not limited to:

(1) An overall vision section that serves as the direction for the other sections of the plan. This section shall contain a set of statements which articulates the desires of the public relative to the future. It shall contain a set of guiding principles and priorities to implement that vision, with special emphasis on maximizing the smart growth principles in RSA 9-B.

(2) A land use section which examines the state's role in land development and in funding projects and programs which affect land uses.

(3) A transportation section which considers all pertinent modes of transportation and provides a framework of policies and actions which will

provide for a safe and adequate transportation system to serve the needs of the state.

(4) A public facilities section which examines the projected needs of state institutions and coordinates with other governmental units, whether federal, county, local, special districts, or school districts, as to their needs as well.

(5) A housing section which sets forth approaches to meeting the need for affordable housing.

(6) An economic development section which proposes actions and policies to suit the state's economic goals and needs, based on the current and projected economic strengths and weaknesses.

(7) A natural resources section which identifies trends in land protection, open space, farm land preservation and protection, and proposes policies and actions necessary at the state level to protect those resources which are perceived to be of statewide significance.

(8) A natural hazards section which identifies actions to improve the ability of the state to minimize damages from future disasters that affect land and property subject to such disasters.

(9) A recreation section which assesses current and future recreation needs within the foreseeable future and identifies policies and a plan of action to support them at the state level.

(10) A utility and public service section which details state level policies and actions necessary to assure adequate service to the citizens of the state.

(11) A regional concerns section which describes specific areas of the state with potentially unique concerns and identifies policies and actions which may reasonably be undertaken to assist in addressing those issues.

(12) A section which identifies state policies and actions necessary to protect cultural and historic resources of statewide significance and assist in their rehabilitation or preservation, and generally assure their availability for future generations of state citizens.

(13) An implementation section, which is a long range action program for assessing the effectiveness of each section of the plan.

IV. The comprehensive development plan shall serve as the basis for policy and program development by the various departments of state government. State agencies shall develop and regional planning commissions and local planning boards are encouraged to develop plans which are consistent with the policies and priorities established in the comprehensive development plan.

V. The comprehensive development plan shall be renewed or revised every 4 years, beginning on October 1, 2003.

Source.

1985, 270:4, eff. June 10, 1985. 2000, 292:5, eff. Aug. 20, 2000. 2002, 229:4, eff. July 1, 2002.

Amendments
—2002. Paragraph I: Added the second sentence.
Paragraph II: Inserted "physical, social, and economic growth" following "orderly".
Paragraph III: Rewritten to the extent that a detailed comparison would be impracticable.
Paragraph IV: Substituted "and regional planning commissions and local planning boards are encouraged to develop" for "program" in the second sentence.
Paragraph V: Added.

—2000. Paragraph III: Added subpar. (d) and made stylistic changes in subpars. (b) and (c).

Cross References.
Preparation of plan generally, see RSA 4-C:2.

9-A:2. Office of Energy and Planning.

The office of energy and planning, under the direction of the governor, shall:

I. Assist the governor in preparing, publishing and revising the comprehensive development plan.

II. Develop and maintain a technical data base of information to support statewide policy development and planning.

III. Coordinate and monitor the planning efforts of various state agencies and departments to ensure that program plans published by such agencies are consistent with the policies and priorities established in the comprehensive development plan.

IV. Coordinate and monitor the planning efforts of the regional planning commissions.

Source.
1985, 270:4, eff. June 10, 1985. 2002, 229:5, eff. July 1, 2002. 2003, 319:9, eff. July 1, 2003. 2004, 257:44, eff. July 1, 2004.

Amendments
—2004. Substituted "office of energy and planning" for "office of state planning and energy programs" in the section heading and introductory paragraph.

—2003. Substituted "office of state planning and energy programs" for "office of state planning" in the section catchline and in the introductory paragraph.

—2002. Paragraph IV: Added.

Cross References.
Powers and duties of office of state planning generally, see RSA 4-C:1.

9-A:3. Transmittal of Plan.

The governor shall transmit the comprehensive development plan, establishing executive priorities as specified in RSA 9-A:1, to the general court by July 1 of each even numbered year. The first comprehensive development plan shall be transmitted to the general court by July 1, 1988.

Source.
1985, 270:4, eff. June 10, 1985.

9-A:4. Consultation With Other Agencies.

I. In preparing the state development plan, the office of energy and planning shall consult with the chief executive officers of the various departments and agencies of state government with responsibilities which are relevant to economic development.

II. The office may also consult with officials of regional and local planning and development agencies and representatives of business and industry.

III. All state agencies and departments shall provide the office of energy and planning with such information and assistance required by the office to fulfill its responsibilities under RSA 9-A:2. The office shall maintain the confidentiality of any information which is protected by law.

Source.

1985, 270:4, eff. June 10, 1985. 2003, 319:9, eff. July 1, 2003. 2004, 257:44, eff. July 1, 2004.

Amendments

—2004. Paragraphs I and III: Substituted "office of energy and planning" for "office of state planning and energy programs".

—2003. Substituted "office of state planning and energy programs" for "office of state planning" in pars. I and III.

Cross References.

Preparation of plan generally, see RSA 4-C:2.

CHAPTER 9-B

STATE ECONOMIC GROWTH, RESOURCE PROTECTION, AND PLANNING POLICY

9-B:1. Findings.

The general court finds that:

I. In addition to clean water and air, productive mountain, forest, and agricultural open space land is one of the state's most valuable assets, and is necessary for the economy and health and welfare of the citizens. The maintenance of this asset is vital if the state is to provide future generations with the same quality of life and environment that we have traditionally enjoyed.

II. Economic development is essential to the well-being and prosperity of our citizens. However, when haphazard development sprawls across the state's landscape, our collective well-being suffers. Fortunately, economic development can take place in a form that maximizes smart growth.

III. The state can encourage development in accordance with this chapter by regularly reviewing its operating procedures, granting policies, and regulatory framework.

IV. A coordinated and comprehensive planning effort by state agencies on future development in the state is needed, which will not only improve our economy, but also encourages smart growth by locating development in appropriate growth areas and thus retaining as much open space land as possible for the long-term.

Source.
2000, 292:6, eff. Aug. 20, 2000.

9-B:2. Policy.

It shall be the policy of the state of New Hampshire that state agencies act in ways that encourage smart growth.

Source.
2000, 292:6, eff. Aug. 20, 2000.

9-B:3. Definition.

In this chapter, "smart growth" means the control of haphazard and unplanned development and the use of land which results over time, in the inflation of the amount of land used per unit of human development, and of the degree of dispersal between such land areas. "Smart growth" also means the development and use of land in such a manner that its physical, visual, or audible consequences are appropriate to the traditional and historic New Hampshire landscape. Smart growth may include denser development of existing communities, encouragement of mixed uses in such communities, the protection of villages, and planning so as to create ease of movement within and among communities. Smart growth preserves the integrity of open space in agricultural, forested, and undeveloped areas. The results of smart growth may include, but shall not be limited to:

I. Vibrant commercial activity within cities and towns.

II. Strong sense of community identity.

III. Adherence to traditional settlement patterns when siting municipal and public buildings and services.

IV. Ample alternate transportation modes.

V. Uncongested roads.

VI. Decreased water and air pollution.

VII. Clean aquifer recharge areas.

VIII. Viable wildlife habitat.

IX. Attractive views of the landscape.

X. Preservation of historic village centers.

Source.
2000, 292:6, eff. Aug. 20, 2000.

9-B:4. Expenditure of State or Federal Funds.

All state agencies shall give due consideration to the state's policy on smart growth under RSA 9-B:2 when providing advice or expending state or federal funds, for their own use or as pass-through grants, for public works, transportation, or major capital improvement projects, and for the construction, rental, or lease of facilities. The intent of this action is that new investments and grants for existing sites and buildings in existing community centers will be given preference over investments in outlying areas where that is a practical solution for the use and community in question.

Source.
2000, 292:6, eff. Aug. 20, 2000.

9-B:5. Procedures for Review.

The governor shall review actions taken by state agencies relative to the provisions of RSA 9-B:4 to ensure compliance with this chapter. The governor shall establish procedures for review no later than December 1, 2000.

Source.
2000, 292:6, eff. Aug. 20, 2000.

9-B:6. Report to the General Court and the Governor.

By October 1 of 2001, and every 4 years thereafter, the council on resources and development, established in RSA 162-C, shall report to the general court and the governor on the following:

I. Progress by state agencies in complying with the expenditure requirements under RSA 9-B:4.

II. Progress by the state agencies represented on the council in coordinating the activities to encourage smart growth.

III. Efforts made to encourage development in accordance with this chapter by regular review of state operating procedures, granting policies, and regulatory framework.

IV. Suggested policy changes or legislation that the council believes would strengthen the state's ability to achieve the smart growth goal of RSA 9-B:2.

V. An assessment of how state agencies are complying with the goals and objectives established in the statewide development plan, under RSA 9-A, and an identification of any suggested changes.

Source.

2000, 292:6, eff. Aug. 20, 2000. 2002, 229:6, 7, eff. July 1, 2002.

Amendments
—2002. Substituted "2001, and every 4 years thereafter" for "each year, beginning in the year 2000" in the introductory paragraph and added par. V.

CHAPTER 12-K

DEPLOYMENT OF PERSONAL WIRELESS SERVICE FACILITIES

Redesignation of chapter; revision of internal references.

RSA 12-K was originally enacted as RSA 12-J by 2000, 240:1, but was redesignated, pursuant to 2000, 240:7, in light of the enactment of RSA 12-J by 2000, 204:2. All internal references to RSA 12-J appearing in this chapter have been revised to refer to RSA 12-K pursuant to 2000, 240:7.

12-K:1. Goals; Purpose.

I. The federal Telecommunications Act of 1996 regulates the deployment of wireless services in the United States. Its purpose is to make these services available to the American people quickly and in a very competitive manner. Nothing in this chapter is intended to preempt the federal Telecommunications Act of 1996.

II. The visual effects of tall antenna mounts or towers may go well beyond the physical borders between municipalities, and should be addressed so as to require that all affected parties have the opportunity to be heard.

III. Carriers wishing to build personal wireless service facilities (PWSFs) in New Hampshire should consider commercially available alternative PWSFs to tall cellular towers, which may include the use of the following:

(a) Lower antenna mounts which do not protrude as far above the surrounding tree canopies.

(b) Disguised PWSFs such as flagpoles, artificial tree poles, light poles, and traffic lights, which blend in with their surroundings.

(c) Camouflaged PWSFs mounted on existing structures and buildings.

(d) Custom designed PWSFs to minimize the visual impact of a PWSF on its surroundings.

(e) Other available technology.

IV. A PWSF map is necessary to allow for the orderly and efficient deployment of wireless communication services in New Hampshire, and so that local communities have adequate information with which to consider appropriate siting and options to mitigate the visual effects of PWSFs.

V. Municipalities will benefit from state guidance regarding provisions to be considered in zoning ordinances relative to the deployment of wireless communications facilities, including one or more model ordinances.

VI. Nothing in this chapter shall be construed as altering any municipal zoning ordinance, and this chapter itself shall not be construed as a zoning ordinance.

Source.
2000, 240:1, eff. Aug. 7, 2000.

12-K:2. Definitions.

In this chapter:

I. "Antenna" means the equipment from which wireless radio signals are sent and received by a PWSF.

II. "Average tree canopy height" means the average height found by inventorying the height above ground level of all trees over a specified height within a specified radius.

III. "Camouflaged" means for a personal wireless service facility one that is disguised, hidden, part of an existing or proposed structure, or placed within an existing or proposed structure.

IV. "Carrier" means a person that provides personal wireless services.

V. "Director" means the director of the office of energy and planning.

VI. "Disguised" means, for a PWSF, designed to look like a structure which may commonly be found in the area surrounding a proposed PWSF such as, but not limited to, flagpoles, light poles, traffic lights, or artificial tree poles.

VII. "Equipment shelter" means an enclosed structure, cabinet, shed vault, or box near the base of a mount within which are housed equipment for PWSFs, such as batteries and electrical equipment.

VIII. "Height" means the height above ground level from the natural grade of a site to the highest point of a structure.

IX. "Mount" means the structure or surface upon which antennas are mounted and include roof-mounted, side-mounted, ground-mounted, and structure-mounted types.

X. "Municipality" means any city, town, unincorporated town, or unorganized place within the state.

XI. "Personal Wireless Service Facility" or "PWSF" or "facility" means any "PWSF" as defined in the federal Telecommunications Act of 1996, 47 U.S.C. section 332(c)(7)(C)(ii), including facilities used or to be used by a licensed provider of personal wireless services.

XII. "Personal Wireless Services" means any wireless telecommunications services, and commercial mobile services including cellular telephone services, personal communications services, and mobile and radio paging services as defined in the federal Telecommunications Act of 1996, 47 U.S.C. section 332 (c)(7)(C)(i).

XIII. "Radio frequency radiation" means the emissions from personal wireless service facilities.

Source.
2000, 240:1, eff. Aug. 7, 2000. 2003, 319:9, eff. July 1, 2003. 2004, 257:44, eff. July 1, 2004.

Amendments
—**2004.** Paragraph V: Substituted "office of energy and planning" for "office of state planning and energy programs".

—**2003.** Paragraph V: Substituted "office of state planning and energy programs" for "office of state planning".

12-K:3. Wireless Carriers Doing Business in this State.

All wireless carriers or their appointed agents doing business, or seeking to do business, in this state shall:

I. Be allowed to construct new ground-mounted PWSFs, provided that these PWSFs comply with municipal regulations for maximum height or maximum allowed height above the average tree canopy height, subject to any exceptions, waivers, or variances allowed or granted by the municipality.

II. Comply with all applicable state and municipal land use regulations.

III. Comply with all federal, state and municipal statutes, rules and regulations, including federal radio frequency radiation emission regulations and the National Environmental Policy Act of 1969, as amended.

IV. Provide information at the time of application to construct an externally visible PWSF, or prior to construction if no approval is required, to the municipality in which the facility is to be constructed and to the office of energy and planning, as follows:

(a) A copy of their license from the Federal Communications Commission (FCC) proving that they are eligible to deploy their systems in this geographical area and that this deployment falls under the jurisdiction of the federal Telecommunications Act of 1996; or a copy of their contract with a person with such a license, and a copy of that license.

(b) Upon request, detailed maps showing all of the carrier's current externally visible tower and monopole PWSF locations in the state within a 20 mile radius of the proposed externally visible PWSF, both active and inactive.

(c) Upon request, site descriptions for each of the above locations showing the antenna height and diameter, and showing all externally visible structures.

(d) Upon request, a description of why less visually intrusive alternatives for this facility were not proposed.

Source.
2000, 240:1, eff. Aug. 7, 2000. 2003, 319:9, eff. July 1, 2003. 2004, 257:44, eff. July 1, 2004.

Amendments
—**2004.** Paragraph IV: Substituted "office of energy and planning" for "office of state plan-

ning and energy programs" in the introductory paragraph.

—**2003.** Paragraph IV: Substituted "office of state planning and energy programs" for "office of state planning".

12-K:4. Payment of Costs.

A wireless carrier seeking approval to deploy a wireless communication facility may be required to pay reasonable fees, including regional notification costs, imposed by the municipality in accordance with RSA 676:4, I(g).

Source.
2000, 240:1, eff. Aug. 7, 2000.

12-K:5. Fall Zones.

Zoning ordinances may include provisions for fall zones for PWSFs to the extent necessary to protect public safety.

Source.
2000, 240:1, eff. Aug. 7, 2000.

12-K:6. Personal Wireless Services Facilities Map.

The director of the office of energy and planning shall develop a personal wireless service facilities map for the state. This map shall include all externally visible tower and monopole PWSF locations in the state, both active and inactive, for all carriers. This map shall also include for each of the above locations a site description as described in RSA 12-K:3, IV(c). Upon request of the director, any wireless carrier or its appointed agent doing business in this state shall provide a map of all of its existing externally visible tower and monopole PWSF locations in the state and a site description of each as described in RSA 12-K:3, IV(c).

Source.
2000, 240:1, eff. Aug. 7, 2000. 2003, 319:9, eff. July 1, 2003. 2004, 257:44, eff. July 1, 2004.

Amendments
—**2004.** Substituted "office of energy and planning" for "office of state planning and energy programs" in the first sentence.

—**2003.** Substituted "office of state planning and energy programs" for "office of state planning" in the first sentence.

12-K:7. Regional Notification.

I. (a) Any municipality or state authority or agency which receives an application to construct a PWSF which will be visible from any other New Hampshire municipality within a 20 mile radius shall provide written notification of such application and pending action to such other municipality within the 20 mile radius.

(b) This notification shall include sending a letter to the governing body of the municipality within the 20 mile radius detailing the pending action on the application and shall also include publishing a notice in a newspaper customarily used for legal notices by such municipality within the 20 mile radius, stating the specifics of the application, the pending action, and the date of the next public hearing on the application. Such notice shall be published not less than 7 days nor more than 21 days prior to the public hearing date.

II. (a) Any person, prior to constructing a new PWSF in any location where no approval is required but which will be visible from any other New Hampshire municipality within a 20 mile radius, shall provide written notification of such planned construction to such other municipality within the 20 mile radius.

(b) This notification shall include sending a letter to the governing body of the municipality within the 20 mile radius detailing the planned construction and shall also include publishing a notice in a newspaper customarily used for legal notices by such municipality within a 20 mile radius, outlining the planned construction.

III. Municipalities within the 20 mile radius described in paragraphs I or II and their residents shall be allowed to comment at any public hearing related to the application. Regional notification and comments from other municipalities or their residents shall not be construed to imply legal standing to challenge any decision.

Source.
2000, 240:1, eff. Aug. 7, 2000.

12-K:8. Model Ordinances and Guidance.

The director of the office of energy and planning shall develop a set of model municipal ordinances relative to the deployment of personal wireless communications facilities. Prior to development, the director shall hold one or more public hearings and solicit comments from interested parties. The office of energy and planning shall provide a copy of the set of model ordinances to any New Hampshire municipality that requests it.

Source.
2000, 240:1, eff. Aug. 7, 2000. 2003, 319:9, eff. July 1, 2003. 2004, 257:44, eff. July 1, 2004.

Amendments
—**2004.** Substituted "office of energy and planning" for "office of state planning and energy programs" in the first and third sentences.

—**2003.** Substituted "office of state planning and energy programs" for "office of state planning".

12-K:9. Rulemaking.

The director of the office of energy and planning, after holding a public hearing, shall adopt rules under RSA 541-A as necessary to implement this act and to provide sufficient information to municipalities, other state agencies, wireless companies doing business or seeking to do business in this state, and the public.

Source.
2000, 240:1, eff. Aug. 7, 2000. 2003, 319:9, eff. July 1, 2003. 2004, 257:44, eff. July 1, 2004.

Amendments
—**2004.** Substituted "office of energy and planning" for "office of state planning and energy programs".

—**2003.** Substituted "office of state planning and energy programs" for "office of state planning".

CHAPTER 21

STATUTORY CONSTRUCTION

21:21. Land; Real Estate.

I. The words "land," "lands" or "real estate" shall include lands, tenements, and hereditaments, and all rights thereto and interests therein.

II. Manufactured housing as defined by RSA 674:31 shall be included in the term "real estate."

Source.
RS 1:17. CS 1:17. GS 1:20. GL 1:20. PS 2:21. PL 2:21. RL 7:21. RSA 21:21. 1983, 230:1, eff. Aug. 17, 1983.

Amendments
—1983. Designated the existing provisions of the section as par. I and added par. II.

Revision note.
Substituted "RSA 674:31" for "RSA 31:118" in par. II. 1983, 447:5, III, repealed RSA 31:118.

NOTES TO DECISIONS

Analysis

1. Construction with Bankruptcy Code
2. Construction with other law

1. Construction with Bankruptcy Code

Debtors' mobile home was 14' x 80' and clearly fit within the definition of manufactured housing in RSA 674:31, and since mobile home was manufactured housing it thus was real estate for purposes of federal bankruptcy law. In re Smith, 176 B.R. 298, 1994 Bankr. LEXIS 2099 (Bankr. D.N.H. 1994).

2. Construction with other law

Provision in ninety-nine-year lease, in which town covenanted with lessee and its successors and assigns not to tax the property or any part thereof during term of lease, was intended to eliminate uncertainty of the law in 1898 with regard to taxability of leasehold interests, and was not a promise to relieve owner of the fee from the burden of taxation. Hampton Beach Casino v. Town of Hampton, 140 N.H. 785, 674 A.2d 979, 1996 N.H. LEXIS 30 (1996).

Cited:
Cited in Webster v. Blodgett, 59 N.H. 120, 1879 N.H. LEXIS 163 (1879); Winnipiseogee Lake Cotton & Woolen Mfg. Co. v. Gilford, 64 N.H. 337, 10 A. 849, 1887 N.H. LEXIS 11 (1887); Amoskeag Manufacturing Co. v. Town of Concord, 66 N.H. 562, 34 A. 241, 1891 N.H. LEXIS 76, 32 L.R.A. 621 (1891); French v. Lyme, 77 N.H. 63, 86 A. 823, 1913 N.H. LEXIS 13 (1913); Whitefield Village Fire District v. Bobst, 93 N.H. 229, 39 A.2d 566, 1944 N.H. LEXIS 132 (1944); Cotter v. Cotter, 103 N.H. 551, 176 A.2d 316, 1961 N.H. LEXIS 89 (1961); Apte v. Department of Revenue Administration, 121 N.H. 1045, 437 A.2d 319, 1981 N.H. LEXIS 459 (1981); In re Fountain, 197 B.R. 748, 1996 Bankr. LEXIS 869 (Bankr. D.N.H. 1996).

RESEARCH REFERENCES

New Hampshire Practice.
7 N.H.P. Wills, Trusts and Gifts §§ 16-14, 16-22.

21:34-a. Farm, Agriculture, Farming.

I. The word "farm" means any land, buildings, or structures on or in which agriculture and farming activities are carried out or conducted and shall include the residence or residences of owners, occupants, or employees located on such land. Structures shall include all farm outbuildings used in the care of livestock, and in the production and storage of fruit, vegetables, or nursery stock; in the production of maple syrup; greenhouses for the production of annual or perennial plants; and any other structures used in operations named in paragraph II of this section.

II. The words "agriculture" and "farming" mean all operations of a farm, including:

(a)(1) The cultivation, conservation, and tillage of the soil.

(2) The storage, use of, and spreading of commercial fertilizer, lime, wood ash, sawdust, compost, animal manure, septage, and, where permitted by municipal and state rules and regulations, other lawful soil amendments.

(3) The use of and application of agricultural chemicals.

(4) The raising and sale of livestock, which shall include, but not be limited to, dairy cows and the production of milk, beef animals, swine, sheep, goats, as well as domesticated strains of buffalo or bison, llamas, alpacas, emus, ostriches, yaks, elk (Cervus elephus canadensis), fallow deer (Dama dama), red deer (Cervus elephus), and reindeer (Rangifer tarandus).

(5) The breeding, boarding, raising, training, riding instruction, and selling of equines.

(6) The commercial raising, harvesting, and sale of fresh water fish or other aquaculture products.

(7) The raising, breeding, or sale of poultry or game birds.

(8) The raising of bees.

(9) The raising, breeding, or sale of domesticated strains of fur-bearing animals.

(10) The production of greenhouse crops.

(11) The production, cultivation, growing, harvesting, and sale of any agricultural, floricultural, forestry, or horticultural crops including, but not limited to, berries, herbs, honey, maple syrup, fruit, vegetables, tree fruit, flowers, seeds, grasses, nursery stock, sod, trees and tree products, Christmas trees grown as part of a commercial Christmas tree operation, trees grown for short rotation tree fiber, compost, or any other plant that can be legally grown and harvested extensively for profit or subsistence.

(b) Any practice on the farm incident to, or in conjunction with such farming operations, including, but not necessarily restricted to:

(1) Preparation for market, delivery to storage or to market, or to carriers for transportation to market of any products or materials from the farm.

(2) The transportation to the farm of supplies and materials.

(3) The transportation of farm workers.

(4) Forestry or lumbering operations.

(5) The marketing or selling at wholesale or retail, on-site and off-site, where permitted by local regulations, any products from the farm.

(6) Irrigation of growing crops from private water supplies or public water supplies where not prohibited by state or local rule or regulation.

(7) The use of dogs for herding, working, or guarding livestock, as defined in RSA 21:34-a, II(a)(4).

(8) The production and storage of compost and the materials necessary to produce compost, whether such materials originate, in whole or in part, from operations of the farm.

III. A farm roadside stand shall remain an agricultural operation and not be considered commercial, provided that at least 35 percent of the product sales in dollar volume is attributable to products produced on the farm or farms of the stand owner.

IV. Practices on the farm shall include technologies recommended from time to time by the university of New Hampshire cooperative extension, the New Hampshire department of agriculture, markets, and food, and appropriate agencies of the United States Department of Agriculture.

V. The term "farmers' market" means an event or series of events at which 2 or more vendors of agricultural commodities gather for purposes of offering for sale such commodities to the public. Commodities offered for sale must include, but are not limited to, products of agriculture, as defined in paragraphs I-IV. "Farmers' market" shall not include any event held upon any premises owned, leased, or otherwise controlled by any individual vendor selling therein.

VI. The term "agritourism" means attracting visitors to a working farm for the purpose of eating a meal, making overnight stays, enjoyment of the farm environment, education on farm operations, or active involvement in the activity of the farm which is ancillary to the farm operation.

Source.

1961, 140:1. 1977, 95:1. 1979, 60:1. 1985, 6:1, eff. May 31, 1985. 1997, 250:1, eff. Aug. 18, 1997. 1999, 191:2, eff. Sept. 4, 1999. 2005, 107:1, eff. August 14, 2005. 2006, 11:5, eff. March 3, 2006. 2006, 326:1, eff. August 25, 2006. 2007, 157:1, eff. June 18, 2007.

Amendments

—**2007.** Paragraph VI: Added.

—**2006.** Paragraph II: Chapter 326 inserted "storage" following "the" at the beginning of subpar. (a)(2), inserted "compost" following "tree fiber" in subpar. (a)(11), and added subpar. (b)(8).

Paragraph II(b)(7): Added by Chapter 11.

—**2005.** Paragraph V: Added.

—**1999.** Rewritten to the extent that a detailed comparison would be impracticable.

—**1997.** Inserted "short rotation tree fiber farming as defined in RSA 79:1, VI" following "greenhouse operations" in the second sentence.

—**1985.** Deleted "and/" preceding "or buildings" in the first sentence and inserted "sod" following "floricultural" in the second sentence.

—**1979.** Inserted "fresh water fish" preceding "or poultry" in the second sentence.

—**1977.** Deleted "the removal of sand, gravel, clay, soil or earth" following "lumbering operations" in the second sentence.

NOTES TO DECISIONS

Cited:
Cited in State v. Qualters, 121 N.H. 484, 431
A.2d 780, 1981 N.H. LEXIS 355 (1981).

21:35. Time, How Reckoned; Days Included and Excluded.

Except where specifically stated to the contrary, when a period or limit of
time is to be reckoned from a day or date, that day or date shall be excluded
from and the day on which an act should occur shall be included in the
computation of the period or limit of time.

Source.
RS 1:25. CS 1:25. GS 1:33. GL 1:32. PS 2:34.
PL 2:34. RL 7:34. RSA 21:35. 1994, 348:1, eff.
July 1, 1994.

Amendments
—**1994.** Rewritten to the extent that a detailed comparison would be impracticable.

NOTES TO DECISIONS

Analysis

1. Purpose
2. Application

1. Purpose
The purpose of this section was to establish a
uniform rule of computation. Ricker v. Blanchard, 45 N.H. 39, 1863 N.H. LEXIS 9 (1863).

2. Application
Because RSA 21:35 provides that the general
rule for computing a time period does not apply
if the statute in question specifically states a
contrary rule, the general rule of computing a
time period by excluding the first day from
which a period is to be determined does not
apply to RSA 677:2, which specifically states
that the time period for filing a motion for a
rehearing of a zoning board's decision begins to
run on the date of a zoning board's vote. Pelletier v. City of Manchester, 150 N.H. 687, 844
A.2d 484, 2004 N.H. LEXIS 54 (2004).
The terms of this section are general, and
apply equally whether the time is to be reckoned backward or forward from the specified
day or act. Bernard v. Martel, 68 N.H. 466, 41
A. 183, 1896 N.H. LEXIS 28 (1896).
The fact that this section provides that the
day from which time is to be reckoned is to be
excluded in computing the time within which
an act must be done tends to the conclusion

that that is the only day to be excluded in
making the computation. Clough v. Wilton, 79
N.H. 66, 104 A. 453, 1918 N.H. LEXIS 24
(1918).

Cited:
Cited in Osgood v. Blake, 21 N.H. 550, 1850
N.H. LEXIS 89 (1850); OPINION declaring the
soldiers' voting bill a valid & binding statute of
the state, 45 N.H. 607, 1864 N.H. LEXIS 87
(1864); Fairgraves v. Stark Mills, 77 N.H. 215,
90 A. 510, 1914 N.H. LEXIS 16 (1914); Drowne
v. Lovering, 93 N.H. 195, 37 A.2d 190, 1944
N.H. LEXIS 122 (1944); Larochelle v. Birch, 98
N.H. 190, 96 A.2d 573, 1953 N.H. LEXIS 46
(1953); Ware v. Champagne's Super Market,
Inc., 99 N.H. 19, 104 A.2d 736, 1954 N.H.
LEXIS 6 (1954); Opinion of the Justices, 101
N.H. 536, 133 A.2d 506, 1957 N.H. LEXIS 59
(1957); HIK Corp. v. City of Manchester, 103
N.H. 378, 172 A.2d 368, 1961 N.H. LEXIS 55
(1961); Hunter v. Department of Employment
Sec., 107 N.H. 365, 222 A.2d 214, 1966 N.H.
LEXIS 192 (1966); Rafferty v. State, 107 N.H.
387, 222 A.2d 823, 1966 N.H. LEXIS 197
(1966); Bridgham v. City of Keene, 112 N.H. 84,
289 A.2d 392, 1972 N.H. LEXIS 148 (1972);
Ayotte v. Department of Employment Security,
114 N.H. 147, 317 A.2d 16, 1974 N.H. LEXIS
226 (1974); Dustin v. Cruise Craft, Inc., 487 F.
Supp. 67, 1980 U.S. Dist. LEXIS 10668 (D.N.H.
1980); Brent v. Paquette, 132 N.H. 415, 567
A.2d 976, 1989 N.H. LEXIS 123 (1989).

RESEARCH REFERENCES

ALR.
Excess of payment for one period as applicable to subsequent period under contract or mortgage providing for periodic payments. 89 A.L.R.3d 947.

21:45. "Bylaw" or "Ordinance".

The term "bylaw" when used in reference to legislative action taken by a city, town, county or village district shall have the same meaning as an ordinance and shall be subject to the same procedures for enactment.

Source.
1975, 300:1, eff. Aug. 6, 1975.

21:46. Mobile Homes.

The words "mobile home" shall mean manufactured housing as defined by RSA 674:31.

Source.
1983, 230:2, eff. Aug. 17, 1983.

Revision note.
Substituted "RSA 674:31" for "RSA 31:118". RSA 31:118 was repealed by 1983, 447:5, III.

21:47. Legislative Body.

When used to refer to a municipality, and in the absence of applicable chapter or subdivision definitions, the term "legislative body" shall mean a town meeting, school district meeting, village district meeting, city or town council, mayor and council, mayor and board of aldermen, or, when used to refer to unincorporated towns or unorganized places, or both, the county convention.

Source.
1989, 205:1, eff. July 21, 1989.

NOTES TO DECISIONS

Construction
Trial court properly granted the two school districts' cross-motion for summary judgment and properly denied the taxpayers summary judgment motion on the taxpayers' claim that voters were required to approve the three-year agreement for the one school district to educate the other school district's students in return for a specified per pupil payment, as the taxpayers did not show anything in the relevant statute, RSA 194:22, that required a school district to obtain prior approval from the district's voters to enter a contract; furthermore, the taxpayers' argument overlooked the fact that school districts were authorized to make necessary contracts through its governing body, the school board, and that it was authorized to raise and appropriate money necessary to fund the approved contracts through its legislative body, the school district meeting. Foote v. Manchester Sch. Dist., 152 N.H. 599, 883 A.2d 283, 2005 N.H. LEXIS 145 (2005).

RESEARCH REFERENCES

New Hampshire Practice.
15 N.H.P. Land Use Planning and Zoning § 27.01.

21:48. Governing Body.

When used to refer to a municipality, and in the absence of applicable chapter or subdivision definitions, the term "governing body" shall mean the board of selectmen in a town, the board of aldermen or council in a city or town with a town council, the school board in a school district or the village district commissioners in a village district, or when used to refer to unincorporated towns or unorganized places, or both, the county commissioners.

Source.
1989, 205:1, eff. July 21, 1989.

NOTES TO DECISIONS

Construction

Trial court properly granted the two school districts' cross-motion for summary judgment and properly denied the taxpayers summary judgment motion on the taxpayers' claim that voters were required to approve the three-year agreement for the one school district to educate the other school district's students in return for a specified per pupil payment, as the taxpayers did not show anything in the relevant statute, RSA 194:22, that required a school district to obtain prior approval from the district's voters to enter a contract; furthermore, the taxpayers' argument overlooked the fact that school districts were authorized to make necessary contracts through its governing body, the school board, and that it was authorized to raise and appropriate money necessary to fund the approved contracts through its legislative body, the school district meeting. Foote v. Manchester Sch. Dist., 152 N.H. 599, 883 A.2d 283, 2005 N.H. LEXIS 145 (2005).

TITLE II

COUNTIES

CHAPTER 28

COUNTY COMMISSIONERS

Section
28:7-b.   Planning and Zoning in Unincorpo-
            rated Towns and Unorganized
            Places.

28:7-b. Planning and Zoning in Unincorporated Towns and Unorganized Places.

For each unincorporated town or unorganized place, the county in which it is located and its commissioners shall have the same responsibilities and powers to exercise planning, zoning, subdivision and related regulations as city and local land use boards. Regulations shall be exercised in accordance with the provisions of RSA 672-677 to the extent practical, in order to ensure reasonable development and planning in the unincorporated town or unorganized place.

Source.
    1983, 161:1. 1986, 31:1. 1989, 266:2, eff. July 1, 1989.

Amendments
    —1989. Rewritten to the extent that a detailed comparison would be impracticable.

—1986. Rewritten to the extent that a detailed comparison would be impracticable.

TITLE III

TOWNS, CITIES, VILLAGE DISTRICTS, AND UNINCORPORATED PLACES

CHAPTER 31

POWERS AND DUTIES OF TOWNS

Power to Make Bylaws

31:39. Purpose and Penalties.

I. Towns may make bylaws for:

(a) The care, protection, preservation and use of the public cemeteries, parks, commons, libraries and other public institutions of the town;

(b) The prevention of the going at large of horses and other domestic animals in any public place in the town;

(c) The observance of Memorial Day, whereby interference with and disturbance of the exercises for such observance, by processions, sports, games or other holiday exercises, may be prohibited;

(d) Regulation of the use of mufflers upon boats and vessels propelled by gasoline, oil or naphtha and operating upon the waters within the town limits;

(e) The kindling, guarding and safekeeping of fires, and for removing all combustible materials from any building or place, as the safety of property in the town may require;

(f) The collection, removal and destruction of garbage, snow and other waste materials;

(g) Regulating the operation of vehicles, except railroads as common carriers, upon their streets;

(h) Regulating the conduct of public dances;

(i) Regulating the conduct of roller skating rinks;

(j) Regulating the sanitary conditions of restaurants within town limits in accordance with the provisions of RSA 147:1;

(k) Issuing a license for the operation of a restaurant and other food serving establishments within the town limits and charging a reasonable fee for same;

(*l*) Making and ordering their prudential affairs;

(m) Issuing permits for tattooing facilities and charging a fee for the permit; and

(n) Regulating noise.

(*o*) Requiring the reporting of contributions to, and expenditures by, any candidate or political committee made for the purpose of influencing the election of any candidate for local elective office, or any person or committee for the purpose of influencing the vote on any local ballot or referendum question.

II. Towns may appoint all such officers as may be necessary to carry the bylaws into effect.

III. Towns may enforce the observance of the bylaws by suitable penalties not exceeding $1,000 for each offense to enure to such uses as the town may direct.

Source.

RS 31:6, 7. 1845, 242:1. CS 32:6, 7, 8. GS 34:5, 6, 7; 45:5. GL 37:5, 6, 7; 49:6. PS 40:7, 8. 1901, 5:1. 1909, 94:1. 1919, 86:3. 1925, 140:1. PL 42:30. 1937, 84:1. RL 51:32. 1949, 133:4. RSA 31:39. 1969, 68:1. 1971, 93:1; 512:8. 1981, 211:1. 1983, 166:1. 1985, 71:1. 1993, 306:1, eff. Aug. 22, 1993. 2007, 43:1, eff. July 20, 2007.

Amendments

—2007. Paragraph I(o): Added.

—1993. Subparagraph I(*l*): Deleted "and" following "affairs".

Subparagraph I(m): Added "and" following "permit".

Subparagraph I(n): Added.

—1985. Paragraph I(*l*): Added "and" following "affairs".

Paragraph I(m): Added.

—1983. Paragraph III: Substituted "$1,000" for "$100" preceding "for each offense".

—1981. Rewritten to the extent that a detailed comparison would be impracticable.

—1971. Chapter 93 inserted "snow" following "garbage" in the first sentence.

Chapter 512 substituted "one hundred" for "the fifty" preceding "dollars" in the second sentence.

—1969. Substituted "fifty" for "ten" preceding "dollars" in the second sentence.

Contingent 1999 amendment.

1999, 278:16, eff. July 14, 1999, provided: "If a constitutional amendment to the New Hampshire constitution providing that municipalities shall have home rule authority to exercise any powers not specifically prohibited by the state or federal constitutions is adopted by the voters in the 2000 general election, then sections 1-15 of this act [which amended this section and RSA 41:11; 47:17; 143-A:5, I, III; 149-M:17, II(b); 179:19, V; 231:132-a, Intro. par.; 266:24, I; 466:30-b, V; 502:14; and 502-A:8, enacted RSA 31:39-b and 47:17-a, and repealed RSA 31:39-a; 31:40-43], shall take effect January 1, 2001. If such a constitutional amendment is not adopted, then sections 1-15 of this act shall not take effect."

Contingent 1999 amendment; outcome of 2000 general election.

In the 2000 general election, the voters of New Hampshire rejected the constitutional amendment, referred to above, which would have provided that municipalities would have home rule authority to exercise any powers not specifically prohibited by the state or federal constitutions. Consequently, sections 1-15 of 1999, 278:16 [which amended this section and

41:11; 47:17; 143-A:5, I, III; 149-M:17, II(b); 179:19, V; 231:132-a, Intro par.; 266:24, I; 466:30-b, V; 502:14; 502-A:8; enacted RSA 31:39-b and 47:17-a, and repealed 31:39-a; 31:40-43] did not take effect.

Cross References.
Animals running at large, see RSA 467.
Cemeteries generally, see RSA 289.
Establishment and discontinuance of parks, see RSA 50.
Fire hazard regulations, see RSA 154:18 et seq.
Motorboat noise levels, see RSA 270:36 et seq.

Muffling devices on boats, see RSA 270:25.
Muzzling and restraining dogs, see RSA 466:29 et seq.
Police attendance at public dances, see RSA 105:9.
Power to regulate registration, sale, transportation or use of pesticides as exception, see RSA 430:49.
Public libraries generally, see RSA 202-A.
Solid waste management generally, see RSA 149-M.
State food service licenses, see RSA 143-A.
Traffic rules and regulations, see RSA 265.

NOTES TO DECISIONS

Analysis

1. State laws regulating subject matter
2. Garbage and waste disposal
3. Traffic control
4. Prudential affairs
5. Surfing
6. Buildings
7. Mobile homes
8. Rent control
9. Setback
10. Zoning
11. Subdivisions
12. Growth control
13. Enforcement
14. Penalties

1. State laws regulating subject matter
Town by-laws may not be inconsistent with statutory law of state. State v. Jenkins, 102 N.H. 545, 162 A.2d 613, 1960 N.H. LEXIS 76 (1960).
Town by-law which prohibited hunting and discharge of firearms throughout the town unless written permission was obtained from the landowner was inconsistent with statutory law of state regulating hunting and discharge of firearms and hence was invalid. State v. Jenkins, 102 N.H. 545, 162 A.2d 613, 1960 N.H. LEXIS 76 (1960).

2. Garbage and waste disposal
Although a dump ordinance may incidentally affect the use of land, such incidental effect is not comprehensive enough to require that the ordinance be adopted pursuant to the zoning statutes rather than pursuant to this section. Derry Sand & Gravel, Inc. v. Town of Londonderry, 121 N.H. 501, 431 A.2d 139, 1981

N.H. LEXIS 358 (1981).
Regulation of the disposal of garbage and waste by local dump ordinance was valid. Derry Sand & Gravel, Inc. v. Town of Londonderry, 121 N.H. 501, 431 A.2d 139, 1981 N.H. LEXIS 358 (1981).

3. Traffic control
Where record suggested that town fathers were acting to relieve traffic congestion, not to impinge upon rights of private entrepreneurs, when they adopted ordinance to keep certain street vendors out of certain high traffic areas, challenged ordinance was valid as a traffic control ordinance, a proper exercise of the police power delegated to the town by the legislature. Piane v. Town of Conway, 118 N.H. 883, 395 A.2d 517, 1978 N.H. LEXIS 312 (1978).

4. Prudential affairs
Provision in this section allowing municipalities to enact bylaws for "making and ordering their prudential affairs" is not a general grant of authority giving municipalities any significant independent legislative authority; language is more properly construed to grant powers that are necessary and proper in execution of powers that have been specifically granted. Op. Atty. Gen. #0-93-6.
The term "prudential affairs" should not be used as substitute means of granting authority when express grants of power are more desirable to attain that end. Girard v. Town of Allenstown, 121 N.H. 268, 428 A.2d 488, 1981 N.H. LEXIS 295 (1981).
The language of the "prudential affairs" clause of this section does not constitute a

separate and distinct grant of legislative authority; rather, it is more suggestive of merely granting those powers that are "necessary and proper" in the execution of the powers that have been specifically granted to towns. Girard v. Town of Allenstown, 121 N.H. 268, 428 A.2d 488, 1981 N.H. LEXIS 295 (1981).

5. Surfing
Although the regulation of surfing is not specifically authorized by this section, an ordinance prohibiting surfing in the ocean in a certain area and at certain times is implicitly permitted by the grant of authority to make by-laws for the use of the public parks, commons and other public institutions to the town. State v. Zetterberg, 109 N.H. 126, 244 A.2d 188, 1968 N.H. LEXIS 135 (1968).

6. Buildings
Ordinances regulating setback, space between buildings and height of buildings are valid exercises of the police power granted by this section. Piper v. Meredith, 110 N.H. 291, 266 A.2d 103, 1970 N.H. LEXIS 156 (1970).

An ordinance establishing a height and setback limitation for buildings in a portion of a town came within the police powers of this section and did not have to be adopted as a zoning ordinance. Piper v. Meredith, 110 N.H. 291, 266 A.2d 103, 1970 N.H. LEXIS 156 (1970).

A municipal ordinance prohibiting the erection of any building or trailer within one-fourth mile of the town common unless the selectmen approve the plans for construction and location "in order that the atmosphere of the Town . . . may be maintained" was a valid exercise of the police power granted by this section, and the fact that no zoning ordinance of general application had been adopted by the town and that the regulation applied to a limited area of town does not invalidate the ordinance. Town of Deering v. Tibbetts, 105 N.H. 481, 202 A.2d 232, 1964 N.H. LEXIS 106 (1964).

An ordinance requiring approval by the selectmen of plans for construction and location of proposed building sought to be erected in the regulated area "in order that the atmosphere of the Town . . . may be maintained" furnished a sufficient guide for determination of whether a building was compatible and appropriate in the typical environment and characteristic setting of the town common. Town of Deering v. Tibbetts, 105 N.H. 481, 202 A.2d 232, 1964 N.H. LEXIS 106 (1964).

7. Mobile homes
The regulation of mobile homes is a proper exercise of a town's police power. Village House, Inc. v. Town of Loudon, 114 N.H. 76, 314 A.2d 635, 1974 N.H. LEXIS 211 (1974).

A town may properly seek to regulate and restrict the location of mobile homes under the police power provisions of this section. Town of Weare v. Stone, 114 N.H. 80, 314 A.2d 638, 1974 N.H. LEXIS 212 (1974).

Where town building code regulated setback, minimum floor size and lot size, required sanitary facilities to conform to state regulations and required a building permit, the code, together with mobile home ordinance did not have to be enacted in compliance with the zoning statutes, and mobile home ordinance could be enacted under the police power. Village House, Inc. v. Town of Loudon, 114 N.H. 76, 314 A.2d 635, 1974 N.H. LEXIS 211 (1974).

A town may, under the police power, restrict the total number of trailer units to be located within the town. Riverview Park, Inc. v. Town of Hinsdale, 113 N.H. 693, 313 A.2d 733, 1973 N.H. LEXIS 353 (1973).

This section furnished adequate authorization for town ordinance regulating the location of a mobile home within the town, under which selectmen would decide whether permit would be issued, after notice to abutters and by publication, and after hearing, and under which no permit would issue unless selectmen found that the mobile home's location and maintenance, inter alia, would advance public health, safety and morals, conserve private property values, encourage appropriate land use and preserve general attractiveness and welfare of town. Town of New Boston v. Coombs, 111 N.H. 359, 284 A.2d 920, 1971 N.H. LEXIS 201 (1971).

Town ordinance requiring permit by selectmen after notice and hearing in order to locate mobile home within town could properly require selectmen to consider opinions of all persons taking a position at the hearing and give particular significance to the consent or objections of owners of neighboring property. Town of New Boston v. Coombs, 111 N.H. 359, 284 A.2d 920, 1971 N.H. LEXIS 201 (1971).

8. Rent control
This section does not convey to towns authority to adopt and enforce a rent control ordinance. Girard v. Town of Allenstown, 121 N.H. 268, 428 A.2d 488, 1981 N.H. LEXIS 295 (1981).

9. Setback

Town setback ordinance, requiring septic systems to be placed at least 125 feet from edge of water, was enacted in order to prevent further pollution of lake and such ordinance was reasonable exercise of the general police power granted to municipalities by this section. Freedom v. Gillespie, 120 N.H. 576, 419 A.2d 1090, 1980 N.H. LEXIS 361 (1980).

10. Zoning

General police power delegated to a municipality pursuant to this section may not be used as a usual and expedient mechanism for effecting zoning regulations which would otherwise fall within the zoning enabling statutes. Beck v. Town of Raymond, 118 N.H. 793, 394 A.2d 847, 1978 N.H. LEXIS 296 (1978).

When legislation attempts to control population growth through definite and detailed control of land development, it must be enacted in accordance with the zoning statutes, rather than pursuant to this section. Beck v. Town of Raymond, 118 N.H. 793, 394 A.2d 847, 1978 N.H. LEXIS 296 (1978).

A town ordinance containing comprehensive regulations which sought to restrict the use of three areas of a town to single and two-family residential buildings, to regulate the use of buildings, the size and percentage of lots and indirectly to regulate the size of yards and other open spaces and the density of population, and which contemplated that permits would be granted for nonconforming uses, was a zoning ordinance which could not be legally enacted except in compliance with the statute authorizing zoning regulations and could not be justified under this section. Bisson v. Town of Milford, 109 N.H. 287, 249 A.2d 688, 1969 N.H. LEXIS 136 (1969).

11. Subdivisions

Town's "slow growth" subdivision ordinance, providing that no owner of land of record could subdivide his land into more than five building lots in any one calendar year, was an impermissible and invalid attempt to exercise its police power under this section to regulate a subject

matter that requires compliance with statutes governing zoning regulation. Stoney-Brook Development Corp. v. Town of Pembroke, 118 N.H. 791, 394 A.2d 853, 1978 N.H. LEXIS 295 (1978).

12. Growth control

A growth control ordinance, enacted as a general ordinance, was not a valid exercise of the police power delegated to a municipality pursuant to this section. Stoney-Brook Development Corp. v. Town of Fremont, 124 N.H. 583, 474 A.2d 561, 1984 N.H. LEXIS 348 (1984).

13. Enforcement

Town could delegate enforcement of ordinance to its planning board. Freedom v. Gillespie, 120 N.H. 576, 419 A.2d 1090, 1980 N.H. LEXIS 361 (1980).

14. Penalties

Penalty of $10 for each day a mobile home was located within town in violation of ordinance was specifically authorized by this section and not unconstitutional on its face. Town of New Boston v. Coombs, 111 N.H. 359, 284 A.2d 920, 1971 N.H. LEXIS 201 (1971).

Town may not enact bylaws to provide for penalties in excess of its statutory authority. State v. Jenkins, 102 N.H. 545, 162 A.2d 613, 1960 N.H. LEXIS 76 (1960).

Cited:

Cited in State v. Wimpfheimer, 69 N.H. 166, 38 A. 786, 1897 N.H. LEXIS 9 (1897); Chung Mee Restaurant Co. v. Healy, 86 N.H. 483, 171 A. 263, 1934 N.H. LEXIS 89 (1934); State v. Guertin, 89 N.H. 126, 193 A. 237, 1937 N.H. LEXIS 25 (1937); McMahon v. Town of Salem, 104 N.H. 219, 182 A.2d 463, 1962 N.H. LEXIS 54 (1962); Robbins Auto Parts v. Laconia, 117 N.H. 235, 371 A.2d 1167, 1977 N.H. LEXIS 308 (1977); Garofoli v. Town of Henniker, 121 N.H. 153, 427 A.2d 35, 1981 N.H. LEXIS 270 (1981); Grondin v. Town of Hinsdale, 122 N.H. 882, 451 A.2d 1299, 1982 N.H. LEXIS 485 (1982); Stablex Corp. v. Town of Hooksett, 122 N.H. 1091, 456 A.2d 94, 1982 N.H. LEXIS 539 (1982).

RESEARCH REFERENCES

New Hampshire Practice.
15 N.H.P. Land Use Planning and Zoning §§ 5.13, 13.01, 15.02, 26.02.

New Hampshire Bar Journal.
Slow growth zoning ordinances, 20 N.H.B.J. 257 (July 1979).

ALR.
Construction and application of ordinances relating to unrestrained dogs, cats, or other domesticated animals. 1 A.L.R.4th 994.

Validity and construction of ordinance prohibiting roof signs. 76 A.L.R.3d 1162.
Validity of local regulation of hazardous waste. 67 A.L.R.4th 822.

31:39-a. Conflict of Interest Ordinances.

The legislative body of a town or city may adopt an ordinance defining and regulating conflicts of interest for local officers and employees, whether elected or appointed. Any such ordinance may include provisions requiring disclosure of financial interests for specified officers and employees, establishing incompatibility of office requirements stricter than those specified by state law or establishing conditions under which prohibited conflicts of interest shall require removal from office. Any such ordinance shall include provisions to exempt affected officers and employees who are in office or employed at the time the ordinance is adopted for a period not to exceed one year from the date of adoption. The superior court shall have jurisdiction over any removal proceedings instituted under an ordinance adopted under this section.

Source.
1981, 221:1, eff. Aug. 10, 1981.

Contingent 1999 repeal.
1999, 278:16, eff. July 14, 1999, provided: "If a constitutional amendment to the New Hampshire constitution providing that municipalities shall have home rule authority to exercise any powers not specifically prohibited by the state or federal constitutions is adopted by the voters in the 2000 general election, then sections 1-15 of this act [which repealed this section and RSA 31:40-43 and amended RSA 31:39; 41:11; 47:17; 143-A:5, I, III; 149-M:17, II(b); 179:19, V; 231:132-a, Intro. par.; 266:24, I; 466:30-b, V; and 502-A:8, and enacted RSA 31:39-b and 47:17-a], shall take effect January 1, 2001. If such a constitutional amendment is not

adopted, then sections 1-15 of this act shall not take effect."

Contingent 1999 repeal; outcome of 2000 general election.
In the 2000 general election, the voters of New Hampshire rejected the constitutional amendment, referred to above, which would have provided that municipalities would have home rule authority to exercise any powers not specifically prohibited by the state or federal constitutions. Consequently, sections 1-15 of 1999, 278:16 [which repealed this section and RSA 31:40-43 and amended RSA 31:39; 41:11; 47:17; 143-A:5, I, III; 149-M:17, II(b); 179:19, V; 231:132-a, Intro. par.; 266:24, I; 466:30-b, V; and 502-A:8, and enacted RSA 31:39-b and 47:17-a] did not take effect.

RESEARCH REFERENCES

New Hampshire Practice.
15 N.H.P. Land Use Planning and Zoning § 20.07.

31:41. Open-Air Motion Picture Theatres.

Towns shall have the power to make bylaws relating to the regulation and licensing of open-air motion picture theatres within the limits of the town, and may fix reasonable fees for the operation of said theatres, and failure to conform to such bylaws shall constitute a violation and any fines collected hereunder shall inure to such uses as said towns may direct.

Source.

1949, 252:1, par. 32-b. RSA 31:41. 1973, 531:5, eff. at 11:59 p.m., Oct. 31, 1973.

Amendments

—1973. Substituted "failure to conform to such by-laws shall constitute a violation and any fines collected hereunder shall" for "may enforce the observance of such by-laws by suitable penalties not exceeding twenty-five dollars for each offense, to" preceding "inure".

Contingent 1999 repeal.

1999, 278:16, eff. July 14, 1999, provided: "If a constitutional amendment to the New Hampshire constitution providing that municipalities shall have home rule authority to exercise any powers not specifically prohibited by the state or federal constitutions is adopted by the voters in the 2000 general election, then sections 1-15 of this act [which repealed this section and RSA 31:39-a, 40, 41-a-43 and amended RSA 31:39; 41:11; 47:17; 143-A:5, I, III; 149-M:17, II(b); 179:19, V; 231:132-a, Intro. par.; 266:24, I; 466:30-b, V; and 502-A:8, and enacted RSA 31:39-b and 47:17-a], shall take effect January

1, 2001. If such a constitutional amendment is not adopted, then sections 1-15 of this act shall not take effect."

Contingent 1999 repeal; outcome of 2000 general election.

In the 2000 general election, the voters of New Hampshire rejected the constitutional amendment referred to above, which would have provided that municipalities would have home rule authority to exercise any powers not specifically prohibited by the state or federal constitutions. Consequently, sections 1-15 of 1999, 278:16 [which repealed this section and RSA 31:39-a, 40, 41-a-43 and amended RSA 31:39; 41:11; 47:17; 143-A:5, I, III; 149-M:17, II(b); 179:19, V; 231:132-a, Intro. par.; 266:24, I; 466:30-b, V; and 502-A:8, and enacted RSA 31:39-b and 47:17-a] did not take effect.

Cross References.

Classification of crimes, see RSA 625:9.

Regulation by selectmen prior to adoption of bylaws, see RSA 31:42.

Sentences, see RSA 651.

NOTES TO DECISIONS

Analysis

1. Purpose
2. Fees

1. Purpose

In enacting this section the legislature intended to grant towns merely a police power to regulate and license open-air motion picture theatres in the interest of the public good. Hooksett Drive-in Theatre v. Hooksett, 110 N.H. 287, 266 A.2d 124, 1970 N.H. LEXIS 155 (1970).

2. Fees

A fee of $500 for each showing of a picture rated "X" bore no reasonable relationship to the

cost of administering and enforcing an ordinance adopted under this section and was therefore confiscatory and rendered the ordinance invalid and unenforceable. Hooksett Drive-in Theatre v. Hooksett, 110 N.H. 287, 266 A.2d 124, 1970 N.H. LEXIS 155 (1970).

Cited:

Cited in Mason v. Town of Salem, 103 N.H. 166, 167 A.2d 433, 1961 N.H. LEXIS 7 (1961); State v. Sukoff, 105 N.H. 70, 192 A.2d 622, 1963 N.H. LEXIS 19 (1963).

RESEARCH REFERENCES

ALR.

Liability of owner or operator of drive-in

movie theater for injury or death to patron or frequenter. 50 A.L.R.2d 1457; 26 A.L.R.3d 1314.

31:41-a. Motor Vehicle Race Tracks.

Towns shall have the power to make bylaws relating to the regulation and licensing of motor vehicle race tracks within the limits of the town, and may fix fees not to exceed $100 annually for the operation of such race tracks, and failure to observe such bylaws shall constitute a violation and any fines collected hereunder shall inure to such uses as said towns may direct. For the purposes of this section, a motor vehicle shall be defined as any self-propelled vehicle, except tractors, activated by an internal combustion engine and not operated exclusively on stationary tracks.

Source.
1967, 149:1. 1973, 531:6, eff. at 11:59 p.m., Oct. 31, 1973.

Amendments
—1973. Substituted "failure to observe such by-laws shall constitute a violation and any fines collected hereunder shall" for "may enforce the observance of such by-laws by suitable penalties not exceeding twenty-five dollars for each offense, to" preceding "inure" in the first sentence.

Contingent 1999 repeal.
1999, 278:16, eff. July 14, 1999, provided: "If a constitutional amendment to the New Hampshire constitution providing that municipalities shall have home rule authority to exercise any powers not specifically prohibited by the state or federal constitutions is adopted by the voters in the 2000 general election, then sections 1-15 of this act [which repealed this section and RSA 31:39-a, 40, 41, 41-b-43 and amended RSA 31:39; 41:11; 47:17; 143-A:5, I, III; 149-M:17, II(b); 179:19, V; 231:132-a, Intro. par.; 266:24, I; 466:30-b, V; and 502-A:8, and enacted RSA 31:39-b and 47:17-a], shall take effect January 1, 2001. If such a constitutional amendment is not adopted, then sections 1-15 of this act shall not take effect."

Contingent 1999 repeal; outcome of 2000 general election.
In the 2000 general election, the voters of New Hampshire rejected the constitutional amendment, referred to above, which would have provided that municipalities would have home rule authority to exercise any powers not specifically prohibited by the state or federal constitutions. Consequently, sections 1-15 of 1999, 278:16 [which repealed this section and RSA 31:39-a, 40, 41, 41-b-43 and amended RSA 31:39; 41:11; 47:17; 143-A:5, I, III; 149-M:17, II(b); 179:19, V; 231:132-a, Intro. par.; 266:24, I; 466:30-b, V; and 502-A:8, and enacted RSA 31:39-b and 47:17-a] did not take effect.

Cross References.
Classification of crimes, see RSA 625:9.
Regulation by selectmen prior to adoption of by-laws, see RSA 31:42.
Sentences, see RSA 651.

31:41-b. Hazardous Embankments.

Towns shall have the power to make bylaws regulating hazardous embankments, including the removal, stabilization, or fencing thereof, for the protection of the health and safety of the public. Whoever violates any such bylaw shall be guilty of a violation for each offense and the penalty therefor shall inure to such uses as the town may direct. Regulation of "excavation" as defined in RSA 155-E:1, II shall be in accordance with RSA 155-E, but any hazardous embankment resulting from excavation, whether undertaken prior to, on, or after August 4, 1989, may be subject to bylaws made under the authority of this section.

Source.
1971, 212:1. 1973, 531:7. 1989, 363:16. 1991, 310:2, eff. Aug. 23, 1991.

Amendments
—1991. Added "but any hazardous embankment resulting from excavation, whether undertaken prior to, on, or after August 4, 1989, may be subject to bylaws made under the authority of this section" following "with RSA 155-E" in the third sentence.

—1989. Substituted "Embankments" for "Pits" in the section catchline, "hazardous embankments, including the removal, stabilization, or fencing thereof" for "land excavation" following "regulating" in the first sentence, and "the" for "said" preceding "town" in the second sentence, and added the third sentence.

—1973. Rewritten to the extent that a detailed comparison would be impracticable.

Contingent 1999 repeal.
1999, 278:16, eff. July 14, 1999, provided: "If a constitutional amendment to the New Hampshire constitution providing that municipalities shall have home rule authority to exercise any powers not specifically prohibited by the state or federal constitutions is adopted by the voters in the 2000 general election, then sections 1-15 of this act [which repealed this section and RSA 31:39-a, 40-41-a, 41-c-43 and amended RSA 31:39; 41:11; 47:17; 143-A:5, I, III; 149-M:17, II(b); 179:19, V; 231:132-a, Intro. par.; 266:24, I; 466:30-b, V; and 502-A:8, and enacted RSA 31:39-b and 47:17-a], shall take effect January 1, 2001. If such a constitutional amendment is not adopted, then sections 1-15 of this act shall not take effect."

Contingent 1999 repeal; outcome of 2000 general election.
In the 2000 general election, the voters of New Hampshire rejected the constitutional amendment, referred to above, which would have provided that municipalities would have home rule authority to exercise any powers not specifically prohibited by the state or federal constitutions. Consequently, sections 1-15 of 1999, 278:16 [which amended this section and RSA 31:39; 41:11; 47:17; 143-A:5, I, III; 149-M:17, II(b); 170:19, V; 231:132-a, Intro par.; 266:24, I; 466:30-b, V; 502:14; 502-A:8; enacted RSA 31:39-b and 47:17-a, and repealed RSA 31:39-a; 31:40-43] did not take effect.

Cross References.
Classification of crimes, see RSA 625:9.
Sentences, see RSA 651.

NOTES TO DECISIONS

Construction with other laws
This section and RSA 155-E, granting authority to local governing bodies to regulate a specific land use, namely earth excavation, exist as grants of authority independent of the zoning enabling legislation. Town of Goffstown v. Thibeault, 129 N.H. 454, 529 A.2d 930, 1987 N.H. LEXIS 184 (1987).

Cited:
Cited in Flanagan v. Town of Hollis, 112 N.H. 222, 293 A.2d 328, 1972 N.H. LEXIS 181 (1972); Town of Surry v. Starkey, 115 N.H. 31, 332 A.2d 172, 1975 N.H. LEXIS 215 (1975).

RESEARCH REFERENCES

New Hampshire Practice.
15 N.H.P. Land Use Planning and Zoning §§ 36.01, 36.22.

Miscellaneous

31:95-a. Tax Maps.

I. Every city and town shall, prior to January 1, 1980, have a tax map, so-called, drawn. Each tax map shall:

(a) Show the boundary lines of each parcel of land in the city or town and shall be properly indexed.

(b) Accurately represent the physical location of each parcel of land in the city or town.

(c) Show on each parcel of land the road or water frontage thereof.

II. (a) The scale on a tax map shall be meaningful and adequately represent the land contained on the map, taking into consideration the urban or rural character of the land. The scale shall be sufficient to allow the naming and numbering of, and the placement of dimensions within, if possible, the parcel represented in the individual plat.

(b) Nothing in this paragraph shall apply to any city or town which, prior to the imposition of such scale requirements, has drawn a tax map, appropriated funds or contracted with any person or firm to prepare a tax map or expended funds in the initial phase of preparing a tax map.

III. Each parcel shall be identified by a map and parcel number and shall be indexed alphabetically by owner's name and numerically by parcel number.

IV. Tax maps shall be updated at least annually to indicate ownership and parcel size changes.

V. Each tax map shall be open to public inspection in a city or town office during regular business hours.

Source.
1971, 426:1. 1975, 402:1, eff. Aug. 15, 1975. 2004, 203:10, eff. June 11, 2004.

Amendments
—**2004.** Paragraph II(a): Inserted "if possible" following "dimensions within" in the second sentence.

Paragraph III: Amended without change.
Paragraph IV: Deleted "continually" preceding "updated" and inserted "at least annually" thereafter.

—**1975.** Rewritten to the extent that a detailed comparison would be impracticable.

Liability for Damages Limited, Indemnification, Insurance

31:104. Liability of Municipal Executives.

Notwithstanding any provisions of law to the contrary, no member of the governing board of any municipal corporation or political subdivision; no member of any other board, commission, or bureau of any municipal corporation or political subdivision created or existing pursuant to a statute or charter, and no chief executive officer of such municipal corporation or political subdivision, including but not limited to city councilors and aldermen, selectmen, county convention members, members of boards of adjustment, members of planning boards, school board members, mayors, city managers, town managers, county commissioners, regional planning commissioners, and school superintendents shall be held liable for civil damages for any vote, resolution or decision made by said person acting in his official capacity in good faith and within the scope of his authority.

Source.
1973, 595:1. 1991, 72:1, eff. July 12, 1991.

Revision note.
Substituted "subdivision" for "subdivisions" preceding "including" to correct a grammatical error.

Amendments
—**1991.** Inserted "regional planning commissioners" following "county commissioners".

Cross References.
Civil suits against municipal officials, see RSA 491:24.

Pleading

Trial court properly dismissed claims against board of selectmen occasioned by a culvert positioned in a public way so as to allegedly cause an accumulation of water on the plaintiffs' land, where, even with conclusory references to "wanton" conduct by the selectmen, there were insufficient allegations of bad faith to take the claims against the selectmen out of the protection of this section. Cannata v. Town of Deerfield, 132 N.H. 235, 566 A.2d 162, 1989 N.H. LEXIS 97 (1989).

Cited:

Cited in Coussoule v. Redden, 118 N.H. 4, 381 A.2d 1200, 1978 N.H. LEXIS 330 (1978); Win-Tasch Corp. v. Town of Merrimack, 120 N.H. 6, 411 A.2d 144, 1980 N.H. LEXIS 222 (1980); Marino v. Goss, 120 N.H. 511, 418 A.2d 1271, 1980 N.H. LEXIS 335 (1980); Adams v. Bradshaw, 135 N.H. 7, 599 A.2d 481, 1991 N.H. LEXIS 131 (1991).

RESEARCH REFERENCES

ALR.

Payment of attorneys' services in defending action brought against officials individually as within power or obligation of public body. 47 A.L.R.5th 553.

31:105. Indemnification for Damages.

A city, town, county, village district or precinct, school district, charter school, school administrative unit, or any other municipal corporation or political subdivision may by a vote of the governing body indemnify and save harmless for loss or damage occurring after said vote any person employed by it and any member or officer of its governing board, administrative staff or agencies including but not limited to selectmen, school board members, charter school trustees, city councilors and aldermen, town and city managers, regional planning commissioners, and superintendents of schools from personal financial loss and expense including reasonable legal fees and costs, if any, arising out of any claim, demand, suit, or judgment by reason of negligence or other act resulting in accidental injury to a person or accidental damage to or destruction of property if the indemnified person at the time of the accident resulting in the injury, damage, or destruction was acting in the scope of employment or office.

Source.

1973, 595:1. 1991, 72:2. 1995, 260:2, eff. July 1, 1995.

Amendments

—1995. Substituted "charter school, school administrative unit" for "supervisory union"

following "school district", inserted "charter school trustees" preceding "city councilors" and deleted "his" preceding "employment".

—1991. Inserted "regional planning commissioners" following "city managers".

Cited:

Cited in Win-Tasch Corp. v. Town of Merrimack, 120 N.H. 6, 411 A.2d 144, 1980 N.H. LEXIS 222 (1980); City of Manchester v. General Reinsurance Corp., 127 N.H. 806, 508 A.2d 1063, 1986 N.H. LEXIS 245 (1986).

RESEARCH REFERENCES

ALR.

Municipal liability for negligent performance of building inspector's duties. 24 A.L.R.5th 200.

Validity and construction of statute authorizing or requiring governmental unit to indemnify public officer or employee for liability arising out of performance of public duties. 71

A.L.R.3d 90.

Validity and construction of statute authorizing or requiring governmental unit to procure liability insurance covering public officers or employees for liability arising out of performance of public duties. 71 A.L.R.3d 6.

Oil Refinery Siting

31:109. Local Option for Oil Refinery Siting in Towns.

Notwithstanding the provisions of any other law, an oil refinery shall not be located in any town without a vote of approval of a majority of the voters present and voting on the question at an annual meeting or a special town meeting called for such purpose. All votes on the question shall be taken by written ballot. The following question shall be placed on the ballot "Shall an oil refinery be permitted within the town of (____)?" Said question shall be printed in the form prescribed by RSA 59:12-a. If a majority of those voting on the question shall vote in the affirmative, approval of the location of the oil refinery in the town shall be deemed granted. If a majority of those voting on the question shall vote in the negative, such approval shall be deemed not granted and no oil refinery may be located in such town unless approval is subsequently granted in accord with this section. Nothing in this section shall be construed as changing, modifying or affecting in any way the provisions of RSA 31 and RSA 36 relating to zoning regulations.

Source.

1974, 36:1, eff. April 5, 1974.

References in text.

RSA 59:12-a, referred to in this section, was repealed by 1979, 436:7, I, eff. July 1, 1979. For present provision prescribing the form of local option questions, see RSA 656:13.

The provisions of RSA 31 and RSA 36 relating to zoning regulations, referred to at the end of this section, were repealed by 1983, 447:5, eff. Jan. 1, 1984. For present provisions relating to zoning regulations, see RSA 674.

Manufactured Housing Foundations

31:116. Manufactured Housing Foundations.

No town shall impose requirements that manufactured housing, as defined by RSA 674:31, which is located in parks be placed on other than the structural carriers designed for that purpose.

Source.

1977, 481:1. 1983, 230:3, eff. Aug. 17, 1983.

Revision note.

Substituted "RSA 674:31" for "RSA 31:118". RSA 31:118 was repealed by 1983, 447:5, III.

Amendments

—1983. Substituted "Manufactured Housing" for "Mobile Home" in the section catchline and "manufactured housing, as defined by RSA 31:118, which is located in parks" for "mobile homes" preceding "be placed" in the text.

Cross References.
Manufactured housing parks generally, see RSA 205-A.

Zoning of manufactured housing, see RSA 674:32.

NOTES TO DECISIONS

Particular foundations
Town building code requiring that mobile homes be set on solid foundations of masonry walls, which conflicted with this section, which clearly and unambiguously prohibits towns from requiring anything in the way of foundation for mobile homes beyond the structural carriers designed for that purpose, was invalid. Town of Nottingham v. Harvey, 120 N.H. 889,

424 A.2d 1125, 1980 N.H. LEXIS 428 (1980).
Under this section, if solid masonry wall was in fact not a "structural carrier" designed for mobile homes, then to extent that injunction was aimed at enforcing the solid-foundation requirement the injunction must be dissolved. Town of Nottingham v. Lee Homes, Inc., 118 N.H. 438, 388 A.2d 940, 1978 N.H. LEXIS 434 (1978).

Validity of Municipal Legislation

Cross References.
Legalization of procedurally defective actions of municipal legislative bodies, see RSA 31:5-b.

31:126. Presumption of Procedural Validity.

Municipal legislation, after 5 years following its enactment, shall, without further curative act of the legislature, be entitled to a conclusive presumption of compliance with statutory enactment procedure. Any claim that municipal legislation is invalid for failure to follow statutory enactment procedure, whether that claim is asserted as part of a cause of action or as a defense to any action, may be asserted within 5 years of the enactment of the legislation and not afterward.

Source.
1988, 33:1, eff. May 23, 1988.

Effect of origin of warrant articles on validity of action, see RSA 31:131.

Cross References.
Effect of non-conforming language on validity of municipal legislation, see RSA 31:130.

31:127. Definitions.

In this subdivision:

I. "Enactment procedure" includes any required notice, copying, filing, service, reporting, publication, posting, public hearing, voting procedure, vote count, ballots, or the form or timing of any of these.

II. "Municipal legislation" means any charter, ordinance, code, bylaw, vote, resolution or regulation enacted by, or any condition or requirement imposed by, a properly authorized official, board, governing body or legislative body of any city, town or village district. It shall not include an "election" as defined in RSA 652:1.

Source.
1988, 33:1, eff. May 23, 1988.

31:128. Certified Copy of Legislation Prima Facie Evidence of Enactment.

A certified copy of the municipal legislation, or a certified code, codification or compilation which includes the legislation, shall constitute prima facie evidence that the legislation was enacted on or prior to the date of certification. Certification shall be by the town or city clerk, or by the official enacting the legislation, or by the chairman, secretary or clerk of the board or body enacting the municipal legislation. The copy or code shall specify, by name or title, which officer, board or body of the municipality enacted the legislation. This method of proving municipal legislation shall not be exclusive.

Source.
1988, 33:1, eff. May 23, 1988.

31:129. Limitation.

This subdivision shall not affect any claim of invalidity which is founded upon the substance of the municipal legislation, or upon the lack of authority of the municipality or its officials, under the federal and state constitutions and laws, to enact such legislation.

Source.
1988, 33:1, eff. May 23, 1988.

31:130. Conformity With Enabling Statute.

The forms of questions prescribed by municipal enabling statutes shall be deemed advisory only, and municipal legislation shall not be declared invalid for failure to conform to the precise wording of any question prescribed for submission to voters, so long as the action taken is within the scope of, and consistent with the intent of, the enabling statute or statutes.

Source.
1991, 113:2, eff. July 13, 1991.

Cross References.
Presumption of procedural validity, see RSA 31:126.

RESEARCH REFERENCES

New Hampshire Practice.
13 N.H.P. Local Government Law § 218.

31:131. Origin of Warrant Articles.

Any question which an enabling statute authorizes to be placed in the warrant for a town meeting by petition may also be inserted by the selectmen, even in the absence of any petition. So long as the subject matter of an action taken at a town meeting was distinctly stated in the warrant, no defect in the process by which such subject matter came to appear in the warrant shall affect the validity of such action.

Source.
1991, 113:2, eff. July 13, 1991.

Cross References.
Presumption of procedural validity, see RSA 31:126.

RESEARCH REFERENCES

New Hampshire Practice.
13 N.H.P. Local Government Law §§ 225, 1284.

Records Storage and Management

31:132. Records Storage.

A municipality may offer storage space for paper records and associated records management services to any agency of the United States government, political subdivisions of the state, and qualified non-profit organizations operating under Internal Revenue Code section 501(c). A municipality, by written agreement, shall establish a rate for service that is no higher than the actual expense of operation and associated capital costs.

Source.
2004, 62:1, eff. May 3, 2004.

31:133. Liability Limitation.

A municipality shall employ the highest standards in record management practices. However, a municipality's liability for loss, damage, delay, improper delivery, or non-delivery shall be limited to the actual value of the storage container and the value of the paper contained within the storage container.

Source.
2004, 62:1, eff. May 3, 2004.

CHAPTER 36

REGIONAL PLANNING COMMISSIONS

Regional Planning Commissions

36:45. Purposes.

The purpose of this subdivision shall be to enable municipalities and counties to join in the formation of regional planning commissions whose duty it shall be to prepare a coordinated plan for the development of a region, taking into account present and future needs with a view toward encouraging the most appropriate use of land, such as for agriculture, forestry, industry, commerce, and housing; the facilitation of transportation and communication; the proper and economic location of public utilities and services; the development of adequate recreational areas; the promotion of good civic design; and the wise and efficient expenditure of public funds. The aforesaid plan shall be made in order to promote the health, safety, morals and general welfare of the region and its inhabitants. To promote these purposes the office of energy and planning shall delineate planning regions for the state so that each municipality of the state will fall within a delineated region and shall have the opportunity of forming or joining the regional planning commission for that planning region. In determining these regions the office shall consider such factors as community of interest and homogeneity, existing metropolitan and regional planning agencies, patterns of communication and transportation, geographic features and natural boundaries, extent of urban development, relevancy of the region for provision of governmental services and functions and its use for administering state and federal programs, the existence of physical, social and economic problems of a regional character, and other related characteristics. To accommodate changing conditions, the office may adjust the boundaries of the planning regions, after consultation with the respective regional planning commissions.

Source.

1969, 324:1, eff. Aug. 29, 1969. 2000, 200:2, eff. July 29, 2000. 2003, 319:9, eff. July 1, 2003. 2004, 257:44, eff. July 1, 2004.

Revision note.

In the third sentence, substituted "office of state planning" for "state office of planning and research of the department of resources and economic development" pursuant to 1970, 53:1.

Amendments

—2004. Substituted "office of energy and

planning" for "office of state planning and energy programs" in the third sentence.

—2003. Substituted "office of state planning and energy programs" for "office of state planning" in the third sentence.

—2000. Added "after consultation with the respective regional planning commissions" at the end of the fifth sentence.

RESEARCH REFERENCES

ALR.

Applicability of zoning regulations to governmental projects or activities. 53 A.L.R.5th 1.

36:46. Formation of Regional Planning Commissions.

I. If no regional planning commission exists in any specific planning region as delineated by the office of energy and planning, then 2 or more municipalities in said planning region and having planning boards may, by ordinance or resolution adopted by the respective legislative bodies of said municipalities, form a regional planning commission.

II. If a regional planning commission already exists in any specific planning region as delineated by the office of energy and planning, then any municipality in said planning region and having a planning board may, by ordinance or resolution adopted by the respective legislative body of said municipality, become a member of the regional planning commission. A regional planning commission may also include municipalities located in an adjacent state.

III. Each municipality which shall become a member of a regional planning commission shall be entitled to 2 representatives on said commission. A municipality with a population of over 10,000 but less than 25,000 shall be entitled to have 3 representatives on said commission and a municipality with a population of over 25,000 shall be entitled to have 4 representatives on said commission. Population as set forth in this section shall be deemed to be determined by the last federal census. Representatives to a regional planning commission shall be nominated by the planning board of each municipality from the residents thereof and shall be appointed by the municipal officers of each municipality. Representatives may be elected or appointed officials of the municipality or county. In any county or counties in which a regional planning commission has been formed, the county may, by resolution of its county commissioners, become a member of said regional planning commission and shall be entitled to appoint 2 representatives on said commission. The terms of office of members of a regional planning commission shall be for 4 years, but initial appointments shall be for 2 and 4 years. In municipalities entitled to 3 or more representatives, initial appointment shall be for 2, 3 and 4 years. Vacancies shall be filled for the remainder of the unexpired term in the same manner as original appointments. Municipalities and counties may also appoint alternate representatives. A representative to a regional planning commission shall, when acting within the scope of his official duties and authority, be deemed to be acting as an agent of both the regional planning commission and of the municipality or county which he represents. In addition, regional planning commissions are encouraged to consult, at their discretion, with agencies and institutions operating within the region whose activities influence planning and development in that region.

Source.
   1969, 324:1. 1991, 72:4, eff. July 12, 1991. 2000, 200:3, eff. July 29, 2000. 2003, 319:9, eff. July 1, 2003. 2004, 257:44, eff. July 1, 2004.

Revision note.
   In pars. I and II, substituted "office of state planning" for "state office of planning and research of the department of resources and economic development" pursuant to 1970, 53:1.

Amendments
   —**2004.** Paragraphs II and II: Substituted "office of energy and planning" for "office of state planning and energy programs".

   —**2003.** Substituted "office of state planning and energy programs" for "office of state planning" in pars. I and II.

   —**2000.** Paragraph III: Added the twelfth sentence.

   —**1991.** Paragraph III: Added the eleventh sentence.

Cross References.
   Liability and indemnification for damages of regional planning commissioners, see RSA 31:104-106.

36:47. General Powers and Duties.

   I. A regional planning commission's powers shall be advisory, and shall generally pertain to the development of the region within its jurisdiction as a whole. Nothing in this subdivision shall be deemed to reduce or limit any of the powers, duties or obligations of planning boards in individual municipalities. The area of jurisdiction of a regional planning commission shall include the areas of the respective municipalities within the delineated planning region. It shall be the duty of a regional planning commission to prepare a comprehensive master plan for the development of the region within its jurisdiction, including the commission's recommendations, among other things, for the use of land within the region; for the general location, extent, type of use, and character of highways, major streets, intersections, parking lots, railroads, aircraft landing areas, waterways and bridges, and other means of transportation, communication, and other purposes; for the development, extent, and general location of parks, playgrounds, shore front developments, parkways, and other public reservations and recreation areas; for the location, type, and character of public buildings, schools, community centers, and other public property; and for the improvement, redevelopment, rehabilitation, or conservation of residential, business, industrial and other areas; including the development of programs for the modernization and coordination of buildings, housing, zoning and subdivision regulations of municipalities and their enforcement on a coordinated and unified basis. A regional planning commission may authorize its employees or consultants to render assistance on local planning problems to any municipality or county which is not a member of said regional planning commission. The cost of such assistance shall be paid entirely by the municipality or county to which the service is rendered or partly by said municipality or county and partly by any gift, grant, or contribution which may be available for such work or by combination thereof. Said commission shall keep a strict account of the cost of such assistance and shall provide such municipality or county with an itemized statement.

II. For the purpose of assisting municipalities in complying with RSA 674:2, III(m), each regional planning commission shall compile a regional housing needs assessment, which shall include an assessment of the regional need for housing for persons and families of all levels of income. The regional housing needs assessment shall be updated every 5 years and made available to all municipalities in the planning region.

III. In preparing a comprehensive plan for the development of the region within its jurisdiction, each regional planning commission may use the framework for the state's comprehensive development plan in RSA 9-A:1, III as the basis for its plan. Such plan shall be updated every 5 years or sooner if desired by the regional planning commission. Prior to its adoption, the plan shall be distributed to every library, planning board, and board of selectmen/aldermen/city council in each of the communities within the region, and to the office of energy and planning. The regional planning commission shall address in writing all comments received prior to the publication of a final draft. A public hearing shall be held by the regional planning commission with 30 days' notice published in all newspapers of general circulation in the region, and shall state where the document can be viewed, the time and place of the public hearing, and shall allow for written comments. For each regional plan, the office of energy and planning shall offer comments as to its consistency with the state plan. The first regional development plans affected by this statute shall be adopted within 5 years of the effective date of this paragraph and renewed at least every 5 years thereafter.

IV. Regional planning commissions shall make a good faith effort to inform and respond to their local communities regarding the purposes and progress of their work in developing the regional development plan.

Source.
1969, 324:1. 1988, 270:2, eff. July 1, 1988. 2002, 178:6, eff. July 14, 2002; 229:8, eff. July 1, 2002. 2003, 319:9, eff. July 1, 2003. 2004, 257:44, eff. July 1, 2004.

Amendments
—2004. Paragraph III: Substituted "office of energy and planning" for "office of state planning and energy programs" in the second and fifth sentences.

—2003. Paragraph III: Substituted "office of state planning and energy programs" for "office of state planning" in the second and fifth sentences.

—2002. Paragraph II: Chapter 178 inserted "(m)" following "RSA 674:2, III" and substituted "an assessment" for "as assessment" in the first sentence.
Paragraphs III and IV: Added by ch. 229.

—1988. Designated existing provisions of section as par. I and added par. II.

RESEARCH REFERENCES

ALR.
Validity, construction, and application of statutes requiring assessment of environmental information prior to grants of entitlements for private land use. 76 A.L.R.3d 388.

36:48. Organization, Officers, and Bylaws.

A regional planning commission shall elect annually from among its members a chairman, vice-chairman, and such other officers as it deems necessary. Meetings shall be held at the call of the chairman and at such other time as the commission may determine. A commission shall keep minutes of its proceedings and such minutes shall be filed in the office of the commission and shall be a public record. A commission may adopt such bylaws as it deems necessary to the conduct of its business.

Source.
1969, 324:1, eff. Aug. 29, 1969.

Cross References.
Access to public records, see RSA 91-A.

36:49. Finances.

A regional planning commission shall determine on a reasonable and equitable basis the proportion of its costs to be borne respectively by each municipality or county which is a member of said commission. A commission may accept and receive in furtherance of its functions, funds, grants, and services from the federal government or its agencies, from departments, agencies and instrumentalities of state, municipal or local government or from private and civic sources. Such funds may be used in conjunction with other funds from federal or state governments or from gifts, grants or contributions available for such work. Municipalities or counties are hereby authorized to appropriate funds to the use of a regional planning commission and to furnish a regional planning commission legal or other services which it may deem reasonable. Failure upon the part of any municipality or county to pay its proportionate annual share of the cost as determined by a regional planning commission shall constitute a termination of such municipality's or county's vote in the commission's affairs until such annual share is paid. Municipalities or counties are hereby authorized to enter into contracts with a regional planning commission for the furnishing of funds or services in connection with the preparation of a comprehensive regional master plan and any special planning work to be done by a regional planning commission for any member municipality or county. Within the amounts appropriated to it or placed at its disposal by gift, grant, or contribution, a regional planning commission may engage employees, contract with professional consultants, rent offices, and obtain such other goods, or services and incur short-term operating debt, not to exceed a term of one year and/or a line of credit secured by the assets of the commission, as are necessary to it in the carrying out of its proper function. Member municipalities and counties shall not be liable for any debt or line of credit incurred by a regional planning commission. Any private gifts or funds when received shall be deemed a contribution to the regional planning commission for a public purpose within the meaning of any federal or state laws relative to tax exemptions.

Source.
1969, 324:1, eff. Aug. 29, 1969. 2000, 200:4, eff. July 29, 2000.

Amendments
—**2000.** In the seventh sentence, inserted

"and incur short-term operating debt, not to exceed a term of one year and/or a line of credit secured by the assets of the commission" preceding "as are necessary to it" and added the eighth sentence.

36:49-a. Status as a Political Subdivision.

Regional planning commissions are political subdivisions of the state. However, regional planning commissions have only that power and authority expressly provided for in RSA 36.

Source.
2000, 200:6, eff. July 29, 2000.

36:50. Relationship To Local Planning Boards.

A regional planning commission may assist the planning board of any municipality within the delineated region to carry out any regional plan or plans developed by said commission. A regional planning commission may also render assistance on local planning problems. A regional planning commission may make recommendations on the basis of its plans and studies to any planning board, to the legislative body of any city and to the selectmen of any town within its region, to the county commissioners of the county or counties in which said region is located and to any state or federal authorities. Upon completion of a comprehensive master plan for the region or any portion of said comprehensive master plan, a regional planning commission may file certified copies of said comprehensive master plan or portion thereof with the planning board of any member municipality. Such planning boards may adopt all or any part of such comprehensive master plan which pertains to the areas within its jurisdiction as its own master plan, subject to the requirements of RSA 674:1-4.

Source.
1969, 324:1, eff. Aug. 29, 1969. 2000, 200:5, eff. July 29, 2000.

tions 13, 14, and 15, chapter 36 of the Revised Statutes Annotated" at the end of the fifth sentence.

Amendments
—**2000.** Substituted "RSA 674:1-4" for "sec-

36:51. Assistance to Urban Renewal by Municipalities and Other Public Bodies.
[Repealed 2000, 200:8, I, eff. July 29, 2000.]

Former section(s).
Former RSA 36:51, relating to assistance to

urban renewal by municipalities and other public bodies, was derived from 1969, 324:1.

36:52. Workable Programs.

[Repealed 2000, 200:8, II, eff. July 29, 2000.]

Former section(s).
  Former RSA 36:52, which was derived from
1969, 324:1, related to workable programs.

36:53. Additional Powers and Duties of Regional Planning Commissions.

In order to implement any of the provisions of a regional plan, which has been adopted or is in preparation, a regional planning commission may, in addition to its powers and duties under RSA 36:47 undertake studies and make specific recommendations on economic, industrial and commercial development within the region and carry out, with the cooperation of municipalities and/or counties within the region, economic development programs for the full development, improvement, protection and preservation of the region's physical and human resources.

Source.
  1969, 324:1, eff. Aug. 29, 1969.

Revision note.
  Substituted "RSA 36:47" for "section 47" to conform reference to citation style of LEXIS New Hampshire Revised Statutes Annotated.

Review of Developments of Regional Impact

Cross References.
  Planning and zoning generally, see RSA 672 et seq.

Regional planning commissions, see RSA 36:45 et seq.

36:54. Purpose.

The purpose of this subdivision is to:

I. Provide timely notice to potentially affected municipalities concerning proposed developments which are likely to have impacts beyond the boundaries of a single municipality.

II. Provide opportunities for the regional planning commission and the potentially affected municipalities to furnish timely input to the municipality having jurisdiction.

III. Encourage the municipality having jurisdiction to consider the interests of other potentially affected municipalities.

Source.
  1991, 300:1, eff. Jan. 1, 1992.

36:55. Definition.

In this subdivision "development of regional impact" means any proposal before a local land use board which in the determination of such local land use board could reasonably be expected to impact on a neighboring municipality, because of factors such as, but not limited to, the following:

I. Relative size or number of dwelling units as compared with existing stock.

II. Proximity to the borders of a neighboring community.

III. Transportation networks.

IV. Anticipated emissions such as light, noise, smoke, odors, or particles.

V. Proximity to aquifers or surface waters which transcend municipal boundaries.

VI. Shared facilities such as schools and solid waste disposal facilities.

Source.
1991, 300:1, eff. Jan. 1, 1992.

RESEARCH REFERENCES

New Hampshire Practice.
15 N.H.P. Land Use Planning and Zoning §§ 28.09, 29.12, 32.04.

36:56. Review Required.

A local land use board, as defined in RSA 672:7, upon receipt of an application for development, shall review it promptly and determine whether or not the development, if approved, reasonably could be construed as having the potential for regional impact. Doubt concerning regional impact shall be resolved in a determination that the development has a potential regional impact.

Source.
1991, 300:1, eff. Jan. 1, 1992.

RESEARCH REFERENCES

New Hampshire Practice.
15 N.H.P. Land Use Planning and Zoning § 21.12.

36:57. Procedure.

I. Upon determination that a proposed development has a potential regional impact, the local land use board having jurisdiction shall afford the regional planning commission and the affected municipalities the status of abutters as defined in RSA 672:3 for the limited purpose of providing notice and giving testimony.

II. Within 144 hours of reaching a decision regarding a development of regional impact, the local land use board having jurisdiction shall, by certified mail, furnish the regional planning commission and the affected municipalities with copies of the minutes of the meeting at which the decision was made. The local land use board shall, at the same time, submit an initial set of plans to the regional planning commission, the cost of which shall be borne by the applicant.

III. At least 14 days prior to public hearing, the local land use board shall notify, by certified mail, all affected municipalities and the regional planning commission of the date, time, and place of the hearing and their right to testify concerning the development.

Source.
1991, 300:1, eff. Jan. 1, 1992. 2003, 220:1, eff. Aug. 30, 2003. 2005, 39:1, eff. July 16, 2005.

Amendments
—2005. Paragraph II: Substituted "144 hours" for "72 hours" in the first sentence.

—2003. Paragraph II: Added the second sentence.

NOTES TO DECISIONS

Construction
Town notified abutting towns of pending public hearings on retail mall, and notice specifically informed abutter towns that it served as notice with respect to potential regional impact and that abutter towns were legally entitled to attend hearing and offer input; abutter towns thus received proper statutory notice of potential regional impact, notwithstanding fact that town failed to mail minutes of hearing to abutter towns. Mountain Valley Mall Assocs. v. Municipality of Conway, 144 N.H. 642, 745 A.2d 481, 2000 N.H. LEXIS 1 (2000).

RESEARCH REFERENCES

New Hampshire Practice.
15 N.H.P. Land Use Planning and Zoning §§ 21.12-21.14, 29.12, 32.04.

36:58. Applicability.

The provisions of this subdivision shall supersede any contrary or inconsistent provisions of local land use regulations enacted under RSA 155-E and RSA 674.

Source.
1991, 300:1, eff. Jan. 1, 1992.

CHAPTER 36-A

CONSERVATION COMMISSIONS

Cross References.

Connecticut River Valley resource commission, see RSA 227-E.

Land conservation investment program, see RSA 162-C:6 et seq.

Soil conservation and farmland preservation, see RSA 432.

NOTES TO DECISIONS

Cited:

Cited in Claridge v. New Hampshire Wetlands Board, 125 N.H. 745, 485 A.2d 287, 1984 N.H. LEXIS 307 (1984).

36-A:1. Method of Adoption.

Any city by vote of its city council, and any town at any duly warned meeting, may adopt the provisions of this chapter.

Source.

1963, 168:1, eff. Aug. 20, 1963.

36-A:2. Conservation Commission.

A city or town which accepts the provisions of this chapter may establish a conservation commission, hereinafter called the commission, for the proper utilization and protection of the natural resources and for the protection of watershed resources of said city or town. Such commission shall conduct researches into its local land and water areas and shall seek to coordinate the activities of unofficial bodies organized for similar purposes, and may advertise, prepare, print and distribute books, maps, charts, plans and pamphlets which in its judgment it deems necessary for its work. It shall keep an index of all open space and natural, aesthetic or ecological areas within the city or town, as the case may be, with the plan of obtaining information pertinent to proper utilization of such areas, including lands owned by the state or lands owned by a town or city. It shall keep an index of all marshlands, swamps and all other wet lands in a like manner, and may recommend to the city council or selectmen or to the department of resources and economic development a program for the protection, development or better utilization of all such areas. It shall keep accurate records of its meetings and actions and shall file an annual report which shall be printed in the annual town or municipal report.

The commission may appoint such clerks and other employees or subcommittees as it may from time to time require.

Source.
1963, 168:1. 1973, 550:1, eff. Sept. 3, 1973.

Amendments
—1973. Rewritten to the extent that a detailed comparison would be impracticable.

36-A:3. Composition of Commission.

The commission shall consist of not less than 3 nor more than 7 members. In a town which has a planning board, one member of the commission may also be on the planning board. In a city which has a planning board, one member of the commission may be on the planning board. In cities, the members of the commission shall be appointed by the mayor subject to the provisions of the city charter, and in towns the members of the commission shall be appointed by the selectmen. Alternate members may be appointed in a like manner and when the alternate serves in the absence or disqualification of a regular member, the alternate shall have full voting powers. When a commission is first established, terms of the members shall be for one, 2, or 3 years, and so arranged that the terms of approximately ⅓ of the members will expire each year, and their successors shall be appointed for terms of 3 years each. Any member of a commission so appointed may, after a public hearing, if requested, be removed for cause by the appointing authority. A vacancy occurring otherwise than by expiration of a term shall be filled for the unexpired term in the same manner as an original appointment. Members of a conservation commission shall be residents of the city or town which they represent. Members of a conservation commission also may serve on other municipal boards and commissions, including, but not limited to a historic district commission established under RSA 673:4, and a heritage commission established under RSA 673:4-a.

Source.
1963, 168:1. 1973, 550:2. 1974, 44:2. 1987, 318:1. 1995, 138:1, eff. July 23, 1995. 1997, 31:1, eff. June 27, 1997.

Amendments
—1997. Added the next to last sentence.

—1995. Substituted "the alternate" for "his" following "regular member" in the fifth sentence and added the last sentence.

—1987. Inserted the fifth sentence and made other minor stylistic changes.

—1974. Rewrote the second sentence, inserted the third sentence, deleted "remaining" following "cities, the" and following "towns the" in the fourth sentence and inserted "of the commission" preceding "shall be appointed by the selectmen" at the end of that sentence.

—1973. Inserted the second sentence and "remaining" following "cities, the" in the third sentence and following "terms of the" in the fourth sentence and substituted "the remaining members" for "they" following "towns" in the third sentence.

36-A:4. Powers.

Said commission may receive gifts of money and property, both real and personal, in the name of the city or town, subject to the approval of the local governing body, such gifts to be managed and controlled by the commission for the purposes of this section. Said commission may acquire in the name of the town or city, subject to the approval of the local governing body, by gift, purchase, grant, bequest, devise, lease, or otherwise, the fee in such land or water rights, or any lesser interest, development right, easement, covenant, or other contractual right including conveyances with conditions, limitations or reversions, as may be necessary to acquire, maintain, improve, protect, or limit the future use of or otherwise conserve and properly utilize open spaces and other land and water areas within their city or town, and shall manage and control the same, but the city or town or commission shall not have the right to condemn property for these purposes.

Source.
1963, 168:1. 1973, 550:3. 1995, 138:2, eff. July 23, 1995.

—1973. Inserted "in the name of the town or city" following "acquire" in the second sentence.

Amendments
—1995. Substituted "local governing body" for "city council in a city or the selectmen in a town" in the first sentence and inserted "subject to the approval of the local governing body" preceding "by gift" in the second sentence.

Cross References.
Acquisition of trails by conservation commission, see RSA 231-A:5.

RESEARCH REFERENCES

ALR.
Local use zoning of wetlands or flood plains

as taking without compensation. 19 A.L.R.4th 756.

36-A:5. Appropriations Authorized.

I. A town or city, having established a conservation commission as authorized by RSA 36-A:2, may appropriate money as deemed necessary for the purpose of this chapter. The whole or any part of money so appropriated in any year and any gifts of money received pursuant to RSA 36-A:4 may be placed in a conservation fund and allowed to accumulate from year to year. Money may be expended from said fund by the conservation commission for the purposes of this chapter without further approval of the town meeting.

II. The town treasurer, pursuant to RSA 41:29, shall have custody of all moneys in the conservation fund and shall pay out the same only upon order of the conservation commission. The disbursement of conservation funds shall be authorized by a majority of the conservation commission. Prior to the use of such funds for the purchase of any interest in real property, the conservation commission shall hold a public hearing with notice in accordance with RSA 675:7.

III. In the municipality that has adopted the provisions of RSA 79-A:25, II, the specified percentage of the revenues received pursuant to RSA 79-A shall be placed in the conservation fund.

Source.
1963, 168:1. 1973, 550:4. 1987, 318:2. 1988, 120:1, eff. June 18, 1988.

Amendments
—**1988.** Paragraph III: Added.

—**1987.** Designated the existing provisions of the section as par. I, in that paragraph rewrote the first sentence, inserted "and any gifts of money received pursuant to RSA 36-

A:4" preceding "may be placed" in the second sentence and "by the conservation commission" preceding "for the purposes of this chapter" and "without further approval of the town meeting" thereafter in the third sentence, and added par. II.

—**1973.** Deleted "development and" preceding "better utilization" in the first sentence.

36-A:6. Commissioner of Resources and Economic Development.

The commissioner of the department of resources and economic development may establish a program to assist, at their request, the cities and towns which have adopted the provisions of this chapter, in acquiring land and in planning of use and structures as described in RSA 36-A:2.

Source.
1963, 168:1, eff. Aug. 20, 1963.

Revision note.
At the end of the section, substituted "RSA

36-A:2" for "section 2" to conform reference to citation style of LEXIS New Hampshire Revised Statutes Annotated.

CHAPTER 39

TIME FOR HOLDING TOWN MEETINGS AND WARNING THEREOF

39:3. Articles.

Upon the written application of 25 or more registered voters or 2 percent of the registered voters in town, whichever is less, although in no event shall fewer than 10 registered voters be sufficient, presented to the selectmen or one of them not later than the fifth Tuesday before the day prescribed for an annual meeting, the selectmen shall insert in their warrant for such meeting the petitioned article with only such minor textual changes as may be required. For the purposes of this section, the number of registered voters in a town shall be the number of voters registered prior to the last state general election. The right to have an article inserted in the warrant conferred by this section shall not be invalidated by the provisions of RSA 32. In towns with fewer than 10,000 inhabitants upon the written application of 50 or more voters or ¼ of the voters in town, whichever is fewer, and in towns with 10,000 or more inhabitants upon the written application of 5 percent of the registered voters in the town, so presented not less than 60 days before the next annual meeting, the selectmen shall warn a special meeting to act upon any question specified in such application. The checklist for an annual or special town meeting shall be corrected by the supervisors of the checklist as provided in RSA 654:25-31. Those persons qualified to vote whose names are on the corrected checklist shall be entitled to vote at the meeting. The same checklist used at a recessed town meeting shall be used at any reconvened session of the same town meeting. In no event shall a special town meeting be held on the biennial election day.

Source.
RS 32:3. CS 34:3. GS 35:3. GL 38:3. PS 41:3. PL 45:3. 1937, 40:1. RL 57:3. 1947, 21:1. RSA 39:3. 1969, 59:1. 1971, 79:1. 1975, 160:1. 1981, 454:1. 1987, 299:1. 1990, 192:1. 1991, 223:1; 370:5. 1994, 197:1, eff. July 23, 1994. 1998. 194:1, eff. Aug. 17, 1998.

Amendments
—1998. Deleted "except that the session 3 weeks before the meeting shall not be required" following "RSA 654:25-31" in the fifth sentence.

—1994. In the fourth sentence, added "in towns with fewer than 10,000 inhabitants" preceding "upon" at the beginning of the sentence and inserted "and in towns with 10,000 or more inhabitants upon the written application of 5 percent of the registered voters in the town" preceding "so presented".

—1991. Chapter 223 inserted "although in no event shall fewer than 10 registered voters be sufficient" preceding "presented" in the first sentence.

Chapter 370 deleted "or biennial" following "annual" in the first sentence and added the eighth sentence.

—1990. Substituted "25" for "10", inserted "registered" preceding "voters" in two places, and substituted "2 percent" for "⅛" and "less" for "fewer" preceding "presented" in the first sentence and added the second sentence.

—1987. Substituted "not later than the fifth

66

Tuesday" for "at least 35 days" preceding "before the day" in the first sentence.

—1981. Rewritten to the extent that a detailed comparison would be impracticable.

—1975. Substituted "the petitioned article with only such minor textual changes as may be required" for "any subject specified in such application" following "such meeting" at the end of the first sentence.

—1971. Added the fourth sentence.

—1969. Substituted "thirty-five" for "twenty-five" preceding "days" in the first sentence.

Cross References.
Abolition of planning board or zoning commission, see RSA 39:3-c.
Application to court for insertion of article in warrant, see RSA 39:9.
Consideration of warrant articles in towns with 10,000 or more inhabitants, see RSA 40:11.
Penalty for refusal to insert article in warrant, see RSA 39:3-b.
Publication of warrant for special town meeting, see RSA 39:4.

NOTES TO DECISIONS

Analysis

1. Insertion of articles
2. Subject of articles
3. Special meetings

1. Insertion of articles

Selectmen have no discretion whether to insert in a warrant an article presented to them in compliance with this section. Woodside v. Selectmen of Derry, 116 N.H. 606, 366 A.2d 210, 1976 N.H. LEXIS 424 (1976).

2. Subject of articles

This section is of general but not all-inclusive application and is not applicable where the legislature has treated a subject specified in an application in a special, exclusive and different manner. Town of Seabrook v. Perkins, 112 N.H. 37, 288 A.2d 688, 1972 N.H. LEXIS 138 (1972).

3. Special meetings

Town selectmen may exercise a certain amount of judgment in determining whether to schedule a special town meeting when petitioned to do so by voters, but selectmen do not have unbridled discretion to frustrate the voters' attempts to call a special town meeting. Winchester Taxpayers' Ass'n v. Board of Selectmen, 118 N.H. 144, 383 A.2d 1125, 1978 N.H. LEXIS 361 (1978).

Town selectmen are under no obligation to warn a special meeting if the issue to be considered is prohibited or limited in scope by statute. Winchester Taxpayers' Ass'n v. Board of Selectmen, 118 N.H. 144, 383 A.2d 1125, 1978 N.H. LEXIS 361 (1978).

Where selectmen of town had been empowered to sell and convey certain town land and had advertised sale by public auction to be held on specified date, there was no requirement as matter of law that selectmen postpone the sale and call special town meeting to see if town would vote to retain such land where petition by requisite number of voters under provisions of this section was filed within four days of date of sale and sufficient time did not permit compliance with the notice requirements of RSA 39:4 and 39:5. Preston v. Gillam, 104 N.H. 279, 184 A.2d 462, 1962 N.H. LEXIS 68 (1926).

Cited:
Cited in Curtis v. Berry, 68 N.H. 18, 40 A. 393, 1894 N.H. LEXIS 9 (1894); Moulton v. Beals, 98 N.H. 461, 102 A.2d 489, 1954 N.H. LEXIS 88 (1954); McDonnell v. Town of Derry, 116 N.H. 3, 350 A.2d 620, 1976 N.H. LEXIS 247 (1976); Levasseur v. Board of Selectmen of Hudson, 116 N.H. 340, 358 A.2d 665, 1976 N.H. LEXIS 349 (1976).

RESEARCH REFERENCES

New Hampshire Practice.
15 N.H.P. Land Use Planning and Zoning § 35.14.

39:3-b. Penalty.

A board of selectmen is guilty of a violation if it refuses to insert an article in the warrant, after being petitioned to do so in accordance with RSA 39:3.

Source.
1971, 79:4. 1977, 588:26, eff. Sept. 16, 1977.

Amendments
—**1977.** Rewritten to the extent that a detailed comparison would be impracticable.

Cross References.
Classification of crimes, see RSA 625:9.
Penalty for failure to give notice of meeting or election, see RSA 39:13.
Sentences, see RSA 651.

NOTES TO DECISIONS

Cited:
Cited in Town of Seabrook v. Perkins, 112 N.H. 37, 288 A.2d 688, 1972 N.H. LEXIS 138 (1972); Woodside v. Selectmen of Derry, 116 N.H. 606, 366 A.2d 210, 1976 N.H. LEXIS 424 (1976); Winchester Taxpayers' Ass'n v. Board of Selectmen, 118 N.H. 144, 383 A.2d 1125, 1978 N.H. LEXIS 361 (1978).

39:3-c. Limitation.

Any petitioned article, which if adopted, would abolish a planning board, or zoning commission shall not be included in the warrant, unless such petition meets the requirements established by RSA 673:18, II.

Source.
1971, 396:1. 1985, 103:1, eff. Jan. 1, 1986.

Amendments
—**1985.** Substituted "RSA 673:18, II" for "RSA 31:63-c" following "established by".

CHAPTER 40

GOVERNMENT OF TOWN MEETING

**Optional Form of Meeting—Official
Ballot Referenda**

Section
40:13.   Use of Official Ballot.

Optional Form of Meeting—Official Ballot Referenda

40:13. Use of Official Ballot.

I. Notwithstanding RSA 39:3-d, RSA 40:4-e, or any other provision of law, any local political subdivision as defined in RSA 40:12 which has adopted this subdivision shall utilize the official ballot for voting on all issues before the voters.

II. The warrant for any annual meeting shall prescribe the place, day and hour for each of 2 separate sessions of the meeting, and notice shall be given as otherwise provided in this section. Final budgets and ballot questions shall be printed in the annual report made available to the legislative body at least one week before the date of the second session of the annual meeting.

II-a. Notwithstanding any other provision of law, all local political subdivisions which adopt this subdivision, who have not adopted an April or May election date under RSA 40:14, X, shall comply with the following schedule pertaining to notice, petitioned articles, hearings, and warrants for the annual meeting:

(a) The final date for posting notice of budget hearings under RSA 32:5 and RSA 195:12 and hearings under RSA 33:8-a shall be the second Tuesday in January.

(b) The "budget submission date" as defined in RSA 273-A:1, III and the final date for submission of petitioned articles under RSA 39:3 and RSA 197:6 shall be the second Tuesday in January.

(c) Budget hearings under RSA 32:5 and RSA 195:12 and hearings under RSA 33:8-a and RSA 675:3 shall be held on or before the third Tuesday in January.

(d) Warrants under RSA 39:5 and RSA 197:7 and budgets shall be posted and copies available to the general public on or before the last Monday in January.

II-b. Notwithstanding any other provision of law, all political subdivisions which hold their annual meetings in April shall comply with the following schedule pertaining to notice, petitioned articles, hearings, and warrants for the annual meeting.

(a) The final date for posting notice of budget hearings under RSA 32:5 and RSA 195:12 and hearings under RSA 33:8-a shall be the second Tuesday in February.

69

(b) The "budget submission date" as defined in RSA 273-A:1, III and the final date for submission of petitioned articles under RSA 39:3 and RSA 197:6 shall be the second Tuesday in February.

(c) Budget hearings under RSA 32:5 and RSA 195:12 and hearings under RSA 33:8-a and RSA 675:3 shall be held on or before the third Tuesday in February.

(d) Warrants under RSA 39:5 and RSA 197:7 and budgets shall be posted and copies available to the general public on or before the last Monday in February.

II-c. Notwithstanding any other provision of law, all political subdivisions which hold their annual meetings in May shall comply with the following schedule pertaining to notice, petitioned articles, hearings, and warrants for the annual meeting:

(a) The final date for posting notice of budget hearings under RSA 32:5 and RSA 195:12 and hearings under RSA 33:8-a shall be the second Tuesday in March.

(b) The "budget submission date" as defined in RSA 273-A:1, III and the final date for submission of petitioned articles under RSA 39:3 and RSA 197:6 shall be the second Tuesday in March.

(c) Budget hearings under RSA 32:5 and RSA 195:12 and hearings under RSA 33:8-a and RSA 675:3 shall be held on or before the third Tuesday in March.

(d) Warrants under RSA 39:5 and RSA 197:7 and budgets shall be posted and copies available to the general public on or before the last Monday in March.

II-d. The voter checklist shall be updated in accordance with RSA 669:5 for each session of the annual meeting.

III. The first session of the annual meeting, which shall be for the transaction of all business other than voting by official ballot, shall be held between the first and second Saturdays following the last Monday in January, inclusive of those Saturdays; between the first and second Saturdays following the last Monday in February, inclusive of those Saturdays; or between the first and second Saturdays following the last Monday in March, inclusive of those Saturdays at a time prescribed by the local political subdivision's governing body.

IV. The first session of the meeting, governed by the provisions of RSA 40:4, 40:4-a, 40:4-b, 40:4-f, and 40:6-40:10, shall consist of explanation, discussion, and debate of each warrant article. A vote to restrict reconsideration shall be deemed to prohibit any further action on the restricted article until the second session, and RSA 40:10, II shall not apply. Warrant articles may be amended at the first session, subject to the following limitations:

(a) Warrant articles whose wording is prescribed by law shall not be amended.

(b) Warrant articles that are amended shall be placed on the official ballot for a final vote on the main motion, as amended.

V. [Repealed.]

V-a. Any town may vote to require that all votes by an advisory budget committee, a town budget committee, and the governing body or, in towns without a budget committee, all votes of the governing body relative to budget items or warrant articles shall be recorded votes and the numerical tally of any such vote shall be printed in the town warrant next to the affected warrant article.

VI. All warrant articles shall be placed on the official ballot for a final vote, including warrant articles as amended by the first session. All special warrant articles shall be accompanied on the ballot by recommendations as required by RSA 32:5, V, concerning any appropriation or appropriation as amended.

VII. The second session of the annual meeting, to elect officers of the local political subdivision by official ballot, to vote on questions required by law to be inserted on said official ballot, and to vote on all warrant articles from the first session on official ballot, shall be held on the second Tuesday in March, the second Tuesday in April, or the second Tuesday in May, as applicable. Notwithstanding RSA 669:1, 670:1, or 671:2, the second session shall be deemed the annual election date for purposes of all applicable election statutes including, but not limited to, RSA 669:5, 669:19, 669:30, 670:3, 670:4, 670:11, 671:15, 671:19, and 671:30 through 32; and votes on zoning ordinances, historic district ordinances, and building codes under RSA 675.

VIII. The clerk of the local political subdivision shall prepare an official ballot, which may be separate from the official ballot used to elect officers, for all warrant articles. Wording shall be substantively the same as the main motion, as it was made or amended at the first session, with only such minor textual changes as may be required to cast the motion in the form of a question to the voters.

IX. (a) "Operating budget" as used in this subdivision means "budget," as defined in RSA 32:3, III, exclusive of "special warrant articles," as defined in RSA 32:3, VI, and exclusive of other appropriations voted separately.

(b) "Default budget" as used in this subdivision means the amount of the same appropriations as contained in the operating budget authorized for the previous year, reduced and increased, as the case may be, by debt service, contracts, and other obligations previously incurred or mandated by law, and reduced by one-time expenditures contained in the operating budget. For the purposes of this paragraph, one-time expenditures shall be appropriations not likely to recur in the succeeding budget, as determined by the governing body, unless the provisions of RSA 40:14-b are adopted, of the local political subdivision.

X. If no operating budget article is adopted, the local political subdivision either shall be deemed to have approved the default budget or the governing body may hold a special meeting pursuant to paragraph XVI to take up the issue of a revised operating budget only; provided that RSA 31:5 and RSA 197:3 shall not apply to such a special meeting. If no operating budget article is adopted the estimated revenues shall nevertheless be deemed to have been approved.

XI. (a) The default budget shall be disclosed at the first budget hearing held pursuant to RSA 32:5 or RSA 197:6. The governing body, unless the provisions of RSA 40:14-b are adopted, shall complete a default budget form created by the department of revenue administration to demonstrate how the default budget amount was calculated. The form and associated calculations shall, at a minimum, include the following:

(1) Appropriations contained in the previous year's operating budget;

(2) Reductions and increases to the previous year's operating budget; and

(3) One-time expenditures as defined under subparagraph IX(b).

(b) This amount shall not be amended by the legislative body. However, this amount may be adjusted by the governing body, unless the provisions of RSA 40:14-b are adopted, acting on relevant new information at any time before the ballots are printed, provided the governing body, unless the provisions of RSA 40:14-b are adopted, completes an amended default budget form.

(c) The wording of the second session ballot question concerning the operating budget shall be as follows:

"Shall the (local political subdivision) raise and appropriate as an operating budget, not including appropriations by special warrant articles and other appropriations voted separately, the amounts set forth on the budget posted with the warrant or as amended by vote of the first session, for the purposes set forth therein, totaling $_____? Should this article be defeated, the default budget shall be $_____, which is the same as last year, with certain adjustments required by previous action of the (local political subdivision) or by law; or the governing body may hold one special meeting, in accordance with RSA 40:13, X and XVI, to take up the issue of a revised operating budget only."

XII. Voting at the second session shall conform to the procedures for the nonpartisan ballot system as set forth in RSA 669:19-29, RSA 670:5-7 and RSA 671:20-30, including all requirements pertaining to absentee voting, polling place, and polling hours.

XIII. Approval of all warrant articles shall be by simple majority except for questions which require a ⅔ vote by law, contract, or written agreement.

XIV. Votes taken at the second session shall be subject to recount under RSA 669:30-33 and RSA 40:4-c.

XV. Votes taken at the second session shall not be reconsidered.

XVI. The warrant for any special meeting shall prescribe the date, place and hour for both a first and second session. The second session shall be warned for a date not fewer than 28 days nor more than 60 days following the first session. The first and second sessions shall conform to the provisions of this subdivision pertaining to the first and second sessions of annual meetings. Special meetings shall be subject to RSA 31:5, 39:3, 195:13, 197:2, and 197:3, provided that no more than one special meeting may be held to raise and appropriate money for the same question or issue in any one calendar year or fiscal year, whichever applies, and further provided that any special meeting held pursuant to paragraphs X and XI shall not be subject to RSA 31:5 and RSA 197:3 and shall not be counted toward the number of special meetings which may be held in a given calendar or fiscal year.

Source.

1995, 164:1, eff. July 31, 1995. 1996, 276:1, 2, eff. June 10, 1996. 1997, 318:4, 5, 12, eff. Aug. 22, 1997. 1999, 86:1-3, eff. Aug. 2, 1999. 2000, 16:2-5, eff. April 30, 2000. 2001, 71:5-7, eff. July 1, 2001. 2004, 219:1, eff. Aug. 10, 2004. 2007, 305:2, eff. September 11, 2007.

Editor's note.

The introductory paragraph of par. II-a is set out to correct an error as it appears in the 1999 supplement.

Amendments

—2007. Paragraph V-a: Added.

—2004. Paragraph IX: Designated the existing provision as subpar. (a) and added subpar. (b).

Paragraph X: Rewrote the first sentence and deleted the second sentence.

Paragraph XI: Rewritten to the extent that a detailed comparison would be impracticable.

—2001. Paragraph II-a: Substituted "second Tuesday" for "first Tuesday" in subpar. (a).

Paragraph II-b: Substituted "second Tuesday" for "first Tuesday" in subpar. (a).

Paragraph II-c: Substituted "second Tuesday" for "first Tuesday" in subpar. (a).

—2000. Paragraph II: Substituted "as otherwise provided in this section" for "in accordance with paragraph II-a" following "given" in the first sentence and added the second sentence.

Paragraph II-a: Inserted "who have not adopted an April or May election date under RSA 40:14, X" following "subdivision" in the introductory paragraph.

Paragraphs II-a—II-d: Added.

Paragraph III: Inserted "between the first and second Saturdays following the last Monday in February, inclusive of those Saturdays; or between the first and second Saturdays following the last Monday in March, inclusive of those Saturdays" preceding "at a time prescribed".

Paragraph VII: Inserted "the second Tuesday in April, or the second Tuesday in May, as applicable" following "March" in the first sentence.

—1999. Paragraph IV: Rewritten to the extent that a detailed comparison would be impracticable.

Paragraph VI: Added "including warrant articles as amended by the first session" following "final vote" in the first sentence.

Paragraph IX: Added "and exclusive of other appropriations voted separately" following "RSA 32:3, VI".

Paragraph X: Inserted "or reduced by one-time expenditures contained in the operating budget" following "mandated by law" in the first sentence and added the third sentence.

Paragraph XI: Inserted "and other appropriations voted separately" following "warrant articles" and made a minor change in punctuation in the second session ballot question.

—1997. Rewritten to the extent that a detailed comparison would be impracticable.

—1996. Paragraph X: Deleted "notwithstanding any requirement for court petition" preceding "to take up the issue", and added "provided that RSA 31:5 and 197:3 shall not apply to such a special meeting" in the first sentence.

Paragraph XVI: Rewrote the former fourth and fifth sentences as the fourth sentence.

Applicability of 1997 amendment.

1997, 318:13, eff. Aug. 22, 1997, provided: "This act [which amended this section and RSA 31:5; 32:13, 39:2-a, 40:14, 197:1 and 197:3, and added RSA 40:15], shall apply to all local political subdivisions, as defined in RSA 40:20, which adopt RSA 40:13 on or after June 30, 1995."

NOTES TO DECISIONS

Transfer of Funds In Default Budget Proper

When voters failed to pass an operating budget, selectmen in implementing a default budget had the discretionary authority under RSA 32:10(I) to transfer funds within a previously adopted budget, and the 2004 amendment to RSA 40:13 did not restrict this authority. Failure to pass an operating budget was a sufficient change in circumstances to justify the use of the authority, and the transfers, which had not increased the bottom line, did not amount to a revised operating budget under § 40:13. Sullivan v. Town of Hampton Bd. of Selectmen, 153 N.H. 690, 917 A.2d 188, 2006 N.H. LEXIS 93 (2006).

Cited:
Cited in Opinion of the Justices (Municiple Bonds), 145 N.H. 680, 765 A.2d 706, 2001 N.H. LEXIS 6 (2001).

CHAPTER 43

HEARINGS BEFORE TOWN OR CERTAIN OTHER LOCAL OFFICERS

NOTES TO DECISIONS

School boards

This chapter did not apply to hearings, under RSA 189:14-a, before school board on teacher's failure to be renominated to teach the coming year. Farrelly v. Timberlane Regional School District, 114 N.H. 560, 324 A.2d 723, 1974 N.H. LEXIS 323 (1974); Hawthorne v. Dresden School District, 114 N.H. 567, 324 A.2d 728, 1974 N.H. LEXIS 324 (1974).

Cited:

Cited in Merrill v. City of Manchester, 124 N.H. 8, 466 A.2d 923, 1983 N.H. LEXIS 352 (1983).

RESEARCH REFERENCES

New Hampshire Practice.

13 N.H.P. Local Government Law § 551 et seq.

43:1. Hearings by Selectmen.

On petition to the selectmen for the laying out or altering of highways, or for laying out lands for any public use, and generally for the purpose of deciding any question affecting the conflicting rights or claims of different persons, their proceedings shall be governed by the following rules.

Source.

GS 233:1. GL 43:1. PS 45:1. PL 49:1. RL 61:1.

NOTES TO DECISIONS

Cited:

Cited in Lenoix v. Dover, Somersworth & Rochester Street Railway, 72 N.H. 58, 54 A. 1022, 1903 N.H. LEXIS 11 (1903).

43:2. Notice of Hearing.

They shall appoint a time and place of hearing, and order notice thereof to be given to all persons whose property or rights may be directly affected by the proceeding, by giving to them or leaving at their abode an attested copy of the petition and order 14 days at least before such hearing, or, if such persons are nonresidents, by publication. If the owner is under guardianship such notice shall be given to his guardian. If the owner is a minor, or under any legal disability, the judge of probate may appoint a guardian for such person, to whom notice shall be given.

Source.
RS 49:3. CS 52:3. GS 233:2. 1870, 28:1. GL 43:2. PS 45:2. PL 49:2. RL 61:2.

NOTES TO DECISIONS

Analysis

1. Failure to notify
2. Waiver

1. Failure to notify
One to whom notice of hearing was not given and who did not appear is not bound by the determination of fence viewers. Davis v. Hazen, 61 N.H. 383, 1881 N.H. LEXIS 84 (1881), overruled, Horne v. Rochester, 62 N.H. 347, 1882 N.H. LEXIS 69 (1882).

2. Waiver
Appearance without objection to the sufficiency of notice is a waiver of all right to notice and of all exceptions to the regularity of issuing it. School Dist. v. Carr, 55 N.H. 452, 1875 N.H. LEXIS 109 (1875).

Cited:
Cited in Lyford v. Laconia, 75 N.H. 220, 72 A. 1085, 1909 N.H. LEXIS 20, 22 L.R.A. (n.s.) 1062 (1909); Worthen v. Kingsbury, 84 N.H. 304, 149 A. 869, 1930 N.H. LEXIS 83 (1930).

43:3. Posting of Notice.

Notice shall be given to all other persons interested by posting a like copy in one of the most public places in the town or district affected by the petition, and by leaving a like copy at the abode of the clerk of such town or district a like time before the hearing.

Source.
GS 233:3. 1878, 7:1. GL 43:3. PS 45:3. PL 49:3. RL 61:3.

NOTES TO DECISIONS

Failure to post notice
The laying out of a highway by selectmen, upon petition and a hearing before them, is a judgment which cannot be attacked collaterally on account of a failure to order notice by posting a copy of the petition and order of notice, and serving a like copy on the town clerk, as required by this section. Horne v. Rochester, 62 N.H. 347, 1882 N.H. LEXIS 69 (1882).

Cited:
Cited in Lenoix v. Dover, Somersworth & Rochester Street Railway, 72 N.H. 58, 54 A. 1022, 1903 N.H. LEXIS 11 (1903); Worthen v. Kingsbury, 84 N.H. 304, 149 A. 869, 1930 N.H. LEXIS 83 (1930).

43:4. Hearing; Record.

They shall hear all parties who desire to be heard, and examine them and their witnesses under oath, which either of the selectmen may administer; they may adjourn when they deem it necessary; and they shall make their decision in writing, and cause the petition, order of notice, evidence of service and their decision to be filed in the town clerk's office and recorded at length upon the town records; and their decision shall be of no force or effect until the same is done.

Source.
GS 233:4. GL 43:4. PS 45:4. PL 49:4. RL 61:4.

NOTES TO DECISIONS

Analysis

1. Construction with other laws
2. Street railways

1. Construction with other laws
Without compliance with this section and RSA 234:13 there can be no taking of land, but if petition for layout of public parking lot, order of notice and evidence of service have not been filed and recorded, board inaugurated after filing of petition can file and record such documents. Rogers v. City of Concord, 104 N.H. 47, 178 A.2d 509, 1962 N.H. LEXIS 14 (1962).

2. Street railways
Proceedings for the location of a street railway are subject to this provision. Lenoix v. Dover, Somersworth & Rochester Street Railway, 72 N.H. 58, 54 A. 1022, 1903 N.H. LEXIS 11 (1903).

43:5. Hearings by Other Officers.

The same rules shall apply to and govern the proceedings of fence-viewers, school boards, village commissioners, committees appointed by the selectmen and all town officers when they are applied to or appointed to decide any question affecting the rights or claims of individuals, saving that other or shorter notice, when required or allowed by statute, shall be sufficient.

Source.
RS 136:13. CS 77:3; 142:13. GS 233:5. GL 43:5. PS 45:5. PL 49:5. RL 61:5.

NOTES TO DECISIONS

Cited:
Cited in School Dist. v. Carr, 55 N.H. 452, 1875 N.H. LEXIS 109 (1875); Hawthorne v. Dresden School District, 114 N.H. 567, 324 A.2d 728, 1974 N.H. LEXIS 324 (1974).

43:6. Disqualification.

No selectman or other officer shall act, in the decision of any such case, who would be disqualified to sit as a juror for any cause, except exemption from service, in the trial of a civil action in which any of the parties interested in such case was a party.

Source.
GS 233:7. GL 43:7. PS 45:6. PL 49:6. RL 61:6.

NOTES TO DECISIONS

Analysis

1. Construction with other laws
2. Prejudice
3. Effect of disqualification

1. Construction with other laws
In proceedings for condemnation of land required for county uses, legislature did not intend application of juror disqualification standard of this section to selectmen or any other official participating in hearings before county commissioners mandated by RSA 26:1. Brouillard v. Atwood, 116 N.H. 842, 367 A.2d 596, 1976 N.H. LEXIS 484 (1976).

2. Prejudice

Selectmen are disqualified by prejudice from further consideration of a petition for the establishment of boundaries for a village district where the report has been set aside on the ground that they have not acted in good faith. Attorney General v. Littlefield, 78 N.H. 185, 98 A. 38, 1916 N.H. LEXIS 33 (1916).

3. Effect of disqualification

The fact that one of the selectmen before whom a highway petition was brought was disqualified by interest is not a jurisdictional defect which operates to quash the proceedings, but is a voidable irregularity for which appeal furnishes an adequate remedy. Bickford v.

Franconia, 73 N.H. 194, 60 A. 98, 1905 N.H. LEXIS 14 (1905).

The fact that one of the three selectmen signing a notice for a hearing upon a petition for the changing of the lines of a school district is disqualified by interest to act upon the petition does not invalidate the notice. Fifield v. Swett, 56 N.H. 432, 1876 N.H. LEXIS 166 (1876).

Cited:

Cited in Farrelly v. Timberlane Regional School District, 114 N.H. 560, 324 A.2d 723, 1974 N.H. LEXIS 323 (1974); Hawthorne v. Dresden School District, 114 N.H. 567, 324 A.2d 728, 1974 N.H. LEXIS 324 (1974).

43:7. Appointment by Board to Fill Place of Disqualified Officer.

The place of a selectman or other officer so disqualified shall be supplied by appointment, by the other members of the board, of a qualified person who has theretofore holden the same office in the town, or, in the case of committees, by a new appointment.

Source.

GS 233:8. GL 43:8. 1881, 16:1. 1883, 103:1. PS 45:7. PL 49:7. RL 61:7.

NOTES TO DECISIONS

Analysis

1. Generally
2. Duration of office

1. Generally

If there remains one of the board who is qualified, he must appoint. Northern Railroad v. Town of Enfield, 57 N.H. 508, 1876 N.H. LEXIS 126 (1876).

2. Duration of office

An appointment under this section is good only for the special occasion. Hartshorn v. Schoff, 51 N.H. 316, 1871 N.H. LEXIS 34 (1871).

43:8. Appointment by Court Where Whole Board is Disqualified.

If in any case the whole board is disqualified the selectmen shall, in writing, so inform some justice of the superior court, who shall thereupon, with or without notice, appoint a new board for that case from qualified persons who have before holden the same office in the town, if such there be, otherwise from qualified persons, residents of another town, who have holden the same office.

Source.

GL 46:8. 1881, 16:1. 1883, 103:1. PS 45:8. PL 49:8. RL 61:8.

NOTES TO DECISIONS

Cited:
Cited in Attorney General v. Littlefield, 78
N.H. 185, 98 A. 38, 1916 N.H. LEXIS 33 (1916).

CHAPTER 47

POWERS OF CITY COUNCILS

Bylaws and Ordinances

47:17. Bylaws and Ordinances.

The city councils shall have power to make all such salutary and needful bylaws as towns and the police officers of towns and engineers or firewards by law have power to make and to annex penalties, not exceeding $1,000, for the breach thereof; and may make, establish, publish, alter, modify, amend and repeal ordinances, rules, regulations, and bylaws for the following purposes:

I. IN GENERAL.   To carry into effect all the powers by law vested in the city.

II. ORDER AND POLICE DUTY.   To regulate the police of the city; to prevent any riot, noise, disturbance, or disorderly assemblages; to regulate the ringing of bells, blowing of horns or bugles, and crying goods and other things; and to prescribe the powers and duties of police officers and watchmen.

III. DISORDERLY HOUSES AND GAMING.   To suppress and restrain disorderly houses and houses of ill-fame, gambling houses and places, billiard tables, nine or ten pin alleys or tables and ball alleys, and all playing of cards, dice or other games of chance; to restrain and prohibit all descriptions of gaming and fraudulent devices; and to authorize the destruction and demolition of all instruments and devices used for the purpose of gaming.

IV. SALE OF LIQUOR.   To establish regulations for groceries, stores, restaurants, and places of public amusement; to authorize the entry of proper officers into all such places to inspect the same, and the seizure and forfeiture of all liquors and the instruments used or designed to be used in the manufacture or sale of the same, in violation of law.

V. SHOWS.   To regulate or prohibit the exhibitions of natural or artificial curiosities, caravans, circuses, theatrical performances, or other shows.

VI. PORTERS, VEHICLES, ETC.   To license and regulate porters, cartmen and cartage, runners for boats, stages, cars, and public houses, hackney coaches, cabs, and carriages, and their drivers; the care and conduct of all animals, carriages, and teams, standing or moving in the streets; to prevent horse-racing and immoderate riding or driving in streets and on bridges; and to prevent cruelty to animals.

VII. USE OF PUBLIC WAYS.   To regulate all streets and public ways, wharves, docks, and squares, and the use thereof, and the placing or leaving therein any carriages, sleds, boxes, lumber, wood, or any articles or materials, and the deposit of any waste or other thing whatever; the removal of any manure or other material therefrom; the erection of posts, signs, steps, public telephones, telephone booths, and other appurtenances thereto, or awnings; the digging up the ground by traffic thereon or in any other manner, or any other act by which the public travel may be incommoded or the city subjected to expense thereby; the securing by railings or otherwise any well, cellar, or other dangerous place in or near the line of any street; to prohibit the rolling of hoops, playing at ball or flying of kites, or any other amusement or practice having a tendency to annoy persons passing in the streets and sidewalks, or to frighten teams of horses within the same; and to compel persons to keep the snow, ice, and dirt from the sidewalks in front of the premises owned or occupied by them.

(a) TRAFFIC DEVICES AND SIGNALS.   To make special regulations as to the use of vehicles upon particular highways, except as to speed, and to exclude such vehicles altogether from certain ways; to regulate the use of class IV highways within the compact limits and class V highways by establishing stop intersections, by erecting stop signs, yield right of way signs, traffic signals and all other traffic control devices on those highways over which the city council has jurisdiction. The erection, removal and maintenance of all such devices shall conform to applicable state statutes and the latest edition of the Manual on Uniform Traffic Control Devices.

(b) The commissioner of transportation shall only approve the installation and modification of traffic signals as to type, size, installation, and method of operation.

IX. COMBUSTIBLES.   To regulate the keeping, conveying and places of deposit of gunpowder and other combustible and dangerous materials; the use of candles, lights, and matches in barns, stables, and other buildings containing combustible and dangerous materials; to regulate the erection or use of buildings within the most compact part of the city, for any purpose which in the opinion of the city councils shall more immediately expose said city to destruction by fire, and to define the limits of such compact part.

X. STOCK AT LARGE.   To regulate, restrain, or prohibit the keeping or running at large of horses, cattle, sheep, swine, geese, goats and other poultry and animals, or any of them, to create the limits of districts within which the same may be kept and the conditions and restrictions under which they may be kept.

XI. DOGS.   To regulate the keeping of dogs and their running at large, require them to be licensed, and authorize the destruction of those kept or running at large contrary to the ordinance.

XII. MARKETS, SALES.   To establish markets and market-places; regulate the place and manner of selling and weighing hay, selling pickled and other fish, and salted and fresh provisions; selling and measuring wood, lime, coal, and other heavy articles; and to appoint suitable persons to superintend and conduct the same; to prevent and punish forestalling and regrating; and to restrain every kind of fraudulent device and practice.

XIII. VAGRANTS, OBSCENE CONDUCT.   To restrain and punish vagrants, men-
dicants, street beggars, strolling musicians, and common prostitutes, and all
kinds of immoral and obscene conduct, and to regulate the times and places of
bathing and swimming in the canals, rivers and other waters of the city, and
the clothing to be worn by bathers and swimmers.

XIV. NUISANCES.   To abate and remove nuisances; to regulate the location
and construction of slaughterhouses, tallow chandlers' shops, soap factories,
tanneries, stables, barns, privies, sewers, and other unwholesome or nauseous
buildings or places, and the abatement, removal or purification of the same by
the owner or occupant; to prohibit any person from bringing, depositing, or
having within the city any dead carcass or other unwholesome substance; to
provide for the removal or destruction, by any person who shall have the same
upon or near such person's premises, of any such substance, or any putrid or
unsound beef, pork, fish, hides, or skins, and, on such person's default, to
authorize the removal or destruction thereof by some officer of the city; to
authorize and provide for the collection, removal, and destruction of garbage
and other waste material, to make necessary regulations relative thereto, and
to provide for payment therefor by assessment, or appropriation, or both.

XIV-a. INTERFERING WITH VOTERS.   To regulate the distribution of campaign
materials or electioneering or any activity which affects the safety, welfare and
rights of voters at any election held for any purpose in such city. Such power
shall not extend to the display of printed or written matter attached to any
legally parked motor vehicle, nor shall such power extend to activities
conducted wholly on private property so as not to interfere with people
approaching or entering a polling place.

XIV-b. LOCAL ELECTION REPORTING REQUIREMENTS.   Requiring the reporting of
contributions to, and expenditures by, any candidate or political committee
made for the purpose of influencing the election of any candidate for local
elective office, or any person or committee for the purpose of influencing the
vote on any local ballot or referendum question.

XV. MISCELLANEOUS.   Relative to the grade of streets, and the grade and
width of sidewalks; to the laying out and regulating public squares and walks,
commons, and other public grounds, public lights, and lamps; to trees planted
for shade, ornament, convenience, or use, and the fruit of the same; to
trespasses committed on public buildings and other public property, and in
private yards and gardens; in relation to cemeteries, public burial grounds, the
burial of the dead, and the returning and keeping records thereof, and bills of
mortality, and the duties of physicians, sextons and others in relation thereto;
relative to public wells, cisterns, pumps, conduits, and reservoirs; the places of
military parade and rendezvous, and the marching of military companies with
music in the streets of the city; relative to precautions against fire; relative to
oaths and bonds of city officers, and penalties upon those elected to such offices
refusing to serve; and relative to licensing and regulating butchers, petty
grocers, or hucksters, peddlers, hawkers, and common victualers; dealers in
and keepers of shops for the purchase, sale or barter of junk, old metals or
second-hand articles, and pawnbrokers; under such limitations and restric-

tions as to them shall appear necessary. They may make any other bylaws and regulations which may seem for the well-being of the city; but no bylaw or ordinance shall be repugnant to the constitution or laws of the state; and such bylaws and ordinances shall take effect and be in force from the time therein limited, without the sanction or confirmation of any other authority whatever.

XVI. WARNINGS AND CITATIONS. To establish a procedure for the issuance of warnings and citations for the violation of health, fire, planning board, building, licensing, zoning, and housing codes and ordinances.

XVII. DRUG-FREE ZONES. Establish as a drug-free zone any area inclusive of public housing authority property and within 1,000 feet of such public housing authority property. If such drug-free zones are established, the municipality shall publish a map clearly indicating the boundaries of such drug-free zone, which shall be posted in a prominent place in the district or municipal court of jurisdiction, the local police department, and on the public housing authority property. The municipality shall also develop signs or markings for the drug-free zone which shall:

(a) Be posted in one or more prominent places in or near the public housing authority property; and

(b) Indicate that the posted area is a drug-free zone which extends to 1,000 feet surrounding such property; and

(c) Warn that a person who violates RSA 318-B, the controlled drug act, within the drug-free zone, shall be subject to severe criminal penalties under RSA 318-B and a penalty of up to $1,000 under this paragraph.

XVIII. AUTOMOBILE PARKING CONTROLS. The city councils shall have the authority to adopt such bylaws and ordinances as are necessary to control the parking, standing and stopping of automobiles within the city limits, including ordinances allowing for the towing or immobilization of automobiles for nonpayment of parking fines and creating parking fines recoverable by means of civil process.

XIX. BUSINESSES OBTAINING CITY PERMITS. To establish regulations relative to businesses obtaining city permits.

Source.
1846, 384:17. GS 44:11. GL 48:10. PS 50:10. 1905, 10:1. 1907, 35:1. 1915, 55:1; 98:1. 1923, 15:1. PL 54:12. 1935, 117:2. 1941, 35:1. RL 66:13. RSA 47:17. 1961, 26:1. 1971, 512:9. 1981, 298:2. 1983, 166:2. 1986, 102:1. 1991, 74:1; 364:7. 1993, 183:1, eff. Aug. 8, 1993. 1996, 268:1, 5, eff. Aug. 9, 1996. 2006, 202:1, eff. July 30, 2006. 2007, 43:2, eff. July 20, 2007.

Editor's note.
The case annotations below have been set out in this 2001 Advance Code Service because they were inadvertently deleted from RSA 47:17 in the 2001 Replacement volume for titles 3-5 of LEXIS New Hampshire Revised Statutes Annotated.

Amendments
—**2007.** Paragraph XIV-b: Added.

—**2006.** Paragraph XIX: Added.

—**1996.** Paragraph XIV: Substituted "or" for "of" following "provide for the removal" and "such person's" for "his" preceding "premises" and "default".

Paragraph XVI: Inserted "licensing" preceding "zoning and housing codes" and added "and ordinances" thereafter.

—**1993.** Paragraph XVIII: Added.

—**1991.** Paragraph VIII: Rewritten by ch. 74 to the extent that a detailed comparison would be impracticable.

Paragraph XVII: Added by ch. 364.

—**1986.** Paragraph XVI: Added.

—**1983.** Substituted "$1000" for "one hundred dollars" in the introductory paragraph.

—**1981.** Paragraph XIV-a: Added.

—**1971.** Substituted "one hundred" for "twenty" preceding "dollars" in the introductory paragraph.

—**1961.** Paragraph VII: Inserted "public telephones, telephone booths, and other appurtenances thereto" following "steps".

Contingent 1999 amendment.
1999, 278:16, eff. July 14, 1999, provided: "If a constitutional amendment to the New Hampshire constitution providing that municipalities shall have home rule authority to exercise any powers not specifically prohibited by the state or federal constitutions is adopted by the voters in the 2000 general election, then sections 1-15 of this act [which amended this section and RSA 31:39; 41:11; 143-A:5, I, III; 149-M:17, II(b); 179:19, V; 231:132-a, Intro. par.; 266:24, I; 466:30-b; 502:14; and 502-A:8, enacted RSA 31:39-b and 47:17-a, and repealed RSA 31:39-a; 31:40-43], shall take effect January 1, 2001. If such a constitutional amendment is not adopted, then sections 1-15 of this act shall not take effect."

Contingent 1999 amendment; outcome of 2000 general election.
In the 2000 general election, the voters of New Hampshire rejected the constitutional amendment referred to above, which would have provided that municipalities would have home rule authority to exercise any powers not specifically prohibited by the state or federal constitutions. Consequently, sections 1-15 of 1999, 278:16 [which amended this section and RSA 31:39; 41:11; 143-A:5, I, III; 149-M:17, II(b); 179:19, V; 231:132-a, Intro par.; 266:24, I; 466:30-b, V; 502:14; 502-A:8; enacted RSA 31:39-b and 47:17-a, and repealed RSA 31:39-a; 31:40-43] did not take effect.

Cross References.
Animals running at large, see RSA 467.
Burials and disinterments, see RSA 290.
Cemeteries, see RSA 289.
Criminal trespass, see RSA 635:2.
Distributing campaign materials at polling place, see RSA 659:43.
Fire hazard regulations, see RSA 154:18 et seq.
Hawkers and peddlers, see RSA 320.
Interfering with voters, see RSA 659:37.
Licensing dogs, see RSA 466:1 et seq.
Licensing pawnbrokers, see RSA 398:4 et seq.
Licensing shows, open-air meetings, billiard tables and bowling alleys, see RSA 286.
Liquor licenses, see RSA 178.
Muzzling and restraining dogs, see RSA 466:29 et seq.
Nuisances, see RSA 147.
Obscene matter, see RSA 650.
Parking enforcement provisions for municipalities, see RSA 231:132-a.
Power to regulate registration, sale, transportation or use of pesticides as exception, see RSA 430:49.
Public indecency, see RSA 645.
Solid waste management generally, see RSA 149-M.
State food service licensure, see RSA 143-A.
Town bylaws, see RSA 31:39 et seq.
Traffic rules and regulations, see RSA 265.

NOTES TO DECISIONS

Analysis

1. Bowling alleys
2. Sale of liquor
3. Vehicles—Parking
4. —Taxicabs
5. Use of public ways—Moving buildings
6. —Sale or display of merchandise
7. —Snow removal
8. —Discontinuance of highways
9. —State preemption
10. Traffic devices and signals
11. Combustibles
12. Dogs
13. Obscene conduct
14. Adult books and magazines
15. Nuisances
16. Grade of sidewalks
17. Commons
18. Licensing hawkers and peddlers
19. Noise
20. Housing standards
21. Sewers and sewage
22. Terms of officers
23. Limitations

1. Bowling alleys

The power to make ordinances includes the power to adopt a statute restricting the operation of bowling alleys. State v. Noyes, 30 N.H. 279 (1855).

2. Sale of liquor

The legislature may constitutionally authorize a city to enact an ordinance that no intoxicating liquor shall be used or kept in any refreshment saloon or restaurant within the city. State v. Clark, 28 N.H. 176, 1854 N.H. LEXIS 56 (1854).

3. Vehicles—Parking

The power to enact ordinances regulating vehicles authorizes an ordinance limiting the time and places for parking. State v. Sweeney, 90 N.H. 127, 5 A.2d 41, 1939 N.H. LEXIS 28 (1939).

4. —Taxicabs

Such powers as a city has to regulate the wages of common carriers by cab, hack or taxicab within it limits spring from paragraph VI of this section, rather than from the provision giving them the same right to enact bylaws as is conferred upon towns. State v. Guertin, 89 N.H. 126, 193 A. 237, 1937 N.H. LEXIS 25 (1937).

A city has a power to establish rates of fares for taxicabs, operating within the city limits, and as an incident thereof to require their equipment with taximeters. State v. Guertin, 89 N.H. 126, 193 A. 237, 1937 N.H. LEXIS 25 (1937).

An ordinance requiring taxicabs to be equipped with taximeters is not discriminatory or unreasonable because it excepts from such requirements cars for hire used in conveying passengers for attendance at marriages or funerals or christenings, or for use in ceremonial parades, and excludes entirely from the provision fixing rates for the transportation of passengers cars used for sightseeing purposes. State v. Guertin, 89 N.H. 126, 193 A. 237, 1937 N.H. LEXIS 25 (1937).

5. Use of public ways—Moving buildings

An ordinance forbidding the moving of a building through any street without first obtaining a license is within the authority granted in paragraph VII of this section. City of Concord v. Burleigh, 67 N.H. 106, 36 A. 606, 1891 N.H. LEXIS 13 (1891).

6. —Sale or display of merchandise

Although selectmen referred to wrong source of their power to enact ordinance forbidding use of certain streets for sale or display of merchandise, ordinance was still valid because power to enact such an ordinance was contained in paragraph VII of this section. Stamper v. Selectmen, Town of Hanover, 118 N.H. 241, 385 A.2d 1213, 1978 N.H. LEXIS 388 (1978).

7. —Snow removal

Where the highway law makes it the duty of municipalities to keep their highways in repair and free from obstruction by snow or other things that impede travel or render the highway dangerous, and empowers them to raise money for such purposes, a municipal ordinance requiring owners or occupants of abutting property to keep the sidewalks free of snow is valid as making an unequal distribution of a public burden. State v. Jackman, 69 N.H. 318, 41 A. 347, 1898 N.H. LEXIS 7, 42 L.R.A. 438 (1898).

8. —Discontinuance of highways

Selectmen are given broad statutory authority to regulate the use of public highways and sidewalks, but the discontinuance of an established town highway is not favored, and may be accomplished only by vote of the town. Marrone v. Town of Hampton, 123 N.H. 729, 466 A.2d 907, 1983 N.H. LEXIS 363 (1983).

9. —State preemption

Where statute specifically provides that commissioner of public works and highways "may" regulate highways, and where legislature has specifically empowered municipalities to regulate use of vehicles on particular highways within their limits, which includes power to exclude such vehicles from certain highways, legislature has not clearly manifested intent to preempt field of highway regulation. State v. Hutchins, 117 N.H. 924, 380 A.2d 257, 1977 N.H. LEXIS 462 (1977).

Where general court gave commissioner of public works and highways authority to regulate use of class I highways in cities outside compact portions thereof, if commissioner to promulgated regulations under the grant, any conflicting municipal ordinance would be voided. State v. Hutchins, 117 N.H. 924, 380 A.2d 257, 1977 N.H. LEXIS 462 (1977).

10. Traffic devices and signals

Under paragraph VIII of this section the authority to provide for the control of traffic by stop signs and to regulate the use of highways in a city resides exclusively with the city council. Beaule v. Weeks, 95 N.H. 453, 66 A.2d 148, 1949 N.H. LEXIS 196 (1949).

In the absence of municipal regulation with respect to a stop sign legally erected at intersecting city streets, the conduct of a motorist after having brought his vehicle to a stop is to be governed by the statute relating to the right of way of intersections where his vehicle arrives at the intersection at approximately the same instant as another. Beaule v. Weeks, 95 N.H. 453, 66 A.2d 148, 1949 N.H. LEXIS 196 (1949).

A stop sign not shown to have conformed to standards set by the highway commissioner or to have been approved by him, is not legally erected and maintained and failure to stop is therefore not negligence per se but only evidence of negligence. Legere v. Buinicky, 93 N.H. 71, 35 A.2d 508, 1943 N.H. LEXIS 51 (1943).

11. Combustibles

A city ordinance may require one proposing to erect a steam mill or garage to obtain a license therefor. Page v. Brooks, 79 N.H. 70, 104 A. 786, 1918 N.H. LEXIS 27 (1918).

An ordinance enacted in exercise of the power to regulate the keeping of combustibles, which prohibited the use as a blacksmith's shop or other thing or business which shall more immediately expose the precinct to destruction by fire, of any building, within the limits of the precinct, without consent of the commissioners, is void as reserving to the commissioners the right to decide the question of fire risk in each individual case, guided by no general rule or regulation. Hanover Precinct v. Atkins, 78 N.H. 308, 99 A. 293, 1916 N.H. LEXIS 61 (1916).

12. Dogs

Paragraph XI of this section and RSA 466:39 authorized city to enact ordinance allowing chief of police to issue a complaint against one who violates the ordinance by allowing his dog to run at large, and the chief of police is not thereby unlawfully delegated legislative authority. State v. Merski, 115 N.H. 48, 333 A.2d 159, 1975 N.H. LEXIS 220 (1975).

13. Obscene conduct

The authority to restrain all kinds of immoral and obscene conduct extends to an ordinance governing the operation and licensing of centralized music systems and coin-operated music-producing instruments. Marine Corps League v. Benoit, 96 N.H. 423, 78 A.2d 513, 1951 N.H. LEXIS 179 (1951).

14. Adult books and magazines

Although there exists no express authority for city to enact ordinance regulating display of adult books and magazines, paragraph XV of this section, providing that cities may make regulations which may seem for well-being of city and which are not repugnant to state constitution or laws, authorized city to enact type of ordinance in question, in which display of adult books and magazines, defined as being harmful to minors, was regulated. Dover News, Inc. v. City of Dover, 117 N.H. 1066, 381 A.2d 752, 1977 N.H. LEXIS 500 (1977).

Legislature has not seen fit to enter field of controlling display of adult material, and therefore until it does, it leaves it open for cities and towns to do so. Dover News, Inc. v. City of Dover, 117 N.H. 1066, 381 A.2d 752, 1977 N.H. LEXIS 500 (1977).

Where state sought to deal with general problem of sexually explicit materials by enacting RSA 650, relating to obscene matter, and RSA 571-B, generally providing that it shall be unlawful to expose harmful materials to minors, and where legislature failed to enact bill which would have amended RSA 571-B:2 to prohibit person from "openly display[ing] where a minor is present any picture, photograph [etc.] ...", state had not preempted city from acting and city was not precluded from enacting ordinance regulating display of adult books and magazines. Dover News, Inc. v. City of Dover, 117 N.H. 1066, 381 A.2d 752, 1977 N.H. LEXIS 500 (1977).

15. Nuisances

The statutory authority to prohibit any person from bringing, depositing or leaving within the city any dead carcass or unwholesome substance applies only to those substances which cause injury to health. Lane v. Concord, 70 N.H. 485, 49 A. 687, 1900 N.H. LEXIS 51 (1900).

16. Grade of sidewalks

Sidewalks are parts of highways concerning which grades may be established which differ from that of the portion used for vehicular traffic. Hinckley v. Franklin, 69 N.H. 614, 45 A. 643, 1899 N.H. LEXIS 24 (1899).

17. Commons

City councils may permit one to occupy a public common for the purpose of furnishing the public with recreation and, as an incident, to erect the structures necessary to carry on the business, if that would be a reasonable use of the premises. Sherburne v. Portsmouth, 72 N.H. 539, 58 A. 38, 1904 N.H. LEXIS 53 (1904).

18. Licensing hawkers and peddlers

The power to make ordinances relative to licensing hawkers and peddlers is suspended in operation by an act of the legislature upon the same subject. State v. Angelo, 71 N.H. 224, 51 A. 905, 1902 N.H. LEXIS 8 (1902).

19. Noise

Ample statutory authority exists for city to abate noise by emergency vehicles when those vehicles are not responding to emergency calls. State v. Driscoll, 118 N.H. 222, 385 A.2d 218, 1978 N.H. LEXIS 384 (1978).

20. Housing standards

Inclusion in housing standards ordinance of provision that violations shall be punished by a fine not to exceed twenty dollars per day and that each day's failure to comply with the ordinance constitutes a separate violation was consistent with this section and RSA 48-A:8. Davy v. Dover, 111 N.H. 1, 273 A.2d 849, 1971 N.H. LEXIS 108 (1971).

21. Sewers and sewage

Chapter of city ordinances imposing sewer rents on industrial users before their sewage facilities were connected to the city sewer system exceeded its source of authority and was therefore invalid. Seal Tanning Co. v. City of Manchester, 118 N.H. 693, 393 A.2d 1382, 1978 N.H. LEXIS 272 (1978).

22. Terms of officers

A city may establish by ordinance the term of office, within reasonable limits, of those of its officers and agents whose terms are not fixed by law. State v. Wimpfheimer, 69 N.H. 166, 38 A. 786, 1897 N.H. LEXIS 9 (1897).

23. Limitations

Paragraph XV of this section provides that where the legislature has enacted a compre-

hensive regulatory scheme, no actions or ordinances will be permitted to contravene it. Op. Atty. Gen. #0-93-6.

Proposed reserve fund provision in city's voter initiative petition would be inconsistent with general laws of the State, since legislature had enacted specific procedures for adoption, management and use of such appropriated funds. Op. Atty. Gen. #0-93-6.

Where the state has enacted a comprehensive regulatory scheme, paragraph XV of this section provides that no actions or ordinances will be permitted to contravene it. Wasserman v. City of Lebanon, 124 N.H. 538, 474 A.2d 994, 1984 N.H. LEXIS 242 (1984).

Power given to city councils to enact bylaws and ordinances for well being of their cities is not unlimited; local legislation must not be inconsistent with state law. State v. Driscoll, 118 N.H. 222, 385 A.2d 218, 1978 N.H. LEXIS 384 (1978).

The constitutional limits of local legislation are not enlarged by the provision of paragraph XV of this section empowering cities to make bylaws and regulations which "may seem for the well being of the city" and declaring that "no bylaw or ordinance may be repugnant to the constitution or laws of the state". State v. Paille, 90 N.H. 347, 9 A.2d 663, 1939 N.H. LEXIS 74 (1939).

Cited:

Cited in State v. Hogan, 30 N.H. 268 (1855); City of Manchester v. Smyth, 64 N.H. 380, 10 A. 700, 1887 N.H. LEXIS 21 (1887); Eaton v. Burke, 66 N.H. 306, 22 A. 452, 1890 N.H. LEXIS 25 (1890); State v. Wimpfheimer, 69 N.H. 166, 38 A. 786, 1897 N.H. LEXIS 9 (1897); State v. Scott, 82 N.H. 278, 132 A. 685, 1926 N.H. LEXIS 21 (1926); Warren Kay Vantine Studio v. Portsmouth, 95 N.H. 171, 59 A.2d 475, 1948 N.H. LEXIS 207 (1948); Appeal of McKenney, 120 N.H. 77, 412 A.2d 116, 1980 N.H. LEXIS 232 (1980); State v. Yee, 129 N.H. 155, 523 A.2d 116, 1987 N.H. LEXIS 164 (1987); Appeal of Coastal Materials Corp., 130 N.H. 98, 534 A.2d 398, 1987 N.H. LEXIS 280 (1987); State v. Hodgkiss, 132 N.H. 376, 565 A.2d 1059, 1989 N.H. LEXIS 114 (1989); Chouinard v. New Hampshire Speedway, 829 F. Supp. 495, 1993 U.S. Dist. LEXIS 11154 (D.N.H. 1993).

RESEARCH REFERENCES

New Hampshire Practice.

15 N.H.P. Land Use Planning and Zoning § 5.13.

ALR.

Authorization, prohibition, or regulation by municipality of the sale of merchandise on streets or highways, or their use for such purpose. 14 A.L.R.3d 896.

Validity and construction of statute or ordinance prohibiting desecration of church. 90 A.L.R.3d 1128.

Validity and construction of statute or ordinance regulating vehicle towing business. 97 A.L.R.3d 495.

Validity of municipal ordinance regulating time during which restaurant business may be conducted. 53 A.L.R.3d 942.

Validity of regulation providing for reserved parking spaces or parking priority on publicly owned property for members of a designated group. 70 A.L.R.3d 1323.

47:18. Notice and Publication of Ordinances.

All proposed city bylaws and ordinances and all adopted city bylaws and ordinances shall be kept on file at the office of the city clerk and at such other public place as the city council may designate. Notice of proposal and of adoption of a bylaw or an ordinance shall be made by publishing the title and brief description of the bylaw or ordinance in such newspaper or newspapers as the city council shall direct. The sufficiency of the published notice shall not affect the validity of the ordinance.

Source.
   1846, 384:17. GS 44:12. 1877, 72:1. GL 48:11.
PS 50:11. 1925, 41:1. PL 54:13. RL 66:14. RSA
47:18. 1985, 183:1, eff. July 26, 1985.

Amendments
   —1985. Rewritten to the extent that a detailed comparison would be impracticable.

NOTES TO DECISIONS

Analysis

1. Construction
2. Failure to publish

1. Construction
   This provision is directory, and a failure to comply with it does not render an ordinance invalid. State v. Wimpfheimer, 69 N.H. 166, 38 A. 786, 1897 N.H. LEXIS 9 (1897).

2. Failure to publish
   The failure of the city councils to publish a city ordinance as required by this section does not render the ordinance invalid in the absence of a provision in this section that the ordinance shall not be effective until such publication. Dover Housing Board v. Colbath, 106 N.H. 481, 213 A.2d 923, 1965 N.H. LEXIS 195 (1965).

Cited:
   Cited in State v. Sweeney, 90 N.H. 127, 5 A.2d 41, 1939 N.H. LEXIS 28 (1939).

Building Codes

Severability of enactment.
   1945, 105:1, was subject to a severability clause. See 1945, 105:1, par. 23.

Cross References.
   Appointment and terms of members of building code boards of appeals, see RSA 673:3 et seq.

   Building codes to provide for building inspector and building code board of appeals, see RSA 673:1.

Building permits, see RSA 676:11 et seq.

Enactment procedures, see RSA 675.

Energy conservation in new building construction, see RSA 155-D.

Hazardous and dilapidated buildings, see RSA 155-B.

Housing standards, see RSA 48-A.

Powers of building code boards of appeals, see RSA 674:34.

47:22. Grant of Power.

The board of mayor and aldermen, or the corresponding governmental body of any city, is hereby empowered and authorized in the passing and adopting of ordinances, establishing codes, rules and regulations for the construction of buildings, relating to the installation of plumbing, the use of concrete, masonry, metal, iron and wood, and other building material, the installation of electric wiring, and fire protection incident thereto or for the prevention of fires to adopt any additional regulations provided that the regulations are not less stringent than the requirements of the state building code under RSA 155-A or the state fire code under RSA 153; provided, that upon adoption of such ordinance wherein such code, rules and regulations or portions thereof have been incorporated by reference, there shall be filed 3 copies of such codes, rules and regulations in the main office of the municipal department or agency administering the same and 3 copies in the office of the city clerk. All copies of any code, rules and regulations filed as provided herein, shall be for use and examination by the public.

Source.

1945, 105:1, par. 18. RSA 47:22. 1963, 232:1. 1965, 255:1, eff. Aug. 31, 1965. 2002, 8:2, eff. Sept. 14, 2002.

Amendments

—**2002.** Substituted "additional regulations provided that the regulations are not less stringent than the requirements of the state building code under RSA 155-A or the state fire code under RSA 153" for "nationally recognized code, rules and regulations to develop good engineering practice or safety that have been printed as a code in book form or such portions thereof by reference thereto in such ordinance" in the first sentence.

—**1965.** Substituted "in the main office of the municipal department or agency administering the same and three copies in the office of the city clerk" for "in the office of the city clerk, and in the case of a fire prevention code or portions thereof, three copies in the main office of the fire department" at the end of the first sentence.

—**1963.** Substituted "city clerk, and, in the case of a fire prevention code or portion thereof, three copies in the main office of the fire department" for "building inspector and three copies in the office of the city clerk" at the end of the first sentence.

RESEARCH REFERENCES

ALR.

What interest qualifies one as an "owner" for purposes of making application for a building permit. 61 A.L.R.3d 1128.

47:22-a. Manufactured Housing.

The board of mayor and aldermen, or the corresponding governmental body of any city or the local legislative body of any town is hereby empowered and authorized to establish minimum construction standards for manufactured housing used as dwellings in the city or town, by adopting by reference any nationally recognized code for manufactured housing that has been printed as a code or any portions thereof, or any amendments to such code, to apply to all manufactured housing manufactured on or after January 1, 1964; provided that upon adoption of such ordinance wherein such code or portions thereof have been incorporated by reference, there shall be filed 3 copies of such code in the office of the building inspector, if any, and 3 copies in the office of the city or town clerk. All copies of any code filed as provided herein shall be for the use and examination by the public.

Source.
1963, 137:1. 1983, 230:18, eff. Aug. 17, 1983.

Amendments
—**1983.** Substituted "manufactured housing" for "mobile homes and travel trailers" and "mobile homes or travel trailers" in the catchline and in the first sentence of the section.

Cross References.
Zoning of manufactured housing, see RSA 674:32.

NOTES TO DECISIONS

Constitutionality
The regulation of mobile homes is a proper exercise of the police power of a town. Town of Plainfield v. Hood, 108 N.H. 502, 240 A.2d 60, 1968 N.H. LEXIS 200 (1968).

RESEARCH REFERENCES

New Hampshire Practice.
15 N.H.P. Land Use Planning and Zoning § 13.02.

47:22-b. Manufactured Housing Foundations.

The authority granted under RSA 47:22-a to establish minimum construction standards for manufactured housing, as defined by RSA 674:31, shall not extend to imposing requirements that manufactured housing which is located in parks be placed on other than the structural carriers designed for that purpose.

Source.
1977, 481:2. 1983, 230:6, eff. Aug. 17, 1983.

Revision note.
Reference to "RSA 31:118" was changed to "RSA 674:31". RSA 31:118 was repealed by 1983, 447:5, III.

Amendments
—**1983.** Substituted "Manufactured Housing" for "Mobile Homes" in the section catchline, "manufactured housing, as defined in RSA 31:118" for "mobile homes" following "standards for" and "manufactured housing which is located in parks" for "mobile homes" following "requirements that".

Cross References.
Manufactured housing parks generally, see RSA 205-A.

RESEARCH REFERENCES

New Hampshire Practice.
15 N.H.P. Land Use Planning and Zoning § 13.02.

47:23. Amendment.

Any such ordinance may be amended or supplemented in like manner, provided, that 3 copies of such ordinance, as amended or supplemented, shall be filed, as provided in RSA 47:22, in the office of the building inspector and 3 copies filed in the office of the city clerk for use and examination by the public.

Source.
1945, 105:1, par. 19, eff. April 10, 1945.

conform reference to style employed in LEXIS New Hampshire Revised Statutes Annotated.

Revision note.
Substituted "RSA 47:22" for "section 22" to

47:24. Exception.

The provisions of this subdivision shall not be construed to permit the adoption by reference of penalty clauses which may be part of any nationally recognized code, rules and regulations. The said city councils shall have power to annex penalties deemed necessary, not exceeding $1000, for the breach of any violation of any such ordinance.

Source.
1945, 105:1, par. 20, eff. April 10, 1945.

47:25. Examination by Public.

At least 30 days prior to the adoption of any such ordinance or any amendment or supplement thereto, not less than 3 copies of such code or regulation referred to shall have been filed in the office of the building inspector, and 3 copies in the office of the city clerk for the use and examination of the public.

Source.
1945, 105:1, par. 21, eff. April 10, 1945.

47:26. Public Hearing; Notice.

No such ordinance or amendments or supplements thereto, as hereinbefore set forth, shall become effective or be altered until after a public hearing in relation thereto, at which parties in interest and citizens shall have an opportunity to be heard. Notice of the time and place of such hearing shall be published in a paper of general circulation in the state at least 15 days before the holding of said hearing.

Source.
1945, 105:1, par. 22, eff. April 10, 1945.

Oil Refinery Siting

47:27. Local Option for Oil Refinery Siting in Cities.

Notwithstanding the provisions of any other law, an oil refinery shall not be located in any city without a vote of approval by one of the procedures specified in paragraphs I, II or III.

I. A site plan for an oil refinery may be approved by a ⅔ vote of the entire governing body of any city.

II. If the governing body of a city should vote to place the question of whether or not to approve the location of an oil refinery in said city on the ballot for referendum, it may place said question on the ballot to be voted upon at any regular municipal or biennial election, or at a special election called for the purpose of voting on said question. Such special election shall be held at the usual ward polling places by the regular city election officers. Should a referendum be held, the following question shall be placed on the ballot: "Shall an oil refinery be permitted within the city of (-)?" Said question shall be printed in the form prescribed by RSA 59:12-a. If a majority of those voting on the question shall vote in the affirmative, then such approval shall be deemed granted and the governing body of the city shall be bound by the outcome. If a majority of those voting on the question shall vote in the negative, such approval shall be deemed not granted and no oil refinery may be located in such city unless approval is subsequently granted in accordance with this paragraph or paragraph III.

III. Upon submission to the governing body of a city of a petition signed by at least 10 percent of the registered voters of said city requesting a referendum on the question of whether or not an oil refinery should be located in said city, the governing body shall direct that such question appear on the ballot at the next regular municipal or biennial election. If said petition is submitted at any time prior to 2 months before the next regular municipal or biennial election, the governing body shall direct that a special election be called. The election procedure and the form of the question shall be as provided in paragraph II. If a majority of those voting on the question shall vote in the affirmative, then such approval shall be deemed granted and the governing body of the city shall be bound by the outcome. If a majority of those voting on the question shall vote in the negative, such approval shall be deemed not granted and no oil refinery may be located in such city unless approval is subsequently granted in accordance with this paragraph or paragraph II.

IV. Nothing in this section shall be construed as changing, modifying or affecting in any way the provisions of RSA 31 and RSA 36 relating to zoning regulations.

Source.

1974, 36:2, eff. April 5, 1974.

References in text.

RSA 59:12-a, referred to in par. II, was repealed by 1979, 436:7, I, eff. July 1, 1979. For present provisions relating to form of questions on ballots, see RSA 656:13, 663:1.

The provisions of RSA 36 relating to zoning, referred to in par. IV, was repealed by 1983, 447:5. For present provisions, see RSA 672 et seq.

CHAPTER 52

VILLAGE DISTRICTS

Cross References.

Applicability of provisions relating to reconsideration of school district meeting votes, see RSA 40:10.

Village district elections, see RSA 670.

Village district managers, see RSA 37.

NOTES TO DECISIONS

Analysis

1. Constitutionality
2. Power of legislature
3. Reorganization

1. Constitutionality

This chapter, governing formation and operation of village districts, is not contrary either to democratic values or the state constitution. Chasan v. Village Dist. of Eastman, 128 N.H. 807, 523 A.2d 16, 1986 N.H. LEXIS 393 (1986).

2. Power of legislature

Action of legislature in separating certain area from town, unless village district identical with former district was in existence on specific date and thereafter maintained, which was designed to prevent dissolution of such district except by legislative permission was not unconstitutionally arbitrary. Town of Lisbon v. Lisbon

Village District, 104 N.H. 255, 183 A.2d 250, 1962 N.H. LEXIS 62 (1962).

3. Reorganization

Where village district was established by special act of legislature with power to maintain highways and such district dissolved itself and organized itself into a new district under the provisions of this chapter which does not grant power to village districts to maintain highways, such new district was held not to be a district "identical so far as possible to the" former district within the meaning of special act which established original district. Town of Lisbon v. Lisbon Village District, 104 N.H. 255, 183 A.2d 250, 1962 N.H. LEXIS 62 (1962).

Cited:

Cited in Town of Lebanon v. Lebanon Water Works, 98 N.H. 328, 100 A.2d 167, 1953 N.H. LEXIS 74 (1953).

RESEARCH REFERENCES

New Hampshire Practice.
13 N.H.P. Local Government Law § 321 et seq.

New Hampshire Code of Administrative

Rules.
Rules of the Department of Revenue Administration, Rev 2001.01 et seq., New Hampshire Code of Administrative Rules Annotated.

52:1-a. Flood Control Projects.

Any village district organized under the provisions of this chapter may at a regular or special village district meeting vote to cooperate or act jointly with other village districts or with towns to defray expenses and take other appropriate action necessary to protect its interest in connection with federal or interstate flood control projects. Such village district may enter into agreements with other districts or towns for the purposes hereof and in such case the agreement shall be governed by the conditions set.

Source.
1957, 287:3, eff. Oct. 1, 1957.

Cross References.
Agreements between governmental units generally, see RSA 53-A.

State guarantee, see RSA 31:97.
Taxation of municipal flood control property, see RSA 72:11, 11-a.

52:2. Meeting to Consider.

Such selectmen shall also forthwith call a meeting of the voters domiciled in the district to see if they will vote to establish the district, and if so to choose necessary officers therefor. They shall call the meeting and give notice thereof as town meetings are called and warned, excepting that the warrant shall be posted at 2 or more public places in the district.

Source.
1849, 852:2, 3, 4. CS 116:2, 3, 4. GS 97:2. GL 107:2. PS 53:2. PL 57:2. RL 70:2. 2003, 289:15, eff. Sept. 1, 2003.

Amendments
—**2003.** Deleted "legal" preceding "voters"

and substituted "domiciled" for "residing" thereafter in the first sentence.

Cross References.
Warning of town meetings, see RSA 39.

NOTES TO DECISIONS

Cited:
Cited in Attorney General v. Littlefield, 78 N.H. 185, 98 A. 38, 1916 N.H. LEXIS 33 (1916);

Chasan v. Village Dist. of Eastman, 128 N.H. 807, 523 A.2d 16, 1986 N.H. LEXIS 393 (1986).

52:2-a. Budgetary Official Ballot.

Notwithstanding any other provision of law, any village district may vote to raise and appropriate money for the support of the district by official ballot as provided for in RSA 49-D:3, II-a, by following the procedures set forth in RSA 49-B. The village district may also include within its charter a plan for voting by official ballot, pursuant to RSA 49-B and RSA 49-D, on such other warrant articles as the village district may determine. For the purposes of this section, all references in RSA 49-B and RSA 49-D to "municipal," "municipality," "city," and "town" shall mean and include "village district," and all references to "elected body" and "governing body" shall mean and include "district commissioners."

Source.
1995, 53:5, eff. July 8, 1995. 1997, 319:8, eff. Aug. 22, 1997.

inserted "and RSA 49-D" following "RSA 49-B" in the third sentence.

Amendments
—1997. Added the second sentence and

52:3. Procedure and Powers.

I. At such meeting the legal voters may by vote establish the district, give to it a name, and choose necessary officers therefor to hold office until the first annual meeting of the district.

II. The district shall thereupon be a body corporate and politic, and shall have all the powers in relation to the objects for which it was established that towns have or may have in relation to like objects, and all that are necessary for the accomplishment of its purposes.

III. The district may at an annual meeting vote to raise such sums of money as the voters judge necessary for the purpose of reducing an accumulated general fund deficit.

Source.
1849, 852:2-4, 7. CS 116:2-4, 7. GS 97:2, 4. 1874, 11:1. GL 107:2, 4. 1887, 42:1. 1889, 11:1. PS 53:3. PL 57:3. RL 70:3. RSA 52:3. 1994, 147:3, eff. Sept. 22, 1994.

Amendments
—1994. Rewritten to the extent that a detailed comparison would be impracticable.

NOTES TO DECISIONS

Cited:
Cited in Granite State Land Co. v. Town of Hampton, 76 N.H. 1, 79 A. 25, 1911 N.H. LEXIS 137 (1911); Chasan v. Village Dist. of Eastman, 128 N.H. 807, 523 A.2d 16, 1986 N.H. LEXIS 393 (1986).

52:3-a. Commissioners Duties; Acceptance by Municipalities of Roads.

I. In addition to the general powers provided in RSA 52:3, the commissioners of a village district formed for the purposes of RSA 52:1, I(m), shall have the same powers, duties and responsibilities of selectmen of towns which are granted or required pursuant to RSA Title XX; and, where appropriate, selectmen of towns shall be construed to mean commissioners of village districts.

I-a. The commissioners shall publish in the next annual report, or post at the annual meeting, the general fund balance sheet from the most recently completed audited financial statements or from the financial report filed pursuant to RSA 21-J:34, V.

I-b. In the case of an accumulated general fund deficit, the commissioners shall insert an article in the warrant recommending such action as they deem appropriate, which may include, but is not limited to, raising a sum of money for the purpose of reducing that deficit.

II. No town or city shall be required to accept, lay out or maintain any road solely because the road was established or maintained by a village district. Dissolution of a village district under RSA 52:21 shall not affect the powers, duties and responsibilities of a city or town to accept, lay out, maintain or otherwise assume responsibility for any road established by that village district.

Source.
1975, 455:2. 1979, 72:1. 1994, 147:4, eff. July 22, 1994.

Amendments
—**1994.** Added pars. I-a and I-b.

—**1979.** Designated the existing provisions of the section as par. I and added par. II.

52:4. Appropriations.

I. No village district shall raise or appropriate money, or reduce or rescind any appropriation of money previously authorized, at any special meeting of the voters thereof except by vote by ballot, nor unless the ballots cast at such meeting shall be equal in number to at least ½ of the number of voters of such district at the regular meeting next preceding such special meeting; and if a checklist was used at the last preceding regular meeting the same shall be used to ascertain the number of voters in the district; and such checklist, corrected according to law, shall be used at such special meeting upon request of 10 voters. In case of an emergency arising in a district for which immediate expenditure of money is necessary, the district through its commissioners may appeal to the superior court for permission to hold a special district meeting which, if granted, shall give said meeting the same authority as the annual district meeting.

II. Ten days prior to petitioning the superior court, the district commissioners shall notify, by certified mail, the commissioner of the department of revenue administration that an emergency exists by providing the commissioner with a copy of the explanation of the emergency, the warrant article or articles and the petition to be submitted to the superior court. The petition to the superior court shall include a certification that the commissioner of the department of revenue administration has been notified pursuant to this paragraph.

Source.
1907, 121:1. PL 57:4. 1931, 103:1. RL 70:4. 1943, 88:1. RSA 52:4. 1989, 172:2, eff. July 16, 1989. 2003, 289:16, eff. Sept. 1, 2003.

Amendments
—**2003.** Paragraph I: Substituted "voters" for "inhabitants" following "special meeting of the" and deleted "legal" preceding "voters"

wherever it appeared throughout the first sentence.

Paragraph II: Substituted "the commissioner" for "him" preceding "with a copy" in the first sentence.

—1989. Designated the existing provisions of the section as par. I and added par. II.

Cross References.
Municipal Finance Act, see RSA 33.

NOTES TO DECISIONS

Number voting
A district may vote an issue of bonds regardless of the total number present and voting, if two-thirds of those participating vote for the issue. Opinion of Justices, 86 N.H. 604, 171 A. 443, 1934 N.H. LEXIS 105 (1934).

Cited:
Cited in Frost v. Hoar, 85 N.H. 442, 160 A. 51, 1932 N.H. LEXIS 100 (1932); Laconia Water Co. v. Laconia, 99 N.H. 409, 112 A.2d 58, 1955 N.H. LEXIS 37 (1955); Welch v. Read, 100 N.H. 174, 121 A.2d 569, 1956 N.H. LEXIS 24 (1956).

52:4-a. Contingency Fund.

Every village district annually by an article in the warrant may establish a contingency fund to meet the cost of unanticipated expenses that may arise during the year. Such fund shall not exceed one percent of the amount appropriated exclusive of capital expenditures and amortization of debt by such village district during the preceding year. A detailed report of all expenditures from the contingency fund shall be made annually by the commissioners and published with their report.

Source.
1965, 123:3, eff. July 27, 1965.

52:6. Added Powers.

A district established for any of the purposes mentioned in RSA 52:1 may from time to time by vote add thereto any other of said purposes; and from and after such vote it shall have all the powers and rights in relation to the new purposes that it previously had in relation to its original purposes.

Source.
PS 53:5. PL 57:6. RL 70:6.

Revision note.
Substituted "RSA 52:1" for "section 1 hereof"

to conform reference to style employed in LEXIS New Hampshire Revised Statutes Annotated.

52:7. Officers.
[Repealed 1979, 410:2, XIII, eff. July 1, 1979.]

Former section(s).
Former RSA 52:7, relating to village district officers, was derived from 1849, 852:5, 6; CS

116:5, 6; GS 97:3; GL 107:3; PS 53:6; PL 57:7 and RL 70:7. See now RSA 670:2.

52:8. Duties.

The moderator, clerk, treasurer and commissioners shall severally qualify and possess the same powers and perform the same duties in respect to the district's meetings and business affairs that the moderator, clerk, treasurer and selectmen of towns respectively possess and perform in respect to like matters in towns.

Source.

1849, 852:5, 6. CS 116:5, 6. GS 97:3. GL 107:3. PS 53:7. 1905, 99:1. PL 57:8. RL 70:8.

NOTES TO DECISIONS

Cited:
Cited in Granite State Land Co. v. Town of Hampton, 76 N.H. 1, 79 A. 25, 1911 N.H. LEXIS 137 (1911).

52:8-a. Report to Commissioner of Revenue Administration.
[Repealed 1979, 410:2, XIV, eff. July 1, 1979.]

Former section(s).
Former RSA 52:8-a, relating to reporting names and addresses of village district officers, was derived from 1965, 34:2 and 1973, 544:8. See now RSA 670:9.

52:9. Tenure.
[Repealed 1979, 410:2, XV, eff. July 1, 1979.]

Former section(s).
Former RSA 52:9, relating to tenure of village district officers, was derived from 1849, 852:5, 6; CS 116:5, 6; GS 97:3; GL 107:3; PS 53:7; 1905, 99:1; 1911, 10:1; PL 57:9 and RL 70:9. See now RSA 670:2.

52:9-a. Appointment to Fill an Elective Office Vacancy; Tenure.
[Repealed 1979, 410:2, XVI, eff. July 1, 1979.]

Former section(s).
Former RSA 52:9-a, relating to filling vacancies in elective village district offices, was derived from 1975, 132:2. See now RSA 670:12.

52:10. Vacancies.
[Repealed 1979, 410:2, XVII, eff. July 1, 1979.]

Former section(s).
Former RSA 52:10, relating to filling vacancies in the offices of village district clerk, treasurer or commissioner, was derived from 1849, 852:5, 6; CS 116:5, 6; GS 97:3; GL 107:3; PS 53:7; 1905, 99:1; PL 57:10 and RL 70:10. See now RSA 670:12.

52:11-a. Voting at District Meetings.

Votes at district meetings shall be conducted according to the procedures established for town meetings in RSA 40:4-a, 4-b, and 6.

Source.
1971, 524:4, eff. July 7, 1971.

Revision note.
Deleted "40:" preceding "6" at the end of the section to conform reference to style employed in LEXIS New Hampshire Revised Statutes Annotated.

52:12. Annual Meetings.

The annual meeting of each district shall be held between January 1 and May 1 of each year. In the case of a district formed for the purpose of impoundment of water, the annual meeting shall be held at another time of the year if so voted at a previous meeting.

Source.
1849, 852:8. CS 116:8. GS 97:5. GL 107:5. PS 53:8. 1899, 49:1. PL 57:12. RL 70:12. RSA 52:12. 1975, 13:3. 1981, 375:2, eff. Aug. 22, 1981.

Amendments
—1981. Rewrote the first sentence.

—1975. Added the second sentence.

NOTES TO DECISIONS

Errors in proceedings
If basic wishes of electorate can fairly be found, the court should be loath to thwart them because of technical errors in district meeting proceedings or because precise legal phraseology is not used. Sugar Hill Improvement Ass'n v. Town of Lisbon, 104 N.H. 40, 178 A.2d 512, 1962 N.H. LEXIS 13 (1962).

Cited:
Cited in Lower Bartlett Water Precinct v. Murnik, 150 N.H. 690, 845 A.2d 1245, 2004 N.H. LEXIS 55 (2004).

52:13. Warning of Meetings.

In case of a vacancy in the office of commissioners, or of their neglect or refusal to warn a meeting or insert an article in a warrant, or of failure to hold an annual meeting, a meeting of the district may be called and warned in the same manner as in like cases in towns.

Source.
1883, 6:1, 2. PS 53:9. PL 57:13. RL 70:13.

Cross References.
Warning of town meetings, see RSA 39.

NOTES TO DECISIONS

Cited:
Cited in Lower Bartlett Water Precinct v. Murnik, 150 N.H. 690, 845 A.2d 1245, 2004 N.H. LEXIS 55 (2004).

52:14. Special Meetings.

The commissioners when calling a special district meeting shall, within one week after posting the warrant therefor, cause a copy of said warrant to be published once in a newspaper of general circulation in said district.

Source.
1945, 39:2, eff. March 6, 1945.

52:14-a. Financial Reports.
[Repealed 1993, 176:18, eff. Aug. 8, 1993.]

Former section(s).
Former RSA 52:14-a, relating to village dis-

trict financial reports, was derived from 1963, 120:4 and 1973, 544:8.

52:15. Checklist.
[Repealed 1979, 410:2, XVIII, eff. July 1, 1979.]

Former section(s).
Former RSA 51:15, relating to village district checklists, was derived from 1887, 4:2; PS

53:10; PL 57:14 and RL 70:14. See now RSA 670:3.

52:16. Taxation, Procedure.

I. Whenever the district votes to raise money by taxation or otherwise for any of its purposes, the clerk shall, within 10 days thereafter, deliver a certified copy of such vote to the selectmen of each town which contains any part of the district and to the commissioner of revenue administration. Whether or not the district is situated wholly within one town, the selectmen of each town shall assess the tax on that part of the district lying within their own town and commit it to the collector of taxes from their own town. The collectors shall then collect the tax as required by law. The selectmen may make such assessments in the manner provided under RSA 76:4.

II. In the case of districts with annual budgets of less than $200,000, the town treasurer shall distribute the amount of taxes collected and held in trust by the town under paragraph I to the district treasurer no later than December 31 of each calendar year, unless otherwise agreed to in writing by the town and district treasurers. In the case of districts with annual budgets of $200,000 or more, the town treasurer shall distribute the amount of taxes collected and held in trust by the town under paragraph I by distributing to the district treasurer all taxes collected in any given calendar month by the end of the next following month, unless otherwise agreed to in writing by the town and district treasurers. The town treasurer, furthermore, shall turn over to the district treasurer all interest earned on district tax revenues held in trust by the town and all interest collected by the town on the account of any delinquent district taxpayers' district taxes in the same manner as the tax revenues are distributed.

Source.
1849, 852:7. CS 116:7. GS 97:4. 1874, 11:1. GL 107:4. PS 53:11. PL 57:15. RL 70:15. RSA 52:16. 1975, 138:1. 1977, 11:1. 1991, 90:1. 1992, 274:1, eff. May 18, 1992.

Amendments
—1992. Added "unless otherwise agreed to in writing by the town and district treasurers" following "year" in the first sentence and following "following month" in the second sentence.

—1991. Designated the existing provisions of the section as par. I and added par. II.

—1977. Inserted "or otherwise" following "taxation" and added "and to the commissioner of revenue administration" following "district" at the end of the first sentence.

—1975. Rewritten to the extent that a detailed comparison would be impracticable.

RESEARCH REFERENCES

New Hampshire Code of Administrative Rules.
   Rules of the Department of Revenue Admin-istration, Rev 1905.09, New Hampshire Code of Administrative Rules Annotated.

52:17. Abatement of Assessments.

The power to abate and correct the assessment of such taxes shall belong to the board authorized to assess them; and aggrieved parties shall have the same remedies for relief as in case of town taxes.

Source.
   1849, 852:7. CS 116:7. GS 97:4. 1874, 11:1. GL 107:4. PS 53:11. PL 57:16. RL 70:16.

52:19. Joint Board.

If a district, situated in 2 or more towns, adopts the provisions of RSA chapter 252 the selectmen of all the towns as a joint board shall have powers and perform the duties of selectmen in such case.

Source.
   PS 53:13. PL 57:18. RL 70:18.

was recodified as RSA 149-I and RSA 231:111-113 by 1981, 87:1, eff. April 20, 1981.

References in text.
   RSA chapter 252, referred to in this section,

52:21. Dissolution.

Any village district and any district now in existence having the rights and powers of a village district, may, at an annual meeting, by a ⅔ vote of its legal voters, terminate its existence and dispose of its corporate property. Upon the dissolution of any such district, the property, real and personal, which is contained within the former boundaries of the dissolved district shall continue to be subject to taxation and betterment assessments for the purpose of paying any unpaid bonds, notes, bills or other obligations incurred while the district was in existence, in the same manner as if the said district had not been dissolved. The selectmen of the town or towns in which the district was situated shall assess the taxes and betterment assessments in the same manner as if the district had not been dissolved and shall have the duty, authority, and power to pay such bonds, notes, bills or other obligations after the moneys received from such taxes and assessments. Provided, however, that in no case shall the total of any such taxes or assessment exceed the balance necessary to pay said bonds, notes, bills or other obligations after the net income derived from the property disposed of has been applied for the payment of the same.

Source.
   GL 107:8. PS 53:15. PL 57:20. RSA 52:21. 1967, 169:1, eff. June 9, 1967.

Amendments
   —1967. Rewritten to the extent that a detailed comparison would be impracticable.

NOTES TO DECISIONS

Analysis

1. Required vote
2. Checklist
3. Burden of proof
4. Intent of voters

1. Required vote

Requirement of this section that two-thirds vote is needed to terminate district means two-thirds of those present and voting, not two-thirds of all voters in the district. Sugar Hill Improvement Ass'n v. Town of Lisbon, 104 N.H. 40, 178 A.2d 512, 1962 N.H. LEXIS 13 (1962).

2. Checklist

Fact that no checklist had been used before in the village was not material as to validity of list used on vote to dissolve district as law under which district was organized authorized such list but did not require its use. Sugar Hill Improvement Ass'n v. Town of Lisbon, 104 N.H. 40, 178 A.2d 512, 1962 N.H. LEXIS 13 (1962).

3. Burden of proof

Plaintiffs seeking to invalidate dissolution of village district had burden of proving such fraud or irregularities in the proceedings, including improper preparation or use of checklist, as would leave the intent of the voters in doubt or which affected the result of the meeting. Sugar Hill Improvement Ass'n v. Town of Lisbon, 104 N.H. 40, 178 A.2d 512, 1962 N.H. LEXIS 13 (1962).

4. Intent of voters

Record showed original intent of voters was to terminate village district and that intent remained constant throughout the proceedings and fact that it became obvious during proceedings that profitable water division should be retained in new district and that this was done did not as a matter of law indicate original purpose was changed. Sugar Hill Improvement Ass'n v. Town of Lisbon, 104 N.H. 40, 178 A.2d 512, 1962 N.H. LEXIS 13 (1962).

52:21-a. Village Districts in Lisbon.

Notwithstanding the provisions of 1961, 360:7, the provisions of RSA 52:21 shall be applicable to the village district existing in the town of Lisbon at the time of the passage of this act, and to any other village district which may hereafter be established in said town.

Source.
1963, 436:4, eff. Aug. 30, 1963.

References in text.
1961, 360:7, referred to in text, is act to incorporate inhabitants of easterly part of Lisbon into separate town.

Revision note.
Substituted "RSA 52:21" for "section 21" to conform reference to style employed in LEXIS New Hampshire Revised Statutes Annotated.

52:22. Adoption of Provisions.

Village districts and precincts established under the laws heretofore in force may adopt the provisions of this chapter, and thereupon shall have the rights conferred thereby and be governed by the same except as hereinafter provided. Unless they do so, the laws under which they were organized shall continue in force as to them, notwithstanding their repeal in general terms. In any case where a village district or precinct heretofore established by special act is authorized to hold its annual meeting any designated time, the time for such annual meeting so designated in such special act shall govern the holding of such annual meeting unless said village district or precinct shall otherwise vote in adopting the provisions of this chapter.

Source.
  GS 97:7 GL 107:7. PS 53:16. PL 57:21. RL
70:21. 1943, 88:2, eff. March 25, 1943.

52:23. Public Water.

Upon the written application of 10 percent of the registered voters in any village water district, presented to the commissioners or one of them at least 15 days before the day prescribed for an annual meeting of the district, the commissioners shall insert in their warrant for such meeting an article relative to the use of fluoride in the water system for said district, and the district clerk shall prepare a ballot for said meeting with the following question: "Shall fluoride be used in the district water system?" Beside the question shall be printed the word "yes" and the word "no" with the proper boxes for the voter to indicate his or her choice. If a majority of the registered voters in a water system that serves only one municipality does not approve the use of fluoride in the district water system, no fluoride shall be introduced into the district water system; or if fluoride has, prior to said vote, been so introduced, such use shall be discontinued until such time as the registered voters of the district shall, by majority vote, approve of the use of fluoride. After such popular referendum, the commissioners shall not insert an article relative to the use of fluoride in the district water system in the warrant nor shall the district clerk prepare such a ballot for a minimum period of 3 years from the date of the last popular referendum of the district and only upon written application at that time of not less than 10 percent of the registered voters of said district. The procedure for a referendum on the use of fluoride in a village district that is part of a water system serving more than one municipality shall be the procedure in RSA 485:14-a.

Source.
  1959, 273:3. 1979, 335:3, eff. Aug 21, 1979.
2004, 225:5, eff. July 1, 2004.

Amendments
  —2004. Rewritten to the extent that a detailed comparison would be impractical.

  —1979. Provided for a voter petition of 10 percent to place article relative to the use of

fluorides in the public water system for an annual meeting of the village water district and limited resubmission of such article.

Cross References.
  Aid to municipalities for water pollution control, see RSA 486.

  Public hearing on introduction of fluorine into public water supply, see RSA 485:14.

52:24. Filing with Secretary of State.

The selectmen of every town, and the councilors or aldermen of every city, which have a village district established under the provisions of this chapter lying in whole or in part within said town or city, shall file with the secretary of state the following information concerning the village district or districts within their respective municipalities.

I. Within one year of the enactment of this section there shall be filed:
  (a) The name of the village district;

(b) The powers granted to said district; and

(c) The territorial boundaries of the district.

II. Thereafter, within one year of any change in the above, there shall be filed:

(a) Any change in the name, powers or territorial limits of the district; and

(b) Any notice of dissolution of the district.

Source.
1969, 25:1, eff. May 3, 1969.

52:25. Authorized to Contract with the Department of Environmental Services.

Any district formed for the purpose of impoundment of water, organized pursuant to this chapter, may contract with the department of environmental services for the construction, operation and maintenance of any dam located within the district's boundaries. Such contract shall provide for payments to the department of environmental services covering all expenses incurred in connection with such contract. In return for such payments, the department of environmental services shall assume all obligations and liabilities resulting from such construction, operation and maintenance. If the village district terminates its existence or if the contract is terminated, such obligations and liabilities outstanding at the time of such termination shall be outstanding obligations and liabilities of the district and, if the district is terminated, shall be treated in the same manner as under RSA 52:21. All contracts pursuant to this section shall become effective upon the approval of the governor and council.

Source.
1975, 13:4. 1989, 138:1, eff. July 16, 1989; 339:15, eff. Jan. 1, 1990. 1996, 228:108, eff. July 1, 1996.

Amendments
—**1996.** Substituted "department of environmental services" for "division of water resources" in the section catchline and throughout the section.

—**1989.** Chapter 138 substituted "division of water resources" for "water resources board" following "Contract with" in the section catchline and following "contract with the" in the first sentence and "division" for "water resources board" preceding "covering" in the second sentence and preceding "shall assume" in the third sentence.

Chapter 339 inserted "the" preceding "Division" in the section catchline, inserted "of water resources" preceding "covering" and substituted "with such contract" for "therewith" following "connection" in the second sentence, substituted "for such payments" for "therefor" following "return" and inserted "of water resources" preceding "shall assume" in the third sentence.

TITLE V

TAXATION

CHAPTER 79-E

COMMUNITY REVITALIZATION TAX RELIEF INCENTIVE

79-E:1. Declaration of Public Benefit.

I. It is declared to be a public benefit to enhance downtowns and town centers with respect to economic activity, cultural and historic character, sense of community, and in-town residential uses that contribute to economic and social vitality.

II. It is further declared to be a public benefit to encourage the rehabilitation of the many underutilized structures in urban and town centers as a means of encouraging growth of economic, residential, and municipal uses in a more compact pattern, in accordance with RSA 9-B.

III. Short-term property assessment tax relief and a related covenant to protect public benefit as provided under this chapter are considered to provide a demonstrated public benefit if they encourage substantial rehabilitation and use of qualifying structures as defined in this chapter.

Source.
2006, 167:1, eff. April 1, 2006.

79-E:2. Definitions.

In this chapter:

I. "Qualifying structure" means a building located in a district officially designated in a municipality's master plan, or by zoning ordinance, as a downtown, town center, central business district, or village center, or, where no such designation has been made, in a geographic area which, as a result of its compact development patterns and uses, is identified by the governing body as the downtown, town center, or village center for purposes of this chapter.

II. "Substantial rehabilitation" means rehabilitation of a qualifying structure which costs at least 15 percent of the pre-rehabilitation assessed valuation or at least $75,000, whichever is less.

III. "Tax relief" means that for a period of time determined by a local governing body in accordance with this chapter, the property tax on a qualifying structure shall not increase as a result of the substantial rehabilitation thereof.

IV. "Tax relief period" means the finite period of time during which the tax relief will be effective, as determined by a local governing body pursuant to RSA 79-E:5.

Source.
   2006, 167:1, eff. April 1, 2006.

79-E:3. Adoption of Community Revitalization Tax Relief Incentive Program.

I. Any city or town may adopt the provisions of this chapter by voting whether to accept for consideration requests for community revitalization tax relief incentives. Any city or town may do so by following the procedures in this section.

II. In a town, other than a town that has adopted a charter pursuant to RSA 49-D, the question shall be placed on the warrant of a special or annual town meeting, by the governing body or by petition under RSA 39:3.

III. In a city or town that has adopted a charter under RSA 49-C or RSA 49-D, the legislative body may consider and act upon the question in accordance with its normal procedures for passage of resolutions, ordinances, and other legislation. In the alternative, the legislative body of such municipality may vote to place the question on the official ballot for any regular municipal election.

IV. If a majority of those voting on the question vote "yes," applications for community revitalization tax relief incentives may be accepted and considered by the local governing body at any time thereafter, subject to the provisions of paragraph VI of this section.

V. If the question is not approved, the question may later be voted on according to the provisions of paragraph II or III of this section, whichever applies.

VI. The local governing body of any town or city that has adopted this program may consider rescinding its action in the manner described in paragraph II or III of this section, whichever applies. A vote terminating the acceptance and consideration of such applications shall have no effect on incentives previously granted by the city or town, nor shall it terminate consideration of applications submitted prior to the date of such vote.

Source.
   2006, 167:1, eff. April 1, 2006.

79-E:4. Community Revitalization Tax Relief Incentive.

I. An owner of a qualifying structure who intends to substantially rehabilitate such structure may apply to the governing body of the municipality in which the property is located for tax relief. The applicant shall include the address of the property, a description of the intended rehabilitation, any changes in use of the property resulting from the rehabilitation, and an application fee.

II. Upon receipt of an application, the governing body shall hold a duly noticed public hearing to take place no later than 60 days from receipt of the application, to determine whether the structure at issue is a qualifying structure; whether the proposed rehabilitation qualifies as substantial rehabilitation; and whether there is a public benefit to granting the requested tax relief and, if so, for what duration.

III. No later than 45 days after the public hearing, the governing body shall render a decision granting or denying the requested tax relief and, if so granting, establishing the tax relief period.

IV. (a) The governing body may grant the tax relief, provided:

(1) The governing body finds a public benefit under RSA 79-E:7; and

(2) The specific public benefit is preserved through a covenant under RSA 79-E:8; and

(3) The governing body finds that the proposed use is consistent with the municipality's master plan or development regulations.

(b) If the governing body grants the tax relief, the governing body shall identify the specific public benefit achieved under RSA 79-E:7, and shall determine the precise terms and duration of the covenant to preserve the public benefit under RSA 79-E:8.

V. If the governing body, in its discretion, denies the application for tax relief, such denial shall be accompanied by a written explanation. The governing body's decision may be appealed either to the board of tax and land appeals or the superior court in the same manner as provided for appeals of current use classification pursuant to RSA 79-A:9 or 79-A:11 provided, however, that such denial shall be deemed discretionary and shall not be set aside by the board of tax and land appeals or the superior court except for bad faith or discrimination.

Source.
2006, 167:1, eff. April 1, 2006.

79-E:5. Duration of Tax Relief Period.

I. The governing body may grant such tax assessment relief for a period of up to 5 years, beginning with the completion of the substantial rehabilitation.

II. The governing body may, in its discretion, add up to an additional 2 years of tax relief for a project that results in new residential units and up to 4 years for a project that includes affordable housing.

III. The governing body may, in its discretion, add up to an additional 4 years of tax relief for the substantial rehabilitation of a qualifying structure that is listed on or determined eligible for listing on the National Register of Historic Places, state register of historic places, or is located within and important to a locally designated historic district, provided that the substantial rehabilitation is conducted in accordance with the U.S. Secretary of Interior's Standards for Rehabilitation.

Source.
2006, 167:1, eff. April 1, 2006.

79-E:6. Resumption of Full Tax Liability.

Upon expiration of the tax relief period, the property shall be taxed at its market value in accordance with RSA 75:1.

Source.
2006, 167:1, eff. April 1, 2006.

79-E:7. Public Benefit.

The proposed substantial rehabilitation must provide at least one of the following public benefits in order to qualify for tax relief under this chapter:

I. It enhances the economic vitality of the downtown;

II. It enhances and improves a structure that is culturally or historically important on a local, regional, state, or national level, either independently or within the context of an historic district, town center, or village center in which the building is located;

III. It promotes development of municipal centers, providing for efficiency, safety, and a greater sense of community, consistent with RSA 9-B; or

IV. It increases residential housing in urban or town centers.

Source.
2006, 167:1, eff. April 1, 2006.

79-E:8. Covenant to Protect Public Benefit.

I. Tax relief for the substantial rehabilitation of a qualifying structure shall be effective only after a property owner grants to the municipality a covenant ensuring that the structure shall be maintained and used in a manner that furthers the public benefits for which the tax relief was granted.

II. The covenant shall be coextensive with the tax relief period. The covenant may, if required by the governing body, be effective for a period of time up to twice the duration of the tax relief period.

III. The covenant shall include provisions requiring the property owner to obtain casualty insurance, and flood insurance if appropriate. The covenant may include, at the governing body's sole discretion, a lien against proceeds from casualty and flood insurance claims for the purpose of ensuring proper restoration or demolition or damaged structures and property. If the property owner has not begun the process of restoration, rebuilding, or demolition of such structure within one year following damage or destruction, the property owner shall be subject to the termination of provisions set forth in RSA 79-E:9, I.

IV. The local governing body shall provide for the recording of the covenant to protect public benefit with the registry of deeds. It shall be a burden upon the property and shall bind all transferees and assignees of such property.

V. The applicant shall pay any reasonable expenses incurred by the municipality in the drafting, review, and/or execution of the covenant. The applicant also shall be responsible for the cost of recording the covenant.

Source.
2006, 167:1, eff. April 1, 2006.

79-E:9. Termination of Covenant; Reduction of Tax Relief; Penalty.

I. If the owner fails to maintain or utilize the building according to the terms of the covenant, or fails to restore, rebuild, or demolish the structure following damage or destruction as provided in RSA 79-E:8, III, the governing body shall, after a duly noticed public hearing, determine whether and to what extent the public benefit of the rehabilitation has been diminished and shall determine whether to terminate or reduce the tax relief period in accordance with such determination. If the covenant is terminated, the governing body shall assess all taxes to the owner as though no tax relief was granted, with interest in accordance with paragraph II.

II. Any tax payment required under paragraph I shall be payable according to the following procedure:

(a) The commissioner of the department of revenue administration shall prescribe and issue forms to the local assessing officials for the payment due, which shall provide a description of the property, the market value assessment according to RSA 75:1, and the amount payable.

(b) The prescribed form shall be prepared in quadruplicate. The original, duplicate, and triplicate copy of the form shall be given to the collector of taxes for collection of the payment along with a special tax warrant authorizing the collector to collect the payment under the warrant. The quadruplicate copy of the form shall be retained by the local assessing officials for their records.

(c) Upon receipt of the special tax warrant and prescribed forms, the tax collector shall mail the duplicate copy of the tax bill to the owner responsible for the tax as the notice of payment.

(d) Payment shall be due not later than 30 days after the mailing of the bill. Interest at the rate of 18 percent per annum shall be due thereafter on any amount not paid within the 30-day period. Interest at 12 percent per annum shall be charged upon all taxes that would have been due and payable on or before December 1 of each tax year as if no tax relief had been granted.

Source.
2006, 167:1, eff. April 1, 2006.

79-E:10. Lien for Unpaid Taxes.

The real estate of every person shall be held for the taxes levied pursuant to RSA 79-E:9.

Source.
2006, 167:1, eff. April 1, 2006.

79-E:11. Enforcement.

All taxes levied pursuant to RSA 79-E:9 which are not paid when due shall be collected in the same manner as provided in RSA 80.

Source.   **Amendments**
2006, 167:1, eff. April 1, 2006. 2007, 42:3, eff.   **—2007.** Substituted "RSA 80" for "RSA
July 20, 2007.   80:1-80:42-a" at the end.

79-E:12. Rulemaking.

The commissioner of the department of revenue administration shall adopt rules, pursuant to RSA 541-A, relative to the payment and collection procedures under RSA 79-E:9.

Source.
2006, 167:1, eff. April 1, 2006.

79-E:13. Extent of Tax Relief.

I. Tax relief granted under this chapter shall pertain only to assessment increases attributable to the substantial rehabilitation performed under the conditions approved by the governing body and not to those increases attributable to other factors including but not limited to market forces; or

II. Tax relief granted under this chapter shall be calculated on the value in excess of the original assessed value. Original assessed value shall mean the value of the qualifying structure assessed at the time the governing body approves the application for tax relief and the owner grants to the municipality the covenant to protect public benefit as required in this chapter.

Source.
2006, 167:1, eff. April 1, 2006.

79-E:14. Other Programs.

The provisions of this chapter shall not apply to properties whose rehabilitation or construction is subsidized by state or federal grants or funds that do not need to be repaid totaling more than 50 percent of construction costs from state or federal programs.

Source.
2006, 167:1, eff. April 1, 2006.

TITLE VI

PUBLIC OFFICERS AND EMPLOYEES

CHAPTER 91-A

ACCESS TO PUBLIC RECORDS AND MEETINGS

Amendments
—**1986.** 1986, 83:1, eff. Jan. 1, 1987, added "and meetings" following "records" in the chapter heading.

Purpose.
2003, 287:1, eff. July 18, 2003, provided: "The general court hereby establishes a commission to study clarifying the right-to-know law in light of the supreme court's December 31, 2001 decision in *Hawkins v. N.H. Department of Health and Human Services* and in-creasing use of electronic communication in the transaction of governmental business. The general court recognizes that guidance is needed for all government officials as well as for members of the public regarding what meetings and what documentation are considered subject to RSA 91-A, the right-to-know law."

Cross References.
Accountability of government officers; public's right to know, see New Hampshire Constitution, Part 1, Article 8.

NOTES TO DECISIONS

Analysis

1. Purpose
2. Generally
3. Appointments
4. Unofficial tape recording
5. Tax Returns
6. Veterans' needs committee
7. Confidentiality of information
8. Burden of proof

1. Purpose
This chapter was intended to increase public access to governmental proceedings in order to augment popular control of government and encourage administrative agency responsibility. Society for Protection of N.H. Forests v. Water Supply & Pollution Control Comm'n, 115 N.H. 192, 337 A.2d 788, 1975 N.H. LEXIS 257 (1975).

Main purpose of this chapter is based upon theory that public knowledge of the considerations upon which governmental action is based and of the decisions taken is essential to the democratic process. Carter v. City of Nashua, 113 N.H. 407, 308 A.2d 847, 1973 N.H. LEXIS 285 (1973).

2. Generally

This chapter does not necessarily require the state to be placed at a disadvantage when bargaining with the private sector. 1987 Op. Att'y Gen. 122.

3. Appointments

Trial court properly ruled that a government official does not necessarily violate this chapter whenever he or she requests a citizen to make an appointment before reviewing a public record. Brent v. Paquette, 132 N.H. 415, 567 A.2d 976, 1989 N.H. LEXIS 123 (1989).

4. Unofficial tape recording

Trial court properly found that tape recording made by school superintendent during a public meeting was not a public record subject to this chapter, where the tape was unofficial and made solely for the superintendent's personal use. Brent v. Paquette, 132 N.H. 415, 567 A.2d 976, 1989 N.H. LEXIS 123 (1989).

5. Tax Returns

Bank tax returns are not subject to public disclosure under this chapter. 1986 Op. Att'y Gen. 198.

6. Veterans' needs committee

State veterans' needs committee is subject to this chapter. 1986 Op. Att'y Gen. 231.

7. Confidentiality of information

The determination of whether information is confidential for purposes of Right-to-Know Law is assessed objectively, not based upon the subjective expectations of the party generating that information. Goode v. N.H. Office of the Legislative Budget Assistant, 148 N.H. 551, 813 A.2d 381, 2002 N.H. LEXIS 168 (2002).

8. Burden of proof

The burden of proving whether information is confidential rests with the party seeking non-disclosure. Goode v. N.H. Office of the Legislative Budget Assistant, 148 N.H. 551, 813 A.2d 381, 2002 N.H. LEXIS 168 (2002).

Cited:

Cited in State v. LaFrance, 124 N.H. 171, 471 A.2d 340, 1983 N.H. LEXIS 377 (1983); Gomez v. City of Nashua, 126 F.R.D. 432, 1989 U.S. Dist. LEXIS 7406 (D.N.H. 1989); Appeal of Salem Regional Medical Ctr., 134 N.H. 207, 590 A.2d 602, 1991 N.H. LEXIS 47 (1991); Chambers v. Gregg, 135 N.H. 478, 606 A.2d 811, 1992 N.H. LEXIS 62 (1992); Appeal of Atl. Connections, Ltd., 135 N.H. 510, 608 A.2d 861, 1992 N.H. LEXIS 69 (1992); Petition of Keene Sentinel, 136 N.H. 121, 612 A.2d 911, 1992 N.H. LEXIS 146 (1992); Union Leader Corp. v. Fenniman, 136 N.H. 624, 620 A.2d 1039, 1993 N.H. LEXIS 4 (1993).

RESEARCH REFERENCES

New Hampshire Practice.

5 N.H.P. Civil Practice & Procedure § 64.11.

13 N.H.P. Local Government Law § 356.

13 N.H.P. Local Government Law § 651 et seq.

15 N.H.P. Land Use Planning and Zoning §§ 3.04, 21.13, 21.19, 28.10, 28.11.

New Hampshire Bar Journal.

New Hampshire Right to Know Law, 20 N.H.B.J. 98 (March 1979).

The New Hampshire Right to Know Law—An analysis, 16 N.H.B.J. 227 (March 1975).

For article, "The Right to Know Your Privacy: An Analysis of *Petition of Keene Sentinel*," see 34 N.H.B.J. 5 (Sept. 1993).

New Hampshire Trial Bar News.

For article, "How to Acquire Information Under the New Hampshire Right-to-Know Law," see 7 N.H. Trial Bar News 57, 57–61 (Winter 1987).

ALR.

Nature and extent of privilege accorded public statements, relating to subject of legislative business or concern, made by member of state or local legislature or council outside of formal proceedings. 41 A.L.R.4th 1116.

State freedom of information act requests: right to receive information in particular medium or format. 86 A.L.R.4th 786.

Validity, construction, and application of statutes making public proceedings open to the public. 38 A.L.R.3d 1070.

Validity, construction, and application of statutory provisions relating to public access to police records. 82 A.L.R.3d 19.

What constitutes preliminary drafts or notes provided by or for state or local governmental agency, or intra-agency memorandums, exempt from disclosure or inspection under state free-dom of information acts. 26 A.L.R.4th 639; King v. Town of Hanover, 959 F. Supp. 62, 1996 U.S. Dist. LEXIS 20797 (D.N.H. 1996), aff'd, 116 F.3d 965, 1997 U.S. App. LEXIS 16007 (1st Cir. 1997).

91-A:1. Preamble.

Openness in the conduct of public business is essential to a democratic society. The purpose of this chapter is to ensure both the greatest possible public access to the actions, discussions and records of all public bodies, and their accountability to the people.

Source.
1967, 251:1. 1971, 327:1. 1977, 540:1, eff. Sept. 13, 1977.

Amendments
—1977. Rewritten to the extent that a de-tailed comparison would be impracticable.

—1971. Rewritten to the extent that a de-tailed comparison would be impracticable.

NOTES TO DECISIONS

Analysis

Investigatory records
Photographs Taken By Police

Investigatory records
Law enforcement representatives did not meet their burden of justifying their withhold-ing of requested documents that the father sought regarding the disappearance of the fa-ther's daughter following reports that the daughter had been involved in a traffic acci-dent; since police investigative reports were not mentioned in the state law concerning the disclosure of government records, the state su-preme court determined that the six-part test under the corresponding federal law applied and required the law enforcement representa-tives on remand of the case to the trial court to show how disclosure of the requested records could interfere with an ongoing investigation or law enforcement proceeding. Murray v. New

Hampshire Div. of State Police, 154 N.H. 579, 913 A.2d 737, 2006 N.H. LEXIS 201 (2006).

Photographs Taken By Police
Photographs which police took with the con-sent of people who were stopped by police but not arrested were public records, and the trial court's judgment ordering the City of Manches-ter to provide a civil liberties union with access to consensual photographs which police officers took over a five-year period was upheld. N.H. Civil Liberties Union v. City of Manchester, 149 N.H. 437, 821 A.2d 1014, 2003 N.H. LEXIS 61 (2003).

Cited:
Cited in Orford Teachers Ass'n v. Watson, 121 N.H. 118, 427 A.2d 21, 1981 N.H. LEXIS 255 (1981); 1986 Op. Att'y Gen. 220; 1986 Op. Att'y Gen. 231; Brent v. Paquette, 132 N.H. 415, 567 A.2d 976, 1989 N.H. LEXIS 123 (1989); Union Leader Corp. v. City of Nashua, 141 N.H. 473, 686 A.2d 310, 1996 N.H. LEXIS 127 (1996).

RESEARCH REFERENCES

ALR.
Actions brought under Freedom of Informa-tion Act, 5 U.S.C.S. §§ 522 et seq. — Supreme Court cases. 167 A.L.R. Fed. 545.

What constitutes "agency" for purposes of Freedom of Information Act (5 U.S.C.S. § 552). 165 A.L.R. Fed 591.

91-A:1-a. Definition of Public Proceedings.

I. The term "public proceedings" as used in this chapter means the transaction of any functions affecting any or all citizens of the state by any of the following:

(a) The general court including executive sessions of committees; and including any advisory committee established by the general court;

(b) The governor's council and the governor with the governor's council; including any advisory committee established by the governor by executive order or by the governor's council;

(c) Any board or commission of any state agency or authority, including the board of trustees of the university system of New Hampshire and including any advisory committee established by such entities;

(d) Any board, commission, agency or authority, of any county, town, municipal corporation, school district, school administrative unit, charter school, or other political subdivision, or any committee, subcommittee or subordinate body thereof, or advisory committee thereto.

II. For the purposes of this section, "advisory committee" means any committee, council, commission, or other like body whose primary purpose is to consider an issue or issues designated by the appointing authority so as to provide such authority with advice or recommendations concerning the formulation of any public policy or legislation that may be promoted, modified, or opposed by such authority.

Source.

1977, 540:2. 1986, 83:2. 1989, 274:1. 1995, 260:4, eff. July 1, 1995. 2001, 223:1, eff. Jan. 1, 2002.

Amendments

—2001. Redesignated the former introductory paragraph as par. I, redesignated former pars. I through IV as pars. I(a) through I(d), and in par. I(a), inserted "and including any advisory committee established by the general court", in par. I(b), inserted "including any advisory committee established by the governor by executive order or by the governor's council",

and in par. I(c), inserted "and including any advisory committee established by such entities", and added new par. II.

—1995. Paragraph IV: Inserted "school administrative unit, charter school" following "school district".

—1989. Paragraph II: Added "and the governor with the governor's council" at the end of the paragraph.

—1986. Paragraph III: Added "including the board of trustees of the university system of New Hampshire" following "authority".

NOTES TO DECISIONS

Analysis

1. Construction
2. Organizations
3. Special legislative session

1. Construction

Public informational meetings conducted by Department of Transportation were "public proceedings" for purposes of this chapter, and

department was required to give notice to public and to keep brief minutes. Op. Atty. Gen. #0-93-1.

2. Organizations

The New Hampshire Housing Finance Authority is subject to the Right-to-Know Law as the authority performs the essential government function of providing safe and affordable housing to the elderly and low income residents of the state. Union Leader Corp. v. New Hampshire Hous. Fin. Auth., 142 N.H. 540, 705 A.2d 725, 1997 N.H. LEXIS 132 (1997).

Not all organizations that work for or with the government are subject to the right-to-know law. Bradbury v. Shaw, 116 N.H. 388, 360 A.2d 123, 1976 N.H. LEXIS 361 (1976).

Where there was no statute or ordinance establishing mayor's industrial advisory committee consisting of prominent businessmen, newspapermen, and city council members, which met monthly on call of mayor and performed variety of functions including contacting concerns which might locate in city, gathering information which might be useful to potential concerns, discussing of sale of city-owned land to commercial developers and extension of city water and sewer lines and construction of new streets, advisory committee's involvement in governmental programs brought it within scope of right-to-know law. Bradbury v. Shaw, 116 N.H. 388, 360 A.2d 123, 1976 N.H. LEXIS 361 (1976).

Municipal finance committee was an agency of municipal corporation so that its meetings were included in the term "public proceedings" as defined by former RSA 91-A:1. Selkowe v. Bean, 109 N.H. 247, 249 A.2d 35, 1968 N.H. LEXIS 171, 38 A.L.R.3d 1066 (1968).

3. Special legislative session

Assuming arguendo that the due process protections applied to the passage of legislation, an inmate's due process rights were not violated by the enactment of RSA 651:2, II-e, as the session during which this occurred was open to the public, as required by RSA 91-A:1-a, I(a) and 91-A:2, II. Starr v. Governor, 154 N.H. 174, 910 A.2d 1247, 2006 N.H. LEXIS 140 (2006).

Cited:

Cited in Lodge v. Knowlton, 118 N.H. 574, 391 A.2d 893, 1978 N.H. LEXIS 246 (1978); Appeal of Plantier, 126 N.H. 500, 494 A.2d 270, 1985 N.H. LEXIS 341, 51 A.L.R.4th 1129 (1985); 1986 Op. Att'y Gen. 220; 1986 Op. Att'y Gen. 231; 1987 Op. Att'y Gen. 122.

RESEARCH REFERENCES

ALR.

What constitutes an agency subject to application of state freedom of information act. 27 A.L.R.4th 742.

91-A:2. Meetings Open to Public.

I. For the purpose of this section, a "meeting" shall mean the convening of a quorum of the membership of a public body, as provided in RSA 91-A:1-a, to discuss or act upon a matter or matters over which the public body has supervision, control, jurisdiction or advisory power. "Meeting" shall not include:

(a) Any chance meeting or a social meeting neither planned nor intended for the purpose of discussing matters relating to official business and at which no decisions are made; however, no such chance or social meeting shall be used to circumvent the spirit of this chapter;

(b) Strategy or negotiations with respect to collective bargaining;

(c) Consultation with legal counsel; or

(d) A caucus consisting of elected members of a public body of the same political party who were elected on a partisan basis at a state general election or elected on a partisan basis by a town or city which has adopted a partisan ballot system pursuant to RSA 669:12 or RSA 44:2.

II. All public proceedings shall be open to the public, and all persons shall be permitted to attend any meetings of those bodies or agencies. Except for town meetings, school district meetings and elections, no vote while in open session may be taken by secret ballot. Any person shall be permitted to use recording devices, including, but not limited to, tape recorders, cameras and videotape equipment, at such meetings. Minutes of all such meetings, including names of members, persons appearing before the bodies or agencies, and a brief description of the subject matter discussed and final decisions, shall be promptly recorded and open to public inspection not more than 5 business days after the public meeting, except as provided in RSA 91-A:6, and shall be treated as permanent records of any body or agency, or any subordinate body thereof, without exception. Except in an emergency or when there is a meeting of a legislative committee, a notice of the time and place of each such meeting, including a nonpublic session, shall be posted in 2 appropriate places or shall be printed in a newspaper of general circulation in the city or town at least 24 hours, excluding Sundays and legal holidays, prior to such meetings. An emergency shall mean a situation where immediate undelayed action is deemed to be imperative by the chairman or presiding officer of the body or agency who shall employ whatever means are available to inform the public that a meeting is to be held. The minutes of the meeting shall clearly spell out the need for the emergency meeting. When a meeting of a legislative committee is held, publication made pursuant to the rules of the house of representatives or the senate, whichever rules are appropriate, shall be sufficient notice. If the charter of any city or guidelines or rules of order of any body or agency described in RSA 91-A:1-a require a broader public access to official meetings and records than herein described, such charter provisions or guidelines or rules of order shall take precedence over the requirements of this chapter. For the purposes of this paragraph, a business day means the hours of 8 a.m. to 5 p.m. on Monday through Friday, excluding national and state holidays.

Source.
1967, 251:1. 1969, 482:1. 1971, 327:2. 1975, 383:1. 1977, 540:3. 1983, 279:1. 1986, 83:3. 1991, 217:2, eff. Jan. 1, 1992. 2003, 287:7, eff. July 18, 2003. 2007, 59:2, eff. July 31, 2007.

Amendments
—2007. Paragraph II: Substituted "not more than 5 business days after" for "within 144 hours of" preceding "the public meeting" in the fourth sentence and added the tenth sentence.

—2003. Paragraph I: Made minor stylistic changes in subpars. (b) and (c) and added subpar. (d).

—1991. Paragraph II: Substituted "a nonpublic" for "an executive" preceding "session" in the fifth sentence.

—1986. Paragraph I: Added the second sentence.
Paragraph II: Inserted "or the senate, whichever rules are appropriate" following "house of

representatives" in the eighth sentence and made other minor stylistic changes.

—1983. Paragraph II: Substituted "144" for "72" following "inspection within" and deleted "of this chapter" following "91-A:6" in the fourth sentence.

—1977. Deleted "the" preceding "public" in the section catchline, designated existing provisions of the section as par. II, added the second sentence of that paragraph, and added par. I.

—1975. Added the second sentence.

—1971. Inserted "or when there is a meeting of a legislative committee" following "emergency" and substituted "Sundays" for "Sunday" following "excluding" in the third sentence and added the fifth sentence.

—1969. Rewritten to the extent that a detailed comparison would be impracticable.

Cross References.
Executive sessions, see RSA 91-A:3.

Minutes and records available for public inspection, see RSA 91-A:4.

NOTES TO DECISIONS

Analysis

1. Construction
2. Availability of records
3. Public dissemination
4. Notice—Generally
5. —Personal notice
6. —Subsequent meetings
7. Collective bargaining
8. Public Proceedings

1. Construction

Right-to-know law applies only to meetings of a quorum of members of a public body, not to conversations among individual members outside of such meetings. Webster v. Town of Candia, 146 N.H. 430, 778 A.2d 402, 2001 N.H. LEXIS 91 (2001).

Public informational meetings conducted by Department of Transportation were "public proceedings" for purposes of this chapter, and department was required to give notice to public and to keep brief minutes. Op. Atty. Gen. #0-93-1.

2. Availability of records

Where newspaper sought to compel clerk of New Hampshire House of Representatives to turn over to it under Right-to-Know Law a certain tape recording of the proceedings of the house, for the purpose of duplicating and using it for a so-called voice stress analysis, case would not be viewed as a true Right-to-Know Law case because the legislative session in question was open to the public and press, an official journal was prepared of the proceedings, and written transcripts were available if the newspaper or anyone else wished to obtain them. Union Leader Corp. v. Chandler, 119 N.H. 442, 402 A.2d 914, 1979 N.H. LEXIS 336 (1979).

Where newspaper sought to compel clerk of New Hampshire House of Representatives to turn over to it under Right-to-Know Law a certain tape recording of the proceedings of the house, for the purpose of duplicating and using it for a so-called voice stress analysis, house could properly decide, consistent with the right of reasonable public access, that its official tape should not be duplicated or subjected to a voice stress analysis. Union Leader Corp. v. Chandler, 119 N.H. 442, 402 A.2d 914, 1979 N.H. LEXIS 336 (1979).

Verbatim stenographic records of testimony at zoning hearing are not required, nor are they commonly made, unless by the parties themselves. Di Pietro v. City of Nashua, 109 N.H. 174, 246 A.2d 695, 1968 N.H. LEXIS 149 (1968).

3. Public dissemination

This chapter does not mandate that a negotiating party may not be restricted from issuing press releases regarding the status of closed public sector collective bargaining sessions. Appeal of Exeter, 126 N.H. 685, 495 A.2d 1288, 1985 N.H. LEXIS 352 (1985).

This section and RSA 365:8 empower the Public Utilities Commission to regulate all private recordings of its hearings and to deny a news media request to broadcast a recording. 1590 Broadcasting Corporation v. Public Utilities Commission, 113 N.H. 258, 306 A.2d 49, 1973 N.H. LEXIS 248 (1973).

Radio broadcasting corporation had no unrestrained right to gather information through the taping of Public Utilities Commission public hearing on rate increase request, and public's right to be informed was satisfied where the commission, which validly denied radio broadcasting corporation's request that it be allowed to broadcast tapes the commission had allowed it to make for litigation purposes, allowed other reasonable methods of recording and reporting the hearing. 1590 Broadcasting Corporation v. Public Utilities Commission, 113 N.H. 258, 306 A.2d 49, 1973 N.H. LEXIS 248 (1973).

4. Notice—Generally

Where principal's contract was improperly terminated because school board meeting was not preceded by proper notice, trial court would have power, if principal was interested in continuing his position, to order school board to hold a new and open meeting on the question whether the contract should be renewed. Stoneman v. Tamworth School District, 114 N.H. 371, 320 A.2d 657, 1974 N.H. LEXIS 281 (1974).

Fundamental purpose of requirements for notice and hearing is to advise all affected parties of their opportunity to be heard in public meeting and to be apprised of the relief sought. Carter v. City of Nashua, 113 N.H. 407, 308 A.2d 847, 1973 N.H. LEXIS 285 (1973).

Lack of compliance with requirements that hearings be upon notice and open to the public would deprive a zoning board of adjustment of jurisdiction to grant a variance. Carter v. City of Nashua, 113 N.H. 407, 308 A.2d 847, 1973 N.H. LEXIS 285 (1973).

Where counsel for applicant for zoning variance posted the notices required by this section, this ministerial act was properly permitted and complied with statutory requirements. Carter v. City of Nashua, 113 N.H. 407, 308 A.2d 847, 1973 N.H. LEXIS 285 (1973).

5. —Personal notice

Where two probationary teachers employed pursuant to individual written contracts were not offered contracts for the upcoming school year after a regularly scheduled school board meeting, the provisions of this section governing meetings open to the public did not require personal notice to be given for the teachers' nominations; the school board had not agreed to provide such personal notice pursuant to a collective bargaining agreement and the teachers' association was the exclusive representative of the two teachers. Brown v. Bedford School Board, 122 N.H. 627, 448 A.2d 1375, 1982 N.H. LEXIS 414 (1982).

School board which decided not to renew principal's contract would not successfully meet fact it had not given posted or published notice of the meeting with fact principal received notice prior to the meeting. Stoneman v. Tamworth School District, 114 N.H. 371, 320 A.2d 657, 1974 N.H. LEXIS 281 (1974).

6. —Subsequent meetings

Where notice was published in a newspaper of general circulation that town planning board would consider adoption of subdivision regulations on January 5, and at such time only one-half of the proposed regulations were discussed and the hearing was recessed until January 12, recess of hearing without posting of additional notice was not violative of any of defendant's rights under this chapter or under RSA 36:23. Town of Nottingham v. Harvey, 120 N.H. 889, 424 A.2d 1125, 1980 N.H. LEXIS 428 (1980).

Where notice of second meeting of zoning board of adjustment in the matter of a variance application was given 24 hours before the meeting instead of the 72-hour notice required by city ordinance, such failure was not sufficient to affect board's jurisdiction over the matter, which it acquired by its compliance with all notice requirements for the first meeting. Carter v. City of Nashua, 113 N.H. 407, 308 A.2d 847, 1973 N.H. LEXIS 285 (1973).

7. Collective bargaining

This chapter does not mandate that public sector collective bargaining sessions be open to the public when one of the negotiating parties insists upon such a format. Appeal of Exeter, 126 N.H. 685, 495 A.2d 1288, 1985 N.H. LEXIS 352 (1985).

Negotiation sessions between school board and teachers' representative were not within the ambit of this chapter, though any board approval of recommendations arrived at during the negotiations must be given at an open meeting in accordance with this chapter. Talbot v. Concord Union School District, 114 N.H. 532, 323 A.2d 912, 1974 N.H. LEXIS 318 (1974).

8. Public Proceedings

Assuming arguendo that the due process protections applied to the passage of legislation, an inmate's due process rights were not violated by the enactment of RSA 651:2, II-e, as the session during which this occurred was open to the public, as required by RSA 91-A:1-a, I(a) and 91-A:2, II. Starr v. Governor, 154 N.H. 174, 910 A.2d 1247, 2006 N.H. LEXIS 140 (2006).

New Hampshire Department of Fish and Game violated RSA 91-A:2, II by excluding a television station's cameras from a hunting license hearing on grounds that the commotion they would cause would deprive the license applicant of his right to a fair hearing. The Department failed to identify what constitutional interest was at stake; a hunting license had never been found to be a constitutionally protected right. WMUR Channel Nine v. N.H. Dep't of Fish Game, 154 N.H. 46, 908 A.2d 146, 2006 N.H. LEXIS 113 (2006).

Executive Director of the New Hampshire Department of Fish and Game violated RSA 91-A:2, II by excluding a television station's cameras from a hunting license hearing. Even if N.H. Code Admin. R. Ann. Fis. 203.01(b) could be read as authorizing the Director to take such action, a Department regulation could not override the clear directive of RSA 91-A:2, II. WMUR Channel Nine v. N.H. Dep't of Fish Game, 154 N.H. 46, 908 A.2d 146, 2006 N.H. LEXIS 113 (2006).

Though the Executive Director of the New

Hampshire Department of Fish and Game violated RSA 91-A:2, II by excluding a television station's cameras from a hunting license hearing on grounds that the commotion they would cause would deprive the license applicant of his right to a fair hearing, the station was properly denied attorney's fees under RSA 91-A:8. The trial court properly found, given the state of the case law, that the Director neither knew nor should have known that his conduct violated RSA 91-A:2, II. WMUR Channel Nine v. N.H.

Dep't of Fish Game, 154 N.H. 46, 908 A.2d 146, 2006 N.H. LEXIS 113 (2006).

Cited:
Cited in Stoneman v. Tamworth School District, 114 N.H. 371, 320 A.2d 657, 1974 N.H. LEXIS 281 (1974); Orford Teachers Ass'n v. Watson, 121 N.H. 118, 427 A.2d 21, 1981 N.H. LEXIS 255 (1981); 1986 Op. Att'y Gen. 220; Op. Atty. Gen. 231; 1987 Op. Att'y Gen. 122.

RESEARCH REFERENCES

New Hampshire Practice.
15 N.H.P. Land Use Planning and Zoning § 28.05.

ALR.
Attorney-client exception under state law making proceedings by public bodies open to the public. 34 A.L.R.5th 591.

Emergency exception under state law making proceedings by public bodies open to the public. 33 A.L.R.5th 731.

What constitutes newspaper of "general circulation" within meaning of state statutes requiring publication of official notices and the like in such newspaper. 24 A.L.R.4th 822.

91-A:3. Nonpublic Sessions.

I. (a) Bodies or agencies shall not meet in nonpublic session, except for one of the purposes set out in paragraph II. No session at which evidence, information or testimony in any form is received shall be closed to the public, except as provided in paragraph II. No body or agency may enter nonpublic session, except pursuant to a motion properly made and seconded.

(b) Any motion to enter nonpublic session shall state on its face the specific exemption under paragraph II which is relied upon as foundation for the nonpublic session. The vote on any such motion shall be by roll call, and shall require the affirmative vote of the majority of members present.

(c) All discussions held and decisions made during nonpublic session shall be confined to the matters set out in the motion.

II. Only the following matters shall be considered or acted upon in nonpublic session:

(a) The dismissal, promotion or compensation of any public employee or the disciplining of such employee, or the investigation of any charges against him, unless the employee affected (1) has a right to a meeting and (2) requests that the meeting be open, in which case the request shall be granted.

(b) The hiring of any person as a public employee.

(c) Matters which, if discussed in public, would likely affect adversely the reputation of any person, other than a member of the body or agency itself, unless such person requests an open meeting. This exemption shall extend to any application for assistance or tax abatement or waiver of a fee, fine, or other levy, if based on inability to pay or poverty of the applicant.

(d) Consideration of the acquisition, sale or lease of real or personal property which, if discussed in public, would likely benefit a party or parties whose interests are adverse to those of the general community.

(e) Consideration or negotiation of pending claims or litigation which has been threatened in writing or filed against the body or agency or any subdivision thereof, or against any member thereof because of his or her membership in such body or agency, until the claim or litigation has been fully adjudicated or otherwise settled. Any application filed for tax abatement, pursuant to law, with any body or board shall not constitute a threatened or filed litigation against any body, board, or agency for the purposes of this subparagraph.

(f) Consideration of applications by the adult parole board under RSA 651-A.

(g) Consideration of security-related issues bearing on the immediate safety of security personnel or inmates at the county correctional facilities by county correctional superintendents or their designees.

(h) Consideration of applications by the business finance authority under RSA 162-A:7–10 and 162-A:13, where consideration of an application in public session would cause harm to the applicant or would inhibit full discussion of the application.

(i) Consideration of matters relating to the preparation for and the carrying out of emergency functions, including training to carry out such functions, developed by local or state safety officials that are directly intended to thwart a deliberate act that is intended to result in widespread or severe damage to property or widespread injury or loss of life.

III. Minutes of proceedings in nonpublic session shall be kept and the record of all actions shall be promptly made available for public inspection, except as provided in this section. Minutes and decisions reached in nonpublic session shall be publicly disclosed within 72 hours of the meeting, unless, by recorded vote of ⅔ of the members present, it is determined that divulgence of the information likely would affect adversely the reputation of any person other than a member of the body or agency itself, or render the proposed action ineffective, or pertain to terrorism, more specifically, to matters relating to the preparation for and the carrying out of all emergency functions, developed by local or state safety officials that are directly intended to thwart a deliberate act that is intended to result in widespread or severe damage to property or widespread injury or loss of life. This shall include training to carry out such functions. In the event of such circumstances, information may be withheld until, in the opinion of a majority of members, the aforesaid circumstances no longer apply.

Source.

1967, 251:1. 1969, 482:2. 1971, 327:3. 1977, 540:4. 1983, 184:1. 1986, 83:4. 1991, 217:3. 1992, 34:1, 2. 1993, 46:1, eff. June 7, 1993; 335:16, eff. June 29, 1993. 2002, 222:2, 3, eff. Jan. 1, 2003. 2004, 42:1, eff. Jan. 1, 2005.

Amendments
—2004. Paragraph II(c): Added the second sentence.

Paragraph II(d): Amended without change.
Paragraph II(e): Inserted "or her" following "of his" in the first sentence and added the second sentence.

—2002. Paragraph II(i): Added.
Paragraph III: Inserted "or pertain to terrorism, more specifically, to matters relating to the preparation for and the carrying out of all emergency functions, developed by local or

state safety officials that are directly intended to thwart a deliberate act that is intended to result in widespread or severe damage to property or widespread injury or loss of life" following "ineffective" in the second sentence, and added the third sentence.

—1993. Paragraph II(g): Added by ch. 46. Paragraph II(h): Added by ch. 335.

—1992. Paragraph II: Substituted "(1) has a right to a meeting and (2) requests that the meeting be open, in which case the request shall be granted" for "requests an open meeting" at the end of subpar. (a) and inserted "real or personal" preceding "property" in subpar. (d).

—1991. Rewritten to the extent that a detailed comparison would be impracticable.

—1986. Paragraph II: Added the second sentence in the introductory paragraph and added subpars. (e) and (f).

—1983. Paragraph II: Rewrote the introductory paragraph and deleted subpar. (e).

—1977. Rewritten to the extent that a detailed comparison would be impracticable.

—1971. Paragraph II(e): Added.

—1969. Paragraph I: Rewritten to the extent that a detailed comparison would be impracticable.

Cross References.
Dismissal of town officer for breach of confidentiality, see RSA 42:1-a.

NOTES TO DECISIONS

Analysis

1. Construction
2. Construction with other laws
3. Finally approved
4. Employment contracts
5. Budget review
6. Legal advice
7. Minutes
8. Termination of employee

1. Construction

Statutory exemption from public access to executive sessions contained in this chapter, like all other exemptions, must be construed narrowly. Orford Teachers Ass'n v. Watson, 121 N.H. 118, 427 A.2d 21, 1981 N.H. LEXIS 255 (1981).

The 1969 and 1971 amendments to this section indicate a disposition to broaden its scope and application. Herron v. Northwood, 111 N.H. 324, 282 A.2d 661, 1971 N.H. LEXIS 191 (1971).

2. Construction with other laws

Board of Registration in Medicine erred in denying request of doctor for an open hearing, on a complaint filed against the doctor, on the basis of subparagraph II(c) of this section where RSA 329:17, X, relating to disciplinary action against doctors, specifically provided for an open hearing upon request of the doctor. Appeal of Plantier, 126 N.H. 500, 494 A.2d 270, 1985 N.H. LEXIS 341, 51 A.L.R.4th 1129 (1985).

Notwithstanding this chapter, intervenors,

as real party in interest, had available the use of traditional discovery techniques, subject to the exclusion of inquiry into the mental processes of the administrative decision-makers. Society for Protection of N.H. Forests v. Water Supply & Pollution Control Comm'n, 115 N.H. 192, 337 A.2d 788, 1975 N.H. LEXIS 257 (1975).

3. Finally approved

"Finally approved," as used in paragraph I, must be read to connote finality within the scope of the powers delegated to a given board, commission, agency or authority subject to the provisions of the statute. Herron v. Northwood, 111 N.H. 324, 282 A.2d 661, 1971 N.H. LEXIS 191 (1971).

"Finally approved," as used in this section, applied to Budget Committee's submission of budget it had prepared for school district and town expenditures, not to approval of budget by voters, as "finally approved" related to bodies' and agencies' final approval, so that fact final action on the budget was by the voters did not allow Budget Committee, following public hearing, to hold a closed, secret executive session for the purpose of giving its final approval to its recommendations for budget expenditures. Herron v. Northwood, 111 N.H. 324, 282 A.2d 661, 1971 N.H. LEXIS 191 (1971).

4. Employment contracts

School board meeting at which it was voted to terminate principal's contract was not an "executive session" or a meeting at which the "hiring" of the principal was considered, and notice of the meeting should have been given. Stoneman v. Tamworth School District, 114 N.H. 371, 320 A.2d 657, 1974 N.H. LEXIS 281 (1974).

5. Budget review

Under paragraph I of this section, municipal finance committee could properly meet in executive session to review the budget and receive information relating to it, so long as no final action was taken by the committee and no recommendation to the city council was formulated or agreed upon. Selkowe v. Bean, 109 N.H. 247, 249 A.2d 35, 1968 N.H. LEXIS 171, 38 A.L.R.3d 1066 (1968).

6. Legal advice

Where Water Supply and Pollution Control Commission received legal advice regarding issue whether it should grant a permit to Public Service Company, which desired to build nuclear generating electrical units, its failure to pass contents of advice on to party opposing the permit was not a violation of this chapter. Society for Protection of N.H. Forests v. Water Supply & Pollution Control Comm'n, 115 N.H. 192, 337 A.2d 788, 1975 N.H. LEXIS 257 (1975).

7. Minutes

Construing the provisions of the right-to-know law for withholding minutes narrowly, supreme court concluded that there is no blanket exemption for minutes of executive sessions, and that they are public records covered by RSA 91-A:4. Orford Teachers Ass'n v. Watson, 121 N.H. 118, 427 A.2d 21, 1981 N.H. LEXIS 255 (1981).

When there is a question under the right-to-know law whether minutes are exempt from public access, trial judge should conduct an in camera review to determine whether portions of the minutes meet any of the other statutory exemptions. Orford Teachers Ass'n v. Watson, 121 N.H. 118, 427 A.2d 21, 1981 N.H. LEXIS 255 (1981).

8. Termination of employee

Governmental body may not move to go into executive session for the purpose of considering termination of a public employee unless it has previously put that employee on notice that such a motion would be made. Johnson v. Nash, 135 N.H. 534, 608 A.2d 200, 1992 N.H. LEXIS 73 (1992).

Cited:

Cited in Appeal of Exeter, 126 N.H. 685, 495 A.2d 1288, 1985 N.H. LEXIS 352 (1985); Perras v. Clements, 127 N.H. 603, 503 A.2d 843, 1986 N.H. LEXIS 208 (1986); 1986 Op. Att'y Gen. 220; 1986 Op. Att'y Gen. 231.

91-A:4. Minutes and Records Available for Public Inspection.

I. Every citizen during the regular or business hours of all such bodies or agencies, and on the regular business premises of such bodies or agencies, has the right to inspect all public records, including minutes of meetings of the bodies or agencies, and to make memoranda, abstracts, and photographic or photostatic copies of the records or minutes so inspected, except as otherwise prohibited by statute or RSA 91-A:5.

I-a. Records of any payment made to an employee of any public body or agency listed in RSA 91-A:1-a, I(a)–(d), or to the employee's agent or designee, upon the resignation, discharge, or retirement of the employee, paid in addition to regular salary and accrued vacation, sick, or other leave, shall immediately be made available without alteration for public inspection. All records of payments shall be available for public inspection notwithstanding that the matter may have been considered or acted upon in nonpublic session pursuant to RSA 91-A:3.

II. After the completion of a meeting of such bodies or agencies, every citizen, during the regular or business hours of all such bodies or agencies, and on the regular business premises of such bodies or agencies, has the right to inspect all notes, materials, tapes or other sources used for compiling the minutes of such meetings, and to make memoranda, abstracts, photographic or photostatic copies, or tape record such notes, materials, tapes or sources inspected, except as otherwise prohibited by statute or RSA 91-A:5.

III. Each body or agency shall keep and maintain all public records in its custody at its regular office or place of business in an accessible place and, if there is no such office or place of business, the public records pertaining to such body or agency shall be kept in an office of the political subdivision in which such body or agency is located or, in the case of a state agency, in an office designated by the secretary of state.

IV. Each public body or agency shall, upon request for any public record reasonably described, make available for inspection and copying any such public record within its files when such records are immediately available for such release. If a public body or agency is unable to make a public record available for immediate inspection and copying, it shall, within 5 business days of request, make such record available, deny the request in writing with reasons, or furnish written acknowledgment of the receipt of the request and a statement of the time reasonably necessary to determine whether the request shall be granted or denied. If a photocopying machine or other device maintained for use by a body or agency is used by the body or agency to copy the public record or document requested, the person requesting the copy may be charged the actual cost of providing the copy, which cost may be collected by the body or agency. Nothing in this section shall exempt any person from paying fees otherwise established by law for obtaining copies of public records or documents, but if such fee is established for the copy, no additional costs or fees shall be charged.

V. In the same manner as set forth in RSA 91-A:4, IV, any body or agency which maintains its records in a computer storage system may, in lieu of providing original documents, provide a printout of any record reasonably described and which the agency has the capacity to produce in a manner that does not reveal information which is confidential under this chapter or any other law. Access to work papers, personnel data and other confidential information under RSA 91-A:5, IV shall not be provided.

VI. Every agreement to settle a lawsuit against a governmental unit, threatened lawsuit, or other claim, entered into by any political subdivision or its insurer, shall be kept on file at the municipal clerk's office and made available for public inspection for a period of no less than 10 years from the date of settlement.

Source.
1967, 251:1. 1983, 279:2. 1986, 83:5, eff. Jan. 1, 1987. 1997, 90:2, eff. Aug. 2, 1997. 2001, 223:2, eff. Jan. 1, 2002. 2004, 246:2, eff. Aug. 14, 2004.

Amendments
—**2004.** Paragraph VI: Added.

—**2001.** Paragraph I-a: Substituted "I(a)–(d)" for "I–IV" in the first sentence.

—1997. Paragraph I-a: Added.

—1986. Paragraphs III–IV: Added.

—1983. Designated the existing provisions of the section as par. I, made minor stylistic changes in that paragraph, and added par. II.

Cross References.

Access to analysis and compilations of data prepared by cancer registry, see RSA 141-B:9.

Disposition of municipal records, see RSA 33-A.

State records management and archives, see RSA 5:25 et seq.

NOTES TO DECISIONS

Analysis

1. Right to inspect generally
2. Temporarily unavailable records
3. Furnishing of copies
4. Minutes of executive sessions
5. Employment records
6. Real estate records
7. Public utilities
8. Destruction of tapes and notes used to prepare minutes
9. Agency budget materials
10. Records not in final form
11. Work Papers
12. Mootness

1. Right to inspect generally

Trial court erred in considering whether the New Hampshire Department of Resources and Economic Development's (DRED's) conduct in withholding certain requested documents by an organization was reasonable or whether it committed a knowing violation when rejecting the organization's request for costs, which required the trial court's denial of costs to the organization to be vacated. Since the organization's request for costs remained viable only if DRED violated the Right-to-Know Law, the case was remanded to the trial court to consider costs and the lawfulness of the DRED's conduct in its delayed disclosure and retention of documents. ATV Watch v. N.H. Dep't of Res. & Econ. Dev., — N.H. —, 923 A.2d 1061, 2007 N.H. LEXIS 72 (May 11, 2007).

Photographs which police took with the consent of people who were stopped by police but not arrested were public records, and the trial court's judgment ordering the City of Manchester to provide a civil liberties union with access to consensual photographs which police officers took over a five-year period was upheld. N.H. Civil Liberties Union v. City of Manchester, 149 N.H. 437, 821 A.2d 1014, 2003 N.H. LEXIS 61 (2003).

Right to inspect does not depend upon a need, or demonstration of a need, for the information. Mans v. Lebanon School Board, 112 N.H. 160, 290 A.2d 866, 1972 N.H. LEXIS 166 (1972).

2. Temporarily unavailable records

Trial court properly concluded that official did not violate this section by failing to provide requested documents immediately on the basis that the official was "too busy," where documents were sent to citizen two days later. Brent v. Paquette, 132 N.H. 415, 567 A.2d 976, 1989 N.H. LEXIS 123 (1989).

Where the only school official with the authority to respond to request for information was on vacation when the request was made, trial court properly concluded that computation of 5-day period within which official had to respond began on the day this official returned from vacation. Brent v. Paquette, 132 N.H. 415, 567 A.2d 976, 1989 N.H. LEXIS 123 (1989).

Where town resident asked town building inspector for plans for proposed industrial park, the latter said the chairman of the planning board had them out for the day on official business, and town otherwise at all times provided resident with access to the plans, town did not deny resident access to the plans in violation of this section. Gallagher v. Town of Windham, 121 N.H. 156, 427 A.2d 37, 1981 N.H. LEXIS 271 (1981).

3. Furnishing of copies

This section does not contain language imposing an absolute duty on towns or agencies to provide copies of public records to citizens; it contemplates that the records be made available for inspection and reproduction. Gallagher v. Town of Windham, 121 N.H. 156, 427 A.2d 37, 1981 N.H. LEXIS 271 (1981).

Where record did not demonstrate that plaintiff offered to pay town for copies of town records were they provided to her by photocopying them on town's photocopier, and the parties' briefs were silent on the issue, finding below that town did not violate this section when town did not provide copies of the record to plaintiff was amply supported by the evidence. Gallagher v. Town of Windham, 121 N.H. 156, 427 A.2d 37, 1981 N.H. LEXIS 271 (1981).

4. Minutes of executive sessions

Construing the provisions of the right-to-know law for withholding minutes narrowly, supreme court concluded that there is no blanket exemption for minutes of executive sessions, and that they are public records covered by this section. Orford Teachers Ass'n v. Watson, 121 N.H. 118, 427 A.2d 21, 1981 N.H. LEXIS 255 (1981).

5. Employment records

Where public employee labor relations board's orders were within its jurisdiction and were supported by ample evidence in the record, superior court properly ordered enforcement of board's order that school board produce specific salary information for school year so that public employee labor relations board could determine which teachers were entitled to back pay and amount owing to each one under master agreement, because this information was contained in records which any citizen had a right to examine. Rochester School Board v. Public Employee Labor Relations Board, 119 N.H. 45, 398 A.2d 823, 1979 N.H. LEXIS 240 (1979).

Order that school district administrator supply educational association representing striking teacher with the names and addresses of substitute teachers hired during the strike was proper. Timberlane Regional Educational Association v. Crompton, 114 N.H. 315, 319 A.2d 632, 1974 N.H. LEXIS 267 (1974).

Teachers' contracts with school board were public records under this section. Mans v. Lebanon School Board, 112 N.H. 160, 290 A.2d 866, 1972 N.H. LEXIS 166 (1972).

6. Real estate records

Computer tape containing information contained on approximately 35,000 field record cards made out when city had all its real estate revaluated, each card containing, inter alia, details of land, buildings, owners, use, topography, improvements, area trends, construction, value and a sketch of the property, was a public record under this section, and was not exempt from disclosure under RSA 91-A:5; and disclosure to the public would not constitute an unconstitutional invasion of privacy. Menge v. City of Manchester, 113 N.H. 533, 311 A.2d 116, 1973 N.H. LEXIS 311 (1973).

7. Public utilities

Intervenors opposing permit to company planning to build nuclear generating electrical units had right to examine all the evidence relied upon by the commission involved in making its final determination. Society for Protection of N.H. Forests v. Water Supply & Pollution Control Comm'n, 115 N.H. 192, 337 A.2d 788, 1975 N.H. LEXIS 257 (1975).

8. Destruction of tapes and notes used to prepare minutes

School official's practice of routinely destroying tapes and notes used to prepare minutes of public meetings did not violate this section, where the tapes and notes were destroyed only after the minutes of the meetings were approved. Brent v. Paquette, 132 N.H. 415, 567 A.2d 976, 1989 N.H. LEXIS 123 (1989).

9. Agency budget materials

State agency budget requests and income estimates are subject to public scrutiny on October 1, the statutory deadline for their submission to the commissioner of administrative services, unless they are exempt from the provisions of the Right-to-Know Law. Chambers v. Gregg, 135 N.H. 478, 606 A.2d 811, 1992 N.H. LEXIS 62 (1992).

10. Records not in final form

Trial court erred in failing to order disclosure of preliminary materials prepared for, but not expressly incorporated in, agency's final audit report, since Right-to-Know Law did not exempt public records from disclosure simply because they were not in their final form. Goode v. New Hampshire Office of Legislative Budget Assistant, 145 N.H. 451, 767 A.2d 393, 2000 N.H. LEXIS 92 (2000).

11. Work Papers

Even if certain interview materials from an audit by the New Hampshire Legislative Budget Assistant constituted work papers within the meaning of this section, a balancing test for exemption from disclosure applied, just as with other confidential materials, and the materials were not exempt from disclosure under that test, as the government's interest in nondisclosure did not outweigh the public's interest in disclosure, especially where there was no evidence that requiring disclosure of such materials would have caused future auditors to be less honest or complete in recording information. Goode v. N.H. Office of the Legislative Budget Assistant, 148 N.H. 551, 813 A.2d 381, 2002 N.H. LEXIS 168 (2002).

Fact that records are "work papers" within the meaning of RSA 91-A:4, V does not render them categorically exempt from disclosure; rather, as with other asserted confidential information under RSA 91-A:5, IV, a court must balance the competing interests regarding disclosure and non-disclosure. Goode v. N.H. Office of the Legislative Budget Assistant, 148 N.H. 551, 813 A.2d 381, 2002 N.H. LEXIS 168 (2002).

12. Mootness

Trial court erred by dismissing, as moot, the remainder of an organization's Right-to-Know

Law petition requesting all terrain vehicle trail documentation from the New Hampshire Department of Resources and Economic Development as the trial court was required to determine if the state agency's conduct in withholding the documents was unlawful despite the ultimate release of the documents since the organization may have been entitled to a remedy despite the ultimate release of the documents. ATV Watch v. N.H. Dep't of Res. & Econ. Dev., — N.H. —, 923 A.2d 1061, 2007 N.H. LEXIS 72 (May 11, 2007).

Cited:

Cited in 1986 Op. Att'y Gen. 198; New Hampshire Challenge, Inc. v. Commissioner, N.H. Dep't of Educ., 142 N.H. 246, 698 A.2d 1252, 1997 N.H. LEXIS 85 (1997).

RESEARCH REFERENCES

New Hampshire Bar Journal.

For Article, "What Do You Have the Right to Know," see 43 N.H.B.J. 1 (March 2002).

ALR.

What are "records" of agency which must be

made available under state freedom of information act. 27 A.L.R.4th 680.

91-A:5. Exemptions.

The following records are exempted from the provisions of this chapter:

I. Records of grand and petit juries.

II. Records of parole and pardon boards.

III. Personal school records of pupils.

IV. Records pertaining to internal personnel practices; confidential, commercial, or financial information; test questions, scoring keys, and other examination data used to administer a licensing examination, examination for employment, or academic examinations; and personnel, medical, welfare, library user, videotape sale or rental, and other files whose disclosure would constitute invasion of privacy. Without otherwise compromising the confidentiality of the files, nothing in this paragraph shall prohibit a body or agency from releasing information relative to health or safety from investigative files on a limited basis to persons whose health or safety may be affected.

V. Teacher certification records, both hard copies and computer files, in the department of education, provided that the department shall make available teacher certification status information.

VI. Records pertaining to matters relating to the preparation for and the carrying out of all emergency functions, including training to carry out such functions, developed by local or state safety officials that are directly intended to thwart a deliberate act that is intended to result in widespread or severe damage to property or widespread injury or loss of life.

VII. Unique pupil identification information collected in accordance with RSA 193-E:5.

VIII. Any notes or other materials made for personal use that do not have an official purpose, including notes and materials made prior to, during, or after a public proceeding.

IX. Preliminary drafts, notes, and memoranda and other documents not in their final form and not disclosed, circulated, or available to a quorum or a majority of those entities defined in RSA 91-A:1-a.

Source.
1967, 251:1. 1986, 83:6. 1989, 184:2. 1990, 134:1. 1993, 79:1, eff. June 22, 1993. 2002, 222:4, eff. Jan. 1, 2003. 2004, 147:5, eff. Aug. 1, 2004; 246:3, 4, eff. Aug. 14, 2004.

Amendments
—**2004.** Chapter 147 added par. VII.
Chapter 246 inserted "following" preceding "records" and deleted "of the following bodies" thereafter in the introductory paragraph, added "records of" in pars. I and II, and added pars. VIII and IX.

—**2002.** Paragraph VI: Added.

—**1993.** Paragraph V: Added.

—**1990.** Paragraph IV: Inserted "videotape sale or rental" following "library user" in the first sentence.

—**1989.** Paragraph IV: Inserted "library user" following "welfare" in the first sentence.

—**1986.** Paragraph IV: Rewritten to the extent that a detailed comparison would be impracticable.

Purpose of 1989 amendment.
1989, 184:1, eff. July 21, 1989, provided: "The Access to Public Records and Meetings Law, RSA 91-A, or Right-to-Know Law, does not include a definition of what constitutes a public record. The New Hampshire supreme court has applied a balancing test to determine whether a record is public by weighing the benefits of disclosure to the public versus the benefits of nondisclosure. By weighing the benefits of allowing disclosure of library user records against the benefits of denial of disclosure, the general court has determined that the benefits of nondisclosure clearly prevail. This act, therefore, exempts library user records from RSA 91-A to ensure that the individual's right to privacy regarding the nature of the library materials used by the individual is not invaded. To protect the right to privacy of all New Hampshire citizens, both public and other than public library records are protected."

Cross References.
Access to information relating to location of archeological sites, see RSA 227-C:11.
Confidentiality of enhanced 911 system records, see RSA 106-H:14.
Confidentiality of information compiled for statewide 911 system, see RSA 106-H:14.
Confidentiality of videotape rental and sales records, see RSA 351-A:1.
Dismissal of town officer for breach of confidentiality, see RSA 42:1-a.
Confidentiality and disclosure of library user records, see RSA 201-D:11.

NOTES TO DECISIONS

Analysis

1. Construction
2. Factors considered
3. Grand juries
4. Salaries
5. Real estate records
6. Names and addresses of pupils
7. Agency budget materials
8. Internal personnel practices
9. Market analysis
10. Audit interview materials
11. Police Records
12. Mootness

1. Construction
The statute requires an analysis of both whether the information sought is "confidential, commercial, or financial information," and whether disclosure would constitute an invasion of privacy. Union Leader Corp. v. New Hampshire Hous. Fin. Auth., 142 N.H. 540, 705

A.2d 725, 1997 N.H. LEXIS 132 (1997).

In determining whether information is sufficiently "confidential" to justify nondisclosure, the emphasis should be placed on the potential harm that will result from disclosure, rather than simply promises of confidentiality, or whether the information has customarily been regarded as confidential. Union Leader Corp. v. New Hampshire Hous. Fin. Auth., 142 N.H. 540, 705 A.2d 725, 1997 N.H. LEXIS 132 (1997).

When a public entity seeks to avoid disclosure of material under Right-to-Know Law, that entity bears a heavy burden to shift balance toward nondisclosure. Union Leader Corp. v. City of Nashua, 141 N.H. 473, 686 A.2d 310, 1996 N.H. LEXIS 127 (1996).

2. Factors considered

When reviewing exemptions from Right-to-Know Law, court balances public interest in disclosure of requested information against government interest in nondisclosure, and in privacy exemption cases, the individual's privacy interest in nondisclosure. Union Leader Corp. v. City of Nashua, 141 N.H. 473, 686 A.2d 310, 1996 N.H. LEXIS 127 (1996).

Although trial court's ex parte, in camera review of records whose release could cause invasion of privacy was plainly appropriate, court erred in considering plaintiff's motives in seeking disclosure of information. Union Leader Corp. v. City of Nashua, 141 N.H. 473, 686 A.2d 310, 1996 N.H. LEXIS 127 (1996).

3. Grand juries

The legislature has protected the secrecy of grand jury proceedings by specifically exempting them from the purview of this otherwise expansive statute. State v. Purrington, 122 N.H. 458, 446 A.2d 451, 1982 N.H. LEXIS 377 (1982).

4. Salaries

In determining whether teachers' salaries are exempted from the provisions of this chapter as being financial or private information, the benefits of disclosure to the public are to be balanced against the benefits of non-disclosure to the school administration and teachers. Mans v. Lebanon School Board, 112 N.H. 160, 290 A.2d 866, 1972 N.H. LEXIS 166 (1972).

Teachers' salaries are not exempt from inspection. Mans v. Lebanon School Board, 112 N.H. 160, 290 A.2d 866, 1972 N.H. LEXIS 166 (1972).

5. Real estate records

A property owner was not entitled to copies of appraisal reports prepared in connection with condemnation proceedings under the provisions of this chapter since disclosure of information regarding the range of offers of compensation available to the state would put the property owner in an unfair bargaining position. Perras v. Clements, 127 N.H. 603, 503 A.2d 843, 1986 N.H. LEXIS 208 (1986).

Computer tape containing information contained on approximately 35,000 field record cards made out when city had all its real estate revaluated, each card containing, inter alia, details of land, buildings, owners, use, topography, improvements, area trends, construction, value and a sketch of the property, was a public record under RSA 91-A:4, and was not exempt from disclosure under this section; and disclosure to the public would not constitute an unconstitutional invasion of privacy. Menge v. City of Manchester, 113 N.H. 533, 311 A.2d 116, 1973 N.H. LEXIS 311 (1973).

6. Names and addresses of pupils

Names and addresses of children of a public school district are part of the personal school records of the pupils and therefore exempt from public inspection under paragraph III of this section. Brent v. Paquette, 132 N.H. 415, 567 A.2d 976, 1989 N.H. LEXIS 123 (1989).

Providing access to records pertaining to names and addresses of public school students would constitute an invasion of the students' and their parents' privacy under paragraph IV of this section. Brent v. Paquette, 132 N.H. 415, 567 A.2d 976, 1989 N.H. LEXIS 123 (1989).

7. Agency budget materials

State agency budget requests and income estimates are subject to public scrutiny on October 1, the statutory deadline for their submission to the commissioner of administrative services, unless they are exempt from the provisions of the Right-to-Know Law. Chambers v. Gregg, 135 N.H. 478, 606 A.2d 811, 1992 N.H. LEXIS 62 (1992).

To determine whether state agency budget requests and income estimates are exempt from the Right-to-Know Law as confidential, the benefits of disclosure to the public must be weighed against the benefits of nondisclosure to the government. Chambers v. Gregg, 135 N.H. 478, 606 A.2d 811, 1992 N.H. LEXIS 62 (1992).

8. Internal personnel practices

Trial court properly held that an investigatory report was exempt from disclosure under RSA 91-A:5, IV; the report, which resulted from allegations that one water precinct employee was harassing another, could have resulted in disciplinary action and was thus a record pertaining to internal personnel practices. Furthermore, there was no merit to petitioners' argument that the exemption applied only to internal police investigations, and the precinct's release of another report did not create an estoppel because that report related to precinct mismanagement, not internal personnel practices. Hounsell v. N. Conway Water Precinct, 154 N.H. 1, 903 A.2d 987, 2006 N.H. LEXIS 108 (2006).

Certain investigatory documents under the control of the defendants, a police department and the department's chief, were exempt from disclosure as records pertaining to internal personnel practices; the documents in question were compiled during an internal investigation of a department lieutenant accused of making harassing phone calls. Union Leader Corp. v. Fenniman, 136 N.H. 624, 620 A.2d 1039, 1993 N.H. LEXIS 4 (1993).

9. Market analysis

A market analysis of potential condominium sales at a certain location was not exempt as commercial information since the negative competitive impact of disclosing market information regarding potential condominium sales that was gathered in 1987 was blunted by time, and did not, on balance, outweigh the public interest in understanding the market conditions that gave rise to the housing finance authority's role in the project. Union Leader Corp. v. New Hampshire Hous. Fin. Auth., 142 N.H. 540, 705 A.2d 725, 1997 N.H. LEXIS 132 (1997).

10. Audit interview materials

Even if certain interview materials from an audit by the New Hampshire Legislative Budget Assistant constituted confidential information under RSA 91-A:5, IV, the trial court erred in determining that the materials were exempt from disclosure, as the government's interest in nondisclosure did not outweigh the public's interest in disclosure, especially where there was no evidence that requiring disclosure of such materials would have caused future auditors to be less honest or complete in recording

information. Goode v. N.H. Office of the Legislative Budget Assistant, 148 N.H. 551, 813 A.2d 381, 2002 N.H. LEXIS 168 (2002).

11. Police Records

Law enforcement representatives did not meet their burden of justifying their withholding of requested documents that the father sought regarding the disappearance of the father's daughter following reports that the daughter had been involved in a traffic accident; since police investigative reports were not mentioned in the state law concerning the disclosure of government records, the state supreme court determined that the six-part test under the corresponding federal law applied and required the law enforcement representatives on remand of the case to the trial court to show how disclosure of the requested records could interfere with an ongoing investigation or law enforcement proceeding. Murray v. New Hampshire Div. of State Police, 154 N.H. 579, 913 A.2d 737, 2006 N.H. LEXIS 201 (2006).

Photographs which police took with the consent of people who were stopped by police but not arrested were public records, and the trial court's judgment ordering the City of Manchester to provide a civil liberties union with access to consensual photographs which police officers took over a five-year period was upheld. N.H. Civil Liberties Union v. City of Manchester, 149 N.H. 437, 821 A.2d 1014, 2003 N.H. LEXIS 61 (2003).

12. Mootness

Trial court erred by dismissing, as moot, the remainder of an organization's Right-to-Know Law petition requesting all terrain vehicle trail documentation from the New Hampshire Department of Resources and Economic Development as the trial court was required to determine if the state agency's conduct in withholding the documents was unlawful despite the ultimate release of the documents since the organization may have been entitled to a remedy despite the ultimate release of the documents. ATV Watch v. N.H. Dep't of Res. & Econ. Dev., — N.H. —, 923 A.2d 1061, 2007 N.H. LEXIS 72 (May 11, 2007).

Cited:

Cited in Hampton Nat'l Bank v. State, 114 N.H. 38, 314 A.2d 668, 1974 N.H. LEXIS 203 (1974); Orford Teachers Ass'n v. Watson, 121 N.H. 118, 427 A.2d 21, 1981 N.H. LEXIS 255 (1981); Gallagher v. Town of Windham, 121

N.H. 156, 427 A.2d 37, 1981 N.H. LEXIS 271 (1981); Hansen v. Lamontagne, 808 F. Supp. 89, 1992 U.S. Dist. LEXIS 19301 (D.N.H. 1992); Pivero v. Largy, 143 N.H. 187, 722 A.2d 461, 1998 N.H. LEXIS 91 (1998); Goode v. New Hampshire Office of Legislative Budget Assistant, 145 N.H. 451, 767 A.2d 393, 2000 N.H. LEXIS 92 (2000).

RESEARCH REFERENCES

New Hampshire Bar Journal.

For Article, "What Do You Have the Right to Know," see 43 N.H.B.J. 1 (March 2002).

ALR.

Construction and application of FOIA exemption 7(f), 5 U.S.C.S. § 552(b)(7)(F), which permits withholding of information compiled for law enforcement purposes if disclosure could reasonably be expected to endanger life or physical safety. 184 A.L.R. Fed. 435.

Discovery or inspection of state bar records of complaints against or investigations of attorneys. 83 A.L.R.3d 777.

Patient's right to disclosure of her or her own medical records under state freedom of information act. 26 A.L.R.4th 701.

Payroll records of individual government employees as subject to disclosure to public. 100 A.L.R.3d 699.

Restricting access to records of disciplinary proceedings against attorneys. 83 A.L.R.3d 749.

What are interagency or intra-agency memorandums or letters exempt from disclosure under the Freedom of Information Act (5 U.S.C.S.

§ 552(b)). 168 A.L.R. Fed. 143.

What constitutes "confidential source" within Freedom of Information Act exemption permitting nondisclosure of confidential source and, in some instances, of information furnished by confidential source (5 U.S.C.S. § 552(b)). 171 A.L.R. Fed. 193.

What constitutes legitimate research justifying inspection of state or local public records not open to inspection by general public. 40 A.L.R.4th 333.

What constitutes personal matters exempt from disclosure by invasion of privacy exemption under state freedom of information act. 26 A.L.R.4th 666.

What constitutes "trade secrets" exempt from disclosure under state freedom of information act. 27 A.L.R.4th 773.

What matters are exempt from disclosure under Freedom of Information Act (5 U.S.C.S. § 552(b)) as "specifically authorized under criteria established by an executive order to be kept secret in the interest of national defense or foreign policy." 169 A.L.R. Fed. 495.

91-A:5-a. Limited Purpose Release.

Records from non-public sessions under RSA 91-A:3, II(i) or that are exempt under RSA 91-A:5, VI may be released to local or state safety officials. Records released under this section shall be marked "limited purpose release" and shall not be redisclosed by the recipient.

Source.

2002, 222:5, eff. Jan. 1, 2003.

91-A:6. Employment Security.

This chapter shall apply to RSA 282-A, relative to employment security; however, in addition to the exemptions under RSA 91-A:5, the provisions of RSA 282-A:117–123 shall also apply; this provision shall be administered and construed in the spirit of that section, and the exemptions from the provisions of this chapter shall include anything exempt from public inspection under RSA 282-A:117–123 together with all records and data developed from RSA 282-A:117–123.

Source.

1967, 251:1. 1981, 576:5, eff. July 1, 1981.

Revision note.

Pursuant to 1981, 408:9, substituted "RSA 282-A" for "RSA 282" and "RSA 282-A:117–123" for "RSA 282:9(M)".

Substituted a semicolon for a comma following "shall also apply" to correct a grammatical error.

Amendments

—1981. Rewritten to the extent that a detailed comparison would be impracticable.

NOTES TO DECISIONS

Cited:

Cited in 1986 Op. Att'y Gen. 220.

91-A:7. Violation.

Any person aggrieved by a violation of this chapter may petition the superior court for injunctive relief. The courts shall give proceedings under this chapter priority on the court calendar. Such a petitioner may appear with or without counsel. The petition shall be deemed sufficient if it states facts constituting a violation of this chapter, and may be filed by the petitioner or his counsel with the clerk of court or any justice thereof. Thereupon the clerk of court or any justice shall order service by copy of the petition on the person or persons charged. When any justice shall find that time probably is of the essence, he may order notice by any reasonable means, and he shall have authority to issue an order ex parte when he shall reasonably deem such an order necessary to insure compliance with the provisions of this chapter.

Source.

1967, 251:1. 1977, 540:5, eff. Sept. 13, 1977.

Amendments

—1977. Added the third through sixth sentences.

NOTES TO DECISIONS

Review

In order to be heard in supreme court, issue of violation of this chapter must be promptly and properly raised below, especially where it does not appear that the alleged violation was obvious, intentional or prejudicial. Hardiman v.

Dover, 111 N.H. 377, 284 A.2d 905, 1971 N.H. LEXIS 206 (1971).

Cited:

Cited in Perras v. Clements, 127 N.H. 603, 503 A.2d 843, 1986 N.H. LEXIS 208 (1986).

91-A:8. Remedies.

I. If any body or agency or employee or member thereof, in violation of the provisions of this chapter, refuses to provide a public record or refuses access to a public proceeding to a person who reasonably requests the same, such body, agency, or person shall be liable for reasonable attorney's fees and costs incurred in a lawsuit under this chapter provided that the court finds that such lawsuit was necessary in order to make the information available or the proceeding open to the public. Fees shall not be awarded unless the court finds that the body, agency or person knew or should have known that the conduct engaged in was a violation of this chapter or where the parties, by agreement, provide that no such fees shall be paid. In any case where fees are awarded under this chapter, upon a finding that an officer, employee, or other official of a public body or agency has acted in bad faith in refusing to allow access to a public proceeding or to provide a public record, the court may award such fees personally against such officer, employee, or other official.

I-a. The court may award attorneys' fees to a board, agency or employee or member thereof, for having to defend against a person's lawsuit under the provisions of this chapter, when the court makes an affirmative finding that the lawsuit is in bad faith, frivolous, unjust, vexatious, wanton, or oppressive.

II. The court may invalidate an action of a public body or agency taken at a meeting held in violation of the provisions of this chapter, if the circumstances justify such invalidation.

III. In addition to any other relief awarded pursuant to this chapter, the court may issue an order to enjoin future violations of this chapter.

Source.
1973, 113:1. 1977, 540:6. 1986, 83:7, eff. Jan. 1, 1987. 2001, 289:3, eff. July 17, 2001.

Amendments
—2001. Paragraph I-a: Added.

—1986. Designated the existing provisions of the section as par. I, rewrote that paragraph, and added pars. II and III.

—1977. Rewritten to the extent that a detailed comparison would be impracticable.

NOTES TO DECISIONS

Analysis

1. Attorney's fees—Purpose
2. —Liability
3. —Review
4. Injunctive relief
5. Costs

1. Attorney's fees—Purpose

The word "shall" in the statute acts as a mandate if the necessary findings to support an award of attorney's fees are made. New Hampshire Challenge, Inc. v. Commissioner, N.H. Dep't of Educ., 142 N.H. 246, 698 A.2d 1252, 1997 N.H. LEXIS 85 (1997).

Provision for award of attorney's fees is critical to securing rights guaranteed by this section; attorney fee provision was enacted so that public's right-to-know law would not depend upon individual's ability to finance litigation. Bradbury v. Shaw, 116 N.H. 388, 360 A.2d 123, 1976 N.H. LEXIS 361 (1976).

2. —Liability

Though the Executive Director of the New Hampshire Department of Fish and Game violated RSA 91-A:2, II by excluding a television station's cameras from a hunting license hear-

ing on grounds that the commotion they would cause would deprive the license applicant of his right to a fair hearing, the station was properly denied attorney's fees under RSA 91-A:8. The trial court properly found, given the state of the case law, that the Director neither knew nor should have known that his conduct violated RSA 91-A:2, II. WMUR Channel Nine v. N.H. Dep't of Fish Game, 154 N.H. 46, 908 A.2d 146, 2006 N.H. LEXIS 113 (2006).

Where it was clear that a lawsuit by petitioner, the risk management administrator for the New Hampshire Property and Casualty Loss Program, was necessary to make the New Hampshire Legislative Budget Assistant (LBA) disclose certain materials related to an audit of the New Hampshire Property and Casualty Loss Program, the trial court erred in denying the administrator's request for attorney's fees under RSA 91-A:8, simply because the LBA voluntarily disclosed some of the materials after the supreme court found that the materials were not exempt from disclosure; instead, the trial court should have considered whether the LBA knew or should have known that its withholding of the information violated the Right-to-Know Law. Goode v. N.H. Office of the Legislative Budget Assistant, 148 N.H. 551, 813

A.2d 381, 2002 N.H. LEXIS 168 (2002).

The superior court utilized an incorrect legal standard in resolving the plaintiffs' request for attorney's fees when it denied such an award on the basis that the defendants' conduct was not a "knowing violation"; on remand, the court would be required to determine whether the defendants "should have known" that their conduct was improper. New Hampshire Challenge, Inc. v. Commissioner, N.H. Dep't of Educ., 142 N.H. 246, 698 A.2d 1252, 1997 N.H. LEXIS 85 (1997).

In a proceeding arising from the dismissal of the plaintiff police chief by a town, attorney's fees were improperly awarded against the town where (1) the town selectmen consulted with town counsel about what procedure should be followed before dismissing the plaintiff and followed that advice, (2) at the time of the plaintiff's dismissal, it was not generally understood among municipal law practitioners that advance notice was required to an employee that his or her dismissal would be considered in executive session, and (3) the town acted in good faith and the violation of the Right-To-Know Law was not obvious, deliberate, or willful. Voelbel v. Town of Bridgewater, 140 N.H. 446, 667 A.2d 1028, 1995 N.H. LEXIS 168 (1995).

Where defendants did not knowingly violate, or have reason to believe that their refusal to provide documents would violate, the Right-to-Know Law, plaintiff's request for attorney's fees was denied. Chambers v. Gregg, 135 N.H. 478, 606 A.2d 811, 1992 N.H. LEXIS 62 (1992).

Where mayor was sued in his official capacity, award of attorney's fees was properly chargeable to city. Bradbury v. Shaw, 116 N.H. 388, 360 A.2d 123, 1976 N.H. LEXIS 361 (1976).

Where plaintiff petitioned to secure access to records of mayor's industrial advisory committee under this section, and trial court ruled that committee was subject to right-to-know law although certain records of its meetings were exempt from disclosure, plaintiff was substantially successful and thus entitled to recover his counsel fees. Bradbury v. Shaw, 116 N.H. 388, 360 A.2d 123, 1976 N.H. LEXIS 361 (1976).

3. —Review

As the trial court properly denied petitioners' request for documents concerning internal personnel practices, there was no need for the appellate court to consider its denial of petition-

ers' request for attorney's fees. Hounsell v. N. Conway Water Precinct, 154 N.H. 1, 903 A.2d 987, 2006 N.H. LEXIS 108 (2006).

Because no abuse of discretion on the part of the trial court appeared on the record, its decision denying plaintiffs' petition for an award of attorney's fees under this section was affirmed. Orford Teachers Ass'n v. Watson, 122 N.H. 803, 451 A.2d 378, 1982 N.H. LEXIS 467 (1982).

Plaintiff's request for attorney's fees under Right-to-Know Law was properly denied, since agency neither knew nor should have known that its refusal to disclose materials was in violation of statute. Goode v. New Hampshire Office of Legislative Budget Assistant, 145 N.H. 451, 767 A.2d 393, 2000 N.H. LEXIS 92 (2000).

4. Injunctive relief

Trial court did not err by denying injunctive relief to an organization requesting information relating to the New Hampshire Department of Resources and Economic Development's intended purchase of a large tract of land as well as its plan to develop all terrain vehicle and other trails once the land was purchased, because at the time of the organization's Right-to-Know petition, the State did not own the land at issue, the property was not state land and, thus, the provisions of RSA 215-A:41, II(f) did not apply. ATV Watch v. N.H. Dep't of Res. & Econ. Dev., — N.H. —, 923 A.2d 1061, 2007 N.H. LEXIS 72 (May 11, 2007).

5. Costs

Trial court erred in considering whether the New Hampshire Department of Resources and Economic Development's (DRED's) conduct in withholding certain requested documents by an organization was reasonable or whether it committed a knowing violation when rejecting the organization's request for costs, which required the trial court's denial of costs to the organization to be vacated. Since the organization's request for costs remained viable only if DRED violated the Right-to-Know Law, the case was remanded to the trial court to consider costs and the lawfulness of the DRED's conduct in its delayed disclosure and retention of documents. ATV Watch v. N.H. Dep't of Res. & Econ. Dev., — N.H. —, 923 A.2d 1061, 2007 N.H. LEXIS 72 (May 11, 2007).

Cited:

Cited in Johnson v. Nash, 135 N.H. 534, 608 A.2d 200, 1992 N.H. LEXIS 73 (1992); Disabili-

ties Rights Ctr., Inc. v. Commissioner, N.H.
Dep't of Cors., 143 N.H. 674, 732 A.2d 1021,
1999 N.H. LEXIS 56 (1999).

RESEARCH REFERENCES

New Hampshire Practice.
5 N.H.P. Civil Practice & Procedure § 64.11.

New Hampshire Trial Bar News.
For article, "Contingent Fees Attacked," see
16 Trial Bar News 52 (Summer 1994).

ALR.
Allowance of punitive damages in state freedom of information actions. 13 A.L.R.6th 721.

Exhaustion of administrative remedies as
prerequisite to judicial action to compel disclosure under state freedom of information acts.
114 A.L.R.5th 283.

91-A:9. Destruction of Certain Information Prohibited.

A person is guilty of a misdemeanor who knowingly destroys any information with the purpose to prevent such information from being inspected or
disclosed in response to a request under this chapter. If a request for inspection
is denied on the grounds that the information is exempt under this chapter, the
requested material shall be preserved for 90 days or while any lawsuit
pursuant to RSA 91-A:7–8 is pending.

Source.
2002, 175:1, eff. Jan. 1, 2003.

Cross References.
Classification of crimes, see RSA 625:9

Sentences, see RSA 651.

Procedure for Release of Personal Information for Research Purposes

91-A:10. Release of Statistical Tables and Limited Data Sets for Research.

I. In this subdivision:

(a) "Agency" means each state board, commission, department, institution, officer or other state official or group.

(b) "Agency head" means the head of any governmental agency which is
responsible for the collection and use of any data on persons or summary data.

(c) "Cell size" means the count of individuals that share a set of characteristics contained in a statistical table.

(d) "Data set" means a collection of personal information on one or more
individuals, whether in electronic or manual files.

(e) "Direct identifiers" means:

(1) Names.

(2) Postal address information other than town or city, state, and zip
code.

(3) Telephone and fax numbers.

(4) Electronic mail addresses.

(5) Social security numbers.

(6) Certificate and license numbers.

(7) Vehicle identifiers and serial numbers, including license plate numbers.

(8) Personal Internet IP addresses and URLs.

(9) Biometric identifiers, including finger and voice prints.

(10) Personal photographic images.

(f) "Individual" means a human being, alive or dead, who is the subject of personal information and includes the individual's legal or other authorized representative.

(g) "Limited data set" means a data set from which all direct identifiers have been removed or blanked.

(h) "Personal information" means information relating to an individual that is reported to the state or is derived from any interaction between the state and an individual and which:

(1) Contains direct identifiers.

(2) Is under the control of the state.

(i) "Provided by law" means use and disclosure as permitted or required by New Hampshire state law governing programs or activities undertaken by the state or its agencies, or required by federal law.

(j) "Public record" means records available to any person without restriction.

(k) "State" means the state of New Hampshire, its agencies or instrumentalities.

(l) "Statistical table" means single or multi-variate counts based on the personal information contained in a data set and which does not include any direct identifiers.

II. Except as otherwise provided by law, upon request an agency shall release limited data sets and statistical tables with any cell size more than 0 and less than 5 contained in agency files to requestors for the purposes of research under the following conditions:

(a) The requestor submits a written application that contains:

(1) The following information about the principal investigator in charge of the research:

(A) name, address, and phone number;

(B) organizational affiliation;

(C) professional qualification; and

(D) name and phone number of principal investigator's contact person, if any.

(2) The names and qualifications of additional research staff, if any, who will have access to the data.

(3) A research protocol which shall contain:

(A) a summary of background, purposes, and origin of the research;

(B) a statement of the general problem or issue to be addressed by the research;

(C) the research design and methodology including either the topics of exploratory research or the specific research hypotheses to be tested;

(D) the procedures that will be followed to maintain the confidentiality of any data or copies of records provided to the investigator; and

(E) the intended research completion date.

(4) The following information about the data or statistical tables being requested:

(A) general types of information;

(B) time period of the data or statistical tables;

(C) specific data items or fields of information required, if applicable;

(D) medium in which the data or statistical tables are to be supplied; and

(E) any special format or layout of data requested by the principal investigator.

(b) The requestor signs a "Data Use Agreement" signed by the principal investigator that contains the following:

(1) Agreement not to use or further disclose the information to any person or organization other than as described in the application and as permitted by the Data Use Agreement without the written consent of the agency.

(2) Agreement not to use or further disclose the information as otherwise required by law.

(3) Agreement not to seek to ascertain the identity of individuals revealed in the limited data set and/or statistical tables.

(4) Agreement not to publish or make public the content of cells in statistical tables in which the cell size is more than 0 and less than 5 unless:

(A) otherwise provided by law; or

(B) the information is a public record.

(5) Agreement to report to the agency any use or disclosure of the information contrary to the agreement of which the principal investigator becomes aware.

(6) A date on which the data set and/or statistical tables will be returned to the agency and/or all copies in the possession of the requestor will be destroyed.

III. The agency head shall release limited data sets and statistical tables and sign the Data Use Agreement on behalf of the state when:

(a) The application submitted is complete.

(b) Adequate measures to ensure the confidentiality of any person are documented.

(c) The investigator and research staff are qualified as indicated by:

(1) Documentation of training and previous research, including prior publications; and

(2) Affiliation with a university, private research organization, medical center, state agency, or other institution which will provide sufficient research resources.

(d) There is no other state law, federal law, or federal regulation prohibiting release of the requested information.

IV. Within 10 days of a receipt of written application, the agency head, or designee, shall respond to the request. Whenever the agency head denies release of requested information, the agency head shall send the requestor a letter identifying the specific criteria which are the basis of the denial. Should release be denied due to other law, the letter shall identify the specific state law, federal law, or federal regulation prohibiting the release. Otherwise the agency head shall provide the requested data or set a date on which the data shall be provided.

V. Any person violating any provision of a signed Data Use Agreement shall be guilty of a violation.

VI. Nothing in this section shall exempt any requestor from paying fees otherwise established by law for obtaining copies of limited data sets or statistical tables. Such fees shall be based on the cost of providing the copy in the format requested. The agency head shall provide the requestor with a written description of the basis for the fee.

Source.
  2003, 292:2, eff. July 18, 2003.

Right-to-Know Oversight Commission

Prospective repeal of subdivision.
  2005, 3:2, provides for the repeal of this subdivision effective Nov. 1, 2010.

[RSA 91-A:11 repealed on November 1, 2010; see prospective repeal note preceding this section.]

91-A:11. Oversight Commission Established.

There is established an oversight commission to study and oversee the right-to-know law in light of the supreme court's decision in *Hawkins v. N.H. Department of Health and Human Services* and increasing use of electronic communications in the transaction of governmental business.

Source.   **Prospective repeal of subdivision.**
  2005, 3:1, eff. May 3, 2005.   See note set out preceding this section.

[RSA 91-A:12 repealed on November 1, 2010; see prospective repeal note preceding RSA 91-A:11.]

91-A:12. Membership and Compensation.

I. The members of the oversight commission shall be as follows:

(a) Four members of the house of representatives, one from the science, technology and energy committee, one from the municipal and county government committee, one from the judiciary committee, and one other member, appointed by the speaker of the house.

(b) Three members of the senate, appointed by the president of the senate.

(c) Three municipal officials, appointed by the New Hampshire Municipal Association.

(d) One school board member, appointed by the New Hampshire School Boards Association.

(e) One school administrator, appointed by the New Hampshire School Administrators Association.

(f) Two county officials, appointed by the New Hampshire Association of Counties.

(g) Four members of the public, one of whom shall be an attorney who has knowledge of and experience with the right-to-know law, one of whom shall be an information technology professional, and one of whom shall be a telecommunications professional, all appointed by the governor with the consent of the council.

(h) The attorney general, or designee.

II. Legislative members of the commission shall receive mileage at the legislative rate when attending to the duties of the commission.

Source.
2005, 3:1, eff. May 3, 2005.

Prospective repeal of subdivision.
See note set out preceding RSA 91-A:11.

[RSA 91-A:13 repealed on November 1, 2010; see prospective repeal note preceding RSA 91-A:11.]

91-A:13. Duties.

The commission shall study:

I. The need for disclosure requirements or guidelines for email and other electronic communication occurring between and among state, county, and local government appointed and elected officials and employees of governmental entities.

II. The need for disclosure requirements or guidelines for electronic communications with constituents of state, county, and local government appointed and elected officials and employees of governmental entities.

III. Archival requirements for electronic documents.

IV. The status of proprietary data within the definitions of the right-to-know law.

V. The ability to recover costs relative to the retrieval of electronic files and communications.

VI. Issues relative to public records posted to web sites of governmental entities.

VII. Whether a member of a body subject to the right-to-know law may participate in a meeting by teleconference or other electronic means.

VIII. The extent to which the public will be provided access to stored computer data under the right-to-know law.

IX. Any other matter deemed relevant by the commission.

Source.
2005, 3:1, eff. May 3, 2005.

Prospective repeal of subdivision.
See note set out preceding RSA 91-A:11.

[RSA 91-A:14 repealed on November 1, 2010; see prospective repeal note preceding RSA 91-A:11.]

91-A:14. Chairperson; Quorum.

The members of the commission shall elect a chairperson from among the members. Nine members of the commission shall constitute a quorum.

Source.
2005, 3:1, eff. May 3, 2005.

Prospective repeal of subdivision.
See note set out preceding RSA 91-A:11.

[RSA 91-A:15 repealed on November 1, 2010; see prospective repeal note preceding RSA 91-A:11.]

91-A:15. Report.

The commission shall make an annual report beginning on November 1, 2005, together with its findings and any recommendations for proposed legislation to the speaker of the house of representatives, the senate president, and the governor.

Source.
2005, 3:1, eff. May 3, 2005.

Prospective repeal of subdivision.
See note set out preceding RSA 91-A:11.

TITLE XII

PUBLIC SAFETY AND WELFARE

CHAPTER 155-A

NEW HAMPSHIRE BUILDING CODE

Cross References.

Building requirements for accommodation of physically disabled persons, see RSA 155:39-c, 39-d.

Double door safety in buildings open to public, see RSA 155:2-a.

Energy conservation in new building construction, see RSA 155-D.

Energy cost reduction in state facilities, see RSA 21-I:19-a et seq.

155-A:1. Definitions.

In this chapter:

I. "Building" means building as defined and interpreted by the International Code Council's International Building Code 2006.

II. "County" means the local legislative body of a county in which there are unincorporated towns or unorganized places.

III. "Local enforcement agency" means for a municipality that has adopted enforcement provisions or additional regulations under RSA 674:51, the building inspector or other local government official with authority to make inspections and to enforce the laws, ordinances and rules enacted by the state and by local government that establish standards and requirements applicable to the construction, alteration, or repair of buildings.

IV. "New Hampshire building code" or "state building code" means the adoption by reference of the International Building Code 2006, the International Plumbing Code 2006, the International Mechanical Code 2006, the International Energy Conservation Code 2006, and the International Residential Code 2006, as published by the International Code Council, and the National Electric Code 2005. The provisions of any other national code or model code referred to within a code listed in this definition shall not be included in the state building code unless specifically included in the codes listed in this definition.

V. "Person" means any individual or organized group of any kind, including partnerships, corporations, limited liability partnerships, limited liability companies, and other forms of association, as well as federal, state or local instrumentalities, political subdivisions, or officers.

VI. "Structure" means structure as defined and interpreted by the International Code Council's International Building Code 2006.

Source.

2002, 8:3, eff. Sept. 14, 2002. 2003, 245:1, eff. July 14, 2003. 2006, 112:1, eff. July 8, 2006. 2007, 187:1, 2, 3, eff. August 17, 2007.

Amendments

—2007. Paragraph I: Substituted "2006" for "2000" following "International Building Code".

Paragraph IV: Substituted "2006" for "2000" following "Code" throughout the paragraph and "2005" for "2002" following "National Electric Code".

Paragraph VI: Substituted "2006" for "2000" following "International Building Code".

—2006. Paragraph IV: Inserted "and the International Residential Code 2000" following "Conservation Code 2000" in the first sentence.

—2003. Paragraph IV: Substituted "National Electric Code 2002" for "National Electric Code 1999" in the first sentence.

155-A:2. State Building Code.

I. Except as provided in paragraphs II and III, all buildings, building components, and structures constructed in New Hampshire beginning one year after the effective date of the section, shall comply with the state building code and state fire code. The construction, design, structure, maintenance, and use of all buildings or structures to be erected and the alteration, renovation, rehabilitation, repair, maintenance, removal, or demolition of all buildings and structures previously erected shall be governed by the provisions of the state building code.

II. Standards, including definitions, established by the most recent edition of the Life Safety Code, NFPA Doc. No. 101, shall take precedence over all standards in the state building code relative to means of egress.

III. All new buildings shall conform to the requirements of the state fire code adopted pursuant to RSA 153:5 and to the extent that there is any conflict between the state building code and the state fire code, the state fire code shall take precedence unless otherwise determined by the board, subject to the review provisions contained in RSA 155-A:10.

IV. To the extent that it does not conflict with any other provision of law, the issuance of permits and the collection of fees pursuant to the state building code is expressly reserved for counties, towns, cities, and village districts.

V. Except for buildings owned by the state or the university system, the issuance of certificates of occupancy pursuant to the state building code is expressly reserved for counties, towns, cities, and village districts.

VI. Counties, towns, cities, and village districts may adopt by ordinance pursuant to RSA 674:51 any additional regulations provided that such regulations are not less stringent than the requirements of the state building code pursuant to this chapter and the state fire code pursuant to RSA 153.

VII. For any municipality which has not adopted an enforcement mechanism under RSA 674:51, the contractor of the building, building component, or structure shall notify the state fire marshal concerning the type of construction before construction begins excluding one- and 2-family dwellings.

VIII. The contractor of a building, building component, or structure shall be responsible for meeting the minimum requirements of the state building code. No municipality shall be held liable for any failure on the part of a contractor to comply with the provisions of the state building code.

IX. Nothing in this chapter shall be construed as amending, repealing, or superseding any local law, ordinance, code, or regulation, except local building code requirements that are less stringent than the state building code, and all buildings, building components, and structures shall comply with all applicable state or local building and fire code requirements, land use restrictions including but not limited to subdivision regulations, use and location restrictions, density and dimensional limitations, or historic district laws or ordinances.

X. Nothing in this chapter shall be construed to permit or encourage the state to initiate or assume an independent role in the administration and enforcement of the New Hampshire building code for a building or structure that is not owned or operated by the state unless otherwise authorized by law.

XI. No state agency, authority, board, or commission shall modify the state building code, unless approved by the state building code review board pursuant to RSA 155-A. Nothing in this chapter shall affect the statutory authority of the public utilities commission, the state board for the licensing and regulation of plumbers, or the state electricians' board, to administer their respective programs, provided that any changes to codes adopted under the rulemaking authority of these agencies shall not be implemented until approved by the state building code review board.

Source.
2002, 8:3, eff. Sept. 14, 2002. 2003, 245:2, eff. July 14, 2003.

state building code" preceding "under RSA 674:51".

Amendments
—**2003.** Paragraph VII: Deleted "for the

RESEARCH REFERENCES

ALR.
Liability of builder or subcontractor for insufficiency of building resulting from latent defects in materials used. 61 A.L.R.3d 792.

Products liability: cement and concrete. 60 A.L.R.5th 413.

Products liability: construction materials or insulation containing formaldehyde. 45 A.L.R.4th 751.

155-A:3. Local Amendments; Application.

For a municipality which has adopted an enforcement mechanism or additional regulations to the state building code pursuant to RSA 674:51:

I. The municipality may adopt local amendments to the state building code which do not prohibit minimum implementation and enforcement of the state building code.

II. The procedure for amendment shall be in accordance with applicable statutes and local regulations.

III. At a minimum, the municipality shall ensure that implementation and enforcement includes:
  (a) Review and acceptance of appropriate plans.
  (b) Issuance of building permits.
  (c) Inspection of the work authorized by the building permits.
  (d) Issuance of appropriate use and occupancy certificates.

IV. (a) The provisions of this chapter and any local amendments under this section shall not be construed to restrict or encumber the local governing body's authority relative to the appointment, removal, or duties of municipal employees and the organization of municipal departments.

  (b) Any provision of the state building code that conflicts with existing or amended local ordinances, regulations, policies, practices, or procedures regarding the appointment, removal, or duties of municipal employees and the organization of municipal departments, shall not apply.

Source.
2002, 8:3, eff. Sept. 14, 2002.

155-A:4. Permit Required.

Before starting new construction or renovation of schools, halls, theaters or other public buildings the person responsible for such construction shall obtain a permit signed by the board of selectmen, after its due consideration of any written recommendations of the fire chief. In municipalities that have adopted an enforcement mechanism pursuant to RSA 674:51, the permit under this section shall conform to the locally adopted process.

Source.
2002, 8:3, eff. Sept. 14, 2002.

155-A:5. Accessibility of Public Buildings.

Notwithstanding RSA 155-A:2, all new buildings constructed by the state or any of its agencies, and all new schools, halls, theaters, or other public buildings in this state in which more than 100 people can be assembled shall be required to provide at least one entrance and exit designed so that the public areas of the entire building are accessible to persons with disabilities.

Source.
2002, 8:3, eff. Sept. 14, 2002.

RESEARCH REFERENCES

ALR.
Committee on architectural barrier-free design, see RSA 275-C:10 et seq.

155-A:6. Inspection of State Buildings.

The commissioner of safety and the commissioner of transportation shall provide for periodic safety inspection of all occupied public buildings owned by the state.

Source.
2002, 8:3, eff. Sept. 14, 2002.

155-A:7. Enforcement Authority.

I. The local enforcement agency appointed pursuant to RSA 674:51 shall have the authority to enforce the provisions of the state building code, provided, however, that where there is no building inspector, the state fire marshal or the state fire marshal's designee shall have the authority to enforce the provisions of the state building code, subject to the review provisions contained in RSA 155-A:10.

II. Upon the request of a local enforcement agency, state agencies, boards, and commissions may provide advisory services and technical assistance concerning any building or any construction project in the local enforcement agent's jurisdiction.

III. The local enforcement agency appointed to enforce the state building code shall have the authority to inspect all buildings, structures, construction sites, and other places in the jurisdiction. If consent for such inspection is denied or not reasonably obtainable, the local enforcement agency may obtain an administrative inspection warrant under RSA 595-B.

Source.
2002, 8:3, eff. Sept. 14, 2002.

155-A:8. Penalty.

Fines, penalties, and remedies for violations of this chapter shall be the same as for violations of title LXIV, as stated in RSA 676:15 and 676:17.

Source.
2002, 8:3, eff. Sept. 14, 2002.

References in text.
Title LXIV, referred to in this section, is Title

64 of LEXIS New Hampshire Revised Statutes Annotated, which is comprised of chapters 672–677.

155-A:9. Fees.

The municipality may establish fees to defray the costs of administration, implementation, and enforcement of the state building code and any local amendments. Such fees shall be for the general use of the municipality having responsibility over the local enforcement agency.

Source.
2002, 8:3, eff. Sept. 14, 2002.

155-A:10. State Building Code Review Board.

I. There is established a state building code review board consisting of the commissioner of safety or the commissioner's designee, and additional members appointed by the commissioner of safety as follows:

(a) One architect licensed in this state for a minimum of 5 years, nominated by the board of architects established in RSA 310-A:29.

(b) One structural engineer licensed in this state for a minimum of 5 years, nominated by the board of engineers established in RSA 310-A:3.

(c) One mechanical engineer licensed in this state for a minimum of 5 years, nominated by the board of engineers established in RSA 310-A:3.

(d) One electrical engineer licensed in this state for a minimum of 5 years, nominated by the board of engineers established in RSA 310-A:3.

(e) One representative of the state's municipalities, nominated by the New Hampshire Municipal Association.

(f) One municipal building official, nominated by the New Hampshire Building Officials Association.

(g) One municipal fire chief, nominated by the New Hampshire Association of Fire Chiefs.

(h) One active fire prevention officer, nominated by the New Hampshire Association of Fire Chiefs.

(i) One building contractor, primarily engaged in the business of constructing non-residential buildings, nominated by the Associated General Contractors of New Hampshire.

(j) One building contractor primarily engaged in the business of constructing residential buildings, nominated by the New Hampshire Home Builders Association.

(k) One representative from the state energy conservation code office under RSA 155-D, nominated by the New Hampshire public utilities commission.

(l) One master plumber licensed in this state for a minimum of 5 years, nominated by the state board for the licensing and regulation of plumbers established in RSA 329-A.

(m) One mechanical contractor with a minimum of 5 years experience, primarily engaged in the business of mechanical construction, nominated by the New Hampshire Plumbing and Mechanical Contractors Association.

(n) One master electrician licensed in this state for a minimum of 5 years, nominated by the electricians' board established in RSA 319-C.

(o) One representative of the Committee on Architectural Barrier — Free Design nominated by the governor's commission on disability.

(p) One master electrician licensed in this state for a minimum of 5 years, nominated by Electrical Contractors Business Association.

II. The term of each member shall be 3 years. The chair shall be appointed by the commissioner of safety. Board members shall be appointed for no more than 2 consecutive 3-year terms.

III. The board shall be administratively attached to the department of safety under RSA 21-G:10.

IV. The board shall meet to review and assess the application of the state building code and shall recommend legislation, as the board deems necessary, to modify the requirements of the state building code and the state fire code in order to provide consistency with the application of other laws, rules, or regulations, and to promote public safety and best practices.

V. The board may adopt rules to update or change the state building code for the codes described in RSA 155-A:1, IV, to the extent the board deems that such updates or changes are necessary, provided that any such updates or changes are ratified by the adoption of appropriate legislation within 2 years of their adoption. If such updates or changes are not ratified, then the rules shall expire, notwithstanding RSA 541-A:17, I, at the end of the 2-year period. With the approval of the commissioner of safety, the board shall be authorized, pursuant to RSA 541-A, to adopt rules relative to procedures of its operation and appeals to the board.

VI. The board shall review the National Fire Protection Association Building Code and its companion manuals when published, and shall review any other building codes when published, in order to evaluate whether the state should continue with the International Building Codes and its manuals, switch to other codes or adopt a combination of codes.

Source.

2002, 8:3, eff. April 17, 2002. 2003, 245:3, 4, 6, eff. July 14, 2003. 2007, 11:1, 2, eff. July 1, 2007.

Amendments

—2007. Paragraph I(h): Substituted "active fire prevention officer" for "municipal volunteer fire chief".

Paragraph II: Deleted "except that persons initially appointed under subparagraphs I(a), (d), (g), (j) and (m) shall serve one-year terms, and persons initially appointed under subparagraphs I(b), (e), (h), (k) and (n) shall serve 2-year terms" following "3 years" in the first sentence.

—2003. Paragraph I: Deleted "15" preceding "additional members" in the introductory paragraph.

Paragraph I(p): Added.

Paragraph V: Deleted "manuals" following "building code" in the first sentence.

—2002. Paragraph I(n): Substituted "electricians' board established in RSA 319-C" for "New Hampshire Electrical Contractors Business Association".

Initial term of new member.

2003, 245:5, eff. July 14, 2003, provided: "The initial term of the master electrician appointed under RSA 155-A:10, I(p) as inserted by this act shall coincide with the remaining term for the master electrician appointed under RSA 155-A:10, I(n). Subsequent terms shall be for 3 years".

155-A:11. Appeals of Decisions of the State Fire Marshal.

I. The board shall hear appeals of variances or exceptions to the state fire code that have been granted or denied by the state fire marshal or the state fire marshal's designee, and appeals of a decision of the state fire marshal or the state fire marshal's designee, in enforcing provisions of the state building code pursuant to RSA 155-A:7, I.

II. The board shall hold a hearing within 40 days of receipt of a complaint, unless an extension of time has been granted by the board at the written request of one of the parties and shall render a decision within 30 days of the conclusion of a hearing.

Source.
2002, 8:3, eff. Sept. 14, 2002.

NOTES TO DECISIONS

Proper review

Property owner's due process rights were not violated by the procedures used by the fire marshal in reclassifying his property for fire code purposes because N.H. Code Admin. R. Ann. Saf.-C 6006.02 was preempted by the adoption of RSA 155-A:11, which provided that appeals from the marshal's decision would be heard by a board and not by a hearing in front of the fire marshal. Fischer v. N.H. State Bldg. Code Review Bd., 154 N.H. 585, 914 A.2d 1234, 2006 N.H. LEXIS 198 (2006).

155-A:11-a. Appeal of Decisions of the Electricians' Board and the State Board for the Licensing and Regulation of Plumbers.

I. The board shall hear appeals of final decisions of the board established under RSA 319-C:4 and the board established under RSA 329-A:3.

II. The board shall hold a hearing within 40 days of the receipt of an appeal, unless an extension of time has been granted by the board at the written request of one of the parties and shall render a decision within 30 days of the conclusion of the hearing.

Source.
2004, 257:55, eff. June 15, 2004.

155-A:12. Appeal From Board's Decision.

I. A party to the proceeding shall have the right to file a petition in the superior court of the county in which the building or structure is located to review the final order of the board within 30 days of the date of the final order.

II. At the earliest practical time, the court shall review the record as developed before the board, together with any written legal argument presented to the court. Based on that review, the court may affirm or reverse the decision of the board or order that oral argument be held. As justice may require, the court may remand the case to the board for further findings and rulings. The petition for appeal shall set forth all the grounds upon which the final order is sought to be overturned. Issues not raised by the appellant before the board shall not be raised before the superior court. The burden of proof shall be on the appellant to show that the decision of the board was clearly unreasonable or unlawful.

III. No new or additional evidence shall be introduced in the superior court, but the case shall be determined upon the record and evidence transferred, except that in any case, if justice requires the review of evidence which by reason of accident, mistake, or misfortune could not have been offered before the board, the superior court shall remand the case to the board to receive and consider such additional evidence.

Source.
2002, 8:3, eff. Sept. 14, 2002.

NOTES TO DECISIONS

Decision upheld

Under RSA 155-A:12, II, state building code review board properly determined that owner's property no longer qualified as two-family dwellings under state fire code as adopted under N.H. Code Admin. R. Ann. Saf.-C 6008.01, 6008.03 because the regulations were not unconstitutionally retrospective under N.H. Const. pt. I, art. 23, the owner did not have a vested right to continued classification under N.H. Const. pt. I, art. 12, the interpretation fit the purpose of RSA 153:5, and the regulation did not impermissibly discriminate between related and unrelated individuals under the Fourteenth Amendment to the United States Constitution in that there was a rational basis for the classification. Fischer v. N.H. State Bldg. Code Review Bd., 154 N.H. 585, 914 A.2d 1234, 2006 N.H. LEXIS 198 (2006).

CHAPTER 155-E

LOCAL REGULATION EXCAVATIONS

Codification.

This chapter was enacted as RSA 155-D and renumbered as 155-E to avoid conflict with pre-existing RSA 155-D which was added by 1979, 460:1.

State and municipal roles relating to regulation of mining and excavation.

1988, 285:2, eff. May 2, 1988, provided: "It is hereby declared to be the intent of the legislature to clarify the respective roles of state and local governments concerning the regulation of mining and excavation activities in light of the recent Supreme Court decision in Appeal of Coastal Materials Corporation [(1987) 130 NH 98, 534 A2d 398]. The state shall have the power to regulate the extraction of minerals including the removal of dimension stone. The municipalities shall have the power to regulate the removal of earth to be used as construction aggregate."

Cross References.

Hazardous excavations, see RSA 155-B:13.

Mining and reclamation, see RSA 12-E.

NOTES TO DECISIONS

Analysis

1. Construction
2. Construction with other laws
3. Purpose
4. Preemption

1. Construction

This chapter expresses a clear intention that the crushing of granite not be regulated by local authorities. Appeal of Coastal Materials Corp., 130 N.H. 98, 534 A.2d 398, 1987 N.H. LEXIS 280 (1987).

2. Construction with other laws

This chapter and RSA 31:41-b, granting authority to local governing bodies to regulate a specific land use, namely earth excavation, exist as grants of authority independent of the zoning enabling legislation. Town of Goffstown v. Thibeault, 129 N.H. 454, 529 A.2d 930, 1987 N.H. LEXIS 184 (1987).

3. Purpose

Legislature's purpose in enacting this chapter was, in part, to increase supply of construction materials and decrease cost of roads and other governmental infrastructure to the public by curtailing simultaneous state and local regulations of the same activity. Arthur Whitcomb, Inc. v. Town of Carroll, 141 N.H. 402, 686 A.2d 743, 1996 N.H. LEXIS 117 (1996).

4. Preemption

This chapter's exhaustive treatment of the field of excavation manifested a legislative intent to preempt it, although not all local legislation applicable to excavation was therefore void; rather, this chapter preempted only local ordinances and regulations that would have the effect or intent of frustrating state authority. Arthur Whitcomb, Inc. v. Town of Carroll, 141 N.H. 402, 686 A.2d 743, 1996 N.H. LEXIS 117 (1996).

RESEARCH REFERENCES

New Hampshire Practice.   §§ 36.01, 36.03, 36.07, 36.08, 36.14, 36.15,
15 N.H.P. Land Use Planning and Zoning   36.18–36.23, 39.02.

155-E:1. Definitions.

In this chapter:

I. "Earth" means sand, gravel, rock, soil or construction aggregate produced by quarrying, crushing or any other mining activity or such other naturally-occurring unconsolidated materials that normally mask the bedrock.

II. "Excavation" means a land area which is used, or has been used, for the commercial taking of earth, including all slopes.

III. "Regulator" means:

(a) The planning board of a city or town, or if a town at an annual or special meeting duly warned for the purpose so provides, the selectmen of the town or the board of adjustment; or

(b) If there is no planning board, the selectmen of the town or the legislative body of the city; or

(c) The county commissioners if the land area is in an unincorporated place.

IV. "Dimension stone" means rock that is cut, shaped, or selected for use in blocks, slabs, sheets, or other construction units of specified shapes or sizes and used for external or interior parts of buildings, foundations, curbing, paving, flagging, bridges, revetments, or for other architectural or engineering purposes. Dimension stone includes quarry blocks from which sections of dimension stone are to be produced. Dimension stone does not include earth as defined in RSA 155-E:1, I.

V. "Excavation site" means any area of contiguous land in common ownership upon which excavation takes place.

VI. "Excavation area" means the surface area within an excavation site where excavation has occurred or is eligible to occur under the provisions of this chapter.

Source.
1979, 481:2. 1988, 285:6, 7. 1989, 363:2. 1991, 310:3, eff. Aug. 23, 1991. 2002, 103:9, eff. April 1, 2002.

Amendments
—2002. Paragraph VI: Inserted "surface" preceding "area within".

—1991. Paragraph VI: Added.

—1989. Paragraph V: Added.

—1988. Paragraph I: Added "produced by quarrying, crushing or any other mining activity or such other naturally-occurring unconsolidated materials that normally mask the bedrock" following "construction aggregate".
Paragraph IV: Added.

Cited:
Cited in Appeal of Coastal Materials Corp., 130 N.H. 98, 534 A.2d 398, 1987 N.H. LEXIS 280 (1987); Town of Wolfeboro v. Smith, 131 N.H. 449, 556 A.2d 755, 1989 N.H. LEXIS 17 (1989); 1986 Op. Att'y Gen. 193; Town of Barrington v. Gadd, 132 N.H. 650, 569 A.2d 231, 1990 N.H. LEXIS 6 (1990); Arthur Whitcomb, Inc. v. Town of Carroll, 141 N.H. 402, 686 A.2d 743, 1996 N.H. LEXIS 117 (1996).

RESEARCH REFERENCES

New Hampshire Practice.
15 N.H.P. Land Use Planning and Zoning §§ 36.02, 36.05.

155-E:2. Permit Required.

No owner shall permit any excavation of earth on his premises without first obtaining a permit therefor, except as follows:

I. EXISTING EXCAVATIONS. The owner of an excavation which lawfully existed as of August 24, 1979, from which earth material of sufficient weight or volume to be commercially useful has been removed during the 2-year period before August 24, 1979, may continue such existing excavation on the excavation site without a permit, subject to the following:

(a) Such an excavation site shall be exempt from the provisions of local zoning or similar ordinances regulating the location of the excavation site, provided that at the time the excavation was first begun, it was in compliance with such local ordinances and regulations, if any, as were then in effect.

(b) Such an excavation area may not be expanded, without a permit under this chapter, beyond the limits of the town in which it is situated and the area which, on August 24, 1979, and at all times subsequent thereto has been contiguous to and in common ownership with the excavation site as of that date, and has been appraised and inventoried for property tax purposes as part of the same tract as the excavation site of that date, as modified by the limitations of RSA 155-E:4-a, I, II, and II-a. In this paragraph the term "contiguous" means land whose perimeter can be circumscribed without interruption in common ownership except for roads or other easements, in a single town. It is further provided that when such excavation is not allowed in that location by local zoning or similar ordinances in effect on August 4, 1989, or when such ordinances allow such excavation only by special exception, expansion may be restricted or modified with conditions by order of the regulator if after notice to the owner and a hearing, the regulator finds that such expansion will have a substantially different and adverse impact on the neighborhood.

(c) Such an excavation shall be performed in compliance with the express operational standards of RSA 155-E:4-a and the express reclamation standards of RSA 155-E:5 and 155-E:5-a. Any violations of those standards shall be enforceable pursuant to RSA 155-E:10.

(d) The owners or operators of any existing excavation area for which no permit has been obtained under this chapter shall file a report with the local regulator within one year after receiving written notice of this requirement from the regulator and in no case later than 2 years following August 4, 1989. The report shall include:

(1) The location of the excavation and the date the excavation first began;

(2) A description of the limits of permissible expansion, as described in subparagraph (b), which are claimed to apply to the excavation;

(3) An estimate of the area which has been excavated at the time of the report; and

(4) An estimate of the amount of commercially viable earth materials still available on the parcel.

(e) The exemption from local zoning or site location regulations as stated in subparagraph (a) shall include the quarrying or crushing of bedrock for the production of construction aggregate; provided, however, that no owner shall, after August 4, 1989, permit any such quarrying or crushing of bedrock to occur for the first time on any excavation site without first obtaining a permit therefor under this chapter.

II. ABANDONED EXCAVATIONS. The permit and zoning exemptions under RSA 155-E:2, I shall not apply to any abandoned excavation, as defined in subparagraph (a).

(a) For purposes of this section, any excavation, except for excavations or excavation sites described in RSA 155-E:2, III, whether subject to a permit under this chapter or not, for which the affected area has not yet been brought into complete compliance with the reclamation standards of RSA 115-E:5 shall be deemed "abandoned" if:

(1) No earth material of sufficient weight or volume to be commercially useful has been removed from that excavation site during any 2-year period, either before, on, or after August 4, 1989; provided, however, that before the end of such 2-year period, the owner or operator may extend the period by submitting to the regulator a reclamation timetable to be approved by the regulator, and posting a bond or other security with the municipal treasurer in a form and amount prescribed by the regulator, sufficient to secure the reclamation of the entire excavation site in accordance with the standards of RSA 155-E:5; or

(2) The excavation site is in use and is not an excavation or excavation site as described in RSA 155-E:2, III, but does not conform with the incremental reclamation requirement of RSA 155-E:5-a, or the owner or operator has not posted a bond or other security and submitted a reclamation timetable to be approved by the regulator as described in subparagraph (a)(1); or

(3) The owner or operator of the excavation has neither secured a permit pursuant to this chapter nor filed a report of an existing excavation pursuant to subparagraph I(d) within the prescribed period.

(b) In addition to the enforcement remedies of RSA 155-E:10, the regulator may order the owner of any land upon which an abandoned excavation is located to either file a reclamation timetable, to be approved by the regulator, and bond or other security as described in subparagraph II(a)(1), or to complete reclamation in accordance with this chapter within a stated reasonable time. Such an order shall only be made following a hearing for which notice has been given in accordance with RSA 155-E:7, if the regulator finds that the public health, safety, or welfare requires such reclamation. If the owner fails to complete reclamation within the time prescribed in the order, the regulator may request the governing body to cause reclamation to be completed at the expense of the municipality. The municipality's costs shall constitute an assessment against the owner, and shall create a lien against the real estate on which the excavation is located. Such assessment and lien may be enforced and collected in the same manner as provided for real estate taxes.

(c) The site of an excavation which ceased commercially useful operation prior to August 24, 1977, but for which the affected area has not been brought into compliance with the reclamation standards of RSA 155-E:5, may be made subject to the remedy prescribed in RSA 155-E:2, II(b) only if the regulator finds in writing that specified reclamation measures are necessary to eliminate or mitigate an identified hazard to public health or safety.

III. STATIONARY MANUFACTURING PLANTS.

(a) No permit shall be required under this chapter for excavation from an excavation site which on August 4, 1989, was contiguous to or was contiguous land in common ownership with stationary manufacturing and processing plants which were in operation as of August 24, 1979, and which use earth obtained from such excavation site. Such excavation shall be performed in compliance with the operational standards as expressly set forth in RSA 155-E:4-a and the reclamation standards as expressly set forth in RSA 155-E:5 and 155-E:5-a, which express standards shall be the sole standards with which such excavations must comply in order to retain their non-permit status as provided under this paragraph. Loss of such non-permit status shall be preceded by written notice from the regulator that the excavation is not in compliance and the owner shall have failed to bring such excavation into compliance within 30 days of receipt of such notice. Such excavation may be expanded without a permit under this chapter to any contiguous lands which were in common ownership with the site of the plant on August 4, 1989, except as limited by RSA 155-E:4-a, I, II, and III.

(b) No further permit shall be required under this chapter for excavation from a site which on August 4, 1989, was contiguous to or was contiguous land in common ownership with stationary manufacturing and processing plants for which local or state permits have been granted since August 24, 1979, and before August 4, 1989, which use earth obtained from such site. It is further provided that their operation and reclamation shall continue to be regulated by such local or state permits and any renewals or extensions thereof by the permitting authority or authorities.

IV. HIGHWAY EXCAVATIONS.   No permit shall be required under this chapter for excavation which is performed exclusively for the lawful construction, reconstruction, or maintenance of a class I, II, III, IV or V highway by a unit of government having jurisdiction for the highway or an agent of the unit of government which has a contract for the construction, reconstruction, or maintenance of the highway, subject, however, to the following:

(a) A copy of the pit agreement executed by the owner, the agent, and the governmental unit shall be filed with the regulator prior to the start of excavation. The failure to file such agreement, or the failure of the excavator to comply with the terms of such agreement, shall be deemed a violation of this chapter, and may be enforced pursuant to RSA 155-E:10.

(b) Such excavation shall not be exempt from local zoning or other applicable ordinances, unless such an exemption is granted pursuant to subparagraph (c), or from the operational and reclamation standards as expressly set forth in RSA 155-E:4-a, 155-E:5 and 155-E:5-a, which express standards shall be the sole standards with which such excavations must comply in order to retain their non-permit status as provided under this paragraph. Before beginning such excavation, the governmental unit or its agents shall certify to the regulator that:

(1) The excavation shall comply with the operational and reclamation standards of RSA 155-E:4-a, RSA 155-E:5, and 155-E:5-a.

(2) The excavation shall not be within 50 feet of the boundary of a disapproving abutter or within 10 feet of the boundary of an approving abutter, unless requested by said approving abutter.

(3) The excavation shall not be unduly hazardous or injurious to the public welfare.

(4) Existing visual barriers in the areas specified in RSA 155-E:3, III shall not be removed, except to provide access to the excavation.

(5) The excavation shall not substantially damage a known aquifer, so designated by the United States Geological Survey.

(6) All required permits for the excavation from state or federal agencies have been obtained.

(c) The department of transportation or its agent may apply directly to the appeals board created under RSA 21-L to be exempted from the provisions of local zoning or other ordinances or regulations, with respect to the excavation or transportation of materials being used exclusively for the lawful construction, reconstruction, or maintenance of a class I, II, or III highway.

(1) The application shall state whether the applicant has requested any exceptions or variances which may be available at the local level, and shall describe the outcome of such requests.

(2) Prior to acting on the application, the board shall hold a hearing in the municipality whose ordinance or regulation is at issue. At least 7 days prior to such hearing, notice shall be published in a newspaper of general circulation in the municipality, and shall be sent by certified mail to the applicant, the municipality's chief executive officer as defined in RSA 672:9, the chairman of its governing board as defined in RSA 672:6, the chairman of the local regulator as defined in RSA 155-E:1, the chairman of its conservation commission, if any, and, if the proposed exemption concerns an excavation site, to the abutters of that site as defined in RSA 672:3.

(3) Following the hearing, the board shall issue a written decision, copies of which shall be mailed to the applicant and the parties to whom

notice was sent. If an exemption is granted, the written decisions shall include:

(A) A statement of the precise section of the ordinance or regulation from which the applicant is exempted. The applicant shall not be exempt from any section or provisions not so listed.

(B) An identification of the public interest being protected by the ordinance or regulation.

(C) A statement of the state interest involved, and of why, in the opinion of the board, that state interest overrides the interest protected by the ordinance or regulation.

(D) Any conditions to be imposed on the applicant, to protect the public health, safety, or welfare.

(4) The decision of the board may be appealed in the manner provided for zoning decisions in RSA 677:4–14; provided, however, that a decision under this section shall be considered a rehearing under RSA 677, and no further motion for rehearing shall be required.

Source.
1979, 481:2. 1985, 88:2. 1988, 285:8. 1989, 363:3. 1991, 310:4–9, eff. Aug. 23, 1991.

References in text.
The reference to "RSA 115-E:5" in subpar. II(a) appears to be incorrect and should probably be RSA 155-E:5.

Revision note.
Substituted "August 4 1989" for "the effective date of this subparagraph" in subpar. I(e) for purposes of clarity.

Amendments
—1991. Rewritten to the extent that a detailed comparison would be impracticable.

—1989. Rewritten to the extent that a detailed comparison would be impracticable.

—1988. Paragraph IV: Added "for the purpose of producing dimension stone" following "quarry".

—1985. Paragraph VI: Added.

NOTES TO DECISIONS

Analysis

1. Existing excavation exemption
2. Stationary plant exemption
3. Scope of exemption
4. Municipal ordinance not preempted

1. Existing excavation exemption
Where town established that excavations were ongoing and that no permit had been granted, burden was on defendant to prove that their mining activities satisfied requirements for invocation of statutory "grandfather clause." Town of Barrington v. Gadd, 132 N.H. 650, 569 A.2d 231, 1990 N.H. LEXIS 6 (1990).

Party claiming exemption from excavation permit requirement under grandfather clause has burden of proving the "intent" to excavate an area larger than that already excavated prior to effective date of this section. Town of Wolfeboro v. Smith, 131 N.H. 449, 556 A.2d 755,

1989 N.H. LEXIS 17 (1989).

Superior court order based on finding that defendants were entitled to additional excavation on their property without a permit under grandfather clause exemption was reversed and remanded, where evidence was inadequate to manifest the necessary objective "intent" to excavate the acreage in question prior to the effective date of this section. Town of Wolfeboro v. Smith, 131 N.H. 449, 556 A.2d 755, 1989 N.H. LEXIS 17 (1989).

Party who desires to continue excavation operations without a permit under grandfather clause exemption must meet a three-pronged test: first, he must prove that excavation activities were actively being pursued when the law became effective; second, he must prove that the area he desires to excavate was clearly intended to be excavated, as measured by objective manifestations and not by subjective intent; and, third, he must prove that the continued operations do not, and/or will not, have a substantially different and adverse impact on the neighborhood. Town of Wolfeboro v. Smith, 131 N.H. 449, 556 A.2d 755, 1989 N.H. LEXIS 17 (1989).

Municipality requesting that an excavation permit be obtained need only prove that excavations are ongoing and that no permit has been granted; upon this showing, burden of proof shifts to a party desiring to continue excavation operations without a permit under grandfather clause exemption to meet three-pronged test. Town of Wolfeboro v. Smith, 131 N.H. 449, 556 A.2d 755, 1989 N.H. LEXIS 17 (1989).

2. Stationary plant exemption

Assuming compliance with other requirements of subdivision III(a) of this section, contiguity provision allowed new excavation in any area bordering an existing excavation. Arthur Whitcomb, Inc. v. Town of Carroll, 141 N.H. 402, 686 A.2d 743, 1996 N.H. LEXIS 117 (1996).

3. Scope of exemption

Under plain reading of statutory language, exemption in subdivision III(a) of this section applied to plaintiff's blasting operation. Arthur Whitcomb, Inc. v. Town of Carroll, 141 N.H.

402, 686 A.2d 743, 1996 N.H. LEXIS 117 (1996).

Permitting exception found in subdivision III(a) of this section has limited applicability, and blasting operations must comply with State and federal strictures relating to explosives. Arthur Whitcomb, Inc. v. Town of Carroll, 141 N.H. 402, 686 A.2d 743, 1996 N.H. LEXIS 117 (1996).

4. Municipal ordinance not preempted

Goshen, N.H., Zoning Ordinance fit within the scope of permissible municipal regulation under RSA ch. 155-E because, by its terms, it applied only to excavations requiring a permit; it followed that the more stringent requirements set forth in the ordinance were not preempted. Guildhall Sand & Gravel, L.L.C. v. Town of Goshen., — N.H. —, 929 A.2d 199, 2007 N.H. LEXIS 128 (July 20, 2007).

Cited:

Cited in Small v. Zoning Bd. of Adj., Town of Newbury, 121 N.H. 226, 427 A.2d 520, 1981 N.H. LEXIS 284 (1981); Appeal of Coastal Materials Corp., 130 N.H. 98, 534 A.2d 398, 1987 N.H. LEXIS 280 (1987); Town of North Hampton v. Sanderson, 131 N.H. 614, 557 A.2d 643, 1989 N.H. LEXIS 32 (1989).

RESEARCH REFERENCES

New Hampshire Practice.
15 N.H.P. Land Use Planning and Zoning §§ 36.02, 36.05, 36.09, 36.10, 36.23.

155-E:2-a. Other Exceptions.

I. No permit shall be required for the following types of excavations:

(a) Excavation that is exclusively incidental to the construction or alteration of a building or structure or the construction or alteration of a parking lot or way including a driveway on a portion of the premises where the removal occurs; provided, however, that no such excavation shall be commenced without a permit under this chapter unless all state and local permits required for the construction or alteration of the building, structure, parking lot, or way have been issued.

(b) Excavation that is incidental to agricultural or silvicultural activities, normal landscaping, or minor topographical adjustment.

(c) Excavation from a granite quarry for the purpose of producing dimension stone, if such excavation requires a permit under RSA 12-E.

II. A person owning land abutting a site which was taken by eminent domain or by any other governmental taking upon which construction is taking place may stockpile earth taken from the construction site and may remove the earth at a later date after written notification to the appropriate local official.

Source.
   1989, 363:4, eff. Aug. 4, 1989.

RESEARCH REFERENCES

New Hampshire Practice.
   15 N.H.P. Land Use Planning and Zoning §§ 36.02–36.06.

155-E:3. Application for Permit.

Any owner or owner's designee subject to this chapter shall, prior to excavation of his land, apply to the regulator in each city or town involved for a permit for excavation. If the area subject to this chapter is situated in an unincorporated place application shall be made to the county commissioners. The applicant shall also send a copy of the application to the conservation commission, if any, of the city or town. Such application shall be signed and dated by the applicant and shall contain at least the following information:

I. The name and address of the owner of the land to be excavated, the person who will actually do the excavating and all abutters to the premises on which the excavation is proposed;

II. A sketch and description of the location and boundaries of the proposed excavation, the number of acres to be involved in the project and the municipalities and counties in which the project lies;

III. A sketch and description of the access and visual barriers to public highways to be utilized in the proposed excavation;

IV. The breadth, depth and slope of the proposed excavation and the estimated duration of the project;

V. The elevation of the highest annual average groundwater table within or next to the proposed excavation;

VI. A plan for the reclamation of the area affected by the excavation at least in compliance with RSA 155-E:5 and RSA 155-E:5-a. Such plan shall address the effects of the proposed excavation on soil, surface water and groundwater, vegetation, overburden, topography, and fill material, and may address future land use consistent with the approved master plan, and shall include a timetable for reclamation of fully depleted areas within the excavation site during said project;

VI-a. Specific actions to be taken by the applicant on the excavation site relative to fuel and chemical handling and storage, dust control, traffic, noise control and abatement, and comprehensive site safety of unauthorized persons; and

VII. Such other information or other special investigative studies as the regulator may reasonably deem necessary.

Source.
1979, 481:2. 1989, 363:5. 1991, 310:10, 11, eff. Aug. 23, 1991. 1996, 141:2, eff. Jan. 1, 1997.

Revision note.
In par. V, substituted "groundwater" for "ground water" to conform to proper grammatical usage.

Amendments
—1996. Paragraph VII: Inserted "or other special investigative studies" following "infor-

mation," and substituted "deem necessary" for "require."

—1991. Paragraph VI: Rewritten to the extent that a detailed comparison would be impracticable.
Paragraph VI-a: Added.

—1989. Paragraph VI: Substituted "reclamation" for "restoration" following "plan for the".

NOTES TO DECISIONS

Cited:
Cited in Town of Wolfeboro v. Smith, 131 N.H. 449, 556 A.2d 755, 1989 N.H. LEXIS 17 (1989).

RESEARCH REFERENCES

New Hampshire Practice.
15 N.H.P. Land Use Planning and Zoning §§ 36.10, 36.11, 36.13.

155-E:4. Prohibited Projects.

The regulator shall not grant a permit:

I. Where the excavation would violate the operational standards of RSA 155-E:4-a;

II. For excavation within 50 feet of the boundary of a disapproving abutter or within 10 feet of the boundary of an approving abutter unless approval is requested by said abutter;

III. When the excavation is not permitted by zoning or other applicable ordinance, provided, however, that in municipalities which have commercial earth resources on unimproved land within their boundaries, and which do not provide for opportunities for excavation of some of these resources in at least some, but not necessarily all areas within the municipality, or in municipalities which have zoning ordinances which do not address the subject of excavations, excavation shall be deemed to be a use allowed by special exception as provided in RSA 674:33, IV, in any non-residential area of the municipality, and the zoning board of adjustment shall grant such a special exception upon a finding that:

(a) The excavation will not cause a diminution in area property value or unreasonably change the character of the neighborhood;

(b) The excavation will not unreasonably accelerate the deterioration of highways or create safety hazards in the use thereof;

(c) The excavation will not create any nuisance or create health or safety hazards; and

(d) The excavation complies with such other special exception criteria as may be set out in applicable local ordinances.

IV. When the issuance of the permit would be unduly hazardous or injurious to the public welfare;

V. Where existing visual barriers in the areas specified in RSA 155-E:3, III would be removed, except to provide access to the excavation;

VI. Where the excavation would substantially damage a known aquifer, so designated by the United States Geological Survey;

VII. When the excavation requires land use permits from state or federal agencies; but the regulator may approve the application when all necessary land use permits have been obtained; or

VIII. Where the project cannot comply with the reclamation provisions of RSA 155-E:5 and 155-E:5-a.

Source.
1979, 481:2. 1989, 138:5; 363:6–8. 1991, 310:12, 13, eff. Aug. 23, 1991.

Amendments
—1991. Paragraph III: Deleted "reasonable" preceding "opportunities", substituted "these" for "those" preceding "resources", and inserted "in at least some, but not necessarily all areas within the municipality" thereafter and "in any non-residential area of the municipality" following "RSA 674:33, IV" in the introductory paragraph, substituted "a" for "an unreasonable" following "cause" in subpar. (a), deleted "and" following "thereof" in subpar. (b), deleted "unreasonable" preceding "nuisance" and added "and" following "hazards" in subpar. (c) and added subpar. (d).

Paragraph VII: Rewritten to the extent that a detailed comparison would be impracticable.

—1989. Paragraphs I and III: Rewritten by ch. 363 to the extent that a detailed comparison would be impracticable.

Paragraph VII: Chapter 138 substituted "division of water supply and pollution control, the division of water resources, the wetlands board" for "water supply and pollution control commission, the water resources board, the special board on dredge and fill" following "required from the".

Chapter 363 substituted "department of environmental services" for "division of water supply and pollution control, the division of water resources, the wetlands board or other state" following "required from the".

Paragraph VIII: Chapter 363 substituted "reclamation" for "restoration" following "comply with the" and added "and 155-E:5-a" following "RSA 155-E:5".

NOTES TO DECISIONS

Cited:
Cited in Town of North Hampton v. Sanderson, 131 N.H. 614, 557 A.2d 643, 1989 N.H. LEXIS 32 (1989).

RESEARCH REFERENCES

New Hampshire Practice.
15 N.H.P. Land Use Planning and Zoning §§ 36.12, 36.13.

155-E:4-a. Minimum and Express Operational Standards.

It shall be a violation of this chapter for any person to excavate, or for any owner to permit excavation on his excavation site, when such excavation is subject to a permit under this chapter, without complying with the following minimum standards or when such excavation is not subject to a permit under this chapter pursuant to RSA 155-E:2 without complying with the following express standards:

I. No excavation shall be permitted below road level within 50 feet of the right of way of any public highway as defined in RSA 229:1 unless such excavation is for the purpose of said highway.

II. No excavation shall be permitted within 50 feet of the boundary of a disapproving abutter, within 150 feet of any dwelling which either existed or for which a building permit has been issued at the time the excavation is commenced.

II-a. No excavation shall be permitted within 75 feet of any great pond, navigable river, or any other standing body of water 10 acres or more in area or within 25 feet of any other stream, river or brook which normally flows throughout the year, or any naturally occurring standing body of water less than 10 acres, prime wetland as designated in accordance with RSA 482-A:15, I or any other wetland greater than 5 acres in area as defined by the department of environmental services.

III. Vegetation shall be maintained or provided within the peripheral areas required by paragraphs I and II.

IV. Drainage shall be maintained so as to prevent the accumulation of free-standing water for prolonged periods. Excavation practices which result in continued siltation of surface waters or any degradation of water quality of any public or private water supplies are prohibited.

V. No fuels, lubricants, or other toxic or polluting materials shall be stored on-site unless in compliance with state laws or rules pertaining to such materials.

VI. Where temporary slopes will exceed a grade of 1:1, a fence or other suitable barricade shall be erected to warn of danger or limit access to the site.

VII. Prior to the removal of topsoil or other overburden material from any land area that has not yet been excavated, the excavator shall file a reclamation bond or other security as prescribed by the regulator, sufficient to secure the reclamation of the land area to be excavated.

VIII. Nothing in this chapter shall be deemed to supersede or preempt applicable environmental standards or permit requirements contained in other state laws, and no exemption under this chapter shall be construed as an exemption from any other state statute.

Source.

1989, 363:9. 1991, 310:14–17, eff. Aug. 23, 1991. 1996, 296:36, eff. Aug. 9, 1996.

Amendments

—1996. Paragraph II-a: Substituted "department of environmental services" for "wetlands board" at the end of the paragraph.

—1991. Added "Minimum and Express" preceding "Operational" in the section catchline and rewrote the introductory paragraph.

Paragraph II-a: Added.

Paragraph IV: Inserted "continued" preceding "siltation of" and substituted "surface waters or any" for "streams or" thereafter and "water quality of any public or private" for "any" following "degradation of" in the second sentence and deleted the former third and fourth sentences of par. IV.

Paragraph VII: Inserted "overburden" preceding "material from" and substituted "any land area that has not yet been excavated" for "a new excavation area" thereafter and "land area to be excavated" for "site" following "secure the reclamation of the".

Contingent 1996 amendment.
1996, 296:8, provided for amendment of this

section. However, under the terms of 1996, 296:54, eff. Aug. 9, 1996, the amendment did not become effective.

Cross References.
Exceptions, see RSA 155-E:5-b.

NOTES TO DECISIONS

Municipal ordinance not preempted
Goshen, N.H., Zoning Ordinance fit within the scope of permissible municipal regulation under RSA ch. 155-E because, by its terms, it applied only to excavations requiring a permit; it followed that the more stringent requirements set forth in the ordinance were not preempted. Guildhall Sand & Gravel, L.L.C. v.

Town of Goshen., — N.H. —, 929 A.2d 199, 2007 N.H. LEXIS 128 (July 20, 2007).

Cited:
Cited in NBAC Corp. v. Town of Weare, 147 N.H. 328, 786 A.2d 867, 2001 N.H. LEXIS 219 (2001).

RESEARCH REFERENCES

New Hampshire Practice.
15 N.H.P. Land Use Planning and Zoning §§ 36.09, 36.10, 36.12, 36.13.

155-E:5. Minimum and Express Reclamation Standards.

Within 12 months after the expiration date in a permit issued under this chapter, or of the completion of any excavation, whichever occurs first, the owner of the excavated land shall have completed the reclamation of the areas affected by the excavation to meet each of the following minimum standards or when such excavation is not subject to a permit under this chapter pursuant to RSA 155-E:2, to meet each of the following express standards:

I. Except for exposed rock ledge, all areas which have been affected by the excavation or otherwise stripped of vegetation shall be spread with topsoil or strippings, if any, but in any case covered by soil capable of sustaining vegetation, and shall be planted with seedlings or grass suitable to prevent erosion. Areas visible from a public way, from which trees have been removed, shall be replanted with tree seedlings, wet out in accordance with acceptable horticultural practices.

II. Earth and vegetative debris resulting from the excavation shall be removed or otherwise lawfully disposed of.

III. All slopes, except for exposed ledge, shall be graded to natural response for the type of soil of which they are composed so as to control erosion or at a ratio of horizontal to vertical proposed by the owner and approved by the regulator. Changes of slope shall not be abrupt, but shall blend with the surrounding terrain.

IV. The elimination of any standing bodies of water created in the excavation project as may constitute a hazard to health and safety.

V. The topography of the land shall be left so that water draining from the site leaves the property at the original, natural drainage points and in the natural proportions of flow. For excavation projects which require a permit from the department of environmental services pursuant to RSA 485-A:17, the provisions of that statute, and rules adopted under it, shall supersede this paragraph as to areas of excavation sites covered thereby. The excavator shall file a copy of permits issued under RSA 485-A:17 with the regulator.

Source.
1979, 481:2. 1989, 363:10. 1991, 310:18–20, eff. Aug. 23, 1991. 1996, 228:108, eff. July 1, 1996.

Amendments
—1996. Paragraph V: Substituted "department of environmental services" for "division of water supply and pollution control" in the second sentence.

—1991. Added "Minimum and Express" preceding "Reclamation" in the section catchline and deleted "whether subject to permit or not" preceding "whichever" and substituted "standards or when such excavation is not subject to a permit under this chapter pursuant to RSA 155-E:2, to meet each of the following express standards" for "conditions"

following "minimum" in the introductory paragraph.

Paragraph III: Inserted "for" preceding "exposed" and substituted "so as to control erosion or at a ratio of horizontal or vertical proposed by the owner and approved by the regulator" for "but shall not in any case be left steeper than 2:1 without an exception under RSA 155-E:5-a" following "composed" in the first sentence.

Paragraph V: Substituted "RSA 485-A:17" for "RSA 149:8-a" in the second and third sentences.

—1989. Rewritten to the extent that a detailed comparison would be impracticable.

Cross References.
Exceptions, see RSA 155-E:5-b.

NOTES TO DECISIONS

Municipal ordinance not preempted
Goshen, N.H., Zoning Ordinance fit within the scope of permissible municipal regulation under RSA ch. 155-E because, by its terms, it applied only to excavations requiring a permit; it followed that the more stringent requirements set forth in the ordinance were not preempted. Guildhall Sand & Gravel, L.L.C. v.

Town of Goshen., — N.H. —, 929 A.2d 199, 2007 N.H. LEXIS 128 (July 20, 2007).

Cited:
Cited in Town of North Hampton v. Sanderson, 131 N.H. 614, 557 A.2d 643, 1989 N.H. LEXIS 32 (1989).

RESEARCH REFERENCES

New Hampshire Practice.
15 N.H.P. Land Use Planning and Zoning §§ 36.09–36.11, 36.13, 36.16.

155-E:5-a. Incremental Reclamation.

Except for excavation sites of operating stationary manufacturing plants, any excavated area of 5 contiguous acres or more, which is depleted of commercial earth materials, excluding bedrock, or any excavation from which earth materials of sufficient weight or volume to be commercially useful have not been removed for a 2-year period, shall be reclaimed in accordance with RSA 155-E:5, within 12 months following such depletion or 2-year non-use, regardless of whether other excavation is occurring on adjacent land in contiguous ownership. Each operator, other than the operator of stationary manufacturing plants which are exempt from permit requirements pursuant to RSA 155-E:2, III, shall prepare and submit for the regulator's record a reclamation plan for the affected land, including a timetable for reclamation of the depleted areas within the reclamation site.

Source.
1989, 363:11. 1991, 310:21, eff. Aug. 23, 1991.

Amendments
—**1991.** Added "Except for excavation sites of operating stationary manufacturing plants" preceding "any excavated area", deleted "either" preceding "is depleted", and substituted "any excavation from which" for "from which

no" following "bedrock, or" and "of sufficient weight or volume to be commercially useful have not" for "have" preceding "been removed" in the first sentence and added the second sentence.

Cross References.
Exceptions, see RSA 155-E:5-b.

RESEARCH REFERENCES

New Hampshire Practice.
15 N.H.P. Land Use Planning and Zoning §§ 36.09–36.11, 36.13, 36.16.

155-E:5-b. Exceptions.

The regulator, upon application and following a hearing held in accordance with RSA 155-E:7, may grant an exception in writing to the standards contained in RSA 155-E:4-a, 155-E:5 and 155-E:5-a for good cause shown. The written decision shall state specifically what standards, if any, are being relaxed, and include reasonable alternative conditions or standards. The regulator's decision on any request for such exception may be appealed in accordance with RSA 155-E:9.

Source.
1989, 363:11, eff. Aug. 4, 1989.

RESEARCH REFERENCES

New Hampshire Practice.
15 N.H.P. Land Use Planning and Zoning § 36.16.

155-E:6. Application for Amendment.

When the scope of a project for which an excavation permit has been issued is proposed to be altered so as to affect either the size or location of the excavation, the rate of removal or the plan for reclamation, the owner shall submit an application for amendment of his excavation permit which application shall be subject to approval in the same manner as provided for an excavation permit.

Source.
1979, 481:2. 1989, 363:12, eff. Aug. 4, 1989.

Amendments
—**1989.** Substituted "reclamation" for "restoration" following "plan for".

RESEARCH REFERENCES

New Hampshire Practice.
15 N.H.P. Land Use Planning and Zoning
§ 36.11.

155-E:7. Hearing.

Prior to the regulator approving an application for an excavation permit or an application for an amended excavation permit, a public hearing shall be held within 30 days on such application. A notice of said hearing shall be sent to all abutters and shall specify the grounds for the hearing as well as the date, time and place and at least 10 days' notice of the time and place of such hearing shall be published in a paper of general circulation in the city, town or unincorporated place wherein the proposed excavation is to be located and a legal notice thereof shall also be posted in at least 3 public places in such city, town or unincorporated place; the 10 days shall not include the day of publications nor the day of the meeting, but shall include any Saturdays, Sundays and legal holidays within said period. Within 20 days of said hearing or any continuation thereof, the regulator shall render a decision approving or disapproving the application, giving reasons for disapproval.

Source.
1979, 481:2, eff. Aug. 24, 1979. 2002, 89:1, eff. July 2, 2002.

Amendments
—**2002.** Substituted "10 days" for "14 days" twice in the second sentence.

NOTES TO DECISIONS

Burden of proof
Because the owner failed to prove that the evidence lacked credibility, the trial court found a sufficient evidentiary basis for the town's denial of the owner's excavation permit application on the ground that it would be injurious to public welfare. NBAC Corp. v. Town of Weare, 147 N.H. 328, 786 A.2d 867, 2001 N.H. LEXIS 219 (2001).

RESEARCH REFERENCES

New Hampshire Practice.
15 N.H.P. Land Use Planning and Zoning
§§ 36.12, 36.16.

155-E:8. Issuance of Permit.

If the regulator after the public hearing approves the application for a permit and determines it is not prohibited by RSA 155-E:4 it shall, upon receipt of an excavation fee determined by the regulator not to exceed $50 and the posting of a bond or other such surety with the municipal treasurer in an amount, as it requires, reasonably sufficient to guarantee compliance with the permit, grant a permit to the applicant for an excavation. A copy of the permit shall be prominently posted at the excavation site or the principal access thereto. A permit shall not be assignable or transferable without the prior written consent of the regulator. A permit shall specify the date upon which it expires. The regulator may include in a permit such reasonable conditions as are consistent with the purpose of this chapter and may include requirements for a permit for excavation which are more stringent than the standards set forth in this chapter including the provision of visual barriers to the excavation.

Source.
1979, 481:2. 1991, 310:22, eff. Aug. 23, 1991.

Amendments
—**1991.** Inserted "and may include require-ments for a permit for excavation which are more stringent than the standards set forth in this chapter" preceding "including the provi-sion" in the fifth sentence.

NOTES TO DECISIONS

Municipal ordinance not preempted
Goshen, N.H., Zoning Ordinance fit within the scope of permissible municipal regulation under RSA ch. 155-E because, by its terms, it applied only to excavations requiring a permit; it followed that the more stringent require-ments set forth in the ordinance were not preempted. Guildhall Sand & Gravel, L.L.C. v. Town of Goshen., — N.H. —, 929 A.2d 199, 2007 N.H. LEXIS 128 (July 20, 2007).

RESEARCH REFERENCES

New Hampshire Practice.
15 N.H.P. Land Use Planning and Zoning § 36.14.

155-E:9. Appeal.

If the regulator disapproves or approves an application for an excavation permit or an application for an amended permit, any interested person affected by such decision may appeal to the regulator for a rehearing on such decision or any matter determined thereby. The motion for rehearing shall fully specify every ground upon which it is alleged that the decision or order complained of is unlawful or unreasonable and said appeal shall be filed within 10 days of the date of the decision appealed from. The regulator shall either grant or deny the request for rehearing within 10 days, and if the request is granted a rehearing shall be scheduled within 30 days. Any person affected by the regulator's decision on a motion for rehearing to the regulator may appeal in conformity with the procedures specified in RSA 677:4–15.

Source.
1979, 481:2. 1985, 103:2, eff. Jan. 1, 1986.

Amendments
—**1985.** Substituted "RSA 677:4–15" for "RSA 31:77–87" following "specified in" at the end of the fourth sentence.

RESEARCH REFERENCES

New Hampshire Practice.
15 N.H.P. Land Use Planning and Zoning §§ 36.16, 36.17.

155-E:10. Enforcement.

I. The regulator or its duly authorized agent may suspend or revoke the permit of any person who has violated any provision of his permit or this chapter or made a material misstatement in the application upon which his permit was granted. Such suspension or revocation shall be subject to a motion for rehearing thereon and appeal in accordance with RSA 155-E:9

II. Fines, penalties, and remedies for violations of this chapter shall be the same as for violations of RSA title LXIV, as stated in RSA 676:15, 676:17, 676:17-a, and 676:17-b. In addition, the regulator or a person directly affected by such violation may seek an order from the superior court requiring the violator to cease and desist from violating any provision of a permit or this chapter and to take such action as may be necessary to comply with the permit and this chapter. If the superior court issues such an order, the superior court in its discretion may award all costs and attorneys' fees incurred in seeking such an order to the regulator or person directly affected by such violation.

III. To ascertain if there is compliance with this chapter, a permit issued hereunder or an order issued hereunder, the regulator or its duly authorized agent may enter upon any land on which there is reason to believe an excavation is being conducted or has been conducted since August 24, 1979.

IV. [Repealed.]

Source.

1979, 481:2. 1989, 363:13, 18, eff. Aug. 4, 1989. 1996, 141:1, eff. Jan. 1, 1997.

Revision note.

In par. II, substituted "RSA title LXIV" for "RSA title LX" to correct an error in the reference.

At the end of par. III, substituted "August 24, 1979" for "the effective date of this chapter" for purposes of clarity.

Amendments

—**1996.** Paragraph II: Inserted "676:17-a, and 676:17-b" following "676:17" in the first sentence, added the second and third sentences, and made a minor stylistic change.

—**1989.** Paragraph II: Rewritten to the extent that a detailed comparison would be impracticable.

Paragraph IV: Repealed.

NOTES TO DECISIONS

Municipal ordinance not preempted

Goshen, N.H., Zoning Ordinance fit within the scope of permissible municipal regulation under RSA ch. 155-E because, by its terms, it applied only to excavations requiring a permit; it followed that the more stringent requirements set forth in the ordinance were not preempted. Guildhall Sand & Gravel, L.L.C. v. Town of Goshen., — N.H. —, 929 A.2d 199, 2007 N.H. LEXIS 128 (July 20, 2007).

Cited:

Cited in Town of Goffstown v. Thibeault, 129 N.H. 454, 529 A.2d 930, 1987 N.H. LEXIS 184 (1987); Town of North Hampton v. Sanderson, 131 N.H. 614, 557 A.2d 643, 1989 N.H. LEXIS 32 (1989); Town of Barrington v. Gadd, 132 N.H. 650, 569 A.2d 231, 1990 N.H. LEXIS 6 (1990).

155-E:11. Regulations.

I. The regulator may adopt such regulations as may be reasonably necessary to carry out the provisions of this chapter, including adopting a permit fee schedule. Whenever such local regulations differ from the provisions of this chapter, the provision which imposes the greater restriction or higher standard shall be controlling, except that no local regulation shall supersede the sole applicability of express standards under RSA 155-E:2, I, III, and IV.

II. Such regulations may include reasonable provisions for the protection of water resources, consistent with the municipality's local water resources management and protection plan developed under RSA 674:2, III(d). If such regulations prohibit excavations below a stated height above the water table, the regulations shall also contain a procedure whereby an exception to such prohibition shall be granted if the applicant demonstrates that such excavation will not adversely affect water quality, provided, however, that written notice of such exception shall be recorded in the registry of deeds, and one copy filed with the department of environmental services.

III. The regulator may impose reasonable fees to cover the costs of notice under RSA 155-E:7, and to cover its administrative expenses, review of documents, and other matters which may be required by particular applications or proceedings before the regulator under this chapter.

Source.
1979, 481:2. 1989, 363:14. 1991, 310:23, eff. Aug. 23, 1991. 1996, 141:3, eff. Jan. 1, 1997; 228:108, eff. July 1, 1996. 2002, 178:7, eff. July 14, 2002.

Amendments
—**2002.** Paragraph II: Substituted "RSA 674:2, III(d)" for "RSA 674:2, VIII" at the end of the first sentence.

—**1996.** Paragraph II: Chapter 228 substituted "department of environmental services" for "division of water supply and pollution control, department of environmental services" in the second sentence.

Paragraph III: Added by ch. 141.

—**1991.** Paragraph I: Added the second sentence.

—**1989.** Designated existing provisions of section as par. I and added par. II.

NOTES TO DECISIONS

Municipal ordinance not preempted
Goshen, N.H., Zoning Ordinance fit within the scope of permissible municipal regulation under RSA ch. 155-E because, by its terms, it applied only to excavations requiring a permit; it followed that the more stringent requirements set forth in the ordinance were not preempted. Guildhall Sand & Gravel, L.L.C. v. Town of Goshen., — N.H. —, 929 A.2d 199, 2007 N.H. LEXIS 128 (July 20, 2007).

CHAPTER 162-C

COUNCIL ON RESOURCES AND DEVELOPMENT

162-C:1. Council Established.

There is established a council on resources and development which shall include the following members:

I. The director or assistant director of the office of energy and planning who shall serve as chairman of the council.

II. The commissioner or appropriate division director, department of resources and economic development.

III. The commissioner or assistant commissioner, department of environmental services.

IV. The commissioner or appropriate division director, department of agriculture, markets, and food.

V. The executive director or appropriate division director, fish and game department.

VI. The commissioner or assistant commissioner, department of safety.

VII. The director of the division of emergency services, communications, and management.

VIII. The commissioner of the department of health and human services or a member of the senior management team.

IX. The commissioner or assistant commissioner, department of education.

X. The commissioner or assistant commissioner, department of transportation.

XI. The commissioner or appropriate division director, department of cultural resources.

XII. The commissioner or appropriate division director, department of administrative services.

XIII. The executive director or chairman of the New Hampshire housing finance authority.

Source.

1963, 301:1. 1965, 212:1. 1986, 176:3; 202:6, I(c), (f). 1987, 283:5. 1995, 130:4, eff. July 23, 1995; 310:182, eff. Nov. 1, 1995. 1999, 59:1, eff. July 20, 1999. 2001, 249:2, eff. Sept. 11, 2001. 2003, 319:9, eff. July 1, 2003; 319:127, eff. Sept.

4, 2003. 2004. 2004, 171:19, eff. July 24, 2004; 257:44, eff. July 1, 2004.

Amendments

—**2004.** Paragraph I: Chapter 257 substituted "office of energy and planning" for "office of state planning and energy programs".

Paragraph VII: Rewritten by ch. 171 to the extent that a detailed comparison would be impracticable.

—2003. Paragraph I: Substituted "office of state planning and energy programs" for "office of state planning".

Paragraph VII: Substituted "chief of the bureau" for "director or assistant director, office".

—2001. Inserted "or assistant director" in par. I; "or appropriate division director" in pars. II, IV, V, and XI; "or assistant commissioner" in pars. III, VI, IX and X; rewrote par. VII; added "or a member of the senior management team" in par. VIII; and added pars. XII and XIII.

—1999. Paragraph XI: Added.

—1995. Paragraph IV: Chapter 130 substituted "department of agriculture, markets, and food" for "department of agriculture" following "commissioner".

Paragraph VIII: Chapter 310 substituted "commissioner of the department of health and human services" for "director, division of public health services".

—1987. Rewritten to the extent that a detailed comparison would be impracticable.

—1986. Rewritten by ch. 176 to the extent that a detailed comparison would be impracticable.

Chapter 202 substituted "director of the division of water supply and pollution control; director, division of water resources, department of environmental services" for "executive director of the water supply and pollution control commission; chairman of the water resources board".

—1965. Rewritten to the extent that a detailed comparison would be impracticable.

Effective date of amendments
—1986, 202 amendment. 1986, 202:31, I, eff. July 1, 1986, provided that 1986, 202:6, I(c), would take effect when the department of environmental services established by the act became operational on the date set pursuant to 1983, 372:5, II. Pursuant to 1983, 372:5, II, the joint committee on implementation of reorganization and the governor determined the effective date upon which the department became operational to be Jan. 2, 1987.

Severability
—1986 amendment. 1986, 176:3, was subject to a severability clause. See 1986, 176:4.
—1995, 310 amendment. 1995, 310, which amended this section, was subject to a severability clause. See 1995, 310:186.

Construction of amendments
—1995, 310. 1995, 310:187, eff. Nov. 1, 1995, provided:
"Nothing in this act is intended to, nor shall it be construed as, mandating or assigning any new, expanded, or modified program or responsibility for any political subdivision in violation of part I, article 28-a of the constitution of the state of New Hampshire."

Cross References.
Public water access advisory board to serve as advisory committee to council on resources and development, see RSA 233-A:2.

162-C:2. Responsibilities.

The council shall:

I. Consult upon common problems in the fields of environmental protection, natural resources, and growth management including the encouragement of smart growth;

II. Consult with, negotiate with, and obtain information from, any federal or state agency concerned with any of the council's problems, reports, recommendations or studies;

III. Make biennial reports and recommendations, as may be desirable, to the governor and council;

IV. Make studies and recommendations concerning changes to effectively coordinate the work of the agencies which have membership in the council;

V. Resolve differences or conflicts concerning development, resource management, or the encouragement of smart growth which result from the work of any agency represented on the council in developing policies, plans, or programs. The council shall investigate; if possible, resolve the problem; and if appropriate, submit its recommendations to the governor and council or to the general court. If investigation by the council shows that the laws and rules of an agency represented on the council are in conflict with those of another agency, the council shall submit a report with recommendations to the governor and council or to the general court;

VI. Resolve differences and conflicts among the agencies and departments of the state in the implementation of the tourism policy under RSA 12-A:23;

VII. Review the disposal of state owned real property pursuant to RSA 4:40;

VIII. Provide oversight relative to the statewide public boat access program, work with the public water access advisory board and provide recommendations to the governor and executive council regarding public access;

IX. Complete the annual smart growth report required under RSA 9-B:6;

X. Review and coordinate the distribution of funds by state agencies to local and regional entities to encourage consistency with and provide support for New Hampshire's smart growth policies under RSA 9-B:4;

XI. Review the following actions by state agencies and ensure, in consultation with the long range capital planning and utilization committee established by RSA 17-M:1-3, that these actions are taken into consideration in the long range capital improvement program that is updated every 2 years in conjunction with the capital budget process, and provide recommendations to the governor regarding whether the actions are consistent with New Hampshire's smart growth policies under RSA 9-B:5:

(a) Capital budget requests;

(b) Building operation and maintenance plans; and

(c) Facility location and planning; and

XII. Facilitate coordination of state agencies to support local, regional, and state planning efforts consistent with RSA 9-A:1-4.

Source.

1963, 301:2. 1965, 212:2. 1973, 140:7. 1981, 364:1. 1986, 165:3; 224:5. 1987, 283:6, 7. 1992, 265:6, eff. Jan. 1, 1993. 2000, 292:7-9, eff. Aug. 20, 2000. 2001, 249:3, eff. Sept. 11, 2001. 2006, 307:2, eff. July 1, 2006.

Amendments
—2006. Paragraph IV: Deleted the former second sentence.

—2001. Made a minor stylistic change in par. VIII, made a minor change in punctuation in par. IX, and added pars. X-XII.

—2000. Paragraph I: Added "including the encouragement of smart growth" following "management".
Paragraph V: Inserted "or the encourage-

ment of smart growth" following "management" and made a stylistic change in the first sentence.

Paragraphs VII and VIII: Made minor stylistic changes.

Paragraph IX: Added.

—1992. Paragraph VIII: Added.

—1987. Paragraph I: Rewritten to the extent that a detailed comparison would be impracticable.

Paragraph V: Substituted "development or resource management" for "water management and supply" following "concerning" and "policies, plans, or programs" for "a plan or program affecting water allocation" following "developing" in the first sentence.

—**1986.** Paragraph IV: Chapter 224 deleted "and" following "rules" at the end of the paragraph.

Paragraph V: Chapter 224 made minor stylistic changes.

Paragraph VI: Added by ch. 165.

Chapter 224 added "and" following "RSA 12-A:23".

Paragraph VII: Added by ch. 224.

—**1981.** Rewritten to the extent that a detailed comparison would be impracticable.

—**1973.** Substituted "biennial" for "such" following "studies; make" in the first sentence.

—**1965.** Added "or state" after federal in the first sentence.

Contingent 1986 amendment.

1986, 224:2, provided for amendment of this section. However, under the terms of 1986, 224:6, eff. Aug. 5, 1986, the amendment did not become effective.

162-C:3. Tenure of Members.

Members shall serve without compensation, and any member's term of office shall terminate when he ceases to be a member of the state agency he represents.

Source.
1963, 301:3. 1965, 212:3, eff. July 1, 1965.

Amendments
—**1965.** Rewritten to the extent that a detailed comparison would be impracticable.

162-C:4. Meetings.

The council shall meet at least once every 3 months, but may meet more often as it shall determine. The chairman shall prepare and deliver an agenda to all members at least 7 days in advance of each meeting. The council shall provide a copy of the minutes from each meeting to the senate president, the speaker of the house of representatives, the long range capital planning and utilization committee, and the governor and council.

Source.
1963, 301:4. 1965, 212:4. 1987, 283:8, eff. May 25, 1987. 2006, 307:3, eff. July 1, 2006.

Amendments
—**2006.** Added the third sentence.

—**1987.** Rewritten to the extent that a detailed comparison would be impracticable.

—**1965.** Deleted "and who shall prepare and have delivered at least seven days before every meeting of the council an agenda for said meeting" at the end of the first sentence, rewrote the third sentence and deleted the fourth sentence.

162-C:5. Staff.

The council may employ staff needed to carry out its responsibilities.

Source.
1981, 364:2, eff. Aug. 22, 1981.

Land Conservation Investment Program

162-C:6. Purpose; Management.

I. The general court recognizes that in order to maintain New Hampshire's distinctive quality of life, strong economic growth must be balanced with responsible conservation initiatives, and that the history of conservation in New Hampshire has been marked by cooperation among government, business, individuals, and conservation organizations. The general court further recognizes the strong traditions of both public and private land ownership and use, and the need to respect investments in the conservation of natural resource lands in the state for the perpetual use of the people of New Hampshire. In addition, the general court recognizes that the land conservation investment program was undertaken, in part, with significant donations of cash and land value by citizens of the state who intended that the conservation value of these lands be protected in perpetuity.

II. In addition to its other responsibilities, the council shall manage and administer the lands acquired and funds established under the land conservation investment program under the former RSA 221-A, according to the provisions of this subdivision and consistent with agreements entered into with persons with ownership interests in such lands.

III. The council shall manage the lands acquired under the former RSA 221-A so as to preserve the natural beauty, landscape, rural character, natural resources, and high quality of life in New Hampshire. The council shall maintain and protect benefits derived from such lands and maintain public access to such lands, where appropriate. On state-owned lands, whenever the council shall deem it in the best interest of conservation and protection of the values outlined in this section, it may, with the consent of the governor, authorize the exchange of any interest in the property when the conservation values of the property would be degraded if no action were taken. Prior to submitting a request to the governor to exchange any interest in the property, the council shall provide at least 30 calendar days advance notice to the local governing body and conservation commission. Such exchanges shall be reviewed and approved by the council, shall involve lands contiguous to the original acquisition which have equal or greater conservation value, and shall convey only those interests necessary to compensate for the potential degradation.

IV. Notwithstanding paragraphs I-III, the council shall recognize that the interest of public safety and welfare may, from time to time, require minor expansion, minor modification, or minor alteration of existing roads within the state highway system. After review and approval by the council, and notwithstanding RSA 162-C:10, the department of transportation may obtain interests in lands acquired under the former RSA 221-A adjacent to state highways. Permissible expansion, modification, or alterations under this section shall include drainage easements, slope easements, lane widening, the addition of a passing, climbing, or turning lane, or similar adjustments, but shall not include construction of a new highway or portion thereof, construction of a bypass for an existing highway, or similar major alterations. Approval shall not be granted if reasonable and prudent alternatives exist nor if individual or cumulative approvals are likely to materially impair the conservation purposes for which the parcel was originally protected. Projects determined by the council to be outside of the scope permitted by this subdivision shall require approval from the general court.

V. The review and approval process required by paragraph IV shall give full consideration to the management provisions contained in paragraphs I-III. The department of transportation shall submit a written request to the council with plans and supporting documentation to demonstrate compliance with the provisions of this chapter. A quorum of the council, consisting of at least 6 members, shall hold a public hearing within 90 days of receipt of a complete request to release land conservation investment program interests. The council shall provide at least 10 calendar days notice in advance of such hearing. Notification shall be made, at the expense of the department, to the landowner, local governing body and conservation commission, abutters, the Society for the Protection of New Hampshire Forests, The Nature Conservancy, the Audubon Society of New Hampshire, the New Hampshire Wildlife Federation, and the county conservation district, or their successors. Notification of the public hearing shall be published, by the department, in a paper of general circulation in the municipality and shall be posted, by the department, in at least 2 public places. At the hearing or within 15 days after the hearing, a majority of the council members attending the hearing shall vote to approve or deny the application, unless a time extension is requested by the department. Aggrieved parties, which include all parties who must be notified under this paragraph, may appeal the council's decision to the superior court in the same manner as planning board decisions are appealed under RSA 677:15.

VI. Compensation for any interest in land obtained by the state department of transportation under this section shall be at the appraised full fair market value of those property interests at the time of the department's acquisition. Alternative forms of compensation such as replacement land with comparable conservation value, or a combination of monetary compensation and replacement land may be considered in appropriate circumstances provided all parties owning an interest in the property agree to such terms.

VII. Compensation due to the state under this section shall be deposited in the trust fund of the New Hampshire land and community heritage investment program established under RSA 227-M and used for the purposes of that program. Compensation due to municipalities shall be dedicated to the acquisition or monitoring of protected lands consistent with the purposes of this chapter. Compensation due to landowners of conservation easement lands shall be as specified in the conservation easement, deed, or as otherwise negotiated. Any party aggrieved by the amount of compensation may file a petition with the superior court in the same manner as damage appeals are filed from the board of tax and land appeals under RSA 498-A:27.

Source.
  1995, 10:4, eff. April 12, 1995. 1998, 364:1,
eff. Jan. 1, 1999. 2000, 245:2, eff. June 8, 2000.

References in text.
  RSA 221-A, referred to in pars. II–IV, was
repealed by 1995, 10:16, VII, eff. April 12, 1995.

Amendments
  —2000.   Paragraph VII: Rewrote the former
first through third sentences as the present
first sentence.

  —1998.   Rewritten to the extent that a detailed comparison would be impractical.

162-C:7. Powers and Duties.

The council shall oversee, direct, and expend funds in the monitoring
endowment of the former New Hampshire land conservation investment
program in accordance with the purposes of this subdivision and RSA
227-M:12. This includes, but is not limited to, the authority to draw upon funds
for the administrative costs of the endowment.

Source.
  1995, 10:4, eff. April 12, 1995. 2000, 245:3,
eff. June 8, 2000.

Amendments
  —2000.   Inserted "and RSA 227-M:12" following "subdivision" in the first sentence.

162-C:8. Monitoring Endowment.

I. The monitoring endowment established by the board of directors pursuant
to former RSA 221-A:5, III shall be maintained in perpetuity and shall be
utilized by the council only for the purposes of monitoring and enforcing the
property rights of persons with ownership interests in property acquired
through the former land conservation investment program. Additional contributions to the endowment pursuant to RSA 227-M:12, I shall be accounted for
separately and shall be utilized only for the purposes of RSA 227-M:12, II.
Additional gifts, donations, and grants to the endowment may be utilized for
monitoring and enforcing other land conservation interests that may be
acquired by the state of New Hampshire.

II. The principal of the endowment shall be managed by the state treasurer
for the sole purpose of providing a perpetual source of income, as defined by the
state treasurer, for the purposes set forth in this subdivision and RSA
227-M:12.

III. Any income earned on the endowment principal which is not used for the
purposes set forth in this subdivision and RSA 227-M:12 within the fiscal year
in which it is earned shall be nonlapsing. The state treasurer is authorized to
accept gifts, donations, and grants, including federal gifts, donations, and
grants, for the purposes set forth in this chapter, and such gifts, donations and
grants shall be added to the principal amount.

IV. The council shall, pursuant to the monitoring endowment established
under former RSA 221-A:5, III, and the provisions of RSA 162-C:8, I, prepare
an annual report to be presented no later than December 1 of each year to the
speaker of the house, the president of the senate, the governor, the house clerk,
the senate clerk, and the state library. The report shall include a listing of all
lands and interests in lands subject to the monitoring provisions of RSA
162-C:7, I and a complete financial accounting of the funds in the monitoring
endowment including expenditures for the most recent full fiscal year. The

report shall also summarize monitoring activities and findings for each property, as conducted in the most recent full fiscal year.

Source.
1995, 10:4, eff. April 12, 1995. 2000, 245:4, eff. June 8, 2000. 2002, 86:2, eff. July 2, 2002. 2004, 257:47, eff. July 1, 2004. 2007, 151:1, eff. August 17, 2007.

References in text.
RSA 221-A:5, referred to in pars. I and IV, was repealed by 1995, 10:16, VII, eff. April 12, 1995.

Amendments
—**2007.** Paragraph I: Deleted "any interest generated thereon" following "in perpetuity and" the first sentence and substituted "shall be accounted for separately and" for "and any interest generated thereon" in the second sentence.

Paragraph II: Rewritten to the extent that a detailed comparison would be impracticable.

Paragraph III: Substituted "any income earned" for "any interest earned" in the first sentence.

—**2004.** Paragraph I: Inserted "any interest generated thereon" following "perpetuity and" and deleted "and for the purposes of RSA 227-M:12" at the end of the first sentence and added the second and third sentences.

—**2002.** Paragraph III: Substituted "non-lapsing" for "added to the principal amount" following "shall be" in the first sentence.

—**2000.** Paragraph I: Added "and for the purposes of RSA 227-M:12" following "investment program".

Paragraph II: Inserted "and RSA 227-M:12" following "in this subdivision".

Paragraph III: Inserted "and RSA 227-M:12" following "subdivision" in the first sentence.

162-C:9. Management.

I. Each assignment of land under this subdivision to a state agency or a municipality shall be subject to review and reassignment if the council deems it advisable.

II. No lands purchased in fee for permanent state ownership under the former RSA 221-A shall be posted to prohibit hunting or fishing, unless the council, by a majority vote of the voting members, deems such posting to be necessary to protect the interests of the state and the safety of its citizens, or upon recommendation of the fish and game commission or the division of forests and lands.

Source.
1995, 10:4, eff. April 12, 1995. 2006, 307:4, eff. July 1, 2006.

References in text.
RSA 221-A, referred to in par. II, was repealed by 1995, 10:16, VII, eff. April 12, 1995.

Amendments
—**2006.** Paragraph I: Inserted "under this subdivision" following "of land".

162-C:10. Public Trust.

The lands and interests in lands acquired under the former RSA 221-A through the use of the trust fund for the program shall be held in public trust and used and applied for the purposes of this subdivision. Notwithstanding any other provision of law relating to the disposal of publicly-owned real estate, no deviation in the uses of any land or interest in land so acquired to uses or purposes not consistent with the purposes of this subdivision shall be permitted. The sale, transfer, conveyance, or release of any such land or interest in land from public trust is prohibited.

Source.
1995, 10:4, eff. April 12, 1995.

was repealed by 1995, 10:16, VII, eff. April 12, 1995.

References in text.
RSA 221-A, referred to in the first sentence,

162-C:11. Public Access; Liability.

No person, or the person's successor in title, who has granted or sold rights of public access by virtue of an easement, right-of-way, development right, or other means in accordance with the purposes of this subdivision shall be liable to a user of that right of access for injuries suffered on that portion of the access way unless those injuries are caused by the willful or wanton misconduct of the grantor or successor in title.

Source.
1995, 10:4, eff. April 12, 1995.

CHAPTER 162-N

ECONOMIC REVITALIZATION ZONE TAX CREDITS

Repeal and reenactment of chapter.
2007, 263:120, effective July 1, 2007 provided for the repeal and reenactment of RSA 162-N. Original RSA 162-N, consisting of RSA 162-N:1 —162-N:9, was derived from 2003, 301:2, eff. July 1, 2003.

Prospective repeal of chapter.
2007, 263:123, I provides for the repeal of this chapter on July 1, 2011.

[Repealed effective July 1, 2011; see prospective repeal note preceding RSA 162-N:1]

162-N:1. Definition.

In this chapter, "economic revitalization zone" means a zone designated by the commissioner of resources and economic development as an economic revitalization zone in accordance with the provisions of this chapter.

Source.
2007, 263:120, eff. July 1, 2007.

[Repealed effective July 1, 2011; see prospective repeal note preceding RSA 162-N:1]

162-N:2. Designation of Economic Revitalization Zone.

I. "Economic revitalization zone" means a zone with a single continuous boundary, comprised of one or more contiguous census tracts or blocks or smaller recognizable physical areas, designated in accordance with the rules adopted under RSA 162-N:8, and certified by the commissioner of resources and economic development as being a brownfields site as defined under RSA 147-F, or having at least one of the following characteristics:

(a) The population of the municipality or municipalities in which the zone is located, according to the most recent federal census, decreased during the 20 years prior to the census.

(b) The median household income in the census tract or tracts in which the zone is located is less than $40,500 according to the most recent federal decennial census.

(c) At least 20 percent of households in the census tract or tracts in which the zone is located have a median income below the federal poverty level.

(d)(1) The zone contains either:

(A) Unused or underutilized industrial parks; or

(B) Vacant land or structures previously used for industrial, commercial, or retail purposes but currently not so used due to demolition, age, obsolescence, deterioration, relocation of the former occupant's operations, or cessation of operation resulting from unfavorable economic conditions either generally or in a specific economic sector; and

(2) Certification of the zone as an economic revitalization zone would likely result in the reduction of the rate of vacant or demolished structures or the rate of tax delinquency in the zone.

II. Economic revitalization zones shall be designated by the commissioner of resources and economic development only upon petition by the local governing body, as defined by RSA 672:6, or the town council. The commissioner of resources and economic development shall certify that the economic revitalization zone meets the criteria required in paragraph I.

III. The commissioner of resources and economic development is authorized to establish an advisory board for each economic revitalization zone established under this chapter.

Source.
2007, 263:120, eff. July 1, 2007.

[Repealed effective July 1, 2011; see prospective repeal note preceding RSA 162-N:1]

162-N:3. Eligibility Requirements for Business Tax Credits.

No economic revitalization zone tax credits shall be allowed to any taxpayer unless the taxpayer's project receives written certification from the commissioner of resources and economic development that it will expand the commercial or industrial base in a designated economic revitalization zone and will create new jobs in the state.

Source.
2007, 263:120, eff. July 1, 2007.

[Repealed effective July 1, 2011; see prospective repeal note preceding RSA 162-N:1]

162-N:4. Economic Revitalization Zone Tax Credit Agreement.

I. The commissioner of resources and economic development shall enter into a written economic revitalization zone tax credit agreement with each taxpayer; such agreement to be certified by the commissioner of resources and economic development under this section. The agreement shall contain such provisions as the commissioner of resources and economic development determines to be in the public interest, which shall include, but not be limited to:

(a) Quality and quantity of jobs to be created.

(b) Duration of the taxpayer's commitments with respect to the economic revitalization zone.

(c) The amount of the taxpayer's investment in the project.

(d) A precise definition of the location of the facility eligible for the credit.

(e) The maximum amount of the economic revitalization zone tax credit that will be allowed to the business under this agreement for jobs created and for construction or reconstruction expenses.

II. A certified copy of each agreement signed by the commissioner of resources and economic development and the taxpayer shall be provided to the commissioner of revenue administration.

Source.
2007, 263:120, eff. July 1, 2007.

[Repealed effective July 1, 2011; see prospective repeal note preceding RSA 162-N:1]

162-N:5. Limit on Total Economic Revitalization Zone Credits.

The aggregate value of all of economic revitalization zone tax credit agreements that the commissioner of resources and economic development enters into shall not exceed the limit of $825,000 in any fiscal year. Notwithstanding RSA 162-N:6, the maximum credit awarded to a taxpayer in any fiscal year shall not exceed $40,000.

Source.
2007, 263:120, eff. July 1, 2007.

[Repealed effective July 1, 2011; see prospective repeal note preceding RSA 162-N:1]

162-N:6. Determination of Economic Revitalization Zone Tax Credits Eligible Amount.

For the purpose of determining the economic revitalization zone tax credit that the taxpayer is eligible to receive, the amount of the credit to be taken shall be the lesser of the following:

I. The maximum amount of the economic revitalization zone tax credit as stated in the agreement as specified by RSA 162-N:4, I(e); or

II. The sum of the following:

(a) 4 percent of the salary for each new job created in the fiscal year with a wage less than or equal to 1.75 times the then current state minimum wage.

(b) 5 percent of the salary for each new job created in the fiscal year with a wage greater than 1.75 times the then current state minimum wage and less than or equal to 2.5 times the then current state minimum wage.

(c) 6 percent of the salary for each new job created in the fiscal year with a wage greater than 2.5 times the then current state minimum wage.

(d) 4 percent of the lesser of the following:
(1) The actual cost incurred in the fiscal year of creating a new facility or renovating an existing facility, and expenditures for machinery, equipment, or other materials, except inventory.
(2) $20,000 for each new job created in the fiscal year.

Source.
2007, 263:120, eff. July 1, 2007.

[Repealed effective July 1, 2011; see prospective repeal note preceding RSA 162-N:1]

162-N:7. Application of Economic Revitalization Zone Tax Credit.

The economic revitalization zone tax credit shall be applied against the business profits tax under RSA 77-A, and any unused portion thereof may be applied against the business enterprise tax under RSA 77-E. Any unused portion of the credit allowed under this chapter may be carried forward and allowed against taxes due under RSA 77-A or RSA 77-E for 5 taxable periods from the taxable period in which the tax was paid.

Source.
2007, 263:120, eff. July 1, 2007.

[Repealed effective July 1, 2011; see prospective repeal note preceding RSA 162-N:1]

162-N:8. Rules.

The commissioner of revenue administration shall adopt rules, under RSA 541-A, relative to documentation of the credits claimed under this chapter. The commissioner of resources and economic development shall, in consultation with the executive director of the community development finance authority, adopt rules, under RSA 541-A, relative to the administration and implementation of this chapter. The rules adopted by the commissioner of resources and economic development shall include provisions relative to:
I. Establishment and certification of economic revitalization zones.
II. Criteria for and approval of projects in economic revitalization zones, including jobs per dollar thresholds.
III. Fees which the commissioner of resources and economic development may charge to each applicant to cover the reasonable costs of the state's administration of the applicant's participation in the economic revitalization zone tax credit program.

Source.
2007, 263:120, eff. July 1, 2007.

[Repealed effective July 1, 2011; see prospective repeal note preceding RSA 162-N:1]

162-N:9. Reports.

The commissioner of resources and economic development shall file an annual report with the governor, the senate president, the speaker of the house of representatives, and the fiscal committee. The report shall describe the results of the economic revitalization zone tax credit program and shall include any recommendations for further legislation regarding the economic revitalization zone tax credit program.

Source.
2007, 263:120, eff. July 1, 2007.

TITLE XVIII

FISH AND GAME

CHAPTER 215-A

OFF HIGHWAY RECREATIONAL VEHICLES AND TRAILS

Section
215-A:15.   Regulations of Political Subdivisions.

215-A:15. Regulations of Political Subdivisions.

I. With bylaws or ordinances city or town councils and boards of selectmen may regulate the operation of OHRVs within city or town limits, providing they do not conflict with provisions of this chapter.

II, III. [Repealed.]

IV. Speed limits for OHRVs traveling on the frozen surface of Turtle Pond, also known as Turtle Town Pond, in the city of Concord shall not exceed 55 miles per hour.

V. Enforcement of paragraph IV shall be the joint responsibility of the city of Concord and the state of New Hampshire.

VI. [Repealed.]

Source.

1981, 538:3, eff. June 30, 1981. 1996, 41:1, eff. June 30, 1996; 41:2, eff. June 30, 1998. 1999, 48:1, eff. July 20, 1999. 2004, 47:2, eff. July 2, 2004; 243:5, eff. June 15, 2004. 2005, 210:64, VIII, eff. July 1, 2006.

Amendments

—**2005.** Paragraph VI: Repealed.

—**2004.** Paragraph I: Substituted "city or town councils and boards of selectmen" for "any town or city" following "ordinances" and "city or town" for "its" preceding "limits".

Paragraph VI: Added.

—**1999.** Paragraphs IV, V: Added.

—**1996.** Chapter 41:1, designated the existing text of the section as par. I and added pars. II and III.

Chapter 41:2 repealed pars. II and III.

CHAPTER 215-C

SNOWMOBILES

215-C:32. Enforcement.

I. The provisions of this chapter shall be enforced by all duly authorized representatives of the department of fish and game and by every police and law enforcement officer including, but not limited to, members of the state police, sheriffs, deputy sheriffs, policemen, and constables and all persons empowered to make arrests in criminal cases.

II. The commissioner of the department of resources and economic development shall appoint a chief supervisor of the bureau of trails, who shall have additional duties as state parks and forest security officer with authority under RSA 594. The commissioner of the department of resources and economic development shall, at his or her discretion, also appoint bureau of trail area supervisors and foremen, who shall be peace officers for the purposes of RSA 594.

III. The commissioner of the department of resources and economic development may designate employees of the bureau as forest and park patrol officers. The chief supervisors appointed under paragraph II and RSA 215-A:16, II and the forest and park patrol officers shall have the authority of peace officers, as defined under RSA 594:1, to enforce the provisions of this chapter anywhere in the state and all rules of the department of resources and economic development on lands owned by, leased to, or under control of the department of resources and economic development. Forest and park patrol officers shall also have authority as peace officers under RSA 594:1 to enforce laws dealing with trespass, litter, breaking and entering, larceny, and vandalism on lands owned by, leased to, or otherwise being used by the state in connection with official recreational or snowmobile trails.

Source.
2005, 210:1, eff. July 1, 2006.

TITLE XX

TRANSPORTATION

CHAPTER 228

ADMINISTRATION OF TRANSPORTATION LAWS

Commissioner, Deputy and Assistant Commissioners

Section

228:31-a.   Agreements for Telecommunica-

tions-Related Uses of the State Highway System and State-Owned Railroad Rights-of-Way.

Commissioner, Deputy and Assistant Commissioners

228:31-a. Agreements for Telecommunications-Related Uses of the State Highway System and State-Owned Railroad Rights-of-Way.

The commissioner may, with the approval of the governor and council, execute contracts, leases, licenses, and other agreements relating to the use or occupation of state-owned rights-of-way, whether easement or fee-owned, for purposes of allowing the installation and maintenance of commercial mobile radio service devices. Such agreements, which shall be for commercially reasonable value, shall not extend for a period of more than 10 years. Any leases executed pursuant to this section shall be subject to the requirements of RSA 72:23 with regard to properly assessed real estate taxes and subject to local zoning and planning requirements. Said devices shall take into consideration the scenic beauty of the landscape. There shall be no advertising signs on these devices. The provisions of RSA 4:40 shall not apply to this section.

Source.

1998, 337:2, eff. June 26, 1998.

CHAPTER 229

HIGHWAY SYSTEM IN THE STATE

229:1. Highways Defined.

Highways are only such as are laid out in the mode prescribed therefor by statute, or roads which have been constructed for public travel over land which has been conveyed to a city or town or to the state by deed of a fee or easement interest, or roads which have been dedicated to the public use and accepted by the city or town in which such roads are located, or roads which have been used as such for public travel, other than travel to and from a toll bridge or ferry, for 20 years prior to January 1, 1968, and shall include the bridges thereon.

Source.
  RS 53:7. CS 57:7. GS 68:8. GL 74:8. PS 67:1.
PL 74:1. RL 90:1. 1943, 57:1. 1945, 188:1, part
1:1. RSA 230:1. 1967, 283:1. 1981, 87:1, eff.
April 20, 1981.

Cross References.
  Laying out of city, town and village district highways, see RSA 231:1 et seq.
  Laying out of state highways, see RSA 230:8 et seq.

NOTES TO DECISIONS

Analysis

1. Construction with other laws
2. Creation of highways
3. Establishment under statutory author-
    ity—Application for laying out
4. —Authority of selectmen
5. —Private roads
6. —Sidewalks
7. —Presumption
8. —Estoppel
9. Dedication and acceptance
10. Establishment under prescription—Gen-
    erally
11. —Public use
12. —Adverse use
13. —Permissive use
14. —Toll bridge or ferry road
15. —Access road to public property
16. —Sidewalks
17. —Extent of right acquired
18. —Responsibility for maintenance and re-
    pair
19. —Estoppel
20. —Burden of proof
21. —Evidence
22. Bridges

1. Construction with other laws

Under former RSA 234:23, authorizing selectmen to reestablish a highway according to the boundaries which, in their opinion, were those by which that highway had been originally established, precise location of restored boundaries could be determined according to opinion of selectmen, but question whether lost, uncertain, or doubtful boundaries had ever been established remained an issue to be determined not by opinion or reasonable belief in prior establishment but by proof pursuant to this section. Nute v. Town of Wakefield, 117 N.H. 602, 376 A.2d 134, 1977 N.H. LEXIS 391 (1977). (Decided under prior law.)

Where town initiated proceedings under former RSA 234:23 to "reestablish" boundary lines of a certain road involving an extension across plaintiffs' property, and plaintiffs sought temporary and permanent injunctive relief and decree to quiet title, finding of referee denying establishment of highway town sought to "reestablish" would not be disturbed on appeal, since road had never been originally established in accordance with this section. Nute v.

185

Town of Wakefield, 117 N.H. 602, 376 A.2d 134, 1977 N.H. LEXIS 391 (1977). (Decided under prior law.)

The provisions of former RSA 36:26(a) that no building permit shall be issued unless the street shall have been accepted or received the status of a public street contemplates streets and highways as defined in this section. Blevens v. City of Manchester, 103 N.H. 284, 170 A.2d 121, 1961 N.H. LEXIS 33 (1961). (Decided under prior law.)

2. Creation of highways

Public highway may be created in any one of four ways: (1) through taking of land by eminent domain and laying out of a highway by some governmental authority; (2) through construction of a road on public land; (3) through twenty years of use by public; or (4) by dedication and acceptance. Polizzo v. Town of Hampton, 126 N.H. 398, 494 A.2d 254, 1985 N.H. LEXIS 342 (1985).

3. Establishment under statutory authority—Application for laying out

Laying out of a highway by selectmen with out an application for it was invalid. State v. Morse, 50 N.H. 9, 1870 N.H. LEXIS 54 (1870). (Decided under prior law.)

4. —Authority of selectmen

Laying out of a highway by selectmen in the exercise of a judicial power conferred on them could not be impeached or set aside in a collateral proceeding. Bryant v. Tamworth, 68 N.H. 483, 39 A. 431, 1896 N.H. LEXIS 38 (1896). (Decided under prior law.)

Upon a petition to the selectmen for a highway between two fixed bounds, their laying out of a way beginning at one of the bounds but not extending to the other might be valid. Spaulding v. Groton, 68 N.H. 77, 44 A. 88, 1894 N.H. LEXIS 36 (1894). (Decided under prior law.)

Road constructed on courses other than those described in judgment laying it out was not a legal highway. Spaulding v. Groton, 68 N.H. 77, 44 A. 88, 1894 N.H. LEXIS 36 (1894). (Decided under prior law.)

Upon a petition to selectmen to lay out a new highway, they had no jurisdiction to lay out a highway with termini substantially different from those set out in the petition. Eames v. Northumberland, 44 N.H. 67, 1862 N.H. LEXIS 19 (1862). (Decided under prior law.)

5. —Private roads

Laying out of roads in manner prescribed was not limited to creation of new roads, but also included making into public highways of private roads already in existence. Locke Development Corp. v. Town of Barnstead, 115 N.H. 642, 349 A.2d 598, 1975 N.H. LEXIS 385 (1975). (Decided under prior law.)

6. —Sidewalks

Sidewalks could legally be a part of the highway. Hall v. Manchester, 40 N.H. 410, 1860 N.H. LEXIS 167 (1860). (Decided under prior law.)

7. —Presumption

Twenty years of continuous and uninterrupted use gave rise to conclusive presumption that highway had at some previous time been established pursuant to law by the proper authority. Windham v. Jubinville, 92 N.H. 102, 25 A.2d 415, 1942 N.H. LEXIS 31 (1942). (Decided under prior law.)

Presumption that a highway had been laid out agreeably to law did not arise from mere use of it by the public for any period less than 20 years. State v. Morse, 50 N.H. 9, 1870 N.H. LEXIS 54 (1870). (Decided under prior law.)

Compliance with necessary conditions for laying out of a road could be presumed after lapse of nearly 40 years although not shown by the record. State v. Alstead, 18 N.H. 59, 1846 N.H. LEXIS 69 (1846). (Decided under prior law.)

8. —Estoppel

Where a road had not been used for twenty years as a public highway, town was not estopped to show that it had not been legally laid out as a highway. Eames v. Northumberland, 44 N.H. 67, 1862 N.H. LEXIS 19 (1862). (Decided under prior law.)

Town which had acquiesced for more than twenty years in doings of selectmen in laying out a highway was estopped from saying that the road was not legally laid out. State v. Boscawen, 32 N.H. 331, 1855 N.H. LEXIS 214 (1855). (Decided under prior law.)

9. Dedication and acceptance

Town meeting article did not lack a vote of acceptance of relocated road and did not merely constitute an exchange of deeds; when liberally construed, article expressed an intent to both discontinue a portion of road and then accept a new portion, and portion to be discontinued was sufficiently defined in article for voters to make a rational decision. Neville v. Highfields Farm, Inc., 144 N.H. 419, 744 A.2d 89, 1999 N.H. LEXIS 135 (1999).

Dedication and acceptance by the proper authority was sufficient to establish a highway. Perrotto v. Claremont, 101 N.H. 267, 140 A.2d 576, 1958 N.H. LEXIS 15 (1958). (Decided under prior law.)

Where claim of dedication rested upon implication, subsequent use, to constitute an acceptance and ripen it into a title, must have been adverse. Wason v. Nashua, 85 N.H. 192, 155 A. 681, 1931 N.H. LEXIS 99 (1931). (Decided under prior law.)

Twenty years' use of a dedicated highway was conclusive evidence of an acceptance. Stevens v. Nashua, 46 N.H. 192, 1865 N.H. LEXIS 55 (1865); State v. Atherton, 16 N.H. 203, 1844 N.H. LEXIS 43 (1844). (Decided under prior law.)

To constitute acts of selectmen an acceptance or recognition of dedicated highway so as to bind a town, there must have been either an express vote of the town, concurrence of a majority of the selectmen, or such circumstances that actual concurrence could be inferred. State v. Atherton, 16 N.H. 203, 1844 N.H. LEXIS 43 (1844). (Decided under prior law.)

Dedication could be accepted by substituting dedicated way for an ancient highway. State v. Atherton, 16 N.H. 203, 1844 N.H. LEXIS 43 (1844). (Decided under prior law.)

10. Establishment under prescription—Generally

The legislature added the language "prior to January 1, 1968" to allow any roads already acquired by prescription to stand, but restricted any further establishment of public highways by prescription; the legislature did not intend to redefine public roads that had already been acquired by prescription. Mahoney v. Town of Canterbury, 150 N.H. 148, 834 A.2d 227, 2003 N.H. LEXIS 153 (2003).

Highway could be established by prescription when it appeared that the public had used it continuously and uninterruptedly for a period of twenty years. Windham v. Jubinville, 92 N.H. 102, 25 A.2d 415, 1942 N.H. LEXIS 31 (1942). (Decided under prior law.)

11. —Public use

In a zoning appeal and quiet title case, a trial court's determination that an old road was a public road, not acquired by plaintiff through adverse possession, was upheld because the evidence presented at trial showed that the road had been used for public travel since the early 1800s and no evidence that the local municipality ever discontinued the public use of the road was shown. Blagbrough Family Realty Trust v. A & T Forest Prods., 155 N.H. 29, 917 A.2d 1221, 2007 N.H. LEXIS 25 (2007).

One cannot acquire rights in a public highway by adverse possession. Blagbrough Family Realty Trust v. A & T Forest Prods., 155 N.H. 29, 917 A.2d 1221, 2007 N.H. LEXIS 25 (2007).

Where plaintiff lot owners seeking declaratory judgment that roads over which they held easements were public highways, plaintiffs were required to prove the "public," not just the lot owners and guests, acquired adverse possession. Catalano v. Town of Windham, 133 N.H. 504, 578 A.2d 858, 1990 N.H. LEXIS 95 (1990).

12. —Adverse use

Evidence did not support trial court's finding that public use of gravel road was adverse and of such a character as to put landowner on notice of an adverse claim. Town of Warren v. Shortt, 139 N.H. 240, 652 A.2d 140, 1994 N.H. LEXIS 136 (1994).

Criterion designating as public highways "roads which have been used as such for public travel ... for 20 years ..." requires more than a showing of public use for 20 years; the use must additionally be shown to have been adverse. Catalano v. Town of Windham, 133 N.H. 504, 578 A.2d 858, 1990 N.H. LEXIS 95 (1990).

13. —Permissive use

In determining whether a road has become a public highway by prescription, once plaintiffs prove public used road openly and under claim of right for statutory period, burden shifts to the defendant to show permissive use. Catalano v. Town of Windham, 133 N.H. 504, 578 A.2d 858, 1990 N.H. LEXIS 95 (1990).

To establish that a public use was adverse or under a claim of right, either color or title in the public must have been shown or the public use must have been of the character to apprise the owner that it was under a claim of right and not permissive. Wason v. Nashua, 85 N.H. 192, 155 A. 681, 1931 N.H. LEXIS 99 (1931). (Decided under prior law.)

Way by prescription could not be established by permissive use. Burnham v. McQuesten, 48

N.H. 446, 1869 N.H. LEXIS 58 (1869). (Decided under prior law.)

14. —Toll bridge or ferry road

Land thrown open or dedicated to the public would not become a public highway, however long it might be used, if the travel upon it was limited to travel to or from a toll bridge or ferry. Harriman v. Moore, 74 N.H. 277, 67 A. 225, 1907 N.H. LEXIS 42 (1907). (Decided under prior law.)

15. —Access road to public property

Fact that access road which school district intended to construct on land taken by eminent domain, so as to have access to school, would be used by the public to reach the school did not make it a public highway. Wilton-Lyndeboro Cooperative School District v. Gregg, 111 N.H. 60, 274 A.2d 787, 1971 N.H. LEXIS 123 (1971). (Decided under prior law.)

16. —Sidewalks

Right to a sidewalk for foot passengers as part of a highway could be acquired by 20 years' use. Stevens v. Nashua, 46 N.H. 192, 1865 N.H. LEXIS 55 (1865). (Decided under prior law.)

17. —Extent of right acquired

If during alleged period of prescription owner continued to make a use of space above highway, by maintaining overhanging eaves discharging water thereon, public could acquire no title thereto. Woodsville Fire District v. Stahl, 80 N.H. 502, 119 A. 123, 1922 N.H. LEXIS 60, 27 A.L.R. 1144 (1922). (Decided under prior law.)

Right acquired by prescriptive use did not extend to space above highway occupied by a bay window, since as to such space public's use was not adverse and owner's continued occupancy of it amounted to denial of public's claim. Exeter v. Meras, 80 N.H. 132, 114 A. 24, 1921 N.H. LEXIS 44 (1921). (Decided under prior law.)

When highway was established by use alone, it was not necessarily limited to travelled track and ditches on each side, but jury could find that easement extended over whole space marked by fences which had been maintained more than 20 years and which gave about the usual width of a highway. State v. Morse, 50 N.H. 9, 1870 N.H. LEXIS 54 (1870). (Decided under prior law.)

18. —Responsibility for maintenance and repair

Twenty years' use was conclusive evidence of a right to use a highway not only as against the landowner, but also as against the city or town to be charged with its maintenance and repair. Stevens v. Nashua, 46 N.H. 192, 1865 N.H. LEXIS 55 (1865). (Decided under prior law.)

19. —Estoppel

After 20 years' use by the public, city could be estopped to deny that a street was a highway for the defects and insufficiency of which it was liable. Gilbert v. Manchester, 55 N.H. 298, 1875 N.H. LEXIS 76 (1875). (Decided under prior law.)

20. —Burden of proof

When a prescriptive easement is claimed and a landowner's defense to it is that use of property was permissive, burden of proof remains on claimant to prove absence of permission by a preponderance of evidence. Town of Warren v. Shortt, 139 N.H. 240, 652 A.2d 140, 1994 N.H. LEXIS 136 (1994).

Plaintiffs who sought declaratory judgment that roads qualified as public highway under provision of this section designating as such a road held by the public adversely for 20 years, bore burden of proving by a balance of the probabilities that the public used the roads for twenty years under a claim of right without the owner's permission. Catalano v. Town of Windham, 133 N.H. 504, 578 A.2d 858, 1990 N.H. LEXIS 95 (1990).

21. —Evidence

Road was properly deemed a highway established by prescription based on adverse public use for 20 continuous years during either the 1800's or the early 1900's as the public use of the road was without interruption for 20 years prior to January 1, 1968 as required by RSA 229:1 as amended. Mahoney v. Town of Canterbury, 150 N.H. 148, 834 A.2d 227, 2003 N.H. LEXIS 153 (2003).

Plaintiffs made out a prima facie case that roads had become public highways by prescription where public used them under a claim of right for statutory period, there was no evidence in the record that members of the public had ever asked permission, and where no "Private Road" sign had ever been erected; owner knew or ought to have known the road was being used without regard to his consent. Catalano v. Town of Windham, 133 N.H. 504, 578

A.2d 858, 1990 N.H. LEXIS 95 (1990).

Testimony that road had been used by the public as a public highway for at least thirty or forty years and that it was generally used by the public during that time to look for a place to swim showed a use which, while it may have been intermittent and of slight volume, was sufficient to sustain finding that road was established by prescription. Leo Foundation v. State, 117 N.H. 209, 372 A.2d 1311, 1977 N.H. LEXIS 303 (1977), cert. denied, 434 U.S. 890, 98 S. Ct. 264, 54 L. Ed. 2d 176, 1977 U.S. LEXIS 3545 (1977). (Decided under prior law.)

Evidence that stretches of road were discontinued by town meeting vote was evidence that road was a public highway. Leo Foundation v. State, 117 N.H. 209, 372 A.2d 1311, 1977 N.H. LEXIS 303 (1977), cert. denied, 434 U.S. 890, 98 S. Ct. 264, 54 L. Ed. 2d 176, 1977 U.S. LEXIS 3545 (1977). (Decided under prior law.)

Uninterrupted use of a road by those who had occasion to use it as members of the general public under a claim of right and without permission of the owner for more than twenty years, although intermittent and of slight volume, was sufficient to sustain a finding that a highway had been established by prescription. Blake v. Hickey, 93 N.H. 318, 41 A.2d 707, 1945 N.H. LEXIS 122 (1945). (Decided under prior law.)

Evidence that a highway of record became a public highway by reason of 20 years' use was not objectionable on the ground that it was secondary proof. Harriman v. Moore, 74 N.H. 277, 67 A. 225, 1907 N.H. LEXIS 42 (1907). (Decided under prior law.)

Proof that part of an entire highway, the laying out of which was defective, had been used by the public for twenty years, was evidence of a legal highway as to the part so used, although no distinct act of acceptance by the town was shown. State v. Morse, 50 N.H. 9, 1870 N.H. LEXIS 54 (1870). (Decided under prior law.)

Evidence was insufficient to support a finding that plaintiffs' driveway had become public through prescription, since photographs and historical documents failed to support an inference that public used driveway and bridge for a continuous twenty-year period and that such use was adverse. Blagbrough v. Town of Wilton, 145 N.H. 118, 755 A.2d 1141, 2000 N.H. LEXIS 28 (2000).

22. Bridges

A bridge is public if the road it services is public, and private if the road it services is private. Blagbrough v. Town of Wilton, 145 N.H. 118, 755 A.2d 1141, 2000 N.H. LEXIS 28 (2000).

Cited:

Cited in Marrone v. Town of Hampton, 123 N.H. 729, 466 A.2d 907, 1983 N.H. LEXIS 363 (1983); Morin v. City of Somersworth, 131 N.H. 253, 551 A.2d 527, 1988 N.H. LEXIS 109 (1988); Town of Warren v. Shortt, 139 N.H. 240, 652 A.2d 140, 1994 N.H. LEXIS 136 (1994).

RESEARCH REFERENCES

New Hampshire Bar Journal.

For article, "Creation and Termination of Highways in New Hampshire," see 31 N.H.B.J. 33 (1990).

229:5. Classification.

Highways of the state shall be divided into 7 classes as follows:

I. Class I highways shall consist of all existing or proposed highways on the primary state highway system, excepting all portions of such highways within the compact sections of the cities and towns listed in RSA 229:5, V, provided that the portions of the turnpikes and the national system of interstate and defense highways within the compact sections of these cities and towns shall be class I highways.

II. Class II highways shall consist of all existing or proposed highways on the secondary state highway system, excepting all portions of such highways within the compact sections of the cities and towns listed in RSA 229:5, V.

III. Class III highways shall consist of all recreational roads leading to, and within, state reservations designated by the legislature.

III-a. Class III-a highways shall consist of new boating access highways from any existing highway to any public water in this state. All class III-a highways shall be limited access facilities as defined in RSA 230:44. Class III-a highways shall be subject to the layout, design, construction, and maintenance provisions of RSA 230:45–47 and all other provisions relative to limited access facilities, except that the executive director of the fish and game department shall have the same authority for class III-a highways that is delegated to the commissioner of the department of transportation for limited access facilities. A class III-a highway may be laid out subject to the condition that it shall not be maintained during the winter months. A class III-a highway may be laid out subject to gates and bars or restricted to the accommodation of persons on foot, or certain vehicles, or both, if federal funds are not used. The executive director of fish and game may petition the governor and council to discontinue any class III-a highway.

IV. Class IV highways shall consist of all highways within the compact sections of cities and towns listed in RSA 229:5, V. The compact section of any such city or town shall be the territory within such city or town where the frontage on any highway, in the opinion of the commissioner of transportation, is mainly occupied by dwellings or buildings in which people live or business is conducted, throughout the year and not for a season only. Whenever the commissioner reclassifies a section of a class I or class II highway as a class IV highway, the commissioner shall prepare a statement of rehabilitation work which shall be performed by the state in connection with the turnback. No highway reclassification from class I or II to class IV shall take effect until all rehabilitation needed to return the highway surface to reputable condition has been completed by the state. Rehabilitation shall be completed during the calendar year preceding the effective date of the reclassification. A copy of the commissioner's statement of work to be performed by the state shall be attached to the notification of reclassification to class IV, and receipt of said statement shall be acknowledged, in writing, by the selectmen of the town, or the mayor of the city, affected by the reclassification.

V. The commissioner of transportation may establish compact sections in the following cities and towns:

Amherst	Keene
Bedford	Laconia
Berlin	Lebanon
Claremont	Londonderry
Concord	Manchester
Derry	Merrimack
Dover	Milford
Durham	Nashua
Exeter	Pelham
Franklin	Portsmouth
Goffstown	Rochester

Hampton

Hanover

Hudson

Salem

Somersworth

VI. Class V highways shall consist of all other traveled highways which the town has the duty to maintain regularly and shall be known as town roads. Any public highway which at one time lapsed to Class VI status due to 5-years' nonmaintenance, as set forth in RSA 229:5, VII, but which subsequently has been regularly maintained and repaired by the town on more than a seasonal basis and in suitable condition for year-round travel thereon for at least 5 successive years without being declared an emergency lane pursuant to RSA 231:59-a, shall be deemed a Class V highway.

VII. Class VI highways shall consist of all other existing public ways, and shall include all highways discontinued as open highways and made subject to gates and bars, except as provided in paragraph III-a, and all highways which have not been maintained and repaired by the town in suitable condition for travel thereon for 5 successive years or more except as restricted by RSA 231:3, II.

Source.

1925, 110:1. PL 83:22. RL 99:24. 1943, 123:1. 1945, 188:1, part 1:4. 1951, 30:1. RSA 230:4. 1955, 333:2. 1957, 181:1, 2, 3. 1961, 4:2. 1973, 418:1–3. 1975, 249:1–3. 1979, 216:1. 1981, 87:1; 443:1. 1983, 131:1. 1985, 235:1–4; 402:6, I(b)(1). 1992, 265:8–10. 1995, 77:1, eff. June 8, 1995. 1999, 109:1, eff. Aug. 9, 1999. 2000, 24:1, eff. May 28, 2000.

Amendments

—2000. Paragraph III-a: Rewrote the fourth sentence.

—1999. Paragraph VI: Added the second sentence.

—1995. Paragraph VII: Added "except as restricted by RSA 231:3, II" following "more".

—1992. Substituted "7" for "6" preceding "classes" in the introductory paragraph, added par. III-a, and inserted "except as provided in paragraph III-a" following "bars" in par. VII.

—1985. Paragraph I: Chapter 235 inserted "the" preceding "cities or towns" and substituted "listed in RSA 229:5, V" for "of 7,500 inhabitants and over" thereafter and inserted "these" preceding "cities and towns" and deleted "of 7,500 inhabitants and over" thereafter.

Paragraph II: Chapter 235 substituted "the cities and towns listed in RSA 229:5, V" for "cities or towns of 7,500 inhabitants and over" following "sections of".

Paragraph IV: Chapter 235 substituted "and" for "or" preceding "towns" in the first sentence and "listed in RSA 229:5, V" for "of 7,500 inhabitants and over" thereafter.

Chapter 402 substituted "commissioner of transportation" for "highway commissioner" in the second sentence.

Paragraph V: Rewritten by ch. 235 to the extent that a detailed comparison would be impracticable.

Chapter 402 substituted "commissioner of transportation" for "commissioner of public works and highways" in the introductory paragraph.

—1983. Paragraph V: Substituted "the annual city or town population estimate reported by the office of state planning; and, in a case in which" for "those shown by the latest available federal census and where" preceding "the classification" and "in said annual population estimate" for language beginning "by said census; provided" and continuing to the end of the paragraph following "as reported".

Effective date of amendments

—1985, 402. 1985, 402:41, II, provided that 1985, 402:6, I, would take effect when the department of transportation became operational on the date set according to 1983, 372:5, II. Pursuant to 1983, 372:5, II, the joint committee on implementation of reorganization and the governor determined the effective date upon which the department became operational to be Feb. 28, 1986.

Legislative classification of highways—Class I.

The classification of the road in the town of Walpole beginning at the Vermont boundary, running easterly to a junction with Route 12 at Walpole Village was changed from Class V to Class I by 1957, 105:1, eff. July 1, 1957.

A highway to be constructed from the Vilas bridge to a point northerly of the steel arch bridge in North Walpole was designated as a Class I highway by 1957, 127:1, eff. July 1, 1957.

Legislative classification of highways—Class II.

Central Street running from its intersection with New Hampshire routes 10, 11 and 103 for approximately 0.2 miles to its intersection with New Hampshire routes 11 and 103 in the town of Newport was reclassified from a class V highway to a class II highway by 1993, 6:1, eff. May 25, 1993.

The Dublin Road running from the end of the existing class II portion (1.34 miles northerly of N.H. 124) for approximately 1.90 miles to the Dublin town line in the town of Jaffrey was reclassified from a class V highway to a class II highway by 1993, 15:1, eff. May 25, 1993.

The Upper Jaffrey Road beginning at its intersection with New Hampshire route 101 and extending southerly approximately 3.1 miles to the Jaffrey town line in the town of Dublin was reclassified from a class V highway to a class II highway by 1993, 15:1, eff. May 25, 1993.

Easton Road, also known as Whipple Road, in the town of Sugar Hill, beginning 0.25 mile north of the intersection with Toad Hill Road at the end of the existing class V highway, northerly for a distance of 1.00 mile to the beginning of the existing class V highway by 1995, 177:1, eff. Aug. 4, 1995.

Drake Hill Road, in the town of Albany, beginning 1.02 miles north of the intersection with NH route 16 northerly for a distance of 0.65 mile to the existing class V highway by 1995, 177:1, eff. Aug. 4, 1995.

Bald Hill Road, in the town of Albany beginning at the Albany-Madison town line northerly 2.46 miles to the Albany-Conway town line is classified as a class II highway provided, however, that Bald Hill Road shall be reclassified as a class V highway 60 days after completion of the reconstruction to be performed by the department of transportation by 1995, 177:2, eff. Aug. 4, 1995.

—Class II.

The federal forest highway, known as the New Hampshire Forest Highway 8, was classified as a Class II highway by 1957, ch. 268, eff. Aug. 1, 1957, which also limited the duty of maintenance by the department of public works and highways to the completed portions.

The Crotched Mountain Road in the town of Greenfield was classified as a Class II highway by 1959, 14:1, eff. March 11, 1959.

U.S. Route 302 in the town of Haverhill from the junction with Route 10 to the Vermont boundary was classified as a Class II highway by 1959, 17:1, eff. March 11, 1959.

Stratford Hollow highway, from Route 3 to the Vermont state line, was designated as a Class II highway by 1959, 171:1, 2, eff. June 25, 1959, repealing 1955, 31:2.

Newton Junction Road in the town of Kingston was classified to Class II by 1959, 237:5, eff. Aug. 21, 1959.

The Class IV highway in the city of Lebanon designated as Route U.S. 4 from the Vermont boundary on the Connecticut River bridge to the junction of Route 10 in West Lebanon was classified as a Class II highway by 1961, 17:1, eff. April 28, 1961.

The highway in the towns of Bedford and New Boston known as the New Boston road and the Chestnut Hill road running from the Manchester-Bedford line by the missile tracking station in New Boston to the New Boston-Amherst town line was classified as a Class II highway by 1961, 87:1, eff. April 20, 1961.

The highway in the town of Goffstown known as the Goffstown Back Road starting at Route NH 114 in Goffstown village and running easterly to route NH 3A in West Manchester was classified as a Class II highway by 1961, 160:1, eff. Aug. 6, 1961.

That section of the "so-called" East Side River road in the town of Milan (theretofore a Class V highway) beginning at the Berlin-Milan line and extending northerly about three and one-half miles to the Class II highway near the bridge over the Androscoggin River at Milan was classified as a Class II highway by 1961, 170:3, eff. June 14, 1961.

Certain sections of Roberts Road and Front Street in Rollinsford were reclassified from Class V to Class II by 1961, 229:1, eff. Aug. 29, 1961.

In Lyman, a portion of the Class V highway running from Lyman to Tinkerville was reclassified to Class II by 1963, ch. 20, eff. May 10, 1963.

The 0.16 mile of Class V highway in the town of Walpole known as South Street, from its junction with River Road to its junction with Main Street, was classified as a Class II highway by 1965, 94:1, eff. July 17, 1965.

The 2.2 miles of the Tripoli Road, in the town of Waterville, extending northwesterly from its junction with the Class II highway, known as the Waterville Valley road, was classified as a Class II highway by 1967, 4:1, eff. February 9, 1967.

The Class V portion of the Bear Rock Road in the town of Stewartstown beginning at Creampoke Road and running easterly 0.60 mile was classified as a Class II highway by 1967, 140:2, eff. July 21, 1967.

The 1.67 miles of Class V highway in the town of Whitefield known as Airport Road, running from Route 116 easterly 1.67 miles to the Whitefield airport, was classified as a Class II highway by 1967, 318:1, eff. Sept. 1, 1967.

The Bear Notch Road in the towns of Albany and Bartlett extending from the Kancamagus highway to the White Mountain National Forest boundary and 0.55 miles of Class V highway in the town of Bartlett from the White Mountain National Forest boundary to Route U.S. 302 was classified as a Class II highway by 1969, 161:1, eff. July 21, 1969.

A proposed Class II highway, beginning at the end of the state section on Pelham road westerly of interstate Route 93 Pelham road interchange and running one and two-tenths miles to a junction with New Hampshire Route 38, was designated by 1969, 162:1, eff. July 21, 1969.

The 0.77 miles of Class V highway in Jaffrey beginning at the end of Cathedral of the Pines Road at the Rindge town line and running northerly to N.H. Route 124 was classified as a Class II highway by 1969, 259:1, eff. August 19, 1969.

The 0.78 miles of Class V highway at U.S. Route 3 in Thornton and running easterly across the Pemigewasset River to N.H. Route 175 was classified a Class II highway by 1969, 262:1, eff. August 19, 1969.

The 1.1 miles of highway known as the Old North Road, beginning from exit 10 on Route 89 southeast to the entrance of the Kearsarge regional school building was classified as a Class II highway by 1970, 31:1–3, eff. Jan. 1, 1971.

The 0.11 mile section of Gary Avenue between New Hampshire Route 152 and 108 was classified as a Class II highway by 1971, 4:2, 3, eff. April 12, 1971.

The 0.94 miles of Class V highway known as Barnard Ridge Road, beginning at New Hampshire Route 25 and running easterly to Meredith Neck Road was classified as a Class II highway by 1971, 5:2, 3, eff. April 18, 1971.

The 1.1 miles of Class V highway, known as the relocation of North Road, which begins at New Hampshire Route 114 and runs easterly, underpassing interstate 89, to relocated Shaker Street was classified as a Class II highway by 1971, 10:1, 2, eff. May 1, 1971.

The 1.97 miles of Class V highway in the towns of Pelham and Hudson, known as Sherburne Road, beginning at New Hampshire Route 128 in Pelham and running westerly to Old Lowell Road in Hudson, was classified as a Class II highway by 1975, 26:1, eff. May 3, 1975.

The 0.26 miles of Class V highway in the town of Danville, known as the Brown Hill Road, beginning at New Hampshire Route 111 and running northerly to the existing Class II section of the Brown Hill Road, was classified as a Class II highway by 1975, 94:1, eff. June 21, 1975.

All of the Class V highway known as the West road in the town of Clarksville from the easterly side of state Route 3 northeasterly to the westerly side of state Route 145, was classified as a Class II highway by 1975, 126:1, eff. July 5, 1975.

The 0.24 miles of Class V highway known as Sea road, beginning at New Hampshire Route 101D (Atlantic avenue) and running easterly to New Hampshire Route 1A was classified as a Class II highway by 1977, 225:1, eff. Aug. 14, 1977.

The 9.70 miles of Class V highway in the town of Conway, known as East Conway road and Green Hill road beginning at U.S. Route 302 and running easterly thence northerly to the Chatham town line was classified as a Class II highway by 1979, 421:1, eff. Aug. 22, 1979.

The section of Camp Sargent road from the southerly terminus of Continental boulevard, as extended, southerly to its junction with Naticook road, and the section of Naticook road running southerly to New Hampshire Route 101-A, were classified as Class II highways by 1983, 235:4, eff. June 18, 1983.

—Class V.
Depot Street in the town of Boscawen beginning at the intersection with U.S. Routes 3 and 4, easterly for a distance of 0.19 miles to the westerly bridge abutment at the Merrimack River was reclassified from Class II to Class V by 1996, 20:1, I, eff. May 15, 1996.

Central Street in the town of Hampstead beginning at the intersection with N.H. Route 111, easterly for a distance of 1.40 miles to the intersection with N.H. Route 121-A was reclassified from Class II to Class V by 1996, 20:1, II, eff. May 15, 1996.

Kent Farm Road in the town of Hampstead beginning at the intersection with N.H. Route 121, northerly for a distance of 1.50 miles to the existing class V highway was reclassified from Class II to Class V by 1996, 20:1, III, eff. May 15, 1996.

The Stratham Heights Road, in the town of Stratham, beginning at the intersection with N.H. Route 101 easterly 1.12 miles to the intersection of Guinea Road is classified as a Class V highway by 1994, 49:1, eff. December 1, 1994.

—Class V.

The North Groton-Dorchester highway was classified as a class V highway by 1957, 104:1, eff. May 2, 1957.

Classification of the Lempster Road from its junction with Route 31 to the Lempster line was changed to Class V by 1957, 145:1, eff. May 29, 1957.

The Trudeau Road between Routes US 3 and US 302 and the Bethlehem Hollow to Bethlehem Junction Road were transferred from Class II to Class V by 1957, 265:1, eff. Aug. 1, 1957.

Country Pond Road in the town of Kingston was reclassified from Class II to Class V by 1959, 237:5, eff. Aug. 21, 1959.

The highways in Bedford known as the North Amherst road and the Back River road were classified as Class V highways by 1961, 87:2, eff. April 20, 1961.

In Lyman, Class II portion of Monroe Road and Class II portion of Black Valley Road were reclassified to Class V by 1963, 20:1, eff. May 10, 1963.

In Goffstown and Manchester, a portion of Goffstown Back Road was classified as Class V by 1963, 396:1, eff. July 1, 1963.

In Newton, Class II Country Pond Road was reclassified as Class V by 1963, 400:1, eff. July 9, 1963.

The 0.60 mile of Class II highway in the town of Stewartstown known as the Bear Rock Road, beginning at the Guy Placey Road and running southeasterly 0.60 mile was classified as a Class V highway by 1967, 140:1, eff. July 21, 1967.

The 0.27 mile of Class II highway in the town of Plainfield, known as the Lower River Road, beginning at Route N.H. 12A and running southwesterly to the Class V highway section of the Lower River Road, was classified as a Class V highway by 1967, 512:1, eff. April 24, 1967.

The 0.19 mile of Class II highway in the town of Dorchester known as the North Dorchester Road, beginning 0.99 mile southerly of the Wentworth-Dorchester town line and running southerly 0.19 mile, was classified as a Class V highway by 1967, 513:1, eff. April 24, 1967.

The 0.51 mile of Class II highway in the town of Seabrook known as the Folly Mill Road, beginning at U.S. Route 1 and running westerly to the Class V highway section of the Folly Mill Road, was classified as a Class V highway by 1967, 527:1, eff. July 10, 1967.

The 1.04 miles of Class II highway in the town of Moultonboro, known as the Shannon Brook Road, beginning at Route N.H. 109 and running westerly to its end was classified as a Class V highway by 1967, 529:1, eff. July 18, 1967.

The 1.20 miles of Class II highway in Benton

known as the Tunnel Stream Road beginning at road inventory #50 and running easterly 1.20 miles to the town-maintained Class V highway was classified as a Class V highway by 1971, 3:1, 2, eff. April 12, 1971.

The two sections of Ash Swamp Road between straight line diagram station 94+65 and 109+65 and straight line diagram station 154+40 and 191+10, 0.29 miles and 0.70 miles respectively were classified as Class V highways by 1971, 4:1, 3, eff. April 12, 1971.

The 1.11 miles of Class II highway in the town of Meredith, known as Meredith Neck Road or Pleasant Street, beginning at New Hampshire Route 25 and running easterly to Barnard Ridge Road was classified as a Class V highway by 1971, 5:1, 3, eff. April 18, 1971.

The 1.1 miles of Class II highway in the town of Sutton known as Old North Road beginning from exit 10 on N.H. Route I-89 southeast to entrance of Kearsarge Regional High School was classified as a Class V highway by 1971, 538:1, eff. Sept. 5, 1971.

The 1.67 miles of Class II highway in the town of Whitefield known as the airport road, beginning at New Hampshire route 116 and running easterly 1.67 miles to Whitefield airport, was classified as a Class V highway by 1973, 66:1, eff. June 1, 1973.

The 0.77 miles of Class II highway in the town of Jaffrey known as the Prescott Road, beginning at the Rindge town line and running northerly to the junction of New Hampshire Route 124, was classified as a Class V highway by 1973, 105:1, eff. May 8, 1973.

The 0.97 miles of Class II highway in the town of Orange known as the Orange Road, beginning at Burnt Hill Road (road inventory no. 41) and running northerly 0.97 miles to the town-maintained Class V highway, was classified as a Class V highway by 1973, 175:1, eff. July 27, 1973.

The 0.17 miles of Class II highway in the town of Warren, known as Station Road, beginning at New Hampshire Route 25 and running westerly to its end was classified as a Class V highway by 1975, 27:1, eff. May 3, 1975.

The 1.52 miles of Class II highway in the city of Dover, known as Upper Sixth Street, beginning at Jeness Road and running to County Farm Road, was classified as a Class V highway by 1977, 72:1, eff. June 27, 1977.

The 0.16 miles of Class II highway in the town of Amherst beginning at New Hampshire Route 101 and running northwesterly to a junction with Main street was classified as a Class V highway by 1981, 196:1, eff. Aug. 1, 1981.

In Conway, Kearsarge road beginning at the Bartlett town line and running southerly 1.5 miles to the intersection of Mechanic street,

West Side road beginning at the intersection of Crescent drive and running southerly 0.5 of a mile to the Swift River bridge, and Old West Side road beginning at the northerly intersection of the River road and running southerly 0.6 of a mile to the Echo Lake state park were reclassified from Class II to Class V highways by 1983, 90:1, eff. July 23, 1983.

The 0.58 mile of Class II highway in the town of Jefferson, known as the Jefferson Notch road, beginning at U.S. Route 2 and running southerly to the Valley road was classified as a Class V highway by 1983, 97:1, eff. July 23, 1983.

The 0.19 mile of Class II highway in the town of Center Harbor, known as the Squam Lake road, beginning at Center Harbor Neck road and running northerly to the High Haith road was classified as a Class V highway by 1983, 97:2, eff. July 23, 1983.

The 0.89 mile section of Class II highway in the town of Belmont, known as Concord Street and Main Street, beginning at the junction of Route 106 and running northwesterly and northeasterly to the junction of Route 140, was classified as a Class V highway by 1989, 55:2, eff. June 18, 1989.

Railroad Avenue beginning at the intersection with United States Route 1 easterly 0.60 miles to the intersection with Centennial Street, Centennial Street beginning at the intersection with Railroad Avenue southerly 0.71 miles to the intersection with Walton Road, Walton Road beginning at the intersection with United States Route 1 easterly 0.66 miles to the intersection with Centennial Street, Washington Street beginning at the intersection with Walton Road and Centennial Street southerly 0.50 miles to the intersection with New Hampshire Route 286, New Zealand Road extension (Crovetti Road) beginning at the intersection with New Hampshire Route 107 westerly 0.36 mile to the intersection with True Road, and Ocean Road Spur being at the intersection with Route 1-A (Ocean Road) northwesterly 0.08 mile to the intersection of River Street were reclassified from Class II to Class V highways by 1989, 56:1, eff. June 18, 1989.

In New Castle, Oliver Street, beginning at the intersection with NH Route 1-B northeasterly 0.15 mile to the intersection with River Road, River Road, beginning at the intersection with NH Route 1-B westerly 0.16 mile to the intersection with Oliver Street, Cranfield Street, beginning at the intersection with NH Route 1-B northerly 0.11 mile to the intersection with Piscataqua Street, Piscataqua Street, beginning at the intersection with Cranfield Street easterly 0.22 mile to the intersection with Walbach Street, Walbach Street, beginning at the intersection with NH Route 1-B northerly 0.07 then easterly 0.09 mile to the intersection with Wentworth Road, and Wentworth Road, beginning at the intersection with NH Route 1-B northerly 0.07 mile to the intersection with Walbach Street, were reclassified from Class II to Class V highways by 1990, 40:1, eff. May 22, 1990.

In Sandwich, Diamond Ledge Road beginning at the intersection with N.H. Route 113 westerly 2.34 miles to Sandwich Notch Road, Mt. Israel Road beginning 760 feet north of the Diamond Ledge Road intersection northerly 0.44 miles to Dale Road, and Church Street beginning at the junction with N.H. Route 113 easterly 0.17 mile to the reconnection with N.H. route 113 were reclassified from Class II to Class V highways by 1991, 11:1, eff. June 18, 1991.

—Forest service road.

The 1.15 miles of Class II highway in the town of Bethlehem, known as the Gale River Road, beginning at United States Route 3 and running westerly to its intersection with the United States Forest Service road, was classified as a United States Forest Service road by 1975, 120:1, eff. July 5, 1975.

The 3.84 miles of class II highway in the town of Carroll known as the Cherry Mountain Road, beginning at a point 0.49 of a mile north of U.S. Route 302 and running northerly to a point 1.46 miles south of the Jefferson town line, was classified as a United States forest service road by 1989, 55:1, eff. June 18, 1989; provided, however, that should the United States government ever close the road to public use except as necessary on a temporary basis for public safety or to protect the road from damage, title and jurisdiction shall revert to the state of New Hampshire.

—Private road.

The .47 mile of Class II highway in the town of Moultonboro, known as the Birch Hill Road, beginning at Route N.H. 109 and running in a southwesterly direction to its end was discontinued as a public highway and the premises and land contained within the confines and limits of said highway was declared to be the property of, and all rights, title, and interest therein was conveyed to, Suissevale Incorporated of Moultonboro, N.H., a New Hampshire corporation, by 1967, 529:2, eff. July 18, 1967.

Cross References.

Classification of highways between military reservations or defense industries and transportation facilities, see RSA 228:51.

Classification of recreational roads, see RSA 233:2.

Scenic roads, see RSA 231:157 et seq.

NOTES TO DECISIONS

Analysis

1. Reclassification
2. Maintenance and repair
3. Public Use

1. Reclassification

There is no statutory requirement that a highway be reclassified by means of a formal procedure that includes a town meeting. Glick v. Town of Ossipee, 130 N.H. 643, 547 A.2d 231, 1988 N.H. LEXIS 79 (1988).

2. Maintenance and repair

In a property owner's action against a harvester who trespassed onto the owner's land and felled 5000 trees, the owner was properly awarded damages to repair a road that the harvester had damaged because the road had been rendered virtually impassable and because it was a Class VI road, the town had no obligation to maintain it. Berliner v. Clukay, 150 N.H. 80, 834 A.2d 297, 2003 N.H. LEXIS 140 (2003).

Road is not "maintained" or "repaired" for purposes of this section's classification scheme if the only work done consists of snowplowing; other work to protect against yearly erosion by the elements is required. Catalano v. Town of Windham, 133 N.H. 504, 578 A.2d 858, 1990 N.H. LEXIS 95 (1990).

Finding of trial court that defendant town maintained road during applicable time period, and therefore road met standard required for Class V status, would not be overturned where record supported findings of maintenance, even though there was conflicting testimony. Catalano v. Town of Windham, 133 N.H. 504, 578 A.2d 858, 1990 N.H. LEXIS 95 (1990).

Road which had been travelled continuously and was not subject to gates and bars, but which had not been maintained for more than five years, was determined to be a class VI highway. Glick v. Town of Ossipee, 130 N.H. 643, 547 A.2d 231, 1988 N.H. LEXIS 79 (1988).

Trial court erroneously concluded that travelled road was a class V highway that a town had a duty to maintain, where town did not maintain it for travel for more than five successive years. Glick v. Town of Ossipee, 130 N.H. 643, 547 A.2d 231, 1988 N.H. LEXIS 79 (1988).

3. Public Use

On summary judgment in a 42 U.S.C.S. § 1983 suit against a town and its selectmen, a federal district court dismissed a landowner's constitutional claims because he failed to show that the town's denial of a building permit and delay of utility access and its permitting the public use of snowmobiles on the landowner's unpaved access road, which was a Class VI public road under RSA 229:5(VI), were motivated by personal animosity or the result of a conspiracy against the landowner; the selectmen were also qualifiedly immune from liability because there was no clearly established constitutional right to be free from official corruption. Bourne v. Town of Madison, 494 F. Supp. 2d 80, 2007 U.S. Dist. LEXIS 47625 (June 29, 2007).

Cited:

Cited in Orcutt v. Richmond, 128 N.H. 552, 517 A.2d 1160, 1986 N.H. LEXIS 346 (1986); Vachon v. Town of New Durham Zoning Bd. of Adjustment, 131 N.H. 623, 557 A.2d 649, 1989 N.H. LEXIS 29 (1989); Turco v. Town of Barnstead, 136 N.H. 256, 615 A.2d 1237, 1992 N.H. LEXIS 164 (1992); Stevens v. Town of Goshen, 141 N.H. 219, 683 A.2d 814, 1996 N.H. LEXIS 74 (1996); Gill v. Gerrato, 154 N.H. 36, 904 A.2d 576, 2006 N.H. LEXIS 117 (2006).

229:6. Roads Laid Out by Courts of Common Pleas or County Commissioners.

All roads laid out by the courts of common pleas or the county commissioners, which have not been maintained by them for at least 20 years, are town-owned rights-of-way and are legally subject to the actions of the town's legislative body.

Source.
1997, 78:1, eff. Aug. 2, 1997.

CHAPTER 230

STATE HIGHWAYS

**Duty to Construct and Maintain
Highways**

Section
230:6.   Construction and Reconstruction;
              Limitation.

Duty to Construct and Maintain Highways

230:6. Construction and Reconstruction; Limitation.

Notwithstanding any other provision of law to the contrary, the state shall
not perform any new construction or major reconstruction of any class I, II or
III highway, except highways laid out under the provisions of RSA 230:44–54
unless the city or town in which the highway is located has adopted a zoning
ordinance pursuant to RSA 675:2 or 3 or a master plan pursuant to RSA 675:6.
This limitation shall not apply to new construction or major reconstruction of
bridges on class I, II or III highways.

Source.
   RSA 231:10. 1979, 216:2. 1981, 87:1; 363:2.
1985, 103:3, eff. Jan. 1, 1986.

Amendments
—**1985.** Substituted "RSA 675:2 or 3" for

"RSA 31:63 or 63-a" preceding "or a master plan
pursuant to" in the first sentence and "RSA
675:6" for "RSA 36:15" thereafter and made
other minor stylistic changes throughout that
sentence.

CHAPTER 230-A

CORRIDOR PROTECTION

Cross References.

Classification of highways, see RSA 229:5.

Laying out of city, town and village district highways, see RSA 231.

Laying out of state highways, see RSA 230:8 et seq.

RESEARCH REFERENCES

New Hampshire Practice.

14 N.H.P. Local Government Law § 814.

230-A:1. Definitions.

In this chapter:

I. "Corridor protection restriction" means a deeded conservation restriction, as defined by RSA 477:45, I, which conveys to a unit of government having power to lay out highways the right to wholly or partially prohibit development on a described tract of land within a highway planning corridor for a limited time period stated in the restriction, not exceeding 10 years.

II. "Development" means the subdivision of land or erection or construction of any structures or improvements on such land, or expansions or additions to such land, or any other action which will appreciably increase the future cost of acquiring such land, if such acquisition is required for highway purposes.

III. "Development permit" includes subdivision or site plan approval, building or zoning permit, or any other permit required by a unit of government as a prerequisite to development.

IV. "Layout authority" means the governor and council or a commission appointed by the governor in the case of class I and II highways, or the mayor and aldermen of a city, selectmen of a town, or village district commissioners of a village district in the case of class IV or V highways.

V. "Highway planning corridor" means an area of land which has been designated as such under this chapter.

VI. "Return" means a written report of the highway planning corridor designation proceedings, including the findings of occasion, and a detailed map showing the boundaries of such corridor. Such return need not include a full metes and bounds description of the corridor boundary.

Source.
1991, 309:2, eff. Jan. 1, 1992.

230-A:2. Occasion for Layout.

A layout authority may determine upon hearing whether there is occasion for the designation of one or more highway planning corridors. For class I or II highways, the location shall be proposed by the commissioner of the department of transportation. In making such determination the layout authority shall:

I. Identify public transportation needs for the present and foreseeable future.

II. Determine whether the public interest requires development restriction along proposed planning corridors.

III. Allow flexibility in planning the design of the highway.

IV. Consider methods to prevent disruption and relocation of residential neighborhoods, residences, and businesses and interference with utility facilities.

V. Determine the acquisition costs of subsequently developed property if a highway planning corridor is not established.

VI. Establish the termini and width of the proposed highway planning corridor.

Source.
1991, 309:2, eff. Jan. 1, 1992.

230-A:3. Notice of Hearing.

Notice of the hearing, together with a description of the proposed corridor, shall be given to the same parties with respect to such corridor, and in the same manner, as in the case of a highway layout hearing, pursuant to RSA 230:17–18 or 231:9–10, as the case may be, including every owner of land or other property within the proposed planning corridor.

Source.
1991, 309:2, eff. Jan. 1, 1992.

230-A:4. Hearing.

The layout authority, at the time and place appointed for hearing, shall make a personal examination of the proposed corridors, shall hear all parties interested who may attend, and may adjourn as it sees cause.

Source.
1991, 309:2, eff. Jan. 1, 1992.

230-A:5. Appeal.

Any owner of land or other property aggrieved by a finding of the layout authority on the matter of occasion for the layout of a highway planning corridor or alteration thereof, may appeal to the superior court, for the county in which such land or other property is situated, by petition within 60 days after the filing of the return with the secretary of state as provided in RSA 230-A:6. The burden of proof shall be upon the party seeking to set aside any finding of the layout authority to show that such decision is unlawful or unreasonable. All findings of the layout authority upon all questions of fact properly before the court shall be prima facie lawful and reasonable. The decision appealed from shall not be set aside or vacated, except for errors of law, unless the court is persuaded by the balance of probabilities, on the evidence before it, that said finding is unreasonable or unlawful.

Source.
1991, 309:2, eff. Jan. 1, 1992.

230-A:6. Return.

The layout authority shall make a return of the highway planning corridor, including a detailed map identifying the boundaries of such corridor, and file the return with the secretary of state, with every unit of government having the authority to issue development permits for the property located within such corridor and with the registry of deeds for each county in which such corridor is located.

Source.
1991, 309:2, eff. Jan. 1, 1992.

230-A:7. Effect of Corridor.

After the highway planning corridor return has been filed, no person shall subdivide any land, begin any development, or alter or expand any structure or use of land within such corridor, without first obtaining a corridor permit from the layout authority or its designated agent. The layout authority shall adopt by rules pursuant to RSA 541-A the form for corridor permits, and what constitutes submission of a completed application. No existing structure or established use of property within the corridor shall be affected.

Source.
1991, 309:2, eff. Jan. 1, 1992.

230-A:8. Relationship to Other Land Use Permits.

The corridor permit requirement shall be in addition to other federal, state or local permits which may be required for such development, and no development shall be exempt from a corridor permit by reason of any other permit, any grandfather clause, or any other exemption. Authorities issuing other development permits should inform applicants of the corridor permit requirement, but the corridor designation shall not interfere with or delay other development permit procedure, unless agreed to by the applicant. No zoning or other land use ordinance or regulation shall be deemed or required to be altered or modified by the creation of the corridor, but any permits issued under any such ordinance or regulation shall be deemed conditional upon the corridor permit.

Source.
  1991, 309:2, eff. Jan. 1, 1992.

230-A:9. Action on Application.

Within 60 days after receipt of a completed corridor permit application, the layout authority or its designated agent shall:
I. Determine that the impact of the proposed development on highway design planning and impact on the cost of possible acquisition is not substantial, and issue the permit;
II. Notify the applicant of its intent to take an interest in all or part of the land or other property, in which case, the date of notification shall constitute the date of valuation for taking purposes; or
III. Reach agreement with the applicant on some alternative action.

Source.
  1991, 309:2, eff. Jan. 1, 1992.

230-A:10. Payment or Tender of Damages.

Within 180 days after notice of intent to take an interest in property has been delivered under this chapter, the layout authority or its designated agent shall pay or tender damages for a specified interest in the applicant's property. The procedure for the payment or tender, and any appeals of assessments, shall be as set forth in RSA 498-A. If the layout authority fails to make a payment or tender within 180 days, the corridor permit shall be deemed to be granted.

Source.
  1991, 309:2, eff. Jan. 1, 1992.

RESEARCH REFERENCES

ALR.
  Deduction of benefits in determining compensation or damages in proceedings involving opening, widening, or otherwise altering highway. 13 A.L.R.3d 1149.

230-A:11. Corridor Protection Restriction.

All property interests taken under this chapter shall be in the form of a corridor protection restriction, unless the layout authority or its designated agent makes a written finding that the public interest requires taking a greater property interest in the property. Reasons for such a finding may include, but are not limited to, a probable likelihood that the layout will eventually require a taking of greater property interest, or a substantial similarity between the appraised value of the greater property interest and the corridor protection restriction. The layout authority may amend the terms and duration of any corridor protection restriction to meet the needs of its planning process, but the duration of any term thereof shall not exceed 10 years, unless renewed.

Source.
1991, 309:2, eff. Jan. 1, 1992.

230-A:12. Other Acquisitions.

The layout authority may acquire corridor protection restrictions or other property interests within the highway planning corridor, absent the submission of a corridor permit application, provided, that, in its discretion, the layout authority determines that such acquisitions are consistent with the purposes of this chapter.

Source.
1991, 309:2, eff. Jan. 1, 1992.

230-A:13. Corridor Amendments.

The layout authority may add to the land area of any highway planning corridor, provided, however, that written notice shall be given to each owner of land or other property affected by the amendment, and no determination of whether there is occasion for the designation shall be made unless the amendment is based on new or revised findings of transportation needs.

Source.
1991, 309:2, eff. Jan. 1, 1992.

230-A:14. Termination of Corridor.

The highway planning corridor shall terminate:
I. Upon the filing of a return of highway layout and the acquisition of the property necessary for the highway for which the planning corridor was created; or
II. Upon a declaration by the layout authority that the corridor, or any portion thereof, is discontinued. The discontinuance of a highway planning corridor shall not be subject to appeal, and shall not entitle any person to damages.

Source.
1991, 309:2, eff. Jan. 1, 1992.

230-A:15. Notice of Termination of Corridor.

Notice of the corridor termination shall be given by first class mail to all owners of land or other property or their successors in interest, and governmental units to whom notice was sent under RSA 230-A:3.

Source.
1991, 309:2, eff. Jan. 1, 1992.

230-A:16. Remedies.

Penalties and remedies for violations of this chapter shall be the same as for violations of title LXIV, as stated in RSA 676:15 and 676:17; and, if any development occurs on any land within a designated highway planning corridor, without a corridor permit, the layout authority shall be entitled to exclude the value of such development from any compensation otherwise due upon the subsequent layout of a highway.

Source.
1991, 309:2, eff. Jan. 1, 1992.

230-A:17. Municipalities.

The powers granted by this chapter may be exercised by a municipality either independently of, or concurrently with, the creation of an official map pursuant to RSA 674:9–15. The designation of a highway planning corridor by a municipal layout authority shall require the approval of the planning board or local legislative body, under RSA 674:40, III, but such corridor shall not be deemed as a "street" for purposes of title LXIV.

Source.
1991, 309:2, eff. Jan. 1, 1992.

230-A:18. Intergovernmental Agreements.

The powers described in this chapter may be exercised jointly by the state and any municipality, or by 2 or more municipalities, utilizing RSA 53-A or any other lawful means of agreement.

Source.
1991, 309:2, eff. Jan. 1, 1992.

230-A:19. Other Laws.

Nothing in this chapter shall preclude the necessity to comply with the provisions of any other applicable federal, state or local law or regulation.

Source.
1991, 309:2, eff. Jan. 1, 1992.

CHAPTER 231

CITIES, TOWNS AND VILLAGE DISTRICT HIGHWAYS

Laying Out Highways

231:22. Previously Discontinued Highway.

Notwithstanding any other provisions of this chapter to the contrary, any owner who has no access to his land by public highway may petition the selectmen to layout, subject to gates and bars, a highway located where any previously discontinued highway was located. Upon receipt of such a petition, the selectmen shall immediately post notice thereof in 2 public places in the town in which the land is situated and shall mail like notices to the owners of the land over which such highway may pass, postage prepaid, at their last known mail addresses. Unless written objection to such layout is filed with the selectmen within 60 days after the posting and mailing of such notice, the highway shall be laid out, subject to gates and bars, in the location in which it previously existed if the selectmen find that the petitioner in fact has no other access to his land by public highway. The selectmen shall assess the damages sustained by each owner of land or other property taken for such highway, which damages shall be paid by the petitioner. They shall take and cause to be recorded by the town clerk a return as required by RSA 231:16. The petitioner and all those succeeding him in title shall be required to maintain the gates and bars and to maintain the highway so laid out at their own expense. In the event written objection to such layout is filed with the selectmen prior to the expiration of said 60-day period, the petition shall be deemed to be a petition filed for the layout of a new class IV, V or VI highway in accordance with RSA 231:8, and all the provisions of this chapter shall be applicable thereto.

Source.
  RSA 234:18-a. 1963, 274:1. 1981, 87:1, eff. April 20, 1981.

Cross References.
  Liability for expenses for proceedings to re-open highways subject to gates and bars, see RSA 231:10-a.

204

NOTES TO DECISIONS

Nature of remedy

Petitioning selectmen to layout, subject to gates and bars, a highway located "where any previously discontinued highway was located", was an administrative remedy requiring appeal to another body and was not a judicial remedy. Williams v. Babcock, 116 N.H. 819, 368 A.2d 1166, 1976 N.H. LEXIS 477 (1976). (Decided under prior law.)

Plaintiff's remedy to seek right-of-way in a purportedly discontinued highway running through defendant's property and past her property was not an adequate and complete remedy under this section and plaintiff's petition for declaratory judgment and injunctive relief should not have been dismissed. Williams v. Babcock, 116 N.H. 819, 368 A.2d 1166, 1976 N.H. LEXIS 477 (1976). (Decided under prior law.)

Cited:

Cited in Caouette v. Town of New Ipswich, 125 N.H. 547, 484 A.2d 1106, 1984 N.H. LEXIS 396 (1984).

RESEARCH REFERENCES

ALR.

Way of necessity where only part of land is inaccessible. 10 A.L.R.4th 500.

231:22-a. Reclassifying a Class VI Highway.

I. A class VI highway or portion thereof may be reclassified by vote of the town as a class V highway, or as a class IV highway if located within the compact sections of cities and towns as set forth in RSA 229:5, IV and V.

II. The warrant article for such a reclassification may be inserted either by the selectmen pursuant to RSA 39:2, or by petition pursuant to RSA 39:3. The reclassification shall become effective upon a majority vote of the registered voters present and voting at any annual or special meeting, or at such later time as may be specified by vote of the meeting.

III. Any class VI highway may be made subject to reclassification under this section, regardless of whether such class VI status resulted from a layout pursuant to RSA 231:21, a discontinuance subject to gates and bars pursuant to RSA 231:45, or by the failure of the town to maintain and repair such highway in suitable condition for travel thereon for 5 successive years or more as set forth in RSA 229:5, VII.

IV. A town meeting vote to reclassify a class VI highway under this section may provide that the highway be conditionally reclassified upon compliance with betterment assessments, as provided in RSA 231:28–33, even if such condition was not stated as part of the warrant article. The public hearing required by RSA 231:28 shall be held within 90 days of such a vote, or within such longer period as the vote may specify. The owners of property abutting or served by the highway shall have the same rights and remedies as provided in RSA 231:28–33, including the right to submit, within 10 days following the public hearing, a petition not to conditionally reclassify the highway. The costs assessed against the owners by the selectmen shall not reflect construction standards any higher or more stringent than those reflected in the best town highway giving access to the highway or portion thereof being reclassified. However, this paragraph shall not be deemed to limit the authority of the planning board to impose more stringent construction standards as a condition of approving new development.

V. This section shall not be deemed to limit the authority of the selectmen to layout an existing class VI highway as a class IV or V highway upon petition pursuant to RSA 231:8. This section shall not affect the classification of any highway which has been reclassified by other means prior to June 18, 1990.

Source.
1990, 155:1, eff. June 18, 1990.

Revision note.
Substituted "June 18, 1990" for "the effective date of this section" at the end of par. V for purposes of clarity.

Cross References.
Reclassification of class V or VI highways as class A or B trails, see RSA 231-A:2, 3.

231:23. Conditional Layout.

Whenever a highway will be of special advantage to any individual the selectmen may require him to bear such portion of land damages and expenses of constructing and maintaining it, and the gates and bars across it, if any, or any of the same, as they may deem just; and the highway may be laid out subject to such condition.

Source.
1850, 957:1. 1871, 20:1. GL 67:16; 78:4. PS 5:19. RSA 234:19. 1981, 87:1, eff. April 20, 1981.

67:16. PL 74:16. RL 90:17. 1945, 188:1, part

NOTES TO DECISIONS

Analysis

1. Amendment of return
2. Illegal condition
3. Damages

1. Amendment of return
Amendment of return of layout which contained such condition, on the ground that it was not intended at time of laying out highway but was found in form used in making return, was not permissible. Brown's Petition, 51 N.H. 367, 1871 N.H. LEXIS 39 (1871). (Decided under prior law.)

2. Illegal condition
Where permissible condition was illegally imposed, any person appealing from layout

could take advantage of the illegality, notwithstanding individual for whose benefit highway was laid out was willing to assent to the imposition. Underwood v. Bailey, 56 N.H. 187, 1855 N.H. LEXIS 237 (1875). (Decided under prior law.)

3. Damages
Commissioners' finding of damages was required to be accepted unless it was such as no reasonable person could make. Tracy v. Surry, 101 N.H. 438, 146 A.2d 268, 1958 N.H. LEXIS 58 (1958). (Decided under prior law.)

231:28. Conditional Layout for Existing Private Rights-of-Way or Class VI Highways.

Whenever, pursuant to the provisions of this chapter, the selectmen receive a petition to lay out roads over existing private rights-of-way or to lay out a class V highway over an existing class VI highway and such private right-of-way or class VI highway does not conform to construction standards and requirements currently in effect in the town, the selectmen may conditionally lay out roads upon compliance with betterment assessments as provided in this section and in RSA 231:29–33. Prior to commencement of conditional layout, however, a public hearing shall be held, written notice of which shall be given by the appropriate governing board to all owners of property abutting or served by the private right-of-way or class VI highway, at least 14 days before the hearing, at which hearing details of the proposed construction, reconstruction or repairs, and the estimated costs thereof shall be presented by the selectmen. Conditional layout proceedings may commence 10 days following the public hearing unless within that period a petition not to conditionally lay out said thoroughfare signed by a majority of the owners of property abutting or served by the existing private right-of-way or class VI highway is received by the selectmen. If a highway is so laid out, the selectmen may construct, reconstruct, repair or cause to be constructed, reconstructed or repaired such highways, streets, roads, or traveled ways to conform in every way with the highway or street construction standards and regulations previously established by the town. The betterment assessments shall be assessed under the provisions of RSA 231:29.

Source.
RSA 234:23-a. 1979, 166:1. 1981, 87:1. 1989, 134:1, eff. July 16, 1989.

Amendments
—1989. Added "or class VI highways" following "rights-of-way" in the section catchline, inserted "or to lay out a class V highway over an existing class VI highway" preceding "and such private" and substituted "right-of-way or class VI highway does" for "rights-of-way do" thereafter in the first sentence, inserted "or class VI highway" following "right-of-way" in the second and third sentences and made other minor stylistic changes.

NOTES TO DECISIONS

Public benefit
Superior court erred in ruling that occasion existed for town to lay out roadway system in housing development, where it was clear that burden to town of laying out roads far outweighed any benefit public could receive. Rockhouse Mountain Property Owners Ass'n v. Town of Conway, 133 N.H. 130, 574 A.2d 380, 1990 N.H. LEXIS 41 (1990).

Cited:
Cited in Rockhouse Mountain Property Owners Ass'n v. Town of Conway, 127 N.H. 593, 503 A.2d 1385, 1986 N.H. LEXIS 207 (1986).

RESEARCH REFERENCES

New Hampshire Practice.
15 N.H.P. Land Use Planning and Zoning § 26.03.

Liability of Municipalities

231:90. Duty of Town After Notice of Insufficiency.

I. Whenever any class IV or class V highway or bridge or sidewalk thereon in any municipality shall be insufficient, any person may give written notice of such insufficiency to one of the selectmen or highway agents of the town, or the mayor or street commissioners of the city, and a copy of said notice to the town or city clerk. The notice shall be signed and shall set forth in general terms the location of such highway, bridge, or sidewalk and the nature of such insufficiency.

II. For purposes of this subdivision, a highway or sidewalk shall be considered "insufficient" only if:

(a) It is not passable in any safe manner by those persons or vehicles permitted on such sidewalk or highway by state law or by any more stringent local ordinance or regulation; or

(b) There exists a safety hazard which is not reasonably discoverable or reasonably avoidable by a person who is traveling upon such highway at posted speeds or upon such sidewalk, in obedience to all posted regulations, and in a manner which is reasonable and prudent as determined by the condition and state of repair of the highway or sidewalk, including any warning signs, and prevailing visibility and weather conditions.

III. A highway or sidewalk shall not, in the absence of impassability or hidden hazard as set forth in paragraph II, be considered "insufficient" merely by reason of the municipality's failure to construct, maintain or repair it to the same standard as some other highway or sidewalk, or to a level of service commensurate with its current level of public use.

Source.
1893, 59:2. PL 82:8. RL 98:8. 1945, 188:1, part 18:9. RSA 247:9. 1981, 87:1. 1991, 385:3, eff. Jan. 1, 1992.

Amendments
—**1991.** Rewritten to the extent that a detailed comparison would be impracticable.

NOTES TO DECISIONS

Analysis

1. Constitutionality
2. Requirement of notice
3. Effect of notice
4. Traveling
5. Jury instructions

1. Constitutionality

Proposed amendment of this section precluding municipal liability for injury or damage arising out of construction, maintenance or repair of public highways and sidewalks unless such injury or damage was caused by an "insufficiency" was not constitutionally inadequate merely because statute provided that a finding of insufficiency could not be made solely on basis that a highway or sidewalk was not maintained at same level of repair as other highways or sidewalks. Opinion of Justices, 134 N.H. 266, 592 A.2d 180, 1991 N.H. LEXIS 53 (1991).

2. Requirement of notice

Where it was clear that the grassy area where a school visitor tripped and fell was actually a part of the curb, the issue was one of alleged failure to maintain a sidewalk, and the visitor could not prevail in a personal injury action because there was no showing of gross negligence, intentional actions, or failure to respond after receiving notice of a dangerous condition; therefore, summary judgment was properly entered for the school district. Richard v. Pembroke Sch. Dist., 151 N.H. 455, 859 A.2d 1157, 2004 N.H. LEXIS 176 (2004).

Notice of want of repair was necessary to town's liability. Wilder v. Concord, 72 N.H. 259, 56 A. 193, 1903 N.H. LEXIS 61 (1903). (Decided under prior law.)

3. Effect of notice

Notice to town that highway was out of repair or unsafe rendered town liable for accidents which happened subsequent to such notice and prior to repairs by town. Beer v. North Conway Lighting Precinct, 108 N.H. 465, 238 A.2d 8, 1968 N.H. LEXIS 189 (1968). (Decided under prior law.)

4. Traveling

Words "traveling upon a highway or bridge" were added to the statute in 1867 apparently for purpose of showing that it was the object of the statute to give a remedy to persons harmlessly and properly using highway or bridge which town was bound to maintain and keep in suitable repair. Wilder v. Concord, 72 N.H. 259, 56 A. 193, 1903 N.H. LEXIS 61 (1903). (Decided under prior law.)

Person was traveling upon a highway when he was making a reasonable use of the highway as a way, and while this included motion from one place to another more or less distant, continuous movement was not necessary. Varney v. Manchester, 58 N.H. 430, 1878 N.H. LEXIS 125 (1878). (Decided under prior law.)

One could not be said to have been traveling on highway so as to be entitled to recover for loss of a horse, which fell over an unrailed embankment while running away, where he had left horse hitched in the highway and gone elsewhere. Cummings v. Center Harbor, 57 N.H. 17, 1876 N.H. LEXIS 45 (1876). (Decided under prior law.)

Whether a person was a traveler on the highway depended upon the use which he was making of it. Hardy v. Keene, 52 N.H. 370, 1872 N.H. LEXIS 54 (1872). (Decided under prior law.)

5. Jury instructions

RSA 231:90, I, II, and III, standing alone, did not provide a standard of care to be imparted on the city and did not provide immunity to the city, but merely defined "insufficiency," and "written notice." As such, it was not error for the trial court to provide the jury with instructions related to their meaning when the driver claimed that the city was liable to her because of an accident allegedly caused by poor road conditions. Cloutier v. City of Berlin, 154 N.H. 13, 907 A.2d 955, 2006 N.H. LEXIS 118 (2006).

Cited:

Cited in Glick v. Town of Ossipee, 130 N.H. 643, 547 A.2d 231, 1988 N.H. LEXIS 79 (1988); City of Dover v. Imperial Cas. & Indem. Co., 133 N.H. 109, 575 A.2d 1280, 1990 N.H. LEXIS 39 (1990); Boston & Me. Corp. v. Town of Hampton, 987 F.2d 855, 1993 U.S. App. LEXIS 4159 (1st Cir. 1993); Schoff v. City of Somersworth, 137 N.H. 583, 630 A.2d 783, 1993 N.H. LEXIS 124 (1993).

231:91. Municipality to Act; Liability.

I. Upon receipt of such notice of insufficiency, and unless the highway agents or street commissioners determine in good faith that no such insufficiency exists, the municipality shall immediately cause proper danger signals to be placed to warn persons by day or night of such insufficiency, and shall, within 72 hours thereafter, develop a plan for repairing such highway, bridge, or sidewalk and shall implement such plan in good faith and with reasonable dispatch until the highway, bridge, or sidewalk is no longer insufficient, as defined by RSA 231:90, II.

II. If the municipality fails to act as set forth in paragraph I, it shall be liable in damages for all personal injury or property damage proximately caused by the insufficiency identified in the notice, subject to the liability limits under RSA 507-B:4.

Source.

1893, 59:2. PL 82:9. RL 98:9. 1945, 188:1, part 18:10. RSA 247:10. 1981, 87:1. 1991, 385:4, eff. Jan. 1, 1992.

Amendments

—1991. Rewritten to the extent that a detailed comparison would be impracticable.

NOTES TO DECISIONS

Analysis

1. Effect of notice
2. Sidewalks
3. Construction

1. Effect of notice

Notice to town that highway was out of repair or unsafe rendered town liable for accidents which happened subsequent to such notice and prior to repairs by town. Beer v. North Conway Lighting Precinct, 108 N.H. 465, 238 A.2d 8, 1968 N.H. LEXIS 189 (1968). (Decided under prior law.)

2. Sidewalks

Duty to repair, maintain and reconstruct sidewalks which are component parts of highways rested with municipalities. Gossler v. Miller, 107 N.H. 303, 221 A.2d 249, 1966 N.H. LEXIS 180 (1966). (Decided under prior law.)

3. Construction

RSA 231:91, by itself, did not confer any sort of immunity on a municipality because it did not limit the liability of a municipality, but instead, required a municipality to respond to any written notice of an insufficiency or to risk being liable for any such insufficiency. Cloutier v. City of Berlin, 154 N.H. 13, 907 A.2d 955, 2006 N.H. LEXIS 118 (2006).

Cited:

Cited in Glick v. Town of Ossipee, 130 N.H. 643, 547 A.2d 231, 1988 N.H. LEXIS 79 (1988); City of Dover v. Imperial Cas. & Indem. Co., 133 N.H. 109, 575 A.2d 1280, 1990 N.H. LEXIS 39 (1990); Schoff v. City of Somersworth, 137 N.H. 583, 630 A.2d 783, 1993 N.H. LEXIS 124 (1993).

231:92. Liability of Municipalities; Standard of Care.

I. A municipality shall not be held liable for damages in an action to recover for personal injury or property damage arising out of its construction, maintenance, or repair of public highways and sidewalks constructed thereupon unless such injury or damage was caused by an insufficiency, as defined by RSA 231:90, and:

(a) The municipality received a written notice of such insufficiency as set forth in RSA 231:90, but failed to act as provided by RSA 231:91; or

(b) The selectmen, mayor or other chief executive official of the municipality, the town or city clerk, any on-duty police or fire personnel, or municipal officers responsible for maintenance and repair of highways, bridges, or sidewalks thereon had actual notice or knowledge of such insufficiency, by means other than written notice pursuant to RSA 231:90, and were grossly negligent or exercised bad faith in responding or failing to respond to such actual knowledge; or

(c) The condition constituting the insufficiency was created by an intentional act of a municipal officer or employee acting in the scope of his official duty while in the course of his employment, acting with gross negligence, or with reckless disregard of the hazard.

II. Any action to recover damages for bodily injury, personal injury or property damage arising out of municipal construction, repair or maintenance of its public highways or sidewalks constructed on such highways shall be dismissed unless the complaint describes with particularity the means by which the municipality received actual notice of the alleged insufficiency, or the intentional act which created the alleged insufficiency.

III. The acceptance or layout of a private road as a public highway shall not be construed to confer upon the municipality any notice of, or liability for, insufficiencies or defects which arose or were created prior to such layout or acceptance.

IV. The setting of construction, repair, or maintenance standards of levels of service for highways and sidewalks by municipal officials with responsibility therefor, whether accomplished formally or informally, shall be deemed a discretionary, policy function for which the municipality shall not be held liable in the absence of malice or bad faith.

Source.
RS 57:1. CS 61:1, 7. GS 69:1, 2. GL 75:1, 2. PS 76:1. 1893, 59:1. 1915, 48:1. 1921, 107:1. 1925, 52:2, 4. PL 89:1. 1935, 118:1. RL 105:1. 1945, 188:1, part 18:17. RSA 247:17. 1981, 87:1. 1991, 385:5, eff. Jan. 1, 1992.

Amendments
—1991. Rewritten to the extent that a de-

tailed comparison would be impracticable.

Cross References.
Liability of 2 or more towns, see RSA 231:105 et seq.
Venue of actions, see RSA 231:110.

NOTES TO DECISIONS

Analysis

1. Constitutionality
2. Historical
3. Application
4. Standard of care—Municipalities
5. —Travelers
6. Bridges
7. Ice
8. Lowered grade
9. Railings and embankments
10. Turnouts
11. Widened highways
12. Bars
13. Standing to sue
14. Defenses
15. Evidence
16. Questions of jury
17. Damages—Generally
18. —Property
19. —Exemplary
20. Effect of insurance policy

1. Constitutionality

Provision of proposed amendment of this section that labeled setting of road maintenance standards a discretionary policy function for which immunity was extended in absence of malice or bad faith was constitutional, even

though determination of whether acts are discretionary was for court, not legislature, to make, where supreme court agreed with legislative designation. Opinion of Justices, 134 N.H. 266, 592 A.2d 180, 1991 N.H. LEXIS 53 (1991).

Provision of proposed amendment of this section which required plaintiffs claiming municipality had actual notice of statutorily actionable "insufficiency" to specify means by which municipality learned of insufficiency was constitutional, as it did no more than admonish a plaintiff to properly plead case. Opinion of Justices, 134 N.H. 266, 592 A.2d 180, 1991 N.H. LEXIS 53 (1991).

Where proposed amendment of this section provided municipalities with immunity for injury or damage arising out of construction, maintenance or repair of highways and sidewalks except for statutorily delimited "insufficiencies" of which municipality has actual notice, provision that municipality's acceptance or layout of a road does not give it actual notice was constitutional, as one cannot assume municipal officials carefully inspect every foot of a road before the road is made public. Opinion of Justices, 134 N.H. 266, 592 A.2d 180, 1991 N.H. LEXIS 53 (1991).

2. Historical

Provision having effect of making towns liable for damages happening from snow encumbering highway as from any other defect was repealed by act of 1893. Miner v. Hopkinton, 73 N.H. 232, 60 A. 433, 1905 N.H. LEXIS 23 (1905). (Decided under prior law.)

Prior to amendment of 1893, towns and cities were liable for injuries suffered by travelers upon their highways due to their obstruction, insufficiency, or want of repair, provided the defect or insufficiency was one that town or city ought to have remedied and it knew or in the exercise of due care could have known of the defect or insufficiency and remedied it; and this was so whether creation of the defect or insufficiency was due to the act or acts of their agents, public officers, strangers, or to some natural cause. Clair v. Manchester, 72 N.H. 231, 55 A. 935, 1903 N.H. LEXIS 53 (1903). (Decided under prior law.)

While under this section prior to its amendment in 1867, when using any part of highway traveler might have an action, under new language no action was given except to one injured when using parts of the highway enumerated, namely, a bridge, culvert, sluiceway, or embankment. Wilder v. Concord, 72 N.H. 259, 56 A. 193, 1903 N.H. LEXIS 61 (1903). (Decided under prior law.)

Changes introduced in this section in 1867 indicated a purpose to strictly limit liability arising in this way, but not to entirely remove it; for no liability could arise at any portion of highway other than those enumerated and not then because obstruction rendered highway unsuitable unless the matter complained of constituted an obstruction, defect, insufficiency, or want of repair in a structure the defect in which was made a ground of liability. Wilder v. Concord, 72 N.H. 259, 56 A. 193, 1903 N.H. LEXIS 61 (1903). (Decided under prior law.)

Prior to restrictive 1867 amendment, location or character of defect or insufficiency in highway complained of as cause of injury was immaterial; by such amendment liability of towns was limited to damages resulting by reason of any obstruction, defect, insufficiency, or want of repair of a bridge, culvert, or sluiceway or from a dangerous embankment and defective railing which rendered highway unsuitable. Owen v. Derry, 71 N.H. 405, 52 A. 926, 1902 N.H. LEXIS 48 (1902). (Decided under prior law.)

3. Application

Where it was clear that the grassy area where a school visitor tripped and fell was actually a part of the curb, the issue was one of alleged failure to maintain a sidewalk, and the visitor could not prevail in a personal injury action because there was no showing of gross negligence, intentional actions, or failure to respond after receiving notice of a dangerous condition; therefore, summary judgment was properly entered for the school district. Richard v. Pembroke Sch. Dist., 151 N.H. 455, 859 A.2d 1157, 2004 N.H. LEXIS 176 (2004).

The former version of this section did not apply to an action against a town arising from the failure of a police officer to warn of an icy road condition because the road was not a highway which the town had the duty to maintain. Trull v. Town of Conway, 140 N.H. 579, 669 A.2d 807, 1995 N.H. LEXIS 196 (1995).

Municipal liability for personal injuries resulting from hazards in a road flows from control of the road and a duty to maintain them; where there is no duty to correct a condition there is no actionable duty to warn users of a highway that the condition has not been corrected. Trull v. Town of Conway, 140 N.H. 579, 669 A.2d 807, 1995 N.H. LEXIS 196 (1995).

This section applied only to open bridges and highways, not to discontinued bridges. Bancroft v. Town of Canterbury, 118 N.H. 453, 388 A.2d 199, 1978 N.H. LEXIS 437 (1978). (Decided under prior law.)

Operation of this section was limited to defects in structures specified. Bernier v. Whitefield, 80 N.H. 245, 116 A. 133, 1921 N.H. LEXIS 72 (1921). (Decided under prior law.)

Obligation of this section did not extend to fire district. Henry v. Haverhill, 67 N.H. 172, 37 A. 1039, 1891 N.H. LEXIS 35 (1892). (Decided under prior law.)

4. Standard of care—Municipalities

Beyond requirement imposed by this section and within the limits of reason at the least, it was for municipality to determine how fine or perfect its highway should be. Langley v. Brown, 86 N.H. 382, 169 A. 477, 1933 N.H. LEXIS 80 (1933). (Decided under prior law.)

Duty of repairing and maintaining highways included performance of any act reasonably necessary to put and keep them in a condition suitable for travel thereon. Connor v. Manchester, 73 N.H. 233, 60 A. 436, 1905 N.H. LEXIS 24 (1905). (Decided under prior law.)

This section, which imposed liability upon towns, was required to be understood with the qualification that obstructions or want of repairs causing injury existed by some fault or neglect of town. Palmer v. Portsmouth, 43 N.H. 265, 1861 N.H. LEXIS 65 (1861). (Decided under prior law.)

Question of negligence on part of town did not arise except incidentally as it was involved in question whether obstruction, insufficiency or want of repair existed, and this question could depend upon manner in which defect originated and circumstances of its continuance. Johnson v. Haverhill, 35 N.H. 74, 1857 N.H. LEXIS 46 (1857). (Decided under prior law.)

5. —Travelers

Traveler on highway was bound to use ordinary care to avoid any danger which he had reason to apprehend. Cullen v. Littleton, 84 N.H. 373, 150 A. 809, 1930 N.H. LEXIS 94 (1930). (Decided under prior law.)

One was required to use ordinary care and prudence in obtaining treatment of injuries sustained by him. Boynton v. Somersworth, 58 N.H. 321, 1878 N.H. LEXIS 52 (1878). (Decided under prior law.)

Traveler was required to use ordinary care and prudence in selection of a reasonably safe horse, wagon and harness, and was bound to exercise only ordinary care and prudence in their management. Tuttle v. Farmington, 58 N.H. 13, 1876 N.H. LEXIS 10 (1876). (Decided under prior law.)

One injured by reason of defect in highway was not precluded from recovery by proof that defect in his carriage contributed to injury, provided that defect was not known to him and he was in no fault for not knowing it. Clark v. Barrington, 41 N.H. 44, 1860 N.H. LEXIS 38 (1860). (Decided under prior law.)

6. Bridges

Laying of planks lengthwise on a bridge having a substantial slope upon which a pedestrian fell could be found to render city liable for injuries sustained on an icy morning. Leonard v. Manchester, 96 N.H. 115, 70 A.2d 915, 1950 N.H. LEXIS 8 (1950). (Decided under prior law.)

Approach to bridge could be regarded as part of bridge for purpose of determining liability of towns for injuries to highway travelers under this section. Saloshin v. Houle, 86 N.H. 132, 164 A. 767, 1933 N.H. LEXIS 10 (1933); Wilson v. Barnstead, 74 N.H. 78, 65 A. 298, 1906 N.H. LEXIS 71 (1906). (Decided under prior law.)

7. Ice

Temporary accumulation of ice was not within this section. Bernier v. Whitefield, 80 N.H. 245, 116 A. 133, 1921 N.H. LEXIS 72 (1921). (Decided under prior law.)

8. Lowered grade

Town was not liable for injury due to lowering of grade where driveway entered highway. Robertson v. Hillsborough, 78 N.H. 603, 99 A. 1069, 1916 N.H. LEXIS 81 (1916). (Decided under prior law.)

9. Railings and embankments

The 1982 version of the statute provided the plaintiffs with a private cause of action where they alleged that they drove off the end of road which ends in a "cliff-like precipitous drop" within approximately 750 feet of its entrance and that they were unable to see the "No Thru Street" sign intended to alert travelers that the street was a dead end because the sign was small and facing directly opposite the direction in which they were traveling. Schoff v. City of Somersworth, 137 N.H. 583, 630 A.2d 783, 1993 N.H. LEXIS 124 (1993). (Decided under prior law.)

Although some of the acts or omissions for which municipalities may be liable under the 1982 version of the statute, including failure to provide warning signs or guardrails for dangerous embankments, may implicate discretionary functions, the statute permits suit for injuries resulting from such acts or omissions. Schoff v. City of Somersworth, 137 N.H. 583, 630 A.2d 783, 1993 N.H. LEXIS 124 (1993). (Decided under prior law.)

Defective railing was not in legal effect the same thing as none, since it could serve as a guide and warning. Bridgham v. Effingham, 87 N.H. 103, 174 A. 769, 1934 N.H. LEXIS 24 (1934). (Decided under prior law.)

Unrailed embankment could be found to be proximate cause of injury to one who fell over it in consequence of slipping on ice. Prichard v. Boscawen, 78 N.H. 131, 97 A. 563, 1916 N.H. LEXIS 13 (1916). (Decided under prior law.)

Town was liable to traveler for injuries resulting from defective railing of dangerous highway embankment. Seeton v. Dunbarton, 72 N.H. 269, 56 A. 197, 1903 N.H. LEXIS 63 (1903). (Decided under prior law.)

Among facts material to be considered in determining whether an embankment should have been railed were the character and amount of travel, the character of the road itself, its width and general construction, the character and extent of the slope or descent of the bank, the direction of the road at the place, the length of the portion claimed to require a rail, whether the danger was concealed or obvious, and the extent of injury liable to occur therefrom. Seeton v. Dunbarton, 72 N.H. 269, 56 A. 197, 1903 N.H. LEXIS 63 (1903). (Decided under prior law.)

Want of sufficient railing when necessary for security of traveler constituted defect for which town in case of accident could be held liable. Whipple v. Walpole, 10 N.H. 130, 1839 N.H. LEXIS 63 (1839), overruled, Woodman v. Nottingham, 49 N.H. 387, 1870 N.H. LEXIS 30 (1870). (Decided under prior law.)

10. Turnouts

Failure to fence off an unsafe private way in the general direction of public travel on highway was not an actionable defect. Knowlton v. Pittsfield, 62 N.H. 535, 1883 N.H. LEXIS 52 (1883). (Decided under prior law.)

Duty of town to keep highway in repair extended to that part of turnout which it permitted to exist from traveled part of its highway to private way as was within limits of highway. Stark v. Lancaster, 57 N.H. 88, 1876 N.H. LEXIS 55 (1876). (Decided under prior law.)

11. Widened highways

If town suffered traveled part of highway to become widened so as to hold out to travelers that whole width was equally suitable for travel it was answerable for damages growing out of defects in part so widened. Saltmarsh v. Bow, 56 N.H. 428, 1876 N.H. LEXIS 165 (1876). (Decided under prior law.)

12. Bars

Bars across road for purpose of turning water from road into gutters could be so constructed as to constitute an actionable defect. Clark v. Barrington, 41 N.H. 44, 1860 N.H. LEXIS 38 (1860). (Decided under prior law.)

13. Standing to sue

Fireman of city in which he lived had no such relation to it as to prevent his maintaining an action under this section to recover for injuries occasioned by defects in highway while he was hastening to a fire. Palmer v. Portsmouth, 43 N.H. 265, 1861 N.H. LEXIS 65 (1861). (Decided under prior law.)

14. Defenses

Failure to perform statutory duty to keep highways in good repair was not excused by the poverty of town. Winship v. Enfield, 42 N.H. 197, 1860 N.H. LEXIS 23 (1860). (Decided under prior law.)

15. Evidence

Verdict for plaintiff in action based upon defective condition of culvert was vitiated by plaintiff's failure to produce evidence that a standard railing would have prevented the accident. Bridgham v. Effingham, 87 N.H. 103, 174 A. 769, 1934 N.H. LEXIS 24 (1934). (Decided under prior law.)

In an action under this section for failure to rail an embankment, evidence that slope was concealed by bushes and that ground gave way beneath wheels of plaintiff's car warranted conclusion that embankment constituted danger making road unsuitable for travel. Bridgham v. Effingham, 87 N.H. 103, 174 A. 769, 1934 N.H. LEXIS 24 (1934). (Decided under prior law.)

In determining whether traveler exercised sufficient care, evidence of traveler's knowledge or ignorance of condition of road and his choice of tracks thereon could be considered. Griffin v. Auburn, 58 N.H. 121, 1877 N.H. LEXIS 39 (1877). (Decided under prior law.)

In an action under this section it was competent to show that town had paid claim for damages to owner of wagon in which plaintiff was riding at time of accident, even though payment was made with a disclaimer of liability. Coffin v. Plymouth, 49 N.H. 173, 1870 N.H. LEXIS 3 (1870). (Decided under prior law.)

16. Questions of jury

Whether condition complained of rendered highway unsuitable for public travel was for jury. Seeton v. Dunbarton, 72 N.H. 269, 56 A. 197, 1903 N.H. LEXIS 63 (1903). (Decided under prior law.)

Whether plaintiff exercised ordinary care and diligence in traveling upon highway at time and in manner he did, and if not, whether want of such care and diligence contributed to injury, were questions of fact to be found by jury under proper instructions. Palmer v. Portsmouth, 43 N.H. 265, 1861 N.H. LEXIS 65 (1861); Whipple v. Walpole, 10 N.H. 130, 1839 N.H. LEXIS 63 (1839), overruled, Woodman v. Nottingham, 49 N.H. 387, 1870 N.H. LEXIS 30 (1870); Norris v. Litchfield, 35 N.H. 271, 1857 N.H. LEXIS 69 (1857); Stack v. Portsmouth, 52

N.H. 221, 1872 N.H. LEXIS 34 (1872); Sleeper v. Sandown, 52 N.H. 244, 1872 N.H. LEXIS 38 (1872); State v. Manchester & Lawrence Railroad, 52 N.H. 528, 1873 N.H. LEXIS 73 (1873); Daniels v. Lebanon, 58 N.H. 284, 1878 N.H. LEXIS 29 (1878). (Decided under prior law.)

Question whether highway was obstructed, insufficient, or out of repair within meaning of those terms as used in this section was for jury under proper instructions from court as to the meaning of the terms, and in view of all the circumstances of the case in reference to nature and extent of defect, character, ground, amounts and kind of travel, ability and means of town, and other like circumstances tending to show whether highway was or was not reasonably safe and convenient for customary travel and whether or not it ought to have been repaired before accident. Johnson v. Haverhill, 35 N.H. 74, 1857 N.H. LEXIS 46 (1857). (Decided under prior law.)

17. Damages—Generally

Under this section damages were recoverable for probable, proximate or direct consequences of a defect. Whipple v. Walpole, 10 N.H. 130, 1839 N.H. LEXIS 63 (1839), overruled, Woodman v. Nottingham, 49 N.H. 387, 1870 N.H. LEXIS 30 (1870). (Decided under prior law.)

Damages for which private person could maintain suit against town were limited to such as happened in use of highway as such and which were direct and not consequential results of defect complained of. Ball v. Winchester, 32 N.H. 435, 1855 N.H. LEXIS 230 (1855). (Decided under prior law.)

18. —Property

Damages recoverable included those for injury to property as well as to the person.

19. —Exemplary

This section did not contemplate exemplary or vindictive damages to suffering party. Whipple v. Walpole, 10 N.H. 130, 1839 N.H. LEXIS 63 (1839), overruled, Woodman v. Nottingham, 49 N.H. 387, 1870 N.H. LEXIS 30 (1870). (Decided under prior law.)

20. Effect of insurance policy

It was not error for the trial court to instruct the jury concerning the notice and liability requirements of the municipality as set forth in RSA 231:92 even though the municipality had obtained an insurance policy. RSA 231:90 through 231:92 establish "a [statutory] standard of care differing from that of [a] private corporation," within the meaning of RSA 412:3 (1998) (repealed 2002) (current version at RSA 507-B:7-a). The presence or absence of liability insurance does not change the legal duty owed to users of highways, or change the type of conduct that constitutes a breach of such duty. Cloutier v. City of Berlin, 154 N.H. 13, 907 A.2d 955, 2006 N.H. LEXIS 118 (2006).

Cited:

Cited in City of Dover v. Imperial Cas. & Indem. Co., 133 N.H. 109, 575 A.2d 1280, 1990 N.H. LEXIS 39 (1990); Doucette v. Town of Bristol, 138 N.H. 205, 635 A.2d 1387, 1993 N.H. LEXIS 182 (1993); Boston & Me. Corp. v. Town of Hampton, 987 F.2d 855, 1993 U.S. App. LEXIS 4159 (1st Cir. 1993).

231:93. When Municipalities not Liable.

Municipalities shall not be deemed to have any duty of care whatsoever with respect to the construction, maintenance or repair of class I, III, III-a or VI highways, or state maintained portions of class II highways. Upon any highway or other way with respect to which a municipality is found to have a duty of care of any kind, its liability shall be limited as set forth in this subdivision.

Source.

RS 105:4. 1945, 188:1, part 18:18. RSA 247:18. 1981, 87:1. 1991, 385:7. 1992, 265:14, eff. July 1, 1992.

Amendments

—1992. Inserted "III-a" preceding "or VI" and deleted "or highways to public waters laid out by a commission appointed by the governor and council" following "class II highways" in the first sentence.

—1991. Rewritten to the extent that a detailed comparison would be impracticable.

Cross References.
Classification of highways, see RSA 229:5.

Town not liable for damages or injuries caused by use of closed highway or bridge, see RSA 228:37.

NOTES TO DECISIONS

Analysis

1. Constitutionality
2. Reason for immunity
3. Extent of immunity
4. State control

1. Constitutionality

Provision of proposed amendment of this section granting immunity for injuries suffered on classes of highways either maintained solely by the state or not required to be maintained by a municipality did not create unconstitutional classification between private and public tortfeasors; municipalities should not be held responsible for insufficiencies on these classes of highways. Opinion of Justices, 134 N.H. 266, 592 A.2d 180, 1991 N.H. LEXIS 53 (1991).

2. Reason for immunity

Reason for immunity afforded by this section was that control had been taken from town either in whole or in part. Bridgham v. Effingham, 87 N.H. 103, 174 A. 769, 1934 N.H. LEXIS 24 (1934); Hanover v. Burroughs, 215 F. 817, 1914 U.S. App. LEXIS 1293 (C.C.A. 1914). (Decided under prior law.)

3. Extent of immunity

Immunity under this section was effective only for that portion of highway which received benefit of state aid. Bridgham v. Effingham, 87 N.H. 103, 174 A. 769, 1934 N.H. LEXIS 24

(1934). (Decided under prior law.)

Grant of state aid upon application of town affected its liability only as to portions of highways to which aid was so granted, or those as to which at least some official action seeking grant had been taken. Bridgham v. Effingham, 86 N.H. 332, 168 A. 904, 1933 N.H. LEXIS 57 (1933). (Decided under prior law.)

4. State control

Mere formulation of plan that designated road should become state-aided over its entire length did not amount to designation in the legal sense, even if approved by highway commissioner. Bridgham v. Effingham, 87 N.H. 103, 174 A. 769, 1934 N.H. LEXIS 24 (1934). (Decided under prior law.)

Until improvement had begun, or at least a definite portion of highway had been concurrently designated for improvement, there was no state control, and town's liability to travelers continued. Bridgham v. Effingham, 87 N.H. 103, 174 A. 769, 1934 N.H. LEXIS 24 (1934). (Decided under prior law.)

Cited:

Cited in Schoff v. City of Somersworth, 137 N.H. 583, 630 A.2d 783, 1993 N.H. LEXIS 124 (1993); Trull v. Town of Conway, 140 N.H. 579, 669 A.2d 807, 1995 N.H. LEXIS 196 (1995); Berliner v. Clukay, 150 N.H. 80, 834 A.2d 297, 2003 N.H. LEXIS 140 (2003).

Street Names and Markers

231:133. Names; Changes; Signs.

I. In all towns, cities, and those village districts which maintain public highways, every highway and street under the control of the town, city, or village district shall have a name which shall be given it by the governing body. Said name shall be legibly marked on a suitable signboard or other marker and placed in at least 2 conspicuous places on said street. The governing body may change the name of any such street or highway at any time when in its judgment there is occasion for so doing. The governing body may change the name of a private street or highway when the name change is necessary to conform to the requirements of the enhanced 911 telecommunications system. In towns and village districts the governing body may at its discretion provide for public hearing and submit such names for approval at any meeting of the legislative body, and voters may submit a petitioned warrant article for such a name change under the procedure of RSA 39:3.

II. The naming of any new street or highway shall form a part of the return of the layout of the street or highway, or of the acceptance of any dedicated way. The municipality shall not be bound by any name previously assigned to the street or highway by any private owner, developer, or dedicator. No name for a highway or street shall be selected which is already in use, or which is confusingly similar to any such existing name, or which otherwise might delay the locating of any address in an emergency.

III. Whenever a name is assigned to any new street or highway, or a change is made in the name of any street or highway, the governing body shall make a return of the same to the town, city, or village district clerk, who shall make a record of the new name or name change, and shall forward a copy of such record to the commissioner of transportation.

Source.
1911, 79:1. PL 93:5. RL 109:5. 1945, 188:1, part 21:1. RSA 251:1. 1981, 87:1. 1991, 53:1, eff. July 5, 1991. 2005, 113:1, eff. August 14, 2005.

Amendments
—**2005.** Paragraph I: Added the fourth sentence.

—**1991.** Rewritten to the extent that a detailed comparison would be impracticable.

NOTES TO DECISIONS

Historical
Similar provision requiring town under penalty to maintain guide posts at highway intersections was held not to make failure to maintain guide posts at each intersection a separate offense in Clark v. Lisbon (1848) 19 N.H. 286. (Decided under prior law.)

Scenic Roads

231:157. Scenic Roads; Designation.

Any road in a town, other than a class I or class II highway, may be designated as a scenic road in the following manner. Upon petition of 10 persons who are either voters of the town or who own land which abuts a road mentioned in the petition (even though not voters of the town), the voters of such town at any annual or special meeting may designate such road as a scenic road. Such petitioners shall be responsible for providing the town clerk with a list of known property owners whose land abuts any of the roads mentioned in the petition. The town clerk shall notify by regular mail within 10 days of the filing all abutters along the road that lies within the town that a scenic road petition has been filed for and that an article to designate such road as a scenic road will appear in the warrant at the next town meeting. The voters at a regular town meeting may rescind in like manner their designation of a scenic road upon petition as provided above. Notice to the abutting landowners shall also be given as provided above. Each town shall maintain and make available to the public a list of all roads or highways or portions thereof within the town which have been designated as scenic roads. Such list shall be kept current by updating not less than annually and shall contain sufficient information to permit ready identification of the location and extent of each scenic road or portion thereof, by reference to a town map or otherwise.

Source.
RSA 253:17. 1971, 455:1. 1973, 586:1. 1981, 87:1. 1992, 160:3, eff. July 5, 1992.

Amendments
—1992. Added the seventh and eighth sentences.

NOTES TO DECISIONS

Analysis

1. Constitutionality
2. Construction

1. Constitutionality
Scenic road statute is not an impermissible delegation of legislative power because the legislature has deemed scenic roads to be a matter of local concern and has delegated the authority to designate scenic roads to local voters, and the authority to regulate tree and stone wall removal from these roads to the local planning board or other "official municipal body" selected by the voters. Webster v. Town of Candia, 146 N.H. 430, 778 A.2d 402, 2001 N.H. LEXIS 91 (2001).

2. Construction
Trial court erred in finding that removal of scenic road designation, accomplished by vote at town meeting, amounted to a circumvention of planning board's earlier decision denying relocation of portion of road; decisions made by voters and by planning board were not the same, and only entity with jurisdiction to designate or undesignate a road as scenic was the town, through its vote. Neville v. Highfields Farm, Inc., 144 N.H. 419, 744 A.2d 89, 1999 N.H. LEXIS 135 (1999).

Cited:
Cited in Cormier v. Town of Danville Zoning Bd. of Adjustment, 142 N.H. 775, 710 A.2d 401, 1998 N.H. LEXIS 35 (1998).

231:158. Effect of Designation as Scenic Roads.

I. As used in this subdivision, "tree" means any woody plant which has a circumference of 15 inches or more at a point 4 feet from the ground.

II. Upon a road being designated as a scenic road as provided in RSA 231:157, any repair, maintenance, reconstruction, or paving work done with respect thereto by the state or municipality, or any action taken by any utility or other person acting to erect, install or maintain poles, conduits, cables, wires, pipes or other structures pursuant to RSA 231:159–189 shall not involve the cutting, damage or removal of trees, or the tearing down or destruction of stone walls, or portions thereof, except with the prior written consent of the planning board, or any other official municipal body designated by the meeting to implement the provisions of this subdivision, after a public hearing duly advertised as to time, date, place and purpose, 2 times in a newspaper of general circulation in the area, the last publication to occur at least 7 days prior to such hearing, provided, however, that a road agent or his designee may, without such hearing, but only with the written permission of the selectmen, remove trees or portions of trees which have been declared a public nuisance pursuant to RSA 231:145 and 231:146, when such trees or portions of such trees pose an imminent threat to safety or property, and provided, further, that a public utility when involved in the emergency restoration of service, may without such hearing or permission of the selectmen, perform such work as is necessary for the prompt restoration of utility service which has been interrupted by facility damage and when requested, shall thereafter inform the selectmen of the nature of the emergency and the work performed, in such manner as the selectmen may require.

III. Designation of a road as scenic shall not affect the eligibility of the town to receive construction, maintenance or reconstruction aid pursuant to the provisions of RSA 235 for such road.

IV. Designation of a road as a scenic road shall not affect the rights of any landowner with respect to work on his own property, except to the extent that trees have been acquired by the municipality as shade or ornamental trees pursuant to RSA 231:139–156, and except that RSA 472:6 limits the removal or alteration of boundary markers including stone walls.

V. A town may, as part of a scenic road designation under RSA 231:157 or as an amendment to such designation adopted in the same manner, impose provisions with respect to such road which are different from or in addition to those set forth in this section. Such provisions may include, but are not limited to, decisional criteria for the granting of consent by the planning board or other designated municipal body under paragraph II, or protections for trees smaller than those described in paragraph I, designated for the purpose of establishing regenerative growth along the scenic road.

VI. Any person who violates this section or any local provision adopted under this section shall be guilty of a violation and shall be liable for all damages resulting therefrom.

Source.
RSA 253:18. 1971, 455:1. 1973, 586:2. 1981, 87:1. 1983, 122:2. 1991, 134:3, 4. 1992, 160:2, eff. July 5, 1992.

Amendments
—1992. Paragraph II: Rewritten to the extent that a detailed comparison would be impracticable.

—1991. Paragraph II: Rewritten to the extent that a detailed comparison would be impracticable.

Paragraph IV: Added "except to the extent that trees have been acquired by the municipality as shade or ornamental trees pursuant to RSA 231:139–156, and except that RSA 472:6 limits the removal or alteration of boundary markers including stone walls" following "property".

Paragraphs V, VI: Added.

—1983. Paragraph III: Inserted "maintenance" following "construction" in the first sentence and deleted the second sentence.

NOTES TO DECISIONS

Analysis

1. Constitutionality
2. Planning board procedures

1. Constitutionality
This section is not unconstitutionally vague because it is sufficiently clear to warn the average person of the prohibited conduct (cutting trees of a specific circumference or destroying stone walls on designated scenic roads) and that if he or she wishes to engage in the prohibited activity, he or she must first obtain written planning board consent. Webster v.

Town of Candia, 146 N.H. 430, 778 A.2d 402, 2001 N.H. LEXIS 91 (2001).

This section is not void on the basis that it does not apprise an applicant of the standards that planning board, or other official municipal body, will use when reviewing plans to cut trees or destroy stone walls on scenic roads; a law is not necessarily vague because it does not precisely apprise an applicant of the standards by which an administrative board will make its decision. Webster v. Town of Candia, 146 N.H. 430, 778 A.2d 402, 2001 N.H. LEXIS 91 (2001).

This section is not vague on the basis that it does not specify standards planning board will use when reviewing plans for tree cutting or stone wall destruction on designated scenic roads because it is implied that the board will exercise its discretion consistent with the purpose of the road's scenic designation. Webster v. Town of Candia, 146 N.H. 430, 778 A.2d 402, 2001 N.H. LEXIS 91 (2001).

Warrant articles by which a town voted to designate a road as scenic specifying that the purpose of so doing was to "protect and enhance ... the scenic beauty of [the town]" was sufficient notice to developers of relevant standards planning board would use when reviewing plans for tree cutting or stone wall destruction. Webster v. Town of Candia, 146 N.H. 430, 778 A.2d 402, 2001 N.H. LEXIS 91 (2001).

This section was not impermissibly vague as applied to plaintiffs because, under the facts of the case, it gave them adequate warning that they could not cut certain kinds of trees absent planning board consent. Webster v. Town of Candia, 146 N.H. 430, 778 A.2d 402, 2001 N.H. LEXIS 91 (2001).

Scenic road statute is not an impermissible delegation of legislative power because the legislature has deemed scenic roads to be a matter of local concern and has delegated the authority to designate scenic roads to local voters, and the authority to regulate tree and stone wall removal from these roads to the local planning board or other "official municipal body" selected by the voters. Webster v. Town of Candia, 146 N.H. 430, 778 A.2d 402, 2001 N.H. LEXIS 91 (2001).

2. Planning board procedures

In denying plaintiffs' applications to remove trees from a designated scenic road, it was reasonable for planning board to have considered whether there was alternative access to plaintiffs' property since the roads constituting alternative means of access were not designated scenic roads. Webster v. Town of Candia, 146 N.H. 430, 778 A.2d 402, 2001 N.H. LEXIS 91 (2001).

In denying plaintiffs' applications to remove trees from a designated scenic road, planning board's consideration of alternative access did not violate their constitutional rights to due process on the basis that they never received notice that the board would consider the possibility of alternative accesses because they received both adequate notice and an opportunity to be heard on their request to cut trees from the scenic road and this is all the procedure due process requires. Webster v. Town of Candia, 146 N.H. 430, 778 A.2d 402, 2001 N.H. LEXIS 91 (2001).

Notice of planning board's decision denying plaintiffs' applications to remove trees from a designated scenic road was not unreasonable and unlawful on the basis that it did not include reasons for the denial where evidence before the trial court, including approved and unapproved minutes of the meeting, reasonably supported a finding that reasons for the denial were adequately set forth. Webster v. Town of Candia, 146 N.H. 430, 778 A.2d 402, 2001 N.H. LEXIS 91 (2001).

Planning board's reasons for its denial of plaintiffs' request to cut trees on designated scenic road were valid based on its finding that the proposed tree cutting "would lead to the deterioration of the scenic quality of the road," and because the request failed to mark all of the trees to be removed and failed to present a study or documentation about how removing the trees would affect drainage for other trees on the road. Webster v. Town of Candia, 146 N.H. 430, 778 A.2d 402, 2001 N.H. LEXIS 91 (2001).

Cited:

Cited in Cormier v. Town of Danville Zoning Bd. of Adjustment, 142 N.H. 775, 710 A.2d 401, 1998 N.H. LEXIS 35 (1998); Neville v. Highfields Farm, Inc., 144 N.H. 419, 744 A.2d 89, 1999 N.H. LEXIS 135 (1999).

CHAPTER 236

HIGHWAY REGULATION, PROTECTION AND CONTROL REGULATIONS

Excavations and Driveways

236:13. Driveways and Other Accesses to the Public Way.

I. It shall be unlawful to construct, or alter in any way that substantially affects the size or grade of, any driveway, entrance, exit, or approach within the limits of the right-of-way of any class I or class III highway or the state-maintained portion of a class II highway that does not conform to the terms and specifications of a written permit issued by the commissioner of transportation.

II. Pursuant to this section, a written construction permit application must be obtained from and filed with the department of transportation by any abutter affected by the provisions of paragraph I. Before any construction or alteration work is commenced, said permit application shall have been reviewed, and a construction permit issued by said department. Said permit shall:

(a) Describe the location of the driveway, entrance, exit, or approach. The location shall be selected to most adequately protect the safety of the traveling public.

(b) Describe any drainage structures, traffic control devices, and channelization islands to be installed by the abutter.

(c) Establish grades that adequately protect and promote highway drainage and permit a safe and controlled approach to the highway in all seasons of the year.

(d) Include any other terms and specifications necessary for the safety of the traveling public.

221

III. For access to a proposed commercial or industrial enterprise, or to a subdivision, all of which for the purposes of this section shall be considered a single parcel of land, even though acquired by more than one conveyance or held nominally by more than one owner:

(a) Said permit application shall be accompanied by engineering drawings showing information as set forth in paragraph II.

(b) Unless all season safe sight distance of 400 feet in both directions along the highway can be obtained, the commissioner shall not permit more than one access to a single parcel of land, and this access shall be at that location which the commissioner determines to be safest. The commissioner shall not give final approval for use of any additional access until it has been proven to him that the 400-foot all season safe sight distance has been provided.

(c) For the purposes of this section, all season safe sight distance is defined as a line which encounters no visual obstruction between 2 points, each at a height of 3 feet 9 inches above the pavement, and so located as to represent the critical line of sight between the operator of a vehicle using the access and the operator of a vehicle approaching from either direction.

IV. No construction permit shall allow:

(a) A driveway, entrance, exit, or approach to be constructed more than 50 feet in width, except that a driveway, entrance, exit, or approach may be flared beyond a width of 50 feet at its junction with the highway to accommodate the turning radius of vehicles expected to use the particular driveway, entrance, exit or approach.

(b) More than 2 driveways, entrances, exits or approaches from any one highway to any one parcel of land unless the frontage along that highway exceeds 500 feet.

V. The same powers concerning highways under their jurisdiction as are conferred upon the commissioner of transportation by paragraphs I, II, III and IV shall be conferred upon the planning board in cities and towns in which the planning board has been granted the power to regulate the subdivision of land as provided in RSA 674:35, and they shall adopt such regulations as are necessary to carry out the provisions of this section. Such regulations may delegate administrative duties, including actual issuance of permits, to a highway agent, board of selectmen, or other qualified official or body. Such regulations, or any permit issued under them, may contain provisions governing the breach, removal, and reconstruction of stone walls or fences within, or at the boundary of, the public right of way, and any landowner or landowner's agent altering a boundary in accordance with such provisions shall be deemed to be acting under a mutual agreement with the city or town pursuant to RSA 472:6, II(a).

VI. The commissioner of transportation or planning board shall retain continuing jurisdiction over the adequacy and safety of every existing driveway, entrance, exit, and approach to a highway, whether or not such access was constructed or installed pursuant to a permit under this section, and, unless the access is a public highway, the owners of property to which the access is appurtenant shall have continuing responsibility for the adequacy of the access and any grades, culverts, or other structures pertaining to such access, whether or not located within the public right of way. If any such access is or becomes a potential threat to the integrity of the highway or its surface, ditches, embankments, bridges, or other structures, or a hazard to the safety of the traveling public, by reason of siltation, flooding, erosion, frost action, vegetative growth, improper grade, or the failure of any culvert, traffic control device, drainage structure, or any other feature, the commissioner of transportation or planning board or their designee may issue an order to the landowner or other party responsible for such access to repair or remove such hazardous condition and to obtain any and all permits required therefor. The order shall describe the hazard, prescribe what corrective action or alteration in the location or configuration of such access shall be required, and set a reasonable time within which the action shall be completed. Such an order shall be sent by certified mail, and shall be enforceable to the same extent as a permit issued under this section. If the order is not complied with within the time prescribed, the commissioner or planning board or their designee may cause to be taken whatever action is necessary to protect the highway and the traveling public, and the owner or other responsible party shall be civilly liable to the state or municipality for its costs in taking such action.

Source.

1939, 109:1. RL 107:4. 1945, 188:1, part 19:12. 1950, 5:1, part 9:1, par. 2. RSA 249:17. 1969, 254:1. 1971, 302:1. 1981, 87:1. 1985, 103:4, eff. Jan. 1, 1986; 402:6, I(a)(7), (b)(7). 1997, 52:1, 2, eff. July 18, 1997.

Revision note.

Substituted a comma for a semicolon following "commenced" in the second sentence of par. II to correct a grammatical error.

Amendments

—1997. Paragraph V: Substituted "in which" for "wherein" following "cities and towns" in the first sentence and added the second and third sentences.

Paragraph VI: Added.

—1985. Paragraph I: Chapter 402 substituted "commissioner of transportation" for "commissioner of public works and highways" at the end of the paragraph.

Paragraph II: Chapter 402 substituted "department of transportation" for "department of public works and highways" in the first sentence of the introductory paragraph.

Paragraph V: Chapter 103 substituted "RSA 674:35" for "RSA 36:19" following "provided in" and "adopt" for "promulgate" preceding "such" and deleted "rules and" thereafter and made other minor stylistic changes throughout the paragraph.

Chapter 402 substituted "commissioner of transportation" for "commissioner of public works and highways".

Effective date of amendments

—1985, 402. See note preceding RSA 236:1 regarding effective date of 1985, 402:6, I.

Cross References.

Exemption of rules adopted under this section from provisions of Administrative Procedure Act, see RSA 541-A:21.

NOTES TO DECISIONS

Analysis

1. State preemption
2. Powers of commissioner
3. Safe sight distance
4. Damages
5. Exceptions.

1. State preemption

Since New Hampshire legislature had given

commissioner of public works and highways broad powers to regulate driveways and other means of access to state highways and had made it unlawful for anyone to construct or alter any entrance onto a state highway without complying with the terms of a permit obtained from the commissioner, state had preempted control of access to state highways. J. E. D. Assocs. v. Sandown, 121 N.H. 317, 430 A.2d 129, 1981 N.H. LEXIS 332 (1981). (Decided under prior law.)

2. Powers of commissioner

New Hampshire Department of Transportation's (DOT's) three driveway rule neither conflicts with the standards in the driveway statute, RSA 236:13, nor oversteps the limited discretion granted to the DOT concerning driveway permits. Appeal of New Hampshire DOT, 152 N.H. 565, 883 A.2d 272, 2005 N.H. LEXIS 139 (Sept. 2, 2005).

Basic design and function of limited access highway was to allow for optimum mobility of through traffic by permitting owners and occupants of abutting land to have only restricted right of physical access to and from roadway and only at points planned and controlled by official highway plan, but such control must have been exercised in a reasonable and nonarbitrary manner in any action by commissioner of public works and highways. Treat v. State, 117 N.H. 6, 369 A.2d 214, 1977 N.H. LEXIS 253 (1977). (Decided under prior law.)

3. Safe sight distance

Four-hundred-foot safe sight distance at a highway intersection required by subparagraph III(b) of this section applied when more than one access to a single parcel of land was involved. J. E. D. Assocs. v. Sandown, 121 N.H. 317, 430 A.2d 129, 1981 N.H. LEXIS 332 (1981). (Decided under prior law.)

4. Damages

Subjecting 50-foot wide right of access to limited access highway reserved to abutting landowners to reasonable control of commissioner of public works and highways was regulation under police power of state to promote public safety and general welfare and was not taking by eminent domain of private property, because it was useful to public and was not compensable. Treat v. State, 117 N.H. 6, 369 A.2d 214, 1977 N.H. LEXIS 253 (1977). (Decided under prior law.)

Power to regulate access to highways conferred upon commissioner applied to all abutters on limited access highways and to abutters on certain other highways; thus, abutting landowners shared hardship resulting from regulation with all other abutters, and damages, not being peculiar to them, constituted general damages and were not compensable. Treat v. State, 117 N.H. 6, 369 A.2d 214, 1977 N.H. LEXIS 253 (1977). (Decided under prior law.)

5. Exceptions.

New Hampshire Transportation Appeals Board erred by requiring the New Hampshire Department of Transportation (DOT) to present evidence that respondent's proposed driveway would create a specific safety issue. It was the owner who sought an exception from the DOT's three driveway rule, and the burden remained with him to establish all requirements to warrant the grant of an exception. Appeal of New Hampshire DOT, 152 N.H. 565, 883 A.2d 272, 2005 N.H. LEXIS 139 (Sept. 2, 2005).

Cited:

Cited in Diversified Properties, Inc. v. Town of Hopkinton Planning Board, 125 N.H. 419, 480 A.2d 194, 1984 N.H. LEXIS 262 (1984); Collier v. Redbones Tavern & Restaurant, Inc., 601 F. Supp. 927, 1985 U.S. Dist. LEXIS 22951 (D.N.H. 1985); Dumont v. Town of Wolfeboro, 137 N.H. 1, 622 A.2d 1238, 1993 N.H. LEXIS 28 (1993).

236:14. Penalty.

Any person who violates any provision of this subdivision or the rules and regulations made under authority thereof shall be guilty of a violation if a natural person, or guilty of a misdemeanor if any other person; and, in addition, shall be liable for the cost of restoration of the highway to a condition satisfactory to the person empowered to give such written permission.

Source.
1917, 96:3. PL 91:3. 1939, 109:2. RL 107:5. 1945, 188:1, part 19:13. RSA 249:18. 1973, 530:26. 1981, 87:1, eff. April 20, 1981.

Cross References.
Classification of crimes, see RSA 625:9. Sentences, see RSA 651.

Outdoor Advertising

236:73-a. "RV Friendly" Markers.

I. Subject to the prior approval of the Federal Highway Administration, the department of transportation shall incorporate the use of "RV friendly" markers on specific business directional signs for business establishments that cater to the needs of persons driving recreational vehicles. A business establishment that qualifies for a business directional sign and that also qualifies as "RV friendly" may request that an "RV friendly" marker be displayed immediately adjacent to such establishment's business logo sign on the appropriate background sign panel. The business applicant shall pay all costs of the "RV friendly" marker. For purposes of this section, the "RV friendly" marker to be displayed shall be such marker as may be approved by the Federal Highway Administration in the Manual on Uniform Traffic Control Devices.

II. In accordance with the provisions of RSA 21-L:12, and subject to the approval of the Federal Highway Administration, the department shall adopt rules, pursuant to RSA 541-A, necessary to implement the provisions of this section, including rules setting forth the minimum requirements for business establishments to qualify as "RV friendly." Such requirements shall include, but shall not be limited to:

(a) Roadways shall be hard surface, such as gravel, compacted stone dust, pavement, or other firm surface, and at least 12 feet wide with a minimum swing radius of 50 feet for entering and exiting the facility.

(b) Roadway access and parking facilities shall be free of any obstructions up to 14 feet above the surface.

(c) Facilities requiring short-term parking shall have 2 or more spaces that are 12 feet wide and 65 feet long with a swing radius of 50 feet to enter and exit the spaces.

(d) Fueling facilities with canopies shall have a 14-foot clearance and facilities selling diesel fuel shall have pumps with non-commercial nozzles.

(e) Fueling facilities shall allow for pull-through with a swing radius of 50 feet.

(f) Campgrounds shall have 2 or more spaces that are 18 feet wide and 45 feet long.

Source.
2007, 87:1, eff. August 10, 2007.

Motor Vehicle Recycling Yards and Junk Yards

Amendments
—1992. 1992, 88:11, eff. Jan. 1, 1993, substituted "Recycling" for "Junk" following "Vehicle" in the subdivision heading.

Cross References.

Control of junk yards and automotive recycling yards adjacent to interstate highways, federal aid highways and turnpikes, see RSA 236:90 et seq.

Licensing of junk dealers, see RSA 322.

Motor vehicle junk dealers, see RSA 261:123 et seq.

Prohibition against siting of junk yards under Groundwater Protection Act, see RSA 485-C:12.

Transporting of junk motor vehicles, see RSA 266:69.

RESEARCH REFERENCES

ALR.

Validity, construction, and application of zoning ordinance relating to operation of junk yard or scrap metal processing plant. 50 A.L.R.3D 837.

236:111. Purposes.

This subdivision is adopted under the police power of the state to conserve and safeguard the public safety, health, morals, and welfare, and to further the economic growth and stability of the people of the state through encouragement to the development of the tourist industry within the state. A clean, wholesome, attractive environment is declared to be of importance to the health and safety of the inhabitants and the safeguarding of their material rights against unwarrantable invasion. In addition, such an environment is considered essential to the maintenance and continued development of the tourist and recreational industry which is hereby declared to be of significant and proven importance to the economy of the state and the general welfare of its citizens. At the same time, it is recognized that the maintenance of junk yards as defined in this subdivision, is a useful and necessary business and ought to be encouraged when not in conflict with the express purposes of this subdivision.

Source.

RSA 267-A:1. 1965, 372:1. 1981, 87:1, eff. April 20, 1981. 1999, 288:2, eff. Sept. 14, 1999. 2002, 27:1, eff. July 1, 2002.

Amendments

—**2002.** Deleted the fifth sentence.

—**1999.** Rewrote the last sentence.

NOTES TO DECISIONS

Analysis

1. Applicability
2. Preemption

1. Applicability

The local licensing provisions of RSA 236:111–236:129 did not apply to a junkyard located adjacent to an interstate highway. Co-

rey v. Town of Merrimack, 140 N.H. 426, 666 A.2d 1359, 1995 N.H. LEXIS 164 (1995).

2. Preemption

The trial court erred by ruling that the town's licensing requirements were per se arbitrary and unreasonable because the town lacked authority to license the junkyard under the legislature's bifurcated scheme; the statutory scheme was concerned with the location and effective control of junkyards near certain highways, but did not purport to be a comprehensive regulatory scheme. Corey v. Town of Merrimack, 140 N.H. 426, 666 A.2d 1359, 1995 N.H. LEXIS 164 (1995).

236:111-a. Scope.

I. Except as provided by paragraphs II and III, the provisions of this subdivision shall apply to all junk yards, as defined by RSA 236:112, I, including those approved under RSA 149-M and those subject to regulation under RSA 236:90–110.

II. The provisions of this subdivision shall not apply to any junk yard that is also a type of solid waste management facility listed below and approved under RSA 149-M, including any such solid waste management facility approved prior to May 1, 1989:

(a) Landfills;

(b) Incinerators and other processing or treatment facilities, not including automotive recycling yards; and

(c) Transfer stations that collect, store, and transfer municipal solid waste, whether or not they also collect:

(1) Source separated waste derived from motor vehicles, such as tires, lead acid batteries, or used oil; and/or

(2) Common household or commercial machinery, such as appliances, office equipment, or lawn mowers.

III. The provisions of this subdivision shall not apply to any noncommercial antique motor vehicle restoration activities involving antique motor vehicles over 25 years old, where the owner or lessee demonstrates that each of the following requirements are met:

(a) All antique motor vehicles kept on the premises are owned by the property owner or lessee; and

(b) All antique motor vehicles and parts of antique motor vehicles are kept out of view of the public and abutters by means of storage inside a permanent structure, or by suitable fencing which complies with the fencing requirements of RSA 236:123, or by trees or shrubbery sufficient to block visual access year round; and

(c) Any combination of antique motor vehicles or parts of antique motor vehicles that are not stored inside a permanent structure shall otherwise comply with the requirements of this section and shall not exceed a total amount of 5 vehicles. For purposes of this section, the sum of the parts of antique motor vehicles that equal in bulk to one antique motor vehicle shall be counted as one antique motor vehicle; and

(d) All mechanical repairs and modifications are performed out of view of the public and abutters; and

(e) Not more than one unregistered and uninspected motor vehicle that is not over 25 years old shall be kept on the premises; and

(f) The use of the premises is in compliance with all municipal land use ordinances and regulations.

Source.

1989, 95:1, eff. May 1, 1989. 2002, 27:2, eff. July 1, 2002; 228:1, 2, eff. at 12:01 a.m, July 1, 2002.

Revision note.

Substituted "May 1, 1989" for "the effective date of this section" for purposes of clarity.

Amendments

—2002. Chapter 27:2 rewrote the section to the extent that a detailed comparison would be impracticable.

Chapter 228:1 substituted "paragraphs II and III" for "paragraph II" in par. I.

Chapter 228:2 added par. III.

236:112. Definitions.

For the purposes of this subdivision:

I. "Junk yard" means a place used for storing and keeping, or storing and selling, trading, or otherwise transferring old or scrap copper, brass, rope, rags, batteries, paper, trash, rubber debris, waste, or junked, dismantled, or wrecked motor vehicles, or parts thereof, iron, steel, or other old or scrap ferrous or nonferrous material. As used in this subdivision, the term includes, but is not limited to, the following types of junk yards:

(a) Automotive recycling yards, meaning a motor vehicle junk yard, as identified in subparagraph (c), the primary purpose of which is to salvage multiple motor vehicle parts and materials for recycling or reuse;

(b) Machinery junk yards, as defined in paragraph III; and

(c) Motor vehicle junk yards, meaning any place, not including the principal place of business of any motor vehicle dealer registered with the director of motor vehicles under RSA 261:104 and controlled under RSA 236:126, where the following are stored or deposited in a quantity equal in bulk to 2 or more motor vehicles:

(1) Motor vehicles which are no longer intended or in condition for legal use according to their original purpose including motor vehicles purchased for the purpose of dismantling the vehicles for parts or for use of the metal for scrap; and/or

(2) Used parts of motor vehicles or old iron, metal, glass, paper, cordage, or other waste or discarded or secondhand material which has been a part, or intended to be a part, of any motor vehicle.

II. "Local governing body" means the mayor and board of aldermen or the council of a city, the selectmen of a town, or the commissioners of a village district.

III. "Machinery junk yard" means any yard or field used as a place of storage in which there is displayed to the public view, junk machinery or scrap metal that occupies an area of 500 square feet.

IV. "Motor vehicle" means "motor vehicle" as defined by RSA 259:60, I, namely, any self-propelled vehicle not operated exclusively upon stationary tracks, including ski area vehicles.

V. "Motor vehicle dealer."

(a) "New motor vehicle dealer" means every person principally engaged in the business of buying, selling or exchanging new and secondhand motor vehicles, or tractors on commission or otherwise who maintains in operating condition, and in operation, and at which the dealer does a major portion of his business a place of business capable of housing indoors in one building in an area of 1200 square feet, 5 average-sized automobiles, devoted to the motor vehicle, or tractor business and gives mechanical service on the same and who holds a written contract with a manufacturer giving such person selling rights for new motor vehicles, or tractors, or with a distributor of such vehicles who, as such distributor, holds a manufacturer's franchise or contract giving selling rights on new motor vehicles, or tractors.

(b) "Used motor vehicle dealer" means every person or firm principally engaged in the business of buying, selling and exchanging secondhand motor vehicles or tractors, who maintains in operating condition and in operation and at which the dealer does the major portion of his business a place of business capable of housing indoors in one building, in an area of at least 1200 square feet, 5 average-sized motor vehicles devoted to the used motor vehicles, or tractor business, and gives mechanical service on the same and at which the repair of used motor vehicles, or tractors is subordinate or incidental to the business of buying, selling and exchanging the same.

(c) "Junk motor vehicle dealer" means any person or firm who has an established place of business at which he is engaged in the business of buying secondhand motor vehicles for the purpose of taking the same apart, or buying, and selling parts of secondhand motor vehicles, or tires, for the assembling of secondhand motor vehicle parts.

Source.

1939, 50:1. RL 165:22. RSA 267:1(b); 267-A:2. 1955, 275:1, par. 22. 1965, 372:1. 1967, 372:2. 1981, 87:1. 1985, 103:7, eff. Jan. 1, 1986. 2002, 27:3, 4, eff. July 1, 2002.

Amendments
—2002. Paragraph I: Rewritten to the extent that a detailed comparison would be impracticable.

Paragraph IV: Inserted "'motor vehicle' as defined by RSA 259:60, I, namely" following "means" and substituted "including ski area vehicles" for "originally intended for the use on public highways".

—1985. Paragraph II: Substituted "local governing" for "legislative" preceding "body" at the beginning of the paragraph.

NOTES TO DECISIONS

Analysis

Relation to Other Laws
Used motor vehicle dealers

Relation to Other Laws
In order to qualify as a motor vehicle junkyard under the city ordinance, the property had to contain two or more vehicles that were both unregistered and no longer intended for legal use on the public highways, and thus, Rochester, N.H. General Ordinances § 42.6(a)(32) effectively made it more difficult for a property to be classified as a motor vehicle junkyard because it contained an extra requirement not present in RSA 236:112, I(c)(1). Therefore, there was an actual conflict between RSA

236:112, I(c)(1) and N.H. General Ordinances § 42.6(a)(32), and since the express language of RSA 236:124 provided that state statutes in that particular field were intended to aid local ordinances, the city's ordinance, § 42.6(a)(32), controlled over the conflicting statutory provision set forth in RSA 236:112, I(c)(1). City of Rochester v. Corpening, 153 N.H. 571, 907 A.2d 383, 2006 N.H. LEXIS 73 (2006).

Used motor vehicle dealers
On petition for mandatory injunction ordering defendants to remove all junk from their property so as to comply with provisions relative to junk yards along federally funded highways, trial court erred in finding that defendants were entitled to exemption for used

motor vehicle dealers; in order to qualify for such exception under RSA 236:91, IV, used vehicle dealer must satisfy definition set forth in subparagraph V(b) of this section in order to be controlled under RSA 236:126. State v. Autoware, Inc., 133 N.H. 465, 578 A.2d 351, 1990 N.H. LEXIS 85 (1990).

236:113. Minimum Area Waiver Authorized.

The director of motor vehicles may in his discretion and after a public hearing waive the minimum 1200 square foot requirement specified in RSA 236:112, V(a) and (b).

Source.
RSA 267-A:2-a. 1975, 121:2. 1981, 87:1, eff. April 20, 1981.

236:114. Requirement for Operation or Maintenance.

A person shall not operate, establish, or maintain a junk yard or machinery junk yard until he (1) has obtained a license to operate a junk yard business and (2) has obtained a certificate of approval for the location of the junk yard.

Source.
RSA 267-A:3. 1965, 372:1. 1981, 87:1, eff. April 20, 1981.

NOTES TO DECISIONS

Cited:
Cited in Town of Henniker v. Homo, 136 N.H. 88, 612 A.2d 360, 1992 N.H. LEXIS 132 (1992).

236:115. Application for License and Certificate of Approval.

Application for the license and the certificate of approved location shall be made in writing to the local governing body of the municipality where it is proposed to locate the junk yard or automotive recycling yard. In municipalities having a zoning ordinance and a zoning board of adjustment, the application must be accompanied by a certificate from the board of adjustment that the proposed location is not within an established district restricted against such uses or otherwise contrary to the prohibitions of the zoning ordinance. The application shall include:

I. A description of the land to be included within the junk yard or automotive recycling yard, by reference to so-called permanent boundary markers.

II. Certification of compliance with best management practices established by the department of environmental services, for applications to establish automotive recycling yards and motor vehicle junk yards.

Source.
RSA 267-A:4. 1965, 372:1. 1981, 87:1. 1985, 103:8. 1992, 88:12, eff. Jan. 1, 1993. 2006, 100:1, eff. January 1, 2007.

Amendments
—**2006.** Rewritten to the extent that a detailed comparison would be impracticable.

—**1992.** Added "or automotive recycling yard" following "junk yard" in the first and third sentences.

—**1985.** Substituted "local governing" for "legislative" preceding "body" in the first sentence.

236:116. Time of Hearing.

A hearing on the application shall be held within the municipality not less than 2 nor more than 4 weeks from the date of the receipt of the application by the local governing body. Notice of the hearing shall be given to the applicant by mail, postage prepaid, to the address given in the application and the notice shall be published once in a newspaper having a circulation within the municipality, which publication shall be not less than 7 days before the date of the hearing.

Source.
RSA 267-A:5. 1965, 372:1. 1981, 87:1. 1985, 103:9, eff. Jan. 1, 1986.

Amendments
—**1985.** Substituted "local governing" for

"legislative" preceding "body" at the end of the first sentence.

236:117. License Requirements.

At the time and place set for hearing, the local governing body shall hear the applicant and all other persons wishing to be heard on the application for a license to operate, establish, or maintain the junk yard or automotive recycling yard. In passing upon the application, it shall take into account the suitability of the applicant with reference to his ability to comply with the fencing requirements or other reasonable regulations concerning the proposed junk yard or automotive recycling yard, to any record of convictions for any type of larceny or receiving of stolen goods, and to any other matter within the purposes of this subdivision.

Source.
RSA 267-A:6. 1965, 372:1. 1981, 87:1. 1985, 103:10. 1992, 88:13, eff. Jan. 1, 1993.

Amendments
—**1992.** Added "or automotive recycling

yard" following "junk yard" in the first and second sentences.

—**1985.** Substituted "local governing" for "legislative" preceding "body" in the first sentence.

236:118. Location Requirements.

At the time and place set for hearing, the local governing body shall hear the applicant and all other persons wishing to be heard on the application for certificate of approval for the location of the junk yard or automotive recycling yard. In passing upon the application, after proof of legal ownership or right to the use of the property by the applicant for the license period, it shall take into account the nature and development of surrounding property, such as the proximity of churches, schools, hospitals, public buildings or other places of public gatherings; and whether or not the use of the proposed location can be reasonably prevented from affecting the public health, safety, or morals by reason of offensive or unhealthy odors or smoke, or of other causes. In no case may a license be granted for a new junk yard or automotive recycling yard located less than 660 feet from the right-of-way lines of class I, class II, class III, or class III-a highways or located less than 300 feet from the right-of-way lines of class IV, class V and class VI highways.

Source.
RSA 267-A:7. 1965, 372:1. 1981, 87:1. 1985, 103:11. 1992, 265:18, eff. July 1, 1992; 265:21, eff. Jan. 1, 1993.

Amendments
—1992. Chapter 265:18 deleted "and" preceding "class III" and inserted "or class III-a" thereafter in the third sentence.

Chapter 265:21 inserted "or automotive recycling yard" following "junk yard" in the first and third sentences.

—1985. Substituted "local governing" for "legislative" preceding "body" in the first sentence and made other minor stylistic changes throughout the section.

Nullification of 1992 amendment.
1992, 88:14, provided for the amendment of this section; however, under the terms of 1992, 265:22, the amendment did not take effect.

Cross References.
Classification of highways, see RSA 229:5.

236:119. Nuisance.

Any junk yard or machinery junk yard located or maintained in violation of the provisions of this subdivision is hereby declared a nuisance, and the same may be abated on complaint of any prosecuting officer as provided in RSA 236:128.

Source.
1939, 50:3. RL 165:24. RSA 267:3. 1955, 275:1, par. 24. 1981, 87:1, eff. April 20, 1981. 2003, 118:1, eff. Jan. 1, 2004.

Amendments
—2003. Added "as provided in RSA 236:128" following "prosecuting officer".

236:120. Aesthetic Considerations.

At the hearing regarding location of the junk yard or automotive recycling yard, the local governing body may also take into account the clean, wholesome, and attractive environment which has been declared to be of vital importance to the continued stability and development of the tourist and recreational industry of the state and the general welfare of its citizens by considering whether or not the use of the proposed location can be reasonably prevented from having an unfavorable effect thereon. In this connection the local governing body may consider collectively the type of road servicing the junk yard or automotive recycling yard or from which the junk yard or automotive recycling yard may be seen, the natural or artificial barriers protecting the junk yard or automotive recycling yard from view, the proximity of the proposed junk yard or automotive recycling yard to established tourist and recreational areas or main access routes thereto, as well as the reasonable availability of other suitable sites for the junk yard or automotive recycling yard.

Source.

RSA 267-A:8. 1965, 372:1. 1981, 87:1. 1985, 103:12. 1992, 88:15, eff. Jan. 1, 1993.

Amendments

—1992. Inserted "or automotive recycling yard" following "junk yard" wherever it appeared.

—1985. Substituted "local governing" for "legislative" preceding "body" in the first and second sentences.

236:121. Grant or Denial of Application; Renewal; Appeal.

I. After the hearing the local governing body shall, within 2 weeks, make a finding as to whether or not the application should be granted, giving notice of their finding to the applicant by mail, postage prepaid, to the address given on the application. If approved, the license, including the certificate of approved location, shall be forthwith issued to remain in effect until the following April 1. Approval is personal to the applicant and is not assignable.

II. Licenses shall be renewed thereafter upon payment of the annual license fee without a hearing, if all provisions of this subdivision are complied with during the license period, if the junk yard does not become a public nuisance under the common law or is not a nuisance under RSA 236:119, and if the applicant is not convicted of any type of larceny or of receiving stolen goods. In addition, applications to renew a license to operate an automotive recycling yard or motor vehicle junk yard shall include certification of compliance with best management practices established by the department of environmental services for the automobile salvage industry.

III. A writ of certiorari lies from the denial of the application to the superior court of the county in which the proposed location is situated.

Source.

RSA 267-A:9. 1965, 372:1. 1981, 87:1. 1985, 103:13, eff. Jan. 1, 1986. 2006, 100:2, eff. January 1, 2007.

—1985. Substituted "local governing" for "legislative" preceding "body" in the first sentence.

Amendments

—2006. Rewritten to the extent that a detailed comparison would be impracticable.

236:122. License Fees.

The annual license fee is not more than $250 to be paid at the time the application is made and annually thereafter in the event of renewal. If the application is not granted, the fee shall be returned to the applicant.

Source.

RSA 267-A:10. 1965, 372:1. 1981, 87:1, eff. April 20, 1981. 2006, 71:1, eff. April 25, 2006.

Amendments

—2006. Substituted "fee is not more than $250" for "fee is $25".

236:123. Fencing.

Before use, a new junk yard or automotive recycling yard shall be completely surrounded with a solidly constructed fence at least 6 feet in height which substantially screens the area and with a suitable gate which shall be closed and locked except during the working hours of the junk yard or automotive recycling yard or when the applicant or his agent is within. All motor vehicles and parts stored or deposited by the applicant shall be kept within the enclosure of the junk yard or automotive recycling yard except as removal is necessary for its transportation in the reasonable course of the business. All wrecking or other work on such motor vehicles and parts and all burning of vehicles shall be accomplished within the enclosure. Where the topography, natural growth of timber, a natural barrier, or other considerations accomplish the purposes of this subdivision in whole or in part, the fencing requirements hereunder may be reduced by the local governing body, upon granting the license. Any citizen of the municipality may apply for writ of certiorari to the superior court for the county in which the new junk yard or automotive recycling yard is located to review the action of the local governing body.

Source.
RSA 267-A:11. 1965, 372:1. 1981, 87:1. 1985, 103:14. 1992, 88:16, eff. Jan. 1, 1993.

Amendments
—**1992.** Inserted "or automotive recycling yard" following "junk yard" in two places in the first sentence and in the second and fifth sentences.

—**1985.** Substituted "local governing" for "legislative" preceding "body" wherever it appeared in the second paragraph.

236:124. Effect of Local Ordinances.

This subdivision is not in derogation of zoning ordinances or ordinances for the control of junk yards now or hereafter established within the proper exercise of the police power granted to municipalities, but rather is in aid thereof. Specific local ordinances shall control when in conflict with this subdivision.

Source.
RSA 267-A:12. 1965, 372:1. 1981, 87:1, eff. April 20, 1981.

NOTES TO DECISIONS

Cited:
Cited in Town of Henniker v. Homo, 136 N.H. 88, 612 A.2d 360; 1992 N.H. LEXIS 132 (1992).

236:125. Established Junk Yards or Automotive Recycling Yards.

For the purposes of this subdivision the location of junk yards or automotive recycling yards already established are considered approved by the local governing body of the municipality where located and the owner of the yard considered suitable for the issuance of a license. Within 60 days from the passage of this subdivision, however, the owner shall furnish the local governing body the information as to location which is required in an application, together with the license fee, and the local governing body shall issue him a license valid until April 1, 1966, at which time the owner may apply for a renewal. The owner shall comply with all other provisions of this subdivision including the fencing requirements set forth in RSA 236:123.

Source.

RSA 267-A:13. 1965, 372:1. 1981, 87:1. 1985,
103:15. 1992, 88:17, eff. Jan. 1, 1993.

References in text.

The date of passage of this subdivision, referred to in the second sentence, was April 20,
1981.

Amendments

—**1992.** Added "or automotive recycling
yards" following "junk yards" in the section
catchline and in the first sentence.

—**1985.** Substituted "local governing" for
"legislative" preceding "body" throughout the
first and second sentences.

236:126. Motor Vehicle Dealers.

Both new and used car dealers are hereby required to remove from their
premises registered with the director of motor vehicles as their principal place
of business any motor vehicle which is of the type referred to in RSA 236:112,
I, under the definition of junk yard, within at least 160 days from the date of
its original entrance thereon. Any other location within the same community
used by such dealer shall be subject to the terms of this subdivision if in its
operation it falls within the confines of the definition of the term junk yard as
defined in this subdivision.

Source.

RSA 267-A:14. 1965, 372:1. 1969, 189:1.
1981, 87:1, eff. April 20, 1981.

NOTES TO DECISIONS

Used motor vehicle dealers

On petition for mandatory injunction ordering defendants to remove all junk from their
property so as to comply with provisions relative to junk yards along federally funded highways, trial court erred in finding that defendants were entitled to exemption for used
motor vehicle dealers; in order to qualify for
such exception under RSA 236:91, IV, used
vehicle dealer must satisfy definition set forth
in RSA 236:112, V(b) in order to be controlled
under this section. State v. Autoware, Inc., 133
N.H. 465, 578 A.2d 351, 1990 N.H. LEXIS 85
(1990).

236:127. Penalty.

Any person who is in violation of any provisions of this subdivision shall be
guilty of a violation and each day or fraction thereof shall constitute a separate
offense.

Source.

RSA 267-A:15. 1965, 372:1. 1973, 531:89.
1981, 87:1, eff. April 20, 1981.

Cross References.

Classification of crimes, see RSA 625:9.
Sentences, see RSA 651.

NOTES TO DECISIONS

Jury trial

Defendants were not entitled to jury trial
despite imposition of $6,060 in fines where
defendants had committed 606 separate violations of local ordinance against maintaining
unlicensed junk yard, since maximum fine for
any single violation was $100. Town of Henni-
ker v. Homo, 136 N.H. 88, 612 A.2d 360, 1992
N.H. LEXIS 132 (1992).

236:128. Local Enforcement; Injunction; Civil Penalties.

The governing body, elected or appointed officers or other appointed agents of a town, city, or unincorporated place, or a private person pursuant to RSA 236:129 may initiate proceedings for the enforcement of the provisions of this subdivision. In addition to the criminal penalty in RSA 236:127, enforcement may be by the following:

I. The local governing body may obtain a mandatory injunction to end the violation.

II. If the local governing body does not obtain such an injunction the attorney general may obtain an injunction in the name of the state.

III. The local governing body or other enforcement official of the town, city, or unincorporated place, after providing notice, may impose a civil penalty of up to $50 for each day upon any person whose land is deemed a nuisance pursuant to RSA 236:119 until such time as the nuisance is removed or abated to the satisfaction of the governing body, or until the owner of the land acquires a license and is in compliance with the provisions of this subdivision. The building inspector or other local official with the authority to enforce the provisions of this section may commence an action to collect the civil penalty in the district court. Imposition of a civil penalty under this paragraph shall not relieve the owner of any requirement to comply with the provisions of this subdivision, nor shall it preclude the imposition of further actions or remedies under this chapter. The proceeds from the assessment of civil penalties under this section shall be for the use of the town, city, or unincorporated place. This paragraph shall not apply to automotive recycling yards and junkyards properly licensed or pending license renewal under this subdivision.

Source.
RSA 267-A:16. 1965, 372:1. 1981, 87:1. 1985, 103:16, eff. Jan. 1, 1986. 2003, 118:2, eff. Jan. 1, 2004.

—1985. Substituted "local governing" for "legislative" preceding "body" throughout the section.

Amendments
—2003. Rewritten to the extent that a detailed comparison would be impracticable.

NOTES TO DECISIONS

Cited:
Cited in Town of Henniker v. Homo, 136 N.H. 88, 612 A.2d 360, 1992 N.H. LEXIS 132 (1992).

236:129. Private Persons.

Any person owning real property whose property is directly affected by the site of a junk yard or automotive recycling yard maintained in violation of the provisions of this subdivision may in writing addressed to the local governing body request the local governing body to take appropriate action under this subdivision. A copy of the written communication to the local governing body shall be mailed to the person complained of. If the local governing body shall not, within 30 days thereafter, make a determination that a junk yard or automotive recycling yard does exist and issue the appropriate order, such person may, in his own name and in his own right, seek appropriate injunctive relief for the enforcement of this subdivision in the superior court.

Source.
RSA 267-A:17. 1967, 372:1. 1969, 415:1. 1981, 87:1. 1985, 103:17. 1992, 88:18, eff. Jan. 1, 1993.

Amendments
—**1992.** Inserted "or automotive recycling yard" following "junk yard" in the first and third sentences.

—**1985.** Substituted "local governing" for "legislative" preceding "body" throughout the section.

TITLE XXXIX
AERONAUTICS

CHAPTER 424

AIRPORT ZONING

Effective date of amendments

—1985, 402. 1985, 402:41, II, provided that the provisions of 1985, 402:6 which affected this chapter would take effect when the department of transportation became operational on the date set according to 1983, 372:5, II. Pursuant to 1983, 372:5, II, the joint committee on implementation of reorganization and the govern determined the effective date upon which the department became operational to be Feb. 28, 1986.

Separability clause.

1941, 145:1-9 were subject to a separability clause. See 1945, 145:10.

Cross References.

Control of tall structures, see RSA 422-B.
Zoning generally, see RSA 672 et seq.

RESEARCH REFERENCES

ALR.

Liability of owner of wires, poles, or structures struck by aircraft for resulting injury or damage. 49 A.L.R.5th 659.

Validity of municipal regulation of aircraft flight paths or altitudes. 36 A.L.R.3d 1314.

424:1. Definitions.

As used in this chapter unless the context otherwise requires:

I. "Airport" means any area of land or water, whether constructed or not, which has been approved by the commissioner as a site for the landing and taking-off of aircraft or utilized or to be utilized by the public as a point of arrival or departure by air.

II. "Airport hazard" means any structure, tree, smoke, steam, dust or other substance which obstructs the aerial approaches of a publicly owned airport or impairs the reasonable visibility in the vicinity thereof, electrical impulses and disturbances which interfere with radio aids or communications and lights which might result in glare in the vision of pilots of aircraft or be confused with airport lights.

III. An airport is "publicly-owned" if the portion thereof used for the landing and taking-off of aircraft is owned by a governmental body, political subdivision, public agency, or other public corporation.

IV. "Department" means the department of transportation.

V. "Person" means any individual, firm, co-partnership, corporation, company, association, joint stock association or body politic, and includes any trustee, receiver, assignee, or other similar representative thereof.

VI. "Structure" means any object constructed or installed by man, including such objects although regulated or licensed by other provisions of law.

VII. "Tree" means any object of natural growth.

Source.
1941, 145:1; 199:40. RL 51:78. RSA 424:1. 1955, 58:1. 1985, 402:6, I(c)(3), 32.

References in text.
The commissioner referred to in this section is the commissioner of transportation. For provisions relating to the department of transportation, see RSA 21-L.

Amendments
—1985. Paragraph I: Substituted "commis-

sioner" for "director of aeronautics" preceding "as a site".

Paragraph IV: Rewritten to the extent that a detailed comparison would be impracticable.

—1955. Paragraphs I, II: Rewritten to the extent that a detailed comparison would be impracticable.

Effective date of amendments
—1985. See note preceding RSA 424:1 regarding effective date of 1985, 402:6.

424:2. Airport Hazards Not in Public Interest.

It is hereby found and declared that an airport hazard endangers the lives and property of users of the airport and of occupants of land in its vicinity, and also, if of the obstruction type, in effect reduces the size of the area available for the landing, taking-off and maneuvering of aircraft, thus tending to destroy or impair the utility of the airport and the public investment therein, and is therefore not in the interest of the public health, public safety, or general welfare.

Source.
1941, 145:2. RL 51:79.

424:3. Preparation of Airport-Approach Plans.

The department of transportation is hereby empowered and directed to formulate and adopt, and from time to time as may be necessary revise, an airport-approach plan for each publicly-owned airport in the state. Each such plan shall indicate the circumstances in which structures and trees are or would be airport hazards, the area within which measures for the protection of the airport's aerial approaches should be taken, and what the height limits and other objectives of such measures should be. In adopting or revising any such plan, the department shall consider, among other things, the character of the flying operations expected to be conducted at the airport, the nature of the terrain, the height of existing structures and trees above the level of the airport, and the practicability of lowering or removing existing obstructions, and all other material matters, and the department may obtain and consider the views of the agency of the federal government charged with the fostering of civil aeronautics as to the aerial approaches necessary to safe flying operations at the airport.

Source.

1941, 145:3. RL 51:80. RSA 424:3. 1985, 402:6, I(c)(3).

Amendments

—**1985.** Substituted "department of transportation" for "aeronautics commission" at the beginning of the first sentence, "department" for "commission" in two places in the third sentence.

Effective date of amendments

—**1985.** See note preceding RSA 424:1 regarding effective date of 1985, 402:6.

Cross References.

Fees of department of transportation for rendition of services under section, see RSA 422:37.

NOTES TO DECISIONS

Cited:

Cited in Treisman v. Town of Bedford, 132 N.H. 54, 563 A.2d 786, 1989 N.H. LEXIS 75 (1989), A2d 786.

RESEARCH REFERENCES

ALR.

Zoning regulations limiting use of property near airport as taking of property. 18 A.L.R.4th 542.

424:4. Privately-owned Airports.

The department of transportation is hereby empowered and directed to formulate and adopt, and from time to time as may be necessary revise, an airport-approach plan for such airports as are privately owned but which have been licensed for commercial operation, have facilities available for public use and are necessary in the opinion of the department for the maintenance of an effective airway system in the state. Every privately-owned airport so designated by the department is hereby declared to be eligible for zoning protection and for the purposes hereof shall be deemed to be a publicly-owned airport for the purposes of airport zoning as provided in this chapter.

Source.

1949, 53:2. RSA 424:4. 1985, 402:6, I(c)(3).

Amendments

—**1985.** Substituted "department of transportation" for "aeronautics commission" preceding "is hereby" and "department" for "commission" preceding "for the maintenance" in the first sentence and following "designated by the" in the second sentence.

Effective date of amendments

—**1985 amendment.** See note preceding RSA 424:1 regarding effective date of 1985, 402:6.

Cross References.

State airways system, see RSA 422:15.

NOTES TO DECISIONS

Noncommercial heliports

This section did not invalidate town zoning amendment allowing the storage and operation of helicopters, since helicopter amendment applied only to private, noncommercial heliports. Treisman v. Town of Bedford, 132 N.H. 54, 563 A.2d 786, 1989 N.H. LEXIS 75 (1989).

Cited:

Cited in Opinion of the Justices, 95 N.H. 548, 65 A.2d 700, 1949 N.H. LEXIS 221 (1949).

424:5. Adoption of Airport Zoning Regulations.

I. Every town having within its territorial limits an airport, or an area approved as an airport site by the commissioner, shall adopt, administer and enforce, under the police power and in the manner and upon the conditions hereinafter prescribed, airport zoning regulations applicable to such area, which regulations shall divide the area into zones, and, within such zones, specify the land uses permitted, regulate and restrict the height to which structures or trees may be erected or allowed to grow, and regulate and restrict the creation and discharge of smoke, steam, dust or other obstructions to visibility, electrical impulses and disturbances which interfere with radio aids or communication and regulate and restrict lighting as may be necessary to effectuate the safe approach to the airport.

II. In the event that a town has adopted, or hereafter adopts, a general zoning ordinance regulating, among other things, the height of buildings, any airport zoning regulations adopted for the same area or portion thereof under this chapter, may be incorporated in and made a part of such general zoning regulations, and be administered and enforced in connection therewith, but such general zoning regulations shall not limit the effectiveness or scope of the regulations adopted hereunder.

III. Any zoning or other regulations applicable to any area within which, according to an airport-approach plan adopted by the department, measures should be taken for the protection of airport approaches, including not only any airport zoning regulations adopted under this chapter but any zoning or other regulations dealing with the same or similar matters that have been or may be adopted under authority other than that conferred by this chapter, shall be consistent with, and conform to, the department's approach plan for such area, and shall be amended from time to time as may be necessary to conform to any revision of the plan that may be made by the department.

IV. All airport zoning regulations adopted hereunder shall be reasonable, and none shall require the removal, lowering, or other change or alteration of any structure or tree not conforming to the regulations when adopted or amended, or otherwise interfere with the continuance of any nonconforming use, except as provided in RSA 424:6, I.

V. If any city or town fails to adopt within a reasonable time airport zoning regulations, the department may, for the protection of the public safety, adopt and from time to time as may be necessary amend or repeal such regulations for such city or town until airport zoning regulations herein provided for are adopted by such city or town.

Source.
1941, 145:4. RL 51:81. RSA 424:5. 1955, 58:2. 1985, 402:6, I(c)(3).

References in text.
The commissioner referred to in this section is the commissioner of transportation. For provisions relating to the department of transportation, see RSA 21-L.

Amendments
—1985. Paragraph I: Substituted "commissioner" for "director" following "site by the".

Paragraph III: Substituted "department" for "commission" preceding "measures", "department's" for "commission's" following "conform to, the" and "department" for "commission" following "may be made by the".

Paragraph V: Substituted "department" for "commission" preceding "may, for the protection".

—1955. Paragraph I: Rewritten to the extent that a detailed comparison would be impracticable.

Effective date of amendments
—1985. See note preceding RSA 424:1 regarding effective date of 1985, 402:6.

Cross References.
Procedure for adoption of airport zoning regulations, see RSA 424:7.

NOTES TO DECISIONS

Analysis
1. Construction with other laws
2. Noncommercial heliports

1. Construction with other laws
The fact that a town, in adopting a zoning ordinance, had complied with the requirements of this chapter, relating to airport zoning, did not render compliance with RSA 31:60-89 unnecessary, and zoning ordinance which did not provide for board of adjustment required by RSA 31:66 was, therefore, invalid. Town of Jaffrey v. Heffernan, 104 N.H. 249, 183 A.2d 246, 1962 N.H. LEXIS 61 (1962).

2. Noncommercial heliports
This section did not invalidate town zoning amendment allowing the storage and operation of helicopters, since helicopter amendment applied only to private, noncommercial heliports. Treisman v. Town of Bedford, 132 N.H. 54, 563 A.2d 786, 1989 N.H. LEXIS 75 (1989).

Cited:
Cited in Manchester Airport Authority v. Romano, 120 N.H. 166, 412 A.2d 1020, 1980 N.H. LEXIS 255 (1980).

424:6. Permits and Variances.

I. PERMITS.   Where advisable to facilitate the enforcement of zoning regulations adopted pursuant to this chapter, a system may be established for granting permits to establish or construct new structures and other uses and to replace existing structures and other uses or make substantial changes therein or substantial repairs thereof. In any event, before any nonconforming structure or tree may be replaced, substantially altered or repaired, rebuilt, allowed to grow higher, or replanted, a permit must be secured from the administrative agency authorized to administer and enforce the regulations, authorizing such replacement, change or repair. No such permit shall be granted that would allow the structure or tree in question to be made higher or become a greater hazard to air navigation than it was when the applicable regulation was adopted; and whenever the administrative agency determines that a nonconforming structure or tree has been abandoned or more than 80 percent torn down, destroyed, deteriorated, or decayed: (a) no permit shall be granted that would allow said structure or tree to exceed the applicable height limit or otherwise deviate from the zoning regulations, but a permit shall be issued as of right if the structure as erected or altered is in conformance with the regulations or will not constitute a greater hazard than the structure that is replaced or altered; and (b) whether application is made for a permit under this paragraph or not, the said agency may by appropriate action compel the owner of the nonconforming structure or tree to lower, remove, reconstruct, or equip such object as may be necessary to conform to the regulations. Except as indicated, all applications for permits for replacement, change or repair of nonconforming uses shall be granted.

II. VARIANCES.   Any person desiring to erect any structure, or increase the height of any structure, or permit the growth of any tree, or otherwise use his property in violation of airport zoning regulations adopted hereunder may apply to the zoning board of adjustment for a variance from the zoning regulations in question. Such variances shall be allowed where a literal application or enforcement of the regulations would result in practical difficulty or unnecessary hardship and the relief granted would not be contrary to the public interest but do substantial justice and be in accordance with the spirit of the regulations.

III. OBSTRUCTION MARKING AND LIGHTING.   In granting any permit or variance under this section, the administrative agency or zoning board of adjustment may, if it deems such action advisable to effectuate the purposes hereof and reasonable in the circumstances, so condition such permit or variance as to require the owner of the structure or tree in question to permit the political subdivision, at its own expense, to install, operate, and maintain suitable obstruction markers and obstruction lights thereon.

Source.
1941, 145:5. RL 51:82. 2001, 40:1, eff. Aug. 7, 2001.

Amendments
—**2001.** Paragraph II: Substituted "zoning board of adjustment" for "board of appeals, as provided herein" in the first sentence.
Paragraph III: Inserted "zoning board of adjustment" for "board of appeals".

424:6-a. Application of Zoning and Planning Laws.

The provisions of title LXIV shall apply to procedures for adoption of local airport zoning regulations, the administration and enforcement of the requirements of local airport zoning regulations, and procedures for rehearing and appeal from any action taken by a local land use board, building inspector, or the local legislative body with respect to airport zoning regulations.

Source.
2001, 40:2, eff. Aug. 7, 2001.

424:7. Procedure.
[Repealed 2001, 40:3, I, eff. Aug. 7, 2001.]

Former section(s).
Former RSA 424:7, which was derived from 1941, 145:6; and RL 51:83, related to procedure for adoption and administration of airport zoning regulations and board of appeals.

424:8. Applications of Laws.
[Repealed 2001, 40:3, II, eff. Aug. 7, 2001.]

Former section(s).
Former RSA 424:8, which was derived from 1941, 145:7; and RL 51:84, related to applications of laws.

424:9. Enforcement and Remedies.
[Repealed 2001, 40:3, III, eff. Aug. 7, 2001.]

Former section(s).
Former RSA 424:9, which was derived from 1941, 145:8; RL 51:85; RSA 424:9; and 1973, 528:291, related to enforcement and remedies.

424:10. Acquisition of Air Rights.

In any case in which: (1) it is desired to remove, lower, or otherwise terminate a nonconforming use; or (2) the approach protection necessary according to the department's airport-approach plan cannot, because of constitutional limitations, be provided by airport zoning regulations hereunder; or (3) it appears advisable that the necessary approach protection be provided by acquisition of property rights rather than by airport zoning regulations, the town within which the property or nonconforming use is located, the town owning the airport or served by it, or the governor and council, upon recommendation of the department, may acquire, by purchase, grant, or condemnation in the manner provided by law by which towns or the governor and council are authorized to acquire real property for public purposes, such an air right, easement, or other estate or interest in the property or nonconforming use in question, and so may acquire a substitute property, structure and easement and convey the same to anyone whose structures, easements and property are or may be a nonconforming use, as may be necessary to effectuate the purposes hereof.

Source.
1941, 145:9. RL 51:86. RSA 424:10. 1985, 402:6, I(c)(3).

Amendments
—**1985.** Substituted "department's" for "commission's" following "according to the" and "department" for "commission" following "recommendation of the".

Effective date of amendments
—**1985.** See note preceding RSA 424:1 regarding effective date of 1985, 402:6.

Cross References.
Eminent domain procedure generally, see RSA 498-A.
Leasing of air rights, see RSA 48-B.

TITLE XL

AGRICULTURE, HORTICULTURE AND ANIMAL HUSBANDRY

CHAPTER 432

SOIL CONSERVATION AND FARMLAND PRESERVATION

Nuisance Liability of Agricultural Operations

Cross References.
Regulation of nuisances generally, see RSA 147:1 et seq.

432:32. Agricultural Operation.

"Agricultural operation" when used in this subdivision includes any farm, agricultural or farming activity as defined in RSA 21:34-a.

Source.
1985, 72:1, eff. July 1, 1985.

432:33. Immunity from Suit.

No agricultural operation shall be found a public or private nuisance as a result of changed conditions in or around the locality of the agricultural operation, if such agricultural operation has been in operation for one year or more and if it was not a nuisance at the time it began operation. This section shall not apply when any aspect of the agricultural operation is determined to be injurious to public health or safety under RSA 147:1 or RSA 147:2.

Source.
1985, 72:1, eff. July 1, 1985.

432:34. Negligent or Improper Operations.

The provisions of this subdivision shall not apply if a nuisance results from the negligent or improper operation of an agricultural operation. Agricultural operations shall not be found to be negligent or improper when they conform to federal, state and local laws, rules and regulations.

Source.

1985, 72:1, eff. July 1, 1985.

432:35. Limits.

Nothing contained in this subdivision shall be construed to modify or limit the duties and authority conferred upon the department of environmental services under RSA 485 or RSA 485-A or the commissioner of agriculture, markets, and food under any of the chapters in this title.

Source.

1985, 72:1. 1989, 339:27. 1995, 130:5, eff. July 23, 1995. 1996, 228:108, eff. July 1, 1996.

Revision note.

Pursuant to 1986, 202:6, II, substituted "division of water supply and pollution control" for "water supply and pollution control commission".

Amendments

—1996. Substituted "department of environmental services" for "division of water supply and pollution control".

—1995. Substituted "commissioner of agriculture, markets, and food" for "commissioner of agriculture".

—1989. Substituted "RSA 485 or RSA 485-A" for "RSA 148 or RSA 149".

TITLE L
WATER MANAGEMENT AND PROTECTION

CHAPTER 483

NEW HAMPSHIRE RIVERS MANAGEMENT AND PROTECTION PROGRAM

Cross References.
Environmental audits, see RSA 147-E.

RESEARCH REFERENCES

New Hampshire Practice.
15 N.H.P. Land Use Planning and Zoning § 39.05.

New Hampshire Code of Administrative Rules.
Rules of the Department of Environmental

Services—Office of the Commissioner, Env-C 701.01 et seq., New Hampshire Code of Administrative Rules Annotated.

483:1. Statement of Policy.

New Hampshire's rivers and streams comprise one of its most important natural resources, historically vital to New Hampshire's commerce, industry, tourism, and the quality of life of New Hampshire people. It is the policy of the state to ensure the continued viability of New Hampshire rivers as valued economic and social assets for the benefit of present and future generations. The state shall encourage and assist in the development of river corridor management plans and regulate the quantity and quality of instream flow along certain protected rivers or segments of rivers to conserve and protect outstanding characteristics including recreational, fisheries, wildlife, environmental, cultural, historical, archaeological, scientific, ecological, aesthetic, community significance, agricultural, and public water supply so that these valued characteristics shall endure as part of the river uses to be enjoyed by New Hampshire people.

Source.
1989, 339:1. 1990, 233:21, eff. June 26, 1990.

Amendments
—1990. Deleted "and" preceding "commu-

nity significance" and added "agricultural, and public water supply" thereafter in the third sentence.

483:2. Program Established; Intent.

There is established within the department of environmental services the New Hampshire rivers management and protection program. It is the intent of the legislature that the New Hampshire rivers management and protection program shall complement and reinforce existing state and federal water quality laws, and that in-stream flows are maintained along protected rivers, or segments thereof, in a manner that will enhance or not diminish the enjoyment of outstanding river characteristics pursuant to RSA 483:1. It is also the intent of the legislature that, through said program, the scenic beauty and recreational potential of such rivers shall be restored and maintained, that riparian interests shall be respected, and that nothing in this chapter shall be interpreted to preempt any land and zoning authority granted to municipal bodies under RSA title LXIV.

Source.
1989, 339:1. 1990, 233:1, eff. June 26, 1990.

Amendments
—1990. Deleted "and" preceding "that riparian" and added "and that nothing in this

chapter shall be interpreted to preempt any land and zoning authority granted to municipal bodies under RSA title LXIV" following "respected" in the third sentence.

483:3. Rivers Coordinator.

There is established in the department of environmental services, a state rivers coordinator, who shall be a classified employee qualified by reason of education and experience, and who shall administer the New Hampshire rivers management and protection program.

Source.
1989, 339:1, eff. Jan. 1, 1990. 2007, 285:1, eff. September 1, 2007.

Amendments
—2007. Deleted "office of planning" preceding "department".

483:4. Definitions.

In this chapter:

I. "Advisory committee" means the rivers management advisory committee established in RSA 483:8.

II. "Agriculture" means agriculture as defined in RSA 21:34-a.

III. "Breached dam" means any dam which impounds water at less than 80 percent of its original design level at seasonal high flows and for which the original configuration of the dam can still be determined.

IV. "Channel alteration" means any human activity which changes the character of a river or stream channel including, but not limited to, filling, dredging, relocating, excavating, cleaning, deepening, widening, straightening or riprapping.

V. "Commissioner" means the commissioner, department of environmental services.

VI. "Dam" means any artificial barrier, including appurtenant works, across a river which impounds or diverts water.

VII. "Department" means the department of environmental services.

VIII. "Designated river" means that portion of a river which has been specifically designated by the general court pursuant to RSA 483:15.

IX. "Existing dam" means any dam which has not deteriorated or been breached or modified to the point where it no longer impounds water at 80 percent or more of its original design level at seasonal high flows.

IX-a. "Flowage right" means an easement to flow water over the land of others.

X. "Free-flowing," as applied to any river or river segment, means existing or flowing in a natural condition without artificial impoundment, diversion, channel alterations, or other modifications and without consideration of upstream flow management.

XI. "Instream public uses" means those uses which comprise the state's interests in surface waters including, but not limited to: navigation; recreation; fishing; storage; conservation; maintenance and enhancement of aquatic and fish life; fish and wildlife habitat; wildlife; the protection of water quality and public health; pollution abatement; aesthetic beauty; and hydroelectric energy production.

XII. "Interbasin transfer" means any transfer of water for use from one river drainage basin to another.

XIII. "New dam" means any dam which requires the construction or enlargement of any impoundment or diversion structure.

XIV. "New hydroelectric power facilities" means the construction, operation, or installation of electric generating units at dams where no hydroelectric power generation has occurred for a period of 6 years or more.

XV. [Repealed.]

XVI. "Protected instream flow" means a constant minimum stream flow level established to maintain water for present and future instream public uses.

XVII. "River" means a flowing body of water or a segment or tributary of such water body.

XVIII. "River corridor" means the river and the land area located within a distance of 1,320 feet of the normal high water mark or to the landward extent of the 100 year floodplain as designated by the Federal Emergency Management Agency, whichever distance is larger.

XIX. "River drainage basin" means the Androscoggin, Coastal, Connecticut, Merrimack, Piscataqua, and Saco river basins as delineated on a map compiled by the department.

Source.
1989, 339:1. 1990, 233:2. 1992, 261:8, eff. July 14, 1992. 2007, 285:10, eff. September 1, 2007.

Revision note.
Substituted "RSA 483:15" for "RSA 483:14" at the end of par. VIII in light of the redesignation of RSA 483:14 as RSA 483:15.

Amendments
—2007. Paragraph XV: Repealed.

—1992. Paragraph IX-a: Added.

—1990. Rewritten to the extent that a detailed comparison would be impractical.

483:5. Coordination With Federal Statutes.

For the purposes of section 10(a)(2)(A) of the Federal Power Act, those rivers or segments designated under this chapter and any state or local management plans developed pursuant to this chapter shall constitute one element of the state comprehensive plan for river conservation and development. Designated rivers or segments shall constitute protected waterways under the provisions of the Public Utilities Regulatory Policies Act, section 210(j)(2), 16 U.S.C. section 824a-3(j)(2).

Source.
1989, 339:1. 1990, 233:3, eff. June 26, 1990.

References in text.
Section 10(a)(2)(A) of the Federal Power Act, referred to in this section, is classified to 16 U.S.C.S. § 803(a)(2)(A).

Amendments
—1990. Rewrote the first sentence, substituted "designated" for "protected" preceding "rivers or segments" and deleted "of such rivers so designated" thereafter and substituted "under" for "with respect to" preceding "the provi-

sions" in the second sentence and deleted the third sentence.

New dams.
1990, 233:17, II, as amended by 1991, 338:5, eff. June 28, 1991, provided: "Notwithstanding the provisions of RSA 483, but for the purposes of RSA 483:5, no new dams shall be permitted, between June 29, 1988 and July 1, 1993, on the main stem of the Connecticut River, excepting that segment north of the confluence of the Israel River in the town of Lancaster."

483:6. Nominations; Criteria.

I. Any New Hampshire organization or resident may nominate a river or any segment or segments of such river for protection by submitting to the commissioner a description of the river or segment or segments of such river and its values and characteristics. The completed nomination shall be submitted to the rivers coordinator on or before June 1 in order for it to be considered in the next legislative session. This nomination shall include, but not be limited to, an assessment of fisheries; geologic and hydrologic features; vegetation; wildlife; historical and archaeological features; open space and recreation features and potential; water quality and quantity; dams, buildings, and other manmade structures; riparian interests, including flowage rights known by the nominating individual or group, and other pertinent instream and riverbank information. The nominating party shall hold at least one public meeting on the information prior to final submittal to the commissioner. The nominating party shall advertise the meeting in cooperation with the rivers coordinator and shall give written notice to the governing body of any municipality where segments of the river are located. The rivers coordinator shall provide assistance to the nominating party in the presentation of the nomination at the public meeting.

II. The rivers coordinator shall assist and cooperate with the nominator or nominating organization and shall, within 120 days of receipt of a nomination, review the nomination and prepare a recommendation for review by the commissioner under the criteria established in paragraph IV and adopted by rules under RSA 483:11, II.

III. The rivers coordinator, in cooperation with the advisory committee, shall hold at least one public hearing in a community along the nominated river or segment of such river to receive public comment on the nomination. Public hearing comments on the nomination, comments on the nomination from local boards and commissions, factors listed in RSA 483:6, IV(a) as further defined in rules adopted under RSA 483:11, II, and other public comments on the nomination submitted to the rivers coordinator shall be considered by the rivers coordinator and the advisory committee when preparing a recommendation for review by the commissioner.

IV. The commissioner shall review the nomination within 45 days. The commissioner shall, in reviewing a nomination under this chapter, consider the following factors:

(a) Whether the river, or segment or segments of such river, contain or represent either a significant statewide or local example of one or more of the following:

(1) Scenic or recreational resource.

(2) Open space or natural resource.

(3) Fisheries, wildlife, vegetation, and rare species or habitat.

(4) Cultural, historical, or archaeological resource.

(5) Hydrological or geological resource.

(6) Water quality.

(7) Scientific resource.

(8) Community resource.

(9) Current and projected withdrawals, discharges, or both, by public utilities and commercial or industrial users.

(b) Public hearing comments on the nomination and other public comments submitted to the rivers coordinator.

(c) The recommendation of the rivers coordinator.

(d) The recommendation of the advisory committee.

V. If the commissioner, after reviewing a nomination and considering the factors in RSA 483:6, IV, determines that designation of the river, or segment or segments of such river, would be consistent with the purpose of this chapter, the commissioner shall forward the nomination to the general court for review and legislative approval according to RSA 483:7.

Source.
1989, 339:1. 1991, 338:6-8. 1992, 261:4. 1995, 219:1, eff. Aug. 11, 1995.

Revision note.
In par. II, substituted "paragraph IV" for "paragraph V" following "criteria established in" in light of changes made by 1991, 338:7, 8.

Amendments
—**1995.** Paragraph I: Substituted "June 1" for "July 15" in the second sentence.

—**1992.** Paragraph I: Inserted "including flowage rights known by the nominating individual or group" following "interests" in the third sentence, and rewrote the former fifth sentence as the fifth and sixth sentences.

—**1991.** Paragraph I: Added the second, fourth and fifth sentences.
Paragraph III: Added the second sentence.
Paragraph IV: Rewritten to the extent that a detailed comparison would be impracticable.
Paragraph V: Rewritten to the extent that a detailed comparison would be impracticable.

New dams.
1990, 233:17, II, as amended by 1991, 338:5, eff. June 28, 1991, provided: "Notwithstanding the provisions of RSA 483, but for the purposes of RSA 483:5, no new dams shall be permitted, between June 29, 1988 and July 1, 1993, on the main stem of the Connecticut River, excepting that segment north of the confluence of the Israel River in the town of Lancaster."

483:7. Legislative Designation.

I. Any nomination approved by the commissioner shall require review and approval by the general court prior to inclusion in the program. Such action shall be filed as a bill in the next legislative session following the nomination.

II. Any nomination which is forwarded to the general court for review and approval shall include:

(a) A map showing the boundaries of the river or segment;

(b) A report which specifies the values and characteristics which qualify the river or segment for designation; and

(c) The classifications of the proposed designation pursuant to RSA 483:7-a.

Source.
1989, 339:1. 1990, 233:4, eff. June 26, 1990.

Amendments
—**1990.** Designated the existing provisions of the section as par. I and added par. II.

483:7-a. River Classification Criteria; Management.

I. Those rivers or segments designated for inclusion in the program shall be classified as one or more of the following:

(a) Natural rivers are free-flowing rivers or segments characterized by the high quality of natural and scenic resources. River shorelines are in primarily natural vegetation and river corridors are generally undeveloped. Development, if any, is limited to forest management and scattered housing. For natural rivers, the following criteria and management objectives shall apply:

(1) The minimum length of any segment shall be 5 miles.

(2) Existing water quality shall be not lower than Class B level pursuant to the water quality standards established under RSA 485-A:8.

(3) The minimum distance from the river shoreline to a paved road open to the public for motor vehicle use shall be 250 feet, except where a

vegetative or other natural barrier exists which effectively screens the sight and sound of motor vehicles for a majority of the length of the river or segment.

(4) Management of natural rivers and segments shall perpetuate their natural condition as defined in this chapter and shall consider, protect, and ensure the rights of riparian owners to use the river for forest management, agricultural, public water supply, and other purposes which are compatible with instream public uses of the river and the management and protection of the resources for which the river or segment is designated.

(b) Rural rivers are those rivers or segments adjacent to lands which are partially or predominantly used for agriculture, forest management and dispersed or clustered residential development. Some instream structures may exist, including low dams, diversion works and other minor modifications. The following criteria and management objectives shall apply to rural rivers:

(1) The minimum length of any segment shall be 3 miles.

(2) Existing water quality shall be at least Class B level pursuant to the water quality standards established under RSA 485-A:8 or have the potential for restoration to that level.

(3) There shall be no minimum distance from the shoreline to an existing road. Roads may parallel the river shoreline with regular bridge crossings and public access sites.

(4) Management of rural rivers and segments shall maintain and enhance the natural, scenic, and recreational values of the river and shall consider, protect and ensure the rights of riparian owners to use the river for agricultural, forest management, public water supply, and other purposes which are compatible with the instream public uses of the river and the management and protection of the resources for which the river or segment is designated.

(c) Rural-community rivers are those rivers or segments which flow through developed or populated areas of the state and which possess existing or potential community resource values such as those defined in official municipal plans or land use controls. Such rivers have mixed land uses in the corridor reflecting some combination of open space, agricultural, residential, commercial and industrial land uses. Such rivers are readily accessible by road or railroad and may include impoundments or diversions. The following criteria and management objectives shall apply to rural-community rivers:

(1) The minimum length of any segment shall be 3 miles.

(2) Existing water quality shall be at least Class B level pursuant to the water quality standards established under RSA 485-A:8, or have the potential for restoration to that level.

(3) Management of rural-community rivers and segments shall maintain and enhance the natural, scenic, recreational and community values of the river and shall consider, protect, and ensure the rights of riparian owners to use the river for such uses as agricultural, forest management, public water supply, residential, recreational, commercial, industrial, flood control, and other community uses which are compatible with the instream

public uses of the river and the management and protection of the resources for which the river or segment is designated.

(d) Community rivers are those rivers or segments which flow through developed or populated areas of the state and which possess existing or potential community resource values, such as those identified in official municipal plans or land use controls. Such rivers have mixed land uses in the corridor reflecting some combination of open space, agricultural, residential, commercial and industrial land uses. Such rivers are readily accessible by road or railroad, may include existing impoundments or diversions, or potential sites for new impoundments or diversions for hydropower, flood control or water supply purposes, and may include the urban centers of municipalities. The following criteria and management objectives shall apply to community rivers:

(1) The minimum length of any segment shall be one mile.

(2) Existing water quality shall be at least Class B level pursuant to the water quality standards established under RSA 485-A:8, or have the potential for restoration to that level.

(3) Management of community rivers and segments shall maintain and enhance the natural, scenic, recreational and community values of the river and shall consider, protect, and ensure the rights of riparian owners to use the river for such uses as agricultural, forest management, public water supply, residential, recreational, commercial, industrial, flood control and hydroelectric energy production purposes which are compatible with the instream public uses of the river and the management and protection of the resources for which the river or segment is designated.

II. The existence of limited exceptions to the criteria for a certain classification under this section shall not necessarily exclude a river or segment from that classification. The river or segment shall be examined as a whole, and the classification of such river or segment shall be based on the overall values and characteristics of such river or segment.

Source.

1990, 233:5. 1991, 338:10, 11, eff. June 28, 1991.

Revision note.

Redesignated par. (bb), as added by 1991, 338:10, as par. (c) and former par. (c) as par. (d) for purposes of conformity with the numbering scheme generally employed in LEXIS New Hampshire Revised Statutes Annotated.

Amendments

—**1991.** Paragraph I(bb): Added.

Paragraph I(c): Rewrote the introductory paragraph and inserted "such uses as" preceding "agricultural", deleted "and" preceding "industrial" and inserted "flood control and hydroelectric energy production" thereafter in subpar. (3).

483:8. Rivers Management Advisory Committee; Establishment.

There is established a rivers management advisory committee appointed by the governor and council. At least 3 committee members shall represent the North Country and all members shall be New Hampshire residents.

I. The advisory committee shall include:

(a) A representative of public water suppliers who shall be an officer or employee of any municipal or privately owned water works in the state.

(b) A municipal officer nominated by the New Hampshire Municipal Association.

(c) A member of the fish and game commission.

(d) A representative of the Business and Industry Association chosen from a list of 3 nominees.

(e) A representative of the Granite State Hydropower Association chosen from a list of 3 nominees.

(f) A conservation commission member chosen from a list of 3 nominees submitted by the New Hampshire Association of Conservation Commissions.

(g) A representative of the conservation community chosen from a list of 3 nominees submitted by the Society for Protection of New Hampshire Forests, Audubon Society, and the New Hampshire Wildlife Federation.

(h) A representative of recreational interests chosen from a list of 3 nominees submitted by the New Hampshire Rivers Campaign and the Appalachian Mountain Club.

(i) A representative of historic/archaeological interests chosen from a list of 3 nominees submitted by the New Hampshire Historical Society.

(j) A representative of the agricultural community chosen from a list of 3 nominees submitted by the New Hampshire Farm Bureau Federation, the Northeast Organic Farming Association, and the New Hampshire Association of Conservation Districts.

(k) A representative of local river management advisory committees from a list of 3 nominees submitted by the commissioner.

II. The director of the office of energy and planning, the executive director of the fish and game department, the commissioner of resources and economic development, the commissioner of the department of transportation, and the commissioner of the department of agriculture, markets, and food or their designees shall serve as nonvoting members of the committee.

III. The terms of state agency members shall be the same as their terms in office. The members shall serve 3-year terms, except that the terms of the initial members appointed under subparagraphs I(a), (d), and (g) shall be one year, and those appointed under subparagraphs I(b), (e), and (h) shall be 2 years.

IV. The commissioner shall convene the first meeting no later than September 15, 1988. The committee shall elect a chairman and vice chairman. Subsequent meetings shall be at the call of the chair, or at the request of 5 or more committee members. The rivers coordinator under RSA 483:3 shall serve as secretary and staff to the committee.

V. The advisory committee shall advise the commissioner and rivers coordinator in implementing the purposes of this chapter.

VI. No state-owned property adjacent to or providing access to a river or river segment shall be recommended for disposal by the council on resources and development except upon the review and recommendation of the advisory committee established under this section.

Source.
   1989, 339:1. 1990, 233:7, 8. 1995, 130:4, eff.
July 23, 1995. 1999, 14:1, eff. June 25, 1999.
2003, 319:9, eff. July 1, 2003. 2004, 257:44, eff.
July 1, 2004. 2007, 285:2–4 eff. September 1,
2007.

Amendments
   —2007.   Paragraph I(b): Substituted "a" for
"an elected" preceding "municipal".
   Paragraph I(k): Added.
   Paragraph II: Inserted "the commissioner of
the department of transportation" following
"economic development".

   —2004.   Paragraph II: Substituted "office of
energy and planning" for "office of state planning and energy programs".

   —2003.   Paragraph II: Substituted "office of
state planning and energy programs" for "office
of state planning".

   —1999.   Paragraph I(j): Added.

   —1995.   Paragraph II: Substituted "department of agriculture, markets, and food" for
"department of agriculture".

   —1990.   Added "and all members shall be
New Hampshire residents" following "North
Country" in the second sentence of the introductory paragraph, deleted "and" following
"game department" and inserted "and the commissioner of the department of agriculture"
following "economic development" in par. II and
added par. VI.

483:8-a. Local River Management Advisory Committees; Establish-ment; Duties.

I. The commissioner shall appoint a local river management advisory committee for each designated river or segment. Committee members shall be chosen from lists of nominees submitted by the local governing bodies of the municipalities through which the designated river or segment flows. The commissioner shall appoint at least one person from each municipality to the local river management advisory committee. All members of such committees shall be New Hampshire residents.

II. Each committee shall be composed of at least 7 members who represent a broad range of interests in the vicinity of the designated river or segment. These interests shall include, but not be limited to, local government, business, conservation interests, recreation, agriculture, and riparian landowners. If an interest is not represented by the local governing bodies' nominations, the commissioner may appoint a member from the vicinity of the designated river or segment, to the local river management advisory committee who will represent that interest. County commissioners shall be permitted to nominate members to the local river management advisory committee in unincorporated towns or unorganized places. Each member shall serve a term of 3 years.

III. The duties of such committees shall be:

   (a) To advise the commissioner, the advisory committee, and the munici-palities through which the designated river or segment flows on matters pertaining to the management of the river or segment. Municipal officials, boards, and agencies shall inform such committees of actions which they are considering in managing and regulating activities within designated river corridors.

   (b) To consider and comment on any federal, state, or local governmental plans to approve, license, fund or construct facilities that would alter the resource values and characteristics for which the river or segment is designated.

(c) To develop or assist in the development and adoption of local river corridor management plans under RSA 483:10. The local planning board, or, in the absence of a planning board, the local governing body, may adopt such plans pursuant to RSA 675:6 as an adjunct to the local master plan adopted under RSA 674:4. No such plan shall have any regulatory effect unless implemented through properly adopted ordinances.

(d) To report annually to the advisory committee and the commissioner on the status of compliance with federal and state laws and regulations, local ordinances, and plans relevant to the designated river or segment and corridor.

IV. In the case of the Connecticut River, the commissioner shall appoint the New Hampshire Connecticut River Valley resource commission as the local river management advisory committee to work with the Vermont Connecticut River Watershed Advisory Commission as provided in RSA 227-E. A minimum of 5 subcommittees shall be established by the Connecticut River Valley resource commission along the river between Vermont and New Hampshire as provided in RSA 483:8-a, II. Vermont residents may be appointed in an advisory capacity to the local river management advisory committee, except where the Connecticut River is exclusively intrastate.

V. In order to establish the tax exempt status of local river management advisory committees established under this section, such advisory committees are deemed to be governmental instrumentalities having a distinct legal existence separate from the state and shall not be considered as departments of state government. The exercise by a local river management advisory committee of any authority granted by this section shall be deemed to be the performance of public and essential governmental functions not otherwise fulfilled by state government.

Source.
1990, 233:6. 1991, 338:9. 1992, 261:2. 1995, 219:2, eff. Aug. 11, 1995. 1997, 7:1, eff. June 20, 1997; 267:3, eff. Aug. 18, 1997. 2007, 285:5, eff. September 1, 2007.

Amendments
—**2007.** Paragraph III(a): Substituted "river" for "rivers" following "designated" in the second sentence.

—**1997.** Paragraph III(c): Chapter 7 rewrote the second sentence and added the third sentence.

Paragraph V: Chapter 267 added.

—**1995.** Paragraph III(a): Added the second sentence.

—**1992.** Paragraph IV: Added.

—**1991.** Paragraph I: Rewrote the third sentence.
Paragraph II: Added the third and fourth sentences.

483:9. Natural Rivers Protection.

The following protection measures shall apply to a river or segment designated as a natural river:

I. No dam or other structure or improvement that impedes or significantly alters the free-flowing condition or natural character of the river or segment shall be permitted, certified, constructed, or operated in such river or segment.

II. No interbasin transfers of water from a designated natural river or segment shall be permitted.

III. No channel alteration activities shall be permitted, except that the commissioner may approve temporary channel alterations in conjunction with the repair or maintenance of a bridge, road, or riprap which is in place at the time a river or segment is designated.

IV. A protected instream flow level shall be established by the commissioner for each designated natural river or segment and any upstream impoundment or diversion facility which may affect the free-flowing condition or natural character of the designated river or segment pursuant to RSA 483:9-c.

V. Water quality shall be maintained at, or restored to the Class A level, or maintained at the Class B level. Each designated natural river or segment shall constitute an outstanding natural resource water pursuant to the standards adopted under RSA 485-A:8. The department shall review and consider adopted local river corridor management plans prior to issuing any permit under RSA 485-A:13 or RSA 485-A:17.

VI. Any new solid waste storage or treatment facility, as defined in RSA 149-M:4, IX shall be set back a minimum of 250 feet from the normal high water mark of a designated natural river or segment and screened with a vegetative or other natural barrier to minimize visual impact, except:

(a) New solid waste landfills shall not be permitted within the corridor of a designated natural river or segment, or less than 100 feet from the landward extent of the 500 year floodplain, whichever distance is greater, and shall be screened from the river with a vegetative or other natural barrier to minimize visual impact;

(b) Expansion of existing solid waste landfills shall not occur within the 500 year floodplain of a designated natural river or segment and any expansion of such a landfill located within the corridor of a designated natural river or segment shall be set back a minimum of 100 feet from the landward extent of the 500 year floodplain and screened from the river with a vegetative or other natural barrier to minimize visual impact;

VII. No new hazardous waste facilities as defined in RSA 147-A:2 which store hazardous waste for more than 90 days, shall be permitted within the corridor of a designated natural river or segment.

VIII. No motorized watercraft shall be permitted to operate on a designated natural river or segment, except for emergency purposes.

Source.
1989, 339:1. 1990, 233:10. 1991, 58:1, eff. May 6, 1991; 338:2, eff. June 28, 1991. 1996, 251:14, 15, eff. Aug. 9, 1996. 1998, 56:2, eff. May 7, 1998. 2007, 308:1, eff. September 11, 2007.

Amendments
—2007. Paragraph VI: Substituted "IX" for "XI" following "RSA 149-M:4" in the introductory par., added the language beginning with "or less than 100 feet" at the end of subpar. (a), added "Expansion of" in the beginning, deleted "permitted and secure" preceding "solid waste" and substituted "occur" for "be expanded" preceding "within the 500" in subpar. (b).

—1998. Paragraph VI(c): Rewritten to the extent that a detailed comparison would be impracticable.

—1996. Paragraph VI: Substituted "RSA 149-M:4, XI" for "RSA 149-M:1, VIII" in the introductory paragraph and "RSA 149-M:4, XXIV" for "RSA 149-M:1, XIX" in subpar. (c).

—**1991.** Paragraph VI(c): Chapter 58 inserted "or lime or wood ash" following "fertilizer".

Chapter 338 inserted "lime and wood ash" preceding "used for fertilizer" and substituted "and sludge and septage" for "or lime or wood ash" thereafter.

—**1990.** Rewritten to the extent that a detailed comparison would be impracticable.

Applicability of 1998 amendment.

1998, 56:6, eff. May 7, 1998, as amended by 2003, 43:14, eff. May 6, 2003, 302:3, eff. July 18, 2003, by 2005, 141:2, eff. June 30, 2005, and 2007, 287:1, eff. July 1, 2007, provided: "The septage and sludge land application restrictions contained in RSA 483:9, VI(c), RSA 483:9-a, VII(b), RSA 483:9-aa, VII(b), and RSA 483:9-b, VII(b) shall not apply until July 1, 2012 to any land upon which septage or sludge has been spread in accordance with all applicable rules adopted by the federal Environmental Protection Agency and the New Hampshire department of environmental services, during any portion of the 3-year period prior to January 1, 1998. In addition, there shall be no termination of this restriction exemption for qualifying land that is used for scientific research on septage or sludge. Any continued application of septage and sludge pursuant to this section shall comply with all applicable federal and state laws and any best management practices published by the university of New Hampshire cooperative extension."

483:9-a. Rural River Protection.

The following protection measures shall apply to a river or segment designated as a rural river:

I. No new dams shall be permitted, certified, constructed, operated or maintained in such river or segment. The repair of a structural failure of a dam which is in place at the time a river or segment is designated shall not be considered to be a new dam if such dam is repaired or reconstructed at the same location and with the same impoundment level within 6 years of the date of failure.

II. Notwithstanding paragraph I, the department may approve permits and certificates for the construction, operation, or maintenance of new hydroelectric power facilities at existing dams provided that:

(a) The operational mode of any proposed facility shall be run-of-the-river, with project outflow equal to project inflow on an instantaneous basis and the project does not significantly alter the natural flow characteristics of the river; and

(b) The proposed facility does not provide for diversion of the river above or below the existing dam for a significant distance; and

(c) The height of the impoundment is constant and is not raised above the maximum historic level of impoundment at that site.

III. No interbasin transfers of water from a designated rural river or segment shall be permitted.

IV. No new channel alteration activities shall be permitted which interfere with or alter the natural flow characteristics of the river or segment or which adversely affect the resources for which the river or segment is designated. However, the commissioner may approve such channel alterations as may be necessary for the construction, repair, or maintenance of a project, including public water supply intake facilities in the river or river corridor. The department shall encourage the use of native vegetation to stabilize streambanks of designated rural rivers.

V. A protected instream flow level shall be established by the commissioner for each designated rural river or segment and any upstream impoundment or diversion facility which may affect the natural flow characteristics or natural character of the designated river or segment pursuant to RSA 483:9-c.

VI. Water quality shall be restored to or maintained at least at the Class B level. Significant adverse impacts on water quality or other instream public uses shall not be permitted. The department shall review and consider adopted local river corridor management plans prior to issuing any permit under RSA 485-A:13, RSA 485-A:17, or RSA 482-A.

VII. Any new solid waste storage or treatment facility, as defined in RSA 149-M:4, IX shall be set back a minimum of 250 feet from the normal high water mark of a designated rural river or segment and shall be screened with a vegetative or other natural barrier to minimize visual impact, except:

(a) New solid waste landfills shall not be permitted within the corridor of a designated rural river or segment or less than 100 feet from the landward extent of the 500 year floodplain, whichever distance is greater, and shall be screened from the river with a vegetative or other natural barrier to minimize visual impact;

(b) New solid waste landfills may be permitted within the city of Rochester within the corridor of the segment defined in RSA 483:15, XIV(c), and if located in the river corridor shall be set back a minimum of 100 feet from the landward extent of the 500 year floodplain and shall be screened from the river with a vegetative or other natural barrier to minimize visual impact;

(c) Expansion of existing solid waste landfills shall not occur within the 500 year floodplain of a designated rural river or segment, and any expansion of such a landfill shall be set back a minimum of 100 feet from the landward extent of the 500 year floodplain and shall be screened from the river with a vegetative or other natural barrier to minimize visual impact;

(d) Any land application within the river corridor of septage, sludge, or solid waste, as defined in RSA 149-M:4, XXII, shall be set back a minimum of 250 feet from the normal high water mark and shall be immediately incorporated into the soil. The provisions of this subparagraph shall not apply to manure, lime, or wood ash when used for agricultural purposes;

(e) An existing solid waste facility which is located within 250 feet of the normal high water mark of a designated rural river or segment may continue to operate under an existing permit provided it does not cause degradation to an area in excess of that area under permit at the time of designation; and

(f) The department may permit a resource recovery operation at an existing landfill located within 250 feet of the normal high water mark of a designated rural river or segment.

VIII. Any motorized watercraft operating within 150 feet of the shoreline of a designated rural river or segment shall travel at the slowest possible speed necessary to maintain steerage way, but at no time shall exceed 6 miles per hour.

Source.

1990, 233:11. 1991, 58:2, eff. May 6, 1991; 338:3, eff. June 28, 1991. 1996, 251:16, eff. June 10, 1996; 251:17, eff. Aug. 9, 1996. 1998, 56:3, eff. May 7, 1998. 2007, 308:2, eff. September 11, 2007.

Revision note.

In par. VII, substituted "RSA 149-M:4, IX" for "RSA 149-M:4, XI" in the introductory paragraph and "RSA 149-M:4, XXII" for "RSA 149-M:4, XXIV" in subpar. (b) to correct the references pursuant to 1996, 251:28. See RSA 149-M:4.

Amendments

—2007. Paragraph VII: Inserted "shall be" preceding "screened with a vegetative" in the introductory par., rewrote subparagraph (a), added present subparas. (b) and (c), and redesignated former subparas. (b) through (d) as subparas. (d) through (f).

—1998. Paragraph VII(b): Rewritten to the extent that a detailed comparison would be impracticable.

—1996. Paragraph VII: Substituted "RSA 149-M:4, XI" for "RSA 149-M:1, VIII" in the introductory paragraph and "RSA 149-M:4, XXIV" for "RSA 149-M:1, XIX" in subpar. (b).

—1991. Paragraph VII(b): Chapter 58 inserted "or lime or wood ash" following "fertilizer".

Chapter 338 inserted "lime and wood ash" preceding "used for fertilizer" and substituted "and sludge and septage" for "or lime or wood ash" thereafter.

Applicability of 1998 amendment.

1998, 56:6, eff. May 7, 1998, as amended by 2003, 43:14, eff. May 6, 2003, 302:3, eff. July 18, 2003, by 2005, 141:2, eff. June 30, 2005, and 2007, 287:1, eff. July 1, 2007, provided: "The septage and sludge land application restrictions contained in RSA 483:9, VI(c), RSA 483:9-a, VII(b), RSA 483:9-aa, VII(b), and RSA 483:9-b, VII(b) shall not apply until July 1, 2012 to any land upon which septage or sludge has been spread in accordance with all applicable rules adopted by the federal Environmental Protection Agency and the New Hampshire department of environmental services, during any portion of the 3-year period prior to January 1, 1998. In addition, there shall be no termination of this restriction exemption for qualifying land that is used for scientific research on septage or sludge. Any continued application of septage and sludge pursuant to this section shall comply with all applicable federal and state laws and any best management practices published by the university of New Hampshire cooperative extension."

Emergency repair of stream banks.

1990, 233:23, eff. June 26, 1990, provided: "Nothing in this act [which added this section and RSA 483:7-a, 483:8-a, 483:9-b, 483:9-c, 483:10-a, 483:10-b, 483:12-a and 483:15 and amended RSA 4:40, 227-E:7, 483:1, 483:2, 483:4, 483:5, 483:7, 483:8, 483:9 and 483:11] shall be construed to prohibit emergency repair of streambanks made necessary by flood damage or stream bank stabilization by riprapping or other means in rivers or segments designated as rural or community rivers, subject to applicable state and federal laws and regulations."

483:9-aa. Rural-Community Rivers Protection.

The following protection measures shall apply to rivers or segments designated as a rural-community river:

I. No new dams shall be permitted, certified, constructed, operated or maintained in such river or segment. The repair of a structural failure of a dam which is in place at the time a river or segment is designated shall not be considered to be a new dam if repaired or reconstructed at the same location and with the same impoundment level within 6 years of the date of failure.

II. Notwithstanding paragraph I, the department may approve permits and certificates for the construction, operation, or maintenance of new hydroelectric power facilities at existing dams provided that:

(a) The operational mode of any proposed facility shall be run-of-the-river, with project outflow equal to project inflow on an instantaneous basis and the project does not significantly alter the natural flow characteristics of the river; and

(b) The proposed facility does not provide for diversion of the river or segment above or below the existing dam for a significant distance; and

(c) The height of the impoundment is constant and is not raised above the maximum historic level of impoundment at that site.

III. No interbasin transfers of water from a designated rural-community river or segment shall be permitted.

IV. No new channel alteration activities shall be permitted which interfere with or alter the natural flow characteristics of the river or segment or which adversely affect the resources for which the river or segment is designated. However, the commissioner may approve such channel alterations as may be necessary for the construction, repair, or maintenance of a project including public water supply intake facilities in the river or river corridor. The department shall encourage the use of native vegetation to stabilize stream-banks of designated rural-community rivers.

V. A protected instream flow level shall be established by the commissioner for each designated rural-community river or segment and any upstream impoundment or diversion facility which may affect the natural flow charac-teristics of such river or segment pursuant to RSA 483:9-c.

VI. Water quality shall be restored or maintained at least at the Class B level. Significant adverse impacts on water quality or other instream public uses shall not be permitted. The department shall review and consider adopted local river corridor management plans prior to issuing any permit under RSA 485-A:13, RSA 485-A:17 or RSA 482-A.

VII. Any new solid waste storage or treatment facility, as defined in RSA 149-M:4, IX shall be set back a minimum of 250 feet from the normal high water mark of a designated rural-community river or segment and screened with a vegetative or other natural barrier to minimize visual impact, except:

(a) New solid waste landfills shall not be permitted within the 500 year floodplain of a designated rural-community river or segment and any new solid waste landfill located within the corridor of a designated rural-community river or segment shall be set back a minimum of 100 feet from the landward extent of the 500 year floodplain and screened from the river with a vegetative or other natural barrier to minimize visual impact;

(b) Any land application of solid waste as defined in RSA 149-M:4, XXII, except manure, lime and wood ash used for fertilizer, and sludge and septage shall be immediately incorporated into the soil and shall be set back a minimum of 250 feet from the normal high water mark of a designated rural-community river or segment;

(c) An existing solid waste facility which is located within 250 feet of the normal high water mark of a designated rural-community river or segment may continue to operate under an existing permit provided it does not cause degradation to an area in excess of that area under permit at the time of designation; and

(d) The department may permit a resource recovery operation at an existing landfill located within 250 feet of the normal high water mark of a designated rural-community river or segment.

VIII. Any motorized watercraft operating within 150 feet of the shoreline of a designated rural-community river or segment shall travel at the slowest possible speed necessary to maintain steerage way, but at no time shall exceed 6 miles per hour.

Source.

1991, 338:12, eff. June 28, 1991. 1996, 251:18, 19, eff. Aug. 9, 1996. 1998, 56:4, eff. May 7, 1998.

Revision note.

In par. VII, substituted "RSA 149-M:4, IX" for "RSA 149-M:4, XI" in the introductory paragraph and "RSA 149-M:4, XXII" for "RSA 149-M:4, XXIV" in subpar. (b) to correct the references pursuant to 1996, 251:28. See RSA 149-M:4.

Amendments

—1998. Paragraph VII(b): Rewritten to the extent that a detailed comparison would be impracticable.

—1996. Paragraph VII: Substituted "RSA 149-M:4, XI" for "RSA 149-M:1, VIII" in the introductory paragraph and "RSA 149-M:4, XXIV" for "RSA 149-M:1, XIX" in subpar. (b).

Applicability of 1998 amendment.

1998, 56:6, eff. May 7, 1998, as amended by

2003, 43:14, eff. May 6, 2003, 302:3, eff. July 18, 2003, by 2005, 141:2, eff. June 30, 2005, and 2007, 287:1, eff. July 1, 2007, provided: "The septage and sludge land application restrictions contained in RSA 483:9, VI(c), RSA 483:9-a, VII(b), RSA 483:9-aa, VII(b), and RSA 483:9-b, VII(b) shall not apply until July 1, 2012 to any land upon which septage or sludge has been spread in accordance with all applicable rules adopted by the federal Environmental Protection Agency and the New Hampshire department of environmental services, during any portion of the 3-year period prior to January 1, 1998. In addition, there shall be no termination of this restriction exemption for qualifying land that is used for scientific research on septage or sludge. Any continued application of septage and sludge pursuant to this section shall comply with all applicable federal and state laws and any best management practices published by the university of New Hampshire cooperative extension."

483:9-b. Community Rivers Protection.

The following protection measures shall apply to rivers or segments designated as a community river:

I. The department may approve permits for the construction of new dams for public water supply, flood control or hydroelectric energy production purposes if such construction is consistent with management and protection of the resources for which the river or segment is designated.

II. The department may approve permits and certificates for the construction, operation, or maintenance of new hydroelectric power facilities at existing or breached dams provided that:

(a) The operational mode of any proposed facility shall be run-of-the-river, with project outflow equal to project inflow on an instantaneous basis and the project does not significantly alter the natural flow characteristics of the river; and

(b) The proposed facility does not provide for diversion of the river or segment above or below the existing dam for a significant distance; and

(c) The height of the impoundment is constant and, for existing or breached dams, is not raised above the maximum historic level of impoundment at that site.

III. No interbasin transfers of water from a designated community river or segment shall be permitted.

IV. No new channel alteration activities shall be permitted which interfere with or alter the natural flow characteristics of the river or segment or which adversely affect the resources for which the river or segment is designated. However, the commissioner may approve such channel alterations as may be necessary for the construction, repair, or maintenance of a project including public water supply intake facilities in the river or river corridor. The department shall encourage the use of native vegetation to stabilize streambanks of designated community rivers.

V. A protected instream flow level shall be established by the commissioner for each designated community river or segment and any upstream impoundment or diversion facility which may affect the natural flow characteristics of such river or segment pursuant to RSA 483-A:9-c.

VI. Water quality shall be restored or maintained at least at the Class B level. Significant adverse impacts on water quality or other instream public uses shall not be permitted. The department shall review and consider adopted local river corridor management plans prior to issuing any permit under RSA 485-A:13, RSA 485-A:17 or RSA 482-A.

VII. Any new solid waste storage or treatment facility, as defined in RSA 149-M:4, IX shall be set back a minimum of 250 feet from the normal high water mark of a designated community river or segment and screened with a vegetative or other natural barrier to minimize visual impact, except:

(a) New solid waste landfills shall not be permitted within the 500 year floodplain of a designated community river or segment and any new solid waste landfill located within the corridor of a designated community river or segment shall be set back a minimum of 100 feet from the landward extent of the 500 year floodplain and screened from the river with a vegetative or other natural barrier to minimize visual impact;

(b) Any land application within the river corridor of septage, sludge, or solid waste, as defined in RSA 149-M:4, XXII, shall be set back a minimum of 250 feet from the normal high water mark and shall be immediately incorporated into the soil. The provisions of this subparagraph shall not apply to manure, lime, or wood ash when used for agricultural purposes.

(c) An existing solid waste facility which is located within 250 feet of the normal high water mark of a designated community river or segment may continue to operate under an existing permit provided it does not cause degradation to an area in excess of that area under permit at the time of designation; and

(d) The department may permit a resource recovery operation at an existing landfill located within 250 feet of the normal high water mark of a designated community river or segment.

VIII. Any motorized watercraft operating within 150 feet of the shoreline of a designated community river or segment shall travel at the slowest possible speed necessary to maintain steerage way, but at no time shall exceed 6 miles per hour.

Source.
1990, 233:11. 1991, 58:3, eff. May 6, 1991; 338:4, 13, 14, eff. June 28, 1991. 1996, 251:20, 21, eff. Aug. 9, 1996. 1998, 56:5, eff. May 7, 1998.

References in text.
The reference to RSA 483-A:9-c at the end of par. V is incorrect. The reference should be to RSA 483:9-c.

Revision note.
In par. VII, substituted "RSA 149-M:4, IX" for "RSA 149-M:4, XI" in the introductory paragraph and "RSA 149-M:4, XXII" for "RSA 149-M:4, XXIV" in subpar. (b) to correct the references pursuant to 1996, 251:28. See RSA 149-M:4.

Amendments
—1998. Paragraph VII(b): Rewritten to the extent that a detailed comparison would be impracticable.

—1996. Paragraph VII: Substituted "RSA 149-M:4, XI" for "RSA 149-M:1, VIII" in the introductory paragraph and "RSA 149-M:4, XXIV" for "RSA 149-M:1, XIX" in subpar. (b).

—1991. Paragraph I: Rewritten by ch. 338 to the extent that a detailed comparison would be impracticable.
Paragraph II: Chapter 338 deleted "notwithstanding paragraph I" preceding "the department" in the introductory paragraph, deleted "or breached" following "existing" in subpar. (b), and inserted "for existing or breached dams" following "constant and" in subpar. (c).
Paragraph IV: Chapter 338 substituted "community" for "rural" following "designated" in the third sentence.
Paragraph VII(b): Chapter 58 inserted "or lime or wood ash" following "fertilizer".
Chapter 338 inserted "lime and wood ash" preceding "used for fertilizer" and substituted "and sludge and septage" for "or lime or wood ash" thereafter.

Applicability of 1998 amendment.
1998, 56:6, eff. May 7, 1998, as amended by 2003, 43:14, eff. May 6, 2003, 302:3, eff. July 18, 2003, by 2005, 141:2, eff. June 30, 2005, and 2007, 287:1, eff. July 1, 2007, provided: "The septage and sludge land application restrictions contained in RSA 483:9, VI(c), RSA 483:9-a, VII(b), RSA 483:9-aa, VII(b), and RSA

483:9-b, VII(b) shall not apply until July 1, 2012 to any land upon which septage or sludge has been spread in accordance with all applicable rules adopted by the federal Environmental Protection Agency and the New Hampshire department of environmental services, during any portion of the 3-year period prior to January 1, 1998. In addition, there shall be no termination of this restriction exemption for qualifying land that is used for scientific research on septage or sludge. Any continued application of septage and sludge pursuant to this section shall comply with all applicable federal and state laws and any best management practices published by the university of New Hampshire cooperative extension."

Emergency repair of stream banks.
1990, 233:23, eff. June 26, 1990, provided: "Nothing in this act [which added this section and RSA 483:7-a, 483:8-a, 483:9-a, 483:9-c, 483:10-a, 483:10-b, 483:12-a and 483:15 and amended RSA 4:40, 227-E:7, 483:1, 483:2, 483:4, 483:5, 483:7, 483:8, 483:9 and 483:11] shall be construed to prohibit emergency repair of streambanks made necessary by flood damage or stream bank stabilization by riprapping or other means in rivers or segments designated as rural or community rivers, subject to applicable state and federal laws and regulations."

Temporary Use Authorization; Time Extended.
2007, 287:1, eff. July 1, provided: "The septage and sludge land application restrictions contained in RSA 483:9, VI(c), RSA 483:9-a, VII(b), RSA 483:9-aa, VII(b), and RSA 483:9-b, VII(b) shall not apply until January 1, 2012 to any land upon which septage or sludge has been spread in accordance with all applicable rules adopted by the federal Environmental Protection Agency and the New Hampshire department of environmental services, during any portion of the 3-year period prior to January 1, 1998. In addition, there shall be no termination of this restriction exemption for qualifying land that is used for scientific research on septage or sludge. Any continued application of septage and sludge pursuant to this section shall comply with all applicable federal and state laws and any best management practices published by the university of New Hampshire cooperative extension."

483:9-c. Establishment of Protected Instream Flows.

I. The commissioner, in consultation with the advisory committee, shall adopt rules under RSA 541-A specifying the standards, criteria, and procedures by which a protected instream flow shall be established and enforced for each designated river or segment. Each protected instream flow shall be established and enforced to maintain water for instream public uses and to protect the resources for which the river or segment is designated. Instream public uses shall include the state's interests in surface waters, including, but not limited to, navigation; recreation; fishing; storage; conservation; maintenance and enhancement of aquatic and fish life; fish and wildlife habitat; wildlife; the protection of water quality and public health; pollution abatement; aesthetic beauty; and hydroelectric energy production.

II. One public hearing shall be held in at least one municipality along the designated river or segment to receive public comment on the establishment of a proposed protected instream flow.

III. The procedure adopted under this section shall include an assessment of the effect of a protected instream flow upon existing hydroelectric power generation, water supply, flood control, and other riparian users. For any portion of a designated river or segment where a protected instream flow would affect the operation of an existing hydroelectric power facility within or upstream from the designated river or segment, the commissioner shall request the assistance of the public utilities commission in order to assess the effect of a protected instream flow upon such facility.

IV. The protected instream flow levels established under this section shall be maintained at all times, except when inflow is less than the protected instream flow level as a result of natural causes or when the commissioner determines that a public water supply emergency exists which affects public health and safety.

V. The maintenance of protected instream flows shall constitute a condition of any permit issued by the department for any project or activity within a designated river or segment and corridor.

VI. Any party who is aggrieved by a determination establishing such protected instream flows may petition the commissioner for a hearing to review such determination within 30 days of the date the determination is issued. The filing of such petition shall stay the implementation of the determination until a final decision has been rendered on the petition or an appeal taken pursuant to RSA 541.

Source.
1990, 233:11, eff. June 26, 1990.

Rulemaking
2000, 242:6, eff. Aug. 7, 2000, provided that notwithstanding any other provision of law, no rules relative to instream flows under par. I of this section shall take effect prior to July 1, 2001.

483:10. Rivers Corridor Management Plans.

I. The rivers coordinator, with the cooperation and assistance of the office of energy and planning, shall develop detailed guidelines for river corridor management plans, including but not limited to model shoreline protection ordinances. The rivers coordinator shall hold a public hearing regarding the proposed guidelines and model ordinances. The rivers coordinator shall provide technical assistance to regional planning commissions, municipalities, and river corridor commissions and shall encourage the development and implementation of river corridor management plans.

II. River corridor management plans developed pursuant to paragraph I shall include, but not be limited to, the following:

(a) Permitted recreational uses and activities.

(b) Permitted non-recreational uses and activities.

(c) Existing land uses.

(d) Protection of flood plains, wetlands, wildlife and fish habitat, and other significant open space and natural areas.

(e) Dams, bridges, and other water structures.

(f) Access by foot and vehicles.

(g) Setbacks and other location requirements.

(h) Dredging, filling, mining, and earth moving.

(i) Prohibited uses.

III. River corridor management plans developed according to this section may include tributary drainage areas as determined by the local river management advisory committee

Source.

1989, 339:1, eff. Jan. 1, 1990. 2003, 319:9, eff. July 1, 2003. 2004, 257:44, eff. July 1, 2004. 2007, 285:6, eff. September 1, 2007.

Amendments

—**2007.** Paragraph III: Added.

—**2004.** Paragraph I: Substituted "office of energy and planning" for "office of state planning and energy programs" in the first sentence.

—**2003.** Paragraph I: Substituted "office of state planning and energy programs" for "office of state planning".

483:10-a. Long-Range River Management Plans.

The department shall prepare and adopt a long-range comprehensive plan for each designated river or segment which shall address the management and protection of instream values and the management of state-owned lands within the corridor and tributary drainage areas thereof. Such state-owned land within the designated river corridor and tributary drainage areas shall be administered and managed in accordance with the plan, and state management of fisheries, streams, waters, wildlife, and boating shall be consistent with the plan. In developing this plan, the department shall cooperate with the department of resources and economic development, the department of fish and game, the office of energy and planning, the department of agriculture, markets, and food, the department of transportation, and the local rivers management advisory committee.

Source.
1990, 233:12. 1995, 130:4, eff. July 23, 1995. 2003, 319:9, eff. July 1, 2003. 2004, 257:44, eff. July 1, 2004. 2007, 285:7, eff. September 1, 2007.

Amendments
—2007. Substituted "the management of state-owned lands within the corridor and tributary drainage areas thereof" for "state lands within the corridor" in the first sentence; "such state-owned land" for "state land" preceding "within the" and inserted "and tributary drainage areas" following "river corridor" in the second sentence; and inserted "the department of transportation" following "and food" in the third sentence.

—2004. Substituted "office of energy and planning" for "office of state planning and energy programs".

—2003. Substituted "office of state planning and energy programs" for "office of state planning".

—1995. Substituted "department of agriculture, markets, and food" for "department of agriculture" in the third sentence.

483:10-b. Withholding of Section 401 Certification.

The general court finds that the development of any dam or channel alteration activities within a natural river or segment or the development of any new dam within a rural or community river or segment, except as provided in RSA 483:9-a, II and RSA 483:9-b, II, will alter the physical and chemical characteristics of that river and will constitute violation of the water quality standards established under RSA 485-A:8. The commissioner shall deny certification of any federally licensed or permitted activity on such designated rivers or segments under section 401 of the Federal Water Pollution Control Act, P.L. 92-500, as amended.

Source.
1990, 233:12, eff. June 26, 1990.

References in text.
Section 401 of the Federal Water Pollution Control Act, P.L. 92-500, referred to in this section, is classified to 33 U.S.C.S. § 1341.

483:11. Rulemaking.

The commissioner, with the advice of the advisory committee, shall adopt rules, pursuant to RSA 541-A, relative to the following:

I. Content and submission of nominations under RSA 483:6, I.

II. Criteria for acceptance of nominations by the commissioner, including criteria listed in RSA 483:6, IV(a).

III. Preparation for legislative designation of nominated rivers or segments of such rivers under RSA 483:7.

IV. Development of standards, criteria, and procedures for establishment and enforcement of protected instream flow levels for designated rivers and segments under RSA 483:9-c.

Source.
1989, 339:1. 1990, 233:13. 1991, 338:15, eff. June 28, 1991.

Amendments
—1991. Paragraph II: Substituted "IV(a)" for "V" following "RSA 483:6".

—1990. Paragraph IV: Added.

483:12. Consistency of State Action.

Upon enactment of this chapter, all state agency actions affecting rivers or segments of such rivers which may be designated for protection under this chapter shall conform to the provisions of this chapter.

Source.
  1989, 339:1, eff. Jan. 1, 1990.

483:12-a. State Action; Notification of Rivers Coordinator; Petition for Review.

I. Any state agency considering any action affecting any river or segment designated under this chapter shall notify the rivers coordinator prior to taking any such action. Such agency shall forward to the rivers coordinator for review and comment copies of all notices of public hearings, or, where a public hearing is not required, a copy of the application for issuance of a permit, certificate, or license within the designated river or corridor under RSA 485-C, RSA 485-A, RSA 483-B, RSA 12-E, RSA 270:12, RSA 482, RSA 482-A, RSA 149-M, or RSA 147-A. If an agency is notified by the rivers coordinator that a proposed activity would violate a protection measure under RSA 483:9, 483:9-a, 483:9-aa, or 483:9-b, such agency shall deny the application.

I-a. The rivers coordinator shall develop, in conjunction with affected state agencies and local river management advisory committees, the procedure by which the state shall notify the appropriate local river management advisory committee when state action is being considered which affects a designated river.

II. If an application is denied solely because the proposed activity would violate a protection measure under RSA 483:9, 483:9-a, 483:9-aa, or 483:9-b, the applicant may petition the commissioner for a review. Within 30 days of receiving such a petition, the commissioner, in consultation with the advisory committee and the appropriate local rivers management advisory committee, shall review the application. If the commissioner determines that the proposed activity is consistent with the character of the designated river or segment or that the proposed activity would provide a public benefit sufficient to outweigh the public benefit of a protection measure under this chapter, the commissioner shall submit to the speaker of the house and the president of the senate a recommendation that the proposed activity be allowed to proceed. Such recommendation shall require review and approval by the general court and shall be filed as a bill in the next legislative session following the petition.

Source.
  1990, 233:14. 1995, 219:3, eff. Aug. 11, 1995.
2007, 285:8, eff. September 1, 2007.

Amendments
  —**2007.** Paragraph I: Inserted "RSA 485-C" preceding "RSA 485-A" and "RSA 483-B" there-

after in the second sentence and "483:9-aa" following "483:9-a" in the third sentence.
  Paragraph II: Inserted "483:9-aa" following "483:9-a" in the first sentence.

  —**1995.** Paragraph I-a: Added.

483:12-b. Subject to Other Laws; Existing Hydroelectric Facilities.

I. Any activities permitted under this chapter shall be subject to all applicable state and federal laws and regulations.

II. Nothing in this chapter shall prohibit the continued operation, repair and maintenance of hydroelectric storage and generation facilities existing on the effective date of this paragraph.

Source.

1990, 233:24. 1992, 261:3, eff. July 14, 1992.

Amendments

—**1992.** Added "Existing Hydroelectric Fa-

cilities" following "laws" in the section catchline, designated the existing provisions of the section as par. I and added par. II.

483:13. Acceptance and Expenditure of Funds.

I. The commissioner may apply for and accept, from any source, gifts; donations of money; grants; federal, local, private, and other matching funds and incentives; and interests in land for the purposes of this chapter.

II. The rivers coordinator, with the approval of the commissioner and the advisory committee, may expend any funds received under paragraph I for the purposes of this chapter, and such funds are hereby appropriated.

III. Local river management advisory committees may apply for and accept, from any source, gifts, grants, and donations of money. The committees may, without further authorization, expend any funds so received to carry out their duties pursuant to RSA 483:8-a.

Source.

1989, 339:1. 1995, 219:4, eff. Aug. 11, 1995.

Amendments

—**1995.** Paragraph III: Added.

483:14. Disposition of State Property.

No state-owned property adjacent to or providing access to a river shall be disposed of by the state except upon the review and recommendation of the advisory committee.

Source.

1990, 118:4, eff. June 18, 1990.

483:15. Rivers Designated for Protection.

The following rivers and river segments are designated as protected:

I. Lamprey River—main stem from the Epping-Lee town line to the Durham-Newmarket town line as a "rural river." Notwithstanding any other provisions of this chapter, the department of environmental services shall not approve the use of flashboards under RSA 482:29 to increase the height of any existing dam within this segment of the Lamprey River.

II. Merrimack River—main stem from the Bedford-Merrimack town line to the New Hampshire-Massachusetts state line as a "community river." Nothing in this chapter shall be construed to limit complete capacity utilization, not to exceed 30 million gallons per day, or any construction or repairs required to achieve such utilization of the existing intake facilities of Pennichuck Water Works situated on the western bank of the Merrimack River in the vicinity of Chase Brook, so-called. This paragraph shall not affect any private right in the Merrimack River and shall not relieve Pennichuck Water Works, or its successors and assigns, from compliance with other laws or rules under the state's police power.

III. Merrimack River—main stem from the confluence of the Winnipesaukee and Pemigewasset Rivers in the city of Franklin to Garvins Falls in the town of Bow as a "rural river."

IV. Saco River—main stem from the base of Saco Lake dam to the southern boundary of Crawford Notch State Park as a "natural river" and from the southern boundary of Crawford Notch State Park to the New Hampshire-Maine state line as a "rural river." Nothing in this chapter shall prohibit the normal repair or maintenance of the Willey House dam in Crawford Notch State Park.

V. Swift River—main stem from its headwaters to the Albany-Conway town line as a "natural river" and from the Albany-Conway town line to its confluence with the Saco River in Conway as a "rural river."

VI. Pemigewasset River:

(a) As a natural river from the outlet of Profile Lake in Franconia to the southern boundary of Franconia Notch State Park.

(b) As a rural river from the Holderness-Ashland town line to the Franklin Falls flood control dam.

(c) As a rural-community river from the northernmost Thornton town line to the I-93 bridge in Plymouth.

(d) As a community river:

(1) From the I-93 bridge in Plymouth to the Holderness-Ashland town line.

(2) From the Franklin Falls flood control dam to its confluence with the Merrimack River.

VII. (a) Contoocook River—main stem:

(1) As a "rural river":

(A) From the Old Sharon Road bridge in Jaffrey to Noone Falls dam in Peterborough.

(B) From the North Peterborough dam to the monument on the Peterborough-Hancock town line.

(C) From the North Bennington Road bridge in Antrim and Bennington to the confluence of the north branch of the Contoocook River in Hillsborough.

(D) From the Hosiery Mill dam in Hillsborough to the twin iron bridges in West Henniker.

(E) From the Henniker-Hopkinton town line to the Riverhill bridge in Penacook.

(2) As a "community river":

(A) From the outlet of Poole Pond in Rindge to Old Sharon Road bridge in Jaffrey.

271

(B) From the Noone Falls dam in Peterborough to North Peterborough dam.

(C) From the monument on the Peterborough-Hancock town line to the North Bennington Road bridge in Antrim and Bennington.

(D) From the confluence of the north branch of the Contoocook River in Hillsborough to the Hosiery Mill dam in Hillsborough.

(E) From the twin iron bridges in West Henniker to the Henniker-Hopkinton town line.

(F) From the Riverhill bridge in Penacook to the confluence with the Merrimack River.

(b) Contoocook River—north branch:

(1) As a "rural river," from the outlet of Rye Pond in Stoddard to the outlet of Franklin Pierce Lake.

(2) As a "community river," from the outlet of Franklin Pierce Lake to the confluence of the Contoocook River.

VIII. Connecticut River:

(a) As a rural river from the outlet of the Fourth Connecticut Lake to a point .3 miles above the Second Connecticut Lake Dam.

(b) As a community river from the point above the Second Connecticut Lake Dam to a point .3 miles below the Second Connecticut Lake Dam.

(c) As a rural river from the point below the Second Connecticut Lake Dam to a point .3 miles above the First Connecticut Lake Dam.

(d) As a community river from the point above the First Connecticut Lake Dam to a point .3 miles below the First Connecticut Lake Dam.

(e) As a rural river from the point below the First Connecticut Lake Dam to a point .3 miles above Murphy Dam.

(f) As a community river from the point above the Murphy Dam to a point 2 miles below the Murphy Dam.

(g) As a rural river from the point 2 miles below the Murphy Dam to Bishop Brook in Stewartstown.

(h) As a community river from Bishop Brook to Leach Creek in Canaan, Vermont.

(i) As a rural river from Leach Creek to the confluence with the Mohawk River.

(j) As a rural community river from the confluence with the Mohawk River to the Columbia-Colebrook town line.

(k) As a rural river from the Columbia-Colebrook town line to Wheeler Stream in Brunswick, Vermont.

(l) As a natural river from Wheeler Stream to the Maidstone-Stratford Bridge.

(m) As a rural river from the Maidstone-Stratford Bridge to a point one mile above the breached Wyoming Valley Dam in Northumberland.

(n) As a community river from one mile above the breached Wyoming Valley Dam site to a point one mile below the Wyoming Valley Dam Site.

(o) As a rural river from one mile below the breached Wyoming Valley Dam site to a point .3 miles above the Simpson Paper Company Dam.

(p) As a community river from the point above the Simpson Paper Company Dam to .3 miles below the Simpson Paper Company.

(q) As a rural river from the point below the Simpson Paper Company Dam to .4 miles above the Moore Dam.

(r) As a community river from the point above the Moore Dam to a point .6 miles below the Moore Dam.

(s) As a rural river from the point below Moore Dam to a point .3 miles above the Comerford Dam.

(t) As a community river from the point above the Comerford Dam to a point .2 miles below McIndoes Falls Dam.

(u) As a rural river from the point below the McIndoes Falls Dam to a point .3 miles above the Ryegate Dam.

(v) As a community river from the point above the Ryegate Dam to a point .2 miles below the Ryegate Dam.

(w) As a rural river from the point below the Ryegate Dam to the Ammonoosuc River in Bath.

(x) As a community river from the Ammonoosuc River to the point where routes 135 and 10 meet in Haverhill.

(y) As a rural river from the intersection of routes 135 and 10 to Storrs Pond Brook in Hanover.

(z) As a rural-community river from Storrs Pond Brook to Dothan Brook outlet in Hartford, Vermont.

(aa) As a community river from the Dothan Brook to .3 miles below the Wilder Dam.

(bb) As a rural-community river from the point below the Wilder Dam to the Lebanon-Plainfield town line.

(cc) As a rural river from the Lebanon-Plainfield town line to the Blow-Me-Down Brook in Cornish.

(dd) As a rural-community river from the Blow-Me-Down Brook to the northern end of Chase Island in Cornish.

(ee) As a rural river from the north end of Chase Island to the southern side of the Williams River in Bellows Falls, Vermont.

(ff) As a community river from the southern side of the Williams River to the Saxtons River in Westminster, Vermont.

(gg) As a rural-community river from the Saxtons River to the bridge between Westminster Station and Walpole.

(hh) As a rural river from the bridge at Westminster Station to the Brattleboro-Dummerston, Vermont town line.

(ii) As a rural-community river from the Brattleboro-Dummerston, Vermont town line to Sprague Brook.

(jj) As a community river from Sprague Brook to a point .3 miles below the Vernon Dam.

(kk) As a rural river from the point below the Vernon Dam to the Massachusetts border.

IX. Ashuelot River:

(a) As a natural river from the dam at Butterfield Pond to and including the falls above Ashuelot Pond.

(b) As a rural river from the falls above Ashuelot Pond to Symondsville Road in Marlow.

(c) As a community river from Symondsville Road in Marlow to the Audio Accessories dam.

(d) As a rural river from below the Audio Accessories dam in Marlow up to the breached Blackstock dam located above the town of Gilsum.

(e) As a community river from the breached Blackstock dam above the town of Gilsum to the stone arch bridge in Gilsum.

(f) As a rural river from the stone arch bridge in Gilsum to the Court Street bridge in Keene.

(g) As a community river from the Court Street bridge in Keene to the Branch River in Keene.

(h) As a rural river from the Branch River in Keene to the unnamed brook entering on the west bank near the intersection of Winchester Street and route 10 in West Swanzey.

(i) As a community river from the unnamed brook on the west bank near the intersection of Winchester Street and route 10 in West Swanzey to the Denman Thompson Bridge.

(j) As a rural river from the Denman Thompson Bridge in West Swanzey to and including the oxbow on the west bank before the A.C. Lawrence building in Winchester.

(k) As a community river from the oxbow on the west bank before the A.C. Lawrence building in Winchester to the route 119 bridge.

(*l*) As a rural river from the route 119 bridge in Winchester to the Winchester dam owned by G.E. Robertson and Company in Hinsdale.

(m) As a community river from the Winchester dam owned by G.E. Robertson and Company in Hinsdale to the route 63 bridge.

(n) As a rural river from the route 63 bridge in Hinsdale to the mouth of the Ashuelot River at the Connecticut River.

X. (a) Piscataquog River—north branch:

(1) As a natural river from the outlet of Deering Lake Dam in Deering, 6.25 miles to the Abijah bridge in Weare.

(2) As a rural river:

(A) From the outlet of Lake Horace Dam in Weare, 8 miles to the Everett Dam flowage in Weare.

(B) From the outlet of Everett Dam in Weare, 8 miles to the river's convergence point with the south branch.

(b) Piscataquog River—middle branch. As a natural river from the natural outlet of Scobie Pond in Francestown to the inlet of the upper cranberry bog at the New Boston town line, approximately 11.5 miles to its mouth in New Boston.

(c) Piscataquog River—south branch:

(1) As a natural river from the outlet of Pleasant Pond in Francestown, 11.5 miles to New Hampshire Route 13 in New Boston.

(2) As a rural river from New Hampshire Route 13 in New Boston, 7 miles to the confluence with the north branch.

(3) As a rural-community river from the confluence with the north branch, 1.7 miles to New Hampshire Route 114 in Goffstown.

(4) As a community river from New Hampshire Route 114 in Goffstown, 1 mile to the Gregg Dam in Goffstown.

(5) As a rural-community river from the Gregg Dam in Goffstown, 6.9 miles to the river's mouth at Bass Island in Manchester.

XI. Exeter River. As a "rural river" from its headwaters at the route 102 bridge in Chester 29.7 miles to its confluence with Great Brook in Exeter.

XII. Cold River:

(a) As a rural river from the outlet of Crescent Lake Dam in Acworth, 20.3 miles to the most downstream crossing of the Langdon-Walpole town line.

(b) As a community river from the most downstream crossing of the Langdon-Walpole town line, 2.1 miles to its confluence with the Connecticut River in Walpole.

XIII. Souhegan River:

(a) As a rural-community river from the confluence of its south and west branches in New Ipswich to a point 0.5 miles above the Otis Dam in Greenville.

(b) As a community river from the point 0.5 miles above the Otis Dam in Greenville to a point 0.5 miles below the Otis Dam.

(c) As a rural river from the point 0.5 miles below the Otis Dam to the Label Arts Dam located approximately 0.3 miles above the confluence with Stony Brook in Wilton.

(d) As a community river from the Label Arts Dam to the Wilton Road bridge near the Pine Valley Mill in west Milford.

(e) As a rural-community river from the Wilton Road bridge to a point 0.5 miles above the route 13 bridge in Milford.

(f) As a community river from the point 0.5 miles above the route 13 bridge to a point 0.5 miles below the route 13 bridge.

(g) As a rural river from the point 0.5 miles below the route 13 bridge to the Everett Turnpike bridge in Merrimack.

(h) As a community river from the Everett Turnpike Bridge to the confluence with the Merrimack River in Merrimack.

XIV. Isinglass River:

(a) As a rural river from the outflow of Bow Lake Dam in Strafford, 0.54 miles to immediately downstream of the route 202A bridge.

(b) As a natural river from immediately downstream of the Route 202A bridge in Strafford, 5.75 miles to immediately upstream of the route 126 bridge in Barrington.

(c) As a rural river from immediately upstream of the route 126 bridge in Barrington, 11.64 miles to its confluence with the Cocheco River in Rochester.

XV. Ammonoosuc River:

(a) As a rural river from the White Mountain National Forest boundary near Lower Falls in Carroll to the Bethlehem-Littleton town line.

(b) As a community river from the Bethlehem-Littleton town line to the Littleton-Lisbon town line.

(c) As a rural-community river from the Littleton-Lisbon town line to the confluence with Pearl Lake Brook in Lisbon.

(d) As a community river from the confluence with the Pearl Lake Brook in Lisbon to the Lisbon-Landaff-Bath town line.

(e) As a rural-community river from the Lisbon-Landaff-Bath town line to a point 0.9 miles above the covered bridge in Bath.

(f) As a community river from the point 0.9 above the covered bridge in Bath to the confluence with Simonds Brook in Bath.

(g) As a rural-community river from the confluence with Simonds Brook in Bath to the confluence with Burton Brook in Bath.

(h) As a community river from the confluence with Burton Brook in Bath to the confluence with the Connecticut River in Haverhill.

Source.

1990, 233:15. 1991, 338:1. 1992, 261:1, 6, 7. 1993, 47:1, eff. June 7, 1993; 132:1, eff. July 16, 1993. 1995, 219:5, eff. Aug. 11, 1995. 1996, 228:108, eff. July 1, 1996. 1999, 64:1, eff. July 20, 1999. 2000, 27:1, eff. May 28, 2000. 2002, 75:1, eff. June 30, 2002. 2007, 66:1, eff. August 10, 2007.

Revision note.

This section was originally enacted as RSA 483:14 and was redesignated pursuant to 1990, 233:25.

Amendments

—**2007.** Paragraph XV: Added.

—**2002.** Paragraph XIV: Added.

—**2000.** Paragraph XIII: Added.

—**1999.** Paragraph XII: Added.

—**1996.** Paragraph I: Substituted "department of environmental services" for "division of water resources" in the second sentence.

—**1995.** Paragraph XI: Added.

—**1993.** Paragraph IX: Added by ch. 47. Paragraph X: Added by ch. 132.

—**1992.** Paragraph VII(a)(1)(E): Added. Paragraph VII(a)(2)(E): Substituted "Henniker-Hopkinton town line" for "confluence with the Merrimack River" following "West Henniker to the". Paragraph VII(a)(2)(F): Added. Paragraph VIII: Added.

—**1991.** Added pars. VI and VII.

Local approval of additional designation of segment of Exeter River as "rural river".

1995, 219:6, eff. Aug. 11, 1995, as amended by 1998, 182:2, eff. June 15, 1998, provided: "Not-

withstanding RSA 483:7, 483:7-a, I(b)(1), and 483:15, XI, the segment of the Exeter River from its confluence with Great Brook 2.3 miles to the base of the Great Dam in Exeter shall be designated as a rural river provided that the selectmen of the town of Exeter, after a public hearing, vote to approve such designation and notify the commissioner of the department of environmental services of such action."

Designation of Connecticut River segment as natural river and effect of designation on solid waste landfill permit applications filed prior to Jan 1, 1993.

1992, 261:9, eff. July 14, 1992, provided: "Notwithstanding RSA 483:15, VIII(l), the segment of the Connecticut River from Wheeler Stream to Paul Stream shall be designated as a natural river on January 1, 1993. Such natural river designation shall not apply to any entity or person who has filed an application with the department of environmental services for a solid waste landfill permit by December 31, 1992, unless such application is withdrawn or is finally denied and all appeals have been exhausted with respect to the application filed by December 31, 1992."

Management and protection of existing and newly designated community rivers.

1991, 338:16, eff. June 28, 1991, provided:

"I. Rivers and river segments designated as community rivers prior to the effective date of this act [June 28, 1991] shall continue to be managed and protected pursuant to the provisions of RSA 483:7-a and RSA 483:9-b under which such rivers and river segments were designated, and pursuant to the values, resources and characteristics addressed in the nomination submitted in support of such designation.

"II. Rivers and river segments designated as community rivers under RSA 483:15,

VII(a)(2)(A)-(D) as inserted by section 1 of this act shall be managed and protected for the values, resources and characteristics addressed in the nomination submitted in support of such designation."

Inclusion of Lamprey River, the Swift River and certain portions of the Merrimack River under the shoreland protection act.

1998, 182:1, eff. June 15, 1998, provided:

"Notwithstanding RSA 483-B:20, the provisions of RSA 483-B, relative to comprehensive shoreland protection, shall apply to the Lamprey River, the Swift River and to those portions of the Merrimack River and the Contoocook River designated as protected under RSA 483:15, I-III, V, and VII."

CHAPTER 483-B

COMPREHENSIVE SHORELAND PROTECTION ACT

Cross References.

Clean lakes program, see RSA 487:15 et seq.

Environmental audits, see RSA 147-E.

Fill and dredge in wetlands, see RSA 482-A.

Lakes management and protection program, see RSA 483-A.

Rivers management and protection program, see RSA 483.

Shore and beach preservation and development generally, see RSA 217.

NOTES TO DECISIONS

Cited:

Cited in Opinion of the Justices (Public Use of Coastal Beaches), 139 N.H. 82, 649 A.2d 604, 1994 N.H. LEXIS 149 (1994).

RESEARCH REFERENCES

New Hampshire Practice.

15 N.H.P. Land Use Planning and Zoning § 39.05.

483-B:1. Purpose.

The general court finds that:

I. The shorelands of the state are among its most valuable and fragile natural resources and their protection is essential to maintain the integrity of public waters.

I-a. A natural woodland buffer, consisting of trees and other vegetation located in areas adjoining public waters, functions to intercept surface runoff, wastewater, subsurface flow, and deeper groundwater flows from upland sources and to remove or minimize the effects of nutrients, sediment, organic matter, pesticides, and other pollutants and to moderate the temperature of the near-shore waters.

II. The public waters of New Hampshire are valuable resources held in trust by the state. The state has an interest in protecting those waters and has the jurisdiction to control the use of the public waters and the adjacent shoreland for the greatest public benefit.

III. There is great concern throughout the state relating to the utilization, protection, restoration and preservation of shorelands because of their effect on state waters.

IV. Under current law the potential exists for uncoordinated, unplanned and piecemeal development along the state's shorelines, which could result in significant negative impacts on the public waters of New Hampshire.

Source.
1991, 303:1. 2002, 263:1, eff. July 17, 2002.

Amendments
—2002. Paragraph I-a: Added.

Effective Date.
1991, 303:8, which is noted in the main volume, and which was subsequently amended by 1992, 157:1, was repealed by 1994, 383:22, III, eff. July 1, 1994. Pursuant to 1991, 303:10, I, as amended by 1994, 383:25, section 1 of

1991, chapter 303, which added this chapter, shall take effect on July 1, 1994.

1991, 303:8, provided that section 1 of the act, which added this chapter, would take effect only after the general court had approved funding of sections 1, 2 and 5 of this act, which added this chapter, amended RSA 4-C:6 and authorized additional staff in the department of environmental services for the administration of RSA 483-B, respectively, after consideration of the implementation plan required under section 7 of the act.

NOTES TO DECISIONS

Cited:
Cited in Bacon v. Town of Enfield, 150 N.H. 468, 840 A.2d 788, 2004 N.H. LEXIS 8 (2004).

RESEARCH REFERENCES

New Hampshire Practice.
15 N.H.P. Land Use Planning and Zoning § 39.05.

483-B:2. Minimum Standards Required.

To fulfill the state's role as trustee of its waters and to promote public health, safety, and the general welfare, the general court declares that the public interest requires the establishment of standards for the subdivision, use, and development of the shorelands of the state's public waters. The development standards provided in this chapter shall be the minimum standards necessary to protect the public waters of the state of New Hampshire. These standards shall serve to:

I. Further the maintenance of safe and healthful conditions.

II. Provide for the wise utilization of water and related land resources.

III. Prevent and control water pollution.

IV. Protect fish spawning grounds, aquatic life, and bird and other wildlife habitats.

V. Protect buildings and lands from flooding and accelerated erosion.

VI. Protect archaeological and historical resources.

VII. Protect commercial fishing and maritime industries.

VIII. Protect freshwater and coastal wetlands.

IX. Control building sites, placement of structures, and land uses.

X. Conserve shoreline cover and points of access to inland and coastal waters.

XI. Preserve the state's lakes, rivers, estuaries and coastal waters in their natural state.

XII. Promote wildlife habitat, scenic beauty, and scientific study.

XIII. Protect public use of waters, including recreation.

XIV. Conserve natural beauty and open spaces.

XV. Anticipate and respond to the impacts of development in shoreland areas.

XVI. Provide for economic development in proximity to waters.

Source.

1991, 303:1. 1992, 235:1, 2. 1994, 383:1, eff. July 1, 1994.

Editor's note.

Although 1992, 235:1, 2 provided for the amendment of par. X and the addition of par XVI effective on Jan. 1, 1993, the amendment did not become effective until July 1, 1994, the date on which this section as originally enacted by 1991, 303:1 became effective under the terms of 1991, 303:10, I, as amended by 1994, 383:25.

Amendments

—1994. Paragraph XI: Inserted "rivers" following "lakes".

—1992. Paragraph X: Substituted "shoreline cover and" for "shore cover, and visual as well as actual" preceding "points".

Paragraph XVI: Added.

Effective Date.

See note under RSA 483-B:1.

RESEARCH REFERENCES

New Hampshire Practice.

15 N.H.P. Land Use Planning and Zoning § 39.05.

483-B:3. Consistency Required.

I. All state agencies shall perform their responsibilities in a manner consistent with the intent of this chapter. State and local permits for work within the protected shorelands shall be issued only when consistent with the policies of this chapter.

II. When the standards and practices established in this chapter conflict with other local or state laws and rules, the more stringent standard shall control.

III. All agricultural activities and operations in the state as defined in RSA 21:34-a and as governed by RSA 430, including the use of animal manure, lime, wood ash, irrigation, and the clearing of land for agricultural utilization, and other agricultural technologies, shall be exempt from the provisions of this chapter, provided such activities and operations are in conformance with the most recent best management practices determined by the United States Department of Agriculture Natural Resources Conservation Service, the United States Department of Agriculture Cooperative Extension Service and the department of agriculture, markets, and food. Persons carrying out such agricultural activities and operations in the protected shoreland shall work directly with the local representatives of the above agencies for their particular property.

Source.
1991, 303:1. 1992, 235:21. 1995, 130:8, eff. July 23, 1995; 206:2, eff. Aug. 11, 1995.

Editor's note.
Although 1992, 235:21 provided for the amendment of par. III effective on Jan. 1, 1993, the amendment did not become effective until July 1, 1994, the date on which this section was originally enacted by 1991, 303:1 became effective under the terms of 1991, 303:10, I, as amended by 1994, 383:25.

Amendments
—1995. Paragraph III: Chapter 130 substituted "and the department of agriculture, markets, and food" for "and the department of agriculture" following "Extension Service" in the first sentence.
Chapter 206 substituted "United States Department of Agriculture Natural Resources Conservation Service" for "United States Department of Agriculture Soil Conservation Service" in the first sentence.

—1992. Paragraph III: Inserted "and the clearing of land for agricultural utilization" following "irrigation" and "the most recent" following "conformance with" in the first sentence and added the second sentence.

Effective Date.
See note under RSA 483-B:1.

NOTES TO DECISIONS

1. Permit
Once a boathouse project was relocated landward of a bank, it lost its status as a water dependent structure because it was no longer located over, on, or in the waters of the State of New Hampshire. It was then located over a dredged inlet, and no longer required a dredge and fill permit so that there was no legal basis for imposing the N.H. Code Admin. R. Ann., Env-Wt 302.03 requirements on the boathouse. Cayten v. N.H. Dep't of Envtl. Servs., — N.H. —, 927 A.2d 494, 2007 N.H. LEXIS 113 (July 13, 2007).

[RSA 483-B:4 effective until April 1, 2008; see also RSA 483-B:4 set out below.]

483-B:4. Definitions.

In this chapter:

I. "Abutter" means any person whose property is located in New Hampshire and adjoins or is directly across the street or stream from the land under consideration by the local land use board. For purposes of receiving testimony only, and not for purposes of notification, the term "abutter" shall include any person who is able to demonstrate that his land will be directly affected by the proposal under consideration.

II. "Accessory structure" means a structure, as defined in paragraph XXII of this section, on the same lot and customarily incidental and subordinate to the primary structure, as defined in paragraph XIV of this section; or a use, including but not limited to paths, driveways, patios, any other improved surface, pump houses, gazebos, woodsheds, garages, or other outbuildings.

III. "Basal area" means the cross sectional area of a tree measured at a height of 4-½ feet above the ground, usually expressed in square feet per acre for a stand of trees.

IV. "Commissioner" means the commissioner of the department of environmental services or designee.

V. "Department" means the department of environmental services.

VI. "Disturbed area" means an area in which natural vegetation is removed, exposing the underlying soil.

VII. "Ground cover" means any herbaceous plant which normally grows to a mature height of 4 feet or less.

VIII. "Lot of record" means a legally created parcel, the plat or description of which has been recorded at the registry of deeds for the county in which it is located.

IX. [Repealed.]

X. "Municipality" means a city, town, village district if specifically authorized to zone by the legislature, or county in respect to unincorporated towns or unorganized places or any combination thereof pursuant to RSA 53-A.

XI. "Natural woodland buffer" means a forested area consisting of various species of trees, saplings, shrubs, and ground covers in any combination and at any stage of growth.

XI-a. "Ordinary high water mark" means the line on the shore, running parallel to the main stem of the river, established by the fluctuations of water and indicated by physical characteristics such as a clear, natural line impressed on the immediate bank, shelving, changes in the character of soil, destruction of terrestrial vegetation, the presence of litter and debris, or other appropriate means that consider the characteristics of the surrounding areas. Where the ordinary high water mark is not easily discernable, the ordinary high water mark may be determined by the department of environmental services.

XII. "Person" means a corporation, company, association, society, firm, partnership or joint stock company, as well as an individual, a state, and any political subdivision of a state or any agency or instrumentality thereof.

XIII. "Primary building line" means a setback from the reference line.

XIV. "Primary structure" means a structure as defined in paragraph XXII of this section that is central to the fundamental use of the property and is not accessory to the use of another structure on the same premises.

XV. "Protected shoreland" means, for natural, fresh water bodies without artificial impoundments, for artificially impounded fresh water bodies, and for coastal waters and rivers, all land located within 250 feet of the reference line of public waters.

XVI. "Public waters" shall include:

(a) All fresh water bodies listed in the official list of public waters published by the department pursuant to RSA 271:20, II, whether they are great ponds or artificial impoundments.

(b) Coastal waters, being all waters subject to the ebb and flow of the tide, including the Great Bay Estuary and the associated tidal rivers.

(c) Rivers, meaning all year-round flowing waters of fourth order or higher, as shown on the now current version of the U.S. Geological Survey 7 ½' topographic maps. Stream order shall be determined using the Strahler method, whereby the highest year-round streams in a watershed are first order streams, their juncture yields second order streams, the juncture of second order streams yields third order streams, et seq. A listing of the streams of fourth order and higher shall be prepared and maintained by the office of energy and planning and delivered to the commissioner 30 days after the effective date of this act.

XVII. "Reference line" means:

(a) For natural fresh water bodies without artificial impoundments, the natural mean high water level as determined by the department of environmental services.

(b) For artificially impounded fresh water bodies with established flowage rights, the limit of the flowage rights, and for water bodies without established flowage rights, the waterline at full pond as determined by the elevation of the spillway crest.

(c) For coastal waters, the highest observable tide line, which means a line defining the furthest landward limit of tidal flow, not including storm events, which can be recognized by indicators such as the presence of a strand line of flotsam and debris, the landward margin of salt tolerant vegetation, or a physical barrier that blocks further flow of the tide.

(d) For rivers, the ordinary high water mark.

XVIII. "Removal or removed" means cut, sawed, pruned, girdled, felled, pushed over, buried, burned, killed, or otherwise destructively altered.

XVIII-a. "Repeat violation" means a violation that occurs within 3 years of notification by the department of a prior violation, as defined in RSA 483-B:18, I, whether on the same site or by the same person or entity on a second site. Each day of continuing violation after notification of that violation shall be considered a repeat violation.

XVIII-b. "Repair" means work conducted to restore an existing, legal structure by partial replacement of worn, broken, or unsound parts or to fix a specific defect, during which all of the exterior dimensions are intact and remain so during construction.

XVIII-c. "Replace in kind" means the substitution of a new structure for an existing legal structure, whether in total or in part, with no change in size, dimensions, footprint, interior square footage, and location, with the exception of changes resulting in an increase in the setback to public waters.

XVIII-d. "Replacement system" means a septic system that is not considered new construction under RSA 485-A:29-44 and rules adopted to implement it.

XIX. "Residential unit" means a structure, or portion thereof, providing complete and independent living facilities, including permanent facilities for living, sleeping, eating, cooking, and sanitation which are used in common by one or more persons.

XX. "Sapling" means any woody plant which normally grows to a mature height greater than 20 feet and has a diameter less than 6 inches at a point 4-½ feet above the ground.

XX-a. "Shoreland frontage" means the average of the distances of the actual natural shoreline footage and a straight line drawn between property lines.

XXI. "Shrub" means any multi-stemmed woody plant which normally grows to a mature height of less than 20 feet.

XXII. "Structure" means anything built for the support, shelter or enclosure of persons, animals, goods, or property of any kind, as well as anything constructed or erected with a fixed location on or in the ground, exclusive of fences.

XXIII. "Subdivision" means subdivision as defined in RSA 672:14.

XXIV. "Tree" means any woody plant which normally grows to a mature height greater than 20 feet and which has a diameter of 6 inches or more at a point 4-½ feet above the ground.

XXV. "Urbanization" means the concentrated development found in the sections of towns or cities where there has been an historic pattern of intensive building for commercial or industrial use, or mixed residential, commercial, and industrial use.

XXVI. "Water dependent structure" means a structure that services and supports activities that require direct access to, or contact with the water, or both, as an operational necessity and that requires a permit under RSA 482-A, including but not limited to a dock, wharf, pier, breakwater, beach, boathouse, retaining wall, or launching ramp.

Source.
1991, 303:1. 1992, 235:3-7, 22. 1994, 383:2-5, 22, I, eff. July 1, 1994. 1996, 17:1, 2, eff. June 14, 1996; 228:65, eff. July 1, 1996. 2002, 169:1, eff. Jan. 1, 2003; 263:2-7, eff. July 17, 2002. 2003, 319:9, eff. July 1, 2003. 2004, 257:44, eff. July 1, 2004.

Editor's note.
Although 1992, 235:3, 5–7, 22 provided for the amendment of pars. IX, XVI, XVII, XIX and XV, respectively, and 1992, 235:4 provided for the addition of par. XI-a effective on Jan. 1, 1993, the amendments to this section did not become effective until July 1, 1994, the date on which this section as originally enacted by 1991, 303:1 became effective under the terms of 1991, 303:10, I, as amended by 1994, 383:25.

Amendments
—2004. Paragraph XVI(c): Substituted "office of energy and planning" for "office of state planning and energy programs".

—2003. Paragraph XVI(c): Substituted "office of state planning and energy programs" for "office of state planning".

—2002. Paragraph II: Rewritten by ch. 263:2 to the extent that a detailed comparison would be impracticable.

Paragraph VIII: Chapter 263:3 inserted "legally created" preceding "parcel".

Paragraph XIV: Rewritten by ch. 263:4 to the extent that a detailed comparison would be impracticable.

Paragraph XVIII-a: Added by chs. 169 and 263:5.

Paragraphs XVIII-b and XVIII-c: Added by ch. 263:5.

Paragraph XX-a: Added by ch. 263:6.

Paragraph XXVI: Added by ch. 263:7.

—1996. Paragraph XIII: Chapter 17 substituted "reference" for "public boundary" preceding "line".

Paragraph XVII(a): Chapter 228 substituted "department of environmental services" for "division of water resources of the department".

Paragraph XVII(b): Rewritten by ch. 17 to the extent that a detailed comparison would be impracticable.

—1994. Paragraph IX: Repealed.

Paragraph X: Added "or any combination

thereof pursuant to RSA 53-A" following "places".

Paragraph XV: Substituted "reference" for "public boundary" preceding "line".

Paragraph XVII: Rewrote the introductory clause and amended subpar. (c) generally.

—1992. Paragraph IX: Inserted "residential" preceding "dwelling".

Paragraph XI-a: Added.

Paragraph XV: Inserted "for natural, fresh water bodies without artificial impoundments, for artificially impounded fresh water bodies, and for coastal waters and rivers" following "means".

Paragraph XVI(c): Added.

Paragraph XVII(c): Substituted "mean high tide established by the U.S. Coastal and Geo-

detic Survey" for "limit of the highest observable tide as determined by the wetlands board" following "waters, the".

Paragraph XVII(d): Added.

Paragraph XIX: Inserted "or portion thereof" preceding "providing", deleted "for one or more persons" preceding "including" and added "which are used in common by one or more persons" following "sanitation".

Effective Date.
See note under RSA 483-B:1.

Redesignation of paragraphs.
Paragraphs XVIII-a--XVIII-c, as added by 2002, 263:5, were redesignated as pars. XVIII-b--XVIII-d pursuant to 2002, 263:13, eff. July 17, 2002.

RESEARCH REFERENCES

New Hampshire Practice.
15 N.H.P. Land Use Planning and Zoning § 39.05.

[RSA 483-B:4 effective April 1, 2008; see bound volume for RSA 483-B:4 as effective until April 1, 2008.]

483-B:4. Definitions.

In this chapter:

I. "Abutter" means any person whose property is located in New Hampshire and adjoins or is directly across the street or stream from the land under consideration by the local land use board. For purposes of receiving testimony only, and not for purposes of notification, the term "abutter" shall include any person who is able to demonstrate that his land will be directly affected by the proposal under consideration.

II. "Accessory structure" means a structure, as defined in paragraph XXII of this section, on the same lot and customarily incidental and subordinate to the primary structure, as defined in paragraph XIV of this section; or a use, including but not limited to paths, driveways, patios, any other improved surface, pump houses, gazebos, woodsheds, garages, or other outbuildings.

III. "Basal area" means the cross sectional area of a tree measured at a height of 4-½ feet above the ground, usually expressed in square feet per acre for a stand of trees.

IV. "Commissioner" means the commissioner of the department of environmental services or designee.

V. "Department" means the department of environmental services.

VI. "Disturbed area" means an area in which natural vegetation is removed, exposing the underlying soil.

VII. "Ground cover" means any herbaceous plant which normally grows to a mature height of 4 feet or less.

VII-a. "Impervious surface" means any modified surface that cannot effectively absorb or infiltrate water. Examples of impervious surfaces include, but are not limited to, roofs, decks, patios, and paved, gravel, or crushed stone driveways, parking areas, and walkways unless designed to effectively absorb or infiltrate water.

VIII. "Lot of record" means a legally created parcel, the plat or description of which has been recorded at the registry of deeds for the county in which it is located.

IX. [Repealed.]

X. "Municipality" means a city, town, village district if specifically authorized to zone by the legislature, or county in respect to unincorporated towns or unorganized places or any combination thereof pursuant to RSA 53-A.

X-a. "Natural ground cover" means any herbaceous plant or any woody seeding or shrub generally less than 3 feet in height. Natural ground cover shall also include naturally occurring leaf or needle litter, stumps, decaying woody debris, stones, and boulders. Natural ground cover shall not include lawns, invasive species as listed by the department of agriculture, markets, and food in accordance with RSA 430:53, III, exotic species as designated by rule of the department of environmental services in accordance with RSA 487:24, VII, Imported organic or stone mulches, or other artificial materials.

XI. "Natural woodland buffer" means a forested area consisting of various species of trees, saplings, shrubs, and ground covers in any combination and at any stage of growth.

XI-a. "Nonconforming lot of record" means an existing lot which does not conform to the provisions of this chapter.

XI-b. "Nonconforming structure" means a structure that, either individually or when viewed in combination with other structures on the property, does not conform to the provisions of this chapter, including but not limited to the impervious surface limits of RSA 483-B:9, V(g).

XI-c. "Ordinary high water mark" means the line on the shore, running parallel to the main stem of the river, established by the fluctuations of water and indicated by physical characteristics such as a clear, natural line impressed on the immediate bank, shelving, changes in the character of soil, destruction of terrestrial vegetation, the presence of litter and debris, or other appropriate means that consider the characteristics of the surrounding areas. Where the ordinary high water mark is not easily discernable, the ordinary high water mark may be determined by the department of environmental services.

XII. "Person" means a corporation, company, association, society, firm, partnership or joint stock company, as well as an individual, a state, and any political subdivision of a state or any agency or instrumentality thereof.

XIII. "Primary building line" means a setback from the reference line.

XIV. "Primary structure" means a structure as defined in paragraph XXII of this section that is central to the fundamental use of the property and is not accessory to the use of another structure on the same premises.

XV. "Protected shoreland" means, for natural, fresh water bodies without artificial impoundments, for artificially impounded fresh water bodies, and for coastal waters and rivers, all land located within 250 feet of the reference line of public waters.

XVI. "Public waters" shall include:

(a) All fresh water bodies listed in the official list of public waters published by the department pursuant to RSA 271:20, II, whether they are great ponds or artificial impoundments.

(b) Coastal waters, being all waters subject to the ebb and flow of the tide, including the Great Bay Estuary and the associated tidal rivers.

(c) Rivers, meaning all year-round flowing waters of fourth order or higher and all rivers and river segments designated as protected under RSA 483:15. Stream order shall be determined using the New Hampshire hydrography dataset archived by the geographically referenced analysis and information transfer system (GRANIT) at the complex systems research center of the university of New Hampshire, and developed by GRANIT in collaboration with the department of environmental services. A listing of the streams of fourth order and higher shall be prepared and periodically updated by the GRANIT at the complex systems research center of the university of New Hampshire and delivered to the commissioner 30 days after the effective date of this section.

XVII. "Reference line" means:

(a) For natural fresh water bodies without artificial impoundments, the natural mean high water level as determined by the department of environmental services.

(b) For artificially impounded fresh water bodies with established flowage rights, the limit of the flowage rights, and for water bodies without established flowage rights, the waterline at full pond as determined by the elevation of the spillway crest.

(c) For coastal waters, the highest observable tide line, which means a line defining the furthest landward limit of tidal flow, not including storm events, which can be recognized by indicators such as the presence of a strand line of flotsam and debris, the landward margin of salt tolerant vegetation, or a physical barrier that blocks further flow of the tide.

(d) For rivers, the ordinary high water mark.

XVIII. "Removal or removed" means cut, sawed, pruned, girdled, felled, pushed over, buried, burned, killed, or otherwise destructively altered.

XVIII-a. "Repeat violation" means a violation that occurs within 3 years of notification by the department of a prior violation, as defined in RSA 483-B:18, I, whether on the same site or by the same person or entity on a second site. Each day of continuing violation after notification of that violation shall be considered a repeat violation.

XVIII-b. "Repair" means work conducted to restore an existing, legal structure by partial replacement of worn, broken, or unsound parts or to fix a specific defect, during which all of the exterior dimensions are intact and remain so during construction.

XVIII-c. "Replace in kind" means the substitution of a new structure for an existing legal structure, whether in total or in part, with no change in size, dimensions, footprint, interior square footage, and location, with the exception of changes resulting in an increase in the setback to public waters.

XVIII-d. "Replacement system" means a septic system that is not considered new construction under RSA 485-A:29-44 and rules adopted to implement it.

XIX. "Residential unit" means a structure, or portion thereof, providing complete and independent living facilities, including permanent facilities for living, sleeping, eating, cooking, and sanitation which are used in common by one or more persons.

XX. "Sapling" means any woody plant which normally grows to a mature height greater than 20 feet and has a diameter less than 6 inches at a point 4-½ feet above the ground.

XX-a. "Shoreland frontage" means the average of the distances of the actual natural shoreline footage and a straight line drawn between property lines.

XXI. "Shrub" means any multi-stemmed woody plant which normally grows to a mature height of less than 20 feet.

XXII. "Structure" means anything built for the support, shelter or enclosure of persons, animals, goods, or property of any kind, as well as anything constructed or erected with a fixed location on or in the ground, exclusive of fences.

XXIII. "Subdivision" means subdivision as defined in RSA 672:14.

XXIV. "Tree" means any woody plant which normally grows to a mature height greater than 20 feet and which has a diameter of 6 inches or more at a point 4-½ feet above the ground.

XXIV-a. "Undisturbed state" means native vegetation allowed to grow without interference.

XXV. "Urbanization" means the concentrated development found in the sections of towns or cities where there has been an historic pattern of intensive building for commercial or industrial use, or mixed residential, commercial, and industrial use.

XXVI. "Water dependent structure" means a structure that is a dock, wharf, pier, breakwater, beach, boathouse, retaining wall, or launching ramp or other similar structure, or any part thereof, built over, on, or in the waters of the state.

Source.
1991, 303:1. 1992, 235:3-7, 22. 1994, 383:2-5, 22, I, eff. July 1, 1994. 1996, 17:1, 2, eff. June 14, 1996; 228:65, eff. July 1, 1996. 2002, 169:1, eff. Jan. 1, 2003; 263:2-7, eff. July 17, 2002. 2003, 319:9, eff. July 1, 2003. 2004, 257:44, eff. July 1, 2004. 2007, 267:1–6, eff. April 1, 2008.

Editor's note.
Although 1992, 235:3, 5–7, 22 provided for the amendment of pars. IX, XVI, XVII, XIX and XV, respectively, and 1992, 235:4 provided for the addition of par. XI-a effective on Jan. 1, 1993, the amendments to this section did not become effective until July 1, 1994, the date on which this section as originally enacted by 1991, 303:1 became effective under the terms of 1991, 303:10, I, as amended by 1994, 383:25.

Amendments
—2007. Paragraph VII-a: Added.
Paragraph X-a: Added.
Paragraph XI-a: Added.
Paragraph XI-b: Added.
Paragraph XI-c: Redesignated from former par. XI-a.
Paragraph XVI(c): Rewritten to the extent that a detailed comparison would be impracticable.
Paragraph XXIV-a: Added.
Paragraph XXVI: Rewritten to the extent that a detailed comparison would be impracticable..

—2004. Paragraph XVI(c): Substituted "office of energy and planning" for "office of state planning and energy programs".

—2003. Paragraph XVI(c): Substituted "office of state planning and energy programs" for "office of state planning".

—2002. Paragraph II: Rewritten by ch. 263:2 to the extent that a detailed comparison would be impracticable.

Paragraph VIII: Chapter 263:3 inserted "legally created" preceeding "parcel".

Paragraph XIV: Rewritten by ch. 263:4 to the extent that a detailed comparison would be impracticable.

Paragraph XVIII-a: Added by chs. 169 and 263:5.

Paragraphs XVIII-b and XVIII-c: Added by ch. 263:5.

Paragraph XX-a: Added by ch. 263:6.

Paragraph XXVI: Added by ch. 263:7.

—1996. Paragraph XIII: Chapter 17 substituted "reference" for "public boundary" preceding "line".

Paragraph XVII(a): Chapter 228 substituted "department of environmental services" for "division of water resources of the department".

Paragraph XVII(b): Rewritten by ch. 17 to the extent that a detailed comparison would be impracticable.

—1994. Paragraph IX: Repealed.

Paragraph X: Added "or any combination thereof pursuant to RSA 53-A" following "places".

Paragraph XV: Substituted "reference" for "public boundary" preceding "line".

Paragraph XVII: Rewrote the introductory clause and amended subpar. (c) generally.

—1992. Paragraph IX: Inserted "residential" preceding "dwelling".

Paragraph XI-a: Added.

Paragraph XV: Inserted "for natural, fresh water bodies without artificial impoundments, for artificially impounded fresh water bodies, and for coastal waters and rivers" following "means".

Paragraph XVI(c): Added.

Paragraph XVII(c): Substituted "mean high tide established by the U.S. Coastal and Geodetic Survey" for "limit of the highest observable tide as determined by the wetlands board" following "waters, the".

Paragraph XVII(d): Added.

Paragraph XIX: Inserted "or portion thereof" preceding "providing", deleted "for one or more persons" preceding "including" and added "which are used in common by one or more persons" following "sanitation".

Effective Date.
See note under RSA 483-B:1.

Redesignation of paragraphs.
Paragraphs XVIII-a--XVIII-c, as added by 2002, 263:5, were redesignated as pars. XVIII-b--XVIII-d pursuant to 2002, 263:13, eff. July 17, 2002.

NOTES TO DECISIONS

Water dependent structure
Once a boathouse project was relocated landward of a bank, it lost its status as a water dependent structure because it was no longer located over, on, or in the waters of the State of New Hampshire. It was then located over a dredged inlet, and no longer required a dredge and fill permit so that there was no legal basis for imposing the N.H. Code Admin. R. Ann., Env-Wt 302.03 requirements on the boathouse. Cayten v. N.H. Dep't of Envtl. Servs., — N.H. —, 927 A.2d 494, 2007 N.H. LEXIS 113 (July 13, 2007).

RESEARCH REFERENCES

New Hampshire Practice.
15 N.H.P. Land Use Planning and Zoning § 39.05.

483-B:5. Enforcement by Commissioner; Duties; Woodland Buffer.

I. The commissioner, with the advice and assistance of the office of energy and planning, department of resources and economic development and department of agriculture, markets, and food, shall enforce the provisions of this chapter.

II. The commissioner or his designee may, for cause, enter upon any land or parcel at any reasonable time to perform oversight and enforcement duties provided for in this chapter.

III. [Repealed.]

IV. To encourage coordination of state and local enforcement measures, the commissioner shall notify, at the time of issuance or filing, the local governing body of enforcement action undertaken by the state in respect to protected shoreland within the municipality by sending it copies of relevant administrative orders issued and pleadings filed.

V. The commissioner may issue an order to any person in violation of this chapter, of rules adopted under this chapter, or of any condition of a permit issued under this chapter.

Source.
1991, 303:1. 1992, 235:8, 9. 1994, 383:6, 22II, eff. July 1, 1994. 1995, 130:4, eff. July 23, 1995. 2003, 319:9, eff. July 1, 2003. 2004, 257:44, eff. July 1, 2004.

Editor's note.
Although 1992, 235:8, 9 provided for the amendment of pars. II and IV, respectively, effective on Jan. 1, 1993, the amendment did not become effective until July 1, 1994, the date on which this section as originally enacted by 1991, 303:1 became effective under the terms of 1991, 303:10, I, as amended by 1994, 383:25.

Amendments
—**2004.** Paragraph I: Substituted "office of energy and planning" for "office of state planning and energy programs".

—**2003.** Paragraph I: Substituted "office of state planning and energy programs" for "office of state planning".

—**1995.** Paragraph I: Substituted "department of agriculture, markets, and food" for "department of agriculture".

—**1994.** Deleted "forest inventory plans" following "buffer" in the section catchline and repealed par. III.

—**1992.** Paragraph II: Inserted "for cause" preceding "enter".
Paragraph IV: Inserted "at the time of issuance or filing" following "notify".

Effective Date.
See note under RSA 483-B:1.

[RSA 483-B:5-a effective April 1, 2008.]

483-B:5-a. Permit Required; Exemption.

I. (a) No person shall commence construction, excavation, or filling activities within the protected shoreland without obtaining a permit from the department to ensure compliance with this chapter.

[Paragraph I(b) repealed effective July 1, 2011; see prospective repeal note set out below.]

(b) The permit application fee shall be $100 plus $.10 per square foot of area affected by the proposed activities and shall be deposited in the wetlands and shorelands review fund established under RSA 482-A:3, III. Such fees shall be capped as follows:

(1) For projects of 0-9,999 square feet, $750.

(2) For projects of 10,000 – 24,999 square feet, $1,875.

(3) For projects of 25,000 square feet or more, $3,750.

II. Timber harvesting operations permitting requirements shall be in accordance with RSA 485-A:17, IV and therefore shall be exempt from the permitting requirement under paragraph I.

[Paragraph III repealed effective July 1, 2011; see prospective repeal note set out below.]

III. Construction of public roads, public utility lines and associated structures and facilities, and public water access facilities shall be exempt from the permitting fees of paragraph I.

IV. Impacts in the protected shoreland that receive a permit in accordance with RSA 482-A shall not require a permit under this section.

V. (a) Within 30 days of receipt of an application for a permit or 75 days of receipt of an application for a permit that will require a variance of the minimum standard of RSA 483-B:9, V or a waiver of the minimum standards of RSA 483-B:9, the department shall request any additional information required to complete its evaluation of the application, and provide the applicant with any written technical comments the department deems necessary. Any request for additional information shall specify that the applicant submit such information as soon as practicable and notify the applicant that if all of the requested information is not received within 60 days of the request, the department shall deny the application.

(b) When the department requests additional information pursuant to subparagraph (a), the department shall, within 30 days of the department's receipt of the information:

(1) Approve the application and issue a permit;

(2) Deny the application, in whole or in part; or

(3) Extend the time for response for good cause and with the written agreement of the applicant.

(c) Where no request for additional information is made, the department shall, within 30 days of receipt of the application for a permit or 75 days of receipt of an application for a permit that will require a variance of the minimum standard of RSA 483-B:9, V or a waiver of the minimum standards of RSA 483-B:9, approve or deny the application, in whole or in part.

(d) If the department fails to render a decision in the time frame provided in this paragraph, the application shall be deemed to be approved and a permit shall be issued.

Source.

2007, 269:1, eff. April 1, 2008. 2007, 267:12, eff. April 1, 2008 at 12:01 a.m. [see contingency note below].

Amendments

—**2007.** Paragraph V: Rewritten by ch. 267 to the extent that a detailed comparison would be impracticable.

Prospective repeal of paragraph I(b).
2007, 269:8, I, provides for the repeal of par. I(b) effective on July 1, 2011.

Prospective repeal of paragraph III.
2007, 269:8, II, provides for the repeal of par. III effective on July 1, 2011.

2007 contingent amendment.
2007, 267:13, eff. June 29, 2007, provided in part: "If HB 663-FN-A [ch. 269] of the 2007 legislative session becomes law, section 12 [which adds RSA 483-B:17, V] shall take effect April 1, 2008 at 12:01 a.m."

483-B:6. Prior Approval; Permits.

I. Within the protected shoreland, any person intending to:

(a) Engage in any earth excavation activity shall obtain all necessary local approvals in compliance with RSA 155-E.

(b) Construct a water-dependent structure, alter the bank, or construct or replenish a beach shall obtain approval and all necessary permits pursuant to RSA 482-A.

(c) Install a septic system as described in RSA 483-B:9, V(b)(1)-(3) shall obtain all permits pursuant to RSA 485-A:29.

(d) Conduct an activity resulting in a contiguous disturbed area exceeding 50,000 square feet shall obtain a permit pursuant to RSA 485-A:17.

(e) Subdivide land as described in RSA 483-B:9, V(d) and (e) shall obtain approval pursuant to RSA 485-A:29.

(f) Conduct an activity regulated under a local zoning ordinance shall obtain all necessary local approvals.

II. In applying for these approvals and permits, such persons shall demonstrate to the satisfaction of the department that the proposal meets or exceeds the development standards of this chapter. The department shall grant, deny, or attach reasonable conditions to a permit listed in subparagraphs I(a)-(e), to protect the public waters or the public health, safety or welfare. Such conditions shall be related to the purposes of this chapter.

Source.
1991, 303:1. 1992, 235:10, eff. Jan. 1, 1993. 1996, 17:3, eff. June 14, 1996. 17:3, eff. June 14, 1996. 2002, 263:8, eff. July 17, 2002.

Editor's note.
Although 1992, 235:10 provided for the amendment of this section effective on Jan. 1, 1993, the amendment did not become effective until July 1, 1994, the date on which this section as originally enacted by 1991, 303:1 became effective under the terms of 1991, 303:10, I, as amended by 1994, 383:25.

Amendments
—2002. Paragraph I(e): Deleted "for residential or non-residential development" following "land".

—1996. Paragraph I(b): Substituted "alter the bank, or construct or replenish a beach" for "as described in RSA 483-B:9, II(c)" following "structure".

—1992. Rewritten to the extent that a detailed comparison would be impracticable.

Effective Date.
See note under RSA 483-B:1.

RESEARCH REFERENCES

New Hampshire Practice.
15 N.H.P. Land Use Planning and Zoning § 39.05.

[RSA 483-B:6 effective April 1, 2008; see bound volume for RSA 483-B:6 as effective until April 1, 2008.]

483-B:6. Other Required Permits and Approvals.

I. Within the protected shoreland, any person intending to:

(a) Engage in any earth excavation activity shall obtain all necessary local approvals in compliance with RSA 155-E.

(b) Construct a water-dependent structure, alter the bank, or construct or replenish a beach shall obtain approval and all necessary permits pursuant to RSA 482-A.

(c) Install a septic system as described in RSA 483-B:9, V(c) shall obtain all permits pursuant to RSA 485-A:29.

(d) Conduct an activity resulting in a contiguous disturbed area exceeding 50,000 square feet shall obtain a permit pursuant to RSA 485-A:17.

(e) Subdivide land as described in RSA 483-B:9, V(e) and (f) shall obtain approval pursuant to RSA 485-A:29.

(f) Conduct an activity regulated under a local zoning ordinance shall obtain all necessary local approvals.

II. In applying for approvals and permits, pursuant to paragraph I, applicants shall demonstrate that the proposal meets or exceeds the development standards of this chapter. The department shall develop minimum standards for information to be required on or with all applications under paragraph I. The department or municipality shall grant, deny, or attach reasonable conditions to approvals or permits listed in subparagraphs I(a)-(f), to protect the public waters or the public health, safety or welfare. Such conditions shall be related to the purposes of this chapter.

III. The commissioner shall have the sole authority to issue variances and waivers of the provisions of this chapter as specifically authorized by this chapter.

IV. No variance, permit, or approval issued by a municipality shall exempt the owner from obtaining any other necessary permit or approval from the department as required by this chapter.

Source.
1991, 303:1. 1992, 235:10, eff. Jan. 1, 1993. 1996, 17:3, eff. June 14, 1996. 17:3, eff. June 14, 1996. 2002, 263:8, eff. July 17, 2002. 2007, 267:7, eff. April 1, 2008.

stituted "RSA 483-B:9, V(c)" for "RSA 483-B:9, V(b)(1)-(3)" in par. I(c), "RSA 483-B:9, V(e) and (f)" for "RSA 483-B:9, V(d) and (e)" in par. I(e); added par. I(f); rewrote par. II; and added pars. III and IV.

Editor's note.
Although 1992, 235:10 provided for the amendment of this section effective on Jan. 1, 1993, the amendment did not become effective until July 1, 1994, the date on which this section as originally enacted by 1991, 303:1 became effective under the terms of 1991, 303:10, I, as amended by 1994, 383:25.

—**2002.** Paragraph I(e): Deleted "for residential or non-residential development" following "land".

—**1996.** Paragraph I(b): Substituted "alter the bank, or construct or replenish a beach" for "as described in RSA 483-B:9, II(c)" following "structure".

Amendments
—**2007.** Rewrote the section heading; sub-

—**1992.** Rewritten to the extent that a detailed comparison would be impracticable.

Effective Date.
See note under RSA 483-B:1.

NOTES TO DECISIONS

Cited:
Cited in Cayten v. N.H. Dep't of Envtl. Servs.,

— N.H. —, 927 A.2d 494, 2007 N.H. LEXIS 113
(July 13, 2007).

RESEARCH REFERENCES

New Hampshire Practice.
15 N.H.P. Land Use Planning and Zoning
§ 39.05.

483-B:7. Reporting; On-Site Inspections; Local Participation.

The department may devise a system whereby municipal officials may voluntarily assist with the permitting process under RSA 483-B:6 and the subsequent enforcement of permit conditions, by performing certain reporting functions relative to on-site inspections. Utilization of such reports shall be at the department's discretion, but may, when appropriate, obviate the need for further on-site review by department staff.

Source.
1991, 303:1. 1992, 235:23, eff. Jan. 1, 1993.

Editor's note.
Although 1992, 235:23 provided for the amendment of this section effective on Jan. 1, 1993, the amendment did not become effective until July 1, 1994, the date on which this section as originally enacted by 1991, 303:1 became effective under the terms of 1991, 303:10, I, as amended by 1994, 383:25.

Amendments
—**1992.** Substituted "department" for "commissioner" preceding "may devise" in the first sentence and "department's" for "commissioner's" preceding "discretion" in the second sentence.

Effective Date.
See note under RSA 483-B:1.

483-B:8. Municipal Authority.

I. Municipalities may adopt land use control ordinances relative to all protected shorelands which are more stringent than the minimum standards contained in this chapter.

II. Municipalities are encouraged to adopt land use control ordinances for the shorelands of water bodies and water courses other than public waters.

III. Municipalities in which protected shoreland is situated may enforce the provisions of this chapter by issuing cease and desist orders and by seeking injunctive relief or civil penalties as provided in RSA 483-B:18, III(a) and (b). Civil penalties and fines collected by the court shall be remitted within 14 days to the treasurer of the municipality prosecuting said violations, for the use of the municipality. Any municipality electing to enforce the provisions of this chapter shall send copies of any pleading to the attorney general at the time of filing. Municipalities bordering the same water body are encouraged to employ jointly a single code enforcement officer to monitor compliance.

IV. The authority granted to municipalities under this chapter shall not be interpreted to extend to RSA 430:28-48.

V. Municipalities bordering the same water body are encouraged to employ jointly a single code enforcement officer to monitor compliance.

Source.
    1991, 303:1. 1992, 235:11, eff. Jan. 1, 1993.

References in text.
    RSA 430:31-a, contained in RSA 430:28-48 in par. IV, was repealed by 1997, 101:1, eff. Aug. 3, 1997.

Editor's note.
    Although 1992, 235:11 provided for the addition of par. V effective on Jan. 1, 1993, the amendment did not become effective until July 1, 1994, the date on which this section as

originally enacted by 1991, 303:1 became effective under the terms of 1991, 303:10, I, as amended by 1994, 383:25.

Amendments
    —1992. Paragraph V: Added.

Effective Date.
    See note under RSA 483-B:1.

Cross References.
    Enforcement of local land use development restrictions generally, see RSA 674:21-a.

RESEARCH REFERENCES

New Hampshire Practice.
    15 N.H.P. Land Use Planning and Zoning § 39.05.

483-B:9. Minimum Shoreland Protection Standards.

I. The standards in this section are designed to minimize shoreland disturbance so as to protect the public waters, while still accommodating reasonable levels of development in the protected shoreland. Development outside the protected shoreland shall conform to local zoning and local ordinances and shall not be subject to standards established in this chapter.

II. Within the protected shoreland the following restrictions shall apply:

(a) The establishment or expansion of salt storage yards, automobile junk yards, and solid or hazardous waste facilities shall be prohibited.

(b) Primary structures shall be set back behind the primary building line which is 50 feet from the reference line.

(c) A water dependent structure, meaning one which is a dock, wharf, pier, breakwater, or other similar structure, or any part thereof, built over, on, or in the waters of the state, shall be constructed only as approved by the department, pursuant to RSA 482-A.

(d) No fertilizer, except limestone, shall be used within 25 feet of the reference line of any property. Twenty-five feet beyond the reference line, low phosphate, slow release nitrogen fertilizer or limestone, may be used on lawns or areas with grass.

III. Public water supply facilities, including water supply intakes, pipes, water treatment facilities, pump stations, and disinfection stations shall be permitted by the commissioner as necessary, consistent with the purposes of this chapter and other state law. Private water supply facilities shall not require a permit.

IV. The placement and expansion of public water and sewage treatment facilities shall be permitted by the commissioner as necessary, consistent with the purposes of this chapter and other state law.

IV-a. Hydro electric facilities, including, but not limited to, dams, dikes, penstocks, and powerhouses, shall be recognized as water dependent, and shall be permitted by the commissioner as necessary, consistent with the purposes of this chapter and other state law.

[Paragraph IV-b effective until April 1, 2008; see also paragraph IV-b set out below.]

IV-b. Public utility lines and associated structures and facilities shall be permitted by the commissioner as necessary, consistent with the purposes of this chapter and other state law.

[Paragraph IV-b effective April 1, 2008; see also paragraph IV-b set out above.]

IV-b. Public utility lines and associated structures and facilities, public roads, and public water access facilities including boat ramps shall be permitted by the commissioner as necessary and consistent with the purposes of this chapter and other state law.

IV-c. An existing solid waste facility which is located within 250 feet of the reference line of public waters under this chapter may continue to operate under an existing permit, provided it does not cause degradation to an area in excess of that area under permit.

IV-d. No solid waste facility shall place solid waste within 250 feet of the reference line of public waters under this chapter except as expressly permitted under RSA 483-B:9, IV-c. However, any solid waste facility may be allowed, subject to permitting conditions under RSA 149-M:9, to erect accessory structures and conduct other activities consistent with the operation of the facility within 250 feet of the reference line of public waters under this chapter, such as filling, grading and installing monitoring wells and other drainage structures as is consistent with its solid waste permit as issued by the department of environmental services. Under no circumstances shall the toe of any slope encroach within 150 feet of the reference line.

[Paragraph V effective until April 1, 2008; see also paragraph V set out below.]

V. The following minimum standards shall apply to the protected shoreland provided that forest management not associated with shoreland development or land conversion, and conducted in compliance with RSA 227-J:9; forestry involving water supply reservoir watershed management; or agriculture conducted in accordance with best management practices; shall be exempt from the provisions of this chapter:

(a) NATURAL WOODLAND BUFFER.

(1) Where existing, a natural woodland buffer shall be maintained within 150 feet of the reference line. The purpose of this buffer shall be to protect the quality of public waters by minimizing erosion, preventing

siltation and turbidity, stabilizing soils, preventing excess nutrient and chemical pollution, maintaining natural water temperatures, maintaining a healthy tree canopy and understory, preserving fish and wildlife habitat, and respecting the overall natural condition of the protected shoreland.

(2) Within the natural woodland buffer of the protected shoreland under conditions defined in RSA 483-B:9, V, all of the following prohibitions and limitations shall apply:

(A) Not more than a maximum of 50 percent of the basal area of trees, and a maximum of 50 percent of the total number of saplings shall be removed for any purpose in a 20-year period. A healthy, well-distributed stand of trees, saplings, shrubs, ground cover, and their living, undamaged root systems shall be left in place.

(B) Any person applying to the department for a septic system construction approval or alteration of terrain permit pursuant to RSA 485-A, or an excavating and dredging permit pursuant to RSA 482-A, within the protected shoreland shall include photographic documentation of the natural woodland buffer.

(C) Structures, as defined in RSA 483-B:4, XXII, within the natural woodland buffer shall be afforded an opening for building construction that shall be excluded when computing the percentage limitations under subparagraph (a)(2)(A).

(D) Dead, diseased, unsafe, or fallen trees, saplings, shrubs, or ground cover may be removed. Their removal shall not be used in computing the percentage limitations under subparagraph (a)(2)(A).

(E) Stumps and their root systems, which are located within 50 feet of the reference line, shall be left intact in the ground, unless removal is specifically approved by the department under RSA 482-A.

(F) Preservation of dead and living trees that provide dens and nesting places for wildlife is encouraged.

(G) Planting efforts that are beneficial to wildlife are encouraged.

(b) SEPTIC SYSTEMS.

(1) All new lots, including those in excess of 5 acres, created within the protected shoreland are subject to subdivision approval by the department of environmental services under RSA 485-A:29.

(2) The following conditions, based on the characteristics of the receiving soil as they relate to U.S. Department of Agriculture, Natural Resources Conservation Service drainage classes, shall dictate the setback requirements for all new leaching portions of new septic systems, as follows:

(A) Adjacent to ponds, lakes, estuaries, and the open ocean.

(i) Where the receiving soil downgradient of the leaching portions of a septic system is a porous sand and gravel material with a percolation rate equal to or faster than 2 minutes per inch, the setback shall be at least 125 feet from the reference line;

(ii) For soils with restrictive layers within 18 inches of the natural soil surface, the setback shall be at least 100 feet from the reference line; and

(iii) For all other soil conditions, the setback shall be at least 75 feet from the reference line.

(B) Adjacent to rivers the setback shall be no less than 75 feet.

(3) The placement of all septic tanks and leaching portions of septic systems for replacement systems shall comply with the requirements of subparagraph (b)(2), to the maximum extent feasible.

(c) EROSION AND SILTATION.

(1) All new structures, modifications to existing structures, and excavation or earth moving within protected shoreland shall be designed and constructed in accordance with rules adopted by the department under RSA 541-A for terrain alteration under RSA 485-A:17, to manage stormwater and control erosion and sediment, during and after construction.

(2) New structures and all modifications to existing structures within the protected shoreland shall be designed and constructed to prevent the release of surface runoff across exposed mineral soils.

(3) A permit under RSA 485-A:17, I shall be required for improved, developed, or subdivided land whenever there is a contiguous disturbed area exceeding 50,000 square feet that is either partially or wholly within protected shoreland.

(d) MINIMUM LOTS AND RESIDENTIAL DEVELOPMENT. In the protected shoreland:

(1) The minimum size for new lots in areas dependent upon on-site septic systems shall be determined by soil type lot size determinations, as established by the department of environmental services under RSA 485-A and rules adopted to implement it.

(2) For projects in areas dependent upon on-site sewage and septic systems, the total number of residential units in the protected shoreland, whether built on individual lots or grouped as cluster or condominium development, shall not exceed:

(A) One unit per 150 feet of shoreland frontage; or

(B) For any lot that does not have direct frontage, one unit per 150 feet of lot width as measured parallel to the shoreland frontage that lies between the lot and the reference line.

(3) No lot dependent upon an on-site septic system, having frontage on public waters, shall be created with less than 150 feet of shoreland frontage.

(4) Lots in areas serviced by municipal sewers shall conform to municipal minimum lot standards, and shall not be subject to any shoreland frontage requirement, except as provided by municipal standards.

(5) Lots and residential units outside of the protected shoreland shall not be subject to this chapter.

(e) MINIMUM LOTS AND NON-RESIDENTIAL DEVELOPMENT. In the protected shoreland:

(1) The minimum size for new non-residential lots in areas dependent upon on-site septic systems shall be determined by soil type lot size determinations, as set forth under rules adopted under RSA 541-A.

(2) Non-residential development requiring on-site water, sewage, and septic systems shall not be constructed on lots less than 150 feet in width.

298

(3) Non-residential lots in areas serviced by municipal sewers shall conform to municipal minimum lot standards.

(4) Non-residential lots outside of the protected shoreland shall not be subject to this chapter.

(f) COMMON OWNERS AND RESIDENTIAL OR NON-RESIDENTIAL DEVELOPMENT.   In the protected shoreland, waterfront parcels held in common by one or more owners of contiguous interior parcels may be developed, but only in a manner consistent with the provisions of this chapter. Care shall be taken for the adequate provision of parking, toilet facilities, and related support systems to minimize the project's impact on the public waters.

(g) The commissioner shall have the authority to grant variances from the minimum standards of this section. Such authority shall be exercised subject to the criteria which govern the grant of a variance by a zoning board of adjustment under RSA 674:33, I(b).

[Paragraph V effective April 1, 2008; see also paragraph V set out above.]

V. The following minimum standards shall apply to areas and activities within the protected shoreland with the exception of forest management that is not associated with shoreland development or land conversion, and is conducted in compliance with RSA 227-J:9; forestry conducted by or under the direction of a water supplier for the purpose of managing a water supply watershed ; and agriculture conducted in accordance with best management practices as required by RSA 483-B:3, III:

(a) MAINTENANCE OF A WATERFRONT BUFFER.

(1) The waterfront buffer shall be those protected shorelands within 50 feet of the reference line. The purpose of this buffer shall be to protect the quality of public waters while allowing homeowner discretion with regard to water access, safety, viewscape maintenance, and lot design.

(2) Within the waterfront buffer all of the following prohibitions and limitations shall apply:

(A) No chemicals, including pesticides of any kind or fertilizers of any kind except those specified in RSA 483-B:9, II(d), shall be applied.

(B) Rocks and stumps and their root systems shall be left intact in the ground unless removal is specifically approved by the department, pursuant to RSA 482-A or RSA 483-B:11, II.

(C) No natural ground cover shall be removed except as necessary for a foot path to water as provided under RSA 483-B:9, V(a)(2)(D)(viii), cutting those portions that have grown over 3 feet in height for the purpose of providing a view, or as specifically approved by the department, pursuant to RSA 482-A or 483-B:11, II.

(D) Starting from the northerly or easterly boundary of the property, and working along the shoreline, the waterfront buffer shall be divided into 50 by 50 foot segments. Within each segment a minimum combined tree and sapling score of at least 50 points shall be maintained. If for any reason there is insufficient area for a full segment, the number of points required to be maintained in that partial segment shall be proportional to that required of a full segment.

(i) Tree and sapling diameters shall be measured at 4½ feet above the ground and are scored as follows: _Diameter Score_ 1 inch to 6 inches 1 greater than 6 inches to 12 inches 5 greater than 12 inches 10

(ii) Dead, diseased, or unsafe trees or saplings shall not be included in scoring.

(iii) If the total tree and sapling score in any 50 foot by 50 foot segment exceeds 50 points, then trees and saplings may be removed as long as the sum of the scores for the remaining trees and saplings in that segment does not total less than 50 points. Trees and saplings may be removed from partial segments provided that the sum of the scores for the remaining trees and saplings in that partial segment is equal to or greater than the proportional point requirement.

(iv) The department may approve applications pursuant to RSA 482-A that include the planting of native trees and saplings as necessary to at least maintain either the existing combined tree and sapling score or the minimum score required. The department shall not approve any application that would result in a combined tree and sapling score less than the minimum score required where the segment initially meets the minimum score or would result in any reduction of the combined tree and sapling score where the segment does not initially meet the minimum score.

(v) Owners of lots that were legally developed prior to April 1, 2008 may maintain but not enlarge cleared areas, including but not limited to existing lawns and beaches, within the waterfront buffer. Conversion to or planting of cleared areas with native species of ground cover, shrubs, saplings, and trees is encouraged but shall not be required unless it is necessary to meet the requirements of subparagraphs (g)(2) or (g)(3), or RSA 483-B:11, II.

(vi) Normal trimming, pruning, and thinning of branches to the extent necessary to protect structures, maintain clearances, and provide views is permitted. Trimming, pruning, and thinning of branches for the purpose of providing views shall be limited to the bottom 1/2 of the trees or saplings.

(vii) When necessary for the completion of construction activities permitted in accordance with RSA 483-B:6, a temporary 12 foot wide access path shall be allowed. The access path shall be completely restored and replanted with native vegetation upon completion of construction except as allowed under subparagraph (viii).

(viii) A permanent 6-foot wide foot path to the water body, configured in a manner that will not concentrate storm water runoff or contribute to erosion, is allowed.

(b) MAINTENANCE OF A NATURAL WOODLAND BUFFER.

(1) A natural woodland buffer shall be maintained within 150 feet of the reference line. The first 50 feet of this buffer is designated the waterfront buffer and is subject to the additional requirements of subparagraph (a). The

purpose of the natural woodland buffer shall be to protect the quality of public waters by minimizing erosion, preventing siltation and turbidity, stabilizing soils, preventing excess nutrient and chemical pollution, maintaining natural water temperatures, maintaining a healthy tree canopy and understory, preserving fish and wildlife habitat, and respecting the overall natural condition of the protected shoreland.

(2) Within the natural woodland buffer of a given lot:

(A) At least 50 percent of the area outside of impervious surfaces shall be maintained in an undisturbed state. Owners of lots legally developed prior to April 1, 2008 that do not comply with this standard are encouraged to, but shall not be required to, increase the percentage of area maintained in an undisturbed state, except as required by the department under RSA 483-B:11, II. The percentage of area maintained in an undisturbed state on nonconforming lots shall not be decreased.

(B) Any person applying to the department for a septic system construction approval or alteration of terrain permit pursuant to RSA 485-A, or an excavating and dredging permit pursuant to RSA 482-A, within the protected shoreland shall include photographic documentation of the natural woodland buffer.

(C) Dead, diseased, or unsafe, trees, saplings, or shrubs that pose an imminent hazard to structures or have the potential to cause personal injury may be removed regardless of any requirements that pertain to the natural woodland buffer under this chapter. Such exemptions shall not be used to contravene the intent of the law.

(D) Preservation of dead and living trees that provide dens and nesting places for wildlife is encouraged.

(E) Native species planting efforts that are beneficial to wildlife are encouraged.

(c) SEPTIC SYSTEMS.

(1) The subdivision of a parcel of land shall be subject to subdivision approval by the department of environmental services under RSA 485-A:29 if any portion of the land to be subdivided is within the protected shoreland.

(2) The following conditions, based on the characteristics of the receiving soil as they relate to U.S. Department of Agriculture, Natural Resources Conservation Service drainage classes, shall dictate the setback requirements for all new leaching portions of new septic systems, as follows:

(A) Adjacent to ponds, lakes, estuaries, and the open ocean.

(i) Where the receiving soil downgradient of the leaching portions of a septic system is a porous sand and gravel material with a percolation rate equal to or faster than 2 minutes per inch, the setback shall be at least 125 feet from the reference line;

(ii) For soils with restrictive layers within 18 inches of the natural soil surface, the setback shall be at least 100 feet from the reference line; and

(iii) For all other soil conditions, the setback shall be at least 75 feet from the reference line.

(B) Adjacent to rivers the setback shall be no less than 75 feet.

(3) The placement of all septic tanks and leaching portions of septic systems for replacement systems shall comply with the requirements of subparagraph (c)(2), to the maximum extent feasible.

(d) EROSION AND SILTATION.

(1) All new structures, modifications to existing structures, and excavation or earth moving within protected shoreland shall be designed and constructed in accordance with rules adopted by the department under RSA 541-A for terrain alteration under RSA 485-A:17, to manage stormwater and control erosion and sediment, during and after construction.

(2) New structures and all modifications to existing structures within the protected shoreland shall be designed and constructed to prevent the release of surface runoff across exposed mineral soils.

(3) A permit under RSA 485-A:17, I shall be required for improved, developed, or subdivided land whenever there is a contiguous disturbed area exceeding 50,000 square feet that is either partially or wholly within protected shoreland.

(e) MINIMUM LOTS AND RESIDENTIAL DEVELOPMENT.   In the protected shoreland:

(1) The minimum size for new lots in areas dependent upon on-site septic systems shall be determined by soil type lot size determinations, as established by the department of environmental services under RSA 485-A and rules adopted to implement it.

(2) For projects in areas dependent upon on-site sewage and septic systems, the total number of residential units in the protected shoreland, whether built on individual lots or grouped as cluster or condominium development, shall not exceed:

(A) One unit per 150 feet of shoreland frontage; or

(B) For any lot that does not have direct frontage, one unit per 150 feet of lot width as measured parallel to the shoreland frontage that lies between the lot and the reference line.

(3) No lot having frontage on public waters, shall be created with less than 150 feet of shoreland frontage.

(4) Lots and residential units outside of the protected shoreland shall not be subject to this chapter.

(f) MINIMUM LOTS AND NON-RESIDENTIAL DEVELOPMENT.   In the protected shoreland:

(1) The minimum size for new non-residential lots in areas dependent upon on-site septic systems shall be determined by soil type lot size determinations, as set forth under rules adopted under RSA 541-A.

(2) No lot having frontage on public water shall be created with less than 150 feet of shoreland frontage.

(3) Non-residential lots outside of the protected shoreland shall not be subject to this chapter.

(g) IMPERVIOUS SURFACES.

(1) No more than 20 percent of the area of a lot located within the protected shoreland shall be composed of impervious surfaces, except as provided in subparagraphs (2) and (3).

(2) The impervious surface area shall not exceed 25 percent provided that in the waterfront buffer, in addition to any other provisions that apply to such area under this chapter, no trees or saplings shall be removed as provided for in RSA 483-B:9, V(a)(2)(D)(iii) and such restriction is recorded in the chain of title for the property. In addition, if the natural tree and sapling cover in the waterfront buffer does not meet the 50-point minimum score of RSA 483-B:9, V(a)(2)(D) in any segment, then such segment shall be planted, as determined by rule of the department, with native trees, saplings, or natural ground cover in sufficient quantity, type, and location either to meet the minimum score or to provide at least an equivalent level of protection as offered by the minimum score.

(3) The impervious surface area shall not exceed 30 percent provided the conditions of subparagraph (2) are satisfied and a stormwater management system designed to ensure that post-development total runoff volume shall not exceed the pre-development total runoff volume, and approved by the department, shall be implemented and maintained.

(4) Property owners and developers are encouraged to seek creative solutions that utilize low impact development techniques.

(h) COMMON OWNERS AND RESIDENTIAL OR NON-RESIDENTIAL DEVELOPMENT.   In the protected shoreland, waterfront parcels held in common by one or more owners of contiguous interior parcels may be developed, but only in a manner consistent with the provisions of this chapter. Care shall be taken for the adequate provision of parking, toilet facilities, and related support systems to minimize the project's impact on the public waters.

(i) The commissioner shall have the authority to grant variances from the minimum standards of this section. Such authority shall be exercised subject to the criteria which govern the grant of a variance by a zoning board of adjustment under RSA 674:33, I(b).

Source.

1991, 303:1. 1992, 235:12-18, 28, I. 1994, 383:7-14, eff. July 1, 1994. 1995, 32:1, eff. April 24, 1995; 206:2, eff. Aug. 11, 1995; 299:16, eff. Jan. 1, 1996. 1996, 17:4, 5, eff. June 14, 1996; 100:1, eff. May 15, 1996; 228:66, 108, eff. July 1, 1996; 251:22, eff. Aug. 9, 1996; 296:52, 53, eff. Aug. 9, 1996. 2002, 114:1, eff. July 2, 2002; 263:9, eff. July 17, 2002. 2007, 267:8, 9 eff. April. 1, 2008.

Editor's note.

Although 1992, 235:12-17, 28, I, provided for the amendment of pars. I, II(c), III, IV, V(a)-(d) and added pars. IV-a-IV-d effective on Jan. 1, 1993, the amendment did not become effective

until July 1, 1994, the date on which this section as originally enacted by 1991, 303:1 became effective under the terms of 1991, 303:10, I, as amended by 1994, 383:25.

Amendments

—**2007.** Paragraph IV-b: Inserted "public roads, and public water access facilities including boat ramps" following "facilities" and "and" following "as necessary".

Paragraph V: Rewritten to the extent that a detailed comparison would be impracticable.

—**2002.** Paragraph II(b): Rewritten by ch. 114 to the extent that a detailed comparison would be impracticable.

Paragraph V: Rewritten by ch. 263 to the extent that a detailed comparison would be impracticable.

—1996. Paragraph II(c): Chapter 296 substituted "department" for "wetlands board".

Paragraph II(d): Rewritten by ch. 100 to the extent that a detailed comparison would be impracticable.

Paragraph IV-d: Chapter 251 substituted "RSA 149-M:9" for "RSA 149-M:10" in the second sentence.

Paragraph V(a)(2)(D): Chapter 17 deleted "noxious" following "unsafe" in the first sentence.

Paragraph V(a)(2)(E): Chapter 296 substituted "department" for "wetlands board".

Paragraph V(b)(2)(A)(i): Chapter 17 inserted "equal to or" preceding "faster than".

Paragraph V(b)(1): Chapter 228 substituted "department of environmental services" for "division of water supply and pollution control, subsurface systems bureau".

Paragraph V(d)(1): Chapter 228 substituted "department of environmental services" for "water supply and pollution control division".

—1995. Paragraph V: Chapter 299 inserted "forest management not associated with shoreland development nor land conversion and conducted in compliance with RSA 227-J:9" preceding "forestry" and made a minor change in punctuation in the introductory paragraph.

Chapter 32 added "unless removal is specifically approved by the wetlands board pursuant to RSA 482-A" following "ground" in subpar. (a)(2)(E).

Chapter 206 substituted "Natural Resources Conservation Service" for "soil conservation services" following "Agriculture" in the introductory paragraph in subpar. (b)(2).

—1994. Paragraph II(b): Substituted "reference" for "public boundary" preceding "line" in the second sentence.

Paragraph II(d): Inserted "lawns or areas with grass on" preceding "residential".

Paragraph IV-c: Substituted "reference" for "public boundary" preceding "line" and "public" for "protected" preceding "waters".

Paragraph IV-d: Substituted "reference" for "public boundary" preceding "line" wherever it appeared in the paragraph and "public" for "protected" preceding "waters" in the first and second sentences.

Paragraph V(a): Substituted "reference" for "public boundary" preceding "line" in the first sentence of subpars. (1) and (2)(E).

Paragraph V(b)(2): Deleted "septic tanks and" preceding "leaching" in the introductory paragraph and substituted "reference" for "public boundary" preceding "line" in subpars. (A)(i)-(iii).

Paragraph V(d)(2): Deleted the second sentence.

Paragraph V(d)(3): Deleted "and" preceding "frontage".

—1992. Paragraph I: Added the second sentence.

Paragraph II(c): Deleted "The construction of" preceding "a water".

Paragraph III: Added "and other state law" following "chapter" in the first sentence.

Paragraph IV: Added "and other state law" following "chapter".

Paragraphs IV-a-IV-d: Added.

Paragraph V(a)(2)(A): Added the third sentence.

Paragraph V(a)(2)(B): Repealed.

Paragraph V(a)(2)(C): Inserted "accessory" preceding "structures".

Paragraph V(b)(1): Inserted "including those in excess of 5 acres" preceding "created" and deleted "regardless of size" following "RSA 485-A:29".

Paragraph V(b)(2): Rewritten to the extent that a detailed comparison would be impracticable.

Paragraph V(d)(1): Substituted "established by the water supply and pollution control division" for "set forth under rules adopted pursuant to 541-A" following "determinations as".

Paragraph V(d)(2): Substituted "projects" for "new lots" preceding "in areas", inserted "sewage and" preceding "septic", substituted "in the protected shoreland, whether built on individual lots or grouped as" for "including" preceding "cluster" and "or" for "and" thereafter in the first sentence, and added the second sentence.

Effective Date.

See note under RSA 483-B:1.

1991, 303:8, as amended by 1992, 157:2, eff. Jan. 1, 1993, provided that, excluding par. V(b) and (c) of this section, this section as added by 1991, 303:1, shall take effect only after the general court has approved funding of sections 1, 2 and 5 of this act, which added this chapter, amended RSA 4-C:6 and authorized additional staff in the department of environmental services for the administration of RSA 483-B, respectively, after consideration of the implementation plan required under section 7 of the act.

Pursuant to 1991, 303:10, I-a, as added by 1992, 157:2, eff. Jan. 1, 1993, par. V(b) and (c) of this section shall take effect January 1, 1993.

Applicability of 2002, ch. 114 amendment.

2002, 114:2, eff. July 2, 2002, provided: "Municipalities having a setback of less than 50 feet prior to January 1, 2002 may maintain the defined primary building line in that municipality."

Repeal of applicability of 2002, ch. 114 amendment.

2007, 267:14, III, eff. April 1, 2008, provided

for the repeal of 2002, 114:2, eff. July 2, 2002, which had provided: "Municipalities having a setback of less than 50 feet prior to January 1, 2002 may maintain the defined primary building line in that municipality."

Contingent 1996 amendment.

1996, 296:28, 29, provided for the amendment of this section. However, under the terms of 1996, 296:54, eff. Aug. 9, 1996, the amendments did not become effective.

Cross References.

Fee for division review of terrain alteration plans, see RSA 485-A:17.

NOTES TO DECISIONS

Analysis

1. Applicability
2. Minimum setback requirements

1. Applicability

Once a boathouse project was relocated landward of a bank, it lost its status as a water dependent structure because it was no longer located over, on, or in the waters of the State of New Hampshire. It was then located over a dredged inlet, and no longer required a dredge and fill permit so that there was no legal basis for imposing the N.H. Code Admin. R. Ann., Env-Wt 302.03 requirements on the boathouse. Cayten v. N.H. Dep't of Envtl. Servs., — N.H. —, 927 A.2d 494, 2007 N.H. LEXIS 113 (July 13, 2007).

2. Minimum setback requirements

Trial court properly ruled that respondents violated the Comprehensive Shoreland Protection Act, RSA 483-B:9, II(b), by building a home within 50 feet of a lake shore without a permit from the New Hampshire Department of Environmental Services, as RSA 483-B:10, I allowed the Department to impose the condition on the property in question. N.H. Dep't of Envtl. Servs. v. Marino, — N.H. —, 928 A.2d 818, 2007 N.H. LEXIS 120 (July 18, 2007).

Cited:

Cited in Bacon v. Town of Enfield, 150 N.H. 468, 840 A.2d 788, 2004 N.H. LEXIS 8 (2004).

RESEARCH REFERENCES

New Hampshire Practice.
15 N.H.P. Land Use Planning and Zoning § 39.05.

483-B:10. Nonconforming Lots of Record.

Nonconforming, undeveloped lots of record that are located within the protected shoreland shall comply with the following restrictions, in addition to any local requirements:

I. Except when otherwise prohibited by law, present and successive owners of an individual undeveloped lot may construct a single family residential dwelling on it, notwithstanding the provisions of this chapter. Conditions may be imposed which, in the opinion of the commissioner, more nearly meet the intent of this chapter, while still accommodating the applicant's rights.

II. Building on nonconforming lots of record shall be limited to single family residential structures and related facilities, including, but not limited to, docks, piers, boathouses, boat loading ramps, walkways, and other water dependent structures, consistent with state law.

Source.
1991, 303:1. 1992, 235:19. 1994, 383:15, eff. July 1, 1994.

Editor's note.
Although 1992, 235:19 provided for the amendment of par. II effective on Jan. 1, 1993, the amendment did not become effective until July 1, 1994, the date on which this section as originally enacted by 1991, 303:1 became effective under the terms of 1991, 303:10, I, as amended by 1994, 383:25.

Amendments
—1994. Paragraph I: Deleted the second sentence.

—1992. Paragraph II: Substituted "be limited to" for "not be used for structures other than" following "record shall", inserted "and related facilities" preceding "including", and added "consistent with state law" following "dependent structures".

Effective Date.
See note under RSA 483-B:1.

NOTES TO DECISIONS

Analysis

1. Constitutionality
2. Minimum setback requirements

1. Constitutionality
RSA 483-B:10, I lays down basic standards and a reasonably definite policy and thus does not constitute an impermissible delegation of legislative authority in violation of N.H. Const. pt. I, art. 37. N.H. Dep't of Envtl. Servs. v. Marino, — N.H. —, 928 A.2d 818, 2007 N.H. LEXIS 120 (July 18, 2007).

2. Minimum setback requirements
Trial court properly ruled that respondents violated the Comprehensive Shoreland Protec-

tion Act, RSA 483-B:9, II(b), by building a home within 50 feet of a lake shore without a permit from the New Hampshire Department of Environmental Services, as RSA 483-B:10, I allowed the Department to impose the condition on the property in question. The plain meaning of RSA 483-B:10, I allowed the Department to impose conditions on any construction of a single-family home on a nonconforming undeveloped lot of record; the right to build a single-family home on a nonconforming undeveloped lot of record, therefore, was not absolute, but was contingent upon conditions that the DES imposed upon the construction. N.H. Dep't of Envtl. Servs. v. Marino, — N.H. —, 928 A.2d 818, 2007 N.H. LEXIS 120 (July 18, 2007).

RESEARCH REFERENCES

New Hampshire Practice.
15 N.H.P. Land Use Planning and Zoning § 39.05.

[RSA 483-B:11 effective until April 1, 2008; see also RSA 483-B:11 set out below.]

483-B:11. Nonconforming Structures.

I. Except as otherwise prohibited by law, nonconforming structures, erected prior to July 1, 1994, located within the protected shoreland may be repaired, renovated, or replaced in kind using modern technologies, provided the result is a functionally equivalent use. Such repair or replacement may alter the interior design or existing foundation, but no expansion of the existing footprint or outside dimensions shall be permitted. An expansion that increases the sewerage load to an on-site septic system, or changes or expands the use of a septic system or converts a structure to condominiums or any other project identified under RSA 485-A:29-44 and rules adopted to implement it shall require approval by the department. Between the primary building line and the reference line, no alteration shall extend the structure closer to the public water, except that the addition of a deck or open porch is permitted up to a maximum of 12 feet towards the reference line.

II. When reviewing requests for the redevelopment of sites that contain nonconforming structures erected prior to July 1, 1994, the commissioner shall review proposals which are more nearly conforming than the existing structures, and may waive some of the standards specified in RSA 483-B:9, so long as there is at least the same degree of protection provided to the public waters. For the purposes of this section, a proposal that is "more nearly conforming" means a proposal for significant changes to the location or size of existing structures that bring the structures into greater conformity, or a proposal for changes to other aspects of the property, including but not limited to stormwater management, wastewater treatment or traffic volume or flow, or both types of proposal which significantly improve wildlife habitat or resource protection.

Source.

1991, 303:1. 1992, 235:20. 1994, 383:16, 17, eff. July 1, 1994. 1996, 17:6, eff. June 14, 1996. 2002, 263:10, eff. July 17, 2002.

Editor's note.

Although 1992, 235:20 provided for the amendment of par. I effective on Jan. 1, 1993, the amendment did not become effective until July 1, 1994, the date on which this section as originally enacted by 1991, 303:1 became effective under the terms of 1991, 303:10, I, as amended by 1994, 383:25.

Amendments

—**2002.** Rewritten to the extent that a detailed comparison would be impracticable.

—**1996.** Paragraph II: Deleted "variances involving" preceding "the redevelopment" and substituted "there is at least the same" for "the net effect represents an improvement in the overall" preceding "degree".

—**1994.** Deleted "New Primary Structures" at the end of the section catchline and inserted "nonconforming" following "pre-existing" in the first sentence and "an on-site septic system" following "load to" in the second sentence, and substituted "reference" for "public boundary" preceding "line" in two places in the third sentence.

—**1992.** Paragraph I: Substituted "boundary" for "building" preceding "line, no" in the third sentence.

Effective Date.

See note under RSA 483-B:1.

RESEARCH REFERENCES

New Hampshire Practice.

15 N.H.P. Land Use Planning and Zoning § 39.05.

[RSA 483-B:11 effective April 1, 2008; see bound volume for RSA 483-B:11 as effective until April 1, 2008.]

483-B:11. Nonconforming Structures.

I. Except as otherwise prohibited by law, nonconforming structures located within the protected shoreland may be repaired, renovated, or replaced in kind using modern technologies, provided the result is a functionally equivalent use. Such repair or replacement may alter the interior design or existing foundation, but shall result in no expansion of the existing footprint except as authorized by the department pursuant to paragraph II. An expansion that increases the sewerage load to an on-site septic system, or changes or expands the use of a septic system or converts a structure to condominiums or any other project identified under RSA 485-A:29-44 and rules adopted to implement it shall require approval by the department. Between the primary building line and the reference line, no alteration shall extend the structure closer to the public water, except that the addition of a deck or open porch is permitted up to a maximum of 12 feet towards the reference line for nonconforming structures erected prior to July 1, 1994.

II. When reviewing requests for the redevelopment of sites that contain nonconforming structures or any expansions of nonconforming structures the commissioner shall review proposals which are more nearly conforming than the existing structures, and may waive some of the standards specified in RSA 483-B:9, so long as there is at least the same degree of protection provided to the public waters. For the purposes of this section, a proposal that is "more nearly conforming" means a proposal for significant changes to the location or size of existing structures that bring the structures into greater conformity, or a proposal for changes to other aspects of the property, including but not limited to stormwater management, wastewater treatment or traffic volume or flow, or both types of proposal which significantly improve wildlife habitat or resource protection.

Source.

1991, 303:1. 1992, 235:20. 1994, 383:16, 17, eff. July 1, 1994. 1996, 17:6, eff. June 14, 1996. 2002, 263:10, eff. July 17, 2002. 2007, 267:10, eff. April 1, 2008.

Editor's note.

Although 1992, 235:20 provided for the amendment of par. I effective on Jan. 1, 1993, the amendment did not become effective until July 1, 1994, the date on which this section as originally enacted by 1991, 303:1 became effective under the terms of 1991, 303:10, I, as amended by 1994, 383:25.

Amendments

—2007. Paragraph I: Deleted "erected prior to July 1, 1994" following "structures" in the first sentence, inserted "shall result in" preceding "no expansion", substituted "except as authorized by the department pursuant to paragraph II" for "or outside dimensions shall be permitted" following "footprint" in the second sentence and added "for nonconforming structures erected prior to July 1, 1994" following "reference line" at the end of fourth sentence.

Paragraph II: Substituted "or any expansions of nonconforming structures" for "erected prior to July 1, 1994" preceding "the commissioner" in the first sentence.

—2002. Rewritten to the extent that a detailed comparison would be impractical.

—1996. Paragraph II: Deleted "variances involving" preceding "the redevelopment" and substituted "there is at least the same" for "the net effect represents an improvement in the overall" preceding "degree".

—**1994.** Deleted "New Primary Structures" at the end of the section catchline and inserted "nonconforming" following "pre-existing" in the first sentence and "an on-site septic system" following "load to" in the second sentence, and substituted "reference" for "public boundary"

preceding "line" in two places in the third sentence.

—**1992.** Paragraph I: Substituted "boundary" for "building" preceding "line, no" in the third sentence.

Effective Date.
See note under RSA 483-B:1.

RESEARCH REFERENCES

New Hampshire Practice.
15 N.H.P. Land Use Planning and Zoning § 39.05.

483-B:12. Shoreland Exemptions.

I. The governing body of a municipality may, in its discretion, request the commissioner to exempt all or a portion of the protected shoreland within its boundaries from the provisions of this chapter if the governing body finds that special local urbanization conditions exist in the protected shoreland for which the exemption is sought.

II. If the governing body of a municipality requests such an exemption, it shall submit evidence of existing and historical patterns of building and development in the protected shoreland. Such evidence shall address:

(a) Current and past building density.

(b) Commercial or industrial uses.

(c) Municipal or other public utilities.

(d) Current municipal land use regulations which affect the protected shoreland.

(e) Any other information which the commissioner may reasonably require.

III. With the advice of the office of energy and planning, the commissioner shall approve or deny the request for an exemption and shall issue written findings in support of his decision. A request for an exemption shall be approved only if the municipality demonstrates, using the evidence required under paragraph II, that special conditions of urbanization exist along the portion of shoreland to be exempted.

IV. The Pease development authority, division of ports and harbors may request an exemption under this section for all or a portion of any land purchased, leased, or otherwise acquired by it pursuant to RSA 12-G:39.

Source.
1991, 303:1. 2001, 290:15, eff. July 1, 2001. 2003, 319:9, eff. July 1, 2003. 2004, 257:44, eff. July 1, 2004.

Amendments
—**2004.** Paragraph III: Substituted "office of energy and planning" for "office of state planning and energy programs".

—**2003.** Paragraph III: Substituted "office of state planning and energy programs" for "office of state planning".

—**2001.** Paragraph IV: Substituted "Pease development authority, division of ports and harbors" for "state port authority" and "RSA 12-G:39" for "RSA 271-A".

Effective Date.
See note under RSA 483-B:1.

RESEARCH REFERENCES

New Hampshire Practice.
15 N.H.P. Land Use Planning and Zoning § 39.05.

483-B:13. Public Hearing and Notice to Abutter.
[Repealed 1992, 235:28, II, eff. Jan. 1, 1993.]

Former section(s).
Former RSA 483-B:13, which was derived from 1991, 303:1, related to notice of public hearing.

Editor's note.
Although 1992, 235:28, II, provided for the repeal of this section effective on Jan. 1, 1993, the repeal did not become effective until July 1, 1994, the date on which this section as originally enacted by 1991, 303:1 became effective under the terms of 1991, 303:10, I, as amended by 1994, 383:25.

483-B:14. Rehearings and Appeals.

Where the requirements of this chapter amend the existing statutory authority of the department or other agencies relative to certain established regulatory programs and shall be enforced under these established regulatory programs, the existing procedures governing contested cases and hearings and appeals regarding these requirements shall apply. Where requirements of this chapter are new and do not amend existing statutory authority relative to any established regulatory programs, the procedures set forth in RSA 541-A:31 for contested cases shall apply.

Source.
1991, 303:1. 1992, 235:24. 1994, 412:51, eff. Aug. 9, 1994.

Editor's note.
Although 1992, 235:24 provided for the amendment of this section effective on Jan. 1, 1993, the amendment did not become effective until July 1, 1994, the date on which this section as originally enacted by 1991, 303:1 became effective under the terms of 1991, 303:10, I, as amended by 1994, 383:25.

Amendments
—**1994.** Substituted "RSA 541-A:31" for "RSA 541-A:16" preceding "for contested" in the second sentence.

—**1992.** Rewritten to the extent that a detailed comparison would be impracticable.

Effective Date.
See note under RSA 483-B:1.

RESEARCH REFERENCES

New Hampshire Practice.
15 N.H.P. Land Use Planning and Zoning § 39.05.

483-B:15. Gifts, Grants and Donations.

The department is authorized to solicit, receive, and expend any gifts, grants, or donations made for the purposes of this chapter. Gifts of land or easements shall be assigned to the department of resources and economic development for management or assignment to another state agency or other public body, as appropriate.

Source.
1991, 303:1, eff. July, 1994.

Effective Date.
See note under RSA 483-B:1.

483-B:16. Assistance to Municipalities; Office of State Planning and Energy Programs.

The office of energy and planning may assist municipalities with the implementation of local ordinances under this chapter, upon the request of an individual municipality.

Source.
1991, 303:1, effective July 1, 1994. 2003, 319:9, eff. July 1, 2003. 2004, 257:44, eff. July 1, 2004.

Amendments
—**2004.** Substituted "office of energy and planning" for "office of state planning and energy programs".

—**2003.** Substituted "office of state planning and energy programs" for "office of state planning" in the section catchline and in the paragraph.

Effective Date.
See note under RSA 483-B:1.

483-B:17. Rulemaking.

The commissioner shall adopt rules, pursuant to RSA 541-A, relative to:

I. The content and structure of all forms, applications and permits to be received or issued by the department under this chapter, including information and other materials to be submitted by an applicant.

II. Procedures for filing and review of requests for urbanized shoreland exemptions and standards for granting urbanized shoreland exemptions, including time frames for decisions.

III. Implementation and enforcement of the minimum shoreland standards, including methods and timing of inspection and coordination with municipalities.

IV. Procedures and criteria for the placement of small accessory structures such as storage sheds and gazebos, the size, placement, and construction of which is consistent with the intent of this chapter, between the reference line and the primary building line.

V. Criteria governing the assessment of administrative fines.

VI. Criteria governing low phosphate, slow release nitrogen fertilizer.

VII. A methodology for identifying unsafe trees.

VIII. Defining the opening for building construction.

IX. Definitions of terms not defined in this chapter.

X. Procedures and criteria for permitting under RSA 483-B:5-a, including permit by notification and the identification of those activities that may be conducted without obtaining a permit, all consistent with the provisions of this chapter.

Source.

1991, 303:1. 1992, 235:25. 1994, 383:18, eff. July 1, 1994. 1996, 100:2, eff. May 15, 1996. 2002, 263:11, eff. July 17, 2002. 2007, 267:11, eff. July 1, 2007; 269:2, eff. July 1, 2007.

Revision note.

Paragraph XI, as added by 269:2, was redesignated as par. X in light of the previous amendments to this section by 2007, 267:11.

Editor's note.

Although 1992, 235:25 provided for the amendment of this section effective on Jan. 1, 1993, the amendment did not become effective until July 1, 1994, the date on which this section as originally enacted by 1991, 303:1 became effective under the terms of 1991, 303:10, I, as amended by 1994, 383:25.

Amendments

—2007. Chapter 267 added "implementation and" at the beginning of par. III; deleted former par. VII; and redesignated former pars. VIII-X as present pars. VII-IX.

Chapter 269 added par. X.

—2002. Paragraphs VII-X: Added.

—1996. Paragraph VI: Added.

—1994. Paragraph IV: Substituted "reference" for "public boundary" preceding "line".

—1992. Deleted former pars. II and III, redesignated former par. IV as par. II and added "including time frames for decisions" at the end of that paragraph, redesignated former pars. V and VI as pars. III and IV respectively, deleted former par. VII, redesignated former par. VIII as par. V, and deleted former par. IX.

Effective Date.

See note under RSA 483-B:1.

Limitation of commencement of rulemaking process.

1991, 303:8, provided: "The commissioner shall not activate the rulemaking process pursuant to RSA 483-B:17 until the general court has approved funding of sections 1, 2, and 5 of this act [which added this chapter, amended RSA 4-C:6 and authorized additional staff in the department of environmental services for the administration of this chapter, respectively] after consideration of thie implementation plan required under section 7 of this act."

RESEARCH REFERENCES

New Hampshire Practice.
15 N.H.P. Land Use Planning and Zoning § 39.05.

483-B:18. Penalties.

I. The following shall constitute a violation of this chapter:

(a) Failure to comply with the provisions of this chapter.

(b) Failure to obey an order of the commissioner or a municipality issued relative to activities regulated or prohibited by this chapter.

(c) Misrepresentation by any person of a material fact made in connection with any activity regulated or prohibited by this chapter.

II. Any person who violates this chapter and any person who purchases land affected by a violation of this chapter who knew or had reason to know of the violation shall be liable for remediation or restoration of the land affected.

III. Persons violating the provisions of this chapter shall be subject to the following:

(a) Upon petition of the attorney general or of the municipality in which the violation occurred, the superior court may levy upon any person violating this chapter a civil penalty in an amount not to exceed $20,000 for each day of each continuing violation. The superior court shall have jurisdiction to restrain a continuing violation of this chapter, and to require remediation.

(b) Any person who knowingly violates any provision of this chapter, or any rule adopted or order issued under this chapter or any condition of any permit issued under this chapter shall be guilty of a misdemeanor if a natural person, or guilty of a felony if any other person, and, notwithstanding RSA 651:2, may in addition to any sentence of imprisonment, probation or conditional discharge, be fined not more than $20,000 for each violation if found guilty pursuant to this section. Each day of violation shall constitute a separate offense.

(c) The commissioner, after notice and hearing pursuant to RSA 541-A, shall impose an administrative fine of up to $5,000 for each offense upon any person who violates this chapter. Rehearings and appeals relating to such fines shall be governed by RSA 541. Imposition of an administrative fine under this section shall not preclude the imposition of further civil or criminal penalties under this chapter.

(d) Notwithstanding the $5000 fine limit in subparagraph (c), the administrative fine for each repeat violation of this chapter may be multiplied by a factor of 2 for every previous violation committed by the person or entity.

Source.
1991, 303:1. 1994, 383:19, eff. July 1, 1994. 2002, 169:2, eff. Jan. 1, 2003.

Amendments
—**2002.** Paragraph III(c): Substituted "shall impose" for "may impose" in the first sentence. Paragraph III(d): Added.

—**1994.** Paragraph III(a): Inserted "or of the municipality in which the violation occurred" following "attorney general" in the first sentence.

Effective Date.
See note under RSA 483-B:1.

Cross References.
Classification of crimes, see RSA 625:9.

RESEARCH REFERENCES

New Hampshire Practice.
5 N.H.P. Civil Practice and Procedure §§ 54.02, 64.28.

15 N.H.P. Land Use Planning and Zoning § 39.05.

[RSA 483-B:19 repealed effective April 1, 2008; see also prospective repeal note set out below.]

483-B:19. Applicability.

I. Subject to paragraph II, the provisions of this chapter shall not apply to any applicant whose land is in a municipality that has adopted a shoreland protection ordinance under RSA 674:16, the provisions of which are at least as stringent as similar provisions in this chapter. The director of the office of energy and planning shall certify to the commissioner that the provisions of a local ordinance are at least as stringent as similar provisions in this chapter.

II. If a municipality has a local ordinance that does not contain a counterpart to all of the provisions of this chapter, the more stringent provisions shall apply.

Source.
1991, 303:1. 1992, 235:26. 1994, 383:20, eff. July 1, 1994. 2002, 263:12, eff. July 17, 2002. 2003, 319:9, eff. July 1, 2003. 2004, 257:44, eff. July 1, 2004.

Editor's note.
Although 1992, 235:26 provided for the amendment of par. II effective on Jan. 1, 1993, the amendment did not become effective until July 1, 1994, the date on which this section as originally enacted by 1991, 303:1 became effective under the terms of 1991, 303:10, I, as amended by 1994, 383:25.

Amendments
—**2004.** Paragraph I: Substituted "office of energy and planning" for "office of state planning and energy programs" in the second sentence.

—**2003.** Paragraph I: Substituted "office of state planning and energy programs" for "office of state planning".

—**2002.** Designated the existing provisions of the section as par. I and in that paragraph

added "subject to paragraph II" in the first sentence, and added par. II.

—**1994.** Rewritten to the extent that a detailed comparison would be impracticable.

—**1992.** Paragraph II: Rewritten to the extent that a detailed comparison would be impracticable.

Effective Date.
See note under RSA 483-B:1.

Prospective repeal of section.
2007, 267:14, I, provides for the repeal of this section on April 1, 2008.

Conditions for review of rivers exemption.
1992, 235:27, eff. Jan. 1, 1993, provided: "In the event that the local river management advisory committees do not fulfill their responsibilities prescribed in RSA 483:8-a, III(c) or that the cities and towns along designated rivers or segments thereof do not adopt the proposals made by their local river management advisory committees, the house and senate shall re-examine the exemption provided in RSA 483-B:19, II(b) and propose minimum standards as defined by this act."

RESEARCH REFERENCES

New Hampshire Practice.
15 N.H.P. Land Use Planning and Zoning § 39.05.

[RSA 483-B:20 repealed effective April 1, 2008; see also prospective repeal note set out below.]

483-B:20. Designated Rivers.

The provisions of this chapter shall not apply to rivers or river segments designated by the general court and approved for management and protection under RSA 483 prior to January 1, 1993 with the exception of the Connecticut River.

Source.
1994, 383:21, eff. July 1, 1994. 2002, 114:3, eff. July 2, 2002.

Amendments
—**2002.** Added "with the exception of the Connecticut River" following "1993".

Prospective repeal of section.
2007, 267:14, II, provides for the repeal of this section on April 1, 2008.

CHAPTER 485

NEW HAMPSHIRE SAFE DRINKING WATER ACT

Cross References.
Aid to public water systems for compliance with Federal Safe Drinking Water Act, see RSA 486-A.

Environmental audits, see RSA 147-E.

Public Water Supply Protection Program

Cross References.
Municipal water systems, see RSA 38.

RESEARCH REFERENCES

New Hampshire Code of Administrative Rules.
Rules of the Department of Environmental Services—Water Supply and Pollution Control Division, Env-Ws 301.01 et seq., New Hampshire Code of Administrative Rules Annotated.

ALR.
Liability of water supplier for damages resulting from furnishing impure water. 54 A.L.R.3d 936.

485:1. Statement of Purpose.

I. The purpose of this chapter is to provide a comprehensive drinking water protection program for the citizens of New Hampshire. It shall be consistent with and at least as stringent as the Federal Safe Drinking Water Act standards.

II. In order to implement a comprehensive drinking water protection program, the department of environmental services shall:

(a) Monitor the water quality of public water supplies.

(b) Provide technical assistance to water operators and the general public.

(c) Review the design of proposed public water systems and alterations for existing systems.

(d) Periodically conduct sanitary surveys of public water systems to make certain of proper safety and operation.

(e) Require that public water supplies comply with all pertinent federal and state statutes and rules.

(f) Educate citizens for the need and methods of providing safe and adequate drinking water.

(g) Approve sources of water used in the manufacture of bottled water.

Source.
1989, 339:1. 1990, 163:1, eff. July 1, 1990.
1996, 228:108, eff. July 1, 1996. 1997, 155:4, eff. Aug. 8, 1997.

References in text.

The Safe Drinking Water Act, referred to in par. I, is classified principally to 42 U.S.C.S. § 300f et seq.

Amendments

—**1997.** Paragraph II(g): Added.

—**1996.** Paragraph II: Substituted "depart-

ment of environmental services" for "division of water supply and pollution control" in the introductory paragraph.

—**1990.** Rewritten to the extent that a detailed comparison would be impracticable.

485:1-a. Definitions.

As used in this chapter, unless the context clearly indicates otherwise, the following words shall have the following meanings:

I. "Community water system" means a public water system which serves at least 15 service connections used by year-round residents or regularly serves at least 25 year-round residents.

II. "Contaminant" means any physical, chemical, biological, or radiological substance or matter in the water.

III. "Department" means the department of environmental services.

IV. "Commissioner" means the commissioner of the department of environmental services.

V. "Feasible" means capable of being done with the use of the best technology, treatment techniques, and other means which the department finds, after examination for efficacy under field as well as laboratory conditions, is available at reasonable cost.

VI. "Household equivalent" means water usage equal to 300 gallons per day.

VII. "Maximum contaminant level" means the maximum permissible level of a contaminant in water which is delivered to the free flowing outlet of the ultimate user of a public water system, except in the case of turbidity where the maximum permissible level is measured at the point of entry to the distribution system. Contaminants added to the water under circumstances controlled by the user, except those resulting from corrosion of piping and plumbing caused by water quality, are excluded from the definition.

VIII. "Maximum contaminant level goal" means that level of a contaminant in water at which no known or anticipated adverse effects on the health of consumers occur and which allows an adequate margin of safety, as determined by federal and state agencies.

IX. "National Drinking Water Regulations" means the drinking water regulations promulgated by the administrator of the U.S. Environmental Protection Agency under the authority of the Safe Drinking Water Act, P.L. 93-523, as amended.

X. "Non-community water system" means a public water system that is not a community water system.

XI. "Non-transient non-community water system" means a system which is not a community water system and which serves the same 25 people, or more, over 6 months per year.

XII. "Operator" means the individual who has direct management responsibility for the routine supervision and operation of a public water system or of

317

a water treatment plant or collection, treatment, storage, or distribution facility or structure that is a part of a system.

XIII. "Person" means any individual, partnership, company, public or private corporation, political subdivision or agency of the state, department, agency, or instrumentality of the United States, or any other legal entity.

XIV. "Political subdivision" means any municipality, county, district, or any portion or combination of 2 or more thereof.

XV. "Public water system" means a system for the provision to the public of piped water for human consumption, if such system has at least 15 service connections or regularly serves an average of at least 25 individuals daily at least 60 days out of the year. Such term includes (1) any collection, treatment, storage, and distribution facilities under control of the operator of such system and used primarily in connection with such system, and (2) any collection or pretreatment storage facilities not under such control which are used primarily in connection with such system. Any water system which meets all of the following conditions is not a public water system:

XV-a. "Source of water" means a spring, artesian well, spa, geyser, drilled well, public water supply, or other source, of any water used in the manufacture of bottled water, which has been inspected and approved by the department.

(a) Consists only of distribution and storage facilities (and does not have any collection and treatment facilities);

(b) Obtains all of its water from, but is not owned or operated by, a public water system; and

(c) Does not sell water to any person.

XVI. "Supplier of water" means any person who controls, owns or generally manages a public water system.

XVII. "Water treatment plant" means that portion of the public water system which is designed to alter the physical, chemical, biological or radiological quality of the water or to remove any contaminants.

XVIII. "Wellhead protection area" means the surface and subsurface area surrounding a water well or wellfield, supplying a public water system, through which contaminants are reasonably likely to move toward and reach such water well or wellfield.

XIX. "Water conservation" means any beneficial reduction in water losses, waste, or use.

Source.
1990, 163:2, eff. July 1, 1990. 1996, 228:68, 106, eff. July 1, 1996. 1997, 155:5, eff. Aug. 8, 1997. 2002, 142:1, eff. July 12, 2002.

References in text.
The Safe Drinking Water Act, P.L. 93-523, referred to in par. IX, is classified principally to 42 U.S.C.S. § 300f et seq.

Amendments
—**2002.** Paragraph XIX: Added.

—**1997.** Paragraph XV-a: Added.

—**1996.** Paragraph IV: Rewritten to the extent that a detailed comparison would be impracticable.
Paragraph V: Substituted "department" for "division".

485:2. Administration.

This chapter shall be administered by the department, which is authorized to:

I. Enter into agreements, contracts or cooperative arrangements under such terms and conditions as it deems appropriate with other state, federal or interstate agencies, municipalities, education institutions, local health departments or other organizations or individuals.

II. Receive financial and technical assistance from the federal government and other public or private agencies.

III. Participate in related programs of the federal government, other states, interstate agencies, or other public agencies or organizations.

IV. Establish adequate fiscal controls and accounting procedures to assure proper disbursement of and accounting for funds.

V. Adopt rules under RSA 541-A to carry out the requirements of this chapter as listed in RSA 485:3.

Source.
1989, 339:1, eff. Jan. 1, 1990. 1996, 228:67, 69, eff. July 1, 1996.

Amendments
—1996. Deleted "with the exception of RSA

485:44, 45, and 46" preceding "shall be administered by the" and substituted "department" for "division" thereafter in the introductory paragraph.

485:3. Drinking Water Rules.

I. The commissioner shall adopt under RSA 541-A, following public hearing, drinking water rules and primary drinking water standards which are necessary to protect the public health and which shall apply to all public water systems. Such rules shall include:

(a) identification of contaminants which may have an adverse effect on the health of persons;

(b) specification for each contaminant of either:

(1) a maximum contaminant level that is acceptable in water for human consumption, if it is feasible to ascertain the level of such contaminant in water in public water systems; or

(2) one or more treatment techniques or methods which lead to a reduction of the level of such contaminant sufficient to protect the public health, if it is not feasible to ascertain the level of such contaminant in water in the public water system; and

(c) criteria and procedures to assure compliance with the levels or methods determined under subparagraph (b), including quality control monitoring and testing procedures and standards to ensure compliance with such levels or methods; criteria and standards to ensure proper operation and maintenance of the system; requirements as to the minimum quality of water which may be delivered to the consumer; and requirements with respect to siting new facilities. Such rules shall be no less stringent than the most recent national Primary Drinking Water Regulations in effect, as issued or promulgated by the United States Environmental Protection Agency.

II. The commissioner may adopt secondary drinking water rules, which are necessary to protect the public welfare. Such rules may apply to any contaminant in drinking water which may adversely affect the color, odor, taste or appearance of the water and consequently may cause a substantial number of persons to discontinue using a public water system, or which may otherwise adversely affect the public welfare. Such rules may vary according to geographic, economic, technical or other relevant circumstances. Such rules shall reasonably assure the protection of the public welfare and the supply of aesthetically adequate drinking water.

III. The commissioner shall adopt under RSA 541-A all rules necessary to implement the requirements of the following sections of this chapter:

(a) RSA 485:42.

(b) RSA 485:43.

IV. The commissioner may adopt rules specifying criteria and procedures for requiring public water systems to conduct monitoring programs for contaminants which are not identified in the national primary drinking water regulations, but which have been identified by the administrator of the United States Environmental Protection Agency as "unregulated contaminants." Such rules shall require monitoring of drinking water supplied by the system and shall vary the frequency and schedule of monitoring requirements for systems. An unregulated contaminant is one for which no maximum contaminant level or treatment technique has been established under paragraph I or II. In developing such rules, the commissioner shall consider materials submitted by the department of health and human services, pursuant to RSA 125-H:3. Rules adopted under this paragraph shall list unregulated contaminants for which public water systems may be required to monitor. Any list established pursuant to this paragraph shall be consistent with, but not limited by, the list of unregulated contaminants identified in regulations promulgated by the administrator of the United States Environmental Protection Agency.

V. The commissioner may adopt rules specifying the criteria under which filtration, including coagulation and sedimentation, as appropriate, is required as a treatment technique for public water systems supplied by surface water sources. In developing such rules the commissioner shall consider the quality of source waters, protection afforded by watershed management, treatment practices such as disinfection and length of water storage and other factors relevant to protection of health. The commissioner may require any public water supply system to assist in determining the necessity of filtration in that system. The commissioner shall provide an opportunity for notice and public hearing prior to implementation of any filtration requirement. Following such hearing, the commissioner shall prescribe, by rule adopted pursuant to RSA 541-A, a compliance schedule for such filtration requirement.

VI. The commissioner may adopt rules requiring disinfection as a treatment technique for all public water systems.

VII. The commissioner may adopt rules specifying the criteria and procedures to be used to identify and notify persons who may be affected by lead contamination of their drinking water when such contamination results from either the lead content in the construction materials of the public water system or the corrosivity of the water supply, or both. The commissioner may also adopt rules prohibiting the use of lead pipes, solder and flux in the installation or repair of any public water system or any plumbing in a residential or nonresidential facility providing water for human consumption. Such rules shall not prohibit the use of leaded joints necessary for the repair of cast iron pipes.

VIII. The commissioner may adopt rules relative to defining the best available technology, treatment techniques, or other means which are feasible for the purpose of meeting the federal maximum contaminant level. In defining the best available technology, treatment technique or other means, the commissioner may consider the number of persons served by the system, other physical conditions related to engineering feasibility and cost of compliance, and information contained in health risk assessments provided by the department of health and human services pursuant to RSA 125-H:3, II and IV. Such rules shall specify all applicable criteria relative to the commissioner's determination.

IX. The commissioner may adopt rules to implement a wellhead protection program pursuant to RSA 485:48.

X. The commissioner may adopt rules to implement the Underground Injection Control Program of the federal Safe Drinking Water Act, 42 U.S.C. section 300f et seq., as well as rules pertaining to permits for the regulation and remediation of contamination from previous discharges or disposal of waste to the groundwater. The commissioner's rules shall include criteria and procedures to ensure that past and present underground injection will not endanger drinking water sources, and shall provide for consideration of varying geologic, hydrologic, or other conditions in different areas within the state.

XI. The commissioner shall adopt rules, pursuant to RSA 541-A, specifying the water quality standards and other criteria and procedures for obtaining a permit to use a source of water for the manufacture of bottled water.

XII. The commissioner may adopt rules to ensure long-term viability of public drinking water systems as required by section 119 of the federal Safe Drinking Water Act Amendments of 1996, 42 U.S.C. section 300g-9 to qualify for full eligibility for federal and state revolving fund capital grants.

XIII. The commissioner shall adopt rules, pursuant to RSA 541-A, relative to new groundwater withdrawals of 57,600 gallons or more in any 24-hour period by public water systems. Such rules shall include:

(a) Criteria and procedures for requiring public water systems to identify and address impacts of withdrawals on surface waters, subsurface waters, water-related natural resources, and public, private, residential, and farm wells within the anticipated zone of contribution to the withdrawal.

(b) Requirements relative to conservation management plans which demonstrate the need for the proposed withdrawals, to be submitted by the public water system seeking approval for a withdrawal.

(c) Procedures by which the department may deny permission for withdrawals or order the applicant to provide a response policy, as provided by department rules, for provision of alternative water supply at no initial capital cost to persons whose wells are adversely affected by the proposed withdrawal or order reduced withdrawals if hydrogeologic data indicate that water-related resources are being adversely affected by the withdrawals.

Source.
1989, 339:1. 1991, 344:3. 1992, 289:53. 1995, 310:181, eff. Nov. 1, 1995. 1996, 228:110, eff. July 1, 1996. 1997, 155:6, eff. Aug. 8, 1997; 271:1, eff. Aug. 18, 1997. 1998, 124:1, eff. Aug. 1, 1998.

Revision note.
Substituted "RSA 485:48" for "RSA 485:50" in par. IX to correct an error in the reference.

Amendments
—**1998.** Paragraph XIII: Added.

—**1997.** Paragraph XI: Added by chs. 155 and 271.

—**1996.** Substituted "commissioner" for "division" wherever it appeared throughout the section and "commissioner's" for "division's" in the third sentence of par. VIII.

—**1995.** Paragraph IV: Deleted "division of public health services" preceding "department of health and human services" in the fourth sentence.
Paragraph VIII: Substituted "department of

health and human services" for "division of public health services" in the second sentence.

—**1992.** Paragraph V: Deleted the sixth sentence.

—**1991.** Paragraph X: Added.

Severability
—**1995 amendment.** 1995, 310, which amended this section, was subject to a severability clause. See 1995, 310:186.

Construction of amendments
—**1995.** 1995, 310:187, eff. Nov. 1, 1995, provided:
"Nothing in this act is intended to, nor shall it be construed as, mandating or assigning any new, expanded, or modified program or responsibility for any political subdivision in violation of part I, article 28-a of the constitution of the state of New Hampshire."

Redesignation of paragraph.
Paragraph XI, as added by 1997, 271:1, was redesignated as par. XII pursuant to 1997, 271:2, eff. Aug. 18, 1997.

RESEARCH REFERENCES

New Hampshire Practice.
14 N.H.P. Local Government Law § 510.

485:3-a. Permit Authority.

The department may grant operational permits for public water systems.

Source.
1990, 163:3, eff. July 1, 1990. 1996, 228:106, eff. July 1, 1996.

Amendments
—**1996.** Substituted "department" for "division".

485:3-b. Site Assessment Review Fee.

I. Any person, except for state and local governments including counties and political subdivisions, that requests an expedited review of environmental site assessment reports by the department shall pay to the department a review fee based on the equalized assessed valuation of the property as determined in rules adopted by the commissioner under RSA 541-A, shall be as follows:

Equalized Assessed Valuation	Fee
$0 to $250,000	$1,800
$250,001 to $500,000	$2,250
$500,001 to $1,000,000	$3,750
greater than $1,000,000	$7,500

II. The department shall provide written comments within 60 days after the date such reports and the required fees are received by the department.

Source.
1993, 289:2, eff. July 1, 1993; 358:93, eff. at 12:01 a.m., July 1, 1993. 2007, 219:9, eff. July 1, 2007.

Amendments
—**2007.** Paragraph I: Substituted "that" for "who" preceding "requests" and inserted "as determined in rules adopted by the commissioner under RSA 541-A, shall be" preceding "as follows" and substituted "$1,800" for "$1,200" and substituted "$2,250" for "$1,500" and "$3,750" for "$2,500" and substituted "$7,500" for "$5,000".

—**1993.** Paragraph I: Substituted "$250,001" for "$250,000" and "$500,001" for "$500,000".

Severability
—**1993 amendment.** 1993, 358 was subject to a severability clause. See 1993, 358:106.

485:3-c. Groundwater Management Permit Fee.

Any person, submitting a permit application under RSA 485:3, X shall pay to the department a groundwater management permit application fee of $2,000. Any person who has paid the environmental site assessment review fee specified in RSA 485:3-b shall be exempt from the groundwater management permit fee. State and local governments including counties and political subdivisions shall be exempt from groundwater management permit application fees, unless eligible for funding under RSA 146-D, RSA 146-E, RSA 146-F, or RSA 146-G.

Source.
1993, 289:2, eff. July 1, 1993. 2007, 219:10, eff. July 1, 2007.

Amendments
—**2007.** Rewritten to the extent that a detailed comparison would be impracticable.

485:3-d. Annual Report Required.

The department of environmental services shall submit an annual report of the status of the environmental site assessment review and groundwater management programs to the speaker of the house, president of the senate and the governor no later than September 1. The first such annual report will be submitted no later than September 1, 1994.

Source.
1993, 289:2, eff. July 1, 1993.

485:4. Power to Require Improvements.

I. The department is empowered to investigate the sanitary conditions and methods pertaining to the source, treatment, and distribution of all public water supplies for domestic use, and to require the application of any treatment or improvement in conditions and methods as it may deem necessary to insure fitness and safety and adequate protection of the public health. If the department determines that improvements are necessary, the municipality, corporation, or person shall be so notified in writing and the requirements so ordered shall be effected pursuant to RSA 38:25 within a reasonable time to be fixed by the department. Appeals of actions of the department may be made as provided in RSA 485:59. The department may set intermediate goals and time frames to assist municipalities, corporations, or persons to abide by an order of the department under this paragraph.

II. Upon complaint of not less than 10 customers of an existing public water system or not less than 10 residents not currently served by a public water supply, the department shall make an investigation of conditions regarding water quality or quantity problems described in the complaint. If, as a result of any such investigation, the department concludes that a significant public health or safety problem exists due to water supply quality or quantity, it shall perform a preliminary analysis of alternatives which address the problem. The department may request additional information from the complainants and nearby public water supply system owners, such as data on water supply quality and quantity, well characteristics, and water distribution system characteristics, as is necessary to perform its investigation and analysis. If the department determines that an extension of water service from an existing public water supply system to the area of impaired water quality or quantity is the most feasible and cost-effective alternative, that the extension is consistent with municipal master planning, local water system policies and rules, RSA 9-B, and RSA 162-C:2, V, and that the existing public water system has adequate water supply and system capacity to serve the problem area, the municipality, corporation, or person who owns the public water system shall be ordered to allow connection to its water distribution system from the identified area, regardless of existing municipal or public water system service area boundaries. The connection so ordered shall be effected pursuant to RSA 38:25 within a reasonable time to be fixed by the department and may contain limitations on water system connections unrelated to the original petition in order to limit unintended land use impacts. Appeals of actions of the department may be made as provided in RSA 485:59. The department may set intermediate goals and time frames to assist municipalities, corporations, or persons to abide by an order of the department under this paragraph. The provisions of this paragraph or of any order issued under this paragraph shall not delegate any costs associated with a connection to the person receiving the order from the department.

Source.

1989, 339:1. 1990, 33:1. 1995, 88:1, eff. Jan. 1, 1996. 1996, 228:106, eff. July 1, 1996. 1997, 206:6, eff. July 1, 1997. 2002, 141:3, eff. May 13, 2002.

Amendments

—2002. Designated the existing provisions of the section as par. I and substituted "paragraph" for "section" in the fourth sentence of that paragraph, and added paragraph II.

—1997. Substituted "RSA 38:25" for "RSA 38:14-a" in the second sentence.

—1996. Substituted "department" for "division" throughout the section.

—1995. Deleted the former second sentence, deleted "after such hearing" preceding "if the division determines" in the present second sentence, and added the third sentence.

—1990. Deleted "Penalty" following "Improvements" in the section catchline and deleted the former fourth sentence.

Severability of enactment.

1997, 206 was subject to a severability clause. See 1997, 206:9.

NOTES TO DECISIONS

Analysis

1. Sewers
2. Reservoirs

1. Sewers

Under this provision the state board of health could require a town to install a sewer in order to preserve a public water supply from contamination. Town of Meredith v. State Board of Health, 94 N.H. 123, 48 A.2d 489, 1946 N.H. LEXIS 161 (1946). (Decided under prior law.)

2. Reservoirs

Water supply and pollution control commis-

sion's order requiring city to cover its high service distribution reservoir because of high bacterial count in the water was not unjust or unreasonable in view of the evidence that for many years city had been urged by the commission to cover the reservoir, which was open to pollution from seagulls, waterfowl and humans and was therefore subject to viral contamination. City of Concord v. Water Supply and Pollution Control Com'n., 115 N.H. 614, 347 A.2d 173, 1975 N.H. LEXIS 377 (1975). (Decided under prior law.)

485:5. Power to Require Acquisition of Land.

The acquisition of adjacent or marginal lands necessary to provide reasonable sanitary control over the quality of a public water supply shall be deemed an improvement in sanitary conditions which is within the power of the department to require under the provisions of RSA 485:4. Municipalities shall comply with such order pursuant to RSA 38:25.

Source.

1989, 339:1, eff. Jan. 1, 1990. 1996, 228:106, eff. July 1, 1996. 1997, 206:6, eff. July 1, 1997.

Revision note.

Substituted "RSA 485:4" for "RSA 485:2" in the first sentence to correct an error in the reference.

Amendments

—1997. Substituted "RSA 38:25" for "RSA 38:14-a" in the second sentence.

—1996. Substituted "department" for "division".

Severability of enactment.

1997, 206 was subject to a severability clause. See 1997, 206:9.

485:6. Disinfection.

Any public water supply system which utilizes any of the surface water of the state, as defined in RSA 485-A, as the source of supply, shall, as a minimum means of treatment, be provided with suitable chlorination or other disinfection facilities installed, operated and maintained in accordance with rules of the department adopted under this chapter.

Source.
1989, 339:1, eff. Jan. 1, 1990. 1996, 228:106, eff. July 1, 1996.

Amendments
—1996. Substituted "department" for "division".

485:7. Penalty.

Any municipality, corporation or person who shall fail to install or to operate and maintain disinfection facilities in accordance with the foregoing requirements shall be guilty of a violation for each day of failure to so install, operate or maintain such equipment. Said penalty shall not be invoked in the event of a bona fide emergency arising from an unavoidable or unforeseen failure or casualty to such treatment facilities. It shall be the duty of the municipality, corporation or person in responsible charge of said public water supply system to give immediate notice of the emergency condition to the department in order that appropriate action to safeguard the public health may be taken.

Source.
1989, 339:1, eff. Jan. 1, 1990. 1996, 228:106, eff. July 1, 1996.

Cross References.
Classification of crimes, see RSA 625:9.
Sentences, see RSA 651.

Amendments
—1996. Substituted "department" for "division" in the third sentence.

485:8. Approval of Construction Plans.

I. No person, proposing to supply water for domestic uses, shall construct any new system, or enlarge any existing system, for supplying water to the public without first submitting detailed plans of the proposed construction to the department and securing its approval of such plans. The department shall examine the topography and the watershed, complete an engineering review of the plans and specifications for said proposed construction, and make chemical and bacteriological analysis of the waters of the proposed supply, before approval is granted.

II. No new construction, addition or alteration involving the source, treatment, distribution or storage of water in any public water system shall be commenced until the plans and specifications have been submitted to and approved in accordance with rules adopted by the department; except, if such construction, addition or alteration is exempted by the department because it will have no effect on public health or welfare, then such submission and approval is not required. In granting approval of plans and specifications, the department may require modifications, conditions or procedures to ensure, as far as feasible, the protection of the public health. The department may require the submission of water samples for analysis to determine the extent of treatment required. Records of construction, including, where possible, plans and descriptions of existing public water systems, shall be maintained by such systems and shall be made available to the department upon request.

III. Any person submitting detailed plans to the department, as provided in this section, for a new public water system, or an existing public water system where conversion from transient use to residential-type use is proposed, shall pay to the department a fee of $45 per residential unit. When usage cannot be apportioned by residential units at new public water systems, the fee shall be based on the flow proportioned equivalent to that of a single family residential unit. The commissioner shall adopt rules pursuant to RSA 541-A defining flow proportioned equivalency.

IV. The fees required under paragraph III shall be for reviewing such detailed plans and making site inspections as may be necessary. The fee shall be paid at the time said detailed plans are submitted and shall be deposited with the state treasurer as unrestricted revenue. The department shall establish by rule, adopted pursuant to RSA 541-A, a minimum threshold below which no fee is required and a maximum level above which the fee will not increase.

V. Any person proposing to install new public sewerage or sewage treatment facilities, or to extend, renovate, replace or substantially repair any such existing facilities, shall submit, at least 30 days in advance of construction, detailed plans and specifications for such facilities to the department and secure its approval of such plans and specifications. The foregoing provisions shall also be applicable to any institution accommodating 30 or more people, which provides its own sewage disposal facilities.

Source.
1989, 339:1, eff. Jan. 1, 1990. 1996, 228:70, 106, eff. July 1, 1996.

Amendments
—**1996.** Paragraphs I, II: Substituted "department" for "division" wherever it appeared in pars. I, II, IV and V and in two places in the first sentence of par. III and "commissioner" for

"division" preceding "shall adopt" in the third sentence of par. III.

Codification.
Pursuant to 1989, 339:34, the amendment to former RSA 148:25, I-a by 1989, 408:16, eff. Aug. 4, 1989, was incorporated in par. III of this section.

NOTES TO DECISIONS

Sewers
Whether water supply and pollution control commission had right to approve or disapprove of city's application to extend combination sanitary and storm sewer line, and what general criteria were to determine its decision, were questions of law on supreme court review of

denial of application. Roy v. Water Supply and Pollution Control Commission, 112 N.H. 87, 289 A.2d 650, 1972 N.H. LEXIS 149 (1972). (Decided under prior law.)

Under the plain language of this section, water supply and pollution control commission had authority to deny city's application to extend sewer line. Roy v. Water Supply and Pollution Control Commission, 112 N.H. 87, 289 A.2d 650, 1972 N.H. LEXIS 149 (1972). (Decided under prior law.)

By the plain language of RSA 125:9 and the commission's history as successor to the state board of health, the water supply and pollution control commission is to judge sewer extension application by the broad criteria of whether extension would be harmful to public health and life. Roy v. Water Supply and Pollution Control Commission, 112 N.H. 87, 289 A.2d 650, 1972 N.H. LEXIS 149 (1972). (Decided under prior law.)

Finding of water supply and pollution control commission that sanitary and storm sewer extension applied for by city to service apartment complex would endanger public health was reasonable where uncontradicted evidence showed that approximately once a year there was overflowing of the sewer in a low area served by it, flooding the land, that it was getting worse and that the extension would increase the dry weather flow of sewage at three points measured in the area by 14, 16 and 30 percent. Roy v. Water Supply and Pollution Control Commission, 112 N.H. 87, 289 A.2d 650, 1972 N.H. LEXIS 149 (1972). (Decided under prior law.)

State board of health may require a town to construct sewerage system to prevent contamination of public water supply. Town of Meredith v. State Board of Health, 94 N.H. 123, 48 A.2d 489, 1946 N.H. LEXIS 161 (1946). (Decided under prior law.)

485:9. Highway Construction.

No public highway, access roads, or private ways of any sort, shall be constructed so as to traverse any watershed tributary to a lake, pond or reservoir used for the storage of public drinking water without first obtaining the approval of the department.

Source.
1989, 339:1, eff. Jan. 1, 1990. 1996, 228:106, eff. July 1, 1996.

Amendments
—1996. Substituted "department" for "division".

485:10. Approval.

No person supplying water to the public for domestic use shall resort to, hold in reserve, or maintain, a connection through which water may be received from any auxiliary or emergency source of supply, unless such source shall have been duly declared to, registered, and approved by the department.

Source.
1989, 339:1, eff. Jan. 1, 1990. 1996, 228:106, eff. July 1, 1996.

Amendments
—1996. Substituted "department" for "division".

485:11. Valve Tests.

Every valve, gate or other device for controlling or preventing the inflow of water of such unapproved character to the public supply pipe system must be constructed to permit efficient inspection and testing, and an actual test of such device shall be made not less than twice annually by the individual, corporation or association furnishing water to the public. If the water supply management shall find that a gate or valve is not working properly, and cannot be readily adjusted, it shall at once notify the department, and, under the advice and direction of said department, shall repair or correct the faulty condition.

Source.
1989, 339:1, eff. Jan. 1, 1990. 1996, 228:106,
eff. July 1, 1996.

Amendments
—1996. Substituted "department" for "division" in two places in the second sentence.

485:12. Sealed Valves.

All valves or gates used in the connection here described, in the case of sources maintained for public fire protection, shall also be subject to the special seal and inspection of the department. Whenever it shall become necessary to break such seal, or to resort to an unapproved emergency source for public fire protection, notice of such action shall, within 24 hours, be sent to the said department by telephone or telegraph and also by mail.

Source.
1989, 339:1, eff. Jan. 1, 1990. 1996, 228:106,
eff. July 1, 1996.

Amendments
—1996. Substituted "department" for "division" wherever it appeared.

485:13. Control of Intakes.

The department shall have general control and oversight of emergency intakes. It may, when feasible and deemed necessary for the protection of the public health, upon reasonable notice, require the abandonment of any existent emergency source and the adoption of other means of supply.

Source.
1989, 339:1, eff. Jan. 1, 1990. 1996, 228:106,
eff. July 1, 1996.

Amendments
—1996. Substituted "department" for "division" in the first sentence.

485:14. Use of Fluoride.

No fluoride shall be introduced into the public water supply unless and until the municipality or municipalities using said waters have held a public hearing as to the introduction of fluoride into the public water supply of said municipality or municipalities, and the registered voters of such municipality or municipalities have approved such action pursuant to RSA 44:16, RSA 31:17-a, RSA 52:23, or RSA 485:14-a. For purposes of this section "municipality" means a municipality that has 100 or more user connections that are served from the public water supply.

Source.
1989, 339:1, eff. Jan. 1, 1990. 2004, 225:1, eff.
July 1, 2004.

Amendments
—2004. Rewritten to the extent that a detailed comparison would be impracticable.

NOTES TO DECISIONS

Analysis

1. Construction
2. Application

1. Construction

City residents were properly awarded summary judgment in their action against a city and the city was required, under the statute, to gain the approval of voters of each municipality in which residents used water provided by a water works before the water works could provide fluoridated water to any residents of the community. Balke v. City of Manchester, 150

N.H. 69, 834 A.2d 306, 2003 N.H. LEXIS 141 (2003).

This section does not require or authorize a city, town or village water district to present a fluoridation proposal to the voters in absence of a petition therefor. Op. Att'y Gen. No. 99-01.

This section does not require approval of voters in towns and cities who may be using water as contract customers of a water supply located in another city. Op. Att'y Gen. No. 99-01.

2. Application

This section applies to privately owned as well as municipally owned utilities. Op. Att'y Gen. No. 99-01.

485:14-a. Referendum Procedure for Public Water Systems Serving More Than One Political Subdivision.

I. Upon the written application of the aggregate of 10 percent of the registered voters in all of the towns served by a water system, presented to the clerk of the town owning the water system at least 90 days before the day prescribed for an annual town meeting or city election, the clerk shall forward a copy of the petition to each town served by the water system. Upon receipt of the petition, the selectmen of the town shall insert on the warrant or the official ballot the following question: "Shall fluoride be used in the public water system?" Beside this question shall be printed the word "yes" and the word "no" with the proper boxes for the voter to indicate his or her choice. If a majority of the registered voters in a water system that serves multiple towns does not approve the use of fluoride in the public water system, no fluoride shall be introduced into the public water system for said towns. After such popular referendum, the selectmen shall not insert an article relative to the use of fluoride in the public water system in the warrant nor shall such question be inserted on the official ballot for a minimum period of 3 years from the date of the last popular referendum and only upon written application at that time of not less than the aggregate of 10 percent of the registered voters of all of the towns.

II. In this section:

(a) "Town" means town as defined in RSA 21:5.

(b) "Selectmen" means selectmen as defined in RSA 21:28.

Source.

2004, 225:2, eff. July 1, 2004.

Effective Date.

2004, 225:6, eff. July 1, 2004, provided: "Any public water system serving more than one municipality which introduced fluoride into the water supply prior to July 1, 2004 may continue the use of fluoride until a referendum under RSA 485:14-a has taken place."

485:15. Appeal.

If the department shall require the abandonment of any such emergency source the person, corporation or association aggrieved by such action shall have an appeal to the superior court, said appeal to be taken within 30 days from the receipt of the order from said department, and said court may make such order on the appeal as justice may require.

Source.
1989, 339:1, eff. Jan. 1, 1990. 1996, 228:106,
eff. July 1, 1996.

Amendments
—**1996.** Substituted "department" for "division" in two places.

RESEARCH REFERENCES

New Hampshire Practice.
5 N.H.P. Civil Practice and Procedure
§ 61.02.

485:16. Penalty.

Whoever violates any of the provisions of RSA 485:8-13, but not RSA 485:8, II, or fails to comply with the lawful orders and requirements of the department duly made pursuant to those sections, or whoever hinders or obstructs any inspector in the pursuit of his lawful duty in respect to such sections, shall be guilty of a misdemeanor if a natural person, or guilty of a felony if any other person.

Source.
1989, 339:1, eff. Jan. 1, 1990. 1996, 228:106,
eff. July 1, 1996.

Cross References.
Classification of crimes, see RSA 625:9.
Sentences, see RSA 651.

Amendments
—**1996.** Substituted "department" for
"division".

Methyl Tertiary Butyl Ether (MTBE)

485:16-a. Drinking Water Standards and Notification.

I. The commissioner, in consultation with the commissioner of health and human services, shall adopt primary and secondary drinking water standards pursuant to RSA 485:3, and ambient groundwater quality standards pursuant to RSA 485-C:6, applicable to MTBE. The commissioner shall not commence rulemaking for these standards until after the department has reviewed the scientific record on the risks posed by the presence of MTBE in drinking water supplies. Such review shall be completed at the earliest possible date, but no later than January 1, 2000. The commissioner shall commence rulemaking no later than January 1, 2000.

II. Any public water system delivering water with greater than 5 parts per billion of MTBE shall notify each customer of the MTBE content.

Source.
1999, 313:2, eff. July 16, 1999.

485:16-b. Authority to Limit MTBE in Gasoline; Penalties.

I. Except as provided for in RSA 485:16-d, the commissioner shall seek all necessary authorizations from the Environmental Protection Agency to opt out of the federal reformulated gasoline program as soon as possible, but in no case later than January 1, 2004. The department of environmental services shall prepare and submit to the Environmental Protection Agency as soon as possible, but in no case later than January 1, 2002, all documentation necessary to accomplish this task.

II. In addition to the provisions of paragraph I, the commissioner, after consultation with the commissioner of health and human services, shall limit to the greatest extent practicable, with the approval of the governor and council, the concentration of MTBE allowed in any gasoline sold in all or part of the state after first holding a public hearing on the issue and certifying to the air pollution advisory committee established in RSA 125-J:11 that gasolines which meet such limit are:

(a) Readily available to New Hampshire consumers at a reasonable price;

(b) Less hazardous overall to humans and the environment than gasoline having higher MTBE concentrations taking into account all exposure routes, including air and water; and

(c) Approved for use in New Hampshire by the Environmental Protection Agency without a requirement to substitute additional air emissions reductions beyond those adopted under RSA 485:16-c.

III. Nothing in this section shall prohibit the commissioner from phasing in any limitations approved under paragraph II.

IV. Retail sellers of gasoline and the suppliers to such retail sellers shall comply with the provisions of paragraph II or be subject to the enforcement provisions of RSA 485:58.

V. The limitations on MTBE concentrations established under the provisions of this section shall be exempt from the requirements of RSA 541-A, the administrative procedure act. The department shall file, however, in the office of legislative services a copy of all rules adopted, amended, or repealed under this section by the department.

Source.
1999, 313:2, eff. July 16, 1999. 2001, 293:2, eff. July 17, 2001.

Amendments
—**2001.** Paragraph I: Rewritten to the extent that a detailed comparison would be impracticable.

Paragraph II: Substituted "provisions of" for "authority to seek waivers under" preceding "paragraph I" and "services, shall limit to the greatest extent practicable, with" for "services, may limit with" in the introductory paragraph and added "beyond those adopted under RSA 485:16-c" in subpar. (c).

485:16-c. Adoption of Other Air Pollution Control Measures.

In order to reduce air emissions and receive federal credit for such reductions, the commissioner shall be authorized to establish limits on the manufacture, use, or sale of consumer products in accordance with RSA 125-C:6, XVII.

Source.
2001, 293:3, eff. July 17, 2001. 2004, 175:5, eff. May 27, 2004.

Amendments
—**2004.** Substituted "to reduce air emissions and receive federal credit for such reduc-

tions" for "to fulfill federal air pollutant emission reduction obligations that may be created by opting out of the federal reformulated gasoline program under RSA 485:16-b or by implementing an alternative regional or federal approach under RSA 485:16-d".

485:16-d. Regional and Federal Efforts.

I. The commissioner is authorized to promote such regional or federal efforts as may be required to reduce the ongoing contamination threat posed by MTBE and other gasoline ethers, including but not limited to efforts to eliminate the federal oxygen mandate in the federal Clean Air Act, secure waivers from federal fuel requirements, or implement cleaner, more protective reformulation of gasoline.

II. If an alternative regional or federal approach to cleaner gasoline is developed which provides equal or greater effectiveness in reducing concentrations of MTBE and other gasoline ethers than opting out of the federal reformulated gasoline program under RSA 485:16-b, I, or does so in a manner that requires less costly substitute emission control measures under RSA 485:16-c, then the commissioner may implement such alternative regional or federal approach. Such alternative regional or federal approach may substitute for opting out of the federal reformulated gasoline program under RSA 485:16-b, I if undertaken prior to January 1, 2004.

Source.
2001, 293:3, eff. July 17, 2001.

Water Pollution Control

Cross References.
Household cleaning products containing phosphates prohibited, see RSA 485-A:56.

485:17. Pollution.

If a person shall place, leave, or cause to be placed or left, in or near a lake, pond, reservoir or stream tributary thereto, from which the domestic water supply of a city, town or village is taken, in whole or in part, any substance or fluid that may cause such water to become impure or unfit for such purposes he shall be guilty of a misdemeanor if a natural person, or guilty of a felony if any other person.

Source.
1989, 339:1, eff. Jan. 1, 1990.

Sentences, see RSA 651.

Cross References.
Classification of crimes, see RSA 625:9.

NOTES TO DECISIONS

Constitutionality
A statute which prohibits the deposit of sawdust in a lake used as a public water supply, and in its tributaries, is not unconstitutional because local in its operation, or as depriving a mill owner of his property without

compensation. State v. Griffin, 69 N.H. 1, 39 A.
260, 1896 N.H. LEXIS 1, 41 L.R.A. 177 (1896).
(Decided under prior law.)

RESEARCH REFERENCES

New Hampshire Practice.
15 N.H.P. Land Use Planning and Zoning
§ 39.01.

485:18. Removal of Polluting Substance.

The health officer of the town, or the water commissioners having charge of
the water supply, or the proprietors of the water supply, may remove such
substance or fluid; and they may recover the expense of removal from the
person who placed the same, or caused it to be placed, in or near the water, in
an action on the case.

Source.
1989, 339:1, eff. Jan. 1, 1990.

485:19. Willful Pollution.

Any person who knowingly and willfully poisons, defiles, pollutes or in any
way corrupts the waters or ice of any well, spring, brook, lake, pond, river or
reservoir, used as the source of a domestic public water or ice supply, or
knowingly corrupts the sources of the water of any water company or of any
city or town supplying its inhabitants with water, or the tributaries of said
sources of supply, in such a manner as to affect the purity of the water or ice
so supplied at the point where the water or ice is taken for such domestic use,
or puts the carcass of any dead animal or other offensive material into said
waters or upon the ice, shall be guilty of a misdemeanor if a natural person, or
guilty of a felony if any other person.

Source.
1989, 339:1, eff. Jan. 1, 1990.

Sentences, see RSA 651.

Cross References.
Classification of crimes, see RSA 625:9.

485:20. Injunctions.

I. The superior court shall have power to issue injunctions restraining any
person from violating the provisions of RSA 485:17 or 485:19.

II. Municipalities may apply to a justice of the superior court for injunctive
relief against existing or impending violations of RSA 485:17 or 485:19. The
municipality shall give notice of any such action to the attorney general and
the commissioner of environmental services, who may take such steps as they
deem necessary to ensure uniform statewide enforcement, including but not
limited to joining the action, assuming sole prosecution of the action, or, as of
right, dismissing the action without prejudice. Such notice shall be given at

least 30 days prior to the commencement of any such action, unless more immediate action is necessary to prevent irreparable environmental damage or other serious public harm, in which case such notice shall be given as soon as practicable, but in no event later than the date of commencement of the action. This paragraph shall not be construed to affect, in any manner, existing authority of municipalities to act based upon the provisions of other statutes or local ordinances.

Source.
1989, 339:1. 1991, 340:3, eff. Jan. 1, 1992.

Amendments
—**1991.** Designated the existing provisions

of the section as par. I, substituted "RSA 485:17 or 485:19" for "the preceding section" following "provisions of" in that paragraph, and added par. II.

RESEARCH REFERENCES

New Hampshire Practice.
14 N.H.P. Local Government Law § 921.
15 N.H.P. Land Use Planning and Zoning § 7.10.

485:21. Fishing; Ice Racing; Penalty.

Said local legislative bodies and officers may also adopt all reasonable rules regarding fishing and the use of boats in and upon any such lake, pond or reservoir, and regarding racing or speeding horses upon the ice of such water body, which they may deem expedient. Any person who shall violate any of said rules after notice of such rules shall be guilty of a misdemeanor.

Source.
1989, 339:1, eff. Jan. 1, 1990.

Sentences, see RSA 651.

Cross References.
Classification of crimes, see RSA 625:9.

485:22. Bathing.

If any person shall bathe in such lake, pond or reservoir, within the limits prescribed for the protection of said water supply by the local board of health or health officer or the department, he shall be guilty of a misdemeanor.

Source.
1989, 339:1, eff. Jan. 1, 1990. 1996, 228:106, eff. July 1, 1996.

Cross References.
Classification of crimes, see RSA 625:9.
Sentences, see RSA 651.

Amendments
—**1996.** Substituted "department" for "division".

485:23. Petition to Protect Water Supplies.

I. Whenever any board of water commissioners, local board of health, local health officer or 10 or more citizens of any town or city have reason to believe that a public water or ice supply is being contaminated or is in danger of contamination, and that the local regulations are not sufficient or effective to prevent such pollution, they may petition the department to investigate the case, and to adopt rules under RSA 541-A as the department may deem necessary for the protection of the said supply against any pollution that in its judgment would endanger the public health. Citizens petitioning under this section shall designate a signatory of the petition as the person to whom the department shall send its response.

II. Whenever any board of water commissioners, local board of health, or other owner of a public water supply has reason to believe that a public water supply is in danger of being contaminated or is otherwise threatened and that an emergency condition exists such that a petition pursuant to paragraph I to the department and the adoption of rules would not adequately protect the water supply, the board or owner may petition the governor to declare a state of emergency for the public water supply. At the request of the governor, the department shall consult with the owner of the water supply and make a recommendation as to emergency protections that may be necessary. If the governor declares a state of emergency for a public water supply, those additional protections that the governor deems necessary shall be effective immediately and for the duration of the emergency. The declaration of a state of emergency for a public water supply shall not exceed 6 months. The governor may renew the declaration one time for up to 6 additional months upon further request by the original petitioner. At such time as any of the emergency protections are to become permanent, the department shall initiate rulemaking in accordance with RSA 485:24. Any protections in the governor's declaration shall be enforced in the same manner as rules adopted pursuant to RSA 485:24 or RSA 485:25 with violations of the protections subject to RSA 485:4 and RSA 485:58.

Source.
1989, 339:1, eff. Jan. 1, 1990. 1996, 228:106, eff. July 1, 1996. 2002, 141:1, eff. May 13, 2002.

—1996. Substituted "department" for "division" wherever it appeared.

Amendments
—2002. Designated the existing provisions of the section as par. I and added par. II.

NOTES TO DECISIONS

Analysis

1. Construction with other laws
2. Procedure

1. Construction with other laws
This and the following section were adopted as a single act and must be read together. Richardson v. Beattie, 98 N.H. 71, 95 A.2d 122, 1953 N.H. LEXIS 17 (1953). (Decided under prior law.)

2. Procedure
State board of health may act without a hearing and on its own inspection and knowledge under this section, provided there is contamination or a threat of contamination of a public water supply. Richardson v. Beattie, 98 N.H. 71, 95 A.2d 122, 1953 N.H. LEXIS 17 (1953). (Decided under prior law.)

In acting upon such a petition the board, if it sees fit, may adopt a summary procedure, and is not bound to grant requests for findings and rulings of law. Willis v. Wilkins, 92 N.H. 400, 32 A.2d 321, 1943 N.H. LEXIS 101 (1943). (Decided under prior law.)

On a petition alleging that a certain source of public water supply was in danger of contamination and asking for regulations "to prohibit swimming or bathing in any part", riparian owners whose rights and privileges would be curtailed thereby are not entitled to a hearing as of right. Willis v. Wilkins, 92 N.H. 400, 32 A.2d 321, 1943 N.H. LEXIS 101 (1943). (Decided under prior law.)

In acting upon such a petition the board may properly act on its own inspection and knowledge; hence it is not necessary that members of the board who participated in the final determination did not hear all the testimony. Willis v. Wilkins, 92 N.H. 400, 32 A.2d 321, 1943 N.H. LEXIS 101 (1943). (Decided under prior law.)

485:23-a. Review of Private Access Facilities.

No private boat access facility shall be constructed to any public waters which serve as a public water supply for a public or private water utility company, without the approval of the department of environmental services upon consultation with the public water access advisory board and notification to the public utilities commission for any water utility under its jurisdiction.

Source.
1996, 224:2, eff. Aug 9, 1996.

485:24. Investigations; Rules.

I. The department shall respond in writing to a petition filed under RSA 485:23, I, after due investigation, but not later than 30 days after receipt of the petition, informing the petitioners of the department's intended action. In response to a petition, or upon its own motion, the department shall adopt such rules under RSA 541-A as it may deem best to protect the water or ice supply against any dangerous contamination. If requested by the department, the local board of water commissioners, the local board of health, or the local health officer, shall enforce such rules in cooperation with the department.

II. In the case of water supplies any part of which may be outside the town or city concerned, the health officer of such town or city may act as an agent of the department for the enforcement of these rules when so designated by the department. The department may empower the board of water commissioners, local board of health, or local health officer and their agents of the affected municipality to enforce rules adopted under the provisions of this section.

Source.
1989, 339:1, eff. Jan. 1, 1990. 1996, 228:106, eff. July 1, 1996. 2002, 141:2, eff. May 13, 2002.

Amendments
—**2002.** Paragraph I: Substituted "RSA 485:23, I" for "RSA 485:23" following "filed under" in the first sentence.

—**1996.** Substituted "department" for "division" throughout the section.

NOTES TO DECISIONS

Analysis

1. Constitutionality
2. Construction with other laws
3. Notice of investigation
4. Hearing
5. Reasonableness of regulations
6. Compensation of landowners

1. Constitutionality

The power to make regulations for the protection of the public health does not involve any unconstitutional delegation of legislative power. State v. Normand, 76 N.H. 541, 85 A. 899, 1913 N.H. LEXIS 47 (1913). (Decided under prior law.)

2. Construction with other laws

This section and the preceding section were adopted as a single act and must be read together. Richardson v. Beattie, 98 N.H. 71, 95 A.2d 122, 1953 N.H. LEXIS 17 (1953). (Decided under prior law.)

3. Notice of investigation

Formal notice of an investigation conducted by the state board of health need not be served upon riparian proprietors, the only provision for notice being posting or publication of regulations. Willis v. Wilkins, 92 N.H. 400, 32 A.2d 321, 1943 N.H. LEXIS 101 (1943). (Decided under prior law.)

4. Hearing

Power to make regulations to protect a public water supply from contamination may be exercised without hearing and upon the state health board's own inspection and knowledge even if such action may seriously impair private as well as public rights. Richardson v. Beattie, 98 N.H. 71, 95 A.2d 122, 1953 N.H. LEXIS 17 (1953). (Decided under prior law.)

Riparian owners whose rights and privileges will be curtailed by a regulation to prohibit swimming or bathing in waters constituting a public water supply are not entitled to a hearing as of right. Willis v. Wilkins, 92 N.H. 400, 32 A.2d 321, 1943 N.H. LEXIS 101 (1943). (Decided under prior law.)

5. Reasonableness of regulations

Regulations adopted must have reasonable connection with protection against dangerous contamination. Richardson v. Beattie, 98 N.H. 71, 95 A.2d 122, 1953 N.H. LEXIS 17 (1953). (Decided under prior law.)

In determining reasonableness of a regulation prohibiting human activity on a lake constituting a source of public water supply, court may determine for itself existence of facts necessary to determine whether regulation is clearly unreasonable; and must balance importance of the public benefit sought to be promoted against seriousness of restriction of private right thereby imposed. Richardson v. Beattie, 98 N.H. 71, 95 A.2d 122, 1953 N.H. LEXIS 17 (1953). (Decided under prior law.)

A regulation prohibiting all human activity upon a part of a lake used as a public water supply was found unreasonable under the circumstances, in Richardson v. Beattie, 98 N.H. 71, 95 A.2d 122, 1953 N.H. LEXIS 17 (1953). (Decided under prior law.)

In determining whether regulations should be adopted prohibiting swimming or bathing in certain waters used as a public supply, and maintenance of any fishing houses on the ice thereof, board should consider the feasibility of a purification system. Willis v. Wilkins, 92 N.H. 400, 32 A.2d 321, 1943 N.H. LEXIS 101 (1943). (Decided under prior law.)

6. Compensation of landowners

If the regulations are reasonable, the resulting loss to riparian owners excluded from swimming or bathing in a source of public water supply does not entitle them to compensation. Willis v. Wilkins, 92 N.H. 400, 32 A.2d 321, 1943 N.H. LEXIS 101 (1943). (Decided under prior law.)

485:25. Interstate Waters.

To protect the purity of interstate waters used as sources of public drinking water supply by adjoining states, the commissioner is authorized, at the request of the state health department of an adjoining state, to adopt rules under RSA 541-A for the protection of the purity of the waters of any lakes, ponds, streams, and reservoirs within any specified drainage area in this state.

Source.
  1989, 339:1, eff. Jan. 1, 1990. 1996, 228:110, eff. July 1, 1996.

Amendments
  —1996. Substituted "commissioner" for "division".

485:26. Penalty for Violation of Rules.

Any person violating rules adopted pursuant to RSA 485:24 or 25 shall be guilty of a misdemeanor if a natural person, or guilty of a felony if any other person.

Source.
  1989, 339:1, eff. Jan. 1, 1990.

Sentences, see RSA 651.

Cross References.
  Classification of crimes, see RSA 625:9.

485:27. Power to Require Improvements in Sewage Treatment.

The department is empowered to investigate the conditions and methods pertaining to existing systems of sewerage and sewage treatment works and to require the application of any treatment, improvement or enlargement of such facilities as will insure their proper operation and provide adequate protection of the public health. Issuance of orders requiring changes or improvements in such sewerage systems or treatment works shall be in the manner as prescribed in RSA 485:4.

Source.
  1989, 339:1, eff. Jan. 1, 1990. 1996, 228:106, eff. July 1, 1996.

Cross References.
  Municipal bond issue for sewage system or treatment works, see RSA 33:5, 5-a-5-c.

Amendments
  —1996. Substituted "department" for "division" in the first sentence.

NOTES TO DECISIONS

Compliance with regulations
  Power of a state board of health to make regulations pertaining to sewage disposal includes the further authority to issue specific orders designed to compel compliance with regulations previously issued but long ignored. Town of Meredith v. State Board of Health, 94 N.H. 123, 48 A.2d 489, 1946 N.H. LEXIS 161 (1946). (Decided under prior law.)

485:28. Power to Require the Installation of Sewage Facilities.

The department is hereby empowered to investigate the conditions and methods relating to the disposal of sewage in any municipality, as set forth in RSA 486:1, and to require the installation of public sewers, as defined in RSA 147:8, whenever such investigation demonstrates that individual sewage disposal systems are inadequate or incapable of protecting the health and welfare of the citizens of the affected municipality or preventing pollution of the surface waters of the state, as defined in RSA 485-A. Before issuing an order requiring the installation of public sewer facilities, the department shall notify the municipality of its findings and shall give the municipality an opportunity to be heard. After such hearing if it shall be determined that said facilities are necessary, the municipality shall be so notified in writing and the requirements so ordered shall be effected pursuant to RSA 38:25 within a reasonable time to be fixed by the department. If any municipality whose duty it is to act shall fail or refuse for a period of 10 days after the expiration of the time fixed by said order, or, in the case of appeal for a period of 10 days after final judgment shall have been entered, to obey the same or in good faith to begin to make the installation as ordered, such municipality so failing shall be fined not more than $1,000 for each day of failure to comply with the order of the department. Said fine shall be paid to the state and may be recovered in an action of debt brought by the attorney general in the name of the state treasurer.

Source.
1989, 339:1, eff. Jan. 1, 1990. 1996, 228:106, eff. July 1, 1996. 1997, 206:7, eff. July 1, 1997.

Amendments
—1997. Substituted "RSA 38:25" for "RSA 38:14-a" in the third sentence.

—1996. Substituted "department" for "division" throughout the section.

Severability of enactment.
1997, 206 was subject to a severability clause. See 1997, 206:9.

485:29. Appeal.

Any person aggrieved by any decision, regulation, ruling or order made by the department pursuant to the provisions of RSA 485:24, 27, and 28 may appeal such decisions pursuant to RSA 21-O:14.

Source.
1989, 339:1, eff. Jan. 1, 1990. 1996, 228:106, eff. July 1, 1996.

Amendments
—1996. Substituted "department" for "division".

485:30. Discharge of Sewage; Penalty.

No person, association or corporation shall cause or permit the discharge of sewage or other deleterious waste from any dwelling, camp, factory, hotel, boardinghouse, or other commercial establishment into any stream, lake, pond, or river not previously polluted, without first submitting detailed plans of said proposed discharge to the department and securing the approval of the said department. Any person who violates the provisions of this section shall be guilty of a misdemeanor if a natural person, or guilty of a felony if any other person.

Source.
1989, 339:1, eff. Jan. 1, 1990. 1996, 228:106, eff. July 1, 1996.

Amendments
—1996. Substituted "department" for "division" in the first sentence.

Cross References.
Classification of crimes, see RSA 625:9.
Sentences, see RSA 651-A.

Sewers

State board of health could require town to construct sewerage system to prevent contamination of public water supply. Town of Meredith v. State Board of Health, 94 N.H. 123, 48 A.2d 489, 1946 N.H. LEXIS 161 (1946). (Decided under prior law.)

485:31. Tampering With Public Water Systems.

I. Any person who tampers with, attempts to tamper with, or makes a threat to tamper with a public water system shall be guilty of a class B felony if a natural person and guilty of a felony if any other person.

II. Notwithstanding RSA 651:2, a natural person may, in addition to any sentence of imprisonment, probation or conditional discharge, be fined not more than $50,000 if found guilty of tampering with a public water system, and not more than $25,000 if found guilty of an attempt to tamper with or making a threat to tamper with a public water system. Each day of violation shall constitute a separate violation.

III. Any person who tampers, attempts to tamper, or makes a threat to tamper with a public water system shall be liable to the state, upon suit brought by the attorney general, for a civil forfeiture not to exceed $50,000 for such tampering or not to exceed $25,000 for such attempt or threat.

IV. In this section, the term "tamper" means:

(a) To introduce a contaminant into a public water system with the purpose of harming persons; or

(b) To otherwise interfere with the operation of a public water system with the purpose of harming persons.

Source.
1989, 339:1, eff. Jan. 1, 1990.

Cross References.
Classification of crimes, see RSA 625:9.

485:32. Injuring Property.

Any person who shall willfully injure any of the property of any water company or of any city or town, used by it in supplying water to its inhabitants, shall be guilty of a misdemeanor if a natural person, or guilty of a felony if any other person, and such person shall also forfeit and pay to such water company, city or town 3 times the amount of actual damages sustained, to be recovered in an action on the case.

Source.
1989, 339:1, eff. Jan. 1, 1990.

Cross References.
Classification of crimes, see RSA 625:9.

Sentences, see RSA 651-A.

Private Water Sources

RESEARCH REFERENCES

ALR.

Measure and elements of damages for pollution of well or spring. 76 A.L.R.4th 629.

485:33. Analyses; Prohibiting Use.

Whenever any well, spring or other water supply is suspected of being polluted by sewage or other matter dangerous to health, the health officer of the town where it is located may cause an analysis of the water to be made by a competent chemist, without expense to the owner. If the analysis shows the water to be unfit for drinking purposes they may, with the approval of the department, prohibit its use, and, if it be from a well, may cause the well to be closed.

Source.

1989, 339:1, eff. Jan. 1, 1990. 1996, 228:106, eff. July 1, 1996.

Amendments

—1996. Substituted "department" for "division" in the second sentence.

485:34. Enforcement.

The department shall have concurrent jurisdiction with local boards and officers to enforce the provisions of this subdivision.

Source.

1989, 339:1, eff. Jan. 1, 1990. 1996, 228:106, eff. July 1, 1996.

Amendments

—1996. Substituted "department" for "division".

485:35. Prohibiting Use; Penalty.

Whenever the department, upon investigation, becomes satisfied that a well, spring or other supply of water, used for domestic purposes, has become polluted so as to endanger the public health, it is authorized to prohibit the person or corporation owning or controlling said supply from furnishing such water for domestic purposes, until it becomes satisfied that said water supply has been purified and made fit for domestic use. Any person who violates the order of the department is guilty of a misdemeanor for each day he continues to furnish water after the order of the department has been served on him.

Source.

1989, 339:1, eff. Jan. 1, 1990. 1996, 228:106, eff. July 1, 1996.

Cross References.

Classification of crimes, see RSA 625:9.

Sentences, see RSA 651-A.

Amendments

—1996. Substituted "department" for "division" wherever it appeared.

485:35-a. Protective Well Radii.

[Repealed 1991, 215:3, eff. Aug. 9, 1991.]

Former section(s).

Former RSA 485:35-a, which was derived from 1989, 191:1, related to protective well radii for private water wells. See now RSA 485-A:30-b.

Effect of repeal on existing rules.

1991, 215:1, II, eff. Aug. 9, 1991, provided: "The rules adopted under former RSA 485:35-a relative to protective well radii shall remain in full force and effect upon enactment of this act [which repealed this section and added RSA 485-A:30-b] to the extent not inconsistent with the provisions of this act. The recodification of the section on protective well radii from RSA 485 to RSA 485-A shall not be construed to affect the validity of such rules otherwise consistent with this act."

485:36. Injunctions to Enforce.

The superior court shall have jurisdiction in equity, upon application of the department, to enforce the orders of the department issued under RSA 485:35.

Source.

1989, 339:1, eff. Jan. 1, 1990. 1996, 228:106, eff. July 1, 1996.

Revision note.

Substituted "RSA 485:35" for "the preceding section" for purposes of clarity in light of the enactment and repeal of RSA 485:35-a.

Amendments

—1996. Substituted "department" for "division".

485:37. Fencing or Covering.

No person who owns or occupies land shall knowingly allow any well which is within 500 feet of a dwelling or within 200 feet of any highway to remain open on such land, unless there is around such well a substantial fence or protection at least 3 feet high so constructed that no child can crawl through or under it. Any such well shall be deemed to be open unless it is protected by a covering strong enough to hold 1,000 pounds and secured so that it cannot be easily removed by children. The term "well" as used in this subdivision shall mean any artificially made hole in the surface of the earth (a) which is more than 4 feet deep and (b) which is more than 8 inches in diameter and less than 16 square feet in area at the top and (c) the sides of which are steeper than a 60 degree slope.

Source.

1989, 339:1, eff. Jan. 1, 1990.

485:38. Nuisance.

Any open well which is not fenced or protected as provided in RSA 485:37 is declared a nuisance and the same may be ordered abated by any court of competent jurisdiction on complaint of any prosecuting officer.

Source.

1989, 339:1, eff. Jan. 1, 1990.

485:39. Penalty.

Whoever violates any provision of RSA 485:37 or RSA 485:38 shall be guilty of a misdemeanor if a natural person, or guilty of a felony if any other person.

Source.
1989, 339:1, eff. Jan. 1, 1990.

Sentences, see RSA 651-A.

Cross References.
Classification of crimes, see RSA 625:9.

485:40. Emergency Planning.

The department shall develop plans, with the advice and assistance of the division of emergency services, communications, and management, and of the public water systems of the state, for emergency conditions and situations that may endanger the public health or welfare by contamination of drinking water. Such plans may include potential sources of contaminants and situations or conditions that could place them in the sources of public drinking water, techniques and methods to be used by public water systems to reduce or eliminate the dangers to public health caused thereby, methods and times for analysis or testing during such emergency conditions or situations, alternate sources of water available to public water systems, and methods of supplying drinking water to consumers if a public water system cannot supply such water.

Source.
1989, 339:1, eff. Jan. 1, 1990. 1996, 228:71, eff. July 1, 1996. 2002, 257:10, eff. July 1, 2002. 2003, 319:128, eff. Sept. 4, 2003. 2004, 171:20, eff. July 24, 2004.

Amendments
—2004. Substituted "division of emergency services, communications, and management" for "bureau of emergency management" in the first sentence.

—2003. Substituted "bureau of emergency

management" for "office of emergency management" in the first sentence.

—2002. Deleted "governor's" preceeding "office of emergency management" in the first sentence.

—1996. Deleted "divisions of water resources, water supply and pollution control" preceding "governor's office" in the first sentence.

485:41. Duties of Department.

The department shall:

I. Monitor the operation and maintenance of new and existing public water systems.

II. Adopt rules governing the maintenance and operation of public water systems to ensure compliance with drinking water standards and to protect the public health.

III. Adopt rules governing the installation of pipes, fixtures and other apparatus which are used to connect the water system to a building. Such rules shall be considered minimum standards. The department shall adopt the International Plumbing Code as published by the International Code Council by reference, provided the department specifies which sections of the code are in force in New Hampshire and makes specific any discretionary provisions in the code subject to approval by the state building code review board. The department shall periodically review the rules adopted under this paragraph to assure that they are no less stringent than the requirements of the current code.

IV. Adopt rules establishing recordkeeping, reporting and testing requirements for public water systems.

V. Enter, and authorize its employees and agents to enter, the premises of all public water systems for the purpose of carrying out inspection and for the purpose of taking water samples, to determine compliance with the provisions of this chapter or rules adopted under it, and to inspect any and all records and facilities of such public water supply in order to determine compliance with this chapter and rules adopted under it.

VI. Undertake long-range planning and studies, within available state and federal funding, relating to the purity of drinking water in the state.

VII. Make available to the public the analytical results of all monitoring and testing undertaken pursuant to this chapter.

VIII. Adopt a fee system in recognition of services provided by the water supply engineering bureau including the issuance of an operational permit for public water systems subject to this chapter. The commissioner shall adopt rules establishing the application process for the issuance of operational permits pursuant to RSA 541-A. The fee category for community systems per year shall be $300, but in no case shall the fee exceed $10 per household or household equivalent. The fee category for non-transient and non-community systems shall be $150 per year. All fees shall be paid to the department for deposit in the operational permits account. Moneys in the operational permits account shall be used to pay the salaries, benefits and expenses of the staff in the department's drinking water supply program. Any revenues generated in excess of the costs of funding the drinking water supply program's expenses, shall lapse to the general fund at the close of each fiscal year to be used to offset the future general fund appropriation for the water supply program.

Source.

1989, 339:1. 1990, 163:4. 1991, 380:3, eff. July 2, 1991. 1996, 228:72, 106, eff. July 1, 1996. 2002, 8:9, eff. Sept. 14, 2002.

Amendments

—2002. Paragraph III: Deleted the former third sentence, substituted "shall adopt the International Plumbing Code as published by the International Code Council" for "may adopt the BOCA code" in the present third sentence, and deleted "BOCA" preceding "code" at the end of the present fourth sentence.

—1996. Substituted "department" for "division" in the section catchline, in the introductory paragraph and throughout par. III, and

"commissioner" for "division" in the second sentence, "department" for "division" in the fifth sentence and "department's" for "division's" in the sixth sentence of par. VIII.

—1991. Paragraph VIII: Substituted "by the water supply engineering bureau including the" for "for the" following "provided" in the first sentence, "$300" for "$600 for all systems serving more than 100 people" following "shall be" in the third sentence and "$150" for "$200" in the fourth sentence, rewrote the sixth sentence, and substituted "drinking water supply program's expenses" for "water supply engineering bureau, operation permits section" preceding "shall lapse" and "water supply program" for "water supply engineering bureau" following "appropriation for the" in the seventh sentence.

—1990. Paragraph VIII: Added.

Exemptions from fees; refunds.

1991, 380:4, eff. July 2, 1991, provided: "Any system owned by a state, county, municipality, town, precinct, or district shall be exempt from water system fees as provided in RSA 485:41, VIII. Any state, county, municipality, town, precinct, or district that has been billed and still has an outstanding account, shall have such outstanding account forgiven. In the event that the entity has already paid, then the sum paid shall be refunded to it. The funds necessary to provide the refunds to the state, county, municipality, town, precinct, or district exempted under RSA 485:41, VIII, are hereby appropriated and shall be a charge against the operational permits account."

485:42. Variances and Exemptions.

I. The department may, after notice and opportunity for hearing, grant one or more variances from an applicable state drinking water regulation to a public water system if the variance will not result in an unreasonable risk to the public health, and if:

(a) Because of the characteristics of the raw water sources reasonably available to the system, the system cannot meet the maximum contaminant levels of such drinking water regulation despite application of the best available technology, treatment techniques or other means. The department's finding of the best available technology treatment, treatment technique or other means may vary depending upon the number of persons served by the system or for other physical conditions related to engineering feasibility and cost of compliance with maximum contaminant levels as considered appropriate by the department; or

(b) Where a specified treatment technique for a contaminant is required by the state drinking water regulations, the system demonstrates to the department's satisfaction that such treatment technique is not required to protect the public health because of the nature of the raw water source. Variances may be conditioned on monitoring, testing, analyzing or other requirements to ensure the protection of the public health, and variances granted under subparagraph (a) shall include a compliance schedule under which the public water system will meet each contaminant level for which a variance is granted as expeditiously as is feasible.

II. The department may, after notice and opportunity for hearing, grant one or more exemptions from an applicable maximum contaminant level or treatment technique in the state drinking water rules to a public water system if:

(a) The exemption will not result in an unreasonable risk to the public health;

(b) The public water system is unable to comply with the rule due to compelling factors, which may include economic factors; and

(c) The public water system was in operation on the earliest effective date, under present or prior law, of the contaminant level or treatment technique requirement. Each exemption shall be conditioned on monitoring, testing, analyzing or other requirements to ensure the protection of the public health, and shall include a compliance schedule under which the public water system will meet each contaminant level or treatment technique for which an exemption is granted as expeditiously as is feasible, but not later than 12 months after the date of issuance of the exemption. The department may extend the final date for compliance provided in any schedule required under this section for a period not to exceed 3 years after the date of the issuance of the exemption if the public water system establishes that:

(1) The system cannot meet the standard without capital improvements which cannot be completed within the period of such exemption;

(2) In the case of a system which needs financial assistance for the necessary improvements, the system has entered into an agreement to obtain such financial assistance; or

(3) The system has entered into an enforceable agreement to become part of a regional public water system; and the system is taking all practicable steps to meet the standards.

If a system serves fewer than 500 service connections and needs financial assistance for necessary improvements, an exemption granted under subparagraph (c)(1) or (c)(2) of this subparagraph may be renewed for one or more additional 2-year periods, if the system establishes that it is taking all practicable steps to meet the requirements of any compliance schedule established under this section.

Source.
1989, 339:1, eff. Jan. 1, 1990. 1996, 228:106, eff. July 1, 1996.

Amendments
—**1996.** Substituted "department" for "division" throughout the section.

485:43. Notification of Noncompliance; Water Quality.

I. A public water system shall, upon granting of a variance or exemption or upon determination of its noncompliance with any primary drinking water standard or any rule adopted under this chapter or with any other requirement of this chapter notify the department of such noncompliance within 48 hours and shall notify its users of such noncompliance in accordance with rules adopted by the department under RSA 485:3.

II. Each community public water system shall annually notify each of its users of the results of water quality tests required by RSA 485:41. Such notification shall be in the form prescribed by rule adopted by the commissioner, pursuant to RSA 541-A, under RSA 485:3, VII. Such notification shall include, but not be limited to, a listing of contaminants identified under rules adopted pursuant to RSA 485:3, I, and the results of testing for various bacteriological agents. Where multiple tests have been conducted, a summary or average level of contaminants or biological agents may be provided.

Source.
1989, 339:1, eff. Jan. 1, 1990. 1996, 228:106, 110, eff. July 1, 1996.

Revision note.
Substituted "RSA 485:41" for "RSA 485:42" in the first sentence of par. II to correct an error in the reference.

Amendments
—**1996.** Paragraph I: Substituted "department" for "division" in two places.

Paragraph II: Substituted "commissioner" for "division" in the first sentence.

Laboratory Accreditation

Amendments
—1998. 1998, 152:1, eff. Aug. 7, 1998, sub-stituted "Accreditation" for "Certification" in the subdivision heading.

RESEARCH REFERENCES

New Hampshire Code of Administrative Rules.
Rules of the Department of Environmental Services—Office of the Commissioner, Env-C 301.01 et seq., New Hampshire Code of Administrative Rules Annotated.

485:44. Water Testing Laboratory Accreditation.

I. Any laboratory conducting water analysis tests for the purpose of determining compliance of a public water supply with the provisions of RSA 485:3 and any laboratory conducting environmental analyses in this state for any other governmental purpose where a requirement of certification or accreditation is specified shall first obtain accreditation.

II. The department shall establish and administer a program to accredit on an annual basis the facilities, equipment, procedures, methods of analysis, analytical assurance and quality control, recordkeeping and traceability, analytical performance, and qualifications of personnel of any laboratory for the purposes of RSA 485:44, I. The program shall be in conformance with and consistent with the national accreditation standards approved by the National Environmental Laboratory Accreditation Conference. The purpose of the accreditation program shall be to ensure that environmental laboratories provide sufficiently accurate, precise, and consistent results of tests, analyses, and measurements.

III. The department shall, upon request of a laboratory accredited pursuant to paragraph II of this section, accredit such laboratory in conformance with and consistent with the national accreditation standards approved by the National Environmental Laboratory Accreditation Conference, provided that such laboratory demonstrates capability to analyze samples with precision and accuracy.

IV. A laboratory may subcontract tests which it is not accredited to perform to another laboratory which is so accredited, provided that the test report clearly indicates which tests were subcontracted and that laboratory test records which specify the name and address of the laboratory which performed the work are maintained and made accessible to the department upon request.

V, VI. [Repealed.]

VII. The department shall accredit laboratories accredited in other states upon request by reciprocity, provided that the accreditation program in such states is in conformance with and consistent with the national accreditation standards approved by the National Environmental Laboratory Accreditation Conference.

VIII. An alternate laboratory test method may be acceptable only if it is in conformance with and consistent with the performance based method requirements set forth in the national accreditation standards approved by the National Environmental Laboratory Accreditation Conference.

IX. Accreditation may be denied, revoked, suspended, or modified as determined by rules of the department. A laboratory which has had accreditation revoked or suspended shall be reaccredited at such time as it again meets criteria for accreditation provided, that such laboratory has not had its accreditation revoked or suspended more than 3 times in the preceding 2 years. Upon notification of the fourth such revocation or suspension, such laboratory shall not be eligible for reaccreditation for one year from the date of such notice, except that, upon appeal by such laboratory, the commissioner may waive such extended period of revocation or suspension if such laboratory can demonstrate to the commissioner good cause for the immediate reaccreditation of such laboratory.

X. Changes in laboratory ownership, location, personnel, methodology, or other factors significantly affecting the performance of analyses for which it was originally accredited shall be reported in writing to the accreditation officer of the department within 5 business days of the change.

XI. The department shall establish by rule, under RSA 541-A, a reasonable time frame for the completion of the accreditation process. The provisions under which any laboratory is certified on January 1, 1990 shall not be affected in any way, except as provided in paragraph IX of this section, before the completion of the accreditation process within the time frame established by the department.

XII. Participation of laboratories in the accreditation program shall be voluntary.

Source.

1989, 339:1. 1992, 191:1, 2, eff. July 11, 1992. 1996, 228:73, eff. July 1, 1996. 1998, 152:3, 4, 8 I, eff. Aug. 7, 1998.

Revision note.

Substituted "RSA 485:3" for "RSA 5:3" in par. I and "RSA 485:44, I" for "RSA 485:42, I" in the first sentence of par. II to correct errors in the references.

Substituted "on January 1, 1990" for "at the time of the effective date of this paragraph" in par. XI for purposes of clarity.

Amendments

—1998. Rewritten to the extent that a detailed comparison would be impracticable.

—1996. Paragraph IX: Substituted "commissioner" for "water supply and pollution control council" and for "council" in the third sentence.

—1992. Paragraph II: In the third sentence inserted "metals by flame AA, metals by furnace AA, metals by ICP" preceding "PCB's, pesticides" and inserted "herbicides" thereafter.

Paragraph VII: Added the third sentence.

485:45. Testing of Water Supplies.

The state laboratory shall make periodic inspections and analyses of the public water supplies of the state and any special investigations of such water supplies that may be called for; also, when requested or as may be deemed by them necessary or expedient in the interests of the public health, make inspections or analyses of sources furnishing water to institutions, schools, hotels, camps, other places of public resort and individuals, and advise in connection with the same.

Source.

1989, 339:1, eff. Jan. 1, 1990.

Cross References.

Fees for analyses, see RSA 131:3-a.

485:46. Fees; Advertising.

I. The department shall adopt rules under RSA 541-A, after public hearing, establishing a schedule of reasonable fees to be paid by any laboratory applying for accreditation.

II. The schedule of fees shall be designed to recover the costs associated with the accreditation services provided under RSA 485:44, and such fees shall be available to the department to be used to defray the expenses for such services. Funds received shall be deposited in a special revolving fund account maintained by the department which shall be continuously appropriated to the department to offset the costs of the accreditation program. Any balance in excess of $1,000 remaining at the end of the fiscal year shall lapse to the general fund.

III. A laboratory shall provide each prospective New Hampshire client with a list which clearly indicates the specific analytes which the laboratory is accredited to test. In the event that a client has paid a fee to a laboratory in anticipation of testing services before the receipt of said test sampling materials, and the client subsequently determines upon receipt of the test materials that the laboratory is not accredited to provide testing services to meet the client's needs, the client may cancel the order for any testing services which have not yet been performed, and the laboratory shall make full refund to the client. Test reports shall clearly identify those specific analytes for which a laboratory has accreditation and shall specifically identify any analyses which were subcontracted to other laboratories.

Source.

1989, 339:1. 1992, 191:3, eff. July 11, 1992. 1998, 152:5, eff. Aug. 7, 1998.

Amendments
—1998. Paragraph I: Substituted "accreditation" for "approval and certification" following "applying for".

Paragraph II: Rewritten to the extent that a detailed comparison would be impracticable.

Paragraph III: Substituted "accredited" for "certified" in the first and second sentences, "accreditation" for "certification" in the third sentence, and "the client's" for "his" preceding "needs" and made a minor stylistic change in the second sentence.

—1992. Paragraph II: In the first sentence inserted "the costs of staff and" following "recover" and "staffing, and the cost of" preceding "travel and associated", in the second sentence inserted "revolving fund" preceding "account", "which shall be continuously appropriated to the department" preceding "to offset" and substituted "certification" for "inspection" preceding "program", in the third sentence inserted "in excess of $1,000" preceding "remaining" and in the fourth sentence "and" preceding "facilities" and deleted "and staff services" thereafter.

485:47. Rulemaking.

The department shall adopt rules, under RSA 541-A, relative to:

I. Procedures and standards for accreditation of laboratories, including but not limited to the form and content of approval and accreditation application forms, analytical techniques to be employed, standard collection and testing procedures, performance on proficiency test samples, as well as qualifications for laboratory personnel. The procedures and standards shall be in conformance with and consistent with the national accreditation standards approved by the National Environmental Laboratory Accreditation Conference.

II. [Repealed.]

III. Procedures and conditions under which accreditation of water testing laboratories may be revoked, suspended, or modified.

IV. Information to be disclosed when tests are subcontracted.

V. Procedures and criteria for laboratory reaccreditation.

VI. Procedures for the accreditation of laboratories which have been accredited by other states.

VII. Procedures for approval of alternate testing methodology.

VIII. Fees for accreditation, including rules for accounting of the fees.

IX. Procedures and standards for testing of water under any expanded accreditation program.

X. A time frame for the completion of the accreditation process.

XI-XIII. [Repealed.]

Source.
1989, 339:1, eff. Jan. 1, 1990. 1998, 152:6, 7, 8 II, 8 III, eff. Aug. 7, 1998.

substituted "reaccreditation" for "recertification" in par. V, and "accredited" for "certified" in par. VI, and repealed pars. XI-XIII.

Amendments
—1998. Substituted "accreditation" for "certification" in pars. I, III, VI, VIII-X, rewrote the second sentence in par. I, repealed par. II,

Cross References.
Certification of laboratories, see RSA 485:44.
Regulation of laboratory advertising and fees, see RSA 485:46.

Wellhead Protection

485:48. Wellhead Protection.

The department may institute a wellhead protection program as described in section 1428 of the federal Safe Drinking Water Amendments of 1986. The program shall be consistent with the provisions of RSA 485-C and shall include, but not be limited to, the following:

I. Determination of the responsibilities of state and local government units, and those of public drinking water supply systems with respect to wellhead protection.

II. Determination of the extent of the wellhead protection area, based on reasonably available hydrogeologic data, groundwater flow, recharge, discharge, and other data the department deems necessary to such determination.

III. Identify within each wellhead protection area all potential anthropogenic sources of contaminants which may have any adverse effect on human health, through consideration of all potential sources of such contaminants.

IV. Technical assistance, financial assistance, implementation of control measures, education, training, and demonstration projects to protect the water supply within wellhead protection areas from such contaminants.

V. Contingency plans for the location and provision of alternate drinking water supplies for each public water system in the event of well or wellfield contamination by such contaminants.

VI. Procedures, including, but not limited to, the establishment of technical and citizens' advisory committees, to encourage the public to participate in developing the protection program for wellhead areas. Such procedures shall include notice and opportunity for public hearing on the state program before it is submitted to the administrator, United States Environmental Protection Agency, for approval.

Source.
1989, 339:1. 1991, 344:2, eff. June 28, 1991. 1996, 228:106, eff. July 1, 1996.

References in text.
Section 1428 of the federal Safe Drinking Water Amendments of 1986, referred to in the introductory paragraph, is classified to 42 U.S.C.S. § 300h-7.

Amendments
—**1996.** Substituted "department" for "division" in the introductory paragraph and in par. II.

—**1991.** Rewrote the introductory paragraph.

Future Supplies of Water for Domestic Use

485:49. Declaration of Need.

It is declared that there is statewide need for long-range planning in order that the health and safety of the people of the state may be protected in respect to adequate water supplies for domestic use.

Source.
1989, 339:1, eff. Jan. 1, 1990.

485:50. Domestic Water Supply Study.

The department of environmental services is authorized and directed to study the probable domestic water supply requirements of groups of towns or cities, or both, which appear likely to have increased industrial and population growths for the next 50 years. In connection with said studies the department shall determine the most feasible and economic sites for sources of water supply for such long-range planning.

Source.
1989, 339:1, eff. Jan. 1, 1990.

485:51. Assistance.

The department of environmental services is authorized, within the limits of the appropriations made therefor, to employ engineers and other assistants to make the studies authorized by this subdivision.

Source.
1989, 339:1, eff. Jan. 1, 1990.

485:52. Reports.

Whenever any study of a group plan for domestic water supply projects is made the department of environmental services shall report the same to the next session of the legislature together with its recommendations to make secure the availability of those sites which the department of environmental services finds will best meet the future needs of the particular locality studied.

Source.
1989, 339:1, eff. Jan. 1, 1990.

485:53. Advice to Municipalities.

Upon request the department of environmental services shall consult with and advise any municipality which is considering a change in its domestic water supply due to an approaching critical situation in the municipality.

Source.
1989, 339:1, eff. Jan. 1, 1990.

Protection of Sources of Ice

485:54. Ice Cutting.

No person shall cut or take ice from any lake, pond or reservoir used as the source of a domestic public water supply, unless he shall first comply in all respects with such reasonable rules regarding the manner and place of such cutting and taking as may be prescribed by the local legislative body, or officers of a water company, who may have charge of the works of any city or town supplying its inhabitants with water from such source.

Source.
1989, 339:1, eff. Jan. 1, 1990.

485:55. Ice; Penalty.

Any person who knowingly or willfully shall cut or take ice for domestic purposes from any waters which are polluted with sewage or other substance deleterious or dangerous to life or health, or from waters which a board of health, local health officer or the department has condemned, shall be guilty of a misdemeanor if a natural person, or guilty of a felony if any other person.

Source.

1989, 339:1, eff. Jan. 1, 1990. 1996, 228:106, eff. July 1, 1996.

Amendments

—**1996.** Substituted "department" for "division".

Cross References.

Classification of crimes, see RSA 625:9.

Sentences, see RSA 651-A.

485:56. Ice Inspection.

Health officers of the cities and towns of the state, and the department of environmental services, shall examine and inspect the sources from which ice is cut, or is proposed to be cut, for domestic use in such cities and towns, and to employ any necessary means to determine whether the waters of such sources of ice supply have been polluted, or whether ice taken from such sources will be deleterious to the public health.

Source.

1989, 339:1, eff. Jan. 1, 1990. 1996, 228:108, eff. July 1, 1996.

Amendments

—**1996.** Substituted "department of envi-

ronmental services" for "division of water supply and pollution control".

485:57. Ice; Notice of Pollution.

If the waters of the sources of ice supplies shall be found so polluted that the ice taken from those sources will be unsafe for domestic use, the local health officer or the department of environmental services shall immediately notify such person who may have taken, or who proposes to take, ice from such polluted source for domestic use, of the dangerous character of the waters inspected, and that the taking of such ice for domestic use must cease.

Source.

1989, 339:1, eff. Jan. 1, 1990. 1996, 228:108, eff. July 1, 1996.

Amendments

—**1996.** Substituted "department of envi-

ronmental services" for "division of water supply and pollution control".

Enforcement; Appeals

485:58. Enforcement and Penalties.

I. If the department determines that a primary standard has violated, or that, in its judgment, a condition exists in a public water system which will cause a violation of a primary standard and may result in a serious risk to public health, it may issue an order requiring:

(a) The prohibition of transportation, sale, distribution or supplying of water;

(b) The repair, installation or operation of purification equipment or methods;

(c) The notification of all potential users of the system, including travelers, of the nature, extent and possible health effects of the imminent hazard, and precautions to be taken by users; or

(d) The testing, sampling or other analytical operations required to determine the nature, extent, duration or termination of the imminent hazard. The superior court shall place any action filed by the department to enforce an order under this section at the top of its calendar of cases and shall provide an expeditious hearing on such order.

II. Any knowing violation of any provision of this chapter, any rule adopted under this chapter, any term or condition of an approval, exemption, variance or order issued under this chapter, or any misstatement of a material fact required to be disclosed under this chapter shall constitute a misdemeanor for a natural person and a felony for any other person. Notwithstanding RSA 651:2, any person, in addition to any sentence of imprisonment, probation, or conditional discharge, may be fined not more than $25,000 for each day of violation.

III. Any person who violates any provision of this chapter or any rule adopted or any term or condition of an approval, exemption, variance or order issued under this chapter shall be liable to the state, upon suit brought by the attorney general, for a civil forfeiture in an amount not to exceed $25,000 for each day of such violation.

IV. The commissioner of environmental services, after notice and hearing pursuant to RSA 541-A, may impose an administrative fine not to exceed $2,000 for each offense upon any person who violates any provision of this chapter including any rule adopted under the provisions of this chapter. Rehearings and appeals from a decision of the commissioner under this paragraph shall be in accordance with RSA 541. Any administrative fine imposed under this section shall not preclude the imposition of further penalties under this chapter. The proceeds of administrative fines levied pursuant to this paragraph shall be deposited by the department in the general fund. The commissioner shall adopt rules, under RSA 541-A, relative to:

(a) A schedule of administrative fines which may be imposed under this paragraph for violations of this chapter as provided above.

(b) Procedures for notice and hearing prior to the imposition of an administrative fine.

V. Any act or failure to act in violation of RSA 485:8, II; 31; 42; 43; 46; or 48; or any rule adopted under RSA 485:2; 3; 4; 40; 41; 44; or 47 may be enjoined.

VI. Notwithstanding RSA 651:2, a natural person may, in addition to any sentence of imprisonment, probation or conditional discharge, be fined not more than $25,000 if found guilty of any violation of paragraph II of this section. Each day of violation shall constitute a separate offense.

Source.   1996; 217:6, eff. Jan. 1, 1996. 1996, 228:106, eff. 1989, 339:1. 1990, 33:2. 1995, 88:2, eff. Jan. 1,   July 1, 1996.

Amendments
—1996. Substituted "department" for "division" in the introductory and concluding paragraphs of par.I, and in the introductory paragraph of par. IV.

—1995. Paragraph I: Chapter 88 deleted the first sentence of the concluding paragraph.
Paragraph IV: Chapter 217 added "including any rule adopted under the provisions of this chapter" at the end of the first sentence and substituted "RSA 541" for "RSA 21-O:14" in the second sentence of the introductory paragraph and substituted "violations" for "violation" preceding "of this chapter" and added "as provided above" thereafter in subpar. (a).

—1990. Paragraph II: Deleted "RSA 485:8, II; 31; 42; 43; 46; or 48 of" following "provision of" and substituted "this chapter" for "RSA 485:2, 3, 40, 41, 44 or 47" following "adopted

under", for "RSA 485:5, II; 31; 42; 43; 46; or 48" following "issued under" and for "such sections" following "disclosed under" in the first sentence and added the second sentence.
Paragraph III: Substituted "this chapter or" for "RSA 485:8, II; 31; 42; 43; 46; or 48" preceding "any rule adopted", deleted "under RSA 485:2, 3, 40, 41, 44, or 47" thereafter and substituted "this chapter" for "RSA 485:8, II; 31; 42; 43; 46; or 48" following "issued under".
Paragraph IV: Substituted "of this chapter" for "set forth in paragraph III of this section" following "provision" in the first sentence of the introductory paragraph.
Paragraph V: Inserted "4" following "RSA 485:2; 3".

Cross References.
Classification of crimes, see RSA 625:9.
Penalties for tampering with public water system, see RSA 485:31.

NOTES TO DECISIONS

Cited:
Cited in Durgin v. Pillsbury Lake Water

Dist., 153 N.H. 818, 903 A.2d 1003, 2006 N.H. LEXIS 110 (2006).

485:59. Appeals.

Actions of the department under RSA 485:1-4; 8, II; 31; 41-44; 46-48, or 58, I may be appealed under RSA 21-O:14.

Source.
1989, 339:1. 1995, 88:3, eff. Jan. 1, 1996. 1996, 228:106, eff. July 1, 1996.

—1995. Substituted "RSA 485:1–4" for "RSA 485:1–3", deleted "or" preceding "46–48" and inserted "or 58, I" thereafter.

Amendments
—1996. Substituted "department" for "division".

485:60. Special Acts.

Nothing in this chapter shall repeal any special act applying to cities and towns.

Source.
1989, 339:1, eff. Jan. 1, 1990.

Rules for Water Conservation

485:61. Rules for Water Conservation.

I. The department shall adopt rules, pursuant to RSA 541-A, for water conservation practices for water users. These rules shall strike a reasonable balance between environmental, energy, and economic impacts and be consistent with current industry standards and practices for different types of water users.

II. The water conservation rules in paragraph I of this section shall apply to all new permit applicants and applications for water withdrawals subject to the provisions of RSA 485:3, RSA 485:48, RSA 485-C:21 and section 401 of the Clean Water Act.

III. Water conservation rules shall be consistent with applicable state or federal rules and regulations.

Source.
2002, 142:2, eff. July 12, 2002.

References in text.
Section 401 of the Clean Water Act, referred to in par. II, is classified to 33 U.S.C.S. § 1341.

Applicability of enactment.
2002, 142:3, eff. July 12, 2002, provided:

"Water conservation rules developed under RSA 485:61 shall apply to all new water withdrawal permit applications approved under RSA 485:61, II on or after the effective date of this act [July 12, 2002]."

TITLE LXIV
PLANNING AND ZONING

Time period for modification of master plans and zoning ordinances to conform with RSA 672–677.

1983, 447:2, eff. Jan. 1, 1984, as amended by 1986, 73:1, eff. May 12, 1986, provided; "Each municipality shall have from January 1, 1984, until July 1, 1986, to make its master plan and its zoning ordinances conform with the relevant provisions of this act."

Terms of office and selection of members of planning boards, zoning boards of adjustment, building code boards of appeals, and historic district commissions.

1983, 447:3, eff. Jan. 1, 1984, provided:

"I. The terms of members of elected planning boards in office on the effective date of this act shall not be affected by this act. The members shall remain in office until the 1984 town election. At the 1984 town election, in any town whose elected planning board member's terms do not conform with the 3 year term established by this act, the town shall elect such members for such terms and the selectmen shall designate an ex officio member as may be necessary to bring the town's planning board into conformity with the provisions of this act. The town clerk, with the approval of the moderator, shall determine the terms to be filled at the 1984 town election and shall notify the existing planning board members accordingly. The vacancies determined to exist shall be filled by election of the voters at the 1984 town election in accordance with the provisions of this act.

"II. The terms of appointed members of planning boards, zoning boards of adjustment, and building code boards of appeals in office on the effective date of this act shall not be affected by this act. However, when the term of each member expires, each new member who. is appointed shall be appointed for a term of 3 years by the appointing authority in order to comply with the provisions of this act.

"III. The terms of members of historic district commissions in office on the effective date of this act shall not be affected by this act."

Cross References.

Acquisition, development and disposal of industrial land and facilities, see RSA 162-G.

Aid to municipalities for water pollution control, see RSA 486.

Airport zoning generally, see RSA 424.

Building and construction standards generally, see RSA 155-A, 155-B.

Condemnation of land for county uses, see RSA 26.

Condominiums, see RSA 356-B.

Conservation and preservation restrictions in conveyances of realty, see RSA 477:45 et seq.

Conservation commissions, see RSA 36-A.

Control of height of structures near airports, see RSA 422-B.

Council on resources and development, see RSA 162-C.

County powers generally, see RSA 23.

Current use taxation, see RSA 79-A.

Eminent domain procedure generally, see RSA 498-A.

Excavation and filling of wetlands, see RSA 483-A.

Hazardous waste facility fees, see RSA 147-D.

Hazardous waste facility review, see RSA 147-C.

Hazardous waste management generally, see RSA 147-A.

Historic preservation, see RSA 227-C.

Home rule powers of municipalities, see RSA 49-B.

Intermunicipal agreements generally, see RSA 53-A.

Interstate regional planning compact, see RSA 36-B.

Interstate water pollution control commission standards for sewage and waste treatment plant personnel, see RSA 484:22 et seq.

Land sales disclosure, see RSA 356-A.

Municipal central business service districts, see RSA 31:120 et seq.

Municipal economic development and revitalization districts, see RSA 162-K.

Municipal housing standards, see RSA 48-A.

New England Interstate Planning Compact, see RSA 163-A.

New England Interstate Water Control Compact, see RSA 484:17 et seq.

Northeastern Water and Related Land Resources Compact, see RSA 484.

Public recreation and park areas, see RSA 35-B.

Regulation of manufactured housing parks, see RSA 205-A.

Review of developments of regional impact, see RSA 36:54 et seq.

Rubbish and waste disposal generally, see RSA 147.

Sewage and waste disposal facilities compacts, see RSA 149-J, 149-K.

Sewage disposal systems, see RSA 485-A:29 et seq.

Siting of electric power plants and transmission lines, see RSA 162-F.

Siting of energy facilities generally, see RSA 162-H.

Solar skyspace easements, see RSA 477:49 et seq.

Solid waste management districts, see RSA 53-B.

Solid waste management generally, see RSA 149-M.

State development plan, see RSA 9-A.

Town powers generally, see RSA 31.

Unit ownership of real property, see RSA 479-A.

Water pollution control generally, see RSA 485-A.

Winnipesaukee river basin control, see RSA 485-A:45 et seq.

NOTES TO DECISIONS

Review of zoning and planning disputes under 42 U.S.C.S. § 1983

Where the state offers a panoply of administrative and judicial remedies, litigants may not ordinarily obtain federal court review of local zoning and planning disputes by means of 42 U.S.C.S. § 1983. Raskiewicz v. Town of New Boston, 754 F.2d 38, 1985 U.S. App. LEXIS 28974, cert. denied, 474 U.S. 845, 106 S. Ct. 135, 88 L. Ed. 2d 111, 1985 U.S. LEXIS 3587 (1985).

RESEARCH REFERENCES

New Hampshire Code of Administrative Rules.

Rules of the Department of Revenue Administration, Rev 101.01 et seq., New Hampshire Code of Administrative Rules Annotated.

Rules of the Department of Environmental Services, Dam Related Programs, Env-Wr 101.01 et seq., New Hampshire Code of Administrative Rules Annotated.

Rules of the Department of Environmental Services, Division of Water, Env-Ws 301.01 et seq., New Hampshire Code of Administrative Rules Annotated.

Rules of the Department of Environmental Services, Wetlands Programs, Env-Wt 101.01 et seq., New Hampshire Code of Administrative Rules Annotated.

New Hampshire Bar Journal.

For Attorney General article, "Department Of Justice's Transportation And Construction Bureau: Trains, Planes And Automobiles," see 45 N.H.B.J. 78 (Spring 2004).

For Article, "The New Zoning Variance Cases: Analyzing Unnecessary Hardship Under RSA 674:33," see 46 N.H.B.J. 40 (Fall 2005).

For Article, "Roads Revisited Creation And Termination Of Highways In New Hampshire - An Update," see , 46 N.H.B.J. 56 (Fall 2005).

For Article, "Unnecessary Hardship Under RSA 674:331(B)," see 46 N.H.B.J. 47 (Fall 2005).

ALR.

Validity and construction of zoning laws setting minimum requirements for floorspace or cubic footage inside residence. 87 A.L.R.4th 294.

Zoning: occupation of less than all dwelling units as discontinuance or abandonment of multifamily dwelling nonconforming use. 40 A.L.R.4th 1012.

CHAPTER 672

GENERAL PROVISIONS

RESEARCH REFERENCES

New Hampshire Bar Journal.

For article, "An Overview of the New Hampshire Land Use Planning and Regulation Statutes, " see 34 N.H.B.J. 6 (June 1993).

ALR.

Applicability of zoning regulations to governmental projects or activities. 53 A.L.R.5th 1.

Purpose

672:1. Declaration of Purpose.

The general court hereby finds and declares that:

I. Planning, zoning and related regulations have been and should continue to be the responsibility of municipal government;

II. Zoning, subdivision regulations and related regulations are a legislative tool that enables municipal government to meet more effectively the demands of evolving and growing communities;

III. Proper regulations enhance the public health, safety and general welfare and encourage the appropriate and wise use of land;

III-a. Proper regulations encourage energy efficient patterns of development, the use of solar energy, including adequate access to direct sunlight for solar energy uses, and the use of other renewable forms of energy, and energy conservation. Therefore, zoning ordinances should not unreasonably limit the installation of solar, wind, or other renewable energy systems or the building of structures that facilitate the collection of renewable energy, except where necessary to protect the public health, safety, and welfare;

III-b. Agriculture makes vital and significant contributions to the food supply, the economy, the environment and the aesthetic features of the state of New Hampshire, and the tradition of using the land resource for agricultural production is an essential factor in providing for the favorable quality of life in the state. Natural features, terrain and the pattern of geography of the state frequently place agricultural land in close proximity to other forms of development and commonly in small parcels. Agricultural activities are a beneficial and worthwhile feature of the New Hampshire landscape and shall not be unreasonably limited by use of municipal planning and zoning powers or by the unreasonable interpretation of such powers;

III-c. Forestry, when practiced in accordance with accepted silvicultural principles, constitutes a beneficial and desirable use of New Hampshire's forest resource. Forestry contributes greatly to the economy of the state through a vital forest products industry; and to the health of the state's forest and wildlife resources through sustained forest productivity, and through improvement of wildlife habitats. New Hampshire's forests are an essential component of the landscape and add immeasurably to the quality of life for the state's citizens. Because New Hampshire is a heavily forested state, forestry activities, including the harvest and transport of forest products, are often carried out in close proximity to populated areas. Further, the harvesting of timber often represents the only income that can be derived from property without resorting to development of the property for more intensive uses, and, pursuant to RSA 79-A:1, the state of New Hampshire has declared that it is in the public interest to encourage preservation of open space by conserving forest and other natural resources. Therefore, forestry activities, including the harvest and transport of forest products, shall not be unreasonably limited by use of municipal planning and zoning powers or by the unreasonable interpretation of such powers;

III-d. For purposes of paragraphs III-b, III-c, and III-e, "unreasonable interpretation" includes the failure of local land use authorities to recognize that agriculture, forestry, and commercial and recreational fisheries, when practiced in accordance with applicable laws and regulations, are traditional, fundamental and accessory uses of land throughout New Hampshire, and that a prohibition upon these uses cannot necessarily be inferred from the failure of an ordinance or regulation to address them;

III-e. All citizens of the state benefit from a balanced supply of housing which is affordable to persons and families of low and moderate income. Establishment of housing which is decent, safe, sanitary and affordable to low and moderate income persons and families is in the best interests of each community and the state of New Hampshire, and serves a vital public need. Opportunity for development of such housing, including so-called cluster development and the development of multi-family structures, should not be prohibited or discouraged by use of municipal planning and zoning powers or by unreasonable interpretation of such powers;

III-f. New Hampshire commercial and recreational fisheries make vital and significant contributions to the food supply, the economy, the environment, and the aesthetic features of the state of New Hampshire, and the tradition of using marine resources for fisheries production is an essential factor in providing for economic stability and a favorable quality of life in the state. Many traditional commercial and recreational fisheries in New Hampshire's rivers and estuarine systems are located in close proximity to coastal development. Such fisheries are a beneficial and worthwhile feature of the New Hampshire landscape and tradition and should not be discouraged or eliminated by use of municipal planning and zoning powers or the unreasonable interpretation of such powers.

IV. The citizens of a municipality should be actively involved in directing the growth of their community;

V. The state should provide a workable framework for the fair and reasonable treatment of individuals;

V-a. The care of up to 6 full-time preschool children and 3 part-time school age children in the home of a child care provider makes a vital and significant contribution to the state's economy and the well-being of New Hampshire families. The care provided through home-based day care closely parallels the activities of any home with young children. Family based care, traditionally relied upon by New Hampshire families, should not be discouraged or eliminated by use of municipal planning and zoning powers or the unreasonable interpretation of such powers; and

VI. It is the policy of this state that competition and enterprise may be so displaced or limited by municipalities in the exercise of the powers and authority provided in this title as may be necessary to carry out the purposes of this title.

Source.

1983, 447:1. 1985, 68:1; 335:3; 369:1. 1989, 42:1; 170:1. 1990, 174:1; 180:1, 2. 1991, 198:1, 2, eff. July 27, 1991. 2002, 73:1, eff. June 30, 2002.

Revision note.

Redesignated par. III-d, as added by 1990, 174:1, as par. III-e, pursuant to 1990, 174:2.

Amendments

—2002. Paragraph III-a: Added the second sentence.

—1991. Paragraph III-d: Deleted "and" preceding "III-c", inserted "and III-e" thereafter, deleted "and" preceding "forestry", inserted "and commercial and recreational fisheries" thereafter and made other minor stylistic changes.

Paragraph III-f: Added.

—1990. Paragraph III-b: Chapter 180 substituted "shall not be unreasonably limited" for "should not be discouraged or eliminated" following "landscape and" in the third sentence.

Paragraph III-c: Chapter 180 rewrote the sixth sentence.

Paragraph III-d: Added by chs. 174 and 180.

—1989. Paragraph III-c: Added by ch. 170.

Paragraph V: Chapter 42 deleted "and" following "individuals".

Paragraph V-a: Added by ch. 42.

—1985. Paragraph III-a: Added by ch. 369.

Paragraph III-b: Added by ch. 335.

Paragraph IV: Chapter 68 deleted "and" following "community".

Paragraph V: Chapter 68 added "and" following "individuals".

Paragraph VI: Added by ch. 68.

Contingent 1985 amendment.

1985, 335:1 provided for amendment of this section. However, under the terms of 1985, 335:4, eff. July 1, 1985, the amendment did not become effective.

Cross References.

Acquisition of agricultural land development rights, see RSA 432:18 et seq.

Conservation and preservation restrictions in conveyances of realty, see RSA 477:45 et seq.

Definitions generally, see RSA 672:2 et seq.

Home rule powers of municipalities, see RSA 49-B.

Solar skyspace easements, see RSA 477:49 et seq.

Town powers generally, see RSA 31.

NOTES TO DECISIONS

Generally

The zoning of property for the health, safety and general welfare of the community is a valid exercise of the police power which states may delegate to municipalities. Town of Chesterfield v. Brooks, 126 N.H. 64, 489 A.2d 600, 1985 N.H. LEXIS 274 (1985).

RESEARCH REFERENCES

New Hampshire Practice.
  15 N.H.P. Land Use Planning and Zoning §§ 2.15, 2.16, 14.06, 18.02.

Words and Phrases Defined

672:2. Definition of Words and Phrases.

The following words and phrases when used in Title LXIV shall have the meanings given to them in this chapter.

Source.
  1983, 447:1, eff. Jan. 1, 1984.

672:3. Abutter.

"Abutter" means any person whose property is located in New Hampshire and adjoins or is directly across the street or stream from the land under consideration by the local land use board. For purposes of receiving testimony only, and not for purposes of notification, the term "abutter" shall include any person who is able to demonstrate that his land will be directly affected by the proposal under consideration. For purposes of receipt of notification by a municipality of a local land use board hearing, in the case of an abutting property being under a condominium or other collective form of ownership, the term abutter means the officers of the collective or association, as defined in RSA 356-B:3, XXIII. For purposes of receipt of notification by a municipality of a local land use board hearing, in the case of an abutting property being under a manufactured housing park form of ownership as defined in RSA 205-A:1, II, the term "abutter" includes the manufactured housing park owner and the tenants who own manufactured housing which adjoins or is directly across the street or stream from the land under consideration by the local land use board.

Source.
  1983, 447:1. 1986, 33:2, eff. June 28, 1986. 2002, 216:1, eff. July 15, 2002.

—1986. Added the third sentence.

Amendments
  —2002. Added the fourth sentence.

NOTES TO DECISIONS

RESEARCH REFERENCES

New Hampshire Practice.
15 N.H.P. Land Use Planning and Zoning
§§ 21.12, 21.13, 32.04, 32.05.

672:4. District Commissioners.

"District commissioners" means the board of commissioners of a village district or precinct.

Source.
1983, 447:1, eff. Jan. 1, 1984.

672:5. Ex Officio Member.

"Ex Officio member" means any member who holds office by virtue of an official position and who shall exercise all the powers of regular members of a local land use board.

Source.
1983, 447:1, eff. Jan. 1, 1984.

RESEARCH REFERENCES

New Hampshire Practice.
15 N.H.P. Land Use Planning and Zoning
§ 27.02.

672:6. Local Governing Body.

"Local governing body" means, in addition to any other appropriate title:
I. Board of selectmen in a town;
II. City council or board of aldermen in a city;
III. Village district commissioners in a village district; or
IV. County commissioners in a county in which there are located unincorporated towns or unorganized places.

Source.
1983, 447:1. 1989, 266:7, eff. July 1, 1989.

Amendments
—1989. Made minor stylistic changes in pars. II and III and added par. IV.

672:7. Local Land Use Board.

"Local land use board" means a planning board, historic district commission, inspector of buildings, building code board of appeals, or zoning board of adjustment established by a local legislative body.

Source.
1983, 447:1, eff. Jan. 1, 1984.

New Hampshire Practice.
15 N.H.P. Land Use Planning and Zoning
§ 19.03.

672:8. Local Legislative Body.

"Local legislative body" means one of the following basic forms of government utilized by a municipality:
I. Council, whether city or town;
II. Mayor—council;
III. Mayor—board of aldermen;
IV. Village district or precinct;
V. Town meeting; or
VI. County convention.

Source.
1983, 447:1. 1985, 103:18. 1989, 266:8, eff. July 1, 1989.

Revision note.
For purposes of conformity with style employed in LEXIS New Hampshire Revised Statutes Annotated, redesignated pars. (a)–(e) as pars. I–V.

Amendments
—**1989.** Made minor stylistic changes in pars. IV and V and added par. VI.

—**1985.** Paragraph IV: Deleted "excluding water and sewer precincts" following "precinct".

NOTES TO DECISIONS

Cited:
Cited in Storms v. Town of Eaton, 131 N.H. 50, 549 A.2d 1208, 1988 N.H. LEXIS 87 (1988);

Blue Jay Realty Trust v. City of Franklin, 132 N.H. 502, 567 A.2d 188, 1989 N.H. LEXIS 128 (1989).

New Hampshire Practice.
15 N.H.P. Land Use Planning and Zoning
§§ 2.11, 20.01, 20.02, 27.01.

672:9. Mayor.

"Mayor" means the chief executive officer of the municipality, whether the official designation of the office is mayor of a city, city or town manager, the board of selectmen of a town, the board of commissioners of a village district, the county commissioners of a county in which there are located unincorporated towns or unorganized places, or any other title or any official designated in the municipal charter to perform the duties of "mayor."

Source.
1983, 447:1. 1989, 266:8. 1991, 377:3, eff. Aug. 31, 1991.

Amendments
—**1991.** Added "or any official designated in the municipal charter to perform the duties of 'mayor'" following "title".

—**1989.** Inserted "the county commissioners of a county in which there are located unincorporated towns or unorganized places" following "village district".

RESEARCH REFERENCES

New Hampshire Practice.
15 N.H.P. Land Use Planning and Zoning §§ 4.01, 27.02, 35.06.

672:10. Municipality.

"Municipality" or "municipal" means, includes and relates to cities, towns, village districts, and counties in which there are located unincorporated towns or unorganized places.

Source.
1983, 447:1. 1989, 266:8, eff. July 1, 1989.

Amendments
—**1989.** Deleted "and" preceding "village districts" and added "and counties in which

there are located unincorporated towns or unorganized places" thereafter.

Cross References.
Town defined generally, see RSA 21:5.

672:11. Planning Board.

"Planning board" means and includes city, town, village district, and county planning boards, in counties which contain unincorporated towns or unorganized places, established under the provisions of RSA 673.

Source.
1983, 447:1. 1989, 266:8, eff. July 1, 1989.

Amendments
—**1989.** Deleted "and" preceding "village

district" and inserted "and county" preceding "planning boards" and "in counties which contain unincorporated towns or unorganized places" thereafter.

672:12. Selectmen.

"Selectmen" means the board of selectmen of a town and the county commissioners of a county in which there are located unincorporated towns or unorganized places.

Source.
1983, 447:1. 1989, 266:8, eff. July 1, 1989.

Amendments
—**1989.** Added "and the county commissioners of a county in which there are located

unincorporated towns or unorganized places" following "selectmen of a town".

Cross References.
Selectmen defined generally, see RSA 21:28.

672:13. Street.

"Street" means, relates to and includes street, avenue, boulevard, road, lane, alley, viaduct, highway, freeway and other ways.

Source.
1983, 447:1, eff. Jan. 1, 1984.

Cross References.
Highway defined generally, see RSA 21:26.

Public way defined generally, see RSA 259:83.

Roadway defined generally, see RSA 259:92.

Way defined generally, see RSA 259:125.

672:14. Subdivision.

I. "Subdivision" means the division of the lot, tract, or parcel of land into 2 or more lots, plats, sites, or other divisions of land for the purpose, whether immediate or future, of sale, rent, lease, condominium conveyance or building development. It includes resubdivision and, when appropriate to the context, relates to the process of subdividing or to the land or territory subdivided.

II. The division of a parcel of land held in common and subsequently divided into parts among the several owners shall be deemed a subdivision under this title.

III. The grant of an easement in gross to a public utility for the purpose of placing and maintaining overhead and underground facilities necessary for its transmission or distribution network such as poles, wires, cable, conduit, manholes, repeaters and supporting apparatus, including any unstaffed structure which is less than 500 square feet, shall not be construed as a subdivision under this title, and shall not be deemed to create any new division of land for any other purpose.

IV. The rent, lease, development, or grant of an easement to a person for the purpose of placing and maintaining a wireless communications facility shall not be construed as a subdivision under this title, and shall not be deemed to create any new division of land for any other purpose. For purposes of this paragraph, "wireless communications facilities" means any towers, poles, antennas, or other unstaffed structure of less than 500 square feet intended for use in connection with licensed transmission or receipt of radio or television signals, or any other licensed spectrum-based transmissions or receptions. This paragraph shall not be deemed to affect other local zoning, site plan, or regulatory authority over wireless communications facilities.

Source.
1983, 447:1. 1988, 75:1, eff. June 14, 1988. 1998, 299:1, 2, eff. June 1, 1999.

Amendments
—1998. Paragraph III: Substituted "unstaffed structure" for "unmanned structure" and "500" for "200".

Paragraph IV: Added.

—1988. Designated the first and second sentences as par. I, the third sentence as par. II and added par. III.

NOTES TO DECISIONS

"Subdivision"

Where property owners applied to town planning board to further subdivide lots that were previously subdivided, the town's planning board and zoning board of adjustment erred in denying the applications on the basis that owners did not adhere to the density requirements of the town's zoning ordinance and because they were not consistent with the original intent of the cluster subdivision approvals because (1) RSA 672:14(I) provided that a resubdivision was included in the term "subdivision," and (2) because the specific density provisions of the local ordinance had been eliminated. Furthermore, inconsistency with the intent of the original subdivision was not a proper ground for denying the applications and the owners were entitled to have their new applications reviewed on their own merits under the applicable regulations, unconstrained by the prior subdivision approval. Feins v. Town of Wilmot, 154 N.H. 715, 919 A.2d 788, 2007 N.H. LEXIS 5 (2007).

Definition of "subdivision" contained in sub-

section I was not intended to apply to conveyance and conversion of an existing apartment unit into a condominium. Bussiere v. Roberge, 142 N.H. 905, 714 A.2d 894, 1998 N.H. LEXIS 57 (1998).

Term "subdivision" in RSA 674:35 authorizing municipal planning board to regulate subdivisions, means only the act of subdividing land; this section's definition of "subdivision" as "land or territory subdivided" is not encompassed within RSA 674:35. Lemm Dev. Corp. v. Town of Bartlett, 133 N.H. 618, 580 A.2d 1082, 1990 N.H. LEXIS 114 (1990).

Cited:

Cited in Town of Plainfield v. Sanville, 125 N.H. 825, 485 A.2d 1052, 1984 N.H. LEXIS 318 (1984); Cohen v. Town of Henniker, 134 N.H. 425, 593 A.2d 1145, 1991 N.H. LEXIS 78 (1991).

A testator's division of property by devise did not fall within the definition of subdivision. In re Estate of Sayewich, 120 N.H. 237, 413 A.2d 581, 1980 N.H. LEXIS 266 (1980). (Decided under prior law.)

RESEARCH REFERENCES

New Hampshire Practice.

15 N.H.P. Land Use Planning and Zoning §§ 29.01, 30.03, 38.04.

CHAPTER 673

LOCAL LAND USE BOARDS

Cross References.

Local land use board review of developments of regional impact, see RSA 36:54 et seq.

Ordinance, regulation and code administration and enforcement generally, see RSA 676.

Ordinance, regulation and code adoption procedures generally, see RSA 675.

Powers and duties of local land use boards generally, see RSA 674.

Rehearing and appeals procedures generally, see RSA 677.

RESEARCH REFERENCES

New Hampshire Practice.

13 N.H.P. Local Government Law § 532.

15 N.H.P. Land Use Planning and Zoning § 35.13.

New Hampshire Bar Journal.

For article, "An Overview of the New Hampshire Land Use Planning and Regulation Statutes," see 34 N.H.B.J. 6 (June 1993).

Establishment of Boards

673:1. Establishment of Local Land Use Boards.

I. Any local legislative body may establish a planning board, the members of which shall be residents of the municipality.

II. Any local legislative body may establish a heritage commission, historic district commission, or both, and may establish an agricultural commission.

III. Any local legislative body may provide for the appointment of an inspector of buildings. The local legislative body may fix the compensation for any inspector who is so appointed.

IV. Every zoning ordinance adopted by a local legislative body shall include provisions for the establishment of a zoning board of adjustment.

V. Every building code adopted by a local legislative body shall include provisions for the establishment of the position of a building inspector, who shall issue building permits, and for the establishment of a building code board of appeals. If no provision is made to establish a separate building code board of appeals, the ordinance shall designate the zoning board of adjustment to act as the building code board of appeals. If there is no zoning board of adjustment, the board of selectmen shall serve as the building code board of appeals.

Source.
1983, 447:1. 1992, 64:5, eff. June 19, 1992. 2007, 266:2, eff. August 28, 2007.

Amendments
—**2007.** Paragraph II: Added "and may establish an agricultural commission" at the end.

—**1992.** Paragraph II: Inserted "heritage commission" preceding "historic district commission" and added "or both" thereafter.

Cross References.
Powers and duties of building code boards of appeals generally, see RSA 674:34.

Powers and duties of building inspectors generally, see RSA 676:11 et seq.

Powers and duties of heritage commissions generally, see RSA 674:44-b et seq.

Powers and duties of historic district commissions generally, see RSA 674:46 et seq.

Powers and duties of planning boards generally, see RSA 674:1 et seq.

Powers and duties of zoning boards of adjustment generally, see RSA 674:33.

NOTES TO DECISIONS

Effect of failure to establish board of adjustment

The failure of a town, in its adoption of a zoning ordinance, to establish a board of adjustment rendered the ordinance invalid. Town of Jaffrey v. Heffernan, 104 N.H. 249, 183 A.2d 246, 1962 N.H. LEXIS 61 (1962). (Decided under former RSA 31:66.)

RESEARCH REFERENCES

New Hampshire Practice.
15 N.H.P. Land Use Planning and Zoning §§ 19.01, 19.03, 20.01, 27.01, 35.06.

Appointment and Terms of Local Land Use Board Members

Cross References.
Designation of alternate members, see RSA 673:11.

Disqualification of members, see RSA 673:14.
Filling of vacancies, see RSA 673:12.
Removal of members, see RSA 673:13.

673:2. Planning Board.

I. (a) In cities, the planning board shall consist of 9 members:

(1) The mayor of the city, or with the approval of the local legislative body the mayor's designee, who shall be an ex officio member;

(2) An administrative official of the city selected by the mayor, who shall be an ex officio member;

(3) A member of the city council selected by the council, who shall be an ex officio member; and

(4) Six persons appointed by the mayor, if the mayor is an elected official, or such other method of appointment or election as shall be provided for by the local legislative body or municipal charter.

(b) Alternatively, the local legislative body in a city with a city council-city manager form of government may establish a planning board with membership as provided in paragraph I-a.

I-a. In cities with a city council-city manager form of government, the planning board may consist of the following 9 members:

(a) The city manager, or with the approval of the local legislative body the city manager's designee, who shall be an ex officio member;

(b) A member of the city council selected by the council, who shall be an ex officio member; and

(c) Seven persons appointed by the mayor, if the mayor is an elected official, or such other method of appointment or election as shall be provided for by the local legislative body or municipal charter.

I-b. In towns which operate under the town council form of government, the planning board shall consist of 7 or 9 members, as determined by the local legislative body or by the municipal charter. If the planning board shall consist of 9 members, the members shall be the persons listed in paragraph I. If the planning board shall consist of 7 members, the members shall be as follows:

(a) A member of the town council or administrative official of the town selected by the town council, who shall be an ex officio member; and

(b) Six persons appointed by the mayor, if the mayor is an elected official, or such other method of appointment or election as shall be provided for by the local legislative body or municipal charter.

II. In other towns, the planning board shall consist of 5 or 7 members as determined by the local legislative body. The membership shall be filled by one of the following procedures:

(a) The selectmen shall designate one selectman or administrative official of the town as an ex officio member and appoint 4 or 6 other persons who are residents of the town, as appropriate; or

(b) The local legislative body may decide, by majority vote at the town meeting, that planning board members shall be elected according to either the procedure in subparagraph (1) or in subparagraph (2). The official ballot shall be used on every referendum for the adoption of RSA 673:2, II(b)(1) or (2), and every subsequent rescission of such adoption pursuant to subparagraph (c). The wording on the official ballot of any referendum for the adoption of RSA 673:2, II(b)(1) or (2) shall specifically state which procedure for electing planning board members is being voted upon. Following the majority vote at town meeting, planning board members shall be elected as follows:

(1) The selectmen shall choose one selectman or administrative official of the town as an ex officio member and the remaining planning board positions shall be filled at the next regular town election pursuant to RSA 669:17. Thereafter, a planning board member shall be elected for the term provided under RSA 673:5, II; or

(2) The selectmen shall choose one selectman or administrative official of the town as an ex officio member and the remaining planning board positions shall be filled on a staggered basis at the subsequent regular town elections pursuant to RSA 669:17 as the term of an appointed member expires, until each member of the board is an elected member. The maximum number of elections to occur annually shall be as provided in RSA 673:5, II. When each planning board member is an elected member, such member shall be elected for the term provided in RSA 673:5, II.

(c) A local legislative body which has voted to elect planning board members may, by majority vote at town meeting, decide to rescind that action and have the planning board appointed in the manner set forth in subparagraph (a). The vote to have planning board members so appointed shall take effect upon adoption by the town meeting, and the selectmen shall forthwith appoint members in accordance with RSA 673:5. The planning board shall, however, continue in existence, and the elected members in office at the time of the town meeting vote to appoint members may continue to serve until their successors are appointed and qualified.

III. In village districts, the planning board shall consist of either 5 or 7 members as determined by the village district meeting. The district commissioners shall:

(a) Designate one district commissioner or administrative official of the district as an ex officio member; and

(b) Appoint 4 or 6 other persons who are residents of the village district, as appropriate.

IV. In counties in which there are located unincorporated towns or unorganized places, the planning board shall consist of 5 or 9 members. The county commissioners shall recommend appointees to the planning board, and the appointees shall be approved by the county delegation. Planning board members shall be residents of the county, and shall be evenly distributed geographically throughout the county. The membership of the planning board shall be as follows:

(a) The chairperson of the board of county commissioners or designee shall be an ex officio member.

(b) A member of the county convention selected by the convention shall be an ex officio member.

(c) An administrative official of the county selected by the chairperson of the board of county commissioners shall be an ex officio member.

(d) Two or 6 persons appointed by the board of county commissioners and approved by the county convention.

(e) One or 3 alternates appointed by the board of county commissioners and approved by the county convention.

Source.
1983, 447:1. 1987, 255:1. 1989, 266:9. 1991, 377:4. 1992, 89:1, 2. 1993, 69:1, eff. June 22, 1993. 1996, 42:1–4, eff. June 23, 1996; 181:1, eff. Aug. 2, 1996. 2000, 107:1, eff. July 7, 2000.

Amendments
—2000. Designated the former introductory paragraph of par. I as present subpar. I(a), redesignated former subpars. I(a)–(d) as subpars. I(a)(1)–(4), and added subpar. (b), added new par. I-a, and redesignated former par. I-a as par. I-b.

—1996. Paragraph I(a): Chapter 42 substituted "the mayor's" for "his" preceding "designee".
Paragraph I-a(a): Chapter 181 inserted "or administrative official of the town" preceding "selected by".
Paragraph II: Chapter 42 added the second sentence in subpar. (b).
Chapter 181 inserted "or administrative official of the town" preceding "as an ex officio" in subpars. (a), (b)(1) and (2).
Paragraph III(a): Chapter 181 inserted "or administrative official of the district" preceding "as an ex officio".
Paragraph IV(a): Chapter 42 substituted "chairperson" for "chairman" preceding "of the board" and deleted "his" preceding "designee".

Paragraph IV(c): Chapter 42 substituted "chairperson" for "chairman" preceding "of the board".

—1993. Paragraph II(b): Rewritten to the extent that a detailed comparison would be impracticable.

—1992. Paragraph I: Deleted "and in towns which operate under the town council form of government" following "cities" in the introductory paragraph and "or town" following "city" in subpars. (a)–(c).
Paragraph I-a: Added.

—1991. Paragraph I(d): Substituted "or such other method of appointment or election as shall be provided for by the local legislative body or municipal charter" for "otherwise appointment shall be as provided for by the local legislative body" following "official".

—1989. Paragraph IV: Added.

—1987. Paragraph I(a): Inserted "or with the approval of the local legislative body his designee" following "town".

Cross References.
Disqualification of members, see RSA 673:14.
Filling of vacancies, see RSA 673:12.
Removal of members, see RSA 673:13.
Terms of office of members, see RSA 673:5.

RESEARCH REFERENCES

New Hampshire Practice.
15 N.H.P. Land Use Planning and Zoning §§ 5.03, 20.02, 27.03–27.05.

673:3. Zoning Board of Adjustment and Building Code Board of Appeals.

I. The zoning board of adjustment shall consist of 5 members. The members of the board shall either be elected in the manner prescribed by RSA 669, or appointed in a manner prescribed by the local legislative body. Each member of the board shall be a resident of the municipality in order to be appointed or elected.

II. Zoning board of adjustment members who are elected shall be elected for the term provided under RSA 673:5, II. The terms of appointed members of zoning boards of adjustment in municipalities in office on the effective date of an affirmative decision to elect such board members shall not be affected by the decision. However, when the term of each member expires, each new member shall be elected at the next regular municipal election for the term provided under RSA 673:5, II.

III. A local legislative body which has provided for the election of zoning board of adjustment members may rescind that action, in which event members shall thereafter be appointed in a manner prescribed by the local legislative body. The elected board shall, however, continue in existence, and the elected members in office may continue to serve until their successors are appointed and qualified.

IV. The building code board of appeals shall consist of 3 or 5 members who shall be appointed in a manner prescribed by the local legislative body; provided, however, that an elected zoning board of adjustment may act as the building code board of appeals pursuant to RSA 673:1, V. Each member of the board shall be a resident of the municipality in order to be appointed.

Source.
1983, 447:1. 1990, 71:1, eff. June 5, 1990.

Amendments
—**1990.** Rewritten to the extent that a detailed comparison would be impracticable.

Cross References.
Disqualification of members, see RSA 673:14.
Filling of vacancies, see RSA 673:12.
Removal of members, see RSA 673:13.
Terms of office of members, see RSA 673:5.

RESEARCH REFERENCES

New Hampshire Practice.
15 N.H.P. Land Use Planning and Zoning § 20.02, 39.11 (supp).

673:3-a. Training.

Within 6 months of assuming office for the first time, any non-ex-officio member of the zoning board of adjustment and the planning board may at the member's option complete at least 6 hours of training for the member's respective position. The training shall be designed and furnished by the office of energy and planning.

Source.
1986, 213:4, eff. Aug. 5, 1986. 1996, 42:5, eff. June 23, 1996. 2003, 319:9, eff. July 1, 2003. 2004, 257:44, eff. July 1, 2004.

Amendments
—**2004.** Substituted "office of energy and planning" for "office of state planning and energy programs" in the second sentence.

—**2003.** Substituted "office of state planning and energy programs" for "office of state planning".

—**1996.** Substituted "the member's" for "his" preceding "option" and "respective" in the first sentence.

New Hampshire Practice.
15 N.H.P. Land Use Planning and Zoning
§ 20.02.

673:4. Historic District Commission.

I. The historic district commission shall consist of not less than 3 members and no more than 7 members who shall be appointed in a manner as prescribed by the local legislative body.

II. Each historic district commission member shall be a resident of the city or town which establishes the district. One commission member shall be a member of the local governing body and one commission member may be a member of the planning board. Not more than 5 alternate members may be appointed. When an alternate sits in absence or disqualification of a regular member, the alternate shall have full voting powers. In determining each member's qualifications, the appointing authority shall take into consideration the appointee's demonstrated interest and ability to understand, appreciate and promote the purposes of the historic district commission.

III. Members of a historic district commission also may serve on other municipal boards and commissions, including but not limited to a conservation commission established under RSA 36-A, and a heritage commission established under RSA 673:4-a.

Source.
1983, 447:1. 1995, 138:3, eff. July 23, 1995.

Amendments
—**1995.** Paragraph I: Substituted "not less than 3 members and no more than 7" for "5 or 7" following "shall consist of".

Paragraph II: Substituted "local governing body" for "board of selectmen or the mayor of the municipality" preceding "and one" in the second sentence and added the third and fourth sentences.

Paragraph III: Added.

Cross References.
Disqualification of members, see RSA 673:14.
Filling of vacancies, see RSA 673:12.
Removal of members, see RSA 673:13.
Terms of office of members, see RSA 673:5.

New Hampshire Practice.
15 N.H.P. Land Use Planning and Zoning
§§ 35.06, 35.07.

673:4-a. Heritage Commissions.

I. The heritage commission shall consist of not less than 3 members and no more than 7 members who shall be appointed in a manner as prescribed by the local legislative body.

II. Each heritage commission member shall be a resident of the city or town which establishes the commission. One commission member shall be a member of the local governing body. One commission member may be a member of the planning board. Not more than 5 alternate members may be appointed. When an alternate sits in absence or disqualification of a regular member, the alternate shall have full voting powers. If there is a historic district commission, one member of this commission shall be an ex officio member of the heritage commission. In determining each member's qualifications, the appointing authority shall take into consideration the appointee's demonstrated interest and ability to understand, appreciate and promote the purpose of the heritage commission.

III. Members of a heritage commission also may serve on other municipal boards and commissions, including but not limited to a conservation commission established under RSA 36-A, and a historic district commission established under RSA 673:4.

Source.
1992, 64:6. 1995, 138:4, eff. July 23, 1995.

Revision note.
Substituted "boards" for "board" following "municipal" in par. III to correct a typographical error.

Amendments
—**1995.** Rewritten to the extent that a detailed comparison would be impracticable.

Cross References.
Heritage commissions generally, see RSA 674:44-a et seq.

RESEARCH REFERENCES

New Hampshire Practice.
15 N.H.P. Land Use Planning and Zoning § 35.17.

673:4-b. Agricultural Commissions.

I. The agricultural commission shall consist of not less than 3 members and no more than 7 members who shall be appointed in a manner as prescribed by the local legislative body.

II. Each agricultural commission member shall be a resident of the city or town which establishes the commission. One commission member may be a member of the local governing body. One commission member may be a member of the planning board. Not more than 5 alternate members may be appointed. When an alternate sits in absence or disqualification of a regular member, the alternate shall have full voting powers. In determining each member's qualifications, the appointing authority shall take into consideration the appointee's demonstrated interest and ability to understand, appreciate, and promote the purpose of the agricultural commission.

III. Members of an agricultural commission also may serve on other municipal boards and commissions, including but not limited to a conservation commission established under RSA 36-A, a historic district commission established under RSA 674:46, or a heritage commission established under RSA 674:44-a.

Source.
2007, 266:3, eff. August 28, 2007.

673:5. Terms of Local Land Use Board Members.

I. (a) Except as provided in subparagraph (b), the term of any ex officio member serving on a local land use board shall coincide with the term for that other office; except that the term of the administrative official appointed by the mayor shall terminate with the term of office of the mayor appointing the official, and that the term of the administrative official appointed by the town council, board of selectmen, or village district commissioners shall be for one year.

(b) A city or town council, board of selectmen, or the village district commissioners may determine that the city or town council member, the selectman member or the village district commission member shall be subject to a 4 month or an annual appointment under such conditions as it determines.

II. The term of an elected or appointed local land use board member shall be 3 years. The initial terms of members first appointed or elected to any local land use board shall be staggered so that no more than 3 appointments or elections occur annually in the case of a 7 or 9 member board and no more than 2 appointments or elections occur annually in the case of a 5 member board, except when required to fill vacancies.

Source.
1983, 447:1, eff. Jan. 1, 1984. 1996, 42:6, eff. June 23, 1996; 181:2, eff. Aug. 2, 1996.

Amendments
—**1996.** Paragraph I(a): Chapter 42 substituted "the official" for "him" following "mayor appointing".

Chapter 181 added "and that the term of the administrative official appointed by the town council, board of selectment, or village district commissioners shall be for one year" following "appointing the official".

Paragraph I(b): Chapter 181 inserted "a 4 month or an" preceding "annual appointment".

Cross References.
Filling of vacancies, see RSA 673:12.
Removal of members, see RSA 673:13.
Terms of officers, see RSA 673:9.

NOTES TO DECISIONS

Terms of ex officio members
The language of the statute to the effect that the terms of office of ex officio members of planning board should "correspond to their respective official tenures" was clear on its face in requiring that a selectman's term as planning board member was to conform to his term as selectman, and a board of selectmen violated the statute when they removed a selectman from a town planning board solely because he had served one year. Silva v. Botsch, 120 N.H. 600, 420 A.2d 301, 1980 N.H. LEXIS 366 (1980). (Decided under former RSA 36:5.)

Because the statute required that a selectman's term on a planning board match, as nearly as possible, his term as a selectman and because the statute did not enumerate length of time served as a criterion for severance, the removal of a selectman from the planning board solely because he had served one year was a violation of the statute. Silva v. Botsch, 120 N.H. 600, 420 A.2d 301, 1980 N.H. LEXIS 366 (1980). (Decided under former RSA 36:5.)

RESEARCH REFERENCES

New Hampshire Practice.
15 N.H.P. Land Use Planning and Zoning §§ 20.03, 27.02, 27.05, 35.07.

673:6. Appointment, Number and Terms of Alternate Members.

I. (a) The local legislative body may provide for the appointment of not more than 5 alternate members to any appointed local land use board, who shall be appointed by the appointing authority. The terms of alternate members shall be 3 years.

(b) In a town which votes to elect its planning board members on a staggered basis according to the provisions of RSA 673:2, II(b)(2), alternate members of the planning board shall continue to be appointed according to the provisions of this paragraph until each member of the board is an elected member. Thereafter, the alternate planning board members shall be appointed according to the provisions of paragraph II.

II. An elected planning board may appoint 5 alternate members for a term of 3 years each, which shall be staggered in the same manner as elected members pursuant to RSA 673:5, II.

II-a. An elected zoning board of adjustment may appoint 5 alternate members for a term of 3 years each, which shall be staggered in the same manner as elected members pursuant to RSA 673:5, II.

III. The alternate for a city or town council member, selectman, or village district commission member shall be appointed by the respective council, board, or commission. The terms of alternate members shall be the same as those of the respective members and may be in addition to the alternates provided for in paragraph I.

IV. Every alternate member appointed to a planning board under this section shall comply with the multiple membership requirements of RSA 673:7, I and II.

Source.
1983, 447:1. 1986, 29:1. 1987, 197:1. 1991, 176:1. 1993, 69:2, eff. June 22, 1993. 1996, 181:3, eff. Aug. 2, 1996; 217:1, eff. Aug. 9, 1996.

Amendments
—1996. Paragraphs II, II-a: Rewritten to the extent that a detailed comparison would be impracticable.

—1993. Paragraph I: Designated the existing provisions of the paragraph as subpar. (a) and added subpar. (b).

—1991. Paragraph II-a: added.

—1987. Paragraph III: Substituted "appointed" for "provided for" following "shall be"

in the first sentence and "those" for "that" preceding "of the respective members and" in the second sentence and "may" for "shall" thereafter.

—1986. Paragraph I: Substituted "5" for "3" preceding "alternate" in the first sentence.

Contingent 1996 amendment.
1996, 181:3, provided for amendment of this section. However, under the terms of 1996, 181:4, eff. Aug. 2, 1996, the amendment did not become effective.

Cross References.
Designation of alternate members, see RSA 673:11.

RESEARCH REFERENCES

New Hampshire Practice.
15 N.H.P. Land Use Planning and Zoning §§ 20.04, 27.07, 35.07.

673:7. Planning Board Members Serving on Other Local Boards.

I. In the case of towns, appointed or elected members of the planning board may also serve on any other municipal board or commission, provided that such multiple membership does not result in 2 planning board members serving on the same board or commission.

II. In cities, appointed members shall not hold any other municipal office, except that:

(a) One of the appointed members may be a member of the zoning board of adjustment;

(b) Either one appointed member or one ex officio member may be a member of the conservation commission if one exists in the city; and

(c) Either one appointed member or one ex officio member may be a member of the heritage commission, the historic district commission, or the agricultural commission, or all 3 if such commissions exist in the city.

III. In counties in which there are located unincorporated towns or unorganized places, the county commissioners shall determine which members of the planning board for those towns and places, if any, may serve on other municipal boards or commissions.

Source.
1983, 447:1. 1989, 266:10. 1992, 64:7, eff. June 19, 1992. 2007, 266:4, eff. August 28, 2007.

Amendments
—2007. Paragraph II(c): Deleted "or" following "heritage commission" and substituted "or the agricultural commission, or all 3 if such commissions exist" for "or both, if such a commission exists".

—1992. Paragraph II(c): Inserted "heritage commission, or the" preceding "historic" and substituted "or both, if such a commission" for "if one" preceding "exists".

—1989. Paragraph III: Added.

Cross References.
Disqualification of members, see RSA 673:14.
Multiple membership of alternates, see RSA 673:6.

RESEARCH REFERENCES

New Hampshire Practice.
15 N.H.P. Land Use Planning and Zoning §§ 20.02, 20.03, 27.06, 27.07.

673:8. Organization.

Each local land use board shall elect its chairperson from the appointed or elected members and may create other offices as it deems necessary.

Source.
1983, 447:1, eff. Jan. 1, 1984. 1996, 42:7, eff. June 23, 1996.

Amendments
—1996. Substituted "chairperson" for "chairman" preceding "from the appointed".

Cross References.
Meetings, see RSA 673:10, 17.
Records, see RSA 673:17.
Staff and finances, see RSA 673:16.

RESEARCH REFERENCES

New Hampshire Practice.
15 N.H.P. Land Use Planning and Zoning §§ 21.01, 28.01, 35.08.

673:9. Term of Chairperson and Officers.

I. The term of every officer and chairperson elected by a local land use board shall be one year. Both the chairperson and officers shall be eligible for reelection.

II. In the case of planning boards, an ex officio member shall not serve as chairperson.

Source.
1983, 447:1, eff. Jan. 1, 1984. 1996, 42:8, eff. June 23, 1996.

Amendments
—**1996.** Substituted "chairperson" for "chairman" wherever it appeared in the section.

Cross References.
Terms of office of members generally, see RSA 673:5.

RESEARCH REFERENCES

New Hampshire Practice.
15 N.H.P. Land Use Planning and Zoning §§ 21.04, 28.04, 35.08.

General Provisions

Cross References.
Appointment and terms of board members generally, see RSA 673:2 et seq.

673:10. Scheduling of Meetings.

I. Meetings of the heritage commission, historic district commission, the agricultural commission, the building code board of appeals, and the zoning board of adjustment shall be held at the call of the chairperson and at such other times as the board may determine.

II. The planning board shall hold at least one regular meeting in each month.

III. A majority of the membership of a local land use board shall constitute the quorum necessary in order to transact business at any meeting of a local land use board.

Source.
1983, 447:1. 1992, 64:8, eff. June 19, 1992. 1996, 42:9, eff. June 23, 1996. 2007, 266:5, eff. August 28, 2007.

Amendments
—**2007.** Paragraph I: Inserted "the agricultural commission" preceding "the building code".

—**1996.** Paragraph I: Substituted "chairperson" for "chairman" following "call of the".

—**1992.** Paragraph I: Inserted "heritage commission" preceding "historic".

Cross References.
Public access to meetings, see RSA 673:17.

RESEARCH REFERENCES

New Hampshire Practice.
15 N.H.P. Land Use Planning and Zoning
§§ 21.03, 21.05, 28.03, 28.05, 35.08.

673:11. Designation of Alternate Members.

Whenever a regular member of a local land use board is absent or whenever a regular member disqualifies himself or herself, the chairperson shall designate an alternate, if one is present, to act in the absent member's place; except that only the alternate designated for the city or town council, board of selectmen, or village district commission member shall serve in place of that member.

Source.
1983, 447:1, eff. Jan. 1, 1984. 1996, 42:10, eff. June 23, 1996.

Amendments
—1996. Inserted "or herself" following "himself" and substituted "chairperson" for "chairman" preceding "shall designate".

Cross References.
Appointment, number and terms of alternate members, see RSA 673:6.
Multiple memberships, see RSA 673:7.

NOTES TO DECISIONS

Failure to designate alternate members
On appeal of planning board decision approving a subdivision, claim concerning the board's failure to appoint alternates was properly dismissed where it was not raised within the 30-day period after the filing of the decision in the office of the planning board, as required by RSA 677:15. Frisella v. Town of Farmington, 131 N.H. 78, 550 A.2d 102, 1988 N.H. LEXIS 94 (1988).

RESEARCH REFERENCES

New Hampshire Practice.
15 N.H.P. Land Use Planning and Zoning
§§ 20.04, 20.07, 21.05, 27.10, 28.06, 35.07.

673:12. Filling Vacancies in Membership.

Vacancies in the membership of a local land use board occurring other than through the expiration of a term of office shall be filled as follows:

I. For an elected member, by appointment by the remaining board members until the next regular municipal election at which time a successor shall be elected to either fill the unexpired term or start a new term, as appropriate.

II. For an appointed, ex officio, or alternate member, by the original appointing or designating authority, for the unexpired term.

Source.
1983, 447:1, eff. Jan. 1, 1984.

Cross References.
Removal of members, see RSA 673:13.

Terms of office of members generally, see RSA 673:5.
Terms of officers, see RSA 673:9.

NOTES TO DECISIONS

Filling of vacancy for elected member

Under the statute, which provided for the filling of a vacancy for an elected member of a planning board by selectmen until the next election, the town's election ballot notified the voters of three openings on the planning board,

but did not mention a fourth opening, a vacancy on the board existed and the selectmen properly made an appointment to fill the vacancy. Town of Derry v. Adams, 121 N.H. 473, 431 A.2d 766, 1981 N.H. LEXIS 354 (1981). (Decided under former RSA 36:7.)

RESEARCH REFERENCES

New Hampshire Practice.

15 N.H.P. Land Use Planning and Zoning §§ 20.05, 27.08.

673:13. Removal of Members.

I. After public hearing, appointed members and alternate members of an appointed local land use board may be removed by the appointing authority upon written findings of inefficiency, neglect of duty, or malfeasance in office.

II. The board of selectmen may, for any cause enumerated in paragraph I, remove an elected member or alternate member after a public hearing.

III. The appointing authority or the planning board shall file with the city or town clerk, the village district clerk, or the clerk for the county commissioners, whichever is appropriate, a written statement of reasons for removal under this section.

IV. The council, selectmen, county commissioners with the approval of the county delegation, or district commissioners may for any cause enumerated in this section remove the members selected by them.

Source.

1983, 447:1. 1989, 266:11, eff. July 1, 1989.

Amendments

—**1989.** Paragraph III: Substituted "the" for "or" preceding "village district clerk" and inserted "or the clerk for the county commissioners" thereafter.

Paragraph IV: Inserted "county commissioners with the approval of the county delegation" following "selectmen".

Cross References.

Filling of vacancies, see RSA 673:12.

NOTES TO DECISIONS

Malfeasance

Trial court erred in upholding city council's removal of a planning board official for acts alleged to constitute malfeasance in office, where the acts relied upon did not relate to the

performance of the official's duties as a planning board member, and therefore did not fall within the scope of malfeasance under this section. Williams v. City of Dover, 130 N.H. 527, 543 A.2d 919, 1988 N.H. LEXIS 33 (1988).

RESEARCH REFERENCES

New Hampshire Practice.

15 N.H.P. Land Use Planning and Zoning §§ 5.03, 20.06, 27.09, 35.07.

673:14. Disqualification of Member.

I. No member of a zoning board of adjustment, building code board of appeals, planning board, heritage commission, historic district commission, or agricultural commission shall participate in deciding or shall sit upon the hearing of any question which the board is to decide in a judicial capacity if that member has a direct personal or pecuniary interest in the outcome which differs from the interest of other citizens, or if that member would be disqualified for any cause to act as a juror upon the trial of the same matter in any action at law. Reasons for disqualification do not include exemption from service as a juror or knowledge of the facts involved gained in the performance of the member's official duties.

II. When uncertainty arises as to the application of paragraph I to a board member in particular circumstances, the board shall, upon the request of that member or another member of the board, vote on the question of whether that member should be disqualified. Any such request and vote shall be made prior to or at the commencement of any required public hearing. Such a vote shall be advisory and non-binding, and may not be requested by persons other than board members, except as provided by local ordinance or by a procedural rule adopted under RSA 676:1.

III. If a member is disqualified or unable to act in any particular case pending before the board, the chairperson shall designate an alternate to act in the member's place, as provided in RSA 673:11.

Source.
 1983, 447:1. 1988, 26:1. 1992, 64:9, eff. June 19, 1992. 1996, 42:11, eff. June 23, 1996. 2007, 266:6, eff. August 28, 2007.

Amendments
 —**2007.** Paragraph I: Deleted "or" following "heritage commission" and inserted "or agricultural commission" following "historic district commission" in the first sentence.

 —**1996.** Paragraph III: Substituted "chairperson" for "chairman" preceding "shall designate" and "the member's" for "his" preceding "place".

 —**1992.** Paragraph I: Inserted "heritage commission" following "planning board" in the first sentence.

 —**1988.** Rewritten to the extent that a detailed comparison would be impracticable.

Cross References.
 Disqualification of member and appointment of alternate member of appeals board for appeals from decisions of commissioner of transportation, see RSA 21-L:14.
 Disqualification of member and appointment of alternate member of railroad appeals board, see RSA 21-L:16.
 Disqualifications of jurors generally, see RSA 500-A:12.
 Multiple memberships, see RSA 673:7.

NOTES TO DECISIONS

Analysis

1. Construction
2. Disqualification not warranted
3. Effect of participation by disqualified member

1. Construction
 The statute does not place restrictions on who may object to the participation of board members; although plaintiffs were not statutorily prohibited from raising the issue, they failed to make a timely objection to board

member's participation. Bayson Props. v. City of Lebanon, 150 N.H. 167, 834 A.2d 202, 2003 N.H. LEXIS 159 (2003).

2. Disqualification not warranted

Trial court did not err in failing to find that planning board member should have recused himself or been disqualified for bias where the only allegation that concerned the member's alleged bias as to plaintiff's request to cut trees on a designated scenic road was that he moved to deny the request; his motion was not evidence of "prejudgment," but of judgment exercised at the appropriate time and place, nor was it evidence of bias. Webster v. Town of Candia, 146 N.H. 430, 778 A.2d 402, 2001 N.H. LEXIS 91 (2001).

A planning board member's discovery of obvious inconsistencies in submitted documents, and subsequent statement to an applicant explaining why such inconsistencies will preclude approval, does not show that the application

has been prejudged so as to require member's disqualification. City of Dover v. Kimball, 136 N.H. 441, 616 A.2d 516, 1992 N.H. LEXIS 187 (1992).

3. Effect of participation by disqualified member

Hearing on request for variance to add addition to county hospital was not rendered unfair, and decision of board was not made illegal, by reason of fact that a member of the board of adjustment worked in the county surplus food program. Sherman v. Town of Brentwood, 112 N.H. 122, 290 A.2d 47, 1972 N.H. LEXIS 157 (1972).

The fact that a disqualified member was present and acting as clerk was immaterial where he took no part in the deliberations or decisions. Gelinas v. City of Portsmouth, 97 N.H. 248, 85 A.2d 896, 1952 N.H. LEXIS 3 (1952). (Decided under prior law.)

RESEARCH REFERENCES

New Hampshire Practice.
15 N.H.P. Land Use Planning and Zoning §§ 20.07, 27.10, 35.07.

ALR.
Disqualification for bias or interest of admin-

istrative officer sitting in zoning proceedings. 10 A.L.R.3d 694.

673:15. Power to Compel Witness Attendance and Administer Oaths.

The chairperson of the zoning board of adjustment or the chairperson of the building code board of appeals or, in the chairperson's absence, the acting chairperson may administer oaths. Whenever the board exercises its regulatory or quasi judicial powers it may, at its sole discretion, compel the attendance of witnesses. All expenses incurred under this section for compelling the attendance of a witness shall be paid by the party or parties requesting that a witness be compelled to attend a meeting of the board.

Source.
1983, 447:1, eff. Jan. 1, 1984. 1996, 42:12, eff. June 23, 1996.

Amendments
—1996. Substituted "chairperson" for "chairman" in three places and "the chairperson's" for "his" preceding "absence" in the first sentence.

Cross References.
Administrative and enforcement procedures generally, see RSA 676.

Summoning witnesses generally, see RSA 516:1 et seq.

RESEARCH REFERENCES

New Hampshire Practice.
15 N.H.P. Land Use Planning and Zoning
§ 21.07.

673:16. Staff; Finances.

I. Each local land use board may appoint such employees as it deems necessary for its work who shall be subject to the same employment rules as other corresponding civil employees of the municipality. Each board may also contract with planners, engineers, architects, and other consultants for such services as it may require. The expenditures of the board, exclusive of gifts, reimbursements, or amounts held pursuant to paragraph II, shall be within the amounts appropriated for the purpose by the local legislative body, which may provide such funds, equipment, and accommodations as it deems necessary or advisable for the board's work. Each board may accept and use gifts, grants, or contributions for the exercise of its functions, in accordance with procedures established for the expenditure of funds within the municipality.

II. Any fee which a local land use board, acting pursuant to this title, collects from an applicant to cover an expense lawfully imposed upon that applicant, including but not limited to the expense of notice, the expense of consultant services or investigative studies under RSA 676:4, I(g), or the implementation of conditions lawfully imposed as part of a conditional approval, may be paid out toward that expense without approval of the local legislative body. Such fees:

(a) Shall, whenever held by the municipality, be placed in the custody of the municipal treasurer, subject to the same investment limitations as for other municipal funds.

(b) Shall be paid out only for the purpose for which the expense was imposed upon the applicant.

(c) Shall be held in a separate, nonlapsing account, and not commingled with other municipal funds; provided, however, that such fees may be used to reimburse any account from which an amount has been paid out in anticipation of the receipt of said fees.

(d) Shall be paid out by the municipal treasurer only upon order of the local land use board or its designated agent for such purpose. This paragraph shall not apply to application, permit, or inspection fees which have been set by the local legislative body as part of an ordinance, or by the selectmen under RSA 41:9-a. Notwithstanding RSA 672:7, a building inspector shall not be considered a "local land use board" for purposes of this section.

Source.

1983, 447:1. 1991, 377:5. 1992, 172:1, 2, eff. July 7, 1992.

Amendments

—**1992.** Paragraph I: Deleted "or" following "gifts" and inserted "or amounts held pursuant to paragraph II" following "reimbursements" in the third sentence.

Paragraph II: Rewrote the introductory paragraph to the extent that a detailed comparison would be impracticable, substituted "shall be paid out" for "may be expended" preceding "only" and "the expense" for "it" preceding "was imposed" in subpar. (b), substituted "paid out" for "spent" preceding "in anticipation" in subpar. (c), and amended subpar. (d) generally.

—**1991.** Designated the existing provisions

of the section as par. I and added par. II.

Cross References.
Municipal budgeting and finances generally, see RSA 32, 33.

RESEARCH REFERENCES

New Hampshire Practice.
15 N.H.P. Land Use Planning and Zoning §§ 21.08, 28.07, 35.09.

673:17. Open Meetings; Records.

Each local land use board shall hold its meetings and maintain its records in accordance with RSA 91-A.

Source.
1983, 447:1, eff. Jan. 1, 1984.

Cross References.
Transfers of records upon abolition of local boards, see RSA 673:21, 22.

NOTES TO DECISIONS

Notice and hearing requirements
The fundamental purpose of the requirements for notice and hearing was to advise all affected parties of their opportunity to be heard in public meeting and to be apprised of the relief sought. Carter v. City of Nashua, 113 N.H. 407, 308 A.2d 847, 1973 N.H. LEXIS 285 (1973). (Decided under prior law.)

A lack of compliance with the requirements that hearing be upon notice and open to the public would deprive a zoning board of adjustment of jurisdiction to grant a variance. Carter v. City of Nashua, 113 N.H. 407, 308 A.2d 847, 1973 N.H. LEXIS 285 (1973). (Decided under prior law.)

Where notice of a second meeting of a zoning board of adjustment in the matter of a variance application was given 24 hours before the meeting instead of the 72-hour notice required by city ordinance, such failure was not sufficient to affect the board's jurisdiction over the matter, which it acquired by its compliance with all notice requirements for the first meeting. Carter v. City of Nashua, 113 N.H. 407, 308 A.2d 847, 1973 N.H. LEXIS 285 (1973). (Decided under prior law.)

RESEARCH REFERENCES

New Hampshire Practice.
15 N.H.P. Land Use Planning and Zoning §§ 21.19, 28.11, 35.08.

Abolition of Boards, Zoning Ordinances, or Building Codes

673:18. Abolishing Planning Board, Heritage Commission, Historic District Commission, or Agricultural Commission.

I. The local legislative body of a city, of a county in which there are located unincorporated towns or unorganized places, or of a town operating under the town council form of government, shall determine the manner in which the planning board, the heritage commission, the historic district commission, or the agricultural commission may be abolished.

II. In all other towns, upon a petition to abolish the planning board, the heritage commission, the historic district commission, or the agricultural commission, signed by 100 or more voters or $\frac{1}{10}$ of the registered voters in town, whichever number is less, the planning board, heritage commission, historic district commission, or agricultural commission shall submit the proposal to the town or village district in the same manner prescribed in RSA 675:4, except that the question put to the voters shall be in substantially the following form: "Are you in favor of abolishing the planning board (heritage commission, historic district commission, or agricultural commission) as proposed by petition of the voters of this town (village district)?"

Source.
1983, 447:1. 1989, 266:12. 1992, 64:10, eff. June 19, 1992. 2007, 266:7, eff. August 28, 2007.

Amendments
—2007. Substituted "commission, historic district commission, or agricultural commission" for "commission or historic district commission" and "commission, the district commission, or agricultural commission" for "commission or the historic district commission" wherever it appeared throughout the section.

—1992. Inserted "Heritage Commission" following "Planning Board" in the section catchline.
Paragraph I: Inserted "the heritage commission" following "planning board".
Paragraph II: Inserted "the heritage commis-

sion" following "abolish the planning board", "heritage commission" following "less, the planning board", "heritage commission, or" preceding "historic" in the parenthetical voter question and made other minor stylistic changes.

—1989. Paragraph I: Inserted "of a county in which there are located unincorporated towns or unorganized places" following "city".

Cross References.
Effect of abolition generally, see RSA 673:19, 20.
Elections generally, see RSA 652 et seq.
Establishment of board or commission, see RSA 673:1.
Home rule powers, see RSA 49-B.
Town elections, see RSA 39, 40, 669.
Transfer of documents of boards or commissions abolished, see RSA 673:21.
Village district elections, see RSA 39, 40, 670.

RESEARCH REFERENCES

New Hampshire Practice.
15 N.H.P. Land Use Planning and Zoning §§ 27.11, 35.14.

673:19. Effect of Abolishing Planning Boards.

Upon the effective date of the abolition of a planning board, all land use control activities in the municipality formerly performed by the planning board shall cease. Existing zoning ordinances shall remain in effect following the abolition date for a period not to exceed 2 years from the date of such action, but no amendment to a zoning ordinance requiring action by the former planning board shall be permitted.

Source.
1983, 447:1, eff. Jan. 1, 1984.

Cross References.
Transfer of records of abolished boards, see
RSA 673:21.

RESEARCH REFERENCES

New Hampshire Practice.
15 N.H.P. Land Use Planning and Zoning
§§ 27.01, 27.12.

673:20. Effect of Abolishing Heritage Commissions, Historic District Commissions, and Agricultural Commissions.

Upon the effective date of the abolition of a heritage commission, historic district commission, or agricultural commission all the powers and duties of such commission shall cease.

Source.
1983, 447:1. 1992, 64:11, eff. June 19, 1992.
2007, 266:8, eff. August 28, 2007.

Amendments
—**2007.** Deleted "and" following "heritage commissions" and added "and agricultural commissions" to the section heading; deleted "or" following "heritage commission" and inserted "or agricultural commission" following "historic dictrict commission".

—**1992.** Inserted "Heritage Commissions and" preceding "Historic District" and substituted "Commissions" for "Commission" thereafter in the section catchline, and in the text of the section, inserted "heritage commission or" following "abolition of a", substituted "such" for "the" following "duties of" and deleted "designed to carry out the purpose of a historic district" preceding "shall cease".

Cross References.
Transfer of records of abolished commissions, see RSA 673:21.

RESEARCH REFERENCES

New Hampshire Practice.
15 N.H.P. Land Use Planning and Zoning
§ 35.14.

673:21. Transfer of Documents Upon Abolition of Planning Board, Heritage Commission, Historic District Commission, and Agricultural Commission.

I. Whenever a heritage commission, historic district commission, or agricultural commission is abolished, the records shall be transferred to the planning board. In a municipality where a planning board does not exist, the records shall be transferred to the city, town, or village district clerk, or to the clerk for the county commissioners, whichever is appropriate.

II. Whenever a planning board is abolished, the records shall be transferred to the city or town clerk, to the clerk of the board of district commissioners, or to the clerk for the county commissioners, whichever is appropriate.

Source.

1983, 447:1. 1989, 266:13. 1992, 64:12, eff. June 19, 1992. 2007, 266:9, eff. August 28, 2007.

Amendments

—2007. Deleted "and" following "heritage commission" and added "and agricultural commission" to the section heading and in par. I deleted "or" following "heritage commission" and inserted "or agricultural commission" following "historic district commission" in the first sentence.

—1992. Inserted "Heritage Commission" following "Planning Board" in the section catchline and "heritage commission or" preceding "historic" in the first sentence of par. I.

—1989. Paragraph I: Inserted "or to the clerk for the county commissioners" preceding "whichever" in the second sentence.

Paragraph II: Deleted "or" following "city or town clerk" and inserted "or to the clerk for the county commissioners" preceding "whichever".

Cross References.

Abolition of boards or commissions generally, see RSA 673:18.

Effect of abolition, see RSA 673:19, 20.

RESEARCH REFERENCES

New Hampshire Practice.

15 N.H.P. Land Use Planning and Zoning §§ 27.13, 35.14.

673:22. Transfer of Documents Upon Abolition of Zoning Ordinance or Building Code.

I. Whenever a zoning ordinance is abolished, the records of the zoning board of adjustment shall be transferred to the planning board.

II. Whenever a building code is abolished, the records of the building code board of appeals shall be transferred to the planning board.

Source.

1983, 447:1, eff. Jan. 1, 1984.

CHAPTER 674

LOCAL LAND USE PLANNING AND REGULATORY POWERS

LOCAL LAND USE PLANNING

Cross References.

Local land use boards generally, see RSA 673.

Local land use board review of development of regional impact, see RSA 36:54 et seq.

Ordinance, regulation and code administration and enforcement generally, see RSA 676.

Ordinance, regulation and code adoption procedures generally, see RSA 675.

Rehearing and appeals procedures generally, see RSA 677.

State development plan, see RSA 9-A.

Town powers generally, see RSA 31.

NOTES TO DECISIONS

Cited:

Cited in Soares v. Town of Atkinson, 128 N.H. 350, 512 A.2d 436, 1986 N.H. LEXIS 298 (1986).

RESEARCH REFERENCES

New Hampshire Practice.

15 N.H.P. Land Use Planning and Zoning § 29.18.

New Hampshire Bar Journal.

For article, "An Overview of the New Hampshire Land Use Planning and Regulation Statutes," see 34 N.H.B.J. 6 (June 1993).

For Attorney General article, "Department Of Justice's Transportation And Construction Bureau: Trains, Planes And Automobiles," see 45 N.H.B.J. 78 (Spring 2004)

For article, "The New Zoning Variance Cases: Analyzing Unnecessary Hardship Under RSA 674:33," see 46 N.H.B.J. 40 (Fall 2005).

For article, "Roads Revisited Creation And Termination Of Highways In New Hampshire - An Update," see 46 N.H.B.J. 56 (Fall 2005).

For article, "Unnecessary Hardship Under RSA 674:331(B)," see 46 N.H.B.J. 47 (Fall 2005).

Master Plan

Cross References.

Emergency temporary zoning and planning ordinances, see RSA 674:24 et seq.

Heritage commissions, see RSA 674:44-a et seq.

Historic districts, see RSA 674:45 et seq.

Manufactured housing regulation, see RSA 674:31 et seq.

Official municipal map, see RSA 674:9 et seq.

Site plan review, see RSA 674:43 et seq.

Subdivision regulation, see RSA 674:35 et seq.

674:1. Duties of the Planning Board.

I. It shall be the duty of every planning board established under RSA 673:1 to prepare and amend from time to time a master plan to guide the development of the municipality. A master plan may include consideration of any areas outside the boundaries of the municipality which in the judgment of the planning board bear a relation to or have an impact on the planning of the municipality. Every planning board shall from time to time update and amend the adopted master plan with funds appropriated for that purpose by the local legislative body. In preparing, amending, and updating the master plan:

(a) The planning board shall have responsibility for promoting interest in, and understanding of, the master plan of the municipality. In order to promote this interest and understanding, the planning board may publish and distribute copies of the master plan, or copies of any report relating to the master plan, and may employ such other means of publicity and education as it may deem advisable.

(b) The planning board shall also have authority to make any investigations, maps and reports, and recommendations which relate to the planning and development of the municipality.

II. The planning board may from time to time report and recommend to the appropriate public officials and public agencies programs for the development of the municipality, programs for the erection of public structures, and programs for municipal improvements. Each program shall include recommendations for its financing. It shall be part of the planning board's duties to consult with and advise public officials and agencies, public utility companies, civic, educational, professional, research and other organizations, and to consult with citizens, for the purposes of protecting or carrying out of the master plan as well as for making recommendations relating to the development of the municipality.

III. Members of the planning board, when duly authorized by the board as a whole, may attend municipal planning conferences or meetings, or hearings upon pending municipal planning legislation. The planning board may by majority vote authorize the payment of reasonable expenses incident to such attendance.

IV. The planning board, and its members, officers, and employees, in the performance of their functions may, by ordinance, be authorized to enter upon any land and make such examinations and surveys as are reasonably necessary and place and maintain necessary monuments and marks and, in the event consent for such entry is denied or not reasonably obtainable, to obtain an administrative inspection warrant under RSA 595-B.

V. The planning board may, from time to time, recommend to the local legislative body amendments of the zoning ordinance or zoning map or additions thereto.

VI. In general, the planning board may be given such powers by the municipality as may be necessary to enable it to fulfill its functions, promote municipal planning, or carry out the purposes of this title.

Source.
1983, 447:1. 1991, 231:12, eff. Aug. 9, 1991.

Amendments
—**1991.** Paragraph IV: Added "and, in the event consent for such entry is denied or not reasonably obtainable, to obtain an administra-

tive inspection warrant under RSA 595-B" following "marks".

Cross References.
Adoption and amendment of master plan, see RSA 674:6.
Preparation of master plan, see RSA 674:3.

NOTES TO DECISIONS

Generally
In absence of special grants of authority, the general function of a planning board was to prepare a master plan for development of the municipality and to investigate, advise, and recommend with respect to municipal planning. Kostreles v. Portsmouth, 104 N.H. 392, 187 A.2d 789, 1963 N.H. LEXIS 62 (1963). (Decided under prior law.)

Cited:
Cited in Rancourt v. Town of Barnstead, 129

N.H. 45, 523 A.2d 55, 1986 N.H. LEXIS 379 (1986); Treisman v. Town of Bedford, 132 N.H. 54, 563 A.2d 786, 1989 N.H. LEXIS 75 (1989); Portsmouth Advocates, Inc. v. City of Portsmouth, 133 N.H. 876, 587 A.2d 600, 1991 N.H. LEXIS 13 (1991); City of Dover v. Kimball, 136 N.H. 441, 616 A.2d 516, 1992 N.H. LEXIS 187 (1992); Caspersen v. Town of Lyme, 139 N.H. 637, 661 A.2d 759, 1995 N.H. LEXIS 70 (1995).

RESEARCH REFERENCES

New Hampshire Practice.
15 N.H.P. Land Use Planning and Zoning §§ 3.02, 26.03, 30.01, 31.01, 32.11.

674:2. Master Plan; Purpose and Description.

I. The purpose of the master plan is to set down as clearly and practically as possible the best and most appropriate future development of the area under the jurisdiction of the planning board, to aid the board in designing ordinances that result in preserving and enhancing the unique quality of life and culture of New Hampshire, and to guide the board in the performance of its other duties in a manner that achieves the principles of smart growth, sound planning, and wise resource protection.

II. The master plan shall be a set of statements and land use and development principles for the municipality with such accompanying maps, diagrams, charts and descriptions as to give legal standing to the implementation ordinances and other measures of the planning board. Each section of the master plan shall be consistent with the others in its implementation of the vision section. The master plan shall be a public record subject to the provisions of RSA 91-A. The master plan shall include, at a minimum, the following required sections:

(a) A vision section that serves to direct the other sections of the plan. This section shall contain a set of statements which articulate the desires of the citizens affected by the master plan, not only for their locality but for the region and the whole state. It shall contain a set of guiding principles and priorities to implement that vision.

(b) A land use section upon which all the following sections shall be based. This section shall translate the vision statements into physical terms. Based on a study of population, economic activity, and natural, historic, and cultural resources, it shall show existing conditions and the proposed location, extent, and intensity of future land use.

III. The master plan may also include the following sections:

(a) A transportation section which considers all pertinent modes of transportation and provides a framework for both adequate local needs and for coordination with regional and state transportation plans. Suggested items to be considered may include but are not limited to public transportation, park and ride facilities, and bicycle routes, or paths, or both.

(b) A community facilities section which identifies facilities to support the future land use pattern of subparagraph II(b), meets the projected needs of the community, and coordinates with other local governments' special districts and school districts, as well as with state and federal agencies that have multi-jurisdictional impacts.

(c) An economic development section which proposes actions to suit the community's economic goals, given its economic strengths and weaknesses in the region.

(d) A natural resources section which identifies and inventories any critical or sensitive areas or resources, not only those in the local community, but also those shared with abutting communities. This section provides a factual basis for any land development regulations that may be enacted to protect natural areas. A key component in preparing this section is to identify any conflicts between other elements of the master plan and natural resources, as well as conflicts with plans of abutting communities. The natural resources section of the master plan should include a local water resources management and protection plan as specified in RSA 4-C:22.

(e) A natural hazards section which documents the physical characteristics, severity, frequency, and extent of any potential natural hazards to the community. It should identify those elements of the built environment at risk from natural hazards as well as extent of current and future vulnerability that may result from current zoning and development policies.

(f) A recreation section which shows existing recreation areas and addresses future recreation needs.

(g) A utility and public service section analyzing the need for and showing the present and future general location of existing and anticipated public and private utilities, both local and regional, including telecommunications utilities, their supplies, and facilities for distribution and storage.

(h) A section which identifies cultural and historic resources and protects them for rehabilitation or preservation from the impact of other land use tools such as land use regulations, housing, or transportation. Such section may encourage the preservation or restoration of stone walls, provided agricultural practices, as defined in RSA 21:34-a, are not impeded.

(i) A regional concern section, which describes the specific areas in the municipality of significant regional interest. These areas may include resources wholly contained within the municipality or bordering, or shared, or both, with neighboring municipalities. Items to be considered may include but are not limited to public facilities, natural resources, economic and housing potential, transportation, agriculture, and open space. The intent of this section is to promote regional awareness in managing growth while fulfilling the vision statements.

(j) A neighborhood plan section which focuses on a specific geographical area of local government that includes substantial residential development. This section is a part of the local master plan and shall be consistent with it. No neighborhood plan shall be adopted until a local master plan is adopted.

(k) A community design section to identify positive physical attributes in a municipality and provide for design goals and policies for planning in specific areas to guide private and public development.

(l) A housing section which assesses local housing conditions and projects future housing needs of residents of all levels of income and ages in the municipality and the region as identified in the regional housing needs assessment performed by the regional planning commission pursuant to RSA 36:47, II, and which integrates the availability of human services with other planning undertaken by the community.

(m) An implementation section, which is a long range action program of specific actions, time frames, allocation of responsibility for actions, description of land development regulations to be adopted, and procedures which the municipality may use to monitor and measure the effectiveness of each section of the plan.

Source.

1983, 447:1. 1986, 167:2. 1988, 270:1. 1989, 339:28, eff. Jan. 1, 1990; 363:15, eff. Aug. 4, 1989. 2002, 178:2, eff. July 14, 2002. 2007, 40:1, eff. July 20, 2007.

Amendments

—2007. Paragraph III(h): Added the second sentence.

—2002. Rewritten to the extent that a detailed comparison would be impracticable.

—1989. Paragraph VIII: Chapter 339 sub-stituted "RSA 4-C:22" for "RSA 4:12-v" in the second sentence.

Paragraph VIII-a: Added by ch. 363.

—1988. Paragraph III: Added "current and" preceding "future housing needs" and added "of residents of all levels of income of the municipality and of the region in which it is located, as identified in the regional housing needs assessment performed by the regional planning commission pursuant to RSA 36:47, II".

—1986. Paragraph VIII: Added the second and third sentences.

Cross References.
Adoption and amendment of master plan, see RSA 674:4.

Preparation of master plan, see RSA 674:3.

NOTES TO DECISIONS

Scope of master plan

A master plan is merely a general guide to aid planning boards in making zoning decisions, and it need not and indeed cannot be particularly detailed in describing future land uses. Treisman v. Town of Bedford, 132 N.H. 54, 563 A.2d 786, 1989 N.H. LEXIS 75 (1989).

Cited:

Cited in Rancourt v. Town of Barnstead, 129

N.H. 45, 523 A.2d 55, 1986 N.H. LEXIS 379 (1986); Portsmouth Advocates, Inc. v. City of Portsmouth, 133 N.H. 876, 587 A.2d 600, 1991 N.H. LEXIS 13 (1991); Zukis v. Town of Fitzwilliam, 135 N.H. 384, 604 A.2d 956, 1992 N.H. LEXIS 46 (1992); Quinlan v. City of Dover, 136 N.H. 226, 614 A.2d 1057, 1992 N.H. LEXIS 159 (1992).

RESEARCH REFERENCES

New Hampshire Practice.
15 N.H.P. Land Use Planning and Zoning §§ 3.02–3.04, 29.02, 36.20.

674:3. Master Plan Preparation.

I. In preparing, revising, or amending the master plan, the planning board may make surveys and studies, and may review data about the existing conditions, probable growth demands, and best design methods to prevent sprawl growth in the community and the region. The board may also consider the goals, policies, and guidelines of any regional or state plans, as well as those of abutting communities.

II. Revisions to the plan are recommended every 5 to 10 years.

III. During the preparation of the various sections of the master plan, the board shall inform the general public, the office of energy and planning, and regional planning commissions and solicit public comments regarding the future growth of the municipality in order to involve citizens in the preparation of the master plan in a way which is most appropriate for the municipality.

Source.
1983, 447:1, eff. Jan. 1, 1984. 2002, 178:3, eff. July 14, 2002; 229:9, eff. July 1, 2002. 2003, 319:9, eff. July 1, 2003. 2004, 257:44, eff. July 1, 2004.

Amendments
—**2004.** Paragraph III: Substituted "office of energy and planning" for "office of state planning and energy programs".

—**2003.** Paragraph III: Substituted "office of state planning and energy programs" for "office of state planning".

—**2002.** Chapter 229:9, eff. July 1, 2002, inserted "and the office of state planning and regional planning commissions" following "general public" in par. III.

Chapter 178:3, eff. July 14, 2002, rewrote pars. I–III.

Cross References.
Contents of master plan generally, see RSA 674:2.

Duties of planning board as to master plan generally, see RSA 674:1.

Cited:
Cited in Rancourt v. Town of Barnstead, 129
N.H. 45, 523 A.2d 55, 1986 N.H. LEXIS 379
(1986).

RESEARCH REFERENCES

New Hampshire Practice.
15 N.H.P. Land Use Planning and Zoning
§ 3.05.

674:4. Master Plan Adoption and Amendment.

The planning board may, according to the procedures required under RSA
675:6, adopt the master plan as a whole, or may adopt successive sections or
parts of the plan. Sections or parts of the plan shall correspond with major
geographical sections or divisions of the municipality, or with the functional
elements of the plan, and may incorporate any amendment, extension, or
addition to the plan.

Source.
1983, 447:1, eff. Jan. 1, 1984.

Cross References.
Preparation of master plan, see RSA 674:3.

NOTES TO DECISIONS

Cited:
Cited in Rancourt v. Town of Barnstead, 129
N.H. 45, 523 A.2d 55, 1986 N.H. LEXIS 379

(1986); Zukis v. Town of Fitzwilliam, 135 N.H.
384, 604 A.2d 956, 1992 N.H. LEXIS 46 (1992).

RESEARCH REFERENCES

New Hampshire Practice.
15 N.H.P. Land Use Planning and Zoning
§§ 3.06, 31.01, 35.17.

Capital Improvements Program

Cross References.
Master plan generally, see RSA 674:1 et seq.
Municipal budgets and finance generally, see
RSA 32-34.

674:5. Authorization.

In a municipality where the planning board has adopted a master plan, the
local legislative body may authorize the planning board to prepare and amend
a recommended program of municipal capital improvement projects projected
over a period of at least 6 years. As an alternative, the legislative body may
authorize the governing body of a municipality to appoint a capital improvement program committee, which shall include at least one member of the
planning board and may include but not be limited to other members of the

planning board, the budget committee, or the town or city governing body, to prepare and amend a recommended program of municipal capital improvement projects projected over a period of at least 6 years. The capital improvements program may encompass major projects being currently undertaken or future projects to be undertaken with federal, state, county and other public funds. The sole purpose and effect of the capital improvements program shall be to aid the mayor or selectmen and the budget committee in their consideration of the annual budget.

Source.

1983, 447:1, eff. Jan. 1, 1984. 2002, 90:1, eff. July 2, 2002.

Amendments

—2002. Added the second sentence and inserted "or selectmen" following "mayor" in the fourth sentence.

Cross References.

Consideration of program by mayor and budget committee, see RSA 674:8.

Preparation of program, see RSA 674:7.

NOTES TO DECISIONS

Construction and application

Other than its management tool capabilities, a capital improvements program has no part to play in review of subdivision applications presented to governmental authorities. Zukis v. Town of Fitzwilliam, 135 N.H. 384, 604 A.2d 956, 1992 N.H. LEXIS 46 (1992).

Cited:

Cited in Rancourt v. Town of Barnstead, 129 N.H. 45, 523 A.2d 55, 1986 N.H. LEXIS 379 (1986).

RESEARCH REFERENCES

New Hampshire Practice.

15 N.H.P. Land Use Planning and Zoning §§ 4.01, 5.09, 17.05, 26.03, 31.02.

674:6. Purpose and Description.

The capital improvements program shall classify projects according to the urgency and need for realization and shall recommend a time sequence for their implementation. The program may also contain the estimated cost of each project and indicate probable operating and maintenance costs and probable revenues, if any, as well as existing sources of funds or the need for additional sources of funds for the implementation and operation of each project. The program shall be based on information submitted by the departments and agencies of the municipality and shall take into account public facility needs indicated by the prospective development shown in the master plan of the municipality or as permitted by other municipal land use controls.

Source.

1983, 447:1, eff. Jan. 1, 1984.

NOTES TO DECISIONS

Construction and application

Other than its management tool capabilities, a capital improvements program has no part to play in review of subdivision applications pre-sented to governmental authorities. Zukis v. Town of Fitzwilliam, 135 N.H. 384, 604 A.2d 956, 1992 N.H. LEXIS 46 (1992).

RESEARCH REFERENCES

New Hampshire Practice.

15 N.H.P. Land Use Planning and Zoning §§ 4.02, 29.02.

674:7. Preparation.

I. In preparing the capital improvements program, the planning board or the capital improvement program committee shall confer, in a manner deemed appropriate by the board or the committee, with the mayor or the board of selectmen, or the chief fiscal officer, the budget committee, other municipal officials and agencies, the school board or boards, and shall review the recommendations of the master plan in relation to the proposed capital improvements program.

II. Whenever the planning board or the capital improvement program committee is authorized and directed to prepare a capital improvements program, every municipal department, authority or agency, and every affected school district board, department or agency, shall, upon request of the planning board or the capital improvement program committee, transmit to the board or committee a statement of all capital projects it proposes to undertake during the term of the program. The planning board or the capital improvement program committee shall study each proposed capital project, and shall advise and make recommendations to the department, authority, agency, or school district board, department or agency, concerning the relation of its project to the capital improvements program being prepared.

Source.

1983, 447:1. 1995, 43:1, eff. July 2, 1995. 2002, 90:2, eff. July 2, 2002.

Amendments

—2002. Paragraph I: Inserted "or the capital improvement program committee" preceding "shall confer" and "or the committee" preceding "with the mayor".

Paragraph II: Inserted "or the capital improvement program committee" following "planning board" in two places and "or committee" preceding "a statement" in the first sentence and "or the capital improvement program committee" preceding "shall study" in the second sentence.

—1995. Paragraph II: Inserted "and every affected school district board, department or agency" preceding "shall, upon request" in the first sentence and deleted "or" following "authority" and inserted "or school district board, department or agency" preceding "concerning" in the second sentence.

Cross References.

Authorization of program, see RSA 674:5.

Contents of program, see RSA 674:6.

RESEARCH REFERENCES

New Hampshire Practice.
15 N.H.P. Land Use Planning and Zoning
§ 4.03.

674:8. Consideration by Mayor and Budget Committee.

Whenever the planning board or the capital improvement program committee has prepared a capital improvements program under RSA 674:7, it shall
submit its recommendations for the current year to the mayor or selectmen
and the budget committee, if one exists, for consideration as part of the annual
budget.

Source.
1983, 447:1, eff. Jan. 1, 1984. 2002, 90:3, eff.
July 2, 2002.

Amendments
—**2002.** Inserted "or the capital improve-

ment program committee" following "planning
board" and "or selectmen" following "mayor".

Cross References.
Authorization of program, see RSA 674:5.
Purpose of program, see RSA 674:6.

RESEARCH REFERENCES

New Hampshire Practice.
15 N.H.P. Land Use Planning and Zoning
§ 4.03.

Official Map of the Municipality

Cross References.
City, town and village district highways, see
RSA 231.
Highway regulations, see RSA 236.
Historic districts, see RSA 674:45 et seq.
Manufactured housing regulation, see RSA
674:31 et seq.

Master plan, see RSA 674:1 et seq.
Powers and duties of county commissioners
as to highways generally, see RSA 232.
Site plan review, see RSA 674:43 et seq.
Subdivision regulation, see RSA 674:35 et
seq.
Zoning generally, see RSA 674:16 et seq.

674:9. Mapping of Street Lines by Planning Board.

At any time after a planning board has adopted a master plan of the
municipality which includes a major street plan or has progressed in its master
planning to the stage of the making and adoption of a major street plan, the
local legislative body may authorize the planning board to make or cause to be
made from time to time surveys for the exact locating of the lines of new,
extended, widened, or narrowed streets in the whole or in any portion of the
municipality. The local legislative body may also empower the planning board
to make and certify to the local legislative body, when completed, a plat of the
area thus surveyed on which are indicated the locations of the lines recommended by the planning board as the planned or mapped lines of future
streets, street extensions, street widenings, or street narrowings. The making
or certifying of a plat by the planning board, under the authorization of the
local legislative body, shall not in and of itself constitute or be deemed to

constitute the opening or establishment of any street or the taking or acceptance of any land for street purposes.

Source.
1983, 447:1, eff. Jan. 1, 1984.

RESEARCH REFERENCES

New Hampshire Practice.
15 N.H.P. Land Use Planning and Zoning §§ 26.03, 31.03.

Termination of Highways in New Hampshire - An Update," see N.H.B.J. 56 (Fall 2005).

New Hampshire Bar Journal.
For article, "Roads Revisited: Creation and

674:10. Establishment of Official Map.

After the planning board of any municipality has adopted a master plan which includes a major street plan, or has progressed in its master planning to the stage of the making and adoption of a major street plan, and has certified a copy of a major street plan to the local legislative body, as provided in RSA 674:9, the local legislative body is hereby empowered and authorized to establish an official map of the municipality showing the location of the exterior lines of streets of the whole or of any parts of the municipality up to that time existing, laid out and established by law as public streets, and may also show the location of the exterior lines of parks. The official map is to be deemed to be final and conclusive with respect to the location and width of streets and the location of parks shown thereon. The official map established under this section shall be established to conserve and promote the public health, safety, convenience or general welfare. The ordinance establishing or adopting the official map shall provide that a certificate, signed by the city or town clerk, the village district clerk, or other duly authorized recording official, giving notice that the municipality has established an official map, including the date of its establishment, shall be filed with the register of deeds of the county or counties in which the municipality is situated. Such certificates shall be accompanied by a certified copy of the official map as adopted or established. Whenever a municipality has established an official map and has filed a certificate to that effect, together with a copy of the official map, with the register of deeds for the county or counties in which the municipality is situated, then no plat of a subdivision of land within the municipality shall thereafter be filed or recorded at the office of the register of deeds until it has been approved by the planning board and such approval entered in writing on the plat by the chairperson or secretary of the planning board.

Source.
1983, 447:1. 1995, 43:2, eff. July 2, 1995.

Amendments
—1995. Substituted "chairperson" for "chairman" preceding "secretary" in the last sentence.

Cross References.
Allowance of buildings and structures in mapped-street locations shown on official map, see RSA 674:12–15.

Subdivision regulation generally, see RSA 674:35 et seq.

RESEARCH REFERENCES

New Hampshire Practice.
  15 N.H.P. Land Use Planning and Zoning
§ 31.03.

674:11. Amendments to Official Map.

The local legislative body is authorized and empowered, whenever and as often as it may deem it advisable or necessary for the public interest, to change or add to the official map of the municipality. Amendments may be made in order to establish the exterior lines of the new streets or parks, or to widen, extend, relocate, narrow, vacate, abandon, or close existing streets or parks, and to indicate the acceptance of, change of use, acquisition of land for, or sale or lease of any street or other public way, ground, place, property, or structure. No change shall become effective until after a public hearing has been held on the change, at which parties in interest and citizens shall have had an opportunity to be heard. Notice of the public hearing shall be given by publishing at least 10 days before the public hearing a notice of such hearing in a newspaper of general circulation in the municipality, and by posting a notice to the same effect at the city or town hall, or in whatever place other notices required by law in connection with municipal affairs are posted or customarily displayed. Before making such addition, amendment, or change, the local legislative body shall refer the matter to the planning board for a report. If the planning board does not make its report within 30 days of such reference, it shall be deemed to have forfeited the right to further suspend action. In the event that the planning board disapproves the proposed addition, amendment, or change, the local legislative body shall not have the right to overrule the planning board's decision, unless by vote of not less than ⅔ of its entire membership in case of a city, or by majority vote of the legal voters present and voting at a regular or special town or district meeting in the case of a town or village district. Such additions, amendments, and changes when adopted shall become a part of the official map of the municipality and shall be deemed to be final and conclusive with respect to the location of the streets and parks shown on the official map. The locating, widening, narrowing, or closing, or the approval of locating, widening, narrowing, or closing, of streets and parks by the municipality under provisions of law other than those contained in this subdivision shall be deemed to be a change or addition to the official map and shall be subject to all the provisions of this subdivision.

Source.
  1983, 447:1, eff. Jan. 1, 1984.

674:12. Refusal of Permit.

A municipality which has established and recorded an official map, as provided in RSA 674:10, may for the purpose of preserving the integrity of such official map provide by ordinance that, from and after the time of such recording, no permit shall be issued for any building or structure, or part thereof, in the bed of or on any land located between the mapped lines of any street as shown or laid out on such official map, except as provided in RSA 674:13.

Source.
   1983, 447:1, eff. Jan. 1, 1984.

Cross References.
   Appeals from denial of permits, see RSA 674:13–15.

674:13. Appeals Where There is a Zoning Ordinance.

I. Any zoning ordinance adopted pursuant to RSA 674:16 shall provide that the board of adjustment created under a local zoning ordinance and having the power to make variances or exceptions in zoning regulations shall have the further power, in specific cases and by vote of a majority of its members, upon an appeal filed with it by the owner of any such land, to grant a permit based on considerations of justice and equity for a building or structure, or part thereof, in a mapped-street location shown on the official map, in any case in which the board of adjustment finds, upon the evidence and arguments presented to it upon appeal:

   (a) That the property of the appellant of which such mapped-street location forms a part will not yield a reasonable return to the owner unless such permit be granted; or

   (b) That, balancing the interest of the municipality in preserving the integrity of the official map and in not increasing too greatly the cost of later opening such street, and the interest of the owner in the use and benefits of the owner's property, the grant of such permit is required by considerations of justice and equity.

II. In the event that the board of adjustment decides to authorize or issue a building permit in such case, it shall have the power to specify the exact location, ground area to be used or occupied, height, and other reasonable details and conditions of extent and character, and also the duration of the building, or part hereof, permitted. Such requirements shall be designed to promote the health, convenience, safety, or general welfare of and shall inure to the benefit of the municipality. The board of adjustment shall refuse a permit if the applicant will not be substantially damaged by placing the applicant's building outside the mapped-street location.

Source.
   1983, 447:1. 1995, 43:3, 4, eff. July 2, 1995.

Amendments
   —1995. Paragraph I(b): Substituted "the owner's" for "his" following "benefits of".
   Paragraph II: Substituted "the applicant's" for "his" following "placing" in the third sentence.

Cross References.
   Appeals from denial of permits in municipalities having no zoning ordinances, see RSA 674:14.
   Denial of permits generally, see RSA 674:12.
   Hearings on appeals, see RSA 674:15.
   Zoning generally, see RSA 674:16 et seq.

674:14. Appeals Where No Zoning Ordinance Exists.

In any municipality, other than a town, in which there is no zoning board of adjustment, the local legislative body, until such time as a board of adjustment may be appointed as a result of the adoption of a zoning ordinance, shall have the same powers as a board of adjustment to act, but only under the circumstances and in such special cases as are specified in RSA 674:13 and 674:41, and shall be subject to the same restrictions as apply to a board of adjustment. For this purpose, the local legislative body is hereby authorized to act as a discretionary administrative or quasi-judicial body. When so acting, it shall not sit as a legislative body but shall sit in a separate meeting for which separate minutes shall be kept. In any town or village district in which there is no board of adjustment, the local governing body is hereby authorized to designate a board of appeals to be composed of 5 members, serving as such without compensation, which shall have the authority of and shall be subject to the same restrictions and regulations as apply to a zoning board of adjustment, but which shall have the power to act only under the circumstances and in such special cases as are specified herein and only until such time as a board of adjustment may be appointed as a result of the adoption of a zoning ordinance.

Source.
1983, 447:1. 1988, 131:1, eff. June 19, 1988.

Amendments
—1988. Substituted "governing body" for "legislative body" preceding "is hereby authorized" in the fourth sentence.

Cross References.
Appeals from denial of permits generally, see RSA 674:13.
Denial of permits generally, see RSA 674:12.
Hearings on appeals, see RSA 674:15.
Zoning generally, see RSA 674:16 et seq.

674:15. Appeals; Public Hearing.

Before taking any action authorized in RSA 674:13, 674:14, and 674:41, the zoning board of adjustment, the legislative body, or the boards of appeal, according to whichever of them is designated by ordinance as the body to which appeals may be made, shall give a hearing at which parties in interest and others shall have an opportunity to be heard. Notice for a public hearing under this section shall be as provided in RSA 675:7.

Source.
1983, 447:1, eff. Jan. 1, 1984.

Cross References.
Appeals procedure generally, see RSA 674:13, 14.

Denial of permits generally, see RSA 674:12.

Zoning

Cross References.
Adoption of bylaws by towns generally, see RSA 31:39 et seq.

Adoption of ordinances and codes generally, see RSA 675.
Airport zoning generally, see RSA 424.

Building codes generally, see RSA 674:51 et seq.

Central business service districts, see RSA 31:120 et seq.

Economic development and revitalization districts, see RSA 162-K.

Emergency temporary zoning and planning ordinances, see RSA 674:24 et seq.

Historic district regulation, see RSA 674:45 et seq.

Site plan review regulations, see RSA 674:44.

Subdivision regulation, see RSA 674:35 et seq.

NOTES TO DECISIONS

Analysis

1. Construction
2. Exercise of municipal power
3. Application

1. Construction

Under power delegated to municipalities to enact zoning ordinances to promote "the general welfare of the community," the term "community" includes the region of which the municipality is a part. Britton v. Town of Chester, 134 N.H. 434, 595 A.2d 492, 1991 N.H. LEXIS 95 (1991).

2. Exercise of municipal power

Ordinance which in effect wrongfully excluded development of low and moderate income housing constituted an invalid exercise of the municipality's power under enabling legislation delegating to the town the power to zone municipality to promote the general welfare of the community, which included not only the municipality itself, but the region in which it was located. Britton v. Town of Chester, 134 N.H. 434, 595 A.2d 492, 1991 N.H. LEXIS 95 (1991).

3. Application

Earth excavation regulations of a town zoning ordinance were not required to be adopted pursuant to this subdivision, since there were other specific enabling statutes for local earth excavation ordinances. Town of Goffstown v. Thibeault, 129 N.H. 454, 529 A.2d 930, 1987 N.H. LEXIS 184 (1987).

674:16. Grant of Power.

I. For the purpose of promoting the health, safety, or the general welfare of the community, the local legislative body of any city, town, or county in which there are located unincorporated towns or unorganized places is authorized to adopt or amend a zoning ordinance under the ordinance enactment procedures of RSA 675:2-5. The zoning ordinance shall be designed to regulate and restrict:

(a) The height, number of stories and size of buildings and other structures;

(b) Lot sizes, the percentage of a lot that may be occupied, and the size of yards, courts and other open spaces;

(c) The density of population in the municipality; and

(d) The location and use of buildings, structures and land used for business, industrial, residential, or other purposes.

II. The power to adopt a zoning ordinance under this subdivision expressly includes the power to adopt innovative land use controls which may include, but which are not limited to, the methods contained in RSA 674:21.

III. In its exercise of the powers granted under this subdivision, the local legislative body of a city, town, or county in which there are located unincorporated towns or unorganized places may regulate and control the timing of development as provided in RSA 674:22.

IV. Except as provided in RSA 424:5 or RSA 422-B or in any other provision of Title XXXIX, no city, town, or county in which there are located unincorporated towns or unorganized places shall adopt or amend a zoning ordinance or regulation with respect to antennas used exclusively in the amateur radio services that fails to conform to the limited federal preemption entitled Amateur Radio Preemption, 101 FCC 2nd 952 (1985) issued by the Federal Communications Commission.

V. In its exercise of the powers granted under this subdivision, the local legislative body of a city, town, or county in which there are located unincorporated towns or unorganized places may regulate and control accessory uses on private land. Unless specifically proscribed by local land use regulation, aircraft take offs and landings on private land by the owner of such land or by a person who resides on such land shall be considered a valid and permitted accessory use.

Source.
1983, 447:1. 1985, 103:19. 1989, 266:14, 15. 1995, 176:1, eff. Aug. 4, 1995. 1996, 218:1, eff. Aug. 9, 1996.

Amendments
—1996. Paragraph V: Added.

—1995. Paragraph IV: Added.

—1989. Paragraph I: Substituted "town, or county in which there are located unincorporated towns or unorganized places" for "or town" following "city" in the first sentence.

Paragraph III: Substituted "town, or county in which there are located unincorporated towns or unorganized places" for "or town" following "city".

—1985. Paragraph IV: Repealed.

Cross References.
Adoption of bylaws by towns generally, see RSA 31:39 et seq.

Applicability of ordinances, see RSA 674:19.

Authority of zoning board of adjustment as to appeals from proceedings for enforcement of zoning ordinances, see RSA 674:33.

Interim growth management regulations, see RSA 674:23.

NOTES TO DECISIONS

Analysis

1. Constitutionality
2. Construction
3. Construction with other laws
4. Substantive Due Process
4.5. Equal protection
5. Facial Invalidity
6. Requirements regarding adoption of ordinances generally
7. Establishment of procedure for administration of ordinances
8. Regulation of particular matters—Lot size
9. —Aesthetic values
10. —Density of population
11. —Location of buildings
12. —Uses of buildings, structures, or land
13. —Rate of growth
14. —Aircraft takeoffs and landings

1. Constitutionality
The statute was a valid exercise of the police power. Sundeen v. Rogers, 83 N.H. 253, 141 A. 142, 1928 N.H. LEXIS 11, 57 A.L.R. 950 (1928); Brady v. Keene, 90 N.H. 99, 4 A.2d 658, 1939 N.H. LEXIS 22 (1939). (Decided under prior law.)

2. Construction
The statute granted localities broad authority to zone in order to promote public health, safety, morals and general welfare. Sanderson v. Town of Greenland, 122 N.H. 1002, 453 A.2d 1285, 1982 N.H. LEXIS 511 (1982). (Decided under prior law.)

3. Construction with other laws
The general police power delegated to a municipality pursuant to RSA 31:39 could not be used as a usual and expedient mechanism for

effecting zoning regulations which would otherwise fall within the scope of RSA 31:60-89. Beck v. Town of Raymond, 118 N.H. 793, 394 A.2d 847, 1978 N.H. LEXIS 296 (1978). (Decided under prior law.)

4. Substantive Due Process

Application of city's zoning ordinance that banned correctional facilities to prohibit applicant from building halfway house that housed federal prisoners still serving out their sentences did not violate applicant's state constitutional right to substantive due process as the ordinance was rationally related to legitimate governmental interests, including concerns that the prisoners to be housed at a residential transition facility would either pose some threat to the surrounding community, engage in recidivism, exacerbate the city's perceived burden in accommodating a disproportionate share of social services or affect surrounding property values. Because the city could reasonably conceive these facts to be true, the ordinance served or could conceivably serve legitimate governmental interests. Cmty. Res. for Justice, Inc. v. City of Manchester, 154 N.H. 748, 917 A.2d 707, 2007 N.H. LEXIS 11 (2007).

Town zoning ordinance, which provided that nonconforming uses that had been destroyed and were not rebuilt within a year had to comply with present zoning requirements, did not violate plaintiff's right to substantive due process as applied to her shed because the ordinance worked to reduce nonconforming uses by establishing a time limit on their reconstruction and the reduction and elimination of nonconforming uses was a legitimate purpose of zoning and so the ordinance's purpose of reducing nonconforming uses was a legitimate governmental interest. Furthermore, the ordinance bore a rational relationship to the legitimate goal since, by imposing a time limit on plaintiff's ability to rebuild her nonconforming shed, the provision reduced the possibility that she would reconstruct her nonconforming shed and increased the possibility that the shed, if rebuilt, would be rebuilt in compliance with the zoning ordinance and, as plaintiff did not rebuild her shed within a year, the efficacy of the time limitation was evident. Mckenzie v. Town of Eaton Zoning Bd. of Adjustment, 154 N.H. 773, 917 A.2d 193, 2007 N.H. LEXIS 14 (2007).

Trial court's ruling that Strafford, N.H., Zoning & Land Use Ordinances, Subdivision Regs., Non-Residential Site Plan Regs., & Bldg. Regs.

ch. 1, § 4.1(F) was unconstitutional was vacated as it could not be determined what standard the trial court applied; the case was remanded for a rational basis review of a developer's substantive due process challenge. Boulders at Strafford v. Town of Strafford, 153 N.H. 633, 903 A.2d 1021, 2006 N.H. LEXIS 82 (2006).

4.5. Equal protection

Intermediate scrutiny was the appropriate standard of review to be applied to applicant's equal protection challenge to application of zoning ordinance that banned correctional facilities to prohibit applicant from building halfway house. As the right to use and enjoy property is an important substantive right, the intermediate scrutiny test is used to review equal protection challenges to zoning ordinances that infringe upon this right. However, because the appellate court departed from its previous intermediate scrutiny standard and developed a new standard, the matter was remanded for further proceedings to apply the new standard. Cmty. Res. for Justice, Inc. v. City of Manchester, 154 N.H. 748, 917 A.2d 707, 2007 N.H. LEXIS 11 (2007).

5. Facial Invalidity

Legislation may not be applied in a particular case if it is facially invalid and cannot constitutionally be applied in any case; thus, to succeed on its facial challenge to Strafford, N.H., Zoning & Land Use Ordinances, Subdivision Regs., Non-Residential Site Plan Regs., & Bldg. Regs. ch. 1, § 4.1(F), a developer had to prove that the ordinance was not rationally related to its intended purpose of protecting the wetlands, but there were many reasons besides scientific data that a town could posit to justify the zoning ordinance and any fair reason that could be assigned for bringing legislation within the town's purview might be sufficient to save it. Boulders at Strafford v. Town of Strafford, 153 N.H. 633, 903 A.2d 1021, 2006 N.H. LEXIS 82 (2006).

6. Requirements regarding adoption of ordinances generally

A town ordinance containing comprehensive regulations which sought to restrict the use of three areas of a town to single and two-family residential buildings, to regulate the use of buildings, the size and percentage of lots and indirectly to regulate the size of yards and other open spaces and the density of population, and which contemplated that permits would be granted for nonconforming uses, was a zoning ordinance which could not be legally enacted except in compliance with the statute authorizing zoning regulations and could not be justified under RSA 31:39. Bisson v. Town of Milford, 109 N.H. 287, 249 A.2d 688, 1969 N.H. LEXIS 136 (1969). (Decided under prior law.)

A town, in adopting a zoning ordinance, was required to comply with the provisions of the enabling statute both in its enactment, and its regulations, including provisions for its administration. Town of Jaffrey v. Heffernan, 104 N.H. 249, 183 A.2d 246, 1962 N.H. LEXIS 61 (1962). (Decided under prior law.) See also Bisson v. Town of Milford, 109 N.H. 287, 249 A.2d 688, 1969 N.H. LEXIS 136 (1969). (Decided under prior law.)

7. Establishment of procedure for administration of ordinances

In accordance with its power to pass zoning regulations and to establish a board of adjustment for the purpose of granting variances and exceptions from the terms of zoning ordinances, a municipality could prescribe reasonable procedures for the board to follow in order to carry out its purposes. Lavallee v. Britt, 118 N.H. 131, 383 A.2d 709, 1978 N.H. LEXIS 358 (1978). (Decided under prior law.)

8. Regulation of particular matters—Lot size

The constitutionality of a zoning ordinance increasing minimum lot sizes could not be decided solely on the basis of whether the new sizes were necessary for health and safety, the test for zoning regulations being whether they had no rational tendency to promote the safety and general welfare of the community or to conserve property values throughout the municipality. Steel Hill Dev., Inc. v. Town of Sanbornton, 338 F. Supp. 301, 1972 U.S. Dist. LEXIS 15050 (D.N.H. 1972), aff'd, 469 F.2d 956, 1972 U.S. App. LEXIS 6564 (1st Cir. 1972). (Decided under prior law.)

The proper test of the validity of an increase in minimum lot sizes was not just the size of the lot, or whether the immediate sale value for the intended purpose of property was depressed, but a balancing of the public objectives promoted by the restriction and the economic burden imposed on the owner of the restricted land. Steel Hill Dev., Inc. v. Town of Sanborn-

ton, 338 F. Supp. 301, 1972 U.S. Dist. LEXIS 15050 (D.N.H. 1972), aff'd, 469 F.2d 956, 1972 U.S. App. LEXIS 6564 (1st Cir. 1972). (Decided under prior law.)

9. —Aesthetic values

Municipalities may validly exercise zoning power solely to advance aesthetic values, since the preservation or enhancement of the visual environment may promote the general welfare. Asselin v. Town of Conway, 137 N.H. 368, 628 A.2d 247, 1993 N.H. LEXIS 89 (1993).

10. —Density of population

Regulating and restricting the density of population were expressly delegated to a town in New Hampshire pursuant to this statute. Beck v. Town of Raymond, 118 N.H. 793, 394 A.2d 847, 1978 N.H. LEXIS 296 (1978). (Decided under prior law.) See also Town of Durham v. White Enterprises, Inc., 115 N.H. 645, 348 A.2d 706, 1975 N.H. LEXIS 386 (1975). (Decided under prior law.)

11. —Location of buildings

Adoption of ordinance requiring newly constructed buildings to be set back stated distance from public highway was within the general police powers of a town. Town of Jaffrey v. Heffernan, 104 N.H. 249, 183 A.2d 246, 1962 N.H. LEXIS 61 (1962). (Decided under prior law.)

12. —Uses of buildings, structures, or land

Trial court properly reversed the zoning adjustment board's decision that affirmed a zoning compliance officer's decision to prohibit the property owners from expanding the use of their seasonal residence to a year-round residence; ordinance drafters did not differentiate between seasonal and full-time residential occupancy and if they had at any point intended to do so, they had available the remedy of amending the ordinance pursuant to RSA 674:16, I, which they did not do. Severance v. Town of Epsom, 155 N.H. 359, 923 A.2d 1057, 2007 N.H. LEXIS 61 (2007).

Municipalities were not authorized under their zoning powers to require the written consent of a certain percentage of abutting owners within a stated distance as a condition precedent to granting of extensions of nonconforming uses. A zoning ordinance was not discriminatory because it permitted the continuation of existing structures and conditions while the creation of new structures or conditions of the same type was prohibited. Ackley v. Nashua, 102 N.H. 551, 163 A.2d 6, 1960 N.H. LEXIS 78 (1960).

A zoning ordinance was not discriminatory because it permitted the continuation of existing structures and conditions while the creation of new structures or conditions of the same type was prohibited. Stone v. Cray, 89 N.H. 483, 200 A. 517, 1938 N.H. LEXIS 60 (1938). (Decided under prior law.)

13. —Rate of growth

The legislative body of any city or town was empowered to regulate and restrict density of population and size, location and use of buildings and land; this power necessarily implied the authority to direct and control population growth. Conway v. Town of Stratham, 120 N.H. 257, 414 A.2d 539, 1980 N.H. LEXIS 269 (1980). (Decided under prior law.)

When towns properly exercised the zoning power delegated to them by the legislature, they could adopt reasonable time controls on population growth. Beck v. Town of Raymond, 118 N.H. 793, 394 A.2d 847, 1978 N.H. LEXIS 296 (1978); Conway v. Town of Stratham, 120 N.H. 257, 414 A.2d 539, 1980 N.H. LEXIS 269 (1980). (Decided under prior law.)

A town's slow-growth ordinance did not improperly infringe upon the jurisdiction of town's planning board since the legislature, by granting growth control power to the town, necessarily limited the power of the planning board. Conway v. Town of Stratham, 120 N.H. 257, 414 A.2d 539, 1980 N.H. LEXIS 269 (1980). (Decided under prior law.)

The authority to enact land use regulations for the purpose of restricting growth was embodied in the power to zone. Beck v. Town of Raymond, 118 N.H. 793, 394 A.2d 847, 1978 N.H. LEXIS 296 (1978). (Decided under prior law.)

14. —Aircraft takeoffs and landings

Because zoning ordinance did not specifically refer to aircraft takeoffs and landings, but generally proscribed all uses not listed, defendants' use of their property for aircraft takeoffs and landings was a valid and permitted accessory use according to land use statute; neighbors' reliance on defeated amendments to ordinance that would have explicitly permitted aircraft takeoffs and landings was misplaced, because legislative history would not be consulted when language of ordinance was plain. Spengler v. Porter, 144 N.H. 163, 737 A.2d 1121, 1999 N.H. LEXIS 92 (1999).

Amended land use statute was not unconstitutional as applied to neighbors abutting private airstrip, where neighbors made no factual allegations that would allow court to conclude that statute effected a taking of their property, or that statute discriminated in favor of airstrip owners; moreover, although neighbors alleged that misrepresentations made to legislators prior to passage of amendment rendered it unconstitutional, neighbors' petition failed to provide any legal theory to support relief sought. Spengler v. Porter, 144 N.H. 163, 737 A.2d 1121, 1999 N.H. LEXIS 92 (1999).

Cited:

Cited in Soares v. Town of Atkinson, 129 N.H. 313, 529 A.2d 867, 1987 N.H. LEXIS 223 (1987); Town of Goffstown v. Thibeault, 129 N.H. 454, 529 A.2d 930, 1987 N.H. LEXIS 184 (1987); Treisman v. Town of Bedford, 132 N.H. 54, 563 A.2d 786, 1989 N.H. LEXIS 75 (1989); Asselin v. Town of Conway, 135 N.H. 576, 607 A.2d 132, 1992 N.H. LEXIS 83 (1992); Asselin v. Town of Conway, 137 N.H. 368, 628 A.2d 247, 1993 N.H. LEXIS 89 (1993); Hurley v. Town of Hollis, 143 N.H. 567, 729 A.2d 998, 1999 N.H. LEXIS 45 (1999); Simonsen v. Town of Derry, 145 N.H. 382, 765 A.2d 1033, 2000 N.H. LEXIS 73 (2000).

RESEARCH REFERENCES

New Hampshire Practice.

15 N.H.P. Land Use Planning and Zoning §§ 2.01, 3.03, 5.14, 7.14, 8.06, 12.03, 14.07, 15.02, 15.04, 15.07, 22.02, 24.12, 30.04, 35.15, 35.16.

New Hampshire Bar Journal.

For article, "The New Zoning Variance Cases: Analyzing Unnecessary Hardship Under RSA 674:33," see N.H.B.J. 40 (Fall 2005).

For article, "Regional Economic Desegregation: *Britton v. Town of Chester*," see 33 N.H.B.J. 486 (1992).

ALR.

Airport operations or flight of aircraft as constituting taking or damaging of property. 22 A.L.R.4th 863.

Applicability of zoning regulations to waste disposal facilities of state or local governmental entities. 59 A.L.R.3d 1244.

Application of zoning regulations to golf courses, swimming pools, tennis courts, or the like. 63 A.L.R.5th 607.

Application of zoning regulations to motels or motor courts. 23 A.L.R.3d 1210.

Application of zoning regulation to radio or television facilities. 81 A.L.R.3d 1086.

Construction and application of zoning laws setting minimum lot size requirements. 2 A.L.R.5th 553.

Construction and application of zoning regulations in connection with funeral homes. 92 A.L.R.3d 328.

Construction and effect of zoning provision permitting accessory use for "professional office." 24 A.L.R.3d 1128.

Exclusionary zoning. 48 A.L.R.3d 1210.

Housing facilities for former patients of mental hospital as violating zoning restrictions. 100 A.L.R.3d 876.

Local use zoning of wetlands or flood plain as taking without compensation. 19 A.L.R.4th 756.

Planned-unit, cluster, or greenbelt zoning. 43 A.L.R.3d 888.

Regulations creating and placing "floating zones". 80 A.L.R.3d 95.

Validity and construction of statute or ordinance regulating commercial video game enterprises. 38 A.L.R.4th 930.

Validity and construction of statute or ordinance regulating or prohibiting self-service gasoline filling stations. 46 A.L.R.3d 1393.

Validity and construction of zoning ordinance regulating architectural style or design of structure. 41 A.L.R.3d 1397.

Validity and construction of zoning ordinance requiring developer to devote specified part of development to low and moderate income housing. 62 A.L.R.3d 880.

Validity and construction of zoning regulation respecting permissible use as affected by division of lot or parcel by zone boundary line. 58 A.L.R.3d 1241.

Validity and construction of zoning regulations expressly referring to hospitals, sanitariums, nursing homes. 27 A.L.R.3d 1022.

Validity, construction, and application of zoning ordinance relating to operation of junkyard or scrap metal processing plant. 50 A.L.R.3D 837.

Validity of local beachfront zoning regulations designed to exclude recreational uses by persons other than beachfront residents. 18 A.L.R.4th 568.

Validity of ordinance restricting number of unrelated persons who can live together in residential zone. 12 A.L.R.4th 238.

Validity of ordinance zoning the entire municipality for residential use. 54 A.L.R.3d 1282.

Validity of "war-zone" ordinances restricting location of "adult entertainment" or sex-oriented businesses. 10 A.L.R.5th 538.

Validity of zoning for senior citizen communities. 83 A.L.R.3d 1084.

Validity of zoning laws setting minimum lot size requirements. 1 A.L.R.5th 622.

What constitutes "church," "religious use," or the like within zoning ordinance. 62 A.L.R.3d 197.

What constitutes "incidental" or "accessory" use of property zoned, and primarily used, for business or commercial purposes. 60 A.L.R.4th 907.

Zoning or licensing regulation prohibiting or restricting location of billiard rooms and bowling alleys. 100 A.L.R.3d 252.

Zoning regulation of intoxicating liquor as pre-empted by state law. 65 A.L.R.4th 555.

Zoning regulations as applied to homes or housing for the elderly. 83 A.L.R.3d 1103.

Zoning regulations as applied to private and parochial schools below the college level. 74 A.L.R.3d 14.

Zoning regulations as applied to public elementary and high schools. 74 A.L.R.3d 136.

Zoning regulations in relation to cemeteries. 96 A.L.R.3d 921.

Zoning regulations limiting use of property near airport as taking of property. 18 A.L.R.4th 542.

Zoning regulations prohibiting or limiting fences, hedges, or walls. 1 A.L.R.4th 373.

Zoning: residential off-street parking requirements. 71 A.L.R.4th 529.

Zoning: what constitutes "incidental" or "accessory" use of property zoned, and primarily used, for residential purposes. 54 A.L.R.4th 1034.

674:17. Purposes of Zoning Ordinances.

I. Every zoning ordinance shall be adopted in accordance with the requirements of RSA 674:18. Zoning ordinances shall be designed:

    (a) To lessen congestion in the streets;

    (b) To secure safety from fires, panic and other dangers;

    (c) To promote health and the general welfare;

    (d) To provide adequate light and air;

    (e) To prevent the overcrowding of land;

    (f) To avoid undue concentration of population;

    (g) To facilitate the adequate provision of transportation, solid waste facilities, water, sewerage, schools, parks, child day care;

    (h) To assure proper use of natural resources and other public requirements;

    (i) To encourage the preservation of agricultural lands and buildings; and

    (j) To encourage the installation and use of solar, wind, or other renewable energy systems and protect access to energy sources by the regulation of orientation of streets, lots, and buildings; establishment of maximum building height, minimum set back requirements, and limitations on type, height, and placement of vegetation; and encouragement of the use of solar skyspace easements under RSA 477. Zoning ordinances may establish buffer zones or additional districts which overlap existing districts and may further regulate the planting and trimming of vegetation on public and private property to protect access to renewable energy systems.

II. Every zoning ordinance shall be made with reasonable consideration to, among other things, the character of the area involved and its peculiar suitability for particular uses, as well as with a view to conserving the value of buildings and encouraging the most appropriate use of land throughout the municipality.

III. Except as provided in RSA 424:5 or RSA 422-B or in any other provision of Title XXXIX, no city, town, or county in which there are located unincorporated towns or unorganized places shall adopt a zoning ordinance or regulation with respect to antennas used exclusively in the amateur radio service that fails to conform to the limited federal preemption entitled Amateur Radio Preemption, 101 FCC 2nd 952 (1985) issued by the Federal Communications Commission.

Source.

  1983, 447:1. 1989, 42:2. 1995, 176:2, eff. Aug. 4, 1995. 2000, 279:2, eff. July 1, 2001. 2002, 73:2, eff. June 30, 2002.

Amendments

  —**2002.** Paragraph I: Made minor changes in phraseology in subpars. (h) and (i) and added subpar. (j).

  —**2000.** Paragraph I: Made minor stylistic changes in subpars. (g) and (h) and added subpar. (i).

  —**1995.** Paragraph III: Added.

  —**1989.** Paragraph I(g): Inserted "child day care" following "parks".

Purpose of 2000 amendment

  2000, 279:1, eff. July 1, 2001, provided: "The purpose of this act [which amended this section and added RSA 674:32-a–674:32-c], is to clarify the requirements of RSA 672:1, III-b, that farming and agriculture, as defined in RSA 21:34-a, shall not be unreasonably limited by the use of municipal planning and zoning powers."

Cross References.
Division of municipality into districts, see RSA 674:20.

Interim growth management regulations, see RSA 674:23.

Uses of innovative land controls, see RSA 674:21.

NOTES TO DECISIONS

Analysis

1. Generally
2. Construction
3. Validity of particular ordinances

1. Generally

Property could be zoned not only to present conditions but also to the requirements of probable and desirable growth. Kimball v. Blanchard, 90 N.H. 298, 7 A.2d 394, 1939 N.H. LEXIS 64 (1939); Edgewood Civic Club v. Blaisdell, 95 N.H. 244, 61 A.2d 517, 1948 N.H. LEXIS 228 (1948). (Decided under prior law.)

2. Construction

This section does not restrict zoning ordinances to be designed only for fire safety. Therefore, fact that antenna structure might not be a fire hazard did not exempt it from height limitation in town zoning ordinance. Carnie v. Town of Richmond, 139 N.H. 21, 648 A.2d 205, 1994 N.H. LEXIS 99 (1994).

3. Validity of particular ordinances

A town could restrict the density of occupancy of premises by a zoning regulation. Town of Durham v. White Enterprises, Inc., 115 N.H. 645, 348 A.2d 706, 1975 N.H. LEXIS 386 (1975). (Decided under prior law.)

A town could constitutionally restrict the density of occupancy of housing by unrelated persons while not restricting persons related by blood, marriage or adoption. Town of Durham v. White Enterprises, Inc., 115 N.H. 645, 348 A.2d 706, 1975 N.H. LEXIS 386 (1975). (Decided under prior law.)

Zoning as residential all properties in a town not zoned as commercial or industrial was valid where the bulk of the land in the town, apart from the sections zoned for business and industry, was rural, used primarily for farming and residential purposes, since it took into account the character of the area involved and its peculiar suitability for particular uses and encouraged the most appropriate use of land. Hudson v. Paradise, 101 N.H. 389, 143 A.2d 421, 1958 N.H. LEXIS 46 (1958). (Decided under prior law.)

The fact that a city might have enacted special regulations for fire protection did not estop it from enacting zoning regulations with a view to securing safety from fire. Sullivan v. Anglo-American Investment Trust, 89 N.H. 112, 193 A. 225, 1937 N.H. LEXIS 22 (1937). (Decided under prior law.)

A zoning regulation requiring that auxiliary buildings, including garages, stables and the like, be placed upon the rear half of the lot was permissible. Sundeen v. Rogers, 83 N.H. 253, 141 A. 142, 1928 N.H. LEXIS 11, 57 A.L.R. 950 (1928). (Decided under prior law.)

Cited:
Cited in Town of Chesterfield v. Brooks, 126 N.H. 64, 489 A.2d 600, 1985 N.H. LEXIS 274 (1985); Treisman v. Town of Bedford, 132 N.H. 54, 563 A.2d 786, 1989 N.H. LEXIS 75 (1989); Buskey v. Town of Hanover, 133 N.H. 318, 577 A.2d 406, 1990 N.H. LEXIS 67 (1990); Asselin v. Town of Conway, 137 N.H. 368, 628 A.2d 247, 1993 N.H. LEXIS 89 (1993).

RESEARCH REFERENCES

New Hampshire Practice.
15 N.H.P. Land Use Planning and Zoning §§ 2.01, 2.02, 2.11, 3.01, 17.02, 24.12.

ALR.
Validity of zoning laws setting minimum lot size requirements. 1 A.L.R.5th 622.

674:18. Adoption of Zoning Ordinance.

The local legislative body may adopt a zoning ordinance under RSA 674:16 only after the planning board has adopted the mandatory sections of the master plan as described in RSA 674:2, I and II.

Source.
1983, 447:1, eff. Jan. 1, 1984. 2002, 178:4, eff. July 14, 2002.

Amendments
—2002. Substituted "mandatory sections" for "general statement of objectives and the land use section" preceding "of the master".

Cross References.
Growth management ordinances, see RSA 674:22, 23.
Innovative land use control ordinances, see RSA 674:21.

NOTES TO DECISIONS

Substantial compliance
Based on doctrine of substantial compliance, otherwise proper amendment to zoning ordinance would not be invalidated based on planning board's failure to certify its master plan. Treisman v. Town of Bedford, 132 N.H. 54, 563 A.2d 786, 1989 N.H. LEXIS 75 (1989).

Cited:
Cited in Hurley v. Town of Hollis, 143 N.H. 567, 729 A.2d 998, 1999 N.H. LEXIS 45 (1999).

RESEARCH REFERENCES

New Hampshire Practice.
15 N.H.P. Land Use Planning and Zoning §§ 2.02, 3.03, 3.04.

674:19. Applicability of Zoning Ordinance.

A zoning ordinance adopted under RSA 674:16 shall not apply to existing structures or to the existing use of any building. It shall apply to any alteration of a building for use for a purpose or in a manner which is substantially different from the use to which it was put before alteration.

Source.
1983, 447:1, eff. Jan. 1, 1984.

Cross References.
Authority to adopt or amend ordinances generally, see RSA 674:16.

Emergency temporary zoning and planning ordinance, see RSA 674:24 et seq.
Interim growth management ordinances, see RSA 674:23.

NOTES TO DECISIONS

Analysis

1. Generally
2. Construction
3. Nonconforming uses
4. Ordinances in compliance
5. Changes in use
6. Particular cases

1. Generally
Nonconforming uses were protected by the statute as well as by the New Hampshire Constitution. Town of Hampton v. Brust, 122 N.H. 463, 446 A.2d 458, 1982 N.H. LEXIS 375 (1982). (Decided under prior law.)
The past use of land might create certain rights to a similar use in the future, and the

413

statute protected an existing use not conforming to later ordinances. Flanagan v. Town of Hollis, 112 N.H. 222, 293 A.2d 328, 1972 N.H. LEXIS 181 (1972). (Decided under prior law.)

2. Construction

Signs were "structures" within the meaning of the provision of this section exempting "existing structures" from regulation through zoning ordinances. Dugas v. Town of Conway, 125 N.H. 175, 480 A.2d 71, 1984 N.H. LEXIS 359 (1984). (Decided under prior law.)

3. Nonconforming uses

The right to maintain nonconforming uses is meant to protect property owners from a retrospective application of zoning ordinances, so that property owners may continue using and enjoying their property when their uses were lawful prior to the enactment of a zoning ordinance. Town of Salem v. Wickson, 146 N.H. 328, 770 A.2d 1120, 2001 N.H. LEXIS 79 (2001).

An established use of land is not disturbed by a subsequent land restriction; to qualify for such protection, a nonconforming use must lawfully exist at time restriction is adopted, and have continually existed since that time. Town of Seabrook v. Vachon Mgmt., Inc., 144 N.H. 660, 745 A.2d 1155, 2000 N.H. LEXIS 7 (2000).

Well established policy of zoning law is to carefully limit enlargement and extension of nonconforming uses, and to reduce them to conformity as completely and rapidly as possible. Hurley v. Town of Hollis, 143 N.H. 567, 729 A.2d 998, 1999 N.H. LEXIS 45 (1999).

Trial court did not err in concluding that use of theater for live performances was substantially different than use of theater to show movies, and that live entertainment was not a preexisting, nonconforming use of property. Conforti v. City of Manchester, 141 N.H. 78, 677 A.2d 147, 1996 N.H. LEXIS 52 (1996).

A zoning ordinance does not apply to a preexisting use unless that use is altered for a purpose or in a manner which is substantially different from the use to which it was put before alteration; when determining whether a nonconforming use is protected, the court will bear in mind that the creation of a nonconforming use depends upon the configuration of specific facts at a certain point in time and, therefore, in order to determine how much a nonconforming use may be expanded or changed, the court will look to the facts existing when the noncon-

forming use was created. Ray's Stateline Market, Inc. v. Town of Pelham, 140 N.H. 139, 665 A.2d 1068, 1995 N.H. LEXIS 111 (1995).

A market owner was properly granted permits to move a coffee counter and to change two sign faces since a permit to build a new coffee counter would not result in a substantial change or an illegal expansion of the nonconforming use and the sign permit would not result in any appreciable effect on the neighborhood. Ray's Stateline Market, Inc. v. Town of Pelham, 140 N.H. 139, 665 A.2d 1068, 1995 N.H. LEXIS 111 (1995).

The right to continue a previously lawful use of one's property after enactment of a zoning ordinance that prohibits such use is a vested right recognized by this section. New London Land Use Ass'n v. New London Zoning Bd. of Adjustment, 130 N.H. 510, 543 A.2d 1385, 1988 N.H. LEXIS 39 (1988).

Nonconforming uses relate to conditions which exist prior to the time a zoning ordinance is passed. New London Land Use Ass'n v. New London Zoning Bd. of Adjustment, 130 N.H. 510, 543 A.2d 1385, 1988 N.H. LEXIS 39 (1988).

4. Ordinances in compliance

Town clearly intended its zoning amendment to codify, not deviate from, existing law concerning expansion of nonconforming uses, and superior court correctly applied this recognized standard in reviewing board's grant of special exception. Hurley v. Town of Hollis, 143 N.H. 567, 729 A.2d 998, 1999 N.H. LEXIS 45 (1999).

A zoning ordinance would be construed to be consistent with the statute as limiting any "extension," "expansion," or "enlargement" of a nonconforming use and prohibiting its change to a "substantially different" nonconforming use. Ray's Stateline Market, Inc. v. Town of Pelham, 140 N.H. 139, 665 A.2d 1068, 1995 N.H. LEXIS 111 (1995).

5. Changes in use

Because the general policy of zoning law is to carefully limit the extension and enlargement of nonconforming uses, provisions that permit the continuance of such uses are strictly construed, and the party asserting that a proposed use is not new or impermissible bears the burden of proof. Town of Salem v. Wickson, 146 N.H. 328, 770 A.2d 1120, 2001 N.H. LEXIS 79 (2001).

An extension and enlargement that substantially changes the nature and purpose of a nonconforming use is impermissible. Town of Salem v. Wickson, 146 N.H. 328, 770 A.2d 1120, 2001 N.H. LEXIS 79 (2001).

Considerations in determining whether there has been a substantial change in the nature or purpose of a preexisting nonconforming use are: (1) the extent the use in question reflects the nature and purpose of the prevailing nonconforming use; (2) whether the use at issue is merely a different manner of utilizing the same use or constitutes a use different in character, nature, and kind; and (3) whether the use will have a substantially different effect on the neighborhood. Town of Salem v. Wickson, 146 N.H. 328, 770 A.2d 1120, 2001 N.H. LEXIS 79 (2001).

Where, at the time a zoning ordinance was enacted, the nature and purpose of a nonconforming use was for pig farming and the stockpiling of manure and earthen materials was incidental thereto, after the property owner abandoned pig farming, and started stockpiling material brought in from off-site, he changed the character and nature of that activity, and the trial court's finding that the nonconforming use had remained essentially unchanged was not supported by the evidence. Town of Salem v. Wickson, 146 N.H. 328, 770 A.2d 1120, 2001 N.H. LEXIS 79 (2001).

Test for expansion of a nonconforming use, where expanded use is determined to be not "substantially different" from existing use, is a more restrictive test than that used to determine "changes of use" sufficient to trigger site plan review. Town of Seabrook v. Vachon Mgmt., Inc., 144 N.H. 660, 745 A.2d 1155, 2000 N.H. LEXIS 7 (2000).

Change in use of leased unit, from a computer retail establishment to a venue for mud wrestling, was effected without required site plan approval and was thus illegal, and therefore the change in use was ineligible to later qualify as a lawful nonconforming use. Town of Seabrook v. Vachon Mgmt., Inc., 144 N.H. 660, 745 A.2d 1155, 2000 N.H. LEXIS 7 (2000).

6. Particular cases

A mere plan to reopen a store, a plan in no way implemented, was not an "existing use" within the meaning of the provision that zoning ordinances were not to apply to existing structures nor to the existing use of any building. Wunderlich v. Town of Webster, 117 N.H. 283, 371 A.2d 1177, 1977 N.H. LEXIS 320 (1977). (Decided under prior law.)

Since the legislature did not give towns authority to regulate existing structures, including large, off-premises signs, a town lacked the power to apply a zoning ordinance requiring removal of all existing nonconforming signs. Town of Jackson v. Town and Country Motor Inn, Inc., 120 N.H. 699, 422 A.2d 1034, 1980 N.H. LEXIS 381 (1980). (Decided under prior law.)

Cited:

Cited in Town of Goffstown v. Thibeault, 129 N.H. 454, 529 A.2d 930, 1987 N.H. LEXIS 184 (1987); Blue Jay Realty Trust v. City of Franklin, 132 N.H. 502, 567 A.2d 188, 1989 N.H. LEXIS 128 (1989); Cohen v. Town of Henniker, 134 N.H. 425, 593 A.2d 1145, 1991 N.H. LEXIS 78 (1991); Conforti v. City of Manchester, 141 N.H. 78, 677 A.2d 147, 1996 N.H. LEXIS 52 (1996); Peabody v. Town of Windham, 142 N.H. 488, 703 A.2d 886, 1997 N.H. LEXIS 121 (1997); North Country Envtl. Servs., Inc. v. Town of Bethlehem, 146 N.H. 348, 772 A.2d 330, 2001 N.H. LEXIS 85 (2001).

RESEARCH REFERENCES

New Hampshire Practice.

15 N.H.P. Land Use Planning and Zoning §§ 2.18, 3.01, 8.02, 8.06, 11.01, 29.03.

New Hampshire Bar Journal.

For article, "'Grandfathered'—The Law of Nonconforming Uses and Vested Rights," see 31 N.H.B.J. 17 (1990).

ALR.

Addition of another activity to existing nonconforming use as violation of zoning ordinance. 61 A.L.R.4th 724.

Alteration, extension, reconstruction, or repair of nonconforming structure or structure devoted to nonconforming use as violation of zoning ordinance. 63 A.L.R.4th 275.

Building in course of construction as establishing valid nonconforming use or vested right to complete construction for intended use. 89 A.L.R.3d 1051.

Change in the type of activity of nonconforming use as violation of zoning ordinance. 61 A.L.R.4th 902.

Change in volume, intensity, or means of performing nonconforming use as violation of zoning ordinance. 61 A.L.R.4th 806.

Classification and maintenance of advertising structures as nonconforming use. 80 A.L.R.3d 630.

Construction of new building or structure on premises devoted to nonconforming use as violation of zoning ordinance. 10 A.L.R.4th 1122.

Retroactive effect of zoning regulation in absence of saving clause, on pending application for building permit. 50 A.L.R.3d 596.

Retroactive effect of zoning regulation, in absence of saving clause, on validly-issued building permit. 49 A.L.R.3d 13.

Right to repair or reconstruct building operating as nonconforming use, after damage or destruction by fire or other casualty. 57 A.L.R.3d 419.

Right to resume nonconforming use of premises after involuntary break in the continuity of nonconforming use caused by difficulties unrelated to governmental activity. 56 A.L.R.3d 14.

Zoning provisions protecting landowners who applied for or received building permit prior to change in zoning. 49 A.L.R.3d 1150.

674:20. Districts.

In order to accomplish any or all of the purposes of a zoning ordinance enumerated under RSA 674:17, the local legislative body may divide the municipality into districts of a number, shape and area as may be deemed best suited to carry out the purposes of RSA 674:17. The local legislative body may regulate and restrict the erection, construction, reconstruction, alteration, repair, or use of buildings, structures, or land within each district which it creates. All regulations shall be uniform for each class or kind of buildings throughout each district, but the regulations in one district may differ from those in other districts.

Source.
1983, 447:1, eff. Jan. 1, 1984.

Cross References.
Authority to adopt or amend ordinances generally, see RSA 674:16.

Historic districts generally, see RSA 674:45 et seq.

Subdivisions generally, see RSA 674:35 et seq.

NOTES TO DECISIONS

Analysis

1. Construction
2. Creation of districts

1. Construction

The provisions of the section were permissive rather than mandatory, and the establishment of a single district for zoning purposes would not for that reason alone invalidate a zoning ordinance. Town of Plainfield v. Hood, 108 N.H. 502, 240 A.2d 60, 1968 N.H. LEXIS 200 (1968). (Decided under prior law.)

2. Creation of districts

The fact that there was but one district did not invalidate a zoning ordinance. Gutoski v. Town of Winchester, 114 N.H. 414, 322 A.2d 4, 1974 N.H. LEXIS 289 (1974). (Decided under prior law.)

The proper zoning of an area as residential would not be affected by any invalid spot zoning of an adjoining area. Mater v. City of Dover, 97 N.H. 13, 79 A.2d 844, 1951 N.H. LEXIS 4 (1951). (Decided under prior law.)

The requirement that a zoning regulation be made in accordance with a comprehensive plan required zoning to be by districts and not be individual pieces of property. Edgewood Civic Club v. Blaisdell, 95 N.H. 244, 61 A.2d 517, 1948 N.H. LEXIS 228 (1948). (Decided under prior law.)

A zoning ordinance did not comply with the statute unless the classification was by districts and not by individual pieces of property. Kimball v. Blanchard, 90 N.H. 298, 7 A.2d 394, 1939 N.H. LEXIS 64 (1939). (Decided under prior law.)

RESEARCH REFERENCES

New Hampshire Practice.
  15 N.H.P. Land Use Planning and Zoning §§ 2.01, 2.11.

ALR.
Validity and construction of zoning regula-

tion respecting permissible use as affected by division of lot or parcel by zone boundary line. 58 A.L.R.3d 1241.

674:21. Innovative Land Use Controls.

I. Innovative land use controls may include, but are not limited to:
  (a) Timing incentives.
  (b) Phased development.
  (c) Intensity and use incentive.
  (d) Transfer of density and development rights.
  (e) Planned unit development.
  (f) Cluster development.
  (g) Impact zoning.
  (h) Performance standards.
  (i) Flexible and discretionary zoning.
  (j) Environmental characteristics zoning.
  (k) Inclusionary zoning.
  (l) Accessory dwelling unit standards.
  (m) Impact fees.
  (n) Village plan alternative subdivision.

II. An innovative land use control adopted under RSA 674:16 may be required when supported by the master plan and shall contain within it the standards which shall guide the person or board which administers the ordinance. An innovative land use control ordinance may provide for administration, including the granting of conditional or special use permits, by the planning board, board of selectmen, zoning board of adjustment, or such other person or board as the ordinance may designate. If the administration of the innovative provisions of the ordinance is not vested in the planning board, any proposal submitted under this section shall be reviewed by the planning board prior to final consideration by the administrator. In such a case, the planning board shall set forth its comments on the proposal in writing and the administrator shall, to the extent that the planning board's comments are not directly incorporated into its decision, set forth its findings and decisions on the planning board's comments.

III. Innovative land use controls must be adopted in accordance with RSA 675:1, II.

IV. As used in this section:

  (a) "Inclusionary zoning" means land use control regulations which provide a voluntary incentive or benefit to a property owner in order to induce the property owner to produce housing units which are affordable to persons or families of low and moderate income. Inclusionary zoning includes, but is not limited to, density bonuses, growth control exemptions, and a streamlined application process.

(b) "Accessory dwelling unit" means a second dwelling unit, attached or detached, which is permitted by a land use control regulation to be located on the same lot, plat, site, or other division of land as the permitted principal dwelling unit.

V. As used in this section "impact fee" means a fee or assessment imposed upon development, including subdivision, building construction or other land use change, in order to help meet the needs occasioned by that development for the construction or improvement of capital facilities owned or operated by the municipality, including and limited to water treatment and distribution facilities; wastewater treatment and disposal facilities; sanitary sewers; storm water, drainage and flood control facilities; public road systems and rights-of-way; municipal office facilities; public school facilities; the municipality's proportional share of capital facilities of a cooperative or regional school district of which the municipality is a member; public safety facilities; solid waste collection, transfer, recycling, processing and disposal facilities; public library facilities; and public recreational facilities not including public open space. No later than July 1, 1993, all impact fee ordinances shall be subject to the following:

(a) The amount of any such fee shall be a proportional share of municipal capital improvement costs which is reasonably related to the capital needs created by the development, and to the benefits accruing to the development from the capital improvements financed by the fee. Upgrading of existing facilities and infrastructures, the need for which is not created by new development, shall not be paid for by impact fees.

(b) In order for a municipality to adopt an impact fee ordinance, it must have enacted a capital improvements program pursuant to RSA 674:5-7.

(c) Any impact fee shall be accounted for separately, shall be segregated from the municipality's general fund, may be spent upon order of the municipal governing body, shall be exempt from all provisions of RSA 32 relative to limitation and expenditure of town moneys, and shall be used solely for the capital improvements for which it was collected, or to recoup the cost of capital improvements made in anticipation of the needs which the fee was collected to meet.

(d) All impact fees imposed pursuant to this section shall be assessed at the time of planning board approval of a subdivision plat or site plan. When no planning board approval is required, or has been made prior to the adoption or amendment of the impact fee ordinance, impact fees shall be assessed prior to, or as a condition for, the issuance of a building permit or other appropriate permission to proceed with development. Impact fees shall be intended to reflect the effect of development upon municipal facilities at the time of the issuance of the building permit. Impact fees shall be collected at the time a certificate of occupancy is issued. If no certificate of occupancy is required, impact fees shall be collected when the development is ready for its intended use. Nothing in this subparagraph shall prevent the municipality and the assessed party from establishing an alternate, mutually acceptable schedule of payment of impact fees in effect at the time of subdivision plat or site plan approval by the planning board. If an alternate schedule of payment is established, municipalities may require developers to post bonds, issue letters of credit, accept liens, or otherwise provide suitable measures of security so as to guarantee future payment of the assessed impact fees.

(e) The ordinance shall establish reasonable times after which any portion of an impact fee which has not become encumbered or otherwise legally bound to be spent for the purpose for which it was collected shall be refunded, with any accrued interest. Whenever the calculation of an impact fee has been predicated upon some portion of capital improvement costs being borne by the municipality, a refund shall be made upon the failure of the legislative body to appropriate the municipality's share of the capital improvement costs within a reasonable time. The maximum time which shall be considered reasonable hereunder shall be 6 years.

(f) Unless otherwise specified in the ordinance, any decision under an impact fee ordinance may be appealed in the same manner provided by statute for appeals from the officer or board making that decision, as set forth in RSA 676:5, RSA 677:2–14, or RSA 677:15, respectively.

(g) The ordinance may also provide for a waiver process, including the criteria for the granting of such a waiver.

(h) The adoption of a growth management limitation or moratorium by a municipality shall not affect any development with respect to which an impact fee has been paid or assessed as part of the approval for that development.

(i) Neither the adoption of an impact fee ordinance, nor the failure to adopt such an ordinance, shall be deemed to affect existing authority of a planning board over subdivision or site plan review, except to the extent expressly stated in such an ordinance.

(j) The failure to adopt an impact fee ordinance shall not preclude a municipality from requiring developers to pay an exaction for the cost of off-site improvement needs determined by the planning board to be necessary for the occupancy of any portion of a development. For the purposes of this subparagraph, "off-site improvements" means those improvements that are necessitated by a development but which are located outside the boundaries of the property that is subject to a subdivision plat or site plan approval by the planning board. Such off-site improvements shall be limited to any necessary highway, drainage, and sewer and water upgrades pertinent to that development. The amount of any such exaction shall be a proportional share of municipal improvement costs not previously assessed against other developments, which is necessitated by the development, and which is reasonably related to the benefits accruing to the development from the improvements financed by the exaction. As an alternative to paying an exaction, the developer may elect to construct the necessary improvements, subject to bonding and timing conditions as may be reasonably required by the planning board. Any exaction imposed pursuant to this section shall be assessed at the time of planning board approval of the development necessitating an off-site improvement. Whenever the calculation of an exaction for an off-site improvement has been predicated upon some portion of the cost of that improvement being borne by the municipality, a refund of any collected exaction shall be made to the payor or payor's successor in interest upon the failure of the local legislative body to appropriate the municipality's share of that cost within 6 years from the date of collection. For the purposes of this subparagraph, failure of local legislative body to appropriate such funding or to construct any necessary off-site improvement shall not operate to prohibit an otherwise approved development.

VI. (a) In this section, "village plan alternative" means an optional land use control and subdivision regulation to provide a means of promoting a more efficient and cost effective method of land development. The village plan alternative's purpose is to encourage the preservation of open space wherever possible. The village plan alternative subdivision is meant to encourage beneficial consolidation of land development to permit the efficient layout of less costly to maintain roads, utilities, and other public and private infrastructures; to improve the ability of political subdivisions to provide more rapid and efficient delivery of public safety and school transportation services as community growth occurs; and finally, to provide owners of private property with a method for realizing the inherent development value of their real property in a manner conducive to the creation of substantial benefit to the environment and to the political subdivision's property tax base.

(b) An owner of record wishing to utilize the village plan alternative in the subdivision and development of a parcel of land, by locating the entire density permitted by the existing land use regulations of the political subdivision within which the property is located, on 20 percent or less of the entire parcel available for development, shall provide to the political subdivision within which the property is located, as a condition of approval, a recorded easement reserving the remaining land area of the entire, original lot, solely for agriculture, forestry, and conservation, or for public recreation. The recorded easement shall limit any new construction on the remainder lot to structures associated with farming operations, forest management operations, and conservation uses. Public recreational uses shall be subject to the written approval of those abutters whose property lies within the village plan alternative subdivision portion of the project at the time when such a public use is proposed.

(c) The submission and approval procedure for a village plan alternative subdivision shall be the same as that for a conventional subdivision. Existing zoning and subdivision regulations relating to emergency access, fire prevention, and public health and safety concerns including any setback requirement for wells, septic systems, or wetland requirement imposed by the department of environmental services shall apply to the developed portion of a village plan alternative subdivision, but lot size regulations and dimensional requirements having to do with frontage and setbacks measured from all new property lot lines, and lot size regulations, as well as density regulations, shall not apply.

(1) The total density of development within a village plan alternate subdivision shall not exceed the total potential development density permitted a conventional subdivision of the entire original lot unless provisions

contained within the political subdivision's land use regulations provide a basis for increasing the permitted density of development within a village plan alternative subdivision.

(2) In no case shall a political subdivision impose lesser density requirements upon a village plan alternative subdivision than the density requirements imposed on a conventional subdivision.

(d) If the total area of a proposed village plan alternative subdivision including all roadways and improvements does not exceed 20 percent of the total land area of the undeveloped lot, and if the proposed subdivision incorporates the total sum of all proposed development as permitted by local regulation on the undeveloped lot, all existing and future dimensional requirements imposed by local regulation, including lot size, shall not apply to the proposed village plan alternative subdivision.

(e) The approving authority may increase, at existing property lines, the setback to new construction within a village plan alternative subdivision by up to 2 times the distance required by current zoning or subdivision regulations, subject to the provisions of subparagraph (c).

(f) Within a village plan alternative subdivision, the exterior wall construction of buildings shall meet or exceed the requirements for fire-rated construction described by the fire prevention and building codes being enforced by the state of New Hampshire at the date and time the property owner of record files a formal application for subdivision approval with the political subdivision having jurisdiction of the project. Exterior walls and openings of new buildings shall also conform to fire protective provisions of all other building codes in force in the political subdivision. Wherever building code or fire prevention code requirements for exterior wall construction appear to be in conflict, the more stringent building or fire prevention code requirements shall apply.

Source.
1983, 447:1. 1988, 149:1, 2. 1991, 283:1, 2. 1992, 42:1. 1994, 278:1, eff. Aug. 5, 1994. 2002, 236:1, 2, eff. July 16, 2002. 2004, 71:1, 2, eff. July 6, 2004; 199:2, eff. June 1, 2005; 199:3, eff. June 7, 2004. 2005, 61:1, 2, eff. July 22, 2005.

Amendments
—**2005.** Paragraph VI(c)–(e): Rewritten to the extent that a detailed comparison would be impracticable.
Paragraph VI(f): Added.

—**2004.** Paragraph I(d): Inserted "density and" preceding "development" by ch. 71.
Paragraph II: Inserted "may be required when supported by the master plan and" in the first sentence by ch. 71.
Paragraph V(d): Rewritten to the extent that a detailed comparison would be impracticable by ch. 199.

Paragraph V(j): Added by ch. 199.

—**2002.** Paragraph I(n): Added.
Paragraph VI: Added.

—**1994.** Paragraph V: Inserted "the municipality's proportional share of capital facilities of a cooperative or regional school district of which the municipality is a member" preceding "public safety" in the first sentence of the introductory paragraph.

—**1992.** Paragraph V(i): Deleted the former first sentence.

—**1991.** Paragraph I: Made minor changes in punctuation in subpars. (a)–(j), deleted "and" following "zoning" in subpar. (k), and added subpar. (m).
Paragraph V: Added.

—**1988.** Paragraph I: Deleted "and" following "zoning" at the end of subpar. (i), made a minor stylistic change at the end of subpar. (j) and added subpars. (k) and (*l*).

Paragraph IV: Added.

Cross References.

Growth management ordinances, see RSA 674:22, 23.

Purposes of zoning ordinances generally, see RSA 674:17.

Subdivision regulation, see RSA 674:35 et seq.

NOTES TO DECISIONS

Analysis

1. Impact fees
2. Growth management ordinances

1. Impact fees

Ordinances that authorized local planning boards to adjust impact fees according to statistical models widely used in New Hampshire contained sufficient standards for adjustments so as to fall within the parameters of a statutory delegation of power. Caparco v. Town of Danville, 152 N.H. 722, 886 A.2d 1045, 2005 N.H. LEXIS 163 (2005).

Because town had not enacted an impact fee ordinance, it lacked authority to condition site plan approval on zoning applicants' payment

for off-site improvements. Simonsen v. Town of Derry, 145 N.H. 382, 765 A.2d 1033, 2000 N.H. LEXIS 73 (2000).

2. Growth management ordinances

Supreme court reversed judgment that held town could not impose both impact fee and growth management ordinances on housing developer; under RSA 674:21, V(h) the growth management ordinance could be imposed since the impact fee had been neither paid nor assessed; neither the town's preliminary estimate of the impact fee nor its receiving an application in which fees were represented constituted a RSA 674:21, V(h) assessment. Monahan-Fortin Props. v. Town of Hudson, 148 N.H. 769, 813 A.2d 523, 2002 N.H. LEXIS 214 (2002).

RESEARCH REFERENCES

New Hampshire Practice.

15 N.H.P. Land Use Planning and Zoning §§ 2.01, 4.02, 15.07, 17.02, 17.05, 18.01, 19.03, 22.02, 26.03, 31.05.

New Hampshire Bar Journal.

For article, "Lex Loci: A Survey of New Hampshire Supreme Court Decisions," see

N.H.B.J. 52 (Winter 2006).

For article, "Municipal Exactions for Development in New Hampshire," see 34 N.H.B.J. 14 (June 1993).

ALR.

Regulations creating and placing "floating zones". 80 A.L.R.3d 95.

674:21-a. Development Restrictions Enforceable.

Any open space designation or other development restriction which is part of a cluster development, planned unit development, village plan alternative subdivision, or other proposal approved under innovative land use controls, or which is lawfully imposed by a local land use board as a condition of subdivision, site plan, variance, or other type of approval, and which has been filed in the records of the local land use board in accordance with its established procedure, shall be deemed to create a conservation restriction as defined in RSA 477:45, I, which shall run with the land, and shall be enforceable by the municipality, or by the owner of any property which would be specially damaged by the violation of such restriction, regardless of whether any deed or other instrument conveying such restriction has been executed or recorded. For purposes of this section, an applicant's statement of intent to restrict development, submitted with or contained in an application which is subsequently approved, shall be deemed a condition of the approval.

Source.
1988, 149:3, eff. June 20, 1988. 2002, 236:3, eff. July 16, 2002.

Amendments
—**2002.** Inserted "village plan alternative

subdivision" following "planned unit development" near the beginning of the first sentence.

RESEARCH REFERENCES

New Hampshire Practice.
15 N.H.P. Land Use Planning and Zoning §§ 18.03, 32.11, 38.06.

674:22. Growth Management; Timing of Development.

The local legislative body may further exercise the powers granted under this subdivision to regulate and control the timing of development. Any ordinance imposing such a control may be adopted only after preparation and adoption by the planning board of a master plan and a capital improvement program and shall be based upon a growth management process intended to assess and balance community development needs and consider regional development needs.

Source.
1983, 447:1, eff. Jan. 1, 1984.

Revision note.
In the second sentence, inserted "plan" following "master" for purposes of clarity.

Cross References.
Authority to adopt or amend ordinances generally, see RSA 674:16.

Capital improvements programs generally, see RSA 674:5 et seq.
Innovative land use controls, see RSA 674:21.
Interim growth management ordinances, see RSA 674:23.
Master plans generally, see RSA 674:1 et seq.

NOTES TO DECISIONS

Analysis
1. Generally
2. Effect of master plan
3. Validity of particular ordinances or plans

1. Generally
This section and RSA 674:23 enable a municipality to adopt an ordinance providing for controlled growth after its planning board has adopted a master plan and a capital improvement program designed to assess and balance community and regional development needs. Rancourt v. Town of Barnstead, 129 N.H. 45, 523 A.2d 55, 1986 N.H. LEXIS 379 (1986).

Growth control ordinances are intended to

regulate and control the timing of development, not the prevention of development. Stoney-Brook Development Corp. v. Town of Fremont, 124 N.H. 583, 474 A.2d 561, 1984 N.H. LEXIS 348 (1984). (Decided under prior law).

2. Effect of master plan
Comprehensive growth control planning assesses and balances the development concerns of the entire community, with less emphasis on the interests of any one particular landowner. Ettlingen Homes v. Town of Derry, 141 N.H. 296, 681 A.2d 97, 1996 N.H. LEXIS 93 (1996).

A planning board may not apply a master plan itself to limit development; it may only apply ordinances adopted pursuant to this section or RSA 674:23 to regulate or control the timing of development. Rancourt v. Town of Barnstead, 129 N.H. 45, 523 A.2d 55, 1986 N.H. LEXIS 379 (1986).

A municipal planning board cannot deny approval of a proposed subdivision on the basis of growth control rates set in a master plan without the municipality's first having enacted an ordinance providing for growth management or the board's having itself enacted a capital improvement program. Rancourt v. Town of Barnstead, 129 N.H. 45, 523 A.2d 55, 1986 N.H. LEXIS 379 (1986).

3. Validity of particular ordinances or plans

A zoning ordinance which required a minimum lot size of 50 acres in a mountain and forest district was not designed to regulate and control the timing of development in the town and, therefore, the statute was not applicable to the plaintiffs' challenge to the ordinance. Caspersen v. Town of Lyme, 139 N.H. 637, 661 A.2d 759, 1995 N.H. LEXIS 70 (1995).

A growth rate of 3% in an article of a town zoning ordinance, enacted in 1975, which required that the number of building permits issued for new dwellings be limited annually to 3% of the number of dwellings in the town at the start of each calendar year, and which limited the number of permits to three per year for each developer or within a subdivision, was an arbitrary figure when it was selected in 1975 as the standard for limitation of new dwelling permits, and selection of an apparently arbitrary figure representing the growth rate at a particular point in time hardly constituted the assessment of community development needs and "careful study" contemplated by either the supreme court's decision in Beck v. Town of Raymond, 118 NH 793, 394 A.2d 847, 1978 N.H. LEXIS 296 (1978), or this section. Stoney-Brook Development Corp. v. Town of Fremont, 124 N.H. 583, 474 A.2d 561, 1984 N.H. LEXIS 348 (1984). (Decided under prior law).

Where a town's community plan, adopted in 1980, assumed a 3% growth rate that had been established in a zoning ordinance adopted in 1975, and where nothing in the record indicated that the community plan committee had made an independent determination that 3% would have been the growth rate unrestricted

by the ordinance itself, the plan was invalid since the appropriateness of any particular growth restriction is premised on a determination of the normal growth rate. Stoney-Brook Development Corp. v. Town of Fremont, 124 N.H. 583, 474 A.2d 561, 1984 N.H. LEXIS 348 (1984). (Decided under prior law).

The record amply supported a master's finding that a town's comprehensive community plan was not a master plan or capital improvement program legally sufficient to support a growth control ordinance enacted pursuant to this section, and that the article of the town's zoning ordinance which required that the number of building permits issued for new dwellings be limited annually to 3% of the number of dwellings in the town at the start of each calendar year, and which limited the number of permits to three per year for each developer or within a subdivision, was illegal and unenforceable since the 3% growth rate was an arbitrary figure when it was selected in 1975 as the standard for the limitation of new dwelling building permits and did not constitute the assessment of community development needs and "careful study" contemplated by either the supreme court's decision in Beck v. Town of Raymond, 118 NH 793, 394 A.2d 847, 1978 N.H. LEXIS 296 (1978), or this section; since the community plan, adopted in 1980, perpetuated the growth rate at that arbitrary figure with no independent determination that 3% would have been the growth rate unrestricted by the ordinance itself; since the plan failed to address the ultimate objective of relaxing or ending growth controls and to articulate the means to accomplish that goal; and since it was unrealistic to suggest that limiting the town's growth indefinitely to 3% per year was guiding the town's growth, as expressed in its community plan, in a "reasonable, responsible and conscientious manner" when, by its own figures, the average growth in the seven abutting towns was almost double that growth rate. Stoney-Brook Development Corp. v. Town of Fremont, 124 N.H. 583, 474 A.2d 561, 1984 N.H. LEXIS 348 (1984). (Decided under prior law).

Cited:

Cited in Zukis v. Town of Fitzwilliam, 135 N.H. 384, 604 A.2d 956, 1992 N.H. LEXIS 46 (1992); Quinlan v. City of Dover, 136 N.H. 226, 614 A.2d 1057, 1992 N.H. LEXIS 159 (1992).

RESEARCH REFERENCES

New Hampshire Practice.
15 N.H.P. Land Use Planning and Zoning
§§ 2.01, 3.04, 4.02, 14.03, 15.02, 15.04–15.06.

ALR.
Validity of zoning ordinance deferring resi-

dential development until establishment of
public services in area. 63 A.L.R.3d 1184.

674:23. Growth Management; Interim Regulation.

I. In unusual circumstances requiring prompt attention and for the purpose of developing or altering a growth management process under RSA 674:22, or a master plan or capital improvement program, a city, town, or county in which there are located unincorporated towns or unorganized places may adopt an ordinance imposing interim regulations upon development as provided in this section.

II. An interim regulation may be proposed by the planning board if it determines that the requirements of paragraph I exist and makes findings of fact so indicating. Any such proposal shall be submitted to the local legislative body as a zoning ordinance and shall be subject to all procedures and provisions relative to enactment of zoning ordinances except that:

(a) There shall be at least one hearing on the interim regulation held by the planning board at which parties in interest and citizens shall have an opportunity to be heard. At least 10 days' notice of the time and place of the hearing shall be published in a paper of general circulation in the municipality, and a legal notice of the hearing shall also be given in accordance with RSA 675:7. The notice shall include either the text or an adequate statement of the proposed regulation. After the hearing, the planning board, by vote, shall determine the final form of the regulation to be submitted to the local legislative body, which form of regulation shall conform, in substance, to the initial proposal and may include editorial revisions and textual modifications resulting from the public hearing which the planning board votes to adopt.

(b) The local legislative body shall act upon the proposed interim regulation not later than 90 days after the posting of the notice for the public hearing under subparagraph (a).

III. An interim regulation adopted under this section shall expire at the earliest of the following occurrences: one year after its adoption by the local legislative body; such earlier time as specified in the ordinance; or upon the effective date of an ordinance adopted under RSA 674:22 which addresses the unusual circumstances.

Source.
1983, 447:1. 1989, 266:16, eff. July 1, 1989.
1997, 15:1, eff. June 21, 1997.

Amendments
—1997. Paragraph II(b): Substituted "90 days" for "45 days".

—1989. Paragraph I: Substituted "town, or county in which there are located unincorporated towns or unorganized places" for "or town" following "program, a city".

Cross References.
Capital improvement programs generally, see RSA 674:5 et seq.

Emergency temporary zoning and planning ordinances, see RSA 674:24 et seq.
Master plans generally, see RSA 674:1 et seq.

NOTES TO DECISIONS

Analysis

1. Generally
2. Effect of master plan

1. Generally

A local interim growth management ordinance, which prohibited zoning and planning boards from formally accepting or acting upon any site plan applications creating a total of more than three lots for a one-year period was valid and not ultra vires where it was enacted pursuant to RSA 674:23, I and in accordance with the decision in Conway v. Stratham, 120 N.H. 257, 414 A.2d 539, 1980 N.H. LEXIS 269 (1980), which upheld the validity of a slow growth ordinance as a temporary measure, when it lasted for no more than one year towards the purpose of developing a comprehensive plan. Weare Land Use Ass'n v. Town of Weare, 153 N.H. 510, 899 A.2d 255, 2006 N.H. LEXIS 69 (2006).

This section and RSA 674:22 enable a municipality to adopt an ordinance providing for controlled growth after its planning board has adopted a master plan and a capital improve-ment program designed to assess and balance community and regional development needs. Rancourt v. Town of Barnstead, 129 N.H. 45, 523 A.2d 55, 1986 N.H. LEXIS 379 (1986).

2. Effect of master plan

A planning board may not apply a master plan itself to limit development; it may only apply ordinances adopted pursuant to this section or RSA 674:22 to regulate or control the timing of development. Rancourt v. Town of Barnstead, 129 N.H. 45, 523 A.2d 55, 1986 N.H. LEXIS 379 (1986).

A municipal planning board cannot deny approval of a proposed subdivision on the basis of growth control rates set in a master plan without the municipality's first having enacted an ordinance providing for growth management or the board's having itself enacted a capital improvement program. Rancourt v. Town of Barnstead, 129 N.H. 45, 523 A.2d 55, 1986 N.H. LEXIS 379 (1986).

Cited:
Cited in Quinlan v. City of Dover, 136 N.H. 226, 614 A.2d 1057, 1992 N.H. LEXIS 159 (1992).

RESEARCH REFERENCES

New Hampshire Practice.
N.H.P. Land Use Planning and Zoning §§ 15.02, 15.03, 15.06.

Emergency Temporary Zoning and Planning Ordinances

Cross References.
Procedure for enactment and adoption of ordinances and building codes generally, see RSA 675:1 et seq.

Procedure for enactment of emergency temporary zoning and planning ordinances in certain towns, see RSA 675:4-a.
Zoning generally, see RSA 674:16 et seq.

NOTES TO DECISIONS

Analysis

1. Construction
2. Exercise of municipal power

1. Construction

Under power delegated to municipalities to enact zoning ordinances to promote "the general welfare of the community," the term "community" includes the region of which the municipality is a part. Britton v. Town of Chester, 134 N.H. 434, 595 A.2d 492, 1991 N.H. LEXIS 95 (1991).

2. Exercise of municipal power

Ordinance which in effect wrongfully excluded development of low and moderate income housing constituted an invalid exercise of the municipality's power under enabling legislation delegating to the town the power to zone municipality to promote the general welfare of the community, which included not only the municipality itself, but the region in which it was located. Britton v. Town of Chester, 134 N.H. 434, 595 A.2d 492, 1991 N.H. LEXIS 95 (1991).

RESEARCH REFERENCES

ALR.

Validity and effect of "interim" zoning ordinance. 30 A.L.R.3d 1196.

674:24. Definitions.

When used in this subdivision the following terms shall have the meanings given to them in this section:

I. "Frontage" means that portion of a lot bordering on a highway, street or right-of-way.

II. "Lot" means a parcel of land at least sufficient in size to meet the minimum requirements for use, coverage and area and to provide required yards and other open spaces. An undersize lot is permissible if it passes state standards for soil conditions and substantially meets the requirements here and if in existence on the date of adoption of this ordinance.

III. "Manufactured housing" means manufactured housing as defined by RSA 674:31.

IV. "Nonconforming" means use of land, building or premise which is not a use permitted by the provisions of this ordinance for the district in which such land, building or premise is situated.

V. "Permanent building" means any building resting upon a foundation or otherwise legally defined as "real estate".

VI. "Permanent resident" means an individual or family using any building continuously as a residence for a period of 6 months or more.

VII. "Right-of-way" means and includes all present and proposed town, state and federal highways and the land on either side of same as covered by statutes to determine the widths of rights-of-way.

VIII. "Setback" means the distance between the nearest portion of a building and a lot or right-of-way line, whichever is closer.

Source.
1983, 447:1, eff. Jan. 1, 1984.

Revision note.
Paragraph III was revised, pursuant to the authority conferred by 1983, 447:4, for pur-

poses of conformity with 1983, 230:5.

Cross References.
Definitions generally, see RSA 672.
State highways, see RSA 230.

NOTES TO DECISIONS

Nonconforming use

Trial court erred in upholding zoning board of adjustment finding that mobile home park was a preexisting nonconforming use under this section where an interim zoning ordinance required a minimum density of one acre per site and mobile home park consisted of twenty-two sites on a single lot with 27.67 acres of developable land. Because the property constituted a single lot, it conformed to the density requirements of the ordinance and was therefore not a nonconforming use. Mudge v. Precinct of Haverhill Corner, 133 N.H. 881, 587 A.2d 603, 1991 N.H. LEXIS 10 (1991).

RESEARCH REFERENCES

New Hampshire Practice.
15 N.H.P. Land Use Planning and Zoning §§ 5.06, 29.16.

674:25. Districting Under Interim Zoning Ordinance.

For the purpose of regulating the use of land and the location and construction of buildings, any town adopting the provisions of an interim zoning ordinance shall be considered as one district with the following regulations and restrictions:

I. It shall be a district of residential agricultural use only. Business, commercial and industrial uses are prohibited in this district except as hereinafter provided.

II. Two apartments for permanent residents shall be the maximum allowable in any one given building.

III. Lots shall be at least one acre minimum in size, or larger, depending on soil and slope conditions, as may be suitable to sustain development according to state standards.

IV. There shall be observed the following setbacks in the construction of new buildings or in the relocation of existing ones:

(a) Minimum distance between any building and the edge of a right-of-way shall be 50 feet.

(b) Minimum distance from a lot's sidelines to any building shall be 30 feet; providing, however, that small detached accessory buildings may, as a special exception, be approved to within 15 feet of a lot line if the board of adjustment finds this would not be detrimental to the neighborhood.

(c) Minimum distance from a lot rearline to any building shall be 40 feet; providing, however, that small detached accessory buildings may, as a special exception, be approved to within 20 feet of a lot rearline, upon a finding of no detriment to the neighborhood.

(d) Maximum height of any building shall be 35 feet, with determination being the vertical distance from the average finished grade surrounding the building to a point midway between the highest and lowest points of the highest roof. Silos, barns and church towers are excepted, as are residential television and radio antennas.

(e) A deviation of 20 percent is allowed for side and rear setbacks in extenuating circumstances, as shall be recommended by the planning board or the selectmen if there is no planning board.

V. Home products and produce may be bought and sold and exposed for sale in this district.

VI. Hotels, motels and tourist homes may be maintained and operated, by special exception, provided that there be adequate parking and traffic provisions, that health standards be maintained, and that there be no detriment to the neighborhood.

VII. Private schools, nursing homes and sanitariums may be maintained by special exception, provided that there be adequate parking and traffic provisions, that health standards be maintained, and that there be no detriment to the neighborhood.

VIII. No building or set of buildings shall occupy more than 30 percent of its lot, nor shall it occupy more than 60 percent of its frontage if its front yard is less than 100 feet deep.

IX. No building, residence, or manufactured housing may be located anywhere in this district unless it meets all of the area and yard requirements of a residence in this district.

X. For the purpose of this ordinance, outdoor advertising shall be classified as commercial use and shall be permitted only if conforming to the following regulations:

(a) An outdoor sign shall not be larger than 6 square feet.

(b) It shall not be placed within 25 feet of a right-of-way nor within 150 feet of an intersection of a right-of-way unless affixed to a building and not extending beyond or above the same by more than 3 feet.

(c) Illumination shall be only by continuous nonflashing noncolored light.

(d) A permit for erection shall be procured from the building inspector, where present, and at the usual fee in accordance with the normal procedures in the community.

XI. Cluster development shall be permitted if the density does not exceed the provisions of paragraph III and if all other provisions of RSA 674:25–29 apply.

Source.
1983, 447:1, eff. Jan. 1, 1984.

Cross References.
Administration of ordinances, see RSA 674:29.

Districting of municipalities generally, see RSA 674:20.

Highways generally, see RSA 229 et seq.

Nonconforming properties and uses, see RSA 674:28.

NOTES TO DECISIONS

Density
Trial court erred in overruling zoning board of adjustment determination that surface area of interior roads should not be included when calculating allowable density under this section. Mudge v. Precinct of Haverhill Corner, 133 N.H. 881, 587 A.2d 603, 1991 N.H. LEXIS 10 (1991).

RESEARCH REFERENCES

New Hampshire Practice.
15 N.H.P. Land Use Planning and Zoning
§ 5.06.

ALR.
Application of zoning regulations to motels or
motor courts. 23 A.L.R.3d 210.
Validity of ordinance zoning the entire mu-

nicipality for residential use. 54 A.L.R.3d 1282.
Validity of zoning laws setting minimum lot
size requirements. 1 A.L.R.5th 622.
Zoning regulations as applied to colleges,
universities, or similar institutions for higher
education. 64 A.L.R.3d 1038.

674:26. Agricultural Use Under Interim Zoning Ordinance.

"Agricultural use" shall mean land used for agriculture, farming, dairying, pasturage, apiculture, horticulture, floriculture, silviculture and animal and poultry husbandry. Any such uses are permitted under an interim zoning ordinance except as restricted below:

I. The slaughtering of animals or poultry, except such as are raised for use of an owner or occupant; and the raising of animals or poultry or both for commercial purposes are permitted only as exceptions and subject to the following regulations:

(a) A lot shall be 8 acres or more in area.

(b) Each lot shall have at least 500 feet in frontage if adjacent to a right-of-way.

(c) A building for these purposes shall be placed at least 100 feet from any right-of-way.

(d) A building shall be located at least 200 feet from side or rear lines.

(e) Before approval by the board of adjustment, a public hearing shall be held with at least 15 days' notice of the time and place of the public hearing published in a paper of general circulation in the town or village district and with a legal notice thereof posted in at least 3 public places in the town or village district.

II. The proposed use shall not be approved if the board finds that it will cause hazard to health, property values or safety through fire, traffic, unsanitary conditions or through excessive noise, vibration, odor or other nuisance feature.

Source.
1983, 447:1, eff. Jan. 1, 1984.

Cross References.
Administration of ordinances, see RSA
674:29.

Commercial uses generally, see RSA 674:27.
Definitions generally, see RSA 674:24.
Permissible uses generally, see RSA 674:25.

RESEARCH REFERENCES

New Hampshire Practice.
15 N.H.P. Land Use Planning and Zoning
§ 5.06.

674:27. Commercial Exceptions Under Interim Zoning Ordinance.

Business, commercial or industrial ventures other than those mentioned in RSA 674:25 or 674:26 may be given special exception by the board of adjustment upon submission and approval of a site plan; provided, however, that the following regulations and restrictions shall be observed:

I. No business, commercial or industrial venture or use shall be permitted which could cause any undue hazard to health, safety or property values or which is offensive to the public because of noise, vibration, excessive traffic, unsanitary conditions, noxious odor, smoke or other similar reason.

II. Sufficient acreage shall be included to allow the following setbacks:

(a) In the front, not less than 75 feet from a right-of-way to any building or parking lot having both an exit and an entrance and with grass or beautification in the buffer area.

(b) Side and rear: Not less than 50 feet from a building or parking lot to the lot line.

(c) Sufficient off-street parking to allow 300 square feet for each 3 anticipated patrons or employees on premises at the same time. In the case of service establishments, one car shall be deemed to contain 4 patrons.

III. On-premise advertising signs in connection with businesses receiving approval shall be exempt from the provisions of RSA 674:25, X and shall be considered as part of the application for commercial exception. They shall be limited to not more than 20 square feet in size and may be illuminated only by noncolored, nonflashing lights. Location may not be within any right-of-way nor within 150 feet of any intersection unless attached to a building.

IV. Before mining, excavation, or removal of soil, rock, sand or gravel or similar material, a special exception shall be received from the board of adjustment, subject to the usual fee permit. Excavation of earth shall be made in accordance with RSA 155-E.

V. All known abutters of any proposed business, commercial, or industrial site shall be notified by the board of adjustment by certified mail at least one week prior to any public hearing regarding the site. The names and addresses of the known abutters shall be supplied by the applicant on a plat plan to be submitted to the board of adjustment.

Source.
1983, 447:1, eff. Jan. 1, 1984.

Cross References.
Administration of ordinances, see RSA 674:29.

Agricultural uses generally, see RSA 674:26.
Permissible uses generally, see RSA 674:25.
Site plan review generally, see RSA 674:43, 44.

NOTES TO DECISIONS

Failure to obtain exception

Trial court improperly denied plaintiff's motion to vacate zoning board of adjustment's upholding of a building permit, where property owner failed to obtain a special exception for a commercial use of premises to be used for expansion of manufactured housing park. Mudge v. Precinct of Haverhill Corner, 133 N.H. 881, 587 A.2d 603, 1991 N.H. LEXIS 10 (1991).

RESEARCH REFERENCES

New Hampshire Practice.
15 N.H.P. Land Use Planning and Zoning § 5.06.

ALR.
Classification and maintenance of advertis-

ing structures as nonconforming use. 80 A.L.R.3d 630.

674:28. Nonconforming Buildings, Land, or Uses Under Interim Zoning Ordinance.

I. All nonconforming properties in active use when an interim ordinance is passed and adopted may continue indefinitely in their present use.

II. Any and all nonconforming property may be altered and expanded as the business and conditions warrant; providing, however, that any such expansion does not make any existing conforming structure nonconforming within the terms of the interim ordinance; nor shall such expansion bring any building within 35 feet of an abutter's building; nor shall the height exceed the limits as defined in RSA 674:25, IV(d); nor shall the use of such property be materially altered in purpose.

III. Any and all nonconforming property which is partially or totally destroyed by reason of obsolescence, fire or other act of God may be restored, remodeled and operated if done within 2 years; providing, however, that proximity to a lot line or right-of-way may be no nearer than the lesser of the original building and the setbacks defined in RSA 674:25, IV(a)–(c), and the height does not exceed the limits set forth in RSA 674:25, IV(d).

Source.
1983, 447:1, eff. Jan. 1, 1984.

Revision note.
Substituted "RSA 674:25, IV(d)" for "RSA 674:25, IV, (d)" in pars. II and III and "RSA 674:25, IV(a)–(c)" for "RSA 674:25, IV, (a)–(c)" in par. III to conform reference to citation style

employed in LEXIS New Hampshire Revised Statutes Annotated.

Cross References.
Agricultural uses generally, see RSA 674:26.
Commercial uses generally, see RSA 674:27.
Permissible uses generally, see RSA 674:25.

RESEARCH REFERENCES

New Hampshire Practice.
15 N.H.P. Land Use Planning and Zoning § 5.06.

ALR.
Addition of another activity to existing nonconforming use as violation of zoning ordinance. 61 A.L.R.4th 724.

Alteration, extension, reconstruction, or repair of nonconforming structure or structure devoted to nonconforming use as violation of zoning ordinance. 63 A.L.R.4th 275.

Change in area or location of nonconforming

use as violation of zoning ordinance. 56 A.L.R.4th 769.

Change in type of activity of nonconforming use as violation of zoning ordinance. 61 A.L.R.4th 902.

Construction of new building or structure on premises devoted to nonconforming use as violation of zoning ordinance. 10 A.L.R.4th 1122.

Provisions protecting landowners who applied for or received building permit prior to change in zoning. 49 A.L.R.3d 1150.

Right to resume nonconforming use of premises after involuntary break in the continuity of nonconforming use caused by difficulties unrelated to governmental activity. 56 A.L.R.3d 14.

Right to resume nonconforming use of premises after involuntary break in the continuity of nonconforming use caused by governmental activity. 56 A.L.R.3d 138.

Right to resume nonconforming use of premises after voluntary or unexplained break in the continuity of nonconforming use. 57 A.L.R.3d 279.

Validity of provisions for amortization of nonconforming uses. 8 A.L.R.5th 391.

Zoning: Right to repair or reconstruct building operating as nonconforming use, after damage or destruction by fire or other casualty. 57 A.L.R.3d 419.

674:29. Board of Adjustment and Administrative Provisions Under Interim Zoning Ordinance.

In any town in which an interim zoning ordinance has been adopted, and while it remains in effect, the board of selectmen shall be the appointing authority for the zoning board of adjustment and shall appoint the first such board forthwith, upon the adoption of interim zoning. Such board shall have all the powers and jurisdiction and be subject to all the duties, requirements and other provisions applicable to zoning boards of adjustment under RSA 673. The board of selectmen, if no building inspector exists, shall act jointly as the building inspector and administrative officer charged with enforcement and may issue building or use permits in the first instance if clearly permitted by law. The applicable provisions of RSA 677 shall govern motions for rehearing, appeals, enforcement, and interpretation. In addition to other remedies, any person convicted of violation of the provisions of RSA 674:25–29 by a court of competent jurisdiction shall be subject to a fine of not more than $50 for each offense. Each day the violation continues shall constitute a separate offense.

Source.
1983, 447:1, eff. Jan. 1, 1984.

Cross References.
Administration and enforcement of ordinances and building codes generally, see RSA 675.

Establishment and composition of zoning boards of adjustment generally, see RSA 673.

Powers of zoning boards of adjustment generally, see RSA 674:33.

RESEARCH REFERENCES

New Hampshire Practice.
15 N.H.P. Land Use Planning and Zoning § 5.06.

674:30. Utility Structures.

Local ordinances, codes, and regulations enacted pursuant to this title shall apply to public utility structures, provided, however, that:

I. Notwithstanding the provisions of any such local ordinance, code, or regulation, a planning board, or its designee pursuant to paragraph II, upon application by a utility, may waive any requirement contained in an ordinance, code, or regulation for any unoccupied structure which is less than 200 square feet in area, which is necessary for the furnishing of utility service for the public health, safety, or general welfare, and for which the utility's siting options are limited by virtue of said structure being a physically integrated component of the utility's transmission or distribution apparatus. Any such waiver shall terminate, without further action by the planning board, if said structure ceases to be used for provisions of utility services.

II. The planning board may adopt regulations, pursuant to RSA 675:6 to ensure that such utility structures do not adversely affect the character of the area or create a hazard to the public. Such regulations may designate the building inspector, municipal engineer, road agent, or other official as agent of the planning board for purposes of this section. Notice shall be given by the planning board to abutters and the public, according to the procedures provided for in RSA 676:4, I(d), 10 days prior to any decision to be issued under such regulations. A hearing shall be held, if requested by the applicant or the abutters at any time prior to issuance of the decision, or if the board determines that a hearing is necessary. Notice of such hearing shall be given as provided in RSA 675:7, and no decision shall be issued until after the hearing.

III. A public utility which uses or proposes to use a structure which does not fit the criteria described in paragraph I, or fits those criteria and has been denied a waiver, or has been granted a waiver with conditions unacceptable to the utility when the waiver was applied for pursuant to paragraph I, may petition the public utilities commission to be exempted from the operation of any local ordinance, code, or regulation enacted under this title. The public utilities commission, following a public hearing, may grant such an exemption if it decides that the present or proposed situation of the structure in question is reasonably necessary for the convenience or welfare of the public and, if the purpose of the structure relates to water supply withdrawal, the exemption is recommended by the department of environmental services.

IV. Except for small power production facilities, as defined in RSA 362-A:1-a, X, and cogeneration facilities, as defined in RSA 362-A:1-a, I-c, owned and operated by a New Hampshire franchised utility, small power production facilities and cogeneration facilities shall not be considered to be public utilities under this section and may not petition the public utilities commission for an exemption from the operation of any regulation under this subdivision.

Source.

1983, 447:1. 1986, 147:1. 1987, 152:1, eff. July 10, 1987. 1998, 124:5, eff. Aug. 1, 1998. 2006, 294:4, eff. August 14, 2006.

Amendments

—2006. Paragraph IV: Substituted "I-c" for "I" preceding "owned and operated".

—1998. Paragraph III: Added "and, if the purpose of the structure relates to water supply withdrawal, the exemption is recommended by the department of environmental services" following "welfare of the public" in the second sentence.

—1987. Rewritten to the extent that a detailed comparison would be impracticable.

—1986. Designated the existing provisions of the section as par. I and added par. II.

Cross References.

Proceedings before public utilities commission generally, see RSA 365:8 et seq.

NOTES TO DECISIONS

Analysis

1. Construction
2. Attachment of conditions to exemption

1. Construction

The special provision in the statute relating to structures of public utilities was not to be construed as authorizing the regulation of governmental activities and uses, since public utilities uses have been commonly privately owned and operated. McGrath v. City of Manchester, 113 N.H. 355, 307 A.2d 830, 1973 N.H. LEXIS 273 (1973). (Decided under prior law.)

2. Attachment of conditions to exemption

The public utilities commission could attach reasonable conditions in consideration of the interests of local residents when it granted a utility's petition for exemption from a zoning ordinance. Appeal of Milford Water Works, 126 N.H. 127, 489 A.2d 627, 1985 N.H. LEXIS 258 (1985). (Decided under prior law.)

The public utilities commission had authority to condition its approval of an exemption from local zoning ordinances under its authority to consider the health and safety of local residents. Appeal of Milford Water Works, 126 N.H. 127, 489 A.2d 627, 1985 N.H. LEXIS 258 (1985). (Decided under prior law.)

The public utilities commission acted within its authority, and rightfully considered the concerns of local residents, when it attached to its order granting a petition to exempt from local zoning ordinances structures related to a well project conditions which were designed to protect local residents against the possible adverse effects of wells on the ground water supply. Appeal of Milford Water Works, 126 N.H. 127, 489 A.2d 627, 1985 N.H. LEXIS 258 (1985). (Decided under prior law.)

There was a reasonable basis in the record for finding that the public welfare and convenience required imposition, upon the grant of a petition for exemption of a well project from local zoning ordinances, of conditions designed to protect local residents against the possible adverse effects of the new wells on the ground water supply since, although expert testimony indicated that the effect of the well project on neighboring wells would be minimal, none of the experts stated that there would be no effect, and since there was testimony that other similar projects had caused depletion of neighboring wells. Appeal of Milford Water Works, 126 N.H. 127, 489 A.2d 627, 1985 N.H. LEXIS 258 (1985). (Decided under prior law.)

Cited:

Cited in In re Public Serv. Co., 88 B.R. 521, 1988 Bankr. LEXIS 1030 (Bankr. D.N.H. 1988).

RESEARCH REFERENCES

New Hampshire Practice.
13 N.H.P. Local Government Law § 510.

ALR.
Applicability of zoning regulations to projects of nongovernmental public utility as affected by utility's power of eminent domain. 87 A.L.R.3d 1265.

Manufactured Housing

Cross References.
Modular building standards, see RSA 205-C.
Regulation of manufactured housing parks generally, see RSA 205-A.

Zoning generally, see RSA 674:16 et seq.

RESEARCH REFERENCES

ALR.
Use of trailer or similar structure for residence purposes as within zoning provision. 96 A.L.R.2d 232; 17 A.L.R.4th 106.

Validity and application of zoning regulations relating to mobile home or trailer parks. 42 A.L.R.3d 598.
Validity of zoning or building regulations

restricting mobile homes or trailers to established mobile home or trailer parks. 17
A.L.R.4th 106.

Validity of zoning ordinances prohibiting or

regulating outside storage of house trailers,
motor homes, campers, vans, and the like, in
residential neighborhoods. 95 A.L.R.3d 378.

674:31. Definition.

As used in this subdivision, "manufactured housing" means any structure,
transportable in one or more sections, which, in the traveling mode, is 8 body
feet or more in width and 40 body feet or more in length, or when erected on
site, is 320 square feet or more, and which is built on a permanent chassis and
designed to be used as a dwelling with or without a permanent foundation
when connected to required utilities, which include plumbing, heating and
electrical heating systems contained therein. Manufactured housing as defined
in this section shall not include presite built housing as defined in RSA
674:31-a.

Source.
1983, 447:1. 1985, 104:1, eff. July 9, 1985.

Amendments
—1985. Added the second sentence.

NOTES TO DECISIONS

Analysis

1. Construction
2. Construction with other law

1. Construction
Although a renter lived on an owner's property, which was not considered a "campground"
under RSA 216-I:1, VII, the trial court did not
reach the issue of whether the renter's camper/
trailer was a "manufactured housing" unit
within the meaning of RSA 205-A:1 and 674:31
before determining if the owner was a "land-
lord"; therefore, the owner's conviction under
RSA 540-A:3, III had to be reversed and remanded for further proceedings. Comeau v.

Vergato, 149 N.H. 508, 823 A.2d 764, 2003 N.H.
LEXIS 74 (2003).

2. Construction with other law
Debtors' mobile home was 14' x 80' and
clearly fit within definition of manufactured
housing. Therefore, it was real estate for purposes of federal bankruptcy law. In re Smith,
176 B.R. 298, 1994 Bankr. LEXIS 2099 (Bankr.
D.N.H. 1994).

Cited:
Cited in Town of Plainfield v. Sanville, 125
N.H. 825, 485 A.2d 1052, 1984 N.H. LEXIS 318
(1984); Town of Chesterfield v. Brooks, 126 N.H.
64, 489 A.2d 600, 1985 N.H. LEXIS 274 (1985).

RESEARCH REFERENCES

New Hampshire Practice.
15 N.H.P. Land Use Planning and Zoning
§ 13.02.

ALR.
What is "mobile home," "house trailer,"

"trailer house," or "trailer" within meaning of
restrictive covenant. 83 A.L.R.5th 651.

674:31-a. Definition; Presite Built Housing.

As used in this subdivision, "presite built housing" means any structure
designed primarily for residential occupancy which is wholly or in substantial
part made, fabricated, formed or assembled in off-site manufacturing facilities

in conformance with the United States Department of Housing and Urban Development minimum property standards and local building codes, for installation, or assembly and installation, on the building site. For the purposes of this subdivision, presite built housing shall not include manufactured housing, as defined in RSA 674:31.

Source.
    1985, 104:2, eff. July 9, 1985.

674:32. Manufactured Housing.

I. Municipalities shall afford reasonable opportunities for the siting of manufactured housing, and a municipality shall not exclude manufactured housing completely from the municipality by regulation, zoning ordinance or by any other police power. A municipality which adopts land use control measures shall allow, in its sole discretion, manufactured housing to be located on individual lots in most, but not necessarily all, land areas in districts zoned to permit residential uses within the municipality, or in manufactured housing parks and subdivisions created for the placement of manufactured housing on individually owned lots in most, but not necessarily all, land areas in districts zoned to permit residential uses within the municipality, or in all 3 types of locations. Manufactured housing located on individual lots shall comply with lot size, frontage requirements, space limitations and other reasonable controls that conventional single family housing in the same district must meet. No special exception or special permit shall be required for manufactured housing located on individual lots or manufactured housing subdivisions unless such special exception or permit is required by the municipality for single family housing located on individual lots or in subdivisions. Municipalities permitting manufactured housing parks shall afford realistic opportunities for the development and expansion of manufactured housing parks. In order to provide such realistic opportunities, lot size and overall density requirements for manufactured housing parks shall be reasonable.

II. Notwithstanding paragraph I or any law or rule to the contrary, no zoning ordinance or bylaw shall prohibit an owner and occupier of a residence which has been damaged by fire or other disaster from placing a manufactured home on the lot of such residence and residing in such structure while the residence is being rebuilt. The period of such occupancy shall expire in 12 months from the placement of such structure or upon the issuance of a certificate of occupancy, whichever occurs first. Any such manufactured home shall be subject to state and local requirements relating to water supply and sewerage disposal. A manufactured home that is placed on a lot under this paragraph shall not attain the status of a vested nonconforming use.

Source.
    1983, 447:1. 1986, 91:2. 1987, 378:1. 1993, 158:1, eff. July 23, 1993.

Amendments
    —1993. Designated the existing provisions of the section as par. I and added par. II.

—1987. Rewritten to the extent that a detailed comparison would be impracticable.

—1986. Rewrote the first sentence and substituted "most" for "some" following "individual lots in" and "manufactured housing" for "mobile home" preceding "parks" and for "mobile homes" preceding "on individually owned lots" in the second sentence.

Legislative findings and purpose of 1986 amendment.

1986, 91:1, eff. July 18, 1986, provided: "In the 1981 legislative session the general court passed chapter 406 relative to zoning of manufactured housing. In the declaration of purpose for that legislation, the general court acknowledged the need and right of individual citizens and families to decent, sanitary housing, and further recognized that the partial or total exclusion of manufactured housing would violate those rights. Since the passage of chapter 406 of the laws of 1981 housing costs have continued to increase substantially, thereby increasing the need for suitable moderately priced housing, such as manufactured housing. The general court reaffirms its findings that manufactured housing, when built in conformance with national codes, is almost indistinguishable from conventional site-built housing, and that the exclusion of manufactured housing is based upon outmoded perceptions. Since the passage of chapter 406, some municipalities across New Hampshire have failed to comply with chapter 406, or have complied by zoning in such a fashion as to relegate manufactured housing to zoning districts where land characteristics or costs effectively eliminate manufactured housing as an alternative to conventional site-built housing. It is the finding of this general court that some municipalities have misunderstood the intent of chapter 406 with the result that the original objective of the law has not been attained. It is the purpose of the general court that the passage of this act will ensure that the municipalities will exercise their authority to zone and regulate manufactured housing in such a manner that reasonable and realistic opportunities will exist for the placement of manufactured housing in all municipalities. To these ends, the purpose of this act is to:

"I. Impose an affirmative duty on municipalities to afford reasonable opportunities for manufactured housing;

"II. Require that manufactured housing on individual lots and in subdivisions be allowed in most, rather than some, zoning districts; or require that manufactured housing be allowed on individual lots in subdivisions and in manufactured housing parks; and

"III. Establish a date by which municipalities must be in compliance with RSA 674:32 or, if not in compliance, must allow manufactured housing in all residential areas within the municipality."

Time period for modification of municipal regulations, ordinances, etc.; effect of noncompliance with section—1987 amendment.

1987, 378:2, eff. May 26, 1987, provided: "Every municipality which regulates manufactured housing by regulation, zoning ordinance, or by any other exercise of the police power shall be in compliance with the provisions of section 1 of this act by July 1, 1988. Any municipality which is not in compliance with the provisions of section 1 of this act by July 1, 1988, shall permit manufactured housing in any area of the municipality in which other residential housing uses are permitted."

—1986 amendment.

1986, 91:3, eff. July 18, 1986, provided: "Every municipality which regulates manufactured housing by regulation, zoning ordinance, or by any other exercise of the police power shall be in compliance with the provisions of section 2 of this act no later than June 1, 1987. Any municipality which is not in compliance with the provisions of section 2 of this act by June 1, 1987, shall allow manufactured housing in all residential areas within the municipality."

NOTES TO DECISIONS

Analysis

1. Validity of zoning ordinance
2. Failure to obtain exception
3. Grandfathered use

1. Validity of zoning ordinance

In a facial attack on a zoning ordinance, the case was remanded with instructions to the trial court to permit the plaintiffs to file a declaratory judgment petition setting forth specifically, clearly, and concisely their argument against the town's ordinance provisions regulating mobile homes. Delude v. Town of Amherst, 137 N.H. 361, 628 A.2d 251, 1993 N.H. LEXIS 90 (1993).

Town ordinance prohibiting expansion of manufactured housing parks did not violate this section. Town was not a "municipality permitting manufactured housing parks" and thus was not subject to this section's requirement that municipalities afford opportunities for development and expansion of parks. Pope v. Town of Hinsdale Planning Bd., 137 N.H. 233, 624 A.2d 1360, 1993 N.H. LEXIS 67 (1993).

Requirement that mobile home parks obtain a special exception for a commercial use is valid and not violative of anti-exclusion protections of this section. Mudge v. Precinct of Haverhill Corner, 133 N.H. 881, 587 A.2d 603, 1991 N.H. LEXIS 10 (1991).

Requirement of zoning ordinance that mobile home parks be limited to areas where city sewer and water is located was reasonable. Jensen's, Inc. v. City of Dover, 130 N.H. 761, 547 A.2d 277, 1988 N.H. LEXIS 60 (1988).

Sufficient compliance with mandate of this section that areas be provided for the siting of manufactured housing was shown where mobile home parks were required to be located in R-40 zones and where vast majority of land areas zoned residential in a municipality were zoned R-40, with mobile homes permitted in subdivisions as of right and mobile home parks by special exception. Jensen's, Inc. v. City of Dover, 130 N.H. 761, 547 A.2d 277, 1988 N.H. LEXIS 60 (1988).

Provision of zoning ordinance requiring a special exception and a finding, for a mobile home park, that it would not adversely affect overall land values, was permissible where the land value inquiry was reasonable, given the permitted density of nearly three times that of other residential development. Jensen's, Inc. v. City of Dover, 130 N.H. 761, 547 A.2d 277, 1988 N.H. LEXIS 60 (1988).

A zoning ordinance which divided a town into two residential zones, and allowed mobile homes to be located in only one of the zones, complied with this section, which forbids total exclusion of such housing from a municipality, but affords wide discretion regarding its regulation. Town of Chesterfield v. Brooks, 126 N.H. 64, 489 A.2d 600, 1985 N.H. LEXIS 274 (1985). (Decided prior to 1986 amendment.)

Where town's zoning and mobile home ordinances did not clearly provide for individual ownership of lots upon which to place mobile homes, they failed to comply with the statute and were, therefore, invalid. Town of Plainfield v. Sanville, 125 N.H. 825, 485 A.2d 1052, 1984 N.H. LEXIS 318 (1984). (Decided under prior law.)

2. Failure to obtain exception

Trial court improperly denied plaintiff's motion to vacate zoning board of adjustment's upholding of a building permit, where property owner failed to obtain a special exception for a commercial use of premises to be used for expansion of manufactured housing park. Mudge v. Precinct of Haverhill Corner, 133 N.H. 881, 587 A.2d 603, 1991 N.H. LEXIS 10 (1991).

Manufactured housing parks are omitted from this section's exemption of manufactured housing from requirement that special exceptions to zoning ordinances be obtained by property owners. Mudge v. Precinct of Haverhill Corner, 133 N.H. 881, 587 A.2d 603, 1991 N.H. LEXIS 10 (1991).

3. Grandfathered use

This section does not require a town to allow expansion of its existing manufactured housing parks. The goal of the legislature in enacting this section was to provide reasonable opportunities for the siting of manufactured housing, but not necessarily manufactured housing parks. Pope v. Town of Hinsdale Planning Bd., 137 N.H. 233, 624 A.2d 1360, 1993 N.H. LEXIS 67 (1993).

Cited:

Cited in Town of Plaistow v. Nadeau, 126 N.H. 439, 493 A.2d 1158, 1985 N.H. LEXIS 320 (1985).

RESEARCH REFERENCES

New Hampshire Practice.
15 N.H.P. Land Use Planning and Zoning §§ 13.02, 14.05.

Agricultural Uses of Land

Purpose.
2000, 279:1, eff. July 1, 2001, provided: "The purpose of this act [which enacted this subdivision and amended RSA 674:17], is to clarify the requirements of RSA 672:1, III-b, that farming and agriculture, as defined in RSA 21:34-a, shall not be unreasonably limited by the use of municipal planning and zoning powers."

674:32-a. Presumption.

In accordance with RSA 672:1, III-d, whenever agricultural activities are not explicitly addressed with respect to any zoning district or location, they shall be deemed to be permitted there, as either a primary or accessory use, so long as conducted in accordance with best management practices adopted by the commissioner of agriculture, markets, and food and with federal and state laws, regulations, and rules.

Source.
2000, 279:3, eff. July 1, 2001.

674:32-b. Existing Agricultural Uses.

Any agricultural use which exists pursuant to RSA 674:32-a may without restriction be expanded, altered to meet changing technology or markets, or changed to another agricultural use, as set forth in RSA 21:34-a, so long as any such expansion, alteration, or change complies with all federal and state laws, regulations, and rules, including best management practices adopted by the commissioner of agriculture, markets, and food; subject, however, to the following limitations:

(a) Any new establishment, re-establishment after disuse, or significant expansion of an operation involving the keeping of livestock, poultry, or other animals may be made subject to special exception, building permit, or other local land use board approval.

(b) Any new establishment, re-establishment after disuse, or significant expansion of a farm stand, retail operation, or other use involving on-site transactions with the public, may be made subject to applicable special exception, building permit, or other local land use board approval and may be regulated to prevent traffic and parking from adversely impacting adjacent property, streets and sidewalks, or public safety.

Source.
2000, 279:3, eff. July 1, 2001.

674:32-c. Other General Provisions.

I. The tilling of soil and the growing and harvesting of crops and horticultural commodities, as a primary or accessory use, shall not be prohibited in any district.

II. Nothing in this subdivision shall exempt new, re-established, or expanded agricultural operations from generally applicable building and site requirements such as dimensional standards, setbacks, driveway and traffic regulations, parking requirements, noise, odor, or vibration restrictions or sign regulations; provided, however, that in circumstances where their literal application would effectively prohibit an agricultural use allowed by this subdivision, or would otherwise be unreasonable in the context of an agricultural use, the board of adjustment, building code board of appeals, or other applicable local board, after due notice and hearing, shall grant a waiver from such requirement to the extent necessary to reasonably permit the agricultural use, unless such waiver would have a demonstrated adverse effect on public health or safety, or the value of adjacent property. Such waiver shall continue only as long as utilized for the permitted agricultural use.

III. Nothing in this subdivision shall apply to any aspect of an agricultural operation determined to be injurious to public health or safety under RSA 147. Nothing in this subdivision shall be deemed to modify or limit the duties and authority of the department of environmental services under RSA 485 or RSA 485-A or the commissioner of the department of agriculture, markets, and food under title XL.

IV. Nothing in this subdivision shall be deemed to affect the regulation of sludge or septage.

Source.
2000, 279:3, eff. July 1, 2001.

Zoning Board of Adjustment and Building Code Board of Appeals

Cross References.
Appointment and terms of members, see RSA 673:3 et seq.
Disqualification of members, see RSA 673:14.
Establishment of boards, see RSA 673:1.
Filling of vacancies, see RSA 673:12.
Meetings, see RSA 673:10, 15, 17.
Ordinance and code administration and enforcement generally, see RSA 676.

Ordinance and code adoption procedures generally, see RSA 675.
Rehearing and appeals procedures generally, see RSA 677.
Removal of members, see RSA 673:13.
Staff, see RSA 673:16.
Transfer of records of boards, see RSA 673:22.

RESEARCH REFERENCES

ALR.
Authority of zoning commission to impose, as condition of allowance of special zoning exception, permit, or variance, requirements as to highway and traffic changes. 49 A.L.R.3d 492.
Construction and application of statute or ordinance requiring notice as prerequisite to granting variance or exception to zoning

requirement. 38 A.L.R.3d 167.
Requirement that zoning variances or exceptions be made in accordance with comprehensive plan. 40 A.L.R.3d 372.
Zoning board's grant of new application for zoning change, variance, or special exception after denial of previous application covering same property or part thereof. 52 A.L.R.3d 494.

674:33. Powers of Zoning Board of Adjustment.

I. The zoning board of adjustment shall have the power to:

(a) Hear and decide appeals if it is alleged there is error in any order, requirement, decision, or determination made by an administrative official in the enforcement of any zoning ordinance adopted pursuant to RSA 674:16; and

(b) Authorize upon appeal in specific cases such variance from the terms of the zoning ordinance as will not be contrary to the public interest, if, owing to special conditions, a literal enforcement of the provisions of the ordinance will result in unnecessary hardship, and so that the spirit of the ordinance shall be observed and substantial justice done.

II. In exercising its powers under paragraph I, the zoning board of adjustment may reverse or affirm, wholly or in part, or may modify the order, requirement, decision, or determination appealed from and may make such order or decision as ought to be made and, to that end, shall have all the powers of the administrative official from whom the appeal is taken.

III. The concurring vote of 3 members of the board shall be necessary to reverse any action of the administrative official or to decide in favor of the applicant on any matter on which it is required to pass.

IV. A local zoning ordinance may provide that the zoning board of adjustment, in appropriate cases and subject to appropriate conditions and safeguards, make special exceptions to the terms of the ordinance. All special exceptions shall be made in harmony with the general purpose and intent of the zoning ordinance and shall be in accordance with the general or specific rules contained in the ordinance.

V. Notwithstanding subparagraph I(b), any zoning board of adjustment may grant a variance from the terms of a zoning ordinance without finding a hardship arising from the condition of a premises subject to the ordinance, when reasonable accommodations are necessary to allow a person or persons with a recognized physical disability to reside in or regularly use the premises, provided that:

(a) Any variance granted under this paragraph shall be in harmony with the general purpose and intent of the zoning ordinance.

(b) In granting any variance pursuant to this paragraph, the zoning board of adjustment may provide, in a finding included in the variance, that the variance shall survive only so long as the particular person has a continuing need to use the premises.

Source.

1983, 447:1. 1985, 103:20. 1987, 256:1, eff. July 17, 1987. 1998, 218:1, eff. Aug. 17, 1998.

Amendments

—1998. Paragraph V: Added.

—1987. Paragraph I(a): Substituted "of" for "thereof or" following "enforcement" and "to RSA 674:16" for "thereto" following "pursuant" and inserted "zoning" preceding "ordinance".

—1985. Paragraph III: Substituted "on" for "or" preceding "any".

NOTES TO DECISIONS

I. Generally

1. Constitutional law

Legislative power was not unconstitutionally conferred by empowering a board of adjustment to grant or refuse variances from compliance with the terms of a zoning ordinance. Sundeen v. Rogers, 83 N.H. 253, 141 A. 142, 1928 N.H. LEXIS 11, 57 A.L.R. 950 (1928); Sundeen v. Rogers, 83 N.H. 253, 141 A. 142, 1928 N.H. LEXIS 11, 57 A.L.R. 950 (1928). (Decided under prior law.)

2. Legislative intent

This statute manifested a legislative intent to vest in a local board, whose members lived close to the circumstances and conditions, authority to determine the public need and the means of meeting it. Vannah v. Bedford, 111 N.H. 105, 276 A.2d 253, 1971 N.H. LEXIS 132 (1971), overruled on other grounds, Cook v. Sanbornton, 118 N.H. 668, 392 A.2d 1201, 1978 N.H. LEXIS 267 (1978), questioned by, Barry v. Amherst, 121 N.H. 335, 430 A.2d 132, 1981 N.H. LEXIS 314 (1981). (Decided under prior law.)

3. Jurisdiction of board of adjustment

The jurisdiction of a town zoning board of adjustment related to the granting of special exceptions and variances and not to the consideration of orders by the selectmen, and, therefore, a zoning board had no jurisdiction to review an order of a board of town selectmen. Town of Derry v. Simonsen, 117 N.H. 1010, 380 A.2d 1101, 1977 N.H. LEXIS 485 (1977). (Decided under prior law.)

4. Rules governing board of adjustment

In accordance with its power to pass zoning regulations and to establish a board of adjustment for the purpose of granting variances and exceptions from the terms of zoning ordinances, a municipality could prescribe reasonable procedures for the board to follow in order to carry out its purposes. Lavallee v. Britt, 118 N.H. 131, 383 A.2d 709, 1978 N.H. LEXIS 358 (1978). (Decided under prior law.)

Pursuant to its power to pass zoning regulations and to establish a board of adjustment for the purpose of granting variances and exceptions from the terms of zoning ordinances, a municipality could impose, by municipal ordinance, a requirement that the board of adjustment record its findings or reasons for granting or refusing to grant a variance. Lavallee v. Britt, 118 N.H. 131, 383 A.2d 709, 1978 N.H. LEXIS 358 (1978). (Decided under prior law.)

The statutory requirement that the board of adjustment adopt rules "in accordance with the provisions of the ordinances" contemplated such rules as related to procedure before the board, and the statutory command that they should conform to the ordinances did not mean that there must have been a provision in the ordinance therefor. Stone v. Cray, 89 N.H. 483, 200 A. 517, 1938 N.H. LEXIS 60 (1938). (Decided under prior law.)

II. Variances

10. Nature of variances

A variance was in the nature of a waiver of the strict letter of a zoning ordinance without sacrifice to its spirit or purpose. New London v. Leskiewicz, 110 N.H. 462, 272 A.2d 856, 1970 N.H. LEXIS 200 (1970). (Decided under prior law.)

11. Purposes of variances

Variances were provided for by zoning statutes so that litigation of constitutional questions could be avoided and a speedy and adequate remedy afforded in cases where special conditions or exceptional environment presented such questions. Bouley v. City of Nashua, 106 N.H. 79, 205 A.2d 38, 1964 N.H. LEXIS 43 (1964). (Decided under prior law.)

12. Ground for variances—Generally

Where the zoning board of adjustment made no explicit findings on the RSA 674:33, I(b) variance factors in granting the variance to the applicant, it implicitly found that the factors were met in granting the variance; therefore, the trial court erred in finding that the requirements for a variance were not met since it could not make factual findings, but the board gave only cursory consideration to the variance issue, so a remand was necessary. Thomas v. Town of Hooksett, 153 N.H. 717, 903 A.2d 963, 2006 N.H. LEXIS 99 (2006).

Where a zoning board specifically found that an owner had not satisfied two of the requirements under RSA 674:33, I(b) in the owner's application for a rehearing of the board's denial of a variance, the owner did not have to raise the conditions that were not specifically denied by the board; therefore, the trial court erred in interpreting RSA 677:3 as requiring the owner to raise all five conditions for a variance in an application for rehearing in order to preserve a right of appeal. Robinson v. Town of Hudson, 149 N.H. 255, 821 A.2d 959, 2003 N.H. LEXIS 33 (2003).

Wrong legal standard was used to deny plaintiffs' request for a variance, where standard placed a higher burden on plaintiffs than was required by statute. Gray v. Seidel, 143 N.H. 327, 726 A.2d 1283, 1999 N.H. LEXIS 5 (1999).

The statutory language authorizes a zoning board of appeals to attach reasonable conditions to variances granted "so that the spirit of the ordinance shall be observed and substantial justice done." Healey v. Town of New Durham Zoning Bd. of Adjustment, 140 N.H. 232, 665 A.2d 360, 1995 N.H. LEXIS 132 (1995).

A variance was properly granted to allow a property owner to build a residence where (1) there was testimony that designing a house to fit on the property without a variance was "functionally not a reasonable thought," and (2) the property's slope, abundance of ledge, and remote location defeated the argument that there were uses for the property other than residential. Husnander v. Town of Barnstead, 139 N.H. 476, 660 A.2d 477, 1995 N.H. LEXIS 36 (1995), overruled on other grounds, Simplex Techs., Inc. v. Town of Newington, 145 N.H. 727, 766 A.2d 713, 2001 N.H. LEXIS 15 (2001).

A zoning board of appeals is authorized to issue a variance from the terms of the zoning ordinance, provided that the variance is not contrary to the public interest, if, owing to special conditions, a literal enforcement of the provisions of the ordinance will result in unnecessary hardship, and so that the spirit of the ordinance will be observed and substantial justice done, and provided that the variance will not result in diminution of surrounding property values. Husnander v. Town of Barnstead, 139 N.H. 476, 660 A.2d 477, 1995 N.H. LEXIS 36 (1995), overruled on other grounds, Simplex Techs., Inc. v. Town of Newington, 145 N.H.

727, 766 A.2d 713, 2001 N.H. LEXIS 15 (2001).

Party seeking zoning variance bears burden of establishing each of the requirements for a variance. Grey Rocks Land Trust v. Town of Hebron, 136 N.H. 239, 614 A.2d 1048, 1992 N.H. LEXIS 162 (1992). (overruled on other grounds, Simplex Techs., Inc. v. Town of Newington, 145 N.H. 727, 766 A.2d 713, 2001 N.H. LEXIS 15 (2001).)

To support a variance, it must have been found that no diminution in value of surrounding properties would be suffered; granting the permit would be of benefit to the public interest; denial of the permit would result in unnecessary hardship to the owner seeking it; granting the permit would do substantial justice; and the use would not be contrary to the spirit of the ordinance. Ouimette v. City of Somersworth, 119 N.H. 292, 402 A.2d 159, 1979 N.H. LEXIS 300 (1979). (Decided under prior law.)

A variance could be granted if the requested use did not diminish the value of the surrounding properties, would benefit the public interest, denial would cause unnecessary hardship to the person seeking it and the use would not be contrary to the spirit of the ordinance. Alcorn v. Rochester Zoning Board of Adjustment, 114 N.H. 491, 322 A.2d 608, 1974 N.H. LEXIS 309 (1974). (Decided under prior law.)

In order to support a variance it was necessary to have found that no diminution in value of surrounding properties would be suffered, that granting of the permit would be of benefit to the public interest, that its denial would result in unnecessary hardship to owner seeking it, that by granting permits substantial justice would be done, and that the use would not be contrary to the spirit of the ordinance. Gelinas v. City of Portsmouth, 97 N.H. 248, 85 A.2d 896, 1952 N.H. LEXIS 3 (1952). (Decided under prior law.)

13. —Unnecessary hardship

When the unnecessary hardship prong of the variance test under RSA 674:33, I(b) is applied to use variances, a court applies Simplex Technologies v. Town of Newington, 145 N.H 727, 766 A.2d 713, 2001 N.H. LEXIS 15 (2001), but when the unnecessary hardship prong is applied to area variances, the factors that should be considered include: (1) whether an area variance is needed to enable the applicant's proposed use of the property given the special conditions of the property; and (2) whether the benefit sought by the applicant can be achieved by some other method reasonably feasible for the applicant to pursue, other than an area variance, and this second factor includes consideration of whether the variance is necessary to avoid an undue financial burden on the owner. Thus, remand was required where the record supported a finding that the variances granted to an intervenor by a city's zoning board of adjustment were needed to enable the proposed use of the property as a hotel, but where it was unclear whether there were reasonably feasible alternative methods to implement the proposed use, without undue financial burden to the landowner. Boccia v. City of Portsmouth, 151 N.H. 85, 855 A.2d 516, 2004 N.H. LEXIS 94 (2004).

State supreme court reversed the superior court's judgment finding that property owners who owned a cabin by a lake were entitled to a variance from a local zoning ordinance so they could expand their cabin because the superior court did not address the factors which the supreme court established in its Boccia decision for determining unnecessary hardship in an area variance application. Shopland v. Town of Enfield, 151 N.H. 219, 855 A.2d 392, 2004 N.H. LEXIS 127 (2004).

In order to establish an unnecessary hardship for variance purposes, an applicant needed to show that the zoning interfered with the reasonable use of the property, considering its unique setting in its environment; the evidence supported the grant of a variance to build a barn. 8 Bonnita Rancourt v. City of Manchester, 149 N.H. 51, 816 A.2d 1011, 2003 N.H. LEXIS 2 (2003).

To establish unnecessary hardship, applicants for variances must prove: "(1) a zoning restriction as applied to their property interferes with their reasonable use of the property, considering the unique setting of the property in its environment; (2) no fair and substantial relationship exists between the general purposes of the zoning ordinance and the specific restriction on the property; and (3) the variance would not injure the public or private rights of others." Town of Plastow Bd. of Selectmen v. Town of Plastow Zoning Bd. of Adjustment, 146 N.H. 263, 769 A.2d 397, 2001 N.H. LEXIS 67 (2001).

The Supreme Court of New Hampshire held that the court's definition of undue hardship had become too restrictive in light of the constitutional protections by which it must be tempered, i.e., the right to acquire, possess, and protect property under N.H. Const. pt. I, arts. 2, 12, and decided to depart from the restrictive

approach that had defined unnecessary hardship and adopted an approach more considerate of the constitutional right to enjoy property. Henceforth, applicants for a variance could establish unnecessary hardship by proof that: (1) a zoning restriction as applied to their property interferes with their reasonable use of the property, considering the unique setting of the property in its environment; (2) no fair and substantial relationship exists between the general purposes of the zoning ordinance and the specific restriction on the property; and (3) the variance would not injure the public or private rights of others. Simplex Techs., Inc. v. Town of Newington, 145 N.H. 727, 766 A.2d 713, 2001 N.H. LEXIS 15 (2001).

Superior court erred by finding hardship necessary to sustain zoning board's award of a zoning variance to individual defendants to build two-car garage; finding that garage was necessary to keep defendant's car free from snow and ice, to enable defendant to make fast and unanticipated wintertime trips to the site of his job as an airline pilot called upon to make emergency flights, established nothing more than a need personal to the landowner, and did not satisfy condition that hardship be unique to applicant's parcel. Crossley v. Pelham, 133 N.H. 215, 578 A.2d 319, 1990 N.H. LEXIS 64 (1990).

A variance from a municipal ordinance could be granted where, owing to special conditions, a literal enforcement of the provisions of the ordinance would result in an unnecessary hardship. Little v. Town of Rye, 120 N.H. 533, 419 A.2d 396, 1980 N.H. LEXIS 347 (1980). (Decided under prior law.)

Where applicant for zoning variance to erect an additional apartment building on property testified that his income from the existing apartments was sufficient to meet expenses and his reason for requesting the variance was to obtain a greater return on his investment, the court properly found that the town's board of adjustment had improperly granted a zoning variance since there was no evidence to demonstrate those "special conditions" which would distinguish applicant's property from other property and warrant a variance based upon unnecessary hardship. Rowe v. Town of Salem, 119 N.H. 505, 403 A.2d 428, 1979 N.H. LEXIS 329 (1979). (Decided under prior law.)

The criterion for unnecessary hardship to warrant the issuance of a zoning variance was not the uniqueness of the plight of the owner but the uniqueness of the land causing the plight. Rowe v. Town of Salem, 119 N.H. 505, 403 A.2d 428, 1979 N.H. LEXIS 329 (1979). (Decided under prior law.)

A "hardship" of the type needed for a zoning variance resulted only if use of the particular property was unduly restricted by the zoning ordinance because of special conditions unique to that property which distinguished it from all others similarly restricted. Ouimette v. City of Somersworth, 119 N.H. 292, 402 A.2d 159, 1979 N.H. LEXIS 300 (1979). (Decided under prior law.)

Inability to use land for one particular purpose was irrelevant to whether a variance should be granted. Ouimette v. City of Somersworth, 119 N.H. 292, 402 A.2d 159, 1979 N.H. LEXIS 300 (1979). (Decided under prior law.)

The language of the statute authorizing a zoning board of adjustment to grant variances did not distinguish between types of variances but instead required a showing of unnecessary hardship whenever an owner of property requested a variance. Ouimette v. City of Somersworth, 119 N.H. 292, 402 A.2d 159, 1979 N.H. LEXIS 300 (1979). (Decided under prior law.)

To warrant the granting of a variance based upon a finding of unnecessary hardship there must have been something special about the applicant's property to distinguish it from other land in the same area with respect to its suitability for the use for which it was zoned. Carbonneau v. Town of Exeter, 119 N.H. 259, 401 A.2d 675, 1979 N.H. LEXIS 289 (1979). (Decided under prior law.)

A variance would be granted when special conditions created a situation in which strict enforcement of a zoning ordinance would result in unnecessary hardship for property owner. Town of Rye v. McMahon, 117 N.H. 857, 379 A.2d 807, 1977 N.H. LEXIS 448 (1977). (Decided under prior law.)

An unnecessary hardship was one suffered as the result of interference with the right to use property as one saw fit even though no public or private rights were injuriously affected by the use. Carter v. City of Nashua, 113 N.H. 407, 308 A.2d 847, 1973 N.H. LEXIS 285 (1973). (Decided under prior law.)

Financial hardship did not alone warrant a variance, but if it was unduly oppressive because of conditions of the property distinguishing it from other properties similarly restricted it could constitute unnecessary hardship. Carter v. City of Nashua, 113 N.H. 407, 308 A.2d 847, 1973 N.H. LEXIS 285 (1973). (Decided under prior law.)

A hardship resulted if a restriction upon use, when applied to a particular property, became arbitrary, confiscatory, or unduly oppressive because of conditions of the property distinguishing it from other properties similarly restricted. Vannah v. Bedford, 111 N.H. 105, 276 A.2d 253, 1971 N.H. LEXIS 132 (1971), overruled on other grounds, Cook v. Sanbornton, 118 N.H. 668, 392 A.2d 1201, 1978 N.H. LEXIS 267 (1978), questioned by, Barry v. Amherst, 121 N.H. 335, 430 A.2d 132, 1981 N.H. LEXIS 314 (1981). (Decided under prior law.)

An unnecessary hardship was one suffered as the result of interference with the right to use property as the owner saw fit, although no public or private rights were injuriously affected thereby. Vannah v. Bedford, 111 N.H. 105, 276 A.2d 253, 1971 N.H. LEXIS 132 (1971), overruled on other grounds, Cook v. Sanbornton, 118 N.H. 668, 392 A.2d 1201, 1978 N.H. LEXIS 267 (1978), questioned by, Barry v. Amherst, 121 N.H. 335, 430 A.2d 132, 1981 N.H. LEXIS 314 (1981). (Decided under prior law.)

The unnecessary hardship referred to in the statute must have related to the owner and not to an option holder. Welch v. City of Nashua, 108 N.H. 92, 227 A.2d 600, 1967 N.H. LEXIS 128 (1967). (Decided under prior law.)

The hardship referred to in the statute must have been one to whom the provision was designed to protect, and the statute was not designed to afford relief to a mere option holder of land as to which use variance was sought. Conery v. Nashua, 103 N.H. 16, 164 A.2d 247, 1960 N.H. LEXIS 3 (1960). (Decided under prior law.)

Financial hardship in and of itself did not warrant the granting of a variance from the terms of a zoning ordinance. St. Onge v. City of Concord, 95 N.H. 306, 63 A.2d 221, 1949 N.H. LEXIS 158 (1948). (Decided under prior law.)

A hardship within the meaning of the statute could result if the restriction upon use, when applied to a particular property, became arbitrary, confiscatory, or unduly oppressive because of conditions of the property distinguishing it from other properties similarly restricted. St. Onge v. City of Concord, 95 N.H. 306, 63 A.2d 221, 1949 N.H. LEXIS 158 (1948). (Decided under prior law.)

In a zoning appeal wherein a trial court reversed a city's denial of an applicant's variance request to build a halfway house on the basis that it was a correctional facility that was not permitted within any of the city's zoning districts, the reviewing court reversed the trial court because no evidence existed in the record that demonstrated how the size and layout of the specific building proposed made the property particularly appropriate for the proposed use, no evidence demonstrated that the proposed site was unique, nor did the evidence reasonably support the trial court's conclusion that the applicant's property was burdened by the restriction in a manner that was distinct from similarly situated property. Thus, the applicant did not satisfy the first prong of the Simplex test to establish unnecessary hardship. Cmty. Res. for Justice, Inc. v. City of Manchester, 154 N.H. 748, 917 A.2d 707, 2007 N.H. LEXIS 11 (2007).

14. Deliberations of board upon application for variance

In arriving at a decision, the members of the board could consider their own knowledge concerning such factors as traffic conditions, surrounding uses, etc., resulting from their familiarity with the area involved. Vannah v. Bedford, 111 N.H. 105, 276 A.2d 253, 1971 N.H. LEXIS 132 (1971), overruled on other grounds, Cook v. Sanbornton, 118 N.H. 668, 392 A.2d 1201, 1978 N.H. LEXIS 267 (1978), questioned by, Barry v. Amherst, 121 N.H. 335, 430 A.2d 132, 1981 N.H. LEXIS 314 (1981). (Decided under prior law.)

The board of adjustment did not have to accept the conclusions of experts, but rather, could properly rely on its own knowledge of the area in which a variance was sought. Vannah v. Bedford, 111 N.H. 105, 276 A.2d 253, 1971 N.H. LEXIS 132 (1971), overruled on other grounds, Cook v. Sanbornton, 118 N.H. 668, 392 A.2d 1201, 1978 N.H. LEXIS 267 (1978), questioned by, Barry v. Amherst, 121 N.H. 335, 430 A.2d 132, 1981 N.H. LEXIS 314 (1981). (Decided under prior law.)

15. Rendition of decision by board

The duty of the board of adjustment to "make such order, or decision, as ought to be made" did not extend to the rendition of an advisory opinion, and was satisfied by a finding that a proposed use was not permissible. Perron v. City of Concord, 102 N.H. 32, 150 A.2d 403, 1959 N.H. LEXIS 11 (1959). (Decided under prior law.)

16. Power of board as to granting of variances—Generally

A board's power to grant variances was not limited to slight variances. Carter v. City of Nashua, 113 N.H. 407, 308 A.2d 847, 1973 N.H. LEXIS 285 (1973). (Decided under prior law.)

17. —Attachment of conditions to variance

While reaffirming its earlier ruling that the plaintiffs' construction business fell within the parameters of a nonconforming use, the zoning board of adjustment properly imposed conditions that (1) no paving materials or vehicles with residual paving materials were to be parked or repaired on the site, (2) equipment on site was limited to 10 pieces; and (3) none of the plaintiffs' vehicles larger than cars or pickup trucks could use the access road to the property. Peabody v. Town of Windham, 142 N.H. 488, 703 A.2d 886, 1997 N.H. LEXIS 121 (1997).

A zoning board, considering an administrative appeal, may impose reasonable conditions to prevent improper expansions of nonconforming uses. Peabody v. Town of Windham, 142 N.H. 488, 703 A.2d 886, 1997 N.H. LEXIS 121 (1997).

A claim that conditions attached to variance were ineffective was an ineffective attack upon a variance for the board of adjustment was not required to anticipate noncompliance or failure of proper public officials to insure that conditions would be met. Carter v. City of Nashua, 113 N.H. 407, 308 A.2d 847, 1973 N.H. LEXIS 285 (1973). (Decided under prior law.)

The broad powers granted boards under the statute included the attachment of reasonable conditions necessary to observance of the spirit of pertinent ordinances, but the conditions were to relate to the use of the land, not the person who was to be using the land. Wentworth Hotel, Inc. v. Town of New Castle, 112 N.H. 21, 287 A.2d 615, 1972 N.H. LEXIS 135 (1972). (Decided under prior law.)

A zoning variance condition requiring compliance with all ordinances and statutes and making all subsequently adopted ordinances applicable to the property would be interpreted as applying only to laws not infringing the vested rights of the party granted the variance and, as so interpreted, was valid. Wentworth Hotel, Inc. v. Town of New Castle, 112 N.H. 21, 287 A.2d 615, 1972 N.H. LEXIS 135 (1972). (Decided under prior law.)

Conditions necessary to observance of the

spirit of a zoning order could be attached to a variance. Vlahos Realty Co. v. Little Boar's Head District, 101 N.H. 460, 146 A.2d 257, 1958 N.H. LEXIS 63 (1958). (Decided under prior law.)

While the statute contained no express provision permitting conditions to be attached to a variance, the board of adjustment was given broad powers and could make "such order, or decision, as ought to be made"; this language was inclusive enough to authorize the power to attach reasonable conditions to the granting of variances. Vlahos Realty Co. v. Little Boar's Head District, 101 N.H. 460, 146 A.2d 257, 1958 N.H. LEXIS 63 (1958). (Decided under prior law.)

III. Special Exceptions

30. Distinction between variances and special exceptions

While in practice a sharp distinction between exceptions and variances may not in all cases be readily made, there is a major difference between the two: there is no necessity for a hardship to exist in order to qualify for a special exception. Stone v. Cray, 89 N.H. 483, 200 A. 517, 1938 N.H. LEXIS 60 (1938); Burr v. City of Keene, 105 N.H. 228, 196 A.2d 63, 1963 N.H. LEXIS 54 (1963). (Decided under prior law.)

A literal enforcement of an ordinance may be disregarded to permit a variance, while the conditions for an exception must be found in the ordinance and may not be varied. Stone v. Cray, 89 N.H. 483, 200 A. 517, 1938 N.H. LEXIS 60 (1938). (Decided under prior law.)

31. Delegation of authority to make special exceptions to ordinances

Under state law, terms of a zoning ordinance and its self-described purposes establish the test for granting special exceptions. Town of Amherst v. Omnipoint Communications Enters., Inc., 173 F.3d 9, 1999 U.S. App. LEXIS 6046 (1st Cir. 1999).

Earth excavation regulation of a town zoning ordinance did not conflict with paragraph IV of this section, vesting authority to grant exceptions in a board of adjustment, since the five listed categories of permissible earth removal activities in the ordinance, which were made subject to the selectmen's control, did not encompass earth removal for sale and were not therefore "exceptions" to the regulation's prohibition of earth removal for sale. Town of Goffstown v. Thibeault, 129 N.H. 454, 529 A.2d 930,

1987 N.H. LEXIS 184 (1987).

As this provision vested in the board of adjustment the power to "make special exceptions to the terms of the ordinance", an ordinance provision purporting to grant such power to a private association and the selectmen of the town, in addition to the board of adjustment, was an unlawful delegation of authority. Fernald v. Bassett, 107 N.H. 282, 220 A.2d 739, 1966 N.H. LEXIS 174 (1966). (Decided under prior law.)

The delegation in a local ordinance of the authority to the municipal zoning board of adjustment to make special exceptions was defective where it failed to establish standards by which the board was to be governed in determining whether an exception should be made. Fernald v. Bassett, 107 N.H. 282, 220 A.2d 739, 1966 N.H. LEXIS 174 (1966). (Decided under prior law.)

32. Power of board as to special exceptions

The zoning board of adjustment has authority under this section to grant special exceptions to zoning ordinance; however, it cannot waive that such special exceptions be obtained by property owners otherwise in violation of the ordinance. Mudge v. Precinct of Haverhill Corner, 133 N.H. 881, 587 A.2d 603, 1991 N.H. LEXIS 10 (1991).

The terms of the ordinance are to define the cases or conditions in or upon which exceptions are allowable; the board's only function in respect to exceptions is to decide if the conditions exist which make the case an appropriate one. Stone v. Cray, 89 N.H. 483, 200 A. 517, 1938 N.H. LEXIS 60 (1938). (Decided under prior law.)

Under the statutory provision relating to special exceptions, the ordinance was to declare when exceptions could be permitted; the language of the statute implied a denial of authority to the board to decide what conditions made an exception expedient. Stone v. Cray, 89 N.H. 483, 200 A. 517, 1938 N.H. LEXIS 60 (1938). (Decided under prior law.)

The purpose and design of the statutory provision relating to the authority to make special exceptions was that only the ordinance could declare the exceptions, leaving it to the board of adjustment to decide their application in particular cases. Stone v. Cray, 89 N.H. 483, 200 A. 517, 1938 N.H. LEXIS 60 (1938). (Decided under prior law.)

33. Manufactured housing parks

Manufactured housing parks are omitted from this section's exemption of manufactured housing from requirement that special exceptions to zoning ordinances be obtained by property owners. Mudge v. Precinct of Haverhill Corner, 133 N.H. 881, 587 A.2d 603, 1991 N.H. LEXIS 10 (1991).

Trial court improperly denied plaintiff's motion to vacate zoning board of adjustment's upholding of a building permit, where property owner failed to obtain a special exception for a commercial use of premises to be used for expansion of manufactured housing park. Mudge v. Precinct of Haverhill Corner, 133 N.H. 881, 587 A.2d 603, 1991 N.H. LEXIS 10 (1991).

Cited:

Cited in Saturley v. Town of Hollis, 129 N.H. 757, 533 A.2d 29, 1987 N.H. LEXIS 256 (1987); Margate Motel, Inc. v. Town of Gilford, 130 N.H. 91, 534 A.2d 717, 1987 N.H. LEXIS 272 (1987); Goslin v. Town of Farmington, 132 N.H. 48, 561 A.2d 507, 1989 N.H. LEXIS 68 (1989); Korpi v. Town of Peterborough, 135 N.H. 37, 599 A.2d 130, 1991 N.H. LEXIS 142 (1991); Olszak v. Town of New Hampton, 139 N.H. 723, 661 A.2d 768, 1995 N.H. LEXIS 81 (1995); Hurley v. Town of Hollis, 143 N.H. 567, 729 A.2d 998, 1999 N.H. LEXIS 45 (1999).

RESEARCH REFERENCES

New Hampshire Practice.

15 N.H.P. Land Use Planning and Zoning §§ 16.01, 19.01, 19.02, 20.04, 21.03, 21.10, 22.01, 22.02, 23.01, 23.05, 24.01, 24.03, 24.04, 24.10, 24.13, 24.16, 24.18, 35.15, 36.13, 36.22, 39.05.

New Hampshire Bar Journal.

For article, "The New Zoning Variance Cases: Analyzing Unnecessary Hardship Under RSA 674:33," see N.H.B.J. 40 (Fall 2005).

For article, "The New Zoning Variance Cases: Analyzing Unnecessary Hardship Under RSA 674:33," see 46 N.H.B.J. 40 (Fall 2005).

For article, "Unnecessary Hardship Under RSA 674:331(B)," see 46 N.H.B.J. 47 (Fall 2005).

674:33-a. Equitable Waiver of Dimensional Requirement.

I. When a lot or other division of land, or structure thereupon, is discovered to be in violation of a physical layout or dimensional requirement imposed by a zoning ordinance enacted pursuant to RSA 674:16, the zoning board of adjustment shall, upon application by and with the burden of proof on the property owner, grant an equitable waiver from the requirement, if and only if the board makes all of the following findings:

(a) That the violation was not noticed or discovered by any owner, former owner, owner's agent or representative, or municipal official, until after a structure in violation had been substantially completed, or until after a lot or other division of land in violation had been subdivided by conveyance to a bona fide purchaser for value;

(b) That the violation was not an outcome of ignorance of the law or ordinance, failure to inquire, obfuscation, misrepresentation, or bad faith on the part of any owner, owner's agent or representative, but was instead caused by either a good faith error in measurement or calculation made by an owner or owner's agent, or by an error in ordinance interpretation or applicability made by a municipal official in the process of issuing a permit over which that official had authority;

(c) That the physical or dimensional violation does not constitute a public or private nuisance, nor diminish the value of other property in the area, nor interfere with or adversely affect any present or permissible future uses of any such property; and

(d) That due to the degree of past construction or investment made in ignorance of the facts constituting the violation, the cost of correction so far outweighs any public benefit to be gained, that it would be inequitable to require the violation to be corrected.

II. In lieu of the findings required by the board under subparagraphs I(a) and (b), the owner may demonstrate to the satisfaction of the board that the violation has existed for 10 years or more, and that no enforcement action, including written notice of violation, has been commenced against the violation during that time by the municipality or any person directly affected.

III. Application and hearing procedures for equitable waivers under this section shall be governed by RSA 676:5 through 7. Rehearings and appeals shall be governed by RSA 677:2 through 14.

IV. Waivers shall be granted under this section only from physical layout, mathematical or dimensional requirements, and not from use restrictions. An equitable waiver granted under this section shall not be construed as a nonconforming use, and shall not exempt future use, construction, reconstruction, or additions on the property from full compliance with the ordinance. This section shall not be construed to alter the principle that owners of land are bound by constructive knowledge of all applicable requirements. This section shall not be construed to impose upon municipal officials any duty to guarantee the correctness of plans reviewed by them or property inspected by them.

Source.
1996, 226:4, eff. Jan. 1, 1997.

674:34. Powers of Building Code Board of Appeals.

The building code board of appeals shall have the power, upon an appeal filed with it by any person aggrieved by a decision of the building inspector dealing with the building code, to vary the application of any provision of the building code to any particular case when, in its opinion, the enforcement of the building code would do manifest injustice and would be contrary to the spirit and purpose of the building code and the public interest.

Source.
1983, 447:1, eff. Jan. 1, 1984.

Requirement and issuance of building permits generally, see RSA 676:11 et seq.

Cross References.
Appeal from and review of building code boards of appeals decisions, see RSA 677:16.

RESEARCH REFERENCES

New Hampshire Practice.
15 N.H.P. Land Use Planning and Zoning §§ 19.03, 29.02.

Regulation of Subdivision of Land

Cross References.
Building codes generally, see RSA 674:51 et seq.
Condominiums, see RSA 356-B.
Emergency temporary zoning and planning ordinances, see RSA 674:24 et seq.
Master plans generally, see RSA 674:1 et seq.

Official municipal maps generally, see RSA 674:9 et seq.
Site plan review, see RSA 674:43 et seq.
Unit ownership of real property, see RSA 479-A.
Zoning generally, see RSA 674:16 et seq.

NOTES TO DECISIONS

Constitutionality
The statute authorizing municipalities to enact ordinances regulating the subdivision of land to promote the orderly and planned growth of relatively undeveloped areas within the municipality was a proper exercise of the police power. Blevens v. City of Manchester, 103

N.H. 284, 170 A.2d 121, 1961 N.H. LEXIS 33 (1961). (Decided under prior law.)

Cited:
Cited in Vachon v. Town of New Durham Zoning Bd. of Adjustment, 131 N.H. 623, 557 A.2d 649, 1989 N.H. LEXIS 29 (1989).

674:35. Power to Regulate Subdivisions.

I. A municipality may by ordinance or resolution authorize the planning board to require preliminary review of subdivisions, and to approve or disapprove, in its discretion, plats, and to approve or disapprove plans showing the extent to which and the manner in which streets within subdivisions shall be graded and improved and to which streets water, sewer, and other utility mains, piping, connections or other facilities within subdivisions shall be installed.

II. The planning board of a municipality shall have the authority to regulate the subdivision of land under the enactment procedures of RSA 675:6. The ordinance or resolution which authorizes the planning board to regulate the subdivision of land shall make it the duty of the city clerk, town clerk, clerk of district commissioners or other appropriate recording official to file with the register of deeds of the county in which the municipality is located a certificate of notice showing that the planning board has been so authorized, giving the date of such authorization.

III. The planning board shall not limit the number of building permits that may be issued except in accordance with an innovative land use control ordinance addressing timing incentives and phased development under RSA 674:21 and adopted under RSA 674:16; or an ordinance to regulate and control the timing of development, adopted under RSA 674:22; or an ordinance to regulate growth via interim regulation, adopted under RSA 674:23. This paragraph shall not be construed to limit the planning board's authority to deny a subdivision application on the basis that it is scattered or premature.

Source.
1983, 447:1, eff. Jan. 1, 1984. 2004, 71:3, eff. July 6, 2004. 2005, 51:1, eff. July 22, 2005.

Amendments
—**2005.** Paragraph III: Added.

—**2004.** Paragraph I: Inserted "to require preliminary review of subdivisions, and" following "planning board".

Cross References.
Adoption of subdivision regulations, see RSA 674:36.

Approval and recording of plats, see RSA 674:37-39.

Development on class V and VI highways, see RSA 674:41.

Effect of section upon existing laws, see RSA 674:42.

Street improvements generally, see RSA 674:40.

NOTES TO DECISIONS

Analysis

1. Construction
2. Definition
3. Construction with other laws
4. Site plan review
5. Necessity for adoption of regulations
6. Conditions for approval of plans—Granting of easements
7. —Offsite improvements
8. Effect of zoning changes upon approved plots or plans

1. Construction

This section grants the town planning board the power to regulate the act of subdividing but not the land that has been subdivided. Lemm Dev. Corp. v. Town of Bartlett, 133 N.H. 618, 580 A.2d 1082, 1990 N.H. LEXIS 114 (1990).

Town planning board's authority to enact subdivision controls is strictly confined to the terms of the enabling legislation. Lemm Dev. Corp. v. Town of Bartlett, 133 N.H. 618, 580 A.2d 1082, 1990 N.H. LEXIS 114 (1990).

Town planning board had no authority under its subdivision regulations to review or control corporation's planned construction of condominium amenities facility on subdivided land, where no division of ownership or physical division of the land was planned. Lemm Dev. Corp. v. Town of Bartlett, 133 N.H. 618, 580 A.2d 1082, 1990 N.H. LEXIS 114 (1990).

2. Definition

Term "subdivision" in this section means only the act of subdividing land; general zoning law provision in RSA 672:14 defining the "subdivision" as "land or territory subdivided" is not encompassed within this section. Lemm Dev. Corp. v. Town of Bartlett, 133 N.H. 618, 580 A.2d 1082, 1990 N.H. LEXIS 114 (1990).

3. Construction with other laws

While it is the state which has the power to regulate access to state highways under RSA 236:13, a town may legitimately consider the impact that increased traffic may have upon the safety of an existing or proposed access in determining whether or not to grant approval of a subdivision plan. Diversified Properties, Inc. v. Town of Hopkinton Planning Board, 125 N.H. 419, 480 A.2d 194, 1984 N.H. LEXIS 262 (1984).

4. Site plan review

To control the construction of condominium amenities facility on subdivided land, planning board must promulgate site plan review regulations. Lemm Dev. Corp. v. Town of Bartlett, 133 N.H. 618, 580 A.2d 1082, 1990 N.H. LEXIS 114 (1990).

5. Necessity for adoption of regulations

The statute authorized municipalities to grant their planning boards discretionary authority to approve or disapprove subdivision plans, but before a board could exercise that authority it was required to adopt subdivision regulations. Durant v. Town of Dunbarton, 121 N.H. 352, 430 A.2d 140, 1981 N.H. LEXIS 318 (1981). (Decided under prior law.)

6. Conditions for approval of plans—Granting of easements

A city planning board could not legally require a landowner, as a condition to approval of a site plan, to grant the city an easement ten feet wide on the edge of his property for highway purposes so that city could use it to widen the road in the future; any taking of such land would require just compensation. Robbins Auto Parts v. Laconia, 117 N.H. 235, 371 A.2d 1167,

1977 N.H. LEXIS 308 (1977). (Decided under prior law.)

7. —Offsite improvements
Where a town planning board conditioned its approval of a developer's application for a subdivision on the developer's upgrading, at its own expense and to standards established by the town, of two roads leading to but located outside the proposed subdivision, and evidence indicated that traffic on the two roads, due to the proposed subdivision, would increase the hazard that an emergency would create, and that there must be improvement to the roads if the subdivision was fully developed, compelling the conclusion that, with respect to the criterion of safety, the proposed subdivision was premature, the town could legitimately condition its approval of the subdivision on the provision of improvements to the offsite access roads. Land/Vest Properties, Inc. v. Town of Plainfield, 117 N.H. 817, 379 A.2d 200, 1977 N.H. LEXIS 440 (1977). (Decided under prior law.)
Where offsite improvements could properly be required of a subdivider by a town planning board, the subdivider could be compelled only

to bear that portion of the cost which bore a rational nexus to the needs created by, and special benefits conferred upon, the subdivision. Land/Vest Properties, Inc. v. Town of Plainfield, 117 N.H. 817, 379 A.2d 200, 1977 N.H. LEXIS 440 (1977). (Decided under prior law.)

8. Effect of zoning changes upon approved plots or plans
In the absence of a statute providing otherwise, final approval of a subdivision plot by a planning board under the statute did not place the lots beyond the authority of zoning changes. R. A. Vachon & Son, Inc. v. City of Concord, 112 N.H. 107, 289 A.2d 646, 1972 N.H. LEXIS 153 (1972). (Decided under prior law.)

Cited:
Cited in Frisella v. Town of Farmington, 131 N.H. 78, 550 A.2d 102, 1988 N.H. LEXIS 94 (1988); Morin v. City of Somersworth, 131 N.H. 253, 551 A.2d 527, 1988 N.H. LEXIS 109 (1988); New England Brickmaster, Inc. v. Town of Salem, 133 N.H. 655, 582 A.2d 601, 1990 N.H. LEXIS 119 (1990); Blevens v. Town of Bow, 887 F. Supp. 38, 1994 U.S. Dist. LEXIS 14408 (D.N.H. 1994).

RESEARCH REFERENCES

New Hampshire Practice.
15 N.H.P. Land Use Planning and Zoning §§ 19.03, 26.03, 29.04, 29.17, 29.19, 29.22, 29.24, 36.20.

New Hampshire Bar Journal.
For article, "Roads Revisited: Creation and Termination of Highways in New Hampshire - An Update," see N.H.B.J. 56 (Fall 2005).

674:36. Subdivision Regulations.

I. Before the planning board exercises its powers under RSA 674:35, the planning board shall adopt subdivision regulations according to the procedures required by RSA 675:6.

II. The subdivision regulations which the planning board adopts may:

(a) Provide against such scattered or premature subdivision of land as would involve danger or injury to health, safety, or prosperity by reason of the lack of water supply, drainage, transportation, schools, fire protection, or other public services, or necessitate the excessive expenditure of public funds for the supply of such services;

(b) Provide for the harmonious development of the municipality and its environs;

(c) Require the proper arrangement and coordination of streets within subdivisions in relation to other existing or planned streets or with features of the official map of the municipality;

(d) Provide for open spaces of adequate proportions;

(e) Require suitably located streets of sufficient width to accommodate existing and prospective traffic and to afford adequate light, air, and access for firefighting apparatus and equipment to buildings, and be coordinated so as to compose a convenient system;

(f) Require, in proper cases, that plats showing new streets or narrowing or widening of such streets submitted to the planning board for approval shall show a park or parks suitably located for playground or other recreational purposes;

(g) Require that proposed parks shall be of reasonable size for neighborhood playgrounds or other recreational uses;

(h) Require that the land indicated on plats submitted to the planning board shall be of such character that it can be used for building purposes without danger to health;

(i) Prescribe minimum areas of lots so as to assure conformance with local zoning ordinances and to assure such additional areas as may be needed for each lot for on-site sanitary facilities;

(j) Include provisions which will tend to create conditions favorable to health, safety, convenience, or prosperity;

(k) Encourage the installation and use of solar, wind, or other renewable energy systems and protect access to energy sources by the regulation of orientation of streets, lots, and buildings; establishment of maximum building height, minimum set back requirements, and limitations on type, height, and placement of vegetation; and encouragement of the use of solar skyspace easements under RSA 477; and

(l) Provide for efficient and compact subdivision development which promotes retention and public usage of open space and wildlife habitat, by allowing for village plan alternative subdivision as defined in RSA 674:21, VI.

(m) Require innovative land use controls on lands when supported by the master plan.

(n) Include provision for waiver of any portion of the regulations in such cases where, in the opinion of the planning board, strict conformity would pose an unnecessary hardship to the applicant and waiver would not be contrary to the spirit and intent of the regulations.

III. The subdivision regulations of the planning board may stipulate, as a condition precedent to the approval of the plat, the extent to which and the manner in which streets shall be graded and improved and to which water, sewer, and other utility mains, piping, connections, or other facilities shall be installed. The regulations or practice of the planning board:

(a) May provide for the conditional approval of the plat before such improvements and installations have been constructed, but any such conditional approval shall not be entered upon the plat.

(b) Shall provide that, in lieu of the completion of street work and utility installations prior to the final approval of a plat, the planning board shall accept a performance bond, irrevocable letter of credit, or other type or types of security as shall be specified in the subdivision regulations; provided that in no event shall the exclusive form of security required by the planning board be in the form of cash or a passbook. As phases or portions of the secured improvements or installations are completed and approved by the planning board or its designee, the municipality shall partially release said security to the extent reasonably calculated to reflect the value of such completed improvements or installations. Cost escalation factors that are applied by the planning board to any bond or other security required under this section shall not exceed 10 percent per year. The planning board shall, within the limitations provided in this subparagraph, have the discretion to prescribe the type and amount of security, and specify a period for completion of the improvements and utilities to be expressed in the bond or other security, in order to secure to the municipality the actual construction and installation of such improvements and utilities. The municipality shall have the power to enforce such bonds or other securities by all appropriate legal and equitable remedies.

(c) May provide that in lieu of the completion of street work and utility installations prior to the final approval of the plat, the subdivision regulations may provide for an assessment or other method by which the municipality is put in an assured position to do said work and to make said alterations at the cost of the owners of the property within the subdivision.

Source.

1983, 447:1. 1986, 200:2. 1988, 3:1, eff. April 19, 1988. 2002, 73:3, eff. June 30, 2002; 236:4, eff. July 16, 2002. 2004, 71:4, eff. July 6, 2004; 199:4, eff. June 7, 2004.

Revision note.

Made minor changes in punctuation at the end of par. II(j) and (k) in light of the amendment to this section by 2002, 236:4.

Amendments

—2004. Paragraph II(m): Added by ch. 71. Paragraph II(n): Added by ch. 199.

—2002. Paragraph II: Chapter 73 made a minor change in phraseology in subpars. (i) and (j) and added subpar. (k).

Chapter 236 added subpar. (*l*).

—1988. Paragraph III(b): Added "provided that in no event shall the exclusive form of security required by the planning board be in the form of cash or a passbook" following "regu-

lations" at the end of the first sentence, added the second and third sentences, inserted "within the limitations provided in this subparagraph" following "planning board shall" and deleted "the bond or other security, require satisfactory evidence of the financial ability of any surety or financial institution to pay such bond or other type of" preceding "security, and specify" in the fourth sentence.

—1986. Paragraph III: Rewritten to the extent that a detailed comparison would be impracticable.

Cross References.

Development on class V and VI highways, see RSA 674:41.

Effect of uncompleted streets or utilities upon applications for building permits, see RSA 676:12.

Revocation of recorded subdivision plat approval, see RSA 676:4-a.

Street improvements generally, see RSA 674:40.

NOTES TO DECISIONS

Analysis

1. Purpose
2. Construction
3. Construction with other laws
4. Access roads
5. Scope of authority
6. Scope of regulations—Generally
7. —Prevention of scattered or premature subdivision of land
8. —Arrangement and coordination of streets

9. —Open space and parks
10. —Lot size
11. Requirement of surety bonds

1. Purpose

This section serves to ensure that the town, through its planning board, retains control over its expenditures on the development, improvement, and maintenance of town services to new subdivisions. Stillwater Condominium Ass'n v. Town of Salem, 140 N.H. 505, 668 A.2d 38, 1995 N.H. LEXIS 177 (1995).

2. Construction

The term "prosperity," as used in the statute, refers to a community's fiscal wellbeing, and not to an individual's financial interest and, therefore, the statute was not intended to protect owners of condominium units from financial harm caused by the developer's failure to construct a municipal water line extension. Stillwater Condominium Ass'n v. Town of Salem, 140 N.H. 505, 668 A.2d 38, 1995 N.H. LEXIS 177 (1995).

3. Construction with other laws

Other than its management tool capabilities, a capital improvements program has no part to play in review of subdivision applications presented to governmental authorities. Zukis v. Town of Fitzwilliam, 135 N.H. 384, 604 A.2d 956, 1992 N.H. LEXIS 46 (1992).

While it is the state which has the power to regulate access to state highways under RSA 236:13, a town may legitimately consider the impact that increased traffic may have upon the safety of an existing or proposed access in determining whether or not to grant approval of a subdivision plan. Diversified Properties, Inc. v. Town of Hopkinton Planning Board, 125 N.H. 419, 480 A.2d 194, 1984 N.H. LEXIS 262 (1984).

Former RSA 36:19 (now covered by RSA 674:35) authorized municipalities to grant their planning boards discretionary authority to approve or disapprove subdivision plans, but before a board could exercise that authority it was required to adopt subdivision regulations. Durant v. Town of Dunbarton, 121 N.H. 352, 430 A.2d 140, 1981 N.H. LEXIS 318 (1981). (Decided under prior law.)

4. Access roads

Planning board may properly consider the present condition of access roads when ruling on a subdivision application, and if a hazard is created by the present level of development, it may find that future development is premature. Zukis v. Town of Fitzwilliam, 135 N.H. 384, 604 A.2d 956, 1992 N.H. LEXIS 46 (1992).

Trial court erred in ruling that preexisting inadequacy of access roads was not a valid basis for planning board's finding that proposed subdivision was premature, since exposing more households to risk that emergency vehicles would be unable to respond when their services were required would magnify existing hazard. Zukis v. Town of Fitzwilliam, 135 N.H. 384, 604 A.2d 956, 1992 N.H. LEXIS 46 (1992).

5. Scope of authority

Where a developer's conservation development subdivision (CDS) approved by a town board, contained a cul-de-sac that serviced seventeen lots, exceeding the 10-lot maximum of the town's subdivision regulations, and the record revealed that the board decided to waive the ten-lot requirement because it preferred the cul-de-sac configuration in the proposed CDS to the loop road configuration in the yield plan, the trial court erred in ruling that the waiver was reasonable under the circumstances, because there was no evidence that a loop road configuration would cause undue hardship or injustice to the developer, as required by RSA 674:36(II)(n).Auger v. Town of Strafford, — N.H.— , — A.2d —, 2007 N.H. LEXIS 142 (Aug. 23, 2007).

Where a developer's yield plan associated with a conservation development subdivision depicted the location of the wetlands, but did not contain detailed information about the proposed disturbances and impact on those wetlands, the plan did not comply with applicable subdivision regulations, which required the plan to show all wetlands and proposed disturbances in sufficient detail so that the board could assess the impact, and to show that the proposed wetlands disturbance would be minimized in accordance with DES requirements. The trial court properly found that the yield plan did not comply with the subdivision regulations, but it improperly remanded the decision to the board to "obtain the information necessary" for determining whether the yield plan complied with the applicable regulations when it should have instead reversed the board's approval of the yield plan.Auger v. Town of Strafford, — N.H.— , — A.2d —, 2007 N.H. LEXIS 142 (Aug. 23, 2007).

Planning board's denial of subdivision proposal on grounds it was "premature" was plainly taken to control growth, and thus exceeded board's statutory authority under subdivision II(a) of this section. Ettlingen Homes v. Town of Derry, 141 N.H. 296, 681 A.2d 97, 1996 N.H. LEXIS 93 (1996).

6. Scope of regulations—Generally

The scope of a municipality's subdivision regulations could be quite broad and generally could include provisions which would tend to create conditions favorable to health, safety, convenience or prosperity. Durant v. Town of Dunbarton, 121 N.H. 352, 430 A.2d 140, 1981 N.H. LEXIS 318 (1981). (Decided under prior law.)

Under the statute, delegation of a municipality's power to regulate subdivisions was quite broad, and the regulation of septic tanks and sewerage systems fell within the purview of the statute. Durant v. Town of Dunbarton, 121 N.H. 352, 430 A.2d 140, 1981 N.H. LEXIS 318 (1981). (Decided under prior law.)

7. —Prevention of scattered or premature subdivision of land

Under the statute, a planning board could promulgate regulations which provided for consideration of off-site factors insofar as they rendered subdivisions "scattered or premature." Garipay v. Town of Hanover, 116 N.H. 34, 351 A.2d 64, 1976 N.H. LEXIS 256 (1976); Land/Vest Properties, Inc. v. Town of Plainfield, 117 N.H. 817, 379 A.2d 200, 1977 N.H. LEXIS 440 (1977). (Decided under prior law.)

The authority of a planning board was not limited to a consideration of streets within a subdivision, but extended to off-site improvements and obligations necessitated by a proposed development, including improvement of a public road abutting the proposed subdivision. KBW, Inc. v. Town of Bennington, 115 N.H. 392, 342 A.2d 653, 1975 N.H. LEXIS 319 (1975); Land/Vest Properties, Inc. v. Town of Plainfield, 117 N.H. 817, 379 A.2d 200, 1977 N.H. LEXIS 440 (1977). (Decided under prior law.)

Where a town planning board conditioned its approval of a developer's application for a subdivision on the developer's upgrading, at its own expense and to standards established by the town, of two roads leading to but located outside the proposed subdivision, and evidence indicated traffic on the two roads, due to the proposed subdivision, would increase the haz-

ard that an emergency would create, and that there must be improvements to the roads if the subdivision was fully developed, compelling the conclusion that, with respect to the criterion of safety, the proposed subdivision was premature, the town could legitimately condition its approval of the subdivision on the provision of improvements to the off-site access roads. Land/Vest Properties, Inc. v. Town of Plainfield, 117 N.H. 817, 379 A.2d 200, 1977 N.H. LEXIS 440 (1977). (Decided under prior law.)

8. —Arrangement and coordination of streets

The statute, which allowed planning boards to regulate the arrangement and coordination of streets within subdivisions in relation to other existing or planned streets, did not give municipalities control over access to state highways. J. E. D. Assocs. v. Sandown, 121 N.H. 317, 430 A.2d 129, 1981 N.H. LEXIS 332 (1981). (Decided under prior law.)

9. —Open space and parks

A planning board could impose conditions, even though there had been compliance with the minimum lot size provisions contained in a zoning ordinance, when the conditions were necessary for "the harmonious development of the municipality and its environs" and for "open spaces of adequate proportion." Town of Seabrook v. Tra-Sea Corporation, 119 N.H. 937, 410 A.2d 240, 1979 N.H. LEXIS 424 (1979). (Decided under prior law.)

The statute authorized planning boards to require open spaces of adequate proportion and parks of reasonable size in subdivisions. Patenaude v. Town of Meredith, 118 N.H. 616, 392 A.2d 582, 1978 N.H. LEXIS 253 (1978). (Decided under prior law.)

10. —Lot size

Town's requirement that lots have a certain minimum contiguous area for building purposes ensured that the lots had proper areas for drainage, conformed with the ordinances, and had sufficient areas for sanitary facilities; thus, Gilmanton, N.H., Subdivision Regulations § VI(C)(2), requiring a minimum lot size, served a legitimate land use purpose. Doyle v. Town of Gilmanton, — N.H. —, 927 A.2d 1211, 2007 N.H. LEXIS 122 (July 19, 2007).

Though subdivision regulations could prescribe minimum lot areas, these prescriptions were required to conform to the local zoning ordinance. Town of Seabrook v. Tra-Sea Corporation, 119 N.H. 937, 410 A.2d 240, 1979 N.H. LEXIS 424 (1979). (Decided under prior law.)

11. Requirement of surety bonds

The statute specifically vested jurisdiction to issue regulations governing performance bonds in the town planning board, and a regulation adopted by a board was defective where it purported to delegate to the town selectmen the authority to determine the amounts and conditions of any surety bonds. Levasseur v. Board of

Selectmen of Hudson, 116 N.H. 340, 358 A.2d 665, 1976 N.H. LEXIS 349 (1976). (Decided under prior law.)

Cited:

Cited in Cutting v. Town of Wentworth, 126 N.H. 727, 497 A.2d 839, 1985 N.H. LEXIS 422 (1985); Mooney v. City of Laconia, 133 N.H. 30, 573 A.2d 447, 1990 N.H. LEXIS 31 (1990); K & P, Inc. v. Town of Plaistow, 133 N.H. 283, 575 A.2d 804, 1990 N.H. LEXIS 50 (1990); State v. Wilson, 140 N.H. 44, 662 A.2d 954, 1995 N.H. LEXIS 91 (1995).

RESEARCH REFERENCES

New Hampshire Practice.

15 N.H.P. Land Use Planning and Zoning §§ 2.18, 12.02, 17.01, 17.02, 26.03, 29.02,

29.05, 29.06, 29.08, 29.10, 29.11, 29.14–29.16, 30.04, 30.08, 32.10, 32.16.

674:37. Recording of Plats.

After the certificate of notice referred to in RSA 674:35, II and the regulations referred to in RSA 674:36 have been filed with the appropriate recording officials, no plat shall be filed or recorded unless it is prepared and certified by a licensed land surveyor since July 1, 1981, or by a registered land surveyor between January 1, 1970 and June 30, 1981, and until it has been approved by the planning board and such approval has been endorsed in writing on the plat in such manner as the planning board may designate, except as provided in RSA 676:18, II and III and RSA 676:4, I(c). The filing or recording of a plat of a subdivision without the requisite approval of the planning board, or which has not been prepared and certified by a licensed land surveyor or by a registered land surveyor as provided in this section, shall be void.

Source.

1983, 447:1. 1988, 233:1. 1990, 275:2. 1995, 303:2, eff. Jan. 1, 1996.

Revision note.

Substituted "of" for "or" preceding "notice" in the first sentence to correct a typographical error.

Amendments

—1995. Inserted "since July 1, 1981, or by a registered land surveyor between January 1, 1970 and June 30, 1981" preceding "and until" in the first sentence and "or by a registered land surveyor as provided in this section" preceding "shall be void" in the second sentence.

—1990. Added "and RSA 676:4, I(c)" following "RSA 676:18, II and III" in the first sentence.

—1988. Substituted "RSA 674:36" for "674:36" preceding "have been filed" and inserted "unless it is prepared and certified by a licensed land surveyor, and" following "filed or recorded" in the first sentence and inserted "or which has not been prepared and certified by a licensed land surveyor" preceding "shall be void" in the second sentence.

Applicability of 1990 amendment.

1990, 275:3, eff. June 27, 1990, provided that the amendment to this section by section 2 of the act shall be prospective only, and shall apply to any application submitted to and accepted as complete by the planning board on or after June 27, 1990.

Cross References.

Development on class V and VI highways, see RSA 674:41.

Effect of approval of plats generally, see RSA 674:38, 39.

Revocation of recorded approval, see RSA 676:4-a.

Street improvements generally, see RSA 674:40.

RESEARCH REFERENCES

New Hampshire Practice.
   15 N.H.P. Land Use Planning and Zoning §§ 29.19, 32.16.

674:37-a. Effect of Subdivision on Tax Assessment and Collection.

The collection of taxes with respect to land being subdivided shall be governed by the following provisions:

I. If approval of a subdivision plat has been granted on or before April 1 of a particular tax year, giving the owner a legal right to sell or transfer the lots, parcels or other divisions of land depicted on the plat without further approval or action by the municipality, then such lots or parcels shall for that tax year be assessed and appraised as separate estates pursuant to RSA 75:9, whether or not any such sale or transfer has actually occurred, and shall continue to be so assessed unless and until subdivision approval is revoked under RSA 676:4-a, or the parcels are merged pursuant to RSA 674:39-a.

II. If subdivision approval does not become final until after April 1, then all assessments, appraisals, and tax warrants for that property during that tax year shall pertain to the entire non-subdivided property as it was configured on April 1, notwithstanding any later sale or transfer of subdivided lots or parcels which may occur during that year.

III. When property has been assessed as a single parcel or estate in accordance with paragraph II, and some subdivided portion of that property is later sold or transferred prior to the payment of all taxes, interest, and costs due for that tax year, the municipality's tax lien shall remain in effect with respect to the entire property, and each lot or parcel transferred or retained shall remain obligated for the entire amount, and shall be subject to all procedures of RSA 80 until that amount is collected.

IV. In order to avoid the liability of subdivided lots or parcels for taxes due on the entire property as set forth in paragraph III, any person with a legal interest may, at the time of subdivision approval or any time thereafter, prepay all taxes to be assessed on the entire property for that tax year. If such prepayment is offered prior to the determination of the property's full tax obligation for that year, the collector shall notify the assessing officials, who shall make a reasonable jeopardy assessment in accordance with the provisions of RSA 76:10-a, and commit it to the collector. After full prepayment the tax collector shall upon request execute a statement identifying the subdivision plat, and stating that all real estate tax obligations for the tax year have been fulfilled with respect to the property shown on the plat. Such a statement may be recorded in the registry of deeds at the expense of the party requesting it.

V. Nothing in this section shall be construed to prevent the parties to a conveyance from making alternative provisions, through privately-held escrow or other means, for the allocation and satisfaction of tax obligations; provided, however, that the municipality shall not, with respect to property assessed as a single parcel or estate pursuant to paragraph II, be required to apportion taxes among subdivided lots, or to release any subdivided portion of such property from the municipality's tax lien unless and until the full tax obligation for the assessed property has been satisfied.

Source.
1998, 39:1, eff. Jan. 1, 1999.

674:38. Status of Plats Approved.

Every plat approved by the planning board shall, by virtue of the board's approval, be deemed to be an amendment of or an addition to or a detail of the official map. Every approved plat shall be a part of the official map. Approval of a plat shall not be deemed to constitute or result in an acceptance by the municipality or the public of the dedication of any street or other ground or open space shown upon the plat.

Source.
1983, 447:1, eff. Jan. 1, 1984.

Cross References.
Effect upon approved plats of subsequent changes in ordinances and regulations, see RSA 674:39.

Master plans generally, see RSA 674:1 et seq.
Official municipal maps generally, see RSA 674:9 et seq.
Revocation of recorded approval, see RSA 676:4-a.

674:39. Four-Year Exemption.

I. Every subdivision plat approved by the planning board and properly recorded in the registry of deeds and every site plan approved by the planning board and properly recorded in the registry of deeds, if recording of site plans is required by the planning board or by local regulation, shall be exempt from all subsequent changes in subdivision regulations, site plan review regulations, impact fee ordinances, and zoning ordinances adopted by any city, town, or county in which there are located unincorporated towns or unorganized places, except those regulations and ordinances which expressly protect public health standards, such as water quality and sewage treatment requirements, for a period of 4 years after the date of approval; provided that:

(a) Active and substantial development or building has begun on the site by the owner or the owner's successor in interest in accordance with the approved subdivision plat within 12 months after the date of approval, or in accordance with the terms of the approval, and, if a bond or other security to cover the costs of roads, drains, or sewers is required in connection with such approval, such bond or other security is posted with the city, town, or county in which there are located unincorporated towns or unorganized places, at the time of commencement of such development;

(b) Development remains in full compliance with the public health regulations and ordinances specified in this section; and

(c) At the time of approval and recording, the subdivision plat or site plan conforms to the subdivision regulations, site plan review regulations, and zoning ordinances then in effect at the location of such subdivision plat or site plan.

II. Once substantial completion of the improvements as shown on the subdivision plat or site plan has occurred in compliance with the approved subdivision plat or site plan or the terms of said approval or unless otherwise stipulated by the planning board, the rights of the owner or the owner's successor in interest shall vest and no subsequent changes in subdivision regulations, site plan regulations, or zoning ordinances, except impact fees adopted pursuant to RSA 674:21 and 675:2–4, shall operate to affect such improvements.

III. The planning board may, as part of its subdivision and site plan regulations or as a condition of subdivision plat or site plan approval, specify the threshold levels of work that shall constitute the following terms, with due regard to the scope and details of a particular project:

(a) "Substantial completion of the improvements as shown on the subdivision plat or site plan," for purposes of fulfilling paragraph II; and

(b) "Active and substantial development or building," for the purposes of fulfilling paragraph I.

IV. Failure of a planning board to specify by regulation or as a condition of subdivision plat or site plan approval what shall constitute "active and substantial development or building" shall entitle the subdivision plat or site plan approved by the planning board to the 4-year exemption described in paragraph I. The planning board may, for good cause, extend the 12-month period set forth in paragraph I(a).

Source.
1983, 447:1. 1989, 266:17, 18. 1991, 331:1, 2. 1995, 43:5, eff. July 2, 1995; 291:7, 8, eff. Aug. 20, 1995. 2004, 199:1, eff. June 7, 2004.

Amendments
—2004. Rewritten to the extent that a detailed comparison would be impracticable.

—1995. Chapter 43 substituted "the owner's" for "his" preceding "successor" in the introductory paragraph and in the first sentence of par. I.

Chapter 291 substituted "the" for "said" following "terms of" in par. I and added par. IV.

—1991. Inserted "or site plan" following "every plat", "site plan review regulations" preceding "and zoning" and "or unless otherwise stipulated by the planning board" preceding "the rights" in the introductory paragraph and inserted "or site plan" preceding "conforms"

and "site plan review regulations" preceding "and zoning" in par. III.

—1989. Substituted "town, or county in which there are located unincorporated towns or unorganized places" for "or town" following "adopted by any city" in the introductory paragraph and following "posted with the city" in par. I.

Legislative purpose of 1991 amendment.
1991, 331:4, eff. Aug. 27, 1991, provided: "The purpose of sections 1–3 of this act [which amended this section and RSA 676:12] is to confirm and re-emphasize the intent of the general court at the time of the enactment of 1986, 229:3 and 1983, 447:1. Municipalities may not retroactively amend local land use regulations or zoning ordinances for the purpose of stopping proposed projects or developments while an application is under consideration by the municipality. This act shall not be

interpreted as changing the intent of any provision of 1986, 229 or 1983, 447."

Cross References.
Development on class V and VI highways, see RSA 674:41.
Effect of approval of plats generally, see RSA 674:38.

Recordation of plats in registry of deeds, see RSA 676:18.
Revocation of recorded approval, see RSA 676:4-a.
Street improvements generally, see RSA 674:40.

NOTES TO DECISIONS

Analysis

1. Applicability
2. "Substantial construction" standard

1. Applicability
Where town ordinance was passed in March authorizing the adoption of a new impact fee schedule and a new fee schedule was approved in August of 2000, where plaintiff developer's first development's approval was recorded before both the March passage of the first town ordinance and the August adoption of the new fees ordinance, it was exempt from the new fees under RSA 674:39; where developer's second development's approval was recorded after the March 2000, amendment, but before the board's adoption of the new fees, the amendment did not affect the developer's RSA 674:39 reliance on the fees existing when the second development's site plan approval was recorded and, as the developer began active or substantial development or building on the developments within 12 months of recording of approvals, it obtained a preliminary 4-year exemption (permanent when substantially completed) from zoning ordinances passed after site plan approval and recording, subject to certain RSA 674:39 exceptions.R.J. Moreau Cos. v. Town of Litchfield, 148 N.H. 773, 813 A.2d 527, 2002 N.H. LEXIS 213 (2002).
This section, providing four-year exemption from lot size restrictions of recently enacted zoning ordinances, was inapplicable as to subdivision plat which was neither approved nor recorded. Chasse v. Town of Candia, 132 N.H. 574, 567 A.2d 999, 1989 N.H. LEXIS 132 (1989).

2. "Substantial construction" standard
Where Town of Hookset officials erroneously told the applicant that the building permit for the gas station would not be revoked under newly enacted zoning laws if the applicant obtained the permit within a year of when the litigation over approval of the gas station ended and if the applicant began building within six months of that, municipal estoppel did not require the reinstatement of the building permit where those statements turned out to be false; the applicant's reliance on the statements of the code enforcement officer and planning board member was not reasonable because a statute, former RSA 674:39, I (see now RSA 674:39, I(a)), required the applicant to begin active and substantial development of the property within one year in order to secure protection from zoning changes. Thomas v. Town of Hooksett, 153 N.H. 717, 903 A.2d 963, 2006 N.H. LEXIS 99 (2006).
Where a developer expended a substantial amount of money on public improvements and constructed six houses, its work was enough to meet the "substantial construction" standard; its right to complete a project permanently vested. AWL Power, Inc. v. City of Rochester, 148 N.H. 603, 813 A.2d 517, 2002 N.H. LEXIS 178 (2002).

Cited:
Cited in Town of Nottingham v. Bonser, 131 N.H. 120, 552 A.2d 58, 1988 N.H. LEXIS 108 (1988); Chasse v. Town of Candia, 132 N.H. 574, 567 A.2d 999, 1989 N.H. LEXIS 132 (1989); Rall v. Town of Belmont, 138 N.H. 172, 635 A.2d 1368, 1993 N.H. LEXIS 185 (1993).

RESEARCH REFERENCES

New Hampshire Practice.
15 N.H.P. Land Use Planning and Zoning §§ 7.14, 11.05, 15.02, 29.23, 30.11, 32.16.

New Hampshire Bar Journal.
For article, "'Grandfathered'—The Law of Nonconforming Uses and Vested Rights," see 31 N.H.B.J. 17 (1990).

ALR.
Construction and application of zoning laws setting minimum lot size requirements. 2 A.L.R.5th 553.

674:39-a. Voluntary Merger.

Any owner of 2 or more contiguous preexisting approved or subdivided lots or parcels who wishes to merge them for municipal regulation and taxation purposes may do so by applying to the planning board or its designee. Except where such merger would create a violation of then-current ordinances or regulations, all such requests shall be approved, and no public hearing or notice shall be required. No new survey plat need be recorded, but a notice of the merger, sufficient to identify the relevant parcels and endorsed in writing by the planning board or its designee, shall be filed for recording in the registry of deeds, and a copy mailed to the municipality's assessing officials. No such merged parcel shall thereafter be separately transferred without subdivision approval.

Source.
1995, 291:9, eff. Aug. 20, 1995.

674:40. Improvements in Unapproved Streets.

I. A municipality which has established and recorded an official map, as provided in RSA 674:10, or has conferred upon a planning board platting jurisdiction in accordance with RSA 674:35 shall not thereafter accept, lay out, open, improve, grade, pave, or light any street or lay or authorize the laying of water mains, sewers, connections, or other facilities or utilities in any street, within any portion of the municipality unless such street:

(a) Has been accepted or opened as, or has otherwise received the legal status of, a public street prior to the conferring of platting jurisdiction upon the planning board; or

(b) Corresponds in its location and lines with a street shown on the official map, or with a street shown on a subdivision plat approved by the planning board, or with a street on a street plat made by and adopted by the board.

II. For the purposes of this section, the word "street" shall not mean or include a discontinued highway.

III. The local legislative body may, however, accept, locate and construct any street not shown on or not corresponding with a street on the official map or on an approved subdivision plat or an approved street plat, provided the ordinance or other measure for the accepting, locating, and construction of such street is first submitted to the planning board for its approval and:

(a) If approved by the board, be approved by a majority vote of those present and voting at a regular or special meeting of the local legislative body; or

(b) If disapproved by the planning board, be approved by not less than ⅔ of those present and voting at a regular or special meeting of the local legislative body.

IV. A street approved under paragraph III shall have the status of an approved street as though it had been originally shown on the official map or on a subdivision plat approved by the planning board or as though it had been originally platted by the planning board.

Source.
1983, 447:1. 1989, 266:19, eff. July 1, 1989. 1998, 344:5, eff. Aug. 25, 1998.

county in which there are located unincorporated towns or unorganized places" preceding "or by majority".

Amendments
—1998. Paragraph III(a): Substituted "those present and voting at a regular or special meeting" for "the entire membership" following "majority vote of".

Paragraph III(b): Rewritten to the extent that a detailed comparison would be impracticable.

—1989. Paragraph III(b): Inserted "or of a

Cross References.
Approval and recording of plats, see RSA 674:37.

Development on class V and VI highways, see RSA 674:41.

Effect of approval of plats generally, see RSA 674:38, 39.

Master plans generally, see RSA 674:1 et seq.

Official municipal maps generally, see RSA 674:9 et seq.

RESEARCH REFERENCES

New Hampshire Practice.
15 N.H.P. Land Use Planning and Zoning § 29.17.

674:40-a. Delegation of Authority to Accept Dedicated Streets.

I. Notwithstanding RSA 674:40, a municipality with the town meeting form of government, which has conferred upon a planning board platting jurisdiction in accordance with RSA 674:35, may, by majority vote at an annual or special meeting, under an article in the warrant inserted by the local governing body, or by petition, delegate to the local governing body the authority to accept dedicated streets. Such a delegation may be rescinded by the municipality in the same manner.

II. If such a delegation is made, the local governing body may vote to accept any dedicated street only if the street corresponds in its location and lines with a street shown on a subdivision plat or site plan approved by the planning board, or on the official map, or on a street plat made and adopted by the board. A street which has not received such prior planning board approval shall not be accepted without a vote of the local legislative body pursuant to RSA 674:40, III.

III. The local governing body shall hold a public hearing on the proposed acceptance prior to taking action.

IV. A street accepted under this section shall have the status of a public highway under RSA 229:1. Such street shall be deemed a class V highway, subject to the municipality's duty of regular maintenance as set forth in RSA 231, unless otherwise designated pursuant to statute.

V. In this section, "dedicated street" means a street which has been dedicated to public use under the New Hampshire common law of dedication.

Source.
1993, 80:1, eff. June 22, 1993.

Construction.
1993, 80:2, eff. June 22, 1993, provided that the provisions of section 1 of the act, which enacted this section, shall not be construed to affect the legal status of any street which was accepted by other means prior to June 22, 1993.

674:41. Erection of Buildings on Streets; Appeals.

I. From and after the time when a planning board shall expressly have been granted the authority to approve or disapprove plats by a municipality, as described in RSA 674:35, no building shall be erected on any lot within any part of the municipality nor shall a building permit be issued for the erection of a building unless the street giving access to the lot upon which such building is proposed to be placed:

(a) Shall have been accepted or opened as, or shall otherwise have received the legal status of, a class V or better highway prior to that time; or

(b) Corresponds in its location and lines with:

(1) A street shown on the official map; or

(2) A street on a subdivision plat approved by the planning board; or

(3) A street on a street plat made by and adopted by the planning board; or

(4) A street located and accepted by the local legislative body of the municipality, after submission to the planning board, and, in case of the planning board's disapproval, by the favorable vote required in RSA 674:40; or

(c) Is a class VI highway, provided that:

(1) The local governing body after review and comment by the planning board has voted to authorize the issuance of building permits for the erection of buildings on said class VI highway or a portion thereof; and

(2) The municipality neither assumes responsibility for maintenance of said class VI highway nor liability for any damages resulting from the use thereof; and

(3) Prior to the issuance of a building permit, the applicant shall produce evidence that notice of the limits of municipal responsibility and liability has been recorded in the county registry of deeds; or

(d) Is a private road, provided that:

(1) The local governing body, after review and comment by the planning board, has voted to authorize the issuance of building permits for the erection of buildings on said private road or portion thereof; and

(2) The municipality neither assumes responsibility for maintenance of said private roads nor liability for any damages resulting from the use thereof; and

(3) Prior to the issuance of a building permit, the applicant shall produce evidence that notice of the limits of municipal responsibility and liability has been recorded in the county registry of deeds for the lot for which the building permit is sought; or

(e) Is an existing street constructed prior to the effective date of this subparagraph and is shown on a subdivision plat that was approved by the local governing body or zoning board of adjustment before the municipality authorized the planning board to approve or disapprove subdivision plats in accordance with RSA 674:35, if one or more buildings have been erected on other lots on the same street.

II. Whenever the enforcement of the provisions of this section would entail practical difficulty or unnecessary hardship, and when the circumstances of the case do not require the building, structure or part thereof to be related to existing or proposed streets, the applicant for such permit may appeal from the decision of the administrative officer having charge of the issuance of permits to the zoning board of adjustment in any municipality which has adopted zoning regulations in accordance with RSA 674, or, in municipalities in which no board of adjustment exists, to the local legislative body, or to a board of appeals, whichever is appropriate, in accordance with RSA 674:14 and 674:15, including the requirement for a public hearing. In a municipality which does not require building permits, direct application may be made to the zoning board of adjustment, or the local legislative body, or the board of appeals for permission to erect the building. In passing on such appeal or application, the board of adjustment, local legislative body, or board of appeals may make any reasonable exception and shall have the power to authorize or issue a permit, subject to such conditions as it may impose, if the issuance of the permit or erection of the building would not tend to distort the official map or increase the difficulty of carrying out the master plan upon which it is based, and if erection of the building or issuance of the permit will not cause hardship to future purchasers or undue financial impact on the municipality. Any such decision made in this connection by a board of adjustment, local legislative body, or by a board of appeals pursuant to this section and RSA 674:14 and 674:15 shall be in writing, together with the reasons for the decision, and shall be subject to review in the manner described in RSA 677.

II-a. Municipalities may except any lot, including island lots for islands served exclusively by boats, from the requirements of paragraphs I and II by an affirmative vote of the local legislative body pursuant to RSA 675, first submitted to the planning board for its approval and:

(a) If approved by the board, approved by a majority of those present and voting at a regular or special meeting of the local legislative body; or

(b) If disapproved by the planning board, approved by not less than ⅔ of those present and voting at a regular or special meeting of the local legislative body.

III. This section shall supersede any less stringent local ordinance, code or regulation, and no existing lot or tract of land shall be exempted from the provisions of this section except in accordance with the procedures expressly set forth in this section. For purposes of paragraph I, "the street giving access to the lot" means a street or way abutting the lot and upon which the lot has frontage. It does not include a street from which the sole access to the lot is via a private easement or right-of-way, unless such easement or right-of-way also meets the criteria set forth in subparagraphs I(a), (b), (c), (d), or (e).

IV. In addition to the requirements for the erection of buildings in paragraph I and notwithstanding the exceptions provided in paragraph II, the planning board for a county in which there are located unincorporated towns or unorganized places shall require every building which is erected on leased land located within an unincorporated town or unorganized place to have a building permit. A building permit shall be required under this paragraph regardless of the proximity of the building to any street or highway. The county shall, by resolution, authorize the planning board to issue building permits under this paragraph.

Source.

1983, 447:1. 1988, 131:2, 3. 1989, 266:20. 1995, 291:10, eff. Aug. 20, 1995. 1998, 344:6, eff. Aug. 25, 1998. 2002, 270:1, eff. July 17, 2002; 270:5, eff. April 17, 2002. 2004, 154:1, 2, eff. July 23, 2004. 2005, 226:1, 2, eff. Sept. 3, 2005.

Amendments

—2005. Paragraph II-a: Inserted "any lot, including" preceding "island lots" and "pursuant to RSA 675" in the introductory paragraph.

Paragraph III: Substituted "subparagraphs I(a), (b), (c), (d), or (e)" for "subparagraphs I(a), (b), or (c)".

—2004. Paragraph I(d)(3): Added "or" to the end of the paragraph.

Paragraph I(e): Added.

—2002. Paragraph I(c)(3): Added "or" following "of deeds".

Paragraph I(d): Added.

—1998. Paragraph II-a: Added.

—1995. Paragraph III: Rewritten to the extent that a detailed comparison would be impracticable.

—1989. Paragraph IV: Added.

—1988. Paragraph II: Substituted "RSA 674:14 and 15" for "RSA 677" following "in accordance with" in the first sentence and preceding "shall be in writing" in the fourth sentence and made other minor stylistic changes.

Paragraph III: Added.

Cross References.

Approval and recording of plats, see RSA 674:37.

Effect of approval of plats generally, see RSA 674:38, 39.

Master plans generally, see RSA 674:1 et seq.

Official municipal maps generally, see RSA 674:9 et seq.

Requirement and issuance of building permits generally, see RSA 676:11 et seq.

NOTES TO DECISIONS

Analysis

1. Construction
2. Purpose

1. Construction

In construing the statute, RSA 674:41, I(c) does not conflict with RSA 674:41, II. Rather, it simply sets forth the procedure to be followed by those applicants who cannot, choose not, or need not, demonstrate a practical difficulty or unnecessary hardship. Blagbrough Family Realty Trust v. A & T Forest Prods., 155 N.H. 29, 917 A.2d 1221, 2007 N.H. LEXIS 25 (2007).

The provisions of this statute, prescribing that no building permit was to be issued unless the street had been accepted or had received the status of a public street, contemplated streets and highways as defined in former RSA 230:1 (now covered by RSA 229:1). Blevens v.

City of Manchester, 103 N.H. 284, 170 A.2d 121, 1961 N.H. LEXIS 33 (1961). (Decided under prior law.)

2. Purpose

Purpose of provision of this section limiting erection of buildings on class III highways, which applies with equal force to building permits and subdivision permits, is to provide against such scattered or premature subdivision as would necessitate excessive expenditure of public funds. Turco v. Town of Barnstead, 136 N.H. 256, 615 A.2d 1237, 1992 N.H. LEXIS 164 (1992).

Plaintiff landowners' subdivision request was not improperly denied by town, where this section, prohibiting building on class VI roads,

applied to subdivision permits, and estoppel did not apply. Turco v. Town of Barnstead, 136 N.H. 256, 615 A.2d 1237, 1992 N.H. LEXIS 164 (1992).

Paragraph I of this section, prohibiting local planning boards from issuing building permits unless the street giving access to the lot qualifies as a class V or better highway, applies to all building permit applications, not just to subdivision applications. Vachon v. Town of New Durham Zoning Bd. of Adjustment, 131 N.H. 623, 557 A.2d 649, 1989 N.H. LEXIS 29 (1989).

Cited:

Cited in Glick v. Town of Ossipee, 130 N.H. 643, 547 A.2d 231, 1988 N.H. LEXIS 79 (1988); Hannigan v. City of Concord, 144 N.H. 68, 738 A.2d 1262, 1999 N.H. LEXIS 70 (1999).

RESEARCH REFERENCES

New Hampshire Practice.
15 N.H.P. Land Use Planning and Zoning § 29.18.

674:42. Status of Existing Platting Statutes.

After a planning board is granted platting jurisdiction by a municipality under RSA 674:35, the planning board's jurisdiction shall be exclusive. All statutory control over plats or subdivisions of land granted by other statutes shall be given effect to the extent that they are in harmony with the provisions of this title. The planning board shall have all statutory control over plats or subdivisions of land. Prior laws which are inconsistent with the powers granted to the planning board and the municipality under this title, and which have expressly by ordinance been adopted by a municipality and made available to a planning board according to the provisions of this title, are hereby declared to have no application, force or effect so long as the powers conferred by this title shall continue to be exercised by a municipality.

Source.
1983, 447:1, eff. Jan. 1, 1984.

Cross References.
Effect of changes in regulations or ordinances upon approved plats, see RSA 674:39.

NOTES TO DECISIONS

Analysis

1. Generally
2. Public streets

1. Generally

Once a municipality created a planning board, that board had exclusive platting and subdivision jurisdiction; the city council retained no general concurrent jurisdiction. Ehrenberg v. City of Concord, 120 N.H. 656, 421 A.2d 128, 1980 N.H. LEXIS 373 (1980). (Decided under prior law.)

2. Public streets

Since former RSA 36:24 expressly stated that approval of a subdivision plan by a planning board did not constitute acceptance of any street shown on the plan, a planning board had

no power to avoid application of RSA 231:51, which released and discharged from all public servitude any street dedicated to public use which had not been open, built or used within 20 years of dedication, and this section could not preempt application of RSA 231:51 to a street never accepted by a municipality. Polizzo v. Town of Hampton, 126 N.H. 398, 494 A.2d 254, 1985 N.H. LEXIS 342 (1985). (Decided under prior law.)

RESEARCH REFERENCES

New Hampshire Practice.
15 N.H.P. Land Use Planning and Zoning § 26.03.

Site Plans

Cross References.
Building codes generally, see RSA 674:51 et seq.
Condominiums generally, see RSA 356-B.
Historic preservation generally, see RSA 227-C.

Subdivision regulation generally, see RSA 674:35 et seq.
Unit ownership of real property, see RSA 479-A.
Zoning generally, see RSA 674:16 et seq.

674:43. Power to Review Site Plans.

I. A municipality, having adopted a zoning ordinance as provided in RSA 674:16, and where the planning board has adopted subdivision regulations as provided in RSA 674:36, may by ordinance or resolution further authorize the planning board to require preliminary review of site plans and to review and approve or disapprove site plans for the development or change or expansion of use of tracts for nonresidential uses or for multi-family dwelling units, which are defined as any structures containing more than 2 dwelling units, whether or not such development includes a subdivision or resubdivision of the site.

II. The ordinance or resolution which authorizes the planning board to review site plans shall make it the duty of the city clerk, town clerk, village district clerk or other appropriate recording official to file with the register of deeds of the county in which the municipality is situated a certificate of notice showing that the planning board has been so authorized, giving the date of such authorization.

III. The local legislative body of a municipality may by ordinance or resolution authorize the planning board to delegate its site review powers and duties in regard to minor site plans to a committee of technically qualified administrators chosen by the planning board from the departments of public works, engineering, community development, planning, or other similar departments in the municipality. The local legislative body may further stipulate that the committee members be residents of the municipality. This special site review committee may have final authority to approve or disapprove site plans reviewed by it, unless the local legislative body deems that final approval shall rest with the planning board, provided that the decision of the committee may be appealed to the full planning board so long as notice of appeal is filed within 20 days of the committee's decision. All provisions of RSA 676:4 shall apply to actions of the special site review committee, except that such a committee shall act to approve or disapprove within 60 days after submissions of applications, subject to extension or waiver as provided in RSA 676:4, I(f). If a municipality authorizes a site review committee in accordance with this paragraph, the planning board shall adopt or amend its regulations specifying application, acceptance and approval procedures and defining what size and kind of site plans may be reviewed by the site review committee prior to authorizing the committee.

IV. The local legislative body of a municipality may by ordinance or resolution establish thresholds based on the size of a project or a tract below which site plan review shall not be required. If a municipality establishes a size limit below which site plan review shall not be required, the planning board shall adopt or amend its regulations to clearly reflect that threshold. Nothing in this paragraph shall preclude the planning board from establishing such thresholds in the absence of action by the legislative body.

Source.

1983, 447:1. 1987, 256:2. 1988, 9:1. 1995, 303:3, eff. Jan. 1, 1996. 2005, 33:1, eff. July 9, 2005.

Amendments

—2005. Paragraph I: Inserted "require preliminary review of site plans and to".

—1995. Paragraph IV: Added.

—1988. Paragraph III: Added.

—1987. Paragraph I: Inserted "or change or expansion of use" following "site plans for the development".

Cross References.

Contents of regulations, see RSA 674:44.

NOTES TO DECISIONS

Analysis

1. Construction with other laws
2. Scope of review
3. Imposition of conditions
4. Imposition of condition subsequent upon approval of application
5. Imposition of moratorium upon site development
6. Effect of zoning changes upon approved plans

1. Construction with other laws

Where an application for approval of a nonresidential use of land was approved subject to the fulfillment of certain conditions, a hearing was not necessary whenever the applicant submitted evidence that he had met a condition; subject to the time limitations imposed by former RSA 36:23, I(c) (now covered by RSA 676:4), governing procedures for approval of such applications, a planning board could wait until the applicant claimed to have fulfilled all conditions, and hold one hearing on all matters of compliance. Sklar Realty, Inc. v. Town of Merrimack, 125 N.H. 321, 480 A.2d 149, 1984 N.H. LEXIS 271 (1984). (Decided under prior law.)

Site plan approvals under this statute were governed by former RSA 36:23 (now covered by RSA 676:4), which regulated the planning board's procedure on approval of plats. Carter v. City of Nashua, 116 N.H. 466, 362 A.2d 191, 1976 N.H. LEXIS 382 (1976), overruled on other grounds, Weeks Restaurant Corp. v. City of Dover, 119 N.H. 541, 404 A.2d 294, 1979 N.H. LEXIS 349 (1979). (Decided under prior law.)

2. Scope of review

Court on appeal from rezoning decision rejected plaintiffs' argument that city council improperly relied on master plan without detailed evidence of physical characteristics of site; zoning ordinance did not require such specific site information, only planning board approval and public hearing were mandated, and site considerations were within province of planning board on site plan review. Quinlan v. City of Dover, 136 N.H. 226, 614 A.2d 1057, 1992 N.H. LEXIS 159 (1992).

3. Imposition of conditions

Planning boards possess the authority to impose conditions in the site plan review process. Morin v. City of Somersworth, 131 N.H. 253, 551 A.2d 527, 1988 N.H. LEXIS 109 (1988).

4. Imposition of condition subsequent upon approval of application

A planning board had authority to impose a condition subsequent upon approval of an application for nonresidential uses of land. Sklar Realty, Inc. v. Town of Merrimack, 125 N.H. 321, 480 A.2d 149, 1984 N.H. LEXIS 271 (1984). (Decided under prior law.)

5. Imposition of moratorium upon site development

When authorized by a municipality pursuant to the statute, a municipal planning board

could pass upon site plans for development of land for nonresidential uses along a highway in accordance with regulations adopted by the board after notice and public hearing and consistent with an official map, but the planning board had no statutory authority to declare a blanket moratorium on site development pending completion of its planning of street changes and inclusion of proposed street changes in the official street map by city council enactment. Leda Lanes Realty, Inc. v. City of Nashua, 112 N.H. 244, 293 A.2d 320, 1972 N.H. LEXIS 187 (1972). (Decided under prior law.)

6. Effect of zoning changes upon approved plans

In the absence of a statute providing otherwise, final approval of a subdivision plat by the planning board under the statute did not place the lots beyond the authority of zoning changes. R. A. Vachon & Son, Inc. v. City of Concord, 112 N.H. 107, 289 A.2d 646, 1972 N.H. LEXIS 153 (1972). (Decided under prior law.)

Cited:

Cited in New England Brickmaster, Inc. v. Town of Salem, 133 N.H. 655, 582 A.2d 601, 1990 N.H. LEXIS 119 (1990).

RESEARCH REFERENCES

New Hampshire Practice.
15 N.H.P. Land Use Planning and Zoning §§ 26.03, 30.01, 30.04, 30.09, 30.10, 35.16.

674:44. Site Plan Review Regulations.

I. Before the planning board exercises its powers under RSA 674:43, it shall adopt site plan review regulations according to the procedures required by RSA 675:6.

II. The site plan review regulations which the planning board adopts may:

(a) Provide for the safe and attractive development or change or expansion of use of the site and guard against such conditions as would involve danger or injury to health, safety, or prosperity by reason of:

(1) Inadequate drainage or conditions conducive to flooding of the property or that of another;

(2) Inadequate protection for the quality of groundwater;

(3) Undesirable and preventable elements of pollution such as noise, smoke, soot, particulates, or any other discharge into the environment which might prove harmful to persons, structures, or adjacent properties; and

(4) Inadequate provision for fire safety, prevention, and control.

(b) Provide for the harmonious and aesthetically pleasing development of the municipality and its environs.

(c) Provide for open spaces and green spaces of adequate proportions.

(d) Require the proper arrangement and coordination of streets within the site in relation to other existing or planned streets or with features of the official map of the municipality;

(e) Require suitably located streets of sufficient width to accommodate existing and prospective traffic and to afford adequate light, air, and access for firefighting apparatus and equipment to buildings, and be coordinated so as to compose a convenient system;

(f) Require, in proper cases, that plats showing new streets or narrowing or widening of such streets be submitted to the planning board for approval;

(g) Require that the land indicated on plats submitted to the planning board shall be of such character that it can be used for building purposes without danger to health;

(h) Include such provisions as will tend to create conditions favorable for health, safety, convenience, and prosperity;

(i) Require innovative land use controls on lands when supported by the master plan; and

(j) Require preliminary review of site plans.

III. The site plan review regulations which the planning board adopts shall:

(a) Provide the procedures which the board shall follow in reviewing site plans;

(b) Define the purposes of site plan review;

(c) Specify the general standards and requirements with which the proposed development shall comply, including appropriate reference to accepted codes and standards for construction;

(d) Include provisions for guarantees of performance, including bonds or other security; and

(e) Include provision for waiver of any portion of the regulations in such cases where, in the opinion of the planning board, strict conformity would pose an unnecessary hardship to the applicant and waiver would not be contrary to the spirit and intent of the regulations.

IV. The site plan review regulations of the planning board may stipulate, as a condition precedent to the approval of the plat, the extent to which and the manner in which streets shall be graded and improved and to which water, sewer, and other utility mains, piping, connections, or other facilities shall be installed. The regulations or practice of the planning board:

(a) May provide for the conditional approval of the plat before such improvements and installations have been constructed, but any such conditional approval shall not be entered upon that plat.

(b) Shall provide that, in lieu of the completion of street work and utility installations prior to the final approval of a plat, the planning board shall accept a performance bond, irrevocable letter of credit, or other type or types of security as shall be specified in the site plan review regulations. The planning board shall have the discretion to prescribe the type and amount of the bond or other security, require satisfactory evidence of the financial ability of any surety or financial institution to pay such bond or other type of security, and specify a period for completion of the improvements and utilities to be expressed in the bond or other security, in order to secure to the municipality the actual construction and installation of such improvements and utilities. The municipality shall have the power to enforce such bonds or other securities by all appropriate legal and equitable remedies.

V. The planning board may, as part of its site plan review regulations, require an applicant to pay all costs for notification of abutters and may provide for the assessment of reasonable fees to cover the board's administrative expenses and costs of special investigation and the review of documents and other matters which may be required by particular applications.

Source.
1983, 447:1. 1985, 103:21. 1986, 200:3. 1987, 256:3, eff. July 17, 1987. 2004, 71:5, eff. July 6, 2004. 2005, 33:2, eff. July 9, 2005.

Amendments
—2005. Paragraph II: Added subpar. (j) and made minor stylistic changes in subpars. (g)–(i).

—2004. Paragraph II(i): Added.

—1987. Paragraph II(a): Inserted "or change or expansion of use" following "development" in the introductory clause.

—1986. Paragraph IV: Rewritten to the extent that a detailed comparison would be impracticable.

—1985. Rewritten to the extent that a detailed comparison would be impracticable.

Cross References.
Effect of uncompleted streets or utilities upon applications for building permits, see RSA 676:12.

Revocation of recorded site plan approval, see RSA 676:4-a.

NOTES TO DECISIONS

Analysis
1. Conditions
2. Definitions
3. Review of site plan
4. Necessity for adoption of regulations
5. Sufficiency of regulations
6. Contributions

1. Conditions
Local planning boards have authority to impose conditions upon the approval of a site plan. New England Brickmaster, Inc. v. Town of Salem, 133 N.H. 655, 582 A.2d 601, 1990 N.H. LEXIS 119 (1990).

2. Definitions
The term "streets" in this section refers to streets both on and off the site, and local planning boards are empowered to promulgate regulations which allow for the conditional approval of a site plan by requiring an applicant to contribute funds to the construction of off-site improvements bearing a rational nexus to the development. New England Brickmaster, Inc. v. Town of Salem, 133 N.H. 655, 582 A.2d 601, 1990 N.H. LEXIS 119 (1990).

3. Review of site plan
Court on appeal from rezoning decision rejected plaintiffs' argument that city council improperly relied on master plan without detailed evidence of physical characteristics of site; zoning ordinance did not require such specific site information, only planning board approval and public hearing were mandated, and site considerations were within province of planning board on site plan review. Quinlan v. City of Dover, 136 N.H. 226, 614 A.2d 1057,

1992 N.H. LEXIS 159 (1992).

Requirement under subparagraph III(a) of this section, that local planning boards shall include "the procedures which the board shall follow in reviewing site plans," does not require that every detail relating to the actions of a planning board be spelled out. New England Brickmaster, Inc. v. Town of Salem, 133 N.H. 655, 582 A.2d 601, 1990 N.H. LEXIS 119 (1990).

4. Necessity for adoption of regulations

To control the construction of condominium amenities facility on subdivided land, planning board must promulgate site plan review regulations. Lemm Dev. Corp. v. Town of Bartlett, 133 N.H. 618, 580 A.2d 1082, 1990 N.H. LEXIS 114 (1990).

The statute, as amended by 1979, 455:3, and 1979, 455:4, the savings clause of the amendatory act, required that any planning board, even one that had been empowered by a zoning ordinance to review site plans before 1979, adopt specific site-plan review regulations prior to its exercise of site-plan review authority. Eddy Plaza Associates v. City of Concord, 122 N.H. 416, 445 A.2d 1106, 1982 N.H. LEXIS 362 (1982). (Decided under prior law.)

Where rules and regulations embodied in a city zoning ordinance were inadequate to meet the requirements of the statute, the city planning board could not continue to exercise site-plan review authority until it adopted specific regulations as prescribed in the statute. Eddy Plaza Associates v. City of Concord, 122 N.H. 416, 445 A.2d 1106, 1982 N.H. LEXIS 362 (1982). (Decided under prior law.)

5. Sufficiency of regulations

Rules and regulations embodied in a city zoning ordinance, which applied to the exercise of the planning board's site review powers relating to large-scale developments, were inadequate to meet the requirement of the statute, as amended in 1979, and the savings clause of the 1979 amendment, that any planning board adopt specific site-plan review regulations prior to its exercise of site-plan review authority where the "regulations" were a statement of general principles and guidelines from which regulations must still have been derived, the "regulations" were not self-implementing, and the "regulations" did not address the items required by the statute, such as notice and hearing requirements, and provisions relative to guarantees for performance, including bonds or other security. Eddy Plaza Associates v. City of Concord, 122 N.H. 416, 445 A.2d 1106, 1982 N.H. LEXIS 362 (1982). (Decided under prior law.)

6. Contributions

In regard to the construction of subdivision, the legislature intended to authorize municipalities to recover fair contributions from subdividers of costs resulting from increased municipal services necessitated by changes to the land. New England Brickmaster, Inc. v. Town of Salem, 133 N.H. 655, 582 A.2d 601, 1990 N.H. LEXIS 119 (1990).

Cited:

Cited in Morin v. City of Somersworth, 131 N.H. 253, 551 A.2d 527, 1988 N.H. LEXIS 109 (1988); Mooney v. City of Laconia, 133 N.H. 30, 573 A.2d 447, 1990 N.H. LEXIS 31 (1990); Lampert v. Town of Hudson, 136 N.H. 196, 612 A.2d 920, 1992 N.H. LEXIS 143 (1992); Town of Pelham v. Browning Ferris Indus., 141 N.H. 355, 683 A.2d 536, 1996 N.H. LEXIS 104 (1996); Town of Seabrook v. Vachon Mgmt., Inc., 144 N.H. 660, 745 A.2d 1155, 2000 N.H. LEXIS 7 (2000); Simonsen v. Town of Derry, 145 N.H. 382, 765 A.2d 1033, 2000 N.H. LEXIS 73 (2000); Bayson Props. v. City of Lebanon, 150 N.H. 167, 834 A.2d 202, 2003 N.H. LEXIS 159 (2003).

RESEARCH REFERENCES

New Hampshire Practice.
15 N.H.P. Land Use Planning and Zoning §§ 26.03, 29.09, 30.06–30.08, 30.09, 32.01, 32.14.

Heritage Commission

Cross References.
Historic districts, see RSA 674:45 et seq.

674:44-a. Heritage Commission.

A heritage commission may be established in accordance with RSA 673 for the proper recognition, use, and protection of resources, tangible or intangible, primarily man-made, that are valued for their historic, cultural, aesthetic, or community significance within their natural, built, or cultural contexts.

Source.
1992, 64:2, eff. June 19, 1992.

RESEARCH REFERENCES

New Hampshire Practice.
15 N.H.P. Land Use Planning and Zoning § 35.17.

674:44-b. Powers.

I. GENERALLY.   Heritage commissions shall have advisory and review authority, specifically, as follows:

(a) Survey and inventory all cultural resources.

(b) Conduct research and publish findings, including reports to establish the legal basis for a district and preparation of historic district ordinances within the municipality prior to its adoption or amendment as provided in RSA 675:6.

(c) Assist the planning board, as requested, in the development and review of those sections of the master plan which address cultural and historic resources.

(d) Advise, upon request, local agencies and other local boards in their review of requests on matters affecting or potentially affecting cultural and historic resources.

(e) Coordinate activities with appropriate service organizations and non-profit groups.

(f) Publicize its activities.

(g) Hire consultants and contractors as needed.

(h) Receive gifts of money and property, both real and personal, in the name of the city or town, subject to the approval of the city council in a city or the board of selectmen in a town, such gifts to be managed and controlled by the commission for its proper purposes.

(i) Hold meetings and hearings necessary to carry out its duties.

II. PROPERTY.   The commission may acquire, in the name of the town or city, subject to the approval of the local governing body, by gift, purchase, grant, bequest, devise, lease, or otherwise, a fee or lesser interest, development rights, covenant, or other contractual right, including conveyances with conditions, limitations, or reversions, as may be necessary to acquire, maintain, improve, protect, limit the future use of, or otherwise conserve and properly use the cultural resources of the city or town, and shall manage and control the same; provided, however, that the city, town, or commission shall not have the right to condemn property for these purposes.

475

III. HISTORIC DISTRICT COMMISSION. Heritage commissions also may assume, if authorized by the local legislative body, the composition and duties of historic district commissions.

Source.
1992, 64:2. 1993, 32:1, eff. June 7, 1993. 1995, 138:5, eff. July 23, 1995.

Amendments
—1995. Paragraph II: Inserted "subject to the approval of the local governing body" following "town or city".

—1993. Paragraph I(i): Added.

Cross References.
Appointment and terms of heritage commission members, see RSA 673:4-a.

RESEARCH REFERENCES

New Hampshire Practice.
15 N.H.P. Land Use Planning and Zoning § 35.17.

674:44-c. Separate Commissions.

A municipality may choose to maintain a separate and distinct heritage commission and historic district commission. In such cases, the heritage commission shall serve in an advisory capacity to the historic district commission as well as to the planning board and other local boards and residents.

Source.
1992, 64:2, eff. June 19, 1992.

RESEARCH REFERENCES

New Hampshire Practice.
15 N.H.P. Land Use Planning and Zoning § 35.17.

674:44-d. Appropriations Authorized.

I. A town or city, having established a heritage commission under this subdivision, may appropriate money as deemed necessary to carry out its purposes. The whole or any part of money so appropriated in any year and any gifts of money received pursuant to RSA 674:44-b shall be placed in a heritage fund and allowed to accumulate from year to year. Money may be expended from such fund by the heritage commission for its purposes without further approval of the local legislative body.

II. The town treasurer, pursuant to RSA 41:29, shall have custody of all moneys in the heritage fund and shall pay out the same only upon order of the heritage commission. The disbursement of heritage funds shall be authorized by a majority of the heritage commission. Prior to the use of such funds for the purchase of any interest in real property, the heritage commission shall hold a public hearing with notice in accordance with RSA 675:7.

Source.
1992, 64:2. 1993, 32:3, eff. June 7, 1993.

Amendments
—1993. Paragraph I: Substituted "local leg-

islative body" for "town meeting" at the end of the third sentence.

Agricultural Commission

674:44-e. Agricultural Commission.

An agricultural commission may be established in accordance with RSA 673 for the proper recognition, promotion, enhancement, encouragement, use, management, and protection of agriculture and agricultural resources, tangible or intangible, that are valued for their economic, aesthetic, cultural, historic, or community significance within their natural, built, or cultural contexts. The word "agriculture" shall include the entirety of RSA 21:34-a, which is the definition of farm, agriculture, and farming.

Source.
2007, 266:1, eff. August 28, 2007.

674:44-f. Powers.

Agricultural commissions shall have advisory and review authority and other duties as follows:

I. Survey and inventory all agricultural resources.

II. Conduct activities to recognize, promote, enhance, and encourage agriculture, agricultural resources, and agricultural-based economic opportunities.

III. Assist the planning board, as requested, in the development and review of those sections of the master plan which address agricultural resources.

IV. Advise, upon request, local agencies and other local boards in their review of requests on matters affecting or potentially affecting agricultural resources.

V. Coordinate activities with appropriate service organizations and non-profit groups.

VI. Publicize and report its activities.

VII. Hire consultants and contractors as needed.

VIII. Receive gifts of money to assist in carrying out its purpose.

IX. Hold meetings and hearings necessary to carry out its duties.

Source.
2007, 266:1, eff. August 28, 2007.

674:44-g. Appropriations Authorized.

I. A town or city, having established an agricultural commission under this subdivision, may appropriate money as deemed necessary to carry out its purposes. The whole or any part of money so appropriated in any year and any

477

gifts of money received pursuant to RSA 674:44-f shall be placed in an agricultural fund and allowed to accumulate from year to year.

II. The town treasurer, pursuant to RSA 41:29, shall have custody of all moneys in the agricultural fund and shall pay out the same only upon order of the agricultural commission. The disbursement of agricultural funds shall be authorized by a majority of the agricultural commission. The use of such funds shall not be for the purchase of any interest in real property.

Source.
2007, 266:1, eff. August 28, 2007.

Historic Districts

Cross References.
Abolition of historic district commissions, see RSA 673:20.

Appointment and terms of members of historic district commissions generally, see RSA 673:4 et seq.

Establishment of historic district commissions, see RSA 673:1.

Filling of vacancies on commissions, see RSA 673:12.

Heritage commission, see RSA 674:44-a et seq.

Historic preservation generally, see RSA 227-C.

Meetings of commissions, see RSA 673:10, 15, 17.

Ordinance administration and enforcement generally, see RSA 676.

Ordinance adoption procedures generally, see RSA 675.

Rehearing and appeals procedures generally, see RSA 677.

Removal of members of commissions, see RSA 673:13.

Staff, see RSA 673:16.

Transfer of records of commissions, see RSA 673:21.

Zoning generally, see RSA 674:16 et seq.

674:45. Purposes.

The preservation of cultural resources, and particularly of structures and places of historic, architectural and community value is hereby declared to be a public purpose. The heritage of the municipality will be safeguarded by:

I. Preserving districts in the municipality which reflect elements of its cultural, social, economic, political, community and architectural history;

II. Conserving property values in such districts;

III. Fostering civic beauty;

IV. Strengthening the local economy; and

V. Promoting the use of historic districts for the education, pleasure and welfare of the citizens of the municipality.

Source.
1983, 447:1. 1992, 64:13, 14, eff. June 19, 1992.

Amendments
—1992. Inserted "cultural resources, and particularly of" preceding "structures", deleted "and" preceding "architectural" and inserted "and community" thereafter in the first sentence of the introductory paragraph.

Paragraph I: Substituted "districts" for "a district" following "preserving", "reflect" for "reflects" preceding "elements" and inserted "community" following "political".

Paragraph II: Substituted "districts" for "district" following "values in such".

Paragraph V: Substituted "historic districts" for "a historic district" preceding "for the education".

NOTES TO DECISIONS

Construction

The statements of purpose in the statute did not impose a burden of proof on any party when a historic district commission considered proposed changes within a historic district. Hanrahan v. City of Portsmouth, 119 N.H. 944, 409 A.2d 1336, 1979 N.H. LEXIS 425 (1979). (Decided under prior law.)

Cited:

Cited in Town of Chesterfield v. Brooks, 126 N.H. 64, 489 A.2d 600, 1985 N.H. LEXIS 274 (1985); Victorian Realty Group v. City of Nashua, 130 N.H. 60, 534 A.2d 381, 1987 N.H. LEXIS 278 (1987); Portsmouth Advocates, Inc. v. City of Portsmouth, 133 N.H. 876, 587 A.2d 600, 1991 N.H. LEXIS 13 (1991).

RESEARCH REFERENCES

New Hampshire Practice.

15 N.H.P. Land Use Planning and Zoning § 35.01.

674:46. Authority Granted.

For the purpose of this subdivision, the local legislative body of any city, town, or county in which there are located unincorporated towns or unorganized places shall have the authority, by ordinance, to establish, change, lay out and define historic districts. Within the district, the municipality is empowered to regulate the construction, alteration, repair, moving, demolition or use of such structures and places.

Source.

1983, 447:1. 1985, 103:22. 1989, 266:21, eff. July 1, 1989.

Amendments

—1989. Substituted "town, or county in which there are located unincorporated towns

or unorganized places" for "or town" following "city" in the first sentence.

—1985. Inserted "by ordinance" following "authority" in the first sentence, made other minor stylistic changes in that sentence and deleted the third and fourth sentences.

NOTES TO DECISIONS

Construction with other laws

City council was not prohibited from rezoning boundary between two historic districts by requirement of RSA 674:46-a that all historic districts and regulations be compatible with master plan and zoning ordinances of the city,

town or county in which they exist; RSA 674:46-a was directed toward local historic district commissions and not municipality's legislative body. Portsmouth Advocates, Inc. v. City of Portsmouth, 133 N.H. 876, 587 A.2d 600, 1991 N.H. LEXIS 13 (1991).

RESEARCH REFERENCES

New Hampshire Practice.

15 N.H.P. Land Use Planning and Zoning §§ 35.02, 35.13.

ALR.

Validity and construction of statute or ordi-

nance protecting historical landmarks. 18 A.L.R.4th 990.

674:46-a. Powers and Duties of the Historic District Commission.

I. For the purpose of establishing a legal basis for the district, the historic district commission may perform research and prepare the content of the historic district ordinance prior to its adoption or amendment as provided in RSA 675:2. In cases in which a municipality chooses to have both a heritage commission and a historic district commission, the historic district commission may request assistance from the heritage commission in performing research and preparing the content of the historic district ordinance.

II. The historic district commission may adopt and amend regulations in the manner provided in RSA 675:6.

III. The historic district commission shall be responsible for administering the ordinance and regulations within the historic district as provided in RSA 676:8–10.

IV. All districts and regulations shall be compatible with the master plan and zoning ordinance of the city, town, or county in which they exist.

V. The historic district commission may assume, if authorized by the local legislative body, the composition and duties of heritage commissions.

Source.
1985, 103:23. 1989, 266:22. 1992, 64:15. 1993, 32:2, eff. June 7, 1993.

Amendments
—**1993.** Paragraph V: Added.

—**1992.** Paragraph I: Added the second sentence.

—**1989.** Paragraph IV: Deleted "or" preceding "town" and inserted "or county" thereafter.

Cross References.
Master plan generally, see RSA 674:1 et seq.
Zoning ordinances generally, see RSA 674:16 et seq.

NOTES TO DECISIONS

Construction with other laws
City council was not prohibited from rezoning boundary between two historic districts by this section, which was directed toward local historic district commissions and not toward municipality's legislative body. Portsmouth Advocates, Inc. v. City of Portsmouth, 133 N.H. 876, 587 A.2d 600, 1991 N.H. LEXIS 13 (1991).

RESEARCH REFERENCES

New Hampshire Practice.
15 N.H.P. Land Use Planning and Zoning §§ 19.03, 35.02, 35.03, 35.06, 35.13, 35.17.

674:47. Abolition of Historic Districts.

I. Except as provided in paragraph II, any district established pursuant to the provisions of this subdivision may be abolished in the following manner: Upon petition of 25 voters, the historic district commission shall hold 2 public hearings at least 15 days apart on the proposal to abolish the historic district, at which hearings citizens shall have an opportunity to be heard. Notice for each public hearing shall be as provided in RSA 675:7. Following the above public hearings, the proposal to abolish a historic district shall be presented for insertion in the warrant of a regular or special town meeting as provided in

RSA 39:3. The historic district shall be abolished upon a vote of ⅔ of the members of the local legislative body present and voting.

II. In counties in which there are located unincorporated towns or unorganized places, the local legislative body shall determine the manner in which any district established pursuant to the provisions of this subdivision may be abolished for those unincorporated towns and unorganized places.

Source.
1983, 447:1. 1989, 266:23, eff. July 1, 1989.

Amendments
—1989. Designated the existing provisions of the section as par. I, added "except as provided in paragraph II" preceding "any district"

in the first sentence of that paragraph, and added par. II.

Cross References.
Abolition of historic district commissions, see RSA 673:18, 20, 21.

674:48. Interpretation.

Nothing in this subdivision shall be construed to prevent ordinary maintenance or repair of any structure or place within any historic district nor to prevent the construction, alteration, repair, moving or demolition of any structure under a permit issued by the building inspector or other duly delegated authority prior to the establishment of any historic district.

Source.
1983, 447:1, eff. Jan. 1, 1984.

RESEARCH REFERENCES

New Hampshire Practice.
15 N.H.P. Land Use Planning and Zoning § 35.05.

674:49. Enforcement.

The enforcement of the provisions of this subdivision shall be made through the zoning ordinance of the municipality. Any local legislative body which has established a historic district commission under RSA 673 shall include provisions for the enforcement of the commission's administrative decisions in the zoning ordinance of the municipality.

Source.
1983, 447:1, eff. Jan. 1, 1984.

Cross References.
Administration and enforcement of ordinances generally, see RSA 676.

RESEARCH REFERENCES

New Hampshire Practice.
15 N.H.P. Land Use Planning and Zoning § 35.13.

674:50. Remedies for Violations.

In case of the violation of any ordinance or regulation made under the authority conferred by this subdivision, the historic district commission, in addition to other remedies, may institute any appropriate action or proceedings to prevent, restrain, correct or abate such violation.

Source.
1983, 447:1, eff. Jan. 1, 1984.

Cross References.
Penalties and remedies generally, see RSA 676:15 et seq.

RESEARCH REFERENCES

New Hampshire Practice.
15 N.H.P. Land Use Planning and Zoning § 35.13.

Building Codes

Cross References.
Appointment and terms of members of building code boards of appeals, see RSA 673:3 et seq.

Building and construction standards generally, see RSA 155-A, 155-B.

Code administration and enforcement generally, see RSA 676.

Code adoption procedures generally, see RSA 675.

Disqualification of members of boards, see RSA 673:14.

Establishment of building code boards of appeals, see RSA 673:1.

Filling of vacancies on boards, see RSA 673:12.

Housing standards, see RSA 48-A.

Meetings of boards, see RSA 673:10, 15, 17.

Modular building standards, see RSA 205-C.

Powers of building code boards of appeals generally, see RSA 674:34.

Rehearing and appeals procedures generally, see RSA 677.

Removal of members of boards, see RSA 673:13.

Staff, see RSA 673:16.

Transfer of records of boards, see RSA 673:22.

RESEARCH REFERENCES

New Hampshire Practice.
15 N.H.P. Land Use Planning and Zoning § 35.13.

674:51. Power to Amend State Building Code and Establish Enforcement Procedures.

I. The local legislative body may enact as an ordinance or adopt, pursuant to the procedures of RSA 675:2–4, additional provisions of the state building code for the construction, remodeling, and maintenance of all buildings and structures in the municipality, provided that such additional regulations are not less stringent than the requirements of the state building code. The local legislative body may also enact a process for the enforcement of the state building code and any additional regulations thereto, and the provisions of a nationally recognized code that are not included in and are not inconsistent with the state building code. Any local enforcement process adopted prior to the effective date of this paragraph shall remain in effect unless it conflicts with the state building code or is amended or repealed by the municipality.

II. Any such ordinance adopted under paragraph I by a local legislative body shall be submitted to the state building code review board for informational purposes.

III. The local ordinance or amendment adopted according to the provisions of paragraph I shall include, at a minimum, the following provisions:

(a) The date of first enactment of any building code regulations in the municipality and of each subsequent amendment thereto.

(b) Provision for the establishment of a building code board of appeals as provided in RSA 673:1, V; 673:3, IV; and 673:5.

(c) Provision for the establishment of the position of building inspector as provided in RSA 673:1, V. The building inspector shall have the authority to issue building permits as provided in RSA 676:11–13 and any certificates of occupancy as enacted pursuant to paragraph III, and to perform inspections as may be necessary to assure compliance with the local building code.

(d) A schedule of fees, or a provision authorizing the governing body to establish fees, to be charged for building permits, inspections, and for any certificate of occupancy enacted pursuant to paragraph III.

IV. The regulations adopted pursuant to paragraph I may include a requirement for a certificate of occupancy to be issued prior to the use or occupancy of any building or structure that is erected or remodeled, or undergoes a change or expansion of use, subsequent to the effective date of such requirement.

Source.
1983, 447:1. 1989, 70:1. 1990, 71:3, eff. June 5, 1990. 2002, 8:10, eff. April 17, 2002. 2003, 245:7, eff. July 14, 2003.

Amendments
—**2003.** Paragraph I: Added the third sentence.

—**2002.** Rewritten to the extent that a detailed comparison would be impracticable.

—**1990.** Subparagraph II(b): Substituted "673:3, IV" for "673:3, II".

—**1989.** Rewritten to the extent that a detailed comparison would be impracticable.

Effect of 1989 amendment on existing local building codes.
1989, 70:3, eff. June 18, 1989, provided that any local building code enacted or amended by a municipality in accordance with existing law prior to June 18, 1989, shall remain in effect until it is amended or repealed; and, provided further, that any local building code enacted or amended by a municipality after June 18, 1989, shall be in conformance with the provisions of this section, as amended by 1989, 70:1.

674:51-a. Local Adoption of Building Codes by Reference.

In addition to the local powers under RSA 674:51 a municipality may adopt by reference any of the codes promulgated by the International Code Conference which are not included in the state building code under RSA 155-A.

Source.
2003, 245:8, eff. July 14, 2003.

674:52. Power to Adopt Building Codes by Reference.
[Repealed 2002, 8:12, II, eff. September 14, 2002.]

Former section(s)
Former RSA 674:52, which was derived from 1983, 447:1; 1989, 70:2, 266:24; 1997, 44:9; and

2000, 195:1 related to local adoption of building codes by reference.

Authority to Order Building Vacated

674:52-a. Ordering Building Vacated.

I. The building inspector shall have the authority to order occupants to vacate a building, structure, or other premises if the inspector determines, based on reasonable information and belief, that there is imminent danger of failure or collapse, or the condition of such premises otherwise constitutes a clear and imminent danger to the life or safety of occupants or other persons and that protection of life or safety requires vacating the premises. Such an order shall be subject to the procedures of RSA 147:16-a, which shall supersede inconsistent provisions contained in any local code or code adopted by reference.

II. The provisions of paragraph I shall not apply to a residence which is occupied by the owner and his or her immediate family, unless the condition of such premises constitutes a clear and imminent danger to the life or health of persons other than the occupant or occupants.

Source.
1998, 318:3, eff. Aug. 25, 1998.

Land Affected by Municipal Boundaries

674:53. Land Affected by Municipal Boundaries.

I. An owner of contiguous land which is located in more than one municipality may treat a municipal boundary line as an existing boundary between lots, tracts, sites or other divisions of land for purposes of this title unless the existing or proposed use of land or arrangement of structures in one of the municipalities requires and is dependent upon land or improvements located in the other municipality or municipalities in order to fulfill the land use ordinances or regulations of the first municipality with respect to such matters as lot size, density, frontage, uses or accessory uses, set-backs or access, or in order to comply with applicable state or federal regulations.

II. Upon receipt of an application for a permit or approval under this title for the subdivision, development, change of use of, or erection or alteration of any structure upon any lot, tract, site or other division of land whose boundary or portion thereof is a municipal boundary line, or whose sole street access or sole maintained street access is via a private road or class IV, V, or VI highway located in an adjoining municipality, the municipality receiving the application shall inquire in writing to the appropriate administrative officials in the adjoining municipality or municipalities as to the existence of facts or regulations which, under paragraphs I, III, or IV of this section or otherwise, would preclude or affect such subdivision, development, construction, or change of use. Response shall be made to such inquiries within the period provided by this title for approval or disapproval of the underlying application. A response which invokes an ordinance or regulation of such adjoining municipality may be appealed in that adjoining municipality in the same manner as any other administrative decision. An adjoining municipality in which is located an existing private road or class VI highway that serves as an applicant's sole means of fulfilling the street access requirements under RSA 674:41 shall have the same regulatory powers under that statute with respect to that road or highway as if the proposed building or development were located within that same municipality.

III. An owner of contiguous land in more than one municipality may treat such contiguous land as a single lot, tract, site, or other division of land for purposes of this title, notwithstanding the municipal boundary line, provided that:

(a) All uses of land, buildings, or structures shall comply with the regulations or ordinances of the municipality in which they are located.

(b) When an owner has fulfilled or proposes to fulfill the requirements of one municipality, through the inclusion of land or improvements located in an adjoining municipality, such owner or the owner's successors shall not thereafter use that land or those improvements in a manner such that those requirements of the first municipality are no longer fulfilled. This paragraph may be enforced by the municipality whose requirements are to be fulfilled.

IV. No plat or plan showing land or streets in more than one municipality in the state shall be deemed approved for purposes of this title unless it has been approved by the planning boards of all included municipalities in which the planning board has been granted authority over approval of that type of plat or plan. In addition, no plat or plan showing land whose sole street access or sole maintained street access is or is planned to be via a private road or class IV, V, or VI highway located in an adjoining municipality shall be deemed approved for purposes of this title unless it has been approved by the planning board, if any, of that adjoining municipality, provided however that the sole issue which may be addressed or regulated by the adjoining municipality shall be the adequacy of such street access, and the impact of the proposal upon it.

V. With respect to a proposal for the use of contiguous land in more than one municipality:

(a) The fact that a lot, tract, or site straddles a municipal boundary, or that the requirements of one municipality are proposed to be fulfilled by the use of land or improvements in an adjoining municipality, shall not be the sole grounds for disapproval of any application.

(b) A planning board may waive or vary its regulations with respect to access or interior roads in order to provide better harmony with the regulations of an adjoining municipality, whenever strict compliance would be unreasonable in light of the overall design of a proposal.

VI. When local land use boards from more than one municipality have jurisdiction over a proposed use, subdivision, or development of property:

(a) The applicant may petition the respective local land use boards of each such municipality to proceed with the application on a joint basis, and upon such petition, joint hearings or meetings shall be held throughout the application process. However, each board may meet separately to confer and take final action upon the application, but may not condition final approval upon the receipt of information not previously requested at a joint hearing or meeting.

(b) Not less than a quorum of each involved land use board shall attend the joint hearing or meeting, and the members who attend the joint hearing or meeting shall have the authority of the full board over that application. In the alternative, the full board may attend the joint hearing or meeting. Each land use board shall be responsible for rendering a decision on the subject matter within its jurisdiction.

(c) The board members present at such a joint meeting or hearing shall select an interim chairperson from among such members, who shall prescribe rules of procedure, subject to alteration by the members present, but consistent with RSA 676.

VII. Whenever a subdivision plat or site plan submitted to a planning board includes land whose only maintained public highway access to the Class I and II highway system is via a Class IV or V highway maintained by another municipality in the state, the local governing body and planning board, if any, of that other municipality shall be deemed "abutters" for purposes of notice under RSA 676:4. A planning board may, by regulation, set forth additional circumstances in which notice to adjoining municipalities is required. A planning board, in determining whether an application satisfies its regulations, may consider the effect of the proposal on adjoining municipalities.

Source.
1989, 381:1. 1995, 43:6, 7, eff. July 2, 1995. 1998, 57:1, 2, eff. July 11, 1998.

Amendments
—1998. Paragraph II: Rewritten to the extent that a detailed comparison would be impracticable.

Paragraph IV: Added the last sentence.

—1995. Paragraph III(b): Substituted "the owner's" for "his" preceding "successors" in the first sentence.

Paragraph VI(c): Substituted "chairperson" for "chairman" following "select an interim".

RESEARCH REFERENCES

New Hampshire Practice.
15 N.H.P. Land Use Planning and Zoning § 29.12.

Governmental Use of Property

Amendments
—1998. 1998, 281:1, eff. Aug. 25, 1998, deleted "Notification to Municipalities of" preceding "Governmental" in the subdivision heading.

674:54. Governmental Land Uses.

I. In this section, "governmental use" means a use, construction, or development of land owned or occupied, or proposed to be owned or occupied, by the state, university system, the community college system of New Hampshire, or by a county, town, city, school district, or village district, or any of their agents, for any public purpose which is statutorily or traditionally governmental in nature.

II. The state, university system, community college system of New Hampshire, county, town, city, school district, or village district shall give written notification to the governing body and planning board, if such exists, of a municipality of any proposed governmental use of property within its jurisdiction, which constitutes a substantial change in use or a substantial new use. Written notification shall contain plans, specifications, explanations of proposed changes available at the time, a statement of the governmental nature of the use as set forth in paragraph I, and a proposed construction schedule. Such notification shall be provided at least 60 days prior to the beginning of construction. Either the governing body or planning board of the municipality may conduct a public hearing relative to the proposed governmental use. Any such hearing shall be held within 30 days after receipt of notice by the governing body or planning board. A representative of the governmental entity which provided notice shall be available to present the plans, specifications, and construction schedule, and to provide explanations. The governing body or planning board may issue nonbinding written comments relative to conformity or nonconformity of the proposal with normally applicable land use regulations to the sponsor of the governmental use within 30 days after the hearing.

II-a. Any use, construction, or development of land occurring on governmentally owned or occupied land, but which is not a governmental use as defined in paragraph I, shall be fully subject to local land use regulations.

II-b. The construction and operation of any solid waste disposal facility on land owned or occupied by any city or town within another city or town shall be subject to local land use regulations to the same extent as if the land were owned and occupied by a private entity. Nothing in this paragraph shall affect the construction and operation of a solid waste facility on land owned by a solid waste management district formed under RSA 53-A or RSA 53-B or any combination of municipalities authorized by an act of the general court, if the land is located within a city or town that is part of the district.

III. This section shall not apply to:

(a) The layout or construction of public highways of any class, or to the distribution lines or transmission apparatus of governmental utilities, provided that the erection of a highway or utility easement across a parcel of land, shall not, in and of itself, be deemed to subdivide the remaining land into 2 or more lots or sites for conveyance for development purposes in the absence of subdivision approval under this title. For purposes of this subparagraph, "transmission apparatus" shall not include wireless communication facilities.

(b) The erection, installation, or maintenance of poles, structures, conduits and cables, or wires in, under, or across any public highways under RSA

231, or licenses or leases for telecommunication facilities in, under, or across railroad rights of way. For purposes of this subparagraph, "structures" shall not include wireless communications facilities.

IV. In the event of exigent circumstances where the delay entailed by compliance with this section would endanger public health or safety, the governor may declare a governmental use exempt from the requirements of this section.

Source.
1996, 262:1, eff. Aug. 9, 1996. 1998, 281:2, eff. Aug. 25, 1998. 2007, 29:1, eff. May 14, 2007; 361:32, eff. July 17, 2007.

Amendments
—**2007.** Paragraph I: Chapter 361 inserted "the community college system of New Hamp-

shire" following "university system".
Paragraph II: Chapter 361 inserted "community college system of New Hampshire" following "university system" in the first sentence.
Paragraph II-b: Added by ch. 29.

—**1998.** Rewrote pars. II and III and added pars. II-a and IV.

Wetlands

674:55. Wetlands.

Wherever the term "wetlands," whether singular or plural, is used in regulations and ordinances adopted pursuant to this chapter, such term shall be given the meaning in RSA 482-A:2, X and the delineation of wetlands for purposes of such regulations and ordinances shall be as prescribed in rules adopted under RSA 482-A. Nothing in this subdivision shall be construed to limit the powers otherwise granted under this chapter for municipalities to plan land use and enact regulations based on consideration of environmental characteristics, vegetation, wildlife habit, open space, drainage, potential for flooding, and protection of natural resources, including critical or sensitive areas or resources and groundwater. In the context of such authority, municipalities may define and delineate resources or environmental characteristics, such as wet soils or areas, and shoreline or buffer areas, in a manner different from the common meaning and delineation of wetlands required herein.

Source.
2004, 243:2, eff. July 1, 2005.

Floodplains

674:56. Floodplain Ordinances.

Municipalities may adopt floodplain ordinances as part of their enrollment in the National Flood Insurance Program. Such ordinances shall be adopted pursuant to the authority granted under RSA 674:16 and 17, and shall be adopted and amended pursuant to the procedures in RSA 675 for the adoption and amendment of zoning ordinances. Municipalities may adopt floodplain ordinances either as an amendment to an existing zoning ordinance or as a separate ordinance. A municipality which adopts a floodplain ordinance which is separate from its zoning ordinance or without otherwise having adopted a zoning ordinance, shall observe all legal and procedural requirements for the floodplain ordinance that would be required for a zoning ordinance, including the creation of a board of adjustment. If a municipality has adopted a zoning ordinance either before or after the adoption of a floodplain ordinance, the board of adjustment shall be the same for both ordinances.

Source.

2006, 176:2, eff. May 25, 2006.

Intent.

2006, 176:1, eff. May 25, 2006, provided: "The intent of this act [which enacted this subdivision] is to clarify the authority of municipalities to adopt floodplain ordinances pursuant to enrolling in the National Flood Insurance Program, to enable the adoption of flood insurance rate map amendments by resolution of the local governing body, and to ratify the past actions of municipalities in adopting local floodplain ordinances and maps. The general court recognizes that municipalities that fail to adopt amendments to the flood insurance rate maps as required for their participation in the National Flood Insurance Program risk suspension from that program by the federal government."

Ratification of Previously Adopted Floodplain Ordinances.

2006, 176:3, eff May 25, 2006, provided:

"The following municipalities and political subdivisions have previously adopted floodplain ordinances and are enrolled in the National Flood Insurance Program (NFIP). The general court hereby ratifies the following previously adopted floodplain ordinances as legal:

"Municipality: Acworth, Albany, Allenstown, Alstead, Alton, Amherst, Andover, Antrim, Ashland, Auburn, Barnstead, Barrington, Bartlett, Bath, Bedford, Belmont, Bennington, Berlin, Bethlehem, Boscawen, Bow, Bradford, Brentwood, Bridgewater, Bristol, Brookfield, Brookline, Campton, Canaan, Canterbury, Carroll, Charlestown, Chester, Chesterfield, Chichester, Claremont, Colebrook, Columbia, Concord, Conway, Cornish, Dalton, Danbury, Danville, Deerfield, Deering, Derry, Dover, Dummer, Dunbarton, Durham, East Kingston, Easton, Enfield, Epping, Epsom, Errol, Exeter, Farmington, Fitzwilliam, Francestown, Franconia, Franklin, Freedom, Fremont, Gilford, Gilsum, Goffstown, Gorham, Goshen, Grantham, Greenfield, Greenland, Greenville, Groton, Hampstead, Hampton, Hampton Falls, Hancock, Hanover, Hart's Location, Haverhill, Hebron, Henniker, Hill, Hillsborough, Hinsdale, Holderness, Hollis, Hooksett, Hopkinton, Hudson, Jackson, Jaffrey, Jefferson, Keene, Kingston, Laconia, Lancaster, Lebanon, Lee, Lincoln, Lisbon, Litchfield, Littleton, Londonderry, Loudon, Lyme, Madison, Manchester, Marlborough, Marlow, Mason, Meredith, Merrimack, Middleton, Milan, Milford, Milton, Moultonborough, Nashua, New Boston, New Castle, New Durham, New Hampton, New Ipswich, New London, Newbury, Newfields, Newmarket, Newport, North Hampton, Northfield, Northumberland, Northwood, Nottingham, Orford, Ossipee, Pelham, Pembroke, Peterborough, Piermont, Pittsfield, Plainfield, Plaistow, Plymouth, Portsmouth, Raymond, Rindge, Rochester, Rollinsford, Roxbury, Rye, Salem, Salisbury, Sanbornton, Sandown, Sandwich, Seabrook, Seabrook Beach Village District, Shelburne, Somersworth, South Hampton, Stark, Stewartstown, Strafford, Stratford, Stratham, Sugar Hill, Sullivan, Sunapee, Sutton, Swanzey, Tamworth, Thornton, Tilton, Troy, Tuftonboro, Wakefield, Walpole, Warner, Warren, Waterville Valley, Weare, Webster, Wentworth, Westmoreland, Whitefield, Wilmot, Wilton, Winchester, Windham, Wolfeboro, and Woodstock."

674:57. Flood Insurance Rate Maps.

In a municipality which has enrolled in the National Flood Insurance Program (NFIP), special flood hazard areas shall be as designated on flood insurance rate maps issued by the Federal Emergency Management Agency. Amendments to the flood insurance rate maps shall apply to local floodplain ordinances upon their adoption by resolution of the local governing body of a municipality and shall require no further action by the local legislative body.

Map amendments are subject to appeal by owners and lessees of affected real property under 44 C.F.R. 67.5.

Source.
2006, 176:2, eff. May 25, 2006.

CHAPTER 675

ENACTMENT AND ADOPTION PROCEDURES

Cross References.

Administration and enforcement of ordinances, regulations and codes generally, see RSA 676.

Adoption of bylaws by towns generally, see RSA 31:39 et seq.

Bylaw defined, see RSA 21:45.

Definitions generally, see RSA 672:2 et seq.

Local land use boards generally, see RSA 673.

Local land use planning and regulatory powers generally, see RSA 674.

Rehearing and appeals procedures generally, see RSA 677.

RESEARCH REFERENCES

New Hampshire Practice.

15 N.H.P. Land Use Planning and Zoning §§ 5.01, et seq.

New Hampshire Bar Journal.

For article, "An Overview of the New

Hampshire Land Use Planning and Regulation Statutes," see 34 N.H.B.J. 6 (June 1993).

General Provisions

675:1. General Requirements.

I. The following shall be adopted under RSA 675:6:

(a) Every master plan or amendment to a master plan proposed under RSA 674:1;

(b) Subdivision regulations proposed under RSA 674:35;

(c) Site plan review regulations proposed under RSA 674:44; and

(d) Historic district regulations proposed under RSA 674:46-a.

II. Zoning ordinances proposed under RSA 674:16, historic district ordinances proposed under RSA 674:46 and building codes proposed under RSA 674:51 shall be adopted in accordance with the procedures required under RSA 675:2–5.

III. If an official map is established, it shall be established according to the procedures required under RSA 674:10.

Source.

1983, 447:1. 1985, 103:24, eff. Jan. 1, 1986.

Amendments

—1985. Paragraph I(b): Deleted "and" following "RSA 674:35".

Paragraph I(c): Added "and" following "RSA 674:44".

Paragraph I(d): Added.

Paragraph II: Inserted "historic district ordinances proposed under RSA 674:46" following "RSA 674:16".

Paragraph III: Substituted "RSA 674:10" for

"RSA 674:9" at the end of the paragraph.

Cross References.

Adoption and amendment of master plan generally, see RSA 674:4.

Adoption of emergency temporary zoning and planning ordinances in certain towns, see RSA 675:4-a.

Adoption of innovative land use controls, see RSA 674:21.

Emergency temporary zoning and planning ordinances generally, see RSA 674:24 et seq.

RESEARCH REFERENCES

New Hampshire Practice.

15 N.H.P. Land Use Planning and Zoning § 15.07.

Zoning Ordinance, Historic District Ordinance and Building Code Enactment Procedures

Cross References.

Building codes generally, see RSA 674:51 et seq.

Emergency temporary zoning and planning ordinances generally, see RSA 674:24 et seq.

Filling of zoning ordinances, historic district ordinances or building codes, see RSA 675:8, 9.

Historic district ordinances generally, see RSA 674:45 et seq.

Master plans generally, see RSA 674:1 et seq.

Official municipal maps generally, see RSA 674:9 et seq.

Site plan review regulations generally, see RSA 674:43 et seq.

Subdivision regulations generally, see RSA 674:35 et seq.

Zoning ordinances generally, see RSA 674:16 et seq.

RESEARCH REFERENCES

ALR.

Adoption of zoning ordinance or amendment thereto as subject of referendum. 72 A.L.R.3d 1030.

Adoption of zoning ordinance or amendment thereto through initiative process. 72 A.L.R.3d 991.

675:2. Method of Enactment in Cities and Towns Operating Under Town Council Form of Government.

I. In cities or in towns operating under the town council form of government, and in counties in which there are located unincorporated towns or unorganized places, the local legislative body shall determine the manner in which a zoning ordinance, historic district ordinance, or a building code is established and amended; provided, however, that any question concerning the establishment and amendment of a zoning ordinance, historic district ordinance, or a building code may be placed on a ballot separate from the ballot used to elect city or town officers. The planning board shall forward to the town clerk all proposed amendments to a zoning ordinance, historic district ordinance, or building code not later than the fifth Tuesday prior to the date for electing city or town officers.

II. No zoning ordinance, historic district ordinance, or building code shall be established or amended until after a public hearing is held in accordance with the procedures required under RSA 675:7 on the proposed zoning ordinance, historic district ordinance, building code or amendment.

Source.
1983, 447:1. 1985, 103:24; 266:1. 1989, 266:25. 1990, 54:1, eff. June 5, 1990.

Amendments
—1990. Paragraph I: Added the second sentence.

—1989. Paragraph I: Inserted "and in counties in which there are located unincorporated towns or unorganized places" following "government".

—1985. Paragraph I: Rewritten by ch. 266 to the extent that a detailed comparison would be impracticable.
Paragraph II: Chapter 103 inserted "historic district ordinance" following "zoning ordinance" wherever it appeared.

Rescinded 1985, 103 amendment.
1985, 103:24 provided for amendment of pars. I and II, effective Jan. 1, 1986. However, 1985, 266:4, eff. Aug. 6, 1985, declared the amendment to par. I made by 1985, 103:24 to be null and void.

Cross References.
Enactment of zoning ordinances, historic district ordinances and building codes pursuant to petition of voters, see RSA 675:4.
Enactment of zoning ordinances, historic district ordinances or building codes by towns not operating under town council form of government and village districts, see RSA 675:3.

NOTES TO DECISIONS

Analysis

1. Purpose of hearings
2. Sufficiency of notice
3. Cure of defects
4. Validity of particular enactments

1. Purpose of hearings
The purpose of public hearings was to insure that the current views of local residents would be taken into account by the council when it considered enactment of a proposed ordinance. Bosse v. City of Portsmouth, 107 N.H. 523, 226 A.2d 99, 1967 N.H. LEXIS 212 (1967). (Decided under prior law.)

2. Sufficiency of notice
While there was no specific statutory requirement that the description of the zones be published, a notice would have been meaningless unless it included some reference to the area involved sufficient to give the reader reasonable warning that his interest might be affected. Schadlick v. City of Concord, 108 N.H. 319, 234 A.2d 523, 1967 N.H. LEXIS 179 (1967). (Decided under prior law.)

3. Cure of defects
A legislative act legalizing the votes and proceedings of a number of town meetings was ineffective to cure the invalidity of a zoning amendment adopted without compliance with the notice provision. Olson v. Litchfield, 112 N.H. 261, 296 A.2d 470, 1972 N.H. LEXIS 191 (1972); Calawa v. Litchfield, 112 N.H. 263, 296 A.2d 124, 1972 N.H. LEXIS 193 (1972). (Decided under prior law.)

4. Validity of particular enactments
A city's adoption of former RSA 156:3-a (now covered by RSA 676:12), allowing building permits to be withheld pending zoning changes, was not subject to the public hearing requirements needed to enact zoning ordinances since former RSA 156:3-a was not a zoning ordinance. Socha v. City of Manchester, 126 N.H. 289, 490 A.2d 794, 1985 N.H. LEXIS 297 (1985). (Decided under prior law.)

Cited:
Cited in Bedford Residents Group v. Town of Bedford, 130 N.H. 632, 547 A.2d 225, 1988 N.H. LEXIS 65 (1988).

RESEARCH REFERENCES

New Hampshire Practice.
15 N.H.P. Land Use Planning and Zoning
§§ 2.01, 5.01–5.04, 35.03, 35.06, 37.06.

675:3. Method of Enactment in Certain Towns and Village Districts.

I. Any town not operating under the town council form of government, or any village district which is specifically authorized by law to enact a zoning ordinance, shall establish and amend a zoning ordinance, historic district ordinance, or building code upon the affirmative vote by ballot of a majority of the legal voters present and voting on the day of the meeting, as provided in paragraph VII. Any proposed zoning ordinance, as submitted by a planning board or any amendment to an existing zoning ordinance as proposed by a planning board, board of selectmen or village district commission shall be submitted to the voters of a town or village district in the manner prescribed in this section.

II. No zoning ordinance, historic district ordinance, or building code shall be established or amended at a town or village district meeting until after the planning board holds at least one public hearing on the proposed ordinance, code or amendment. Notice for the time and place of each public hearing shall be the same as that provided in RSA 675:7.

III. After the public hearing the planning board shall, by vote, determine the final form of the ordinance, amendment, or amendments to be presented to the town or village district, which ordinance or amendment may include editorial revisions and textual modifications resulting from the proceedings of that hearing.

IV. An additional public hearing shall be held if the proposal is substantively altered by the planning board after public hearing. Subsequent public hearings shall be held at least 14 days after the prior public hearing and with the notice provided in RSA 675:7.

V. Official copies of the final proposal to adopt or amend the zoning ordinance, historic district ordinance, or building code shall be placed on file and made available to the public at the town or village clerk's office not later than the fifth Tuesday prior to the date when action is to be taken. An official copy of the proposal shall be on display for the voters at the meeting place on the date of the meeting.

VI. Each village district must be specifically authorized to zone by the legislature.

VII. If the town or village district has adopted an official ballot for the election of its respective officers, the issue as to the adoption of the proposed ordinance, building code, or amendment shall be presented to the voters of the town or village district by having the town or village district clerk prepare an official ballot separate from the official ballot used to elect town or village district officers which shall include the following question, or by including the following question on the official ballot as prepared by the town or village district clerk:

494

"Are you in favor of the adoption of the zoning ordinance, historic district ordinance, or building code (or amendment to the existing town (village district) zoning ordinance, historic district ordinance, or building code) as proposed by the planning board?" In the event that there shall be more than a single proposed amendment to be submitted to the voters at any given meeting, the issue as to the several amendments shall be put in the following manner: "Are you in favor of the adoption of Amendment No. ____ as proposed by the planning board for the town (village district) zoning ordinance (historic district ordinance or building code) as follows: (Here insert topical description of substance of amendment.)?" If such action is to be taken at a meeting other than the one at which officers are to be elected, the clerk shall prepare a special ballot containing the question or questions above stated, and the meeting shall open not later than noon and shall remain open at least 8 hours. If such action is to be taken at a meeting in a town or village district which has not adopted an official ballot, the clerk may prepare a special ballot likewise separate from the ballot used to elect town or village district officers for the use of voters in voting on the question. If a majority of the voters present and voting on any question as herein provided shall vote in the affirmative, the ordinance or amendment thereto shall be declared to have been adopted. When submitting any question to the voters under this section, there shall be 2 squares printed after the question, one with the word "yes" beside it and another with the word "no" beside it.

VIII. If an amendment is submitted by the selectmen or village district commissioners, the ballot shall so indicate. A notation on the ballot stating the planning board's approval or disapproval shall immediately follow the question's description.

IX. The method for amending a zoning ordinance, historic district ordinance or building code, as set forth in this section, may also be utilized to repeal such ordinance or code. The ballot question shall use the word "repeal" in place of the words "adoption" or "amendment."

Source.
1983, 447:1. 1985, 103:24; 266:2. 1990, 54:2, eff. June 5, 1990. 1996, 43:1, eff. June 23, 1996.

Amendments
—**1996.** Paragraph IX: Added.

—**1990.** Paragraph V: Substituted "not later than the fifth Tuesday" for "4 weeks" following "office" in the first sentence.

—**1985.** Paragraph I: Chapter 103 inserted "historic district ordinance" preceding "or building code" in the first sentence and added the second sentence.
Paragraph II: Chapter 103 inserted "historic district ordinance" preceding "or building code" in the first sentence.
Paragraph V: Chapter 103 inserted "historic

district ordinance" preceding "or building code" in the first sentence.
Paragraph VII: Rewritten by ch. 266 to the extent that a detailed comparison would be impracticable.
Paragraph VIII: Added by ch. 103.

Rescinded 1985 amendment.
1985, 103:24 provided for amendment of pars. I, II, V and VII, reenactment of pars. III, IV and V without changes and addition of par. VIII, effective Jan. 1, 1986. However, 1985, 266:4, eff. Aug. 6, 1985, declared the amendment to par. VII made by 1985, 103:24 to be null and void.

Cross References.
Enactment of zoning ordinances, historic district ordinances or building codes by cities and

towns operating under town council form of government, see RSA 675:2.

Enactment of zoning ordinances, historic district ordinances or building codes pursuant to petition of voters, see RSA 675:4.

Filing of zoning ordinances, historic district ordinances or building codes, see RSA 675:8, 9.

NOTES TO DECISIONS

Analysis

1. Constitutionality
2. Applicability of procedure
3. Notice and hearing
4. Records of meeting of planning board
5. Submission of amendments to voters

1. Constitutionality

The submission of a zoning ordinance to the voters under the statute was not an unconstitutional exercise of legislative power by referendum, and the provisions for hearings before the planning board and the restriction of the voters to consideration of only those changes as were proposed was not a delegation of legislative power to the board, but a valid limitation upon the power of the town. Cutter v. Durham, 109 N.H. 33, 241 A.2d 216, 1968 N.H. LEXIS 109 (1968). (Decided under prior law.)

2. Applicability of procedure

Where RSA 675:3, VII and RSA 675:4, I pertained to ballots, not warrant articles, and the trial court conflated warrant articles and ballots, the trial court misapprehended the relevant statutes and the matter had to be remanded for further consideration. Lower Bartlett Water Precinct v. Murnik, 150 N.H. 690, 845 A.2d 1245, 2004 N.H. LEXIS 55 (2004).

Whether or not a particular law was a zoning measure subject to the prerequisites for the enactment of such an ordinance under the statute or was an expression of some other phase of the police power, not so subject, was to be determined by the nature and purpose of the particular enactment. Piper v. Meredith, 110 N.H. 291, 266 A.2d 103, 1970 N.H. LEXIS 156 (1970). (Decided under prior law.)

An ordinance establishing a height and setback limitation for buildings in a portion of a town came within the police powers of RSA 31:39 and did not have to be adopted under the provisions of this statute. Piper v. Meredith, 110 N.H. 291, 266 A.2d 103, 1970 N.H. LEXIS 156 (1970). (Decided under prior law.)

3. Notice and hearing

The provision for public hearing in this statute required a hearing before the legislative body. Towle v. Nashua, 106 N.H. 394, 212 A.2d 204, 1965 N.H. LEXIS 177 (1965). (Decided under prior law.)

4. Records of meeting of planning board

The statute did not require that minutes of the meeting of the planning board be kept, and the lack of precise records of the board did not invalidate the action taken at a town meeting. Collins v. Town of Derry, 109 N.H. 470, 256 A.2d 654, 1969 N.H. LEXIS 181 (1969). (Decided under prior law.)

5. Submission of amendments to voters

The "single subject" rule is applicable to RSA 675:3 and a proposed amendment that includes changes to multiple sections of an ordinance is proper so long as the sections sought to be changed are reasonably germane to the subject of the amendment. Handley v. Town of Hooksett, 147 N.H. 184, 785 A.2d 399, 2001 N.H. LEXIS 192 (2001).

The requirements of the statute were met when all amendments to a zoning ordinance were printed and distributed to all voters, the amendments and the town zoning map were available from the town clerk, and copies of the amendments were displayed in the town. Town of Hampton v. Brust, 122 N.H. 463, 446 A.2d 458, 1982 N.H. LEXIS 375 (1982). (Decided under prior law.)

The provision requiring the planning board to determine the final form in which a proposed amendment was to be presented to the voters, and allowing editorial revisions and textual modifications after a second public hearing, could not be interpreted to allow substantive changes, since such changes would violate the spirit of the statute, the entire purpose of which was to allow the public to participate in the process of amending zoning ordinances. Town of Hampton v. Brust, 122 N.H. 463, 446 A.2d 458, 1982 N.H. LEXIS 375 (1982). (Decided under prior law.)

No substantial amendments could be included in a proposed zoning ordinance after a second public hearing unless an additional third hearing was held because the public must have had an opportunity to discuss the ordinance before it voted. Town of Hampton v. Brust, 122 N.H. 463, 446 A.2d 458, 1982 N.H. LEXIS 375 (1982). (Decided under prior law.)

Where the town planning board added a second sentence to a proposed zoning ordinance defining a penny arcade, after a second public hearing had been held and before the amendment was presented to the voters for approval, the changes made after the second hearing were not editorial revisions or textual modifications permitted by the statute, and the ordinance was void and unenforceable, not having been validly enacted, even though it was submitted to and approved by the voters, since a third hearing had not been held after the planning board added the second sentence. Town of Hampton v. Brust, 122 N.H. 463, 446 A.2d 458, 1982 N.H. LEXIS 375 (1982). (Decided under prior law.)

There was compliance with the statute and the voters were given adequate notice of the proposal on which they were to vote where, although notice of the second public hearing contained only the changes in the original proposal set forth in the notice for the first public hearing and did not contain all the amendments that were being proposed, all amendments to be acted upon were printed in a town report and distributed to all voters, the amendments and the zoning map were on file and copies were available at the town clerk's office two weeks prior to the town meeting, and copies of the amendments were posted in each polling booth and displayed in other places in the town hall. Collins v. Town of Derry, 109 N.H. 470, 256 A.2d 654, 1969 N.H. LEXIS 181 (1969). (Decided under prior law.)

Cited:
Cited in Rall v. Town of Belmont, 138 N.H. 172, 635 A.2d 1368, 1993 N.H. LEXIS 185 (1993).

OPINIONS OF THE ATTORNEY GENERAL

Analysis

1. Notice and hearing
2. Submission of amendments to voters

1. Notice and hearing

Zoning amendments accepted by a planning board were to be fully and legally noticed to inform the public, and if additional amendments were to be considered after the hearing, there were to be further hearings at which such

amendments would be considered before they were placed on the ballot. 1 N.H.Op.A.G. 162. (Decided under prior law.)

2. Submission of amendments to voters

There was nothing in the statute which required all amendments to a zoning ordinance to be presented as one package; therefore, amendments could be submitted to the voters separately. 1 N.H.Op.A.G. 157. (Decided under prior law.)

RESEARCH REFERENCES

New Hampshire Practice.
15 N.H.P. Land Use Planning and Zoning

§§ 5.01, 5.03, 5.04, 5.07, 5.16, 26.03, 31.04, 35.04.

675:4. Method of Enactment by Petition.

I. Twenty-five or more voters may petition for an amendment to a zoning ordinance, historic district ordinance, or a building code. Petitioned amendments shall be voted only at the annual town or village district meeting. A petition to amend a zoning ordinance, historic district ordinance, or a building code shall be submitted to the board of selectmen or the village district commissioners during the period between 120 and 90 days prior to the annual town or village district meeting. The petition shall be in correct warrant article form, as determined by the selectmen or village district commissioners, to amend the zoning ordinance, historic district ordinance, or building code. The selectmen or the village district commissioners shall submit the petitions to the planning board in a timely manner.

II. The planning board at its first regular meeting following the petition period shall set the date of the public hearing for each petitioned amendment which is received and shall hold a public hearing on each petitioned amendment. Notice for the time and place of the public hearing shall be the same as that provided in RSA 675:7.

III. Each petitioned amendment shall be placed on a ballot which may be separate from the ballot used to elect town or village district officers. A notation on the ballot stating the planning board's approval or disapproval shall immediately follow the question's description. Any petitioned question receiving an affirmative vote of a majority of the legal voters present and voting shall be adopted, except as provided in RSA 675:5. The planning board shall forward to the town or village district clerk all proposed amendments to a zoning ordinance, historic district ordinance, or building code under this section not later than the fifth Tuesday prior to the date for electing town or village district officers.

IV. The town or village district clerk shall include each question on a petitioned amendment on the appropriate official or special ballot, or separate official ballot, in the same manner as provided in paragraph III and in RSA 675:3, VII.

V. The method for amending a zoning ordinance, historic district ordinance or building code, as set forth in this section, may also be utilized to repeal such ordinance or code. The ballot question shall use the word "repeal" in place of the word "amendment."

Source.
1983, 447:1. 1985, 103:24; 266:3. 1990, 54:3, eff. June 5, 1990. 1996, 43:2, eff. June 23, 1996.

Amendments
—**1996.** Paragraph V: Added.

—**1990.** Paragraph III: Added the fourth sentence.

—**1985.** Paragraph I: Chapter 103 inserted "historic district ordinance" following "zoning ordinance" in the first, second and third sentences.

Paragraph III: Chapter 266 added "which may be separate from the ballot used to elect town or village district officers" following "ballot" at the end of the first sentence.

Paragraph IV: Chapter 266 inserted "or separate official ballot" preceding "in the same man-

ner as provided in" and "paragraph III and in" thereafter.

Rescinded 1985, 103 amendment.
1985, 103:24 provided for amendment of par. I and reenactment of pars. II-IV without changes, effective Jan. 1, 1986. However, 1985, 266:4, eff. Aug. 6, 1985, declared the amendments to pars. III and IV purportedly made by 1985, 103:24 to be null and void.

Cross References.
Enactment of zoning ordinances, historic district ordinances or building codes generally, see RSA 675:2, 3.

Filing of zoning ordinances, historic district ordinances or building codes, see RSA 675:8, 9.

Warrants for town meetings generally, see RSA 39.

NOTES TO DECISIONS

Analysis

1. Construction with other laws
2. Notice and hearing
3. Petition for repeal

1. Construction with other laws

RSA 39:2, requiring that town selectmen include in the town meeting warrant all subject matter to be considered at the meeting, and this statute, empowering selectmen to determine whether a petition for a zoning amendment was in correct form, did not require that petitions be submitted to the selectmen before submission to the planning board; the petition was to be submitted, but only after the planning board had completed its part in the amending process. Board of Selectmen of Merrimack v. Planning Board of Merrimack, 118 N.H. 150, 383 A.2d 1122, 1978 N.H. LEXIS 362 (1978). (Decided under prior law.)

2. Notice and hearing

Under the terms of the statute, the date from which time is to be reckoned is the date of the town meeting, and the days prior to the meeting date are to be counted not counting the date of the meeting. Miller v. Town of Tilton, 139 N.H. 429, 655 A.2d 409, 1995 N.H. LEXIS 24 (1995).

3. Petition for repeal

Where RSA 675:3, VII and RSA 675:4, I pertained to ballots, not warrant articles, and the trial court conflated warrant articles and ballots, the trial court misapprehended the relevant statutes and the matter had to be remanded for further consideration. Lower Bartlett Water Precinct v. Murnik, 150 N.H. 690, 845 A.2d 1245, 2004 N.H. LEXIS 55 (2004).

RESEARCH REFERENCES

New Hampshire Practice.
15 N.H.P. Land Use Planning and Zoning §§ 5.05–5.07, 5.16, 15.06, 26.03, 27.11, 31.04, 35.02, 35.14.

ALR.
Adoption of zoning ordinance or amendment thereto as subject of referendum. 72 A.L.R.3d 1030.

Adoption of zoning ordinance or amendment thereto through initiative process. 72 A.L.R.3d 991.

675:4-a. Adoption of Emergency Temporary Zoning and Planning Ordinance in Certain Towns.

I. In any town which does not have a planning board, as provided by RSA 674, or a zoning ordinance, as provided in this subdivision, or in any town which has a planning board, but which does not have in effect a zoning ordinance, the selectmen, upon recommendation of the planning board, or upon written application to them for this purpose signed by 5 percent of the voters of the town, shall call a special town meeting, warning the same as provided by law, to act upon the following question: "Shall the town adopt the provisions of RSA 674:24–29 entitled 'Emergency Temporary Zoning and Planning Ordinance'"

II. The provisions of RSA 675 relating to method of enactment shall not apply; provided, however, that there shall be a public hearing, with notice as provided in RSA 675:7, not more than 7 calendar days before the proposed special town meeting. There shall be reasonable opportunity for debate of such question at such town meeting before balloting commences. Voting shall be by ballot, with the use of the checklist used at the most recent annual meeting plus any new registrations, and the polls shall remain open at least 2 hours after debate has ended for the casting of ballots. If the question in paragraph I receives affirmative votes amounting at least to a majority of those present and voting, the provisions of RSA 674:24–29 shall take effect forthwith in the town and shall remain in effect until 2 annual town meetings shall have been held or the voters of the town consider a zoning ordinance as provided for by this chapter, whichever period of time is the lesser.

III. If no zoning ordinance has been considered and no zoning ordinance under the applicable provisions of this chapter has been proposed for action by the time of the second such annual town meeting, the selectmen shall include in the warrant for such meeting the following proposal to be put as a question to be voted upon by ballot after discussion: To see if the town will vote to continue for one additional year the temporary zoning ordinance enacted under the provisions of RSA 674:24–29. If a majority of those present and voting on said article vote in the affirmative, the provisions of RSA 674:24–29 shall remain in effect in the town for one year from the date of such meeting. If a majority of those present and voting on the article vote in the negative, the provisions of RSA 674:24–29 shall cease to be in effect.

Source.
1985, 103:24, eff. Jan. 1, 1986.

Warnings of town meetings generally, see RSA 39.

Cross References.
Filing of zoning ordinances, historic district ordinances or building codes, see RSA 675:8, 9.

675:5. Zoning Ordinance Protest Petition.

I. Zoning regulations, restrictions and boundaries may from time to time be amended or repealed.

I-a. A favorable vote of ⅔ of all the members of the legislative body present and voting shall be required to act upon any amendment or repeal in the case of a protest against such zoning change signed by either:

(a) The owners of 20 percent of the area of the lots included in such proposed change; or

(b) The owners of 20 percent of the area within 100 feet immediately adjacent to the area affected by the change or across a street from such area.

I-b. Paragraph I-a shall apply only to amendments which alter the boundary locations separating previously defined zoning districts, or to amendments which alter the regulations or restrictions of an area not larger than ⅓ of the land area within the municipality.

I-c. The area of streets, commons, or land owned by a governmental entity shall not be included in any calculation under this section.

II. In order to have any protest considered pursuant to paragraph I-a:

(a) The owners signing the petition shall identify themselves on the petition by name and address, and by address of the property involved, or by lot and map number, or by whatever other means is used within the town or village district to identify the land in question, so that the selectmen or commissioners may identify such owners as interested and affected parties; and

(b) The signed protest petition shall be submitted to the selectmen or village district commissioners at least 7 days prior to the town or village district meeting; provided, however, that each protest petition shall apply to only one article on the warrant. A notice of receipt of the protest petition shall be posted at the polling place, and the moderator shall announce at the opening of the town meeting that a protest petition has been received.

Source.
1983, 447:1. 1985, 103:24. 1989, 44:1-3, eff. June 11, 1989.

Amendments
—1989. Paragraph I: Deleted the second sentence.

Paragrahs I-a–I-c: Added.
Paragraph II: Substituted "paragraph I-a" for "paragraph I" in the introductory clause.

—1985. Paragraph I: Rewritten to the extent that a detailed comparison would be impracticable.

NOTES TO DECISIONS

Analysis

1. Generally
2. Protests—Persons who may file protests
3. —Signature of petition
4. —Filing
5. —Determination of validity of protest petition
6. Approval of change by members of legislative body
7. Effect of noncompliance with statutory procedures
8. Cure of defects in proceedings

1. Generally

Preexisting land use regulations were not so comprehensive as to acquire the status of de facto zoning and, therefore, a town properly enacted a zoning ordinance by a simple majority, rather than a two-thirds majority; the preexisting regulations included a mobile home and trailer park ordinance, a sign ordinance, a town beach bylaw, a building permit ordinance, excavation regulations, driveway access regulations, a floodplain ordinance, and a large institutional land ordinance. Caspersen v. Town of Lyme, 139 N.H. 637, 661 A.2d 759, 1995 N.H. LEXIS 70 (1995).

The power to amend a zoning ordinance was not unlimited, but must have been exercised reasonably. Brady v. Keene, 90 N.H. 99, 4 A.2d 658, 1939 N.H. LEXIS 22 (1939). (Decided under prior law.)

Amendments and changes must have been reasonable and in the public interest. Edgewood Civic Club v. Blaisdell, 95 N.H. 244, 61 A.2d 517, 1948 N.H. LEXIS 228 (1948). (Decided under prior law.)

2. Protests—Persons who may file protests

By its plain terms, RSA 675:5, I-a encompasses all land within 100 feet of an area subject to the change by a zoning amendment regardless of whether it is within the same municipality and RSA 675:5, II(a) does not limit protest petitions to owners of land within the municipality in which the petition is filed; in addition, the town's tax maps are more than sufficient to determine whether a protest petition meets the threshold of community support required by RSA 675:5, I-a. Smagula v. Town of Hooksett, 149 N.H. 784, 834 A.2d 333, 2003 N.H. LEXIS 125 (2003).

Where a proposed amendment would rezone from residential to general business use a single tract adjoining a general business district fronting upon a public highway, the statute could properly be interpreted to require protest by the owners of twenty percent of the area extending one hundred feet from the area to be rezoned on all sides except the frontage adjoining the business district on the highway. Towle v. Nashua, 106 N.H. 394, 212 A.2d 204, 1965 N.H. LEXIS 177 (1965). (Decided under prior law.)

3. —Signature of petition

Superior court properly determined that protest petition failed to satisfy requirements of this section and therefore did not require a two-thirds vote for passage of zoning amendment where petition did not contain signatures of the owners of 20 percent of the land adjacent to or across the street from area to be rezoned. Treisman v. Town of Bedford, 132 N.H. 54, 563 A.2d 786, 1989 N.H. LEXIS 75 (1989).

Where land was owned by joint tenants, the

signature of just one of them on the petition was sufficient. Disco v. Board of Selectmen of Amherst, 115 N.H. 609, 347 A.2d 451, 1975 N.H. LEXIS 375 (1975). (Decided under prior law.)

Withdrawal of a name from the protest petition two days after tabulation of the votes was not permissible. Disco v. Board of Selectmen of Amherst, 115 N.H. 609, 347 A.2d 451, 1975 N.H. LEXIS 375 (1975). (Decided under prior law.)

Property owned by trusts, partnerships and cotenants did not have to be represented by the signatures of all the parties having an interest in the properties where those not signing authorized a signing in their behalf. Town of Alton v. Fisher, 114 N.H. 359, 320 A.2d 653, 1974 N.H. LEXIS 278 (1974). (Decided under prior law.)

4. —Filing

Protests against a proposed amendment of the zoning ordinance were to be filed with the board of aldermen. Towle v. Nashua, 106 N.H. 394, 212 A.2d 204, 1965 N.H. LEXIS 177 (1965). (Decided under prior law.)

5. —Determination of validity of protest petition

RSA 675:5 does not mandate a determination of the validity of a protest petition prior to voting. Handley v. Town of Hooksett, 147 N.H. 184, 785 A.2d 399, 2001 N.H. LEXIS 192 (2001). (Decided under prior law.)

6. Approval of change by members of legislative body

The purpose of the requirement that two-thirds of all members of the legislative body of the municipality present and voting adopt a zoning change after a valid protest had been filed was to confer an added protection to property owners against unwanted or ill-considered changes. Disco v. Board of Selectmen of Amherst, 115 N.H. 609, 347 A.2d 451, 1975 N.H.

LEXIS 375 (1975). (Decided under prior law.)

In the case of a protest, a vote of two-thirds of all the members of the legislative body present and voting was required for adoption, and that statutory requirement controlled over the provisions of a local ordinance. Cutter v. Durham, 109 N.H. 33, 241 A.2d 216, 1968 N.H. LEXIS 109 (1968). (Decided under prior law.)

7. Effect of noncompliance with statutory procedures

Since minor deviations from or technical violations of a statutory procedure could be excused if there had been substantial compliance, a town's demurrer to a plaintiff-protestor's petition for injunctive relief arising out of the adoption of a zoning ordinance amendment was properly overruled where the plaintiff established a basis upon which the relief could be granted by pleading substantial compliance. Bourgeois v. Town of Bedford, 120 N.H. 145, 412 A.2d 1021, 1980 N.H. LEXIS 247 (1980). (Decided under prior law.)

8. Cure of defects in proceedings

An act of the state legislature legalizing, ratifying and confirming votes and proceedings of a town meeting could not override a lawful vote of the townspeople defeating a proposed amendment and was without legal effect to make a valid enactment an amendment declared by the moderator to have passed and to be in effect even though it did not receive a two-thirds favorable vote. Drown v. Town of Hudson, 112 N.H. 386, 296 A.2d 897, 1972 N.H. LEXIS 225 (1972). (Decided under prior law.)

Cited:

Cited in Blue Jay Realty Trust v. City of Franklin, 132 N.H. 502, 567 A.2d 188, 1989 N.H. LEXIS 128 (1989); Real Estate Planners, Inc. v. Town of Newmarket, 134 N.H. 696, 597 A.2d 78, 1991 N.H. LEXIS 125 (1991).

RESEARCH REFERENCES

New Hampshire Practice.
15 N.H.P. Land Use Planning and Zoning §§ 5.07–5.12.

ALR.
Validity and construction of provisions of

zoning statute or ordinance regarding protest by neighboring property owners. 7 A.L.R.4th 732.

675:6. Method of Adoption.

Every local master plan, subdivision regulation, site plan review regulation and historic district regulation referred to in this title shall be adopted or amended by the planning board or historic district commission, as appropriate, in the following manner:

I. The board or commission, as appropriate, shall hold a public hearing prior to adoption or amendment. Notice for the time and place of the hearing shall be as provided in RSA 675:7.

II. The board or commission, as appropriate, may adopt or amend the master plan or regulation upon completion of the public hearing by an affirmative vote of a majority of its members.

III. No master plan, regulation, amendment or exception adopted under this section shall be legal or have any force and effect until copies of it are certified by a majority of the board or commission and filed with the city clerk, town clerk, or clerk for the county commissioners.

IV. The historic district commission may adopt or amend regulations only after the commission has held a public hearing within the district. Notice for the time and place shall be as provided in RSA 675:7. The adopted regulations shall be certified by a majority of the historic district commission members and filed with the city clerk, town clerk, or clerk for the county commissioners.

Source.
1983, 447:1. 1985, 103:24. 1989, 266:26, eff. July 1, 1989.

Amendments
—1989. Paragraph III: Substituted "clerk, town clerk, or clerk for the county commissioners" for "or town clerk" following "city".
Paragraph IV: Substituted "clerk, town clerk, or clerk for the county commissioners" for "or town clerk" following "city" in the second sentence.

—1985. Rewritten to the extent that a detailed comparison would be impractical.

Cross References.
Filing of master plans, subdivision regulations, site plan review regulations, and historic district regulations, see RSA 675:8, 9.

NOTES TO DECISIONS

Analysis

1. Construction
2. Uncertified master plan

1. Construction
Because certification and filing of proposed amendment to subdivision regulations had not taken place, amendment was not yet effective, and planning board was thus not entitled to decline jurisdiction over plaintiff's subdivision application for failure to comply with amendment. Rallis v. Town of Hampton Planning Bd., 146 N.H. 18, 766 A.2d 281, 2001 N.H. LEXIS 20 (2001).

2. Uncertified master plan
Master plan adopted by town planning board but not certified by the board before filing with the town clerk did not meet all requirements necessary to give the plan legal effect. Treisman v. Town of Bedford, 132 N.H. 54, 563 A.2d 786, 1989 N.H. LEXIS 75 (1989).

Based on doctrine of substantial compliance, otherwise proper amendment to zoning ordinance would not be invalidated based on planning board's failure to certify its master plan. Treisman v. Town of Bedford, 132 N.H. 54, 563 A.2d 786, 1989 N.H. LEXIS 75 (1989).

Cited:
Cited in Frisella v. Town of Farmington, 131

N.H. 78, 550 A.2d 102, 1988 N.H. LEXIS 94 (1988); New England Brickmaster, Inc. v. Town of Salem, 133 N.H. 655, 582 A.2d 601, 1990 N.H. LEXIS 119 (1990); Rall v. Town of Belmont, 138 N.H. 172, 635 A.2d 1368, 1993 N.H. LEXIS 185 (1993).

RESEARCH REFERENCES

New Hampshire Practice.
15 N.H.P. Land Use Planning and Zoning §§ 3.06, 29.05, 30.05, 35.06, 35.10.

675:7. Notice Requirements for Public Hearing.

I. Notice shall be given for the time and place of each public hearing held under RSA 675:2–4 and RSA 675:6 at least 10 calendar days before the hearing. The notice required under this section shall not include the day notice is posted or the day of the public hearing. Notice of each public hearing shall be published in a paper of general circulation in the municipality and shall be posted in at least 2 public places.

II. The full text of the proposed master plan, zoning ordinance, building code, subdivision regulation, site plan review regulation and historic district regulation, ordinance, or amendment need not be included in the notice if an adequate statement describing the proposal and designating the place where the proposal is on file for public inspection is stated in the notice.

Source.
1983, 447:1. 1985, 103:24, eff. Jan. 1, 1986.

Amendments
—1985. Paragraph II: Inserted "subdivision regulation, site plan review regulation and historic district regulation, ordinance" following "building code", substituted "proposal" for "proposed master plan, zoning ordinance, building code, or amendment" preceding "is on file for public inspection is" and "stated in" for "attached to" thereafter.

NOTES TO DECISIONS

Analysis

1. Constructive notice
2. Sufficiency of notice

1. Constructive notice

While property owners who might be affected by a zoning amendment need not be afforded actual notice of a proposed zoning change, they must be afforded constructive notice sufficient to inform the public of the essence and scope of the zoning regulation under consideration. Bedford Residents Group v. Town of Bedford, 130 N.H. 632, 547 A.2d 225, 1988 N.H. LEXIS 65 (1988).

Publication and posting of documents that indicated planning board would be considering zoning amendments, and further stated that copies of the proposed amendments were on file for public inspection, was not sufficient notice to property owners who might be affected by zoning amendments, since notice did not satisfy requirements of this section for constructive notice because it did not contain even essential information to alert interested parties of the change under consideration. Bedford Residents Group v. Town of Bedford, 130 N.H. 632, 547 A.2d 225, 1988 N.H. LEXIS 65 (1988).

2. Sufficiency of notice

Notice was sufficient where it alerted readers that height, area, or bulk regulations pertaining to one-family or two-family zoning districts might be changed, and accurately noted that such a change would promote consistency between those two districts, and also directed readers to city clerk's office for copies of amendments. Bradley v. City of Manchester, 141 N.H. 329, 682 A.2d 1194, 1996 N.H. LEXIS 100 (1996).

RESEARCH REFERENCES

New Hampshire Practice.
    15 N.H.P. Land Use Planning and Zoning

§§ 3.06, 5.02–5.07, 5.15, 15.06, 21.12, 28.05, 29.05, 30.05, 35.04, 35.10, 35.14.

675:8. Filing of Zoning Ordinances, Historic District Ordinances, Building Codes, Subdivision Regulations, Site Plan Review Regulations, and Amendments.

All zoning ordinances, historic district ordinances, building codes, subdivision regulations, site plan review regulations, historic district regulations and their amendments shall be placed on file with the city, town, or village district clerk, or, in the case of unincorporated towns or unorganized places, with the clerk for the county commissioners for public inspection.

Source.
    1983, 447:1. 1985, 103:24. 1989, 266:27, eff. July 1, 1989.

Amendments
—1989. Inserted "or, in the case of unincorporated towns or unorganized places, with the clerk for the county commissioners" preceding "for public inspection".

—1985. Inserted "historic district ordinances" following "zoning ordinances" and "historic district regulations" preceding "and their".

Cross References.
    Filing of ordinances, codes, regulations and amendments with office of state planning, see RSA 675:9.

RESEARCH REFERENCES

New Hampshire Practice.
    15 N.H.P. Land Use Planning and Zoning §§ 5.13, 29.22, 35.04.

675:9. Place for Filing Documents.

I. A copy of each master plan, zoning ordinance, historic district ordinance, capital improvement plan, building code, subdivision regulation, historic district regulation, site plan review regulation or amendment which is adopted by a municipality shall be placed in a central file with the office of energy and planning; provided, however, that failure to file these documents or amendments with the office of energy and planning shall not affect the validity of the document.

II. [Repealed.]

Source.
    1983, 447:1. 1985, 103:24. 1987, 50:1. 1989, 266:28, eff. July 1, 1989. 2002, 8:12, III, eff. Sept. 14, 2002. 2003, 319:9, eff. July 1, 2003. 2004, 257:44, eff. July 1, 2004.

Amendments
—2004. Paragraph I: Substituted "office of

energy and planning" for "office of state planning and energy programs".

—2003. Paragraph I: Substituted "office of state planning and energy programs" for "office of state planning".

—2002. Paragraph II: Repealed.

—1989. Paragraph II: Inserted "or a county" preceding "adopts".

—1987. Paragraph I: Inserted "capital improvement plan" preceding "building code".

—1985. Paragraph I: Inserted "historic district ordinance" preceding "building code, sub-

division regulation" and "historic district regulation" thereafter.

Cross References.
Filing of ordinances, codes, regulations and amendments with municipal clerks, see RSA 675:8.

New Hampshire Practice.
15 N.H.P. Land Use Planning and Zoning §§ 3.06, 4.03, 5.13, 29.22, 30.05, 35.04.

CHAPTER 676

ADMINISTRATIVE AND ENFORCEMENT PROCEDURES

Revision of organization of chapter.

1987, 256:4, eff. July 17, 1987, amended this chapter by adding the subdivision heading preceding RSA 676:5.

Cross References.

Local land use boards generally, see RSA 673.

Ordinance, regulation and code adoption procedures generally, see RSA 675.

Rehearing and appeal procedures generally, see RSA 677.

RESEARCH REFERENCES

New Hampshire Practice.

15 N.H.P. Land Use Planning and Zoning § 28.08.

New Hampshire Bar Journal.

For article, "An Overview of the New Hampshire Land Use Planning and Regulation Statutes," see 34 N.H.B.J. 6 (June 1993).

ALR.

Right to cross-examination of witnesses in hearings before administrative zoning authorities. 27 A.L.R.3d 1304.

General Provisions

676:1. Method of Adopting Rules of Procedure.

Every local land use board shall adopt rules of procedure concerning the method of conducting its business. Rules of procedure shall be adopted at a regular meeting of the board and shall be placed on file with city, town, village district clerk or clerk for the county commissioners for public inspection.

Source.
1983, 447:1. 1989, 266:29, eff. July 1, 1989.

Amendments
—**1989.** Deleted "or" preceding "village" and inserted "or clerk for the county commission-ers" preceding "for public inspection" in the second sentence.

Cross References.
Meetings and records of boards generally, see RSA 673:10, 17.

RESEARCH REFERENCES

New Hampshire Practice.
15 N.H.P. Land Use Planning and Zoning §§ 20.06, 21.02, 27.10, 28.02, 35.08.

676:2. Joint Meetings and Hearings.

I. An applicant seeking a local permit may petition 2 or more land use boards to hold a joint meeting or hearing when the subject matter of the requested permit is within the responsibilities of those land use boards. Each board shall adopt rules of procedure relative to joint meetings and hearings, and each board shall have the authority on its own initiative to request a joint meeting. Each land use board shall have the discretion as to whether or not to hold a joint meeting with any other land use board. The planning board chair shall chair joint meetings unless the planning board is not involved with the subject matter of the requested permit. In that situation, the appropriate agencies which are involved shall determine which board shall be in charge.

II. Procedures for joint meetings or hearings relating to testimony, notice of hearings, and filing of decisions shall be consistent with the procedures established by this chapter for individual boards.

III. Every local land use board shall be responsible for rendering a decision on the subject matter which is within its jurisdiction.

Source.
1983, 447:1, eff. Jan. 1, 1984.

Cross References.
Adoption of rules of procedure generally, see RSA 676:1.
Issuance of decision generally, see RSA 676:3.

Meetings and records of boards generally, see RSA 673:10, 17.
Powers of boards as to administration of oaths and compulsion of attendance of witnesses generally, see RSA 673:15.

RESEARCH REFERENCES

New Hampshire Practice.
15 N.H.P. Land Use Planning and Zoning § 21.09, 28.08.

676:3. Issuance of Decision.

I. The local land use board shall issue a final written decision which either approves or disapproves an application for a local permit. If the application is not approved, the board shall provide the applicant with written reasons for the disapproval.

II. Whenever a local land use board votes to approve or disapprove an application or deny a motion for rehearing, the minutes of the meeting at which such vote is taken, including the written decision containing the reasons therefor, shall be placed on file in the board's office and shall be made available for public inspection within 144 hours of such vote. Boards in towns that do not have an office of the board that has regular business hours shall file copies of their decisions with the town clerk.

Source.
1983, 447:1, eff. Jan. 1, 1984. 2000, 144:1, eff. Jan. 1, 2001.

Amendments
—**2000.** Paragraph II: Rewritten to the extent that a detailed comparison would be impracticable.

Cross References.
Issuance of decisions in cases involving joint meetings or hearings, see RSA 676:2.
Maintenance of records of boards generally, see RSA 673:17.

RESEARCH REFERENCES

New Hampshire Practice.
15 N.H.P. Land Use Planning and Zoning

§§ 21.14, 21.15, 21.19, 25.01, 28.10, 32.03, 32.07, 33.02, 35.12.

Planning Board

Cross References.
Master plans generally, see RSA 675:1 et seq.
Official municipal maps generally, see RSA 674:9 et seq.
Site plan review regulations generally, see RSA 674:43 et seq.

Subdivision regulation generally, see RSA 674:35 et seq.
Zoning ordinances generally, see RSA 674:16 et seq.

RESEARCH REFERENCES

ALR.
Right to cross-examination of witnesses in

hearings before administrative zoning authorities. 27 A.L.R.3d 1304.

676:4. Board's Procedures on Plats.

I. The procedures to be followed by the planning board when considering or acting upon a plat or application submitted to it for approval under this title shall be as set forth in the board's subdivision regulations, subject to the following requirements:

(a) An application for approval filed with the planning board under this title, other than an application for subdivision approval, shall be subject to the minimum requirements set forth in this section and shall be governed by the procedures set forth in the subdivision regulations, unless the planning board by regulation specifies other procedures for that type of application.

(b) The planning board shall specify by regulation what constitutes a completed application sufficient to invoke jurisdiction to obtain approval. A completed application means that sufficient information is included or submitted to allow the board to proceed with consideration and to make an informed decision. A completed application sufficient to invoke jurisdiction of the board shall be submitted to and accepted by the board only at a public meeting of the board, with notice as provided in subparagraph (d). The applicant shall file the application with the board or its agent at least 15 days prior to the meeting at which the application will be accepted. The application shall include the names and addresses of the applicant, all holders of conservation, preservation, or agricultural preservation restrictions as defined in RSA 477:45, and all abutters as indicated in the town records for incorporated towns or county records for unincorporated towns or unorganized places not more than 5 days before the day of filing. Abutters shall also be identified on any plat submitted to the board. The application shall also include the name and business address of every engineer, architect, land surveyor, or soil scientist whose professional seal appears on any plat submitted to the board.

(c)(1) The board shall, at the next regular meeting or within 30 days following the delivery of the application, for which notice can be given in accordance with the requirements of subparagraph (b), determine if a submitted application is complete according to the board's regulation and shall vote upon its acceptance. Upon determination by the board that a submitted application is incomplete according to the board's regulations, the board shall notify the applicant of the determination in accordance with RSA 676:3, which shall describe the information, procedure, or other requirement necessary for the application to be complete. Upon determination by the board that a submitted application is complete according to the board's regulations, the board shall begin formal consideration and shall act to approve, conditionally approve as provided in subparagraph (i), or disapprove within 65 days, subject to extension or waiver as provided in subparagraph (f). Upon failure of the board to approve, conditionally approve, or disapprove the application, the selectmen or city council shall, upon request of the applicant, immediately issue an order directing the board to act on the application within 30 days. If the planning board does not act on the application within that 30-day time period, then within 40 days of the issuance of the order, the selectmen or city council shall certify on the applicant's application that the plat is approved pursuant to this paragraph, unless within those 40 days the selectmen or city council has identified in writing some specific subdivision regulation or zoning or other ordinance provision with which the application does not comply. Such a certification, citing this paragraph, shall constitute final approval for all purposes including filing and recording under RSA 674:37 and 676:18, and court review under RSA 677:15.

(2) Failure of the selectmen or city council to issue an order to the planning board under subparagraph (1), or to certify approval of the plat upon the planning board's failure to comply with the order, shall constitute grounds for the superior court, upon petition of the applicant, to issue an order approving the application if the court determines that the proposal

complies with existing subdivision regulations and zoning or other ordinances. If the court determines that the failure of the selectmen or the city council to act was not justified, the court may order the municipality to pay the applicant's reasonable costs, including attorney's fees, incurred in securing such order.

(d) Notice to the applicant, holders of conservation, preservation, or agricultural preservation restrictions, abutters, and the public shall be given as follows: The planning board shall notify the abutters, the applicant, holders of conservation, preservation, or agricultural preservation restrictions, and every engineer, architect, land surveyor, or soil scientist whose professional seal appears on any plat submitted to the board by certified mail of the date upon which the application will be formally submitted to the board. Notice shall be mailed at least 10 days prior to submission. Notice to the general public shall also be given at the same time by posting or publication as required by the subdivision regulations. The notice shall include a general description of the proposal which is the subject of the application and shall identify the applicant and the location of the proposal. For any public hearing on the application, the same notice as required for notice of submission of the application shall be given. If notice of public hearing has been included in the notice of submission or any prior notice, additional notice of that hearing is not required nor shall additional notice be required of an adjourned session of a hearing with proper notice if the date, time, and place of the adjourned session was made known at the prior hearing. All costs of notice, whether mailed, posted, or published, shall be paid in advance by the applicant. Failure to pay such costs shall constitute valid grounds for the planning board to terminate further consideration and to disapprove the plat without a public hearing.

(e) Except as provided in this section, no application may be denied or approved without a public hearing on the application. At the hearing, any applicant, abutter, holder of conservation, preservation, or agricultural preservation restriction, or any person with a direct interest in the matter may testify in person or in writing. Other persons may testify as permitted by the subdivision regulations or the board at each hearing. Public hearings shall not be required, unless specified by the subdivision regulations, when the board is considering or acting upon:

(1) Minor lot line adjustments or boundary agreements which do not create buildable lots, except that notice to abutters and holders of conservation, preservation, or agricultural preservation restrictions shall be given prior to approval of the application in accordance with subparagraph (d) and any abutter or holder of conservation, preservation, or agricultural preservation restrictions may be heard on the application upon request; or

(2) Disapprovals of applications based upon failure of the applicant to supply information required by the regulations, including identification of abutters or holders of conservation, preservation, or agricultural preservation restrictions; or failure to meet reasonable deadlines established by the board; or failure to pay costs of notice or other fees required by the board.

(f) The planning board may apply to the selectmen or city council for an extension not to exceed an additional 90 days before acting to approve or disapprove an application. The applicant may waive the requirement for planning board action within the time periods specified in subparagraph (c) and consent to such extension as may be mutually agreeable.

(g) Reasonable fees in addition to fees for notice under subparagraph (d) may be imposed by the board to cover its administrative expenses and costs of special investigative studies, review of documents and other matters which may be required by particular applications.

(h) In case of disapproval of any application submitted to the planning board, the ground for such disapproval shall be adequately stated upon the records of the planning board.

(i) A planning board may grant conditional approval of a plat or application, which approval shall become final without further public hearing, upon certification to the board by its designee or based upon evidence submitted by the applicant of satisfactory compliance with the conditions imposed. Final approval of a plat or application may occur in the foregoing manner only when the conditions are:

(1) Minor plan changes whether or not imposed by the board as a result of a public hearing, compliance with which is administrative and which does not involve discretionary judgment; or

(2) Conditions which are in themselves administrative and which involve no discretionary judgment on the part of the board; or

(3) Conditions with regard to the applicant's possession of permits and approvals granted by other boards or agencies or approvals granted by other boards or agencies.

All other conditions shall require a hearing, and notice as provided in subparagraph I(d), except that additional notice shall not be required of an adjourned session of a hearing with proper notice if the date, time and place of the adjourned session were made known at the prior hearing.

II. A planning board may provide for preliminary review of applications and plats by specific regulations subject to the following:

(a) PRELIMINARY CONCEPTUAL CONSULTATION PHASE. The regulations shall define the limits of preliminary conceptual consultation which shall be directed at review of the basic concept of the proposal and suggestions which might be of assistance in resolving problems with meeting requirements during final consideration. Such consultation shall not bind either the applicant or the board and statements made by planning board members shall not be the basis for disqualifying said members or invalidating any action taken. The board and the applicant may discuss proposals in conceptual form only and in general terms such as desirability of types of development and proposals under the master plan. Such discussion may occur without the necessity of giving formal public notice as required under subparagraph I(d), but such discussions may occur only at formal meetings of the board.

(b) DESIGN REVIEW PHASE. The board or its designee may engage in nonbinding discussions with the applicant beyond conceptual and general discussions which involve more specific design and engineering details; provided, however, that the design review phase may proceed only after identification of and notice to abutters, holders of conservation, preservation, or agricultural preservation restrictions, and the general public as required by subparagraph I(d). Statements made by planning board members shall not be the basis for disqualifying said members or invalidating any action taken.

(c) Preliminary review shall be separate and apart from formal consideration under paragraph I, and the time limits for acting under subparagraph I(c) shall not apply until formal application is submitted under subparagraph I(b).

III. A planning board may, by adopting regulations, provide for an expedited review and approval for proposals involving minor subdivisions which create not more than 3 lots for building development purposes or for proposals which do not involve creation of lots for building development purposes. Such expedited review may allow submission and approval at one or more board meetings, but no application may be approved without the full notice to the abutters, holders of conservation, preservation, or agricultural preservation restrictions, and public required under subparagraph I(d). A hearing, with notice as provided in subparagraph I(d), shall be held if requested by the applicant, abutters, or holders of conservation, preservation, or agricultural preservation restrictions any time prior to approval or disapproval or if the planning board determines to hold a hearing.

IV. Jurisdiction of the courts to review procedural aspects of planning board decisions and actions shall be limited to consideration of compliance with applicable provisions of the constitution, statutes and regulations. The procedural requirements specified in this section are intended to provide fair and reasonable treatment for all parties and persons. The planning board's procedures shall not be subjected to strict scrutiny for technical compliance. Procedural defects shall result in the reversal of a planning board's actions by judicial action only when such defects create serious impairment of opportunity for notice and participation.

Source.
1983, 447:1. 1985, 159:1. 1986, 57:1, 2; 229:1, 2. 1989, 266:30. 1990, 275:1. 1995, 117:1, 2, eff. July 15, 1995. 1997, 142:1–4, eff. Aug. 8, 1997; 249:1, eff. Aug. 18, 1997. 1998, 274:1, eff. Aug. 25, 1998. 2004, 71:6, eff. July 6, 2004. 2005, 33:3, 4, eff. July 9, 2005.

Amendments
—**2005.** Paragraph II: Substituted "preliminary" for "preapplication" in the introductory paragraph and in subpar. (c).

—**2004.** Paragraph II(c): Deleted the former first sentence.

—**1998.** Paragraph I(c)(1): Rewritten to the extent that a detailed comparison would be impracticable.

—**1997.** Paragraph I(b): Inserted "all holders of conservation, preservation, or agricultural preservation restrictions as defined in RSA 477:45" in the fifth sentence.

Paragraph I(c)(1): Substituted "receipt" for "submission" preceding "of the completed application" and added "by the board or its designee" thereafter in the first sentence, added the second sentence, and substituted "receipt of the completed application by the board or its designee" for "submission" following "90 days after" in the third sentence.

Paragraph I(d): Inserted "holders of conservation, preservation, or agricultural preservation restrictions" in two places in the first sentence.

Paragraph I(e): Rewritten to the extent that a detailed comparison would be impracticable.

Paragraph II(b): Inserted "holders of conservation, preservation, or agricultural preservation restrictions" following "abutters" in the first sentence.

Paragraph III: Inserted "holders of conservation, preservation, or agricultural preservation restrictions" in the second and third sentences and made a minor stylistic change in the third sentence.

—1995. Paragraph I(b): Added the seventh sentence.

Paragraph I(d): Deleted "and" following "notify the abutters" and inserted "and every engineer, architect, land surveyor, or soil scientist whose professional seal appears on any plat submitted to the board" preceding "by certified" in the first sentence.

—1990. Paragraph I(c): Rewritten to the extent that a detailed comparison would be impracticable.

—1989. Paragraph I(b): Substituted "the town records for incorporated towns or county records for unincorporated towns or unorganized places" for "town records" preceding "not more than 5 days" in the fifth sentence.

—1986. Paragraph I(c): Chapter 57:2 inserted "conditionally approve as provided in subparagraph (i)" following "approve" in the second sentence and "conditionally approve" following "approve" in the third sentence.

Paragraph I(i) added by ch. 57:1.

Chapter 229:1 deleted "conditionally approved" following "approval of a plat or application" in the introductory clause and "conditions and" preceding "minor plan changes" in clause (1) of the second sentence, substituted "whether or not" for "or conditions or minor plan changes" preceding "imposed by the board" in clause (1) of the second sentence, and rewrote the third sentence.

Paragraph II: Amended generally by ch. 229:2.

—1985. Paragraph I(d): Deleted "return receipt requested" following "mail" in the first sentence.

Applicability of 1990 amendment.

1990, 275:3, eff. June 27, 1990, provided that the amendment to this section by section 1 of the act shall be prospective only and shall apply to any application submitted to and accepted as complete by the planning board on or after June 27, 1990.

Cross References.

Appeals to boards of adjustment, see RSA 676:5 et seq.

Rehearing and appeal procedures generally, see RSA 677.

Conservation restriction assessment, see RSA 79-B.

Soil conservation and farmland preservation, see RSA 432.

NOTES TO DECISIONS

Analysis

0.5. Applicability
1. Construction with other laws
2. Authority of board
3. Preliminary discussions
4. Submission of application
5. Completeness of application
6. Time for action on application—Generally
7. —Effect of revision of application
8. Proceedings upon failure of board to act on application within limitation period
9. Hearings
10. Applicant's right to speak
11. Statement of reasons for denial of application
12. Procedure upon disapproval of application

0.5 Applicability

Plaintiff abutter's claim that trial court had jurisdiction to review procedural aspects of a town planning board's decision granting approval to applicant's site plan determination under RSA 676:4, IV was improper as that provision does not address the process by which one may appeal a planning board decision. RSA 676:4, IV must be read in conjunction with RSA 677:15, which describes that process and requires that such appeal be brought within thirty days of the planning board's decision. Because plaintiff failed to file its appeal within the thirty day window, the superior court had no jurisdiction over the appeal. Prop. Portfolio Group, LLC v. Town of Derry, 154 N.H. 610, 913 A.2d 750, 2006 N.H. LEXIS 206 (Dec. 21, 2006).

1. Construction with other laws

Site plan approvals under former RSA 36:19-a (now covered by RSA 674:43) were governed by this statute regulating the board's procedure for approval of plats. Carter v. City of Nashua, 116 N.H. 466, 362 A.2d 191, 1976 N.H. LEXIS 382 (1976), overruled on other grounds, Weeks Restaurant Corp. v. City of Dover, 119 N.H. 541, 404 A.2d 294, 1979 N.H. LEXIS 349 (1979). (Decided under prior law.)

2. Authority of board

Local planning boards have authority to impose conditions upon the approval of a site plan. New England Brickmaster, Inc. v. Town of Salem, 133 N.H. 655, 582 A.2d 601, 1990 N.H. LEXIS 119 (1990).

The statute provided no power for a planning board to enact a subdivision regulation that required automatic approval of an application for a subdivision. Davis v. Town of Barrington, 127 N.H. 202, 497 A.2d 1232, 1985 N.H. LEXIS 387 (1985). (Decided under prior law.)

3. Preliminary discussions

Planning board is not bound to give final approval to a project based solely upon preliminary discussions, but must act reasonably in both preliminary and formal stages of review. Batakis v. Town of Belmont, 135 N.H. 595, 607 A.2d 956, 1992 N.H. LEXIS 88 (1992).

This section specifically recognizes the need for allowing planning board to separate non-binding consultations from formal review of completed applications. Batakis v. Town of Belmont, 135 N.H. 595, 607 A.2d 956, 1992 N.H. LEXIS 88 (1992).

4. Submission of application

Where a landowner submitted a plat at a planning board meeting, the plat did not meet the requirement that lot sizes be shown in square feet, the board refused to accept the plat and the landowner took it away to have the required information added, the plat had not been submitted within the meaning of the statute for purposes of the provision requiring approval or disapproval of the application within 90 days after submission. Allard v. Thalheimer, 116 N.H. 299, 358 A.2d 395, 1976 N.H. LEXIS 336 (1976). (Decided under prior law.)

5. Completeness of application

Where a subdivision application was not complete in terms of compliance with an ordinance that included a subdivision checklist, the jurisdiction of the planning board could not be invoked and the board was free not to accept the application for consideration. DHB, Inc. v. Town of Pembroke, 152 N.H. 314, 876 A.2d 206, 2005 N.H. LEXIS 99 (2005).

Plaintiff's subdivision application was sufficiently complete for planning board to exercise jurisdiction over it, and fact that plaintiff offered to revise or redesign his plans to satisfy various planning board concerns, after submitting a completed application, did not render his application incomplete for jurisdictional purposes. Rallis v. Town of Hampton Planning Bd., 146 N.H. 18, 766 A.2d 281, 2001 N.H. LEXIS 20 (2001).

6. Time for action on application—Generally

The statute clearly stated that a town planning board had ninety days to act on any plat submitted to it and was required to state its reason for disapproval upon the record, and if an applicant's filing was improper in form, the board had ninety days to disapprove it and was required to state that reason on the record. Savage v. Town of Rye, 120 N.H. 409, 415 A.2d 873, 1980 N.H. LEXIS 303 (1980). (Decided under prior law.)

7. —Effect of revision of application

Revision of a plan subsequent to its submission with an application for subdivision approval could result in a new filing date for purposes of the statutory provision requiring a town planning board to approve or disapprove of a subdivision within ninety days of submission of the application. Savage v. Town of Rye, 120 N.H. 409, 415 A.2d 873, 1980 N.H. LEXIS 303 (1980). (Decided under prior law.)

8. Proceedings upon failure of board to act on application within limitation period

A master properly refused to order approval of a subdivision application as a matter of law because of a planning board's failure to act within the time prescribed by local regulation, since, under the statute, there was no right to automatic approval. Davis v. Town of Barrington, 127 N.H. 202, 497 A.2d 1232, 1985 N.H. LEXIS 387 (1985). (Decided under prior law.)

Where a town planning board failed to approve or disapprove a subdivision application within ninety days of submission of the application, the town was required to certify this failure on the plan, thereby allowing the applicant to record the subdivision plan at the registry of deeds without written endorsement by the planning board. Savage v. Town of Rye, 120 N.H. 409, 415 A.2d 873, 1980 N.H. LEXIS 303 (1980). (Decided under prior law.)

9. Hearings

Where a landowner submitted a site plan for nonresidential use of land to the town zoning board of adjustment and applied for a special exception to the zoning ordinance, the board voted to preliminarily approve the application subject to eleven conditions; and an abutting landowner was not given notice of or an opportunity to be heard at a subsequent compliance hearing, at which the board found that all the conditions had been satisfied and signed the site plan, the failure to allow testimony from the abutting landowner on the issue of compliance with the conditions was a serious impairment of the opportunity for participation under this section, for which reversal was the only effective remedy. Sklar Realty, Inc. v. Town of Merrimack, 125 N.H. 321, 480 A.2d 149, 1984 N.H. LEXIS 271 (1984). (Decided under prior law.)

10. Applicant's right to speak

By its plain language, a public meeting was not the same as a hearing mandated by statute; therefore, a subdivision approval applicant whose application had not been accepted did not have a right to speak at a public meeting that was held on the matter. DHB, Inc. v. Town of Pembroke, 152 N.H. 314, 876 A.2d 206, 2005 N.H. LEXIS 99 (2005).

11. Statement of reasons for denial of application

Letter from a planning board denying a landowner's site plan application was sufficient to start the time for appeal running where the letter discussed three reasons for denial and also enclosed a copy of the minutes of the meeting. Route 12 Books & Video v. Town of Troy, 149 N.H. 569, 825 A.2d 493, 2003 N.H. LEXIS 79 (2003).

Certified record, including minutes of three lengthy public hearings, coupled with a detailed letter sent to the applicant for site plan approval of a shooting range, providing multiple reasons for denial of the application, were adequate to apprise the applicant of planning board's reasons for such denial. Star Vector Corp. v. Town of Windham, 146 N.H. 490, 776 A.2d 138, 2001 N.H. LEXIS 102 (2001).

Purpose of requirement that planning board state adequate reasons on the record for its denial of an application is to insure that the developer receives written reasons for the disapproval, and that a record of the board's reasoning exists so that the decision may be reviewed on appeal. K & P, Inc. v. Town of Plaistow, 133 N.H. 283, 575 A.2d 804, 1990 N.H. LEXIS 50 (1990).

Requirement that planning board state adequate reasons on the record for its denial of an application may be satisfied by a letter from the board to the applicant, together with minutes of board meetings. K & P, Inc. v. Town of Plaistow, 133 N.H. 283, 575 A.2d 804, 1990 N.H. LEXIS 50 (1990).

12. Procedure upon disapproval of application

Subdividers were to receive written reasons for a planning board's disapproval of subdivision plans submitted to the board, and a written record, not limited to the minutes of the planning board meeting, was to exist so that a reviewing authority could hold the board accountable. Patenaude v. Town of Meredith, 118 N.H. 616, 392 A.2d 582, 1978 N.H. LEXIS 253 (1978). (Decided under prior law.)

Planning boards were not required to reiterate their reasons for disapproval of a resubmitted plan that contained the same fundamental defect that proved fatal to the original plan. Patenaude v. Town of Meredith, 118 N.H. 616, 392 A.2d 582, 1978 N.H. LEXIS 253 (1978). (Decided under prior law.)

Letters from planning boards notifying developers of the reasons for plan disapproval met the statutory requirements and were "records" within the meaning of the statute. Patenaude v. Town of Meredith, 118 N.H. 616, 392 A.2d 582, 1978 N.H. LEXIS 253 (1978). (Decided under prior law.)

Where the planning board wrote a landowner that it would approve the plat if one lot was increased to the minimum size, and the letter stated that eight other lots were under consideration and demanded an "affirmative response" to the problem of the undersized lot, the board's letter constituted disapproval under the statute. Allard v. Thalheimer, 116 N.H. 299, 358 A.2d 395, 1976 N.H. LEXIS 336 (1976). (Decided under prior law.)

Cited: Newmarket, 134 N.H. 696, 597 A.2d 78, 1991
  Cited in Real Estate Planners, Inc. v. Town of   N.H. LEXIS 125 (1991).

RESEARCH REFERENCES

New Hampshire Practice.   29.19, 29.23, 30.10, 30.11, 32.01–32.03, 32.05,
  15 N.H.P. Land Use Planning and Zoning   32.06, 32.09, 32.12, 32.13, 32.16, 33.09, 33.10.
§§ 5.04, 11.04, 28.02, 28.05, 28.07–28.11, 29.16,

676:4-a. Revocation of Recorded Approval.

I. A subdivision plat, street plat, site plan or other approval which has been filed with the appropriate recording official under RSA 674:37 may not be revoked, in whole or in part, by the planning board, except pursuant to this section, and only under the following circumstances:

(a) At the request of, or by agreement with, the applicant or the applicant's successor in interest.

(b) When the applicant or successor in interest to the applicant has performed work, erected a structure or structures, or established a use of land, which fails to conform to the statements, plans or specifications upon which the approval was based, or has materially violated any requirement or condition of such approval.

(c) When the applicant or successor in interest to the applicant has failed to perform any condition of the approval within a reasonable time specified in the approval, or, if no such time is specified, within the time periods specified in RSA 674:39.

(d) When the time periods specified in RSA 674:39 have elapsed without any vesting of rights as set forth therein, and the plat, plan or other approval no longer conforms to applicable ordinances or regulations.

(e) When the applicant or successor in interest to the applicant has failed to provide for the continuation of adequate security as provided by RSA 674:36, III(b) and 674:44, III(d) until such time as the work secured thereby has been completed.

II. Prior to recording any revocation under this section, the planning board shall give notice, as provided by RSA 676:4, I(d), to the public, the applicant or the applicant's successor in interest, and all abutters and holders of conservation, preservation, or agricultural preservation restrictions. The notice shall include the board's reasons for the revocation. A hearing with notice as provided in RSA 676:4, I(d) shall be held at the request of any party receiving such notice, submitted within 30 days of receiving such notice, or if the planning board determines to hold a hearing.

III. A declaration of revocation, dated and endorsed in writing by the planning board, and containing reference to the recording information for the plat, plan or other approval being revoked, shall be filed for recording with the register of deeds, no sooner than 30 days after written notification of the revocation is served on the applicant or the applicant's successor in interest, in person or by certified mail, or 30 days after any public hearing, whichever is later. If only part of an approval is revoked, that portion of land subject to revocation shall be clearly identified in the declaration. The declaration shall be recorded under the same name or names as was the original approval, as well as the names of subsequent owners, if any, of the land or part thereof subject to revocation, as identified by the municipality.

IV. A revocation under this section may be appealed pursuant to RSA 677:15. Nothing in this section shall affect the municipality's ability, either before or after such a revocation, to pursue other remedies or penalties as set forth in RSA 676:15–17.

Source.
1991, 237:1, eff. Aug. 9, 1991. 1997, 142:5, eff. Aug. 8, 1997.

of conservation, preservation, or agricultural preservation restrictions" at the end of the first sentence.

Amendments
—**1997.** Paragraph II: Added "and holders

NOTES TO DECISIONS

Analysis

1. Due process
2. Practice and procedure

1. Due process
Planning board's decision to revoke site plan approval for soccer facility was not erroneous as a matter of law or unsupported by record, where town communicated with land owners by letter no less than eight times regarding alleged violations of site plan conditions, and record revealed a recurring pattern of complaints and alleged violations, followed by hearings before board and promises of remedial action by land owners. Brewster v. Town of Amherst, 144 N.H. 364, 742 A.2d 121, 1999 N.H. LEXIS 122 (1999).

2. Practice and procedure
Although neither initial site plan revocation, nor unsubstantiated complaints by abutters contained in record, were appropriate factors for planning board to consider in determining materiality of violations in subsequent revocation determination, board was entitled, once it found that subsequent violations were material, to consider prior violations in determining appropriate sanction or penalty for noncompliance with material conditions. Brewster v. Town of Amherst, 144 N.H. 364, 742 A.2d 121, 1999 N.H. LEXIS 122 (1999).

RESEARCH REFERENCES

New Hampshire Practice.
15 N.H.P. Land Use Planning and Zoning §§ 29.16, 30.08, 32.16.

Zoning Board of Adjustment

676:5. Appeals to Board of Adjustment.

I. Appeals to the board of adjustment concerning any matter within the board's powers as set forth in RSA 674:33 may be taken by any person aggrieved or by any officer, department, board, or bureau of the municipality affected by any decision of the administrative officer. Such appeal shall be taken within a reasonable time, as provided by the rules of the board, by filing with the officer from whom the appeal is taken and with the board a notice of appeal specifying the grounds thereof. The officer from whom the appeal is taken shall forthwith transmit to the board all the papers constituting the record upon which the action appealed from was taken.

II. For the purposes of this section:

(a) The "administrative officer" means any official or board who, in that municipality, has responsibility for issuing permits or certificates under the ordinance, or for enforcing the ordinance, and may include a building inspector, board of selectmen, or other official or board with such responsibility.

(b) A "decision of the administrative officer" includes any decision involving construction, interpretation or application of the terms of the ordinance. It does not include a discretionary decision to commence formal or informal enforcement proceedings, but does include any construction, interpretation or application of the terms of the ordinance which is implicated in such enforcement proceedings.

III. If, in the exercise of subdivision or site plan review, the planning board makes any decision or determination which is based upon the terms of the zoning ordinance, or upon any construction, interpretation, or application of the zoning ordinance, which would be appealable to the board of adjustment if it had been made by the administrative officer, then such decision may be appealed to the board of adjustment under this section; provided, however, that if the zoning ordinance contains an innovative land use control adopted pursuant to RSA 674:21 which delegates administration, including the granting of conditional or special use permits, to the planning board, then the planning board's decision made pursuant to that delegation cannot be appealed to the board of adjustment, but may be appealed to the superior court as provided by RSA 677:15.

Source.

1983, 447:1. 1987, 256:5. 1989, 69:1. 1991, 231:13. 1995, 243:1, eff. Jan. 1, 1996.

Amendments

—1995. Paragraph III: Deleted "the board states" preceding "is based" and "solely" thereafter.

—1991. Paragraph III: Added.

—1989. Designated the existing provisions of the section as par. I and added par. II.

—1987. Inserted "concerning any matter within the board's powers as set forth in RSA 674:33" following "board of adjustment" in the first sentence.

Cross References.

Effect of appeals, see RSA 676:6.

Hearings before boards of adjustment, see RSA 676:7.

Powers of boards of adjustment generally, see RSA 674:33.

Rehearings and appeals procedures generally, see RSA 677.

NOTES TO DECISIONS

Analysis

1. Generally
2. Construction
3. Jurisdiction of court
4. Legislative intent
5. Standing

1. Generally

The provision for administrative review precluded resort to the courts before seeking such review. Carrick v. Langtry, 99 N.H. 251, 108 A.2d 546, 1954 N.H. LEXIS 61 (1954). (Decided under prior law.)

2. Construction

Mere fact that an individual is a taxpaying resident of a town does not give that individual standing to seek mandamus relief requiring the town to enforce its zoning ordinances. Pursuant to RSA 676:5, 677:2, 677:4, an individual can seek relief before a zoning board of appeals or in the courts with regard to a zoning officer's decision only if the individual is an "aggrieved person," which requires a showing that he or she has some direct, definite interest in the outcome of the zoning decision itself, and the mere fact that an individual lives and/or pays taxes to a town, does not, by itself, give that individual a direct, definite interest in town zoning decisions. Goldstein v. Town of Bedford, 154 N.H. 393, 910 A.2d 1158, 2006 N.H. LEXIS 173 (Nov. 22, 2006).

Petitioners had actual or constructive notice of issuance of building permit, as well as respondent's construction activities, and their decision to wait for fifty-five days to file their appeal did not constitute filing within a reasonable time. Tausanovitch v. Town of Lyme, 143 N.H. 144, 722 A.2d 914, 1998 N.H. LEXIS 81 (1998).

3. Jurisdiction of court

Although an applicant for site plan approval had a right to expect the town to assist with the application process, instead of failing to respond to the applicant's communications, the issue was moot; the trial court had lacked jurisdiction over the applicant's appeal from the planning board's action application of its site plan review rules, because of the applicant's failure to seek review within 30 days, and it lacked jurisdiction over the applicant's appeal from the planning board's application of zoning regulations because, in the absence of a ruling by the zoning board of adjustment, there was nothing to appeal to the trial court. Route 12 Books & Video v. Town of Troy, 149 N.H. 569, 825 A.2d 493, 2003 N.H. LEXIS 79 (2003).

Landowners were required to seek zoning adjustment board review of a planning board's decision to apply only an architectural design review to a parking lot application, and failure to seek board review resulted in the reviewing court's lacking jurisdiction to consider the landowners' appeals. Heartz v. City of Concord, 148 N.H. 325, 808 A.2d 76, 2002 N.H. LEXIS 131 (2002).

4. Legislative intent

Where the legislature did not intend to grant standing to request a rehearing to all municipal boards that could initiate an appeal, a town conservation commission lacked standing to request a rehearing or to appeal a zoning board decision. Hooksett Conservation Comm'n v. Hooksett Zoning Bd. of Adjustment, 149 N.H. 63, 816 A.2d 948, 2003 N.H. LEXIS 5 (2003).

5. Standing

Superior court properly dismissed the mandamus petition filed by a town resident, seeking to require the town to enforce its zoning ordinances, because the resident was not an "aggrieved person," which was required for him to have standing under RSA 676:5, I, 677:2, 677:4, to seek administrative review of a zoning officer's decision or to seek judicial review of actions taken by the town's zoning board of adjustment. The mere fact that the resident lived in, and paid taxes to, the town did not give him a direct, definite interest in the zoning decision that he challenged, which pertained to permits obtained by a third party with regard to his nonconforming lots. Goldstein v. Town of Bedford, 154 N.H. 393, 910 A.2d 1158, 2006 N.H. LEXIS 173 (Nov. 22, 2006).

Cited:

Cited in Doggett v. Town of N. Hampton Zoning Bd. of Adjustment, 138 N.H. 744, 645 A.2d 673, 1994 N.H. LEXIS 97 (1994); Babiarz v. Town of Grafton, — N.H. —, 930 A.2d 395, 2007 N.H. LEXIS 127 (July 20, 2007).

RESEARCH REFERENCES

New Hampshire Practice.
15 N.H.P. Land Use Planning and Zoning §§ 7.05, 7.06, 7.17, 16.01, 19.03, 21.10, 22.02, 29.07, 33.01, 33.02, 35.15.

676:6. Effect of Appeal to Board.

The effect of an appeal to the board shall be to maintain the status quo. An appeal of the issuance of any permit or certificate shall be deemed to suspend such permit or certificate, and no construction, alteration, or change of use which is contingent upon it shall be commenced. An appeal of any order or other enforcement action shall stay all proceedings under the action appealed from unless the officer from whom the appeal is taken certifies to the board of adjustment, after notice of appeal shall have been filed with such officer, that, by reason of facts stated in the certificate, a stay would, in the officer's opinion, cause imminent peril to life, health, safety, property, or the environment. In such case, the proceedings shall not be stayed otherwise than by a restraining order which may be granted by the board or by the superior court on notice to the officer from whom the appeal is taken and cause shown.

Source.
    1983, 447:1. 1995, 243:2, eff. Jan. 1, 1996.

Amendments
—**1995.** Rewritten to the extent that a detailed comparison would be impracticable.

—**1985.** Paragraph I(a): Deleted "return receipt requested" following "mail" in the first sentence.

Cross References.
    Appeals procedure generally, see RSA 676:5.

RESEARCH REFERENCES

New Hampshire Practice.
    15 N.H.P. Land Use Planning and Zoning §§ 7.06, 21.11, 35.02.

676:7. Public Hearing; Notice.

I. Prior to exercising its appeals powers, the board of adjustment shall hold a public hearing. Notice of the public hearing shall be given as follows:

(a) The appellant and every abutter and holder of conservation, preservation, or agricultural preservation restrictions shall be notified of the hearing by certified mail stating the time and place of the hearing, and such notice shall be given not less than 5 days before the date fixed for the hearing of the appeal. The board shall hear all abutters and holders of conservation, preservation, or agricultural preservation restrictions desiring to submit testimony and all nonabutters who can demonstrate that they are affected directly by the proposal under consideration. The board may hear such other persons as it deems appropriate.

(b) A public notice of the hearing shall be placed in a newspaper of general circulation in the area not less than 5 days before the date fixed for the hearing of the appeal.

II. The public hearing shall be held within 30 days of the receipt of the notice of appeal.

III. Any party may appear in person or by the party's agent or attorney at the hearing of an appeal.

IV. The cost of notice, whether mailed, posted, or published, shall be paid in advance by the applicant. Failure to pay such costs shall constitute valid grounds for the board to terminate further consideration and to deny the appeal without public hearing.

Source.
1983, 447:1. 1985, 159:2, eff. July 26, 1985. 1996, 226:1, eff. Jan. 1, 1997. 1997, 142:6, eff. Aug. 8, 1997.

Amendments
—1997. Paragraph I(a): Inserted "and holder of conservation, preservation, or agricultural preservation restrictions" in the first sentence and "and holders of conservation, preservation, or agricultural preservation restrictions" in the second sentence.

—1996. Paragraph III: Substituted "the party's" for "his" preceding "agent".

—1985. Paragraph I(a): Deleted "return receipt requested" following "mail" in the first sentence.

Cross References.
Powers of boards of adjustment generally, see RSA 674:33.

NOTES TO DECISIONS

Analysis

1. Application
2. Conditions precedent to hearing
3. Effect of failure to hold timely hearing

1. Application
Where 1987 hearing on landowner's request for variance was conducted without jurisdiction because all abutters had not received notice, and in 1989 zoning board of adjustment ordered landowner to reapply for variance because of lack of notice, 1989 hearing on variance was a new hearing calling for a fresh decision. Hussey v. Town of Barrington, 135 N.H. 227, 604 A.2d 82, 1992 N.H. LEXIS 3 (1992).

2. Conditions precedent to hearing
The absence of any statutory provision specifically authorizing the making of consent of property owners a condition precedent to a hearing for a variance did not preclude a city from imposing such a condition. Robwood Advertising Associates, Inc. v. City of Nashua, 102 N.H. 215, 153 A.2d 787, 1959 N.H. LEXIS 49 (1959). (Decided under prior law.)

3. Effect of failure to hold timely hearing
A party was not entitled to have a variance granted as a matter of law because a zoning board of adjustment had violated the time requirement of the statute by failing to hold a hearing on the application for a variance within thirty days after the application was filed; the legislature had not seen fit to provide that a zoning board's failure to comply with the statute would constitute approval of an application for a variance submitted to it. Barry v. Amherst, 121 N.H. 335, 430 A.2d 132, 1981 N.H. LEXIS 314 (1981). (Decided under prior law.)

RESEARCH REFERENCES

New Hampshire Practice.
15 N.H.P. Land Use Planning and Zoning §§ 5.04, 21.05, 21.12, 21.19, 32.04.

Historic District Commission

Cross References.
Building codes generally, see RSA 674:51 et seq.
Building permits generally, see RSA 676:11 et seq.

Historic districts generally, see RSA 674:45 et seq.
Protection of New Hampshire heritage landmarks from development, see RSA 227-C:24 et seq.

676:8. Issuing Approval for Building Permits.

The historic district commission shall review applications for building permits within the historic district for their impact on the historic district and its objectives by:

I. Requesting reports and recommendations regarding the feasibility of the applicant's proposal from the planning board, fire chief, building inspector, health officer and other administrative officials who may possess information concerning the impact of the proposal on the historic district.

II. Seeking advice from professional, educational, cultural or other groups or persons as may be deemed necessary for the determination of a reasonable decision.

III. Filing with the building inspector or other duly delegated authority either a certificate of approval or a notice of disapproval following the review and determination of the application.

Source.
1983, 447:1, eff. Jan. 1, 1984.

Powers and duties of historic district commission generally, see RSA 674:46-a.

Cross References.
Issuance of certificate of approval or notice of disapproval, see RSA 676:9.

NOTES TO DECISIONS

Basis for decision of commission
The statute placed on the commission the duty to reach a reasoned decision. Hanrahan v. City of Portsmouth, 119 N.H. 944, 409 A.2d 1336, 1979 N.H. LEXIS 425 (1979). (Decided under prior law.)
The statute imposed a duty on district com-

missions to make a group assessment of information that was more than the mere personal opinion of one or more members. Hanrahan v. City of Portsmouth, 119 N.H. 944, 409 A.2d 1336, 1979 N.H. LEXIS 425 (1979). (Decided under prior law.)

RESEARCH REFERENCES

New Hampshire Practice.
15 N.H.P. Land Use Planning and Zoning § 35.11.

676:9. Procedure for Approval of Building Permits.

I. The historic commission district shall file a certificate of approval or a notice of disapproval pursuant to RSA 676:8, III within 45 days after the filing of the application for the certificate, unless the applicant agrees to a longer period of time.

II. No building permit shall be issued until a certificate of approval has been filed with the building inspector; but, in the case of disapproval, notice of disapproval shall be binding upon the building inspector or other duly delegated authority, and no permit shall be issued.

III. Failure to file the certificate within the specified period of time shall constitute approval by the commission.

Source.
1983, 447:1, eff. Jan. 1, 1984.

RESEARCH REFERENCES

New Hampshire Practice.
15 N.H.P. Land Use Planning and Zoning
§ 35.12.

676:10. Enforcement by Historic District Commission.

I. In municipalities which have established one or more historic districts pursuant to RSA 674:46, but which have no local zoning ordinances, the historic district commission shall have within the bounds of the historic district all the authority, powers and duties prescribed in this chapter for planning boards insofar as such authority, powers and duties are within the intent of the historic district commission's grant of power. In such municipalities, the requirement of conformity with the local zoning ordinance, as provided in RSA 674:46, shall not apply.

II. In municipalities which do not have a planning board, the requirements of RSA 674:46 and 676:6 relating to conformity with the master plan and the requirement of RSA 673:4 that one member of the commission may be a planning board member shall not apply.

III. In municipalities which do not have a building inspector, the certificate of approval of the commission, as provided in RSA 676:8, III, shall be the equivalent of a building permit. In municipalities which do not have a zoning board of adjustment, motions for rehearing and appeals from decisions of the historic district commission shall be governed by the provisions of RSA 677, insofar as applicable.

Source.
1983, 447:1, eff. Jan. 1, 1984.

Powers and duties of planning boards generally, see RSA 676:4 et seq.

Cross References.
Powers and duties of historic district commissions generally, see RSA 674:46-a.

RESEARCH REFERENCES

New Hampshire Practice.
15 N.H.P. Land Use Planning and Zoning
§§ 35.02, 35.11, 35.13, 35.15.

Building Permits

Cross References.
Building codes generally, see RSA 674:51 et seq.

Powers of building code boards of appeals generally, see RSA 674:34.

Zoning ordinances generally, see RSA 674:16 et seq.

ALR.
 Liability of governmental entity to builder or developer for negligent issuance of building

permit subsequently suspended or revoked. 41 A.L.R.4th 99.

676:11. Building Permits Required.

After a municipality has adopted a building code, any person who intends to erect or remodel any building in the municipality shall submit the plans to the building inspector for the building inspector's examination and approval prior to commencement of the planned construction.

Source.
 1983, 447:1, eff. Jan. 1, 1984. 1996, 226:2, eff. Jan. 1, 1997.

Amendments
 —1996. Substituted "the building inspector's" for "his" preceding "examination".

676:12. Building Permits to be Withheld in Certain Cases.

I. The building inspector shall not issue any building permit within the 120 days prior to the annual or special town or village district meeting if:

(a) Application for such permit is made after the first legal notice of proposed changes in the building code or zoning ordinance has been posted pursuant to the provisions of RSA 675:7; and

(b) The proposed changes in the building code or the zoning ordinance would, if adopted, justify refusal of such permit.

II. After final action has been taken on the proposed changes in the building code or zoning ordinance, the building inspector shall issue or refuse to issue a permit which has been held in abeyance under this section pursuant to a final action under this section.

III. The provisions of paragraph I shall not be applicable in a city or in a county in which there are located unincorporated towns or unorganized places unless the governing body of the city or the county votes by majority vote to be subject to the provisions of such paragraph.

IV. The building inspector may be authorized by the local legislative body to issue a temporary occupancy permit not to exceed 30 days, which may be extended at the discretion of the building inspector.

V. No building permit shall be denied on the grounds of uncompleted streets or utilities when the construction of such streets or utilities has been secured to the municipality by a bond or other security approved by the planning board pursuant to RSA 674:36, III or RSA 674:44, IV; provided, however, that on land which is part of a subdivision plat or site plan, no building shall be used or occupied prior to the completion of required streets and utilities, except upon such terms as the planning board may have authorized as part of its decision approving the plat or site plan.

VI. The provisions of paragraph I shall not apply to any plat or application which has been the subject of notice by the planning board pursuant to RSA 676:4, I(d) prior to the first legal notice of a proposed change in a building code or zoning ordinance or any amendment thereto. No proposed subdivision or site plan review or zoning ordinance or amendment thereto shall affect a plat or application which has been the subject of notice by the planning board pursuant to RSA 676:4, I(d) so long as said plat or application was the subject of notice prior to the first legal notice of said change or amendment. The provisions of this paragraph shall apply to proposals submitted to a planning board for design review pursuant to RSA 676:4, II(b), provided that a formal application is filed with the planning board within 12 months of the end of the design review process.

Source.

1983, 447:1. 1986, 200:1; 229:3. 1989, 266:31. 1991, 331:3, eff. Aug. 27, 1991. 2003, 134:1, eff. Aug. 13, 2003. 2006, 285:1, eff. August 14, 2006.

Amendments

—2006. Paragraph VI: In the first sentence, substituted "the subject of notice" for "formally accepted" and "which has been the subject of notice" preceding "by the planning board pursuant to RSA 676:4" and substituted "I(d)" for "I(b)", substituted "the subject of notice" for "accepted", and added the second sentence.

—2003. Rewritten to the extent that a detailed comparison would be impracticable.

—1991. Paragraph V: Substituted "or zoning ordinance" for "regulation" following "review" in the second sentence.

—1989. Paragraph II: Inserted "or in a county in which there are located unincorporated towns or unorganized places" preceding "unless" and "or the county" preceding "votes by majority".

—1986. Paragraph IV: Added by ch. 200. Paragraph V: Added by ch. 229.

Legislative purpose of 1991 amendment.

1991, 331:4, eff. Aug. 27, 1991, provided: "The purpose of sections 1–3 of this act [which amended this section and RSA 674:39] is to confirm and re-emphasize the intent of the general court at the time of the enactment of 1986, 229:3 and 1983, 447:1. Municipalities may not retroactively amend local land use regulations or zoning ordinances for the purpose of stopping proposed projects or developments while an application is under consideration by the municipality. This act shall not be interpreted as changing the intent of any provisions of 1986, 229 or 1983, 447."

NOTES TO DECISIONS

Analysis

1. Application of section
2. Purpose
3. Procedure for adoption of section

1. Application of section

Purpose of former RSA 676:12, V (see now 676:12,VI for similar provisions) was to protect a zoning application from any regulatory amendments passed while application was under formal consideration, and since plaintiff's subdivision application had not yet been accepted by planning board, RSA 676:12, V could not be relied upon by board to deny jurisdiction over plaintiff's application. Rallis v. Town of Hampton Planning Bd., 146 N.H. 18, 766 A.2d 281, 2001 N.H. LEXIS 20 (2001).

Former version of this section extended grandfather protection to subdivision appli-cants from certain proposed and adopted land use regulations. However, the 1988 version of this section only provided protection from sub-division and site plan review regulations, not from zoning ordinances. Rall v. Town of Belmont, 138 N.H. 172, 635 A.2d 1368, 1993 N.H. LEXIS 185 (1993).

2. Purpose

The purpose of the statute allowing building permits to be withheld pending proposed zoning changes was not land use regulation, but rather enhancement of the effectiveness of the zoning process by preventing landowners from adopting property uses inconsistent with proposed zoning changes during the zoning deliberation process. Socha v. City of Manchester, 126 N.H. 289, 490 A.2d 794, 1985 N.H. LEXIS 297 (1985). (Decided under prior law.)

3. Procedure for adoption of section

A city's adoption of the statute allowing building permits to be withheld pending zoning changes did not operate as a zoning ordinance where zoning deliberations did not extend beyond a reasonable time; therefore, the adoption of the statute was not subject to the public hearing requirements of former RSA 31:63 (now covered by RSA 675:2) needed to enact zoning ordinances. Socha v. City of Manchester, 126 N.H. 289, 490 A.2d 794, 1985 N.H. LEXIS 297 (1985). (Decided under prior law.)

Cited:

Cited in Real Estate Planners, Inc. v. Town of Newmarket, 134 N.H. 696, 597 A.2d 78, 1991 N.H. LEXIS 125 (1991); State v. Roy, 138 N.H. 97, 635 A.2d 486, 1993 N.H. LEXIS 166 (1993).

RESEARCH REFERENCES

New Hampshire Practice.

15 N.H.P. Land Use Planning and Zoning §§ 7.14, 11.03–11.05, 28.02, 29.23, 30.11, 32.02.

New Hampshire Bar Journal.

For article, "'Grandfathered'—The Law of Nonconforming Uses and Vested Rights," see 31 N.H.B.J. 17 (1990).

676:13. Building Permits Restricted.

I. The building inspector shall not issue any building or occupancy permit for any proposed construction, remodeling, or maintenance which will not comply with any or all zoning ordinances, building codes, or planning board regulations which are in effect.

II. If any building inspector is prosecuted for violation of RSA 643:1 and found guilty of issuing any permit contrary to the provisions of this section, it shall be prima facie evidence that the building inspector has knowingly refrained from performing a duty imposed on the building inspector by law.

III. The building inspector shall adopt a form or set of standards specifying the minimum contents of a completed application for any building permit. Upon the submission of a completed application, the building inspector shall act to approve or deny a building permit within 30 days; provided, however, that nonresidential applications or residential applications encompassing more than 10 dwelling units shall be approved or denied within 60 days.

Source.

1983, 447:1. 1986, 150:1, eff. July 26, 1986. 1996, 226:3, eff. Jan. 1, 1997.

Amendments

—1996. Paragraph II: Substituted "the building inspector" for "he" preceding "has knowingly" and "the building inspector" for "him" preceding "by law".

—1986. Paragraph III: Added.

Cross References.

Penalties for violations of title generally, see RSA 676:17.

RESEARCH REFERENCES

New Hampshire Trial Bar News.

For article, "Presumptions in New Hampshire Law—A Guide Through the Impenetrable Jungle (Part 1)," see 10 N.H. Trial Bar News 55, 60 n.82 (Winter 1990).

Local Conflicts of Law

676:14. Determination of Which Local Ordinance Takes Precedence.

Whenever a local land use ordinance is enacted or a regulation is adopted which differs from the authority of an existing ordinance or other regulation, the provision which imposes the greater restriction or higher standard shall be controlling.

Source.
1983, 447:1, eff. Jan. 1, 1984.

Penalties and Remedies

Cross References.
Fines for violations of RSA 674:25–29, see RSA 674:29.

Remedies for violations of historic district ordinances or regulations generally, see RSA 674:50.

RESEARCH REFERENCES

ALR.
Enforcement of zoning regulations as affected by other violations. 4 A.L.R.4th 462.

Mandamus to compel zoning officials to cancel permit granted in violation of zoning regulation. 68 A.L.R.3d 166.

676:15. Injunctive Relief.

In case any building or structure or part thereof is or is proposed to be erected, constructed, altered, or reconstructed, or any land is or is proposed to be used in violation of this title or of any local ordinance, code, or regulation adopted under this title, or of any provision or specification of an application, plat, or plan approved by, or any requirement or condition of a permit or decision issued by, any local administrator or land use board acting under the authority of this title, the building inspector or other official with authority to enforce the provisions of this title or any local ordinance, code, or regulation adopted under this title, or the owner of any adjacent or neighboring property who would be specially damaged by such violation may, in addition to other remedies provided by law, institute injunction, mandamus, abatement, or any other appropriate action or proceeding to prevent, enjoin, abate, or remove such unlawful erection, construction, alteration, or reconstruction.

Source.
1983, 447:1. 1988, 19:5, eff. Jan. 1, 1989.

Amendments
—**1988.** Rewritten to the extent that a detailed comparison would be impracticable.

Cross References.
Recovery of costs and attorney's fees in actions under section, see RSA 676:17.
Requirement of bond in actions under section, see RSA 676:17.

NOTES TO DECISIONS

Standing

Private landowners who sought relief from alleged zoning violation had standing, where evidence showed that the landowners were specially damaged by the alleged violation. Barton v. H. D. Riders Motorcycle Club, Inc., 131 N.H. 60, 550 A.2d 91, 1988 N.H. LEXIS 89 (1988).

Cited:

Cited in White v. Francoeur, 138 N.H. 307, 638 A.2d 1250, 1994 N.H. LEXIS 27 (1994); Miner v. A & C Tire Co., 146 N.H. 631, 776 A.2d 1286, 2001 N.H. LEXIS 124 (2001).

RESEARCH REFERENCES

New Hampshire Practice.

15 N.H.P. Land Use Planning and Zoning §§ 7.04, 7.08, 7.16, 7.17, 24.06, 32.10, 32.11, 38.18.

ALR.

Laches as defense in suit by governmental entity to enjoin zoning violation. 73 A.L.R.4th 870.

Mandamus to compel zoning officials to cancel permit granted in violation of zoning regulation. 68 A.L.R.3d 166.

Standing of municipal corporation or other governmental body to attack zoning of land lying outside its borders. 49 A.L.R.3d 1126.

Standing of owner of property adjacent to zoned property, but not within territory of zoning authority, to attack zoning. 69 A.L.R.3d 805.

676:16. Penalties for Transferring Lots in Unapproved Subdivisions.

Any owner, or agent of the owner, of any land located within a subdivision in a municipality that has adopted subdivision regulations who transfers or sells any land before a plat of the subdivision has been approved by the planning board and filed with the appropriate recording official under RSA 674:35, II, shall forfeit and pay a civil penalty of $1,000 for each lot or parcel so transferred or sold; and the description by metes and bounds in the instrument of transfer or other document used in the process of selling or transferring shall not exempt the transaction from such penalties. The municipality may enjoin a transfer or sale which violates the provisions of this section and may recover the penalty imposed by civil action. In any action to recover a penalty, the prevailing party may recover reasonable court costs and attorney's fees as may be ordered by the court.

Source.

1983, 447:1, eff. Jan. 1, 1984. 1997, 92:3, eff. Jan. 1, 1998.

Amendments

—1997. Substituted "$1,000" for "$500" in the first sentence.

Cross References.

Filing or recording by registers of deeds of unapproved subdivision plats, see RSA 676:18.

Fines and penalties generally, see RSA 676:17.

Injunctions generally, see RSA 676:15.

NOTES TO DECISIONS

Analysis

1. Conveyance in violation of a subdivision plat

2. Attorney fees
3. Conveyance without planning board approval

1. Conveyance in violation of a subdivision plat

A conveyance in violation of a subdivision plat is not void. White v. Francoeur, 138 N.H. 307, 638 A.2d 1250, 1994 N.H. LEXIS 27 (1994).

2. Attorney fees

Where trial court ruled that defendant had violated this section, it had the power to grant attorney's fees to plaintiff, and it was not required to make a finding of bad faith before awarding attorney's fees. Town of Windham v. Lawrence Sav. Bank, 146 N.H. 517, 776 A.2d 730, 2001 N.H. LEXIS 109 (2001).

Where trial court ruled that defendant had violated this section, it did not abuse its discretion in declining to award attorney's fees based on its consideration of a number of factors including: (1) whether plaintiff town alleged that defendant acted in bad faith; (2) the relative merits of the parties' positions; and (3) the true purpose of the litigation. Town of Windham v. Lawrence Sav. Bank, 146 N.H. 517, 776 A.2d 730, 2001 N.H. LEXIS 109 (2001).

3. Conveyance without planning board approval

Where expandable lands were not separated from other lands by a road or any boundary except that which the developer established when he submitted land to a condominium, and, further, planning board approved a plan that designated the expandable land as a single parcel and never treated the phases of development or the expandable lands as distinct parcels, therefore, conveyance of a portion of the expandable land as a separate lot prior to receiving planning board subdivision approval was in violation of this section. Town of Windham v. Lawrence Sav. Bank, 146 N.H. 517, 776 A.2d 730, 2001 N.H. LEXIS 109 (2001).

Cited:

Cited in Erin Food Service, Inc. v. Derry Motel, Inc., 131 N.H. 353, 553 A.2d 304, 1988 N.H. LEXIS 136 (1988); City of Dover v. Kimball, 136 N.H. 441, 616 A.2d 516, 1992 N.H. LEXIS 187 (1992).

RESEARCH REFERENCES

New Hampshire Practice.
15 N.H.P. Land Use Planning and Zoning § 29.24.

676:17. Fines and Penalties.

I. Any person who violates any of the provisions of this title, or any local ordinance, code, or regulation adopted under this title, or any provision or specification of any application, plat, or plan approved by, or any requirement or condition of a permit or decision issued by, any local administrator or land use board acting under the authority of this title shall be guilty of a misdemeanor if a natural person, or guilty of a felony if any other person; and shall be subject to a civil penalty of $275 for the first offense and $550 for subsequent offenses for each day that such violation is found to continue after the conviction date or after the date on which the violator receives written notice from the municipality that the violator is in violation, whichever is earlier.

II. In any legal action brought by a municipality to enforce, by way of injunctive relief as provided by RSA 676:15 or otherwise, any local ordinance, code or regulation adopted under this title, or to enforce any planning board, zoning board of adjustment or building code board of appeals decision made pursuant to this title, or to seek the payment of any fine levied under paragraph I, the municipality shall recover its costs and reasonable attorney's fees actually expended in pursuing the legal action if it is found to be a prevailing party in the action. For the purposes of this paragraph, recoverable costs shall include all out-of-pocket expenses actually incurred, including but not limited to, inspection fees, expert fees and investigatory expenses.

III. If any violation of a local ordinance, code or regulation, or any violation of a planning board, zoning board of adjustment or building code board of appeals decision, results in the expenditure of public funds by a municipality which are not reimbursed under paragraph II, the court in its discretion may order, as an additional civil penalty, that a violator make restitution to the municipality for such funds so expended.

IV. The superior court may, upon a petition filed by a municipality and after notice and a preliminary hearing as in the case of prejudgment attachments under RSA 511-A, require an alleged violator to post a bond with the court to secure payment of any penalty or remedy or the performance of any injunctive relief which may be ordered or both. At the hearing, the burden shall be on the municipality to show that there is a strong likelihood that it will prevail on the merits, that the penalties or remedies sought are reasonably likely to be awarded by the court in an amount consistent with the bond sought, and that the bond represents the amount of the projected expense of compliance with the injunctive relief sought.

V. The building inspector or other local official with the authority to enforce the provisions of this title or any local ordinance, code, or regulation adopted under this title may commence an action under paragraph I either in the district court pursuant to RSA 502-A:11-a, or in the superior court. The prosecuting official in the official's discretion may, prior to or at the time of arraignment, charge the offense as a violation, and in such cases the penalties to be imposed by the court shall be limited to those provided for a violation under RSA 651:2 and the civil penalty provided in subparagraph I(b) of this section. The provisions of this section shall supersede any inconsistent local penalty provision.

Source.
1983, 447:1. 1985, 103:25; 210:4. 1988, 19:6, 7, eff. Jan. 1, 1989. 1996, 226:5, 6, eff. Jan. 1, 1997. 1997, 92:4, 5, eff. Jan. 1, 1998. 2004, 242:1, eff. Jan. 1, 2005. 2006, 101:1, eff. January 1, 2007.

Amendments
—2006. Paragraph I: Substituted "of $275" for "not to exceed $275".

—2004. Paragraph I: Rewritten to the extent that a detailed comparison would be impracticable.
Paragraph II: Substituted "shall recover" for "may recover" in the first sentence.

—1997. Paragraph I(b): Substituted "$275" for "$100".
Paragraph V: Substituted "subparagraph I(b)" for "subparagraph I(a)" in the second sentence.

—1996. Paragraph I(b): Substituted "the violator" for "he" following "municipality that".
Paragraph V: Substituted "the official's" for "his" preceding "discretion" in the second sentence.

—1988. Paragraph I: Rewritten to the extent that a detailed comparison would be impracticable.
Paragraph V: Added.

—1985. Rewritten by chs. 103 and 210 to the extent that a detailed comparison would be impracticable.

Applicability of 1985 amendment.
1985, 210:3, provided that this section, as amended by 1985, 210, would apply to all actions filed after 12:01 a.m. Jan. 1, 1986.

Contingent 1985 amendment.
1985, 210:2 provided for amendment of this section. However, under the terms of 1985,

210:3, the amendment did not become effective.

Sentences, see RSA 651.

Cross References.
Classification of crimes, see RSA 625:9.

NOTES TO DECISIONS

Analysis

1. Constitutionality
2. Construction
3. Notice of violation
4. Attorney's fees

1. Constitutionality

Trial court did not abuse its discretion by imposing $14,650 in fines and awarding town $6,000 in attorney's fees against property owners who agreed to move two mobile homes by June 15, 1993, but who did not move second mobile home until July 1997. Town of Nottingham v. Newman, 147 N.H. 131, 785 A.2d 891, 2001 N.H. LEXIS 184 (2001).

2. Construction

"Shall be subject to" clause granted the trial court the authority to impose the statutory penalties set forth in RSA 676:17, I(b) rather than the obligation to impose such penalties. Thus, RSA 676:17, I(b) granted the trial court the authority to determine whether or not to impose a penalty and the amount of the penalty should it choose to impose one, and the city's argument that imposition of a statutory penalty was mandatory was rejected. City of Rochester v. Corpening, 153 N.H. 571, 907 A.2d 383, 2006 N.H. LEXIS 73 (2006).

3. Notice of violation

Developer could not be fined with civil penalties under this section unless given reasonable written notice that he was in fact in violation of a town ordinance, and mere reference to RSA chapter 310-A—the licensing statute applicable to architects, engineers, and land surveyors—in town's cease and desist order was not sufficient notice. Town of Swanzey v. Liebeler, 140 N.H. 760, 674 A.2d 968, 1996 N.H. LEXIS 26 (1996).

4. Attorney's fees

Where town sought civil penalties against developer, it was reasonable for him to challenge the basis for imposing them, and since litigation was not unreasonably prolonged by developer's conduct, trial court correctly denied award of attorney's fees to town. Town of Swanzey v. Liebeler, 140 N.H. 760, 674 A.2d 968, 1996 N.H. LEXIS 26 (1996).

Town was not entitled to award of attorney's fees and costs, where its enforcement action was a de minimis portion of its case and trial court's findings did not support an award of fees and costs under subdivision II of this section. White v. Francoeur, 138 N.H. 307, 638 A.2d 1250, 1994 N.H. LEXIS 27 (1994).

RESEARCH REFERENCES

New Hampshire Practice.
14 N.H.P. Local Government Law §§ 920, 925, 926, 929, 981, 982.

15 N.H.P. Land Use Planning and Zoning §§ 7.05–7.07, 7.13, 7.16, 16.06, 24.06, 29.24, 36.18, 36.19.

676:17-a. Cease and Desist Orders.

The building inspector, code enforcement officer, zoning administrator or other official designated as an enforcement authority by ordinance or resolution of the local legislative body may issue a cease and desist order against any violation of this title, any local ordinance, code or regulation adopted under this title, or any provision or specification of an application, plat, or plan approved by, or any requirement or condition of a permit or decision issued by, any local administrator or land use board acting under the authority of this title, subject to the following:

I. The order shall state, in writing:

(a) The precise regulation, provision, specification or condition which is being violated.

(b) The facts constituting the violation, including the date of any inspection from which these facts were ascertained.

(c) The corrective action required, including a reasonable time within which such action shall be taken.

(d) A statement that a motion for summary enforcement of the order shall be made to the court of the district in which the property is situated unless such corrective action is taken within the time provided, or unless an answer is filed within 20 days, as provided in paragraph V.

(e) A statement that failure to either take the corrective action, or to file an answer, may result in corrective action being taken by the municipality, and that if this occurs the municipality's costs shall constitute a lien against the real estate, enforceable in the same manner as real estate taxes, including possible loss of the property if not paid.

II. The order shall be served upon the record owner of the property or the record owner's agent, and upon the person to whom taxes are assessed for the property, if other than the owner, and upon any occupying tenant of the property, and upon any other person known by the enforcing officer to exercise control over the premises in violation, and upon all persons holding mortgages upon such property as recorded in the office of the register of deeds, in the same manner provided for service of a summons in a civil action in district court. Personal service may be made by a sheriff, deputy sheriff, local police officer, or constable. If the owner is unknown or cannot be found, the order shall be served by posting it upon the property and by 4 weeks' publication in a newspaper in general circulation in the municipality.

III. Upon service of the order, the owner or the owner's agent, occupying tenant or the tenant's agent, or any other person who is engaged in development, construction, excavation, or other changes of the land or buildings on the land shall cease immediately such activities, if so provided in the order, until such time as judgment is rendered under paragraphs VI or VII. Failure to cease such activity shall constitute a separate violation of this title in addition to the violation cited in the order, unless such order is annulled as provided in paragraph VII.

IV. A copy of the order with proof of service shall be filed with clerk of the district court of the district in which the property is located not fewer than 5 days prior to the filing of a motion to enforce under paragraph VI.

V. Within 20 days after the date of service, any person upon whom the order is served may serve an answer in the manner provided for the service of an answer in a civil action, specifically denying such facts in the order as are in dispute.

VI. If no answer is served, the enforcement official may move the court for the enforcement of the order. If such a motion is made the court may, upon the presentation of such evidence as it may require, affirm or modify the order and enter judgment accordingly, fixing a time after which the governing body may proceed with the enforcement of the order. The clerk of the court shall mail a copy of the judgment to all persons upon whom the original order was served.

VII. If an answer is filed and served as provided in paragraph V, further proceedings in the action shall be governed by the rules of the district court. If the order is sustained following trial, the court shall enter judgment and shall fix a time within which the corrective action shall be taken, in compliance with the order as originally filed, or as modified by the court. If the order is not sustained, it shall be annulled and set aside. If it appears to the court that the order was frivolous, was commenced in bad faith, or was not based upon information and belief formed after reasonable inquiry or was not well-grounded in fact, then the court shall order the defendant's costs and reasonable attorneys fees to be paid by the municipality. The clerk of the court shall mail a copy of the judgment to the persons upon whom the original order was served.

VIII. If a judgment is not complied with in the time prescribed, the local governing body may cause the corrective action to be taken as set forth in the judgment. The cost to the municipality of taking such corrective action together with its other expenses as provided in paragraph IX, shall be a lien against the real estate on which the violation occurred, which shall continue for 18 months from the date upon which the expense account is allowed by the court, as provided in paragraph IX.

IX. The municipality shall keep an accurate account of the expenses incurred in carrying out the order and of all other expenses in connection with its enforcement, including but not limited to filing fees, service fees, publication fees, the expense of searching the registry of deeds to identify mortgages, witness and expert fees, attorneys fees and traveling expenses. The court shall examine, correct if necessary, and allow the expense account. The municipal governing body, by majority vote, may commit the expense account to the collector of taxes, in which case the mayor, as defined by RSA 672:9, shall direct the expense account, together with a warrant under the mayor's hand and seal, to the municipal tax collector, requiring the tax collector to collect the same from the person to whom real estate taxes are assessed for the premises upon which such corrective action was taken, and to pay the amount so collected to the municipal treasurer. Within 30 days after the receipt of such warrant, the collector shall send a bill as provided in RSA 76:11. Interest as provided in RSA 76:13 shall be charged on any amount not paid within 30 days after the bill is mailed. The collector shall have the same rights and remedies as in the collection of taxes, as provided in RSA 80.

X. A party aggrieved by the judgment of the district court may appeal, within 15 days after the rendering of such judgment, to the superior court.

XI. The remedy provided in this section is supplementary to other enforcement remedies provided by this chapter or local ordinance. At the discretion of the local enforcement official, an action to enforce a cease and desist order under this section may be joined with an action under RSA 676:17, I, and the cease and desist order shall constitute the written notice under RSA 676:17, I(b).

Source.
1991, 328:1, eff. June 28, 1991. 1996, 226:7, 8, eff. Jan. 1, 1997. 1997, 79:1, eff. Jan. 1, 1998.

Amendments
—1997. Paragraph II: Added the second sentence.

—1996. Paragraph II: Substituted "the record owner's" for "his" preceding "agent" in the first sentence.

Paragraph III: Substituted "the owner's" for "his" preceding "agent, occupying tenant or" and substituted "the tenant's" for "his" thereafter.

Paragraph IX: Substituted "the mayor's" for "his" preceding "hand and seal" and "the tax collector" for "him" following "requiring" in the third sentence.

NOTES TO DECISIONS

Attorney fees
Corporation was entitled to attorney's fees and costs under RSA 676:17-a, VII, where a trial court vacated a cease and desist order entered by a town against the corporation's co-generation facility; the town had no author-ity to issue the order as the field of air quality control had been preempted by the State under RSA ch. 125-C. Bio Energy, LLC v. Town of Hopkinton, 153 N.H. 145, 891 A.2d 509, 2005 N.H. LEXIS 188 (2005).

RESEARCH REFERENCES

New Hampshire Practice.
13 N.H.P. Local Government Law §§ 917, 918, 925, 981.

15 N.H.P. Land Use Planning and Zoning §§ 7.05, 7.06, 32.11.

676:17-b. Local Land Use Citations; Pleas by Mail.

A building inspector or other local official with authority to prosecute an offense within the scope of RSA 676:17, and who, prior to or at the time of serving the summons, elects, pursuant to RSA 676:17, V, to charge the offense as a violation, may issue and serve upon the defendant, in addition to the summons, a local land use citation as set forth in this section. The defendant receiving such a citation may plead guilty or nolo contendere by mail by entering that plea as provided herein. If such a plea is accepted by the court, the defendant shall not be required to appear personally or by counsel; otherwise the defendant shall appear as directed by the court. The following procedure shall be used:

I. No local land use citation as set forth in this section shall be served unless the defendant has first been given written notice of the violation by the municipality. If the notice involves or includes a decision which may be appealed to the zoning board of adjustment pursuant to RSA 676:5, or to the building code board of appeals pursuant to RSA 674:34, such notice to the building code board of appeals pursuant to RSA 674:34, such notice shall set forth a reasonable period, as provided by the rules of the respective board, in no case less than 7 days, within which such appeal shall be filed after receipt of the written notice, and the citation shall not be served until after the end of such period. If such an appeal is filed, further proceedings shall be governed by RSA 676:6.

II. The local land use citation shall contain:
(a) The caption: "Local Land Use Citation, Town (City) of _____".

(b) The name of the offender, and address if known to the prosecuting official.

(c) The statute, code, ordinance, regulation, provision, specification, requirement or condition the offender is charged with violating.

(d) The act or circumstances constituting the violation.

(e) The place of the violation.

(f) The date upon which the offender received written notice of the violation by the municipality.

(g) The time and date upon which the violation was witnessed subsequent to such written notice.

(h) The amount of the civil penalty as set forth in RSA 676:17, I(b), which is payable by the offender for each day the violation continued subsequent to such written notice, up to a maximum of 5 days' violation charged in one citation.

(i) Instructions informing the defendant that the defendant may answer the citation by mail or may personally appear in court upon the date on the summons, and instructing the defendant how to enter a plea by mail, together with either the amount of the penalty specified in the citation, or a request for a trial.

(j) The address of the clerk of the district court, where the plea by mail may be entered.

(k) A warning to the defendant that failure to respond to the citation on or before the date on the summons may result in the defendant's arrest as provided in paragraph V.

(*l*) The signature of the prosecuting official.

III. Defendants who are issued a summons and local land use citation and who wish to plead guilty or nolo contendere shall enter their plea on the summons and return it with payment of the civil penalty, as set forth in the citation, to the clerk of the court prior to the arraignment date, or shall appear in court on the date of arraignment.

IV. Civil penalties collected by the district court under this section shall be remitted to the municipality issuing the citation. Whenever a defendant (a) does not enter a plea by mail prior to the arraignment day or does not appear personally or by counsel on or before that date or move for a continuance; or (b) otherwise fails to appear for a scheduled court appearance in connection with a summons for any offense, the defendant shall be defaulted and the court shall determine what the civil penalty would be upon a plea of guilty or nolo contendere and shall impose an administrative processing fee in addition to the civil penalty. Such fee shall be the same as the administrative processing fee under RSA 502-A:19-b, and shall be retained by the court for the benefit of the state.

V. The court may, in its discretion, issue a bench warrant for the arrest of any defendant who:

(a) Is defaulted in accordance with the provisions of paragraph IV of this section;

(b) Fails to pay a fine or other penalty imposed in connection with a conviction under this title which a court has determined the defendant is able to pay, or issues a bad check in payment of a fine or other penalty; or

(c) Fails to comply with a similar order on any matter within the court's discretion.

VI. For cause, the court in its discretion may refuse to accept a plea by mail and may impose a fine or penalty other than that stated in the local land use citation. The court may order the defendant to appear personally in court for the disposition of the defendant's case.

VII. The prosecuting official may serve additional local land use citations, without giving additional written notice or appeal opportunity under paragraph I, if the facts or circumstances constituting the violation continue beyond the date or dates of any prior citation. A plea of guilty or nolo contendere to the prior citation shall not affect the rights of the defendant with respect to a subsequent citation.

VIII. Forms and rules for the local land use citation and summons shall be developed and adopted by the New Hampshire supreme court.

IX. This section is not intended in any way to abrogate other enforcement actions or remedies in the district or superior court pursuant to this title, nor to require written notice as a prerequisite to other types of actions or remedies under this title.

Source.

1991, 374:2, eff. Jan. 1, 1992. 1996, 226:9-13, eff. Jan. 1, 1997.

Revision note.

This section, which was originally enacted as RSA 676:17-a by 1991, 374:2, was redesignated as RSA 676:17-b pursuant to 1991, 374:3.

Substituted "paragraph V" for "paragraph IV" in par. II(k) to correct an error in the reference.

Amendments

—1996. Substituted "the defendant" for "he" preceding "shall appear" in the third sentence of the introductory paragraph.

Paragraph II(i): Substituted "the defendant" for "he" preceding "may answer".

Paragraph II(k): Substituted "the defendant's" for "his" preceding "arrest".

Paragraph V(b): Substituted "the defendant" for "he" following "has determined".

Paragraph VI: Substituted "the defendant's" for "his" following "disposition of" in the second sentence.

RESEARCH REFERENCES

New Hampshire Practice.

13 N.H.P. Local Government Law § 917, 919.

15 N.H.P. Land Use Planning and Zoning §§ 7.06, 32.11.

676:18. Register of Deeds.

I. A register of deeds who files or records a plat of a subdivision without the approval of a planning board shall be guilty of a misdemeanor.

II. Notwithstanding the provisions of paragraph I, the register of deeds shall accept for recording a plat prepared and certified by a licensed land surveyor or by a former registered land surveyor if such plat bears a certificate by a licensed or registered land surveyor that this survey plat is not a subdivision pursuant to this title and that the lines of streets and ways shown are those of public or private streets or ways already established and that no new ways are shown. The recording of any such plat shall not relieve any owner from compliance with the provisions of this chapter.

II-a. Notwithstanding the provisions of paragraph I or II, the register of deeds may accept for recording a plat without the licensed land surveyor's seal if such plat was in existence on December 31, 1969, or if the plat has been incorporated into deeds or other instruments recorded before town zoning ordinances or planning board subdivision regulations, or both, became effective in that particular town.

III. The certificate by a licensed land surveyor shall be in the following form:

"I certify that this survey plat is not a subdivision pursuant to this title and that the lines of streets and ways shown are those of public or private streets or ways already established and that no new ways are shown."

Date: _____

_____
Licensed Land Surveyor

SEAL

IV. Prior to recording any plat in the registry of deeds, the surveyor shall file, for information purposes only, a copy of the survey with the town planning board.

V. All decisions of the district, superior, and supreme courts, which affect property boundaries, shall be recorded by the register of deeds in the registry of deeds for the county in which the site is situated, and, upon recordation, such decision shall run with the land. Subsequent to any probate court decision creating divisions of land, a survey plat shall be prepared by a licensed land surveyor, which, if approved by the probate court, shall be recorded, along with the court's decision, at the registry of deeds without local planning board approval. The recording of such decision or plat, however, shall not be deemed to authorize any transfer or development of the property in violation of any applicable local land use regulations adopted pursuant to this title.

Source.
1983, 447:1. 1985, 103:26. 1988, 233:2. 1989, 120:1, 2. 1990, 64:1, 2. 1995, 303:4, 5, eff. Jan. 1, 1996.

Amendments
—1995. Amended pars. II and III generally.

—1990. Paragraph II-a: Substituted "licensed" for "registered" preceding "land surveyor's", "was" for "has been" preceding "in existence", "on December 31, 1969" for "since December 31, 1958" thereafter, "or" for "and" following "ordinances" and inserted "or both" following "regulations".

Paragraph V: Inserted "and" preceding "supreme", deleted "and probate" thereafter and made a minor change in punctuation in the first sentence, rewrote the second sentence and added the third sentence.

—1989. Paragraph II-a: Added.
Paragraph V: Added.

—1988. Paragraph II: Substituted "a plat prepared and certified by a licensed land surveyor if such plat bears" for "any plat bearing" preceding "a certificate by a" and substituted "licensed" for "registered" thereafter in the first sentence.

—**1985.**   Paragraph IV: Added.

Cross References.
   Classification of crimes, see RSA 625:9.

Sentences, see RSA 651.
   Transfers or sales of land prior to approval of subdivision plats, see RSA 676:16.

NOTES TO DECISIONS

Cited:
   Cited in City of Dover v. Kimball, 136 N.H.

441, 616 A.2d 516, 1992 N.H. LEXIS 187 (1992).

RESEARCH REFERENCES

New Hampshire Practice.
   15 N.H.P. Land Use Planning and Zoning §§ 29.19–29.21, 32.08.

676:19. Penalties.
[Repealed 1985, 103:27, eff. Jan. 1, 1986.]

Former section(s).
   Former RSA 676:19, which was derived from 1983, 447:1, related to penalties for violations

of ordinances, codes or regulations adopted pursuant to this title. See now RSA 676:17.

CHAPTER 677

REHEARING AND APPEAL PROCEDURES

Cross References.

Local land use boards generally, see RSA 673.

Local land use planning and regulatory powers generally, see RSA 674.

Ordinance, regulation and code administration and enforcement generally, see RSA 676.

Ordinance, regulation and code adoption procedure generally, see RSA 675.

Rehearings and appeals generally, see RSA 541.

NOTES TO DECISIONS

Cited:

Cited in Vachon v. Town of New Durham Zoning Bd. of Adjustment, 131 N.H. 623, 557 A.2d 649, 1989 N.H. LEXIS 29 (1989); Blue Jay Realty Trust v. City of Franklin, 132 N.H. 502, 567 A.2d 188, 1989 N.H. LEXIS 128 (1989); Allen v. Wetlands Bd., 133 N.H. 379, 577 A.2d 92, 1990 N.H. LEXIS 71 (1990).

RESEARCH REFERENCES

New Hampshire Practice.

15 N.H.P. Land Use Planning and Zoning §§ 29.18, 35.15.

New Hampshire Bar Journal.

For article, "An Overview of the New Hampshire Land Use Planning and Regulation Statutes," see 34 N.H.B.J. 6 (June 1993).

For article, "The New Zoning Variance Cases: Analyzing Unnecessary Hardship Under RSA 674:33," see 46 N.H.B.J. 40 (Fall 2005).

For article, "Unnecessary Hardship Under RSA 674:331(B)," see 46 N.H.B.J. 47 (Fall 2005).

General Provisions

677:1. Procedure.

Whenever a person or a municipality seeks a rehearing on or an appeal of a zoning-related order or decision, the procedures enacted under this chapter shall be followed.

Source.
1983, 447:1, eff. Jan. 1, 1984.

Rehearing Procedures Before Board of Adjustment, Board of Appeals and Local Legislative Body

Revision note.
Inserted "Board of Appeals" following "Board of Adjustment" in the subdivision heading for purposes of conformity with RSA 677:2 and 677:3, as amended by 1988, 131:4, 5, eff. June 19, 1988.

Cross References.
Appeals from decisions of historic district cimmissions exercising powers of boards of adjustment, see RSA 676:10.

Appeals to boards of adjustment, see RSA 676:5–7.
Ordinance, regulation and code enactment generally, see RSA 675.
Powers of zoning boards adjustment generally, see RSA 674:33.
Rehearings of decisions of historic district commission, see RSA 677:17 et seq.
Zoning ordinances generally, see RSA 674:16 et seq.

677:2. Motion for Rehearing of Board of Adjustment, Board of Appeals, and Local Legislative Body Decisions.

Within 30 days after any order or decision of the zoning board of adjustment, or any decision of the local legislative body or a board of appeals in regard to its zoning, the selectmen, any party to the action or proceedings, or any person directly affected thereby may apply for a rehearing in respect to any matter determined in the action or proceeding, or covered or included in the order, specifying in the motion for rehearing the ground therefor; and the board of adjustment, a board of appeals, or the local legislative body, may grant such rehearing if in its opinion good reason therefor is stated in the motion. This 30-day time period shall be counted in calendar days beginning with the date following the date upon which the board voted to approve or disapprove the application in accordance with RSA 21:35; provided however, that if the moving party shows that the minutes of the meeting at which such vote was taken, including the written decision, were not filed within 144 hours of the vote pursuant to RSA 676:3, II, the person applying for the rehearing shall have the right to amend the motion for rehearing, including the grounds therefor, within 30 days after the date on which the written decision was actually filed. If the decision complained against is that made by a town meeting, the application for rehearing shall be made to the board of selectmen, and, upon receipt of such application, the board of selectmen shall hold a rehearing within 30 days after receipt of the petition. Following the rehearing, if in the judgment of the selectmen the protest warrants action, the selectmen shall call a special town meeting.

Source.
1983, 447:1. 1988, 131:4. 1994, 116:1, eff. July 10, 1994. 1995, 243:3, eff. Jan. 1, 1996. 2000, 144:2, eff. Jan. 1, 2001. 2005, 105:1, eff. Aug. 14, 2005.

Amendments
—2005. Inserted "following the date" preceding "upon which the board voted" and "in accordance with RSA 21:35" following "application" in the second sentence.

—2000. Rewritten to the extent that a detailed comparison would be impracticable.

—1995. Inserted "has been filed and first becomes available for public inspection in the office of the respective board or body or of its clerk or secretary" preceding "the selectmen" in the first sentence.

—1994. Added the second sentence.

—1988. Inserted "Board of Appeals" following "Board of Adjustment" in the section catchline, "or a board of appeals" following "legislative body" and "a board of appeals" following "the board of adjustment" in the first sentence.

NOTES TO DECISIONS

Analysis

1. Generally
2. Application
3. Request for rehearing
4. Persons entitled to request rehearing
5. Requirements of motion for rehearing
6. Amendment of motion for rehearing
7. Motion for rehearing as basis for appeal
8. Timeliness of motion

1. Generally

In the interest of finality of decisions by zoning boards, rehearings were not to be lightly granted. Griauzde v. City of Nashua, 103 N.H. 468, 174 A.2d 432, 1961 N.H. LEXIS 68 (1961). (Decided under prior law.)

2. Application

Affirmative defense of illegality, asserted by developers who signed promissory note, was not barred by appeal provisions of this section and RSA 677:4. Questions of ordinance's legality and ultimately the binding effect of promissory note were not questions of administrative action under these sections, but affirmative defenses relating to underlying legality of legislative action. City of Portsmouth v. Schlesinger, 140 N.H. 733, 672 A.2d 712, 1996 N.H. LEXIS 17 (1996).

In challenge to validity of zoning amendments by petition for declaratory judgment, this section does not apply, and failure to pursue rehearing is no bar to direct relief. Blue Jay Realty Trust v. City of Franklin, 132 N.H. 502, 567 A.2d 188, 1989 N.H. LEXIS 128 (1989).

3. Request for rehearing

Where a zoning board of adjustment denied a property owner's motion for rehearing on her variance application, the owner was not required by RSA 677:2 et seq., to file a second motion for rehearing to preserve for appeal new issues, findings, or rulings first raised by the board's denial order. McDonald v. Town of Effingham Zoning Bd. of Adjustment, 152 N.H. 171, 872 A.2d 1018, 2005 N.H. LEXIS 68 (2005).

There is no statutory requirement that a request for rehearing on a zoning board of adjustment decision come only after a formal vote of the board of selectmen, thus, a town manager could file a rehearing request with the authorization of a majority of the selectmen. Town of Plastow Bd. of Selectmen v. Town of Plastow Zoning Bd. of Adjustment, 146 N.H. 263, 769 A.2d 397, 2001 N.H. LEXIS 67 (2001).

4. Persons entitled to request rehearing

Mere fact that an individual is a taxpaying resident of a town does not give that individual standing to seek mandamus relief requiring the town to enforce its zoning ordinances. Pursuant to RSA 676:5, 677:2, 677:4, an individual can seek relief before a zoning board of appeals or in the courts with regard to a zoning officer's decision only if the individual is an "aggrieved person," which requires a showing that he or she has some direct, definite interest in the outcome of the zoning decision itself, and the mere fact that an individual lives and/or pays taxes to a town, does not, by itself, give that individual a direct, definite interest in town zoning decisions. Goldstein v. Town of Bedford, 154 N.H. 393, 910 A.2d 1158, 2006 N.H. LEXIS 173 (Nov. 22, 2006).

Superior court properly dismissed the mandamus petition filed by a town resident, seeking to require the town to enforce its zoning ordinances, because the resident was not an "aggrieved person," which was required for him to have standing under RSA 677:4 to seek judicial review of actions taken by the town's zoning board of adjustment. The mere fact that the resident lived in, and paid taxes to, the town did not give him a direct, definite interest in the zoning decision that he challenged, which pertained to permits obtained by a third party with regard to his nonconforming lots. Goldstein v. Town of Bedford, 154 N.H. 393, 910 A.2d 1158, 2006 N.H. LEXIS 173 (Nov. 22, 2006).

Where the applicant sought permission to build a gas station, the challengers to the applicant would have been a competing gas station, and the challengers' property was located within 1,000 feet of the applicant's property and within a groundwater conservation district, under which circumstances the amended zoning code barred new gas stations, the challengers had standing under RSA 677:4 to appeal the decision of the zoning board of adjustment, as the challengers were directly affected by the proceedings pursuant to RSA 677:2. Thomas v. Town of Hooksett, 153 N.H. 717, 903 A.2d 963, 2006 N.H. LEXIS 99 (2006).

The citizens of a city were "directly affected" by the action of a zoning board and were thus entitled to move for rehearing and to appeal, at least to the extent that their appeal questioned whether an amendment to a zoning ordinance was validly adopted. Towle v. Nashua, 106 N.H. 394, 212 A.2d 204, 1965 N.H. LEXIS 177 (1965). (Decided under prior law.)

5. Requirements of motion for rehearing

The requirement of former RSA 31:75 (now covered by RSA 677:3) that a party moving for rehearing before a zoning board of adjustment specify in the motion the grounds upon which a rehearing was sought, and the provision that no ground not set forth in the motion could be considered by the superior court on appeal from the board, did not give the moving party the right to control the scope of the proceeding on rehearing; rather, it was intended to ensure that the board had the first opportunity to pass upon errors which it might have made in the first hearing. Fisher v. Town of Boscawen, 121 N.H. 438, 431 A.2d 131, 1981 N.H. LEXIS 348 (1981). (Decided under prior law.)

Compliance with the requirement that a rehearing be applied for within 20 days was mandatory, and failure to comply could not be waived by the board of adjustment. City of

Keene v. Zoning Board of Adjustment, 114 N.H. 744, 329 A.2d 141, 1974 N.H. LEXIS 364 (1974). (Decided under prior law.)

Failure to file a motion for rehearing satisfying the requirements of this statute and former RSA 31:75 (now covered by RSA 677:3) by motion seasonably filed, setting forth "every ground" upon which the plaintiffs claimed the order of the board of adjustment was unlawful or unreasonable, precluded maintenance of their pending appeal. Di Pietro v. City of Nashua, 109 N.H. 174, 246 A.2d 695, 1968 N.H. LEXIS 149 (1968). (Decided under prior law.)

6. Amendment of motion for rehearing

Where a motion for rehearing as originally filed was insufficient, it was not subject to amendment by supplemental filing after the twenty-day limitation had expired. Di Pietro v. City of Nashua, 109 N.H. 174, 246 A.2d 695, 1968 N.H. LEXIS 149 (1968). (Decided under prior law.)

7. Motion for rehearing as basis for appeal

The filing of an application for rehearing on the decision of a zoning board of adjustment was a precondition of appeal to the court by an aggrieved person. Shaw v. City of Manchester, 118 N.H. 158, 384 A.2d 491, 1978 N.H. LEXIS 364 (1978). (Decided under prior law.) But see Metzger v. Brentwood, 115 N.H. 287, 343 A.2d 24, 1975 N.H. LEXIS 289 (1975). (Decided under prior law.)

The statutory scheme for zoning in this state was geared to the proposition that the board of adjustment would have a first opportunity to correct any action it had taken, if correction was necessary, before an appeal to the court was filed; thus a party could not appeal the decision of a board of adjustment to the superior court without first applying for a rehearing before the board under this statute. Bourassa v. City of Keene, 108 N.H. 261, 234 A.2d 112, 1967 N.H. LEXIS 168 (1967). (Decided under prior law.)

8. Timeliness of motion

Language of RSA 677:2 is unambiguous and provides that the 30-day time period for filing a motion for a rehearing of a zoning board's decision begins to run on the date of the decision. Because a variance applicant filed his motion for a rehearing 33 days after the date of the board's vote, the motion was not timely filed. Pelletier v. City of Manchester, 150 N.H.

687, 844 A.2d 484, 2004 N.H. LEXIS 54 (2004).

Because RSA 21:35 provides that the general rule for computing a time period does not apply if the statute in question specifically states a contrary rule, the general rule of computing a time period by excluding the first day from which a period is to be determined does not apply to RSA 677:2, which specifically states that the time period for filing a motion for a rehearing of a zoning board's decision begins to run on the date of a zoning board's vote. Pelletier v. City of Manchester, 150 N.H. 687, 844 A.2d 484, 2004 N.H. LEXIS 54 (2004).

Where the date that a zoning board of adjustment denied an owner's variance was included in calculating the time for an appeal under RSA 677:2, the owner's appeal was due 30 days later on a Friday; because the appeal was filed on the following Monday, it was properly dismissed as untimely under RSA 677:3. Ireland v. Town of Candia, 151 N.H. 69, 851 A.2d 630, 2004 N.H. LEXIS 90 (2004).

Where zoning board of adjustment errone-ously waived appeal period rule to hear an appeal from grant of building permit on the merits, defendant was not required to move for rehearing under this section prior to seeking summary judgment in supreme court; issue of timeliness was jurisdictional and could be raised at any time. Daniel v. B & J Realty, 134 N.H. 174, 589 A.2d 998, 1991 N.H. LEXIS 43 (1991).

Cited:

Cited in Bedford Residents Group v. Town of Bedford, 130 N.H. 632, 547 A.2d 225, 1988 N.H. LEXIS 65 (1988); McGovern v. City of Manchester, 130 N.H. 628, 546 A.2d 1057, 1988 N.H. LEXIS 54 (1988); Hussey v. Town of Barrington, 135 N.H. 227, 604 A.2d 82, 1992 N.H. LEXIS 3 (1992); City of Portsmouth v. Schlesinger, 57 F.3d 12, 1995 U.S. App. LEXIS 14582 (1st. Cir. 1995); Bourne v. Town of Madison, 494 F. Supp. 2d 80, 2007 U.S. Dist. LEXIS 47625 (June 29, 2007).

RESEARCH REFERENCES

New Hampshire Practice.

15 N.H.P. Land Use Planning and Zoning §§ 7.15, 16.01, 21.15, 25.01, 26.03.

ALR.

Standing of civic or property owners' associa-tion to challenge zoning board decision (as aggrieved party). 8 A.L.R.4th 1087.

677:3. Rehearing by Board of Adjustment, Board of Appeals, or Local Legislative Body.

I. A motion for rehearing made under RSA 677:2 shall set forth fully every ground upon which it is claimed that the decision or order complained of is unlawful or unreasonable. No appeal from any order or decision of the zoning board of adjustment, a board of appeals, or the local legislative body shall be taken unless the appellant shall have made application for rehearing as provided in RSA 677:2; and, when such application shall have been made, no ground not set forth in the application shall be urged, relied on, or given any consideration by a court unless the court for good cause shown shall allow the appellant to specify additional grounds.

II. Upon the filing of a motion for a rehearing, the board of adjustment, a board of appeals, or the local legislative body shall within 30 days either grant or deny the application, or suspend the order or decision complained of pending further consideration. Any order of suspension may be upon such terms and conditions as the board of adjustment, a board of appeals, or the local legislative body may prescribe. If the motion for rehearing is against a decision of the local legislative body and if the selectmen, as provided in RSA 677:2, shall have called a special town meeting within 25 days from the receipt of an application for a rehearing, the town shall grant or deny the same or suspend the order or decision complained of pending further consideration; and any order of suspension may be upon such terms and conditions as the town may prescribe.

Source.
1983, 447:1. 1988, 131:5. 1994, 116:2, eff. July 10, 1994.

Amendments
—1994. Paragraph II: Substituted "30" for "10" preceding "days" in the first sentence.

—1988. Inserted "Board of Appeals" following "Board of Adjustment" in the section catchline.
Paragraph I: Inserted "a board of appeals" following "board of adjustment" in the second sentence.
Paragraph II: Inserted "a board of appeals" following "board of adjustment" in the first and second sentences.

NOTES TO DECISIONS

Analysis

1. Purpose of requirement of motion for rehearing
2. Failure to move for rehearing
3. Grounds for rehearing
4. Timeliness of appeal
5. Motion for rehearing as basis for appeal
6. Procedure on rehearing

1. Purpose of requirement of motion for rehearing

The rule requiring exhaustion of administrative remedies before appealing to the courts, embodied in this statute, was based on the reasonable policies of encouraging the exercising of administrative expertise, preserving agency autonomy and promoting judicial efficiency. Metzger v. Brentwood, 115 N.H. 287, 343 A.2d 24, 1975 N.H. LEXIS 289 (1975). (Decided under former RSA 31:75.)

Where the issue before a zoning board of adjustment was a narrow legal one, rigid adherence to the provision of this section requiring an application for a rehearing prior to appealing to the superior court was not necessary. Metzger v. Brentwood, 115 N.H. 287, 343 A.2d 24, 1975 N.H. LEXIS 289 (1975). (Decided under former RSA 31:75.)

2. Failure to move for rehearing

Where a zoning board of adjustment denied a property owner's motion for rehearing on her variance application, the owner was not required by RSA 677:2 et seq., to file a second motion for rehearing to preserve for appeal new issues, findings, or rulings first raised by the board's denial order. McDonald v. Town of Effingham Zoning Bd. of Adjustment, 152 N.H. 171, 872 A.2d 1018, 2005 N.H. LEXIS 68 (2005).

Superior court correctly dismissed plaintiff's appeal contesting special exceptions granted by zoning board of adjustment, where plaintiff failed to file a motion for rehearing and thus its appeal did not satisfy statutory prerequisites. Mountain Valley Mall Assocs. v. Municipality of Conway, 144 N.H. 642, 745 A.2d 481, 2000 N.H. LEXIS 1 (2000).

3. Grounds for rehearing

Trial court's refusal to consider the property owner's vagueness argument concerning a cost condition imposed on the property owner's property as a condition of the property owner being able to obtain a requested variance was not error and the state supreme court would not review that claim for the first time on the property owner's appeal; the property owner was required to, but did not, raise that argument in the motion for rehearing that the property owner filed before the zoning board of appeals. Robinson v. Town of Hudson, 154 N.H. 563, 914 A.2d 239, 2006 N.H. LEXIS 200 (2006).

Where a zoning board specifically found that an owner had not satisfied two of the requirements under RSA 674:33, I(b) in the owner's application for a rehearing of the board's denial of a variance, the owner did not have to raise the conditions that were not specifically denied by the board; therefore, the trial court erred in interpreting RSA 677:3 as requiring the owner to raise all five conditions for a variance in an application for rehearing in order to preserve a right of appeal. Robinson v. Town of Hudson, 149 N.H. 255, 821 A.2d 959, 2003 N.H. LEXIS 33 (2003).

Where plaintiff referenced and attached to its request for rehearing the planning board's memorandum, which listed three specific grounds for a rehearing, the trial court correctly found that incorporation of the memorandum adequately set forth grounds for the rehearing. Town of Plastow Bd. of Selectmen v. Town of Plastow Zoning Bd. of Adjustment, 146 N.H. 263, 769 A.2d 397, 2001 N.H. LEXIS 67 (2001).

The requirement that a party moving for rehearing before a zoning board of adjustment was to specify in the motion the grounds upon which a rehearing was sought, and the provision that no ground not set forth in the motion could be considered by the superior court on appeal from the board, did not give the moving party the right to control the scope of the proceeding on rehearing; rather, it was intended to ensure that the board had the first opportunity to pass upon errors which it might have made in the first hearing. Fisher v. Town of Boscawen, 121 N.H. 438, 431 A.2d 131, 1981 N.H. LEXIS 348 (1981). (Decided under former RSA 31:75.)

The temporary unavailability of the minutes of testimony at a zoning board hearing did not relieve plaintiffs of the necessity of stating the ground of motion for rehearing as they attended the hearing and the nature of the evidence presented must have been ascertainable by counsel retained after the hearing. Di Pietro v. City of Nashua, 109 N.H. 174, 246 A.2d 695, 1968 N.H. LEXIS 149 (1968). (Decided under former RSA 31:75.)

4. Timeliness of appeal

Where the date that a zoning board of adjustment denied an owner's variance was included in calculating the time for an appeal under RSA 677:2, the owner's appeal was due 30 days later on a Friday; because the appeal was filed on the following Monday, it was properly dismissed as untimely under RSA 677:3. Ireland v. Town of Candia, 151 N.H. 69, 851 A.2d 630, 2004 N.H. LEXIS 90 (2004).

5. Motion for rehearing as basis for appeal

The statute required an aggrieved party to file a new motion for rehearing that raised any new issues that were thrust upon the appealing party where a procedural decision was reversed, and the board then issued a decision on the merits consistent with the procedural result, and the aggrieved party remained the same, but following the decision upon rehearing, it was aggrieved by a substantive issue rather than a procedural issue; to hold otherwise would deny the board an opportunity to correct its errors and would limit the court to consideration of the errors alleged in the original rehearing motion. Dziama v. City of Portsmouth, 140 N.H. 542, 669 A.2d 217, 1995 N.H. LEXIS 185 (1995).

In light of the plaintiff's reasonable reliance upon a prior case, the court's holding requiring an aggrieved party to file a new motion for rehearing in certain circumstances would be enforced prospectively only and the plaintiff would be permitted additional time in which to move for rehearing before the board. Dziama v. City of Portsmouth, 140 N.H. 542, 669 A.2d 217, 1995 N.H. LEXIS 185 (1995).

The filing of an application for rehearing on the decision of a zoning board of adjustment was a precondition of appeal to the court by an aggrieved person. Shaw v. City of Manchester, 118 N.H. 158, 384 A.2d 491, 1978 N.H. LEXIS 364 (1978). (Decided under former RSA 31:75.)

It could not be successfully claimed, where a board of adjustment denied a petition without notice or hearing and took no action on the motion for rehearing, that the matter was never before the board and the board took no proper action and that, therefore, there could be no appeal to superior court and the court could not remand to the board. Smith v. Nutter, 113 N.H. 58, 301 A.2d 90, 1973 N.H. LEXIS 200 (1973). (Decided under former RSA 31:75.)

6. Procedure on rehearing

The zoning board of adjustment rehearing process was designed to afford a board an opportunity to correct its own mistakes before appeal to the courts, and a board which denied an application for a special exception, stating its reason, could, upon rehearing, decide that such reason was erroneous and proceed to consider the application again and deny it for another reason. Fisher v. Town of Boscawen, 121 N.H. 438, 431 A.2d 131, 1981 N.H. LEXIS 348 (1981). (Decided under former RSA 31:76.)

Where a zoning board of adjustment denied an application for a special exception on the stated ground that it could not approve the application in the absence of approval of the site by the planning board, and, at a rehearing, decided its ground for denial was erroneous and that planning board approval was not a prerequisite to zoning board of adjustment approval, the zoning board of adjustment was free on the rehearing to consider the application on its merits. Fisher v. Town of Boscawen, 121 N.H. 438, 431 A.2d 131, 1981 N.H. LEXIS 348 (1981). (Decided under former RSA 31:76.)

Cited:
Cited in Bedford Residents Group v. Town of

Bedford, 130 N.H. 632, 547 A.2d 225, 1988 N.H. LEXIS 65 (1988); Blue Jay Realty Trust v. City of Franklin, 132 N.H. 502, 567 A.2d 188, 1989 N.H. LEXIS 128 (1989); Granite State Minerals, Inc. v. City of Portsmouth, 134 N.H. 408, 593 A.2d 1142, 1991 N.H. LEXIS 80 (1991); Prime Fin. Group v. Masters, 141 N.H. 33, 676 A.2d 528, 1996 N.H. LEXIS 43 (1996); NBAC Corp. v. Town of Weare, 147 N.H. 328, 786 A.2d 867, 2001 N.H. LEXIS 219 (2001).

RESEARCH REFERENCES

New Hampshire Practice.
15 N.H.P. Land Use Planning and Zoning §§ 16.01, 21.15, 21.16, 25.03, 33.02.

New Hampshire Bar Journal.
For article, "Lex Loci: A Survey of New

Hampshire Supreme Court Decisions," see N.H.B.J. 46 (Spring 2006).

Appeal and Court Review of Board of Adjustment and Local Legislative Body Decisions

Cross References.
Appeal and review of building code boards of appeals decisions, see RSA 677:16.
Appeal and review of planning board decisions, see RSA 677:15.
Appeal of historic district commission decisions, see RSA 677:17 et seq.

Ordinance, regulation and code enactment generally, see RSA 675.
Procedure for rehearings, see RSA 677:2, 3.
Powers of zoning boards of adjustment generally, see RSA 674:33.
Zoning ordinances generally, see RSA 674:16 et seq.

RESEARCH REFERENCES

ALR.
Standing of zoning board of appeals or simi-

lar body to appeal reversal of its decision. 13 A.L.R.4th 1130.

677:4. Appeal from Decision on Motion for Rehearing.

Any person aggrieved by any order or decision of the zoning board of adjustment or any decision of the local legislative body may apply, by petition, to the superior court within 30 days after the date upon which the board voted to deny the motion for rehearing; provided however, that if the petitioner shows that the minutes of the meeting at which such vote was taken, including the written decision, were not filed within 144 hours of the vote pursuant to RSA 676:3, II, the petitioner shall have the right to amend the petition within 30 days after the date on which the written decision was actually filed. The petition shall set forth that such decision or order is illegal or unreasonable, in whole or in part, and shall specify the grounds upon which the decision or order is claimed to be illegal or unreasonable. For purposes of this section, "person aggrieved" includes any party entitled to request a rehearing under RSA 677:2.

Source.
1983, 447:1. 1994, 116:3, eff. July 10, 1994. 1995, 243:4, eff. Jan. 1, 1996. 1996, 43:3, eff. June 23, 1996. 2000, 144:3, eff. Jan. 1, 2001.

Amendments
—2000. Rewritten to the extent that a detailed comparison would be impracticable.

—1996. Added the third sentence.

—1995. Inserted "by petition" following "body may apply" and substituted "filed and first becomes available for public inspection in the office of the respective board or body or of its

clerk or secretary" for "recorded, by petition" preceding "setting forth" in the first sentence and substituted "filing" for "recording" following "the date of" in the second sentence.

—1994. Added the second sentence.

Cross References.
Effect of filing of appeal, see RSA 677:9.
Furnishing of record on appeal, see RSA 677:12.
Issuance of order of notice by clerk of court, see RSA 677:8.
Joinder of parties, see RSA 677:7.

NOTES TO DECISIONS

Analysis

1. Jurisdiction
2. Applicability
3. Conflict of laws
4. Standing to appeal
5. Prior law
6. Prerequisite for appeal
7. Filing of appeal
8. Statement of grounds for appeal
9. Notification of other parties of filing of appeal—Generally
10. Continuance pending notification of appeal

1. Jurisdiction

Where a zoning board of adjustment denied a property owner's motion for rehearing on her variance application, the owner was not required by RSA 677:2 et seq., to file a second motion for rehearing to preserve for appeal new issues, findings, or rulings first raised by the board's denial order. McDonald v. Town of Effingham Zoning Bd. of Adjustment, 152 N.H. 171, 872 A.2d 1018, 2005 N.H. LEXIS 68 (2005).

Superior court in zoning appeal correctly declined to address propriety of zoning board of adjustment's decision; since plaintiff filed its direct appeal under RSA 677:15, rather than RSA 677:4, superior court lacked jurisdiction beyond evaluating decision of planning board. Mountain Valley Mall Assocs. v. Municipality of Conway, 144 N.H. 642, 745 A.2d 481, 2000 N.H. LEXIS 1 (2000).

Superior court erred by exercising its jurisdiction under this section to review town select-

men's decision to revoke a building permit. Storms v. Town of Eaton, 131 N.H. 50, 549 A.2d 1208, 1988 N.H. LEXIS 87 (1988).

2. Applicability

Affirmative defense of illegality, asserted by developers who signed promissory note, was not barred by appeal provisions of this section and RSA 677:2. Questions of ordinance's legality and ultimately the binding effect of promissory note were not questions of administrative action under these sections, but affirmative defenses relating to underlying legality of legislative action. City of Portsmouth v. Schlesinger, 140 N.H. 733, 672 A.2d 712, 1996 N.H. LEXIS 17 (1996).

Superior court erroneously dismissed petition for declaratory judgment and injunctive relief, challenging validity of amendments to zoning ordinance, based on 30-day requirement of this section. Blue Jay Realty Trust v. City of Franklin, 132 N.H. 502, 567 A.2d 188, 1989 N.H. LEXIS 128 (1989).

3. Conflict of laws

Second suit provision of RSA 508:10 applied to zoning board of adjustment appeal brought pursuant to this section. Since defendants' voluntary nonsuit in their appeal was not a judgment on the merits, RSA 508:10 authorized defendants to revive their appeal if revival would not be manifestly unjust to opposing party. Town of Plaistow v. Riddle, 141 N.H. 307, 681 A.2d 650, 1996 N.H. LEXIS 94 (1996).

Provisions of "second suit" statute set forth in RSA 508:10 applied to appeals originally brought in superior court pursuant to this section. Doggett v. Town of N. Hampton Zoning Bd. of Adjustment, 138 N.H. 744, 645 A.2d 673, 1994 N.H. LEXIS 97 (1994).

4. Standing to appeal

Mere fact that an individual is a taxpaying resident of a town does not give that individual standing to seek mandamus relief requiring the town to enforce its zoning ordinances. Pursuant to RSA 676:5, 677:2, 677:4, an individual can seek relief before a zoning board of appeals or in the courts with regard to a zoning officer's decision only if the individual is an "aggrieved person," which requires a showing that he or she has some direct, definite interest in the outcome of the zoning decision itself, and the mere fact that an individual lives and/or pays taxes to a town, does not, by itself, give that individual a direct, definite interest in town zoning decisions. Goldstein v. Town of Bedford, 154 N.H. 393, 910 A.2d 1158, 2006 N.H. LEXIS 173 (Nov. 22, 2006).

Superior court properly dismissed the mandamus petition filed by a town resident, seeking to require the town to enforce its zoning ordinances, because the resident was not an "aggrieved person," which was required for him to have standing under RSA 677:4 to seek judicial review of actions taken by the town's zoning board of adjustment. The mere fact that the resident lived in, and paid taxes to, the town did not give him a direct, definite interest in the zoning decision that he challenged, which pertained to permits obtained by a third party with regard to his nonconforming lots. Goldstein v. Town of Bedford, 154 N.H. 393, 910 A.2d 1158, 2006 N.H. LEXIS 173 (Nov. 22, 2006).

Where the applicant sought permission to build a gas station, the challengers to the applicant would have been a competing gas station, and the challengers' property was located within 1,000 feet of the applicant's property and within a groundwater conservation district, under which circumstances the amended zoning code barred new gas stations, the challengers had standing under RSA 677:4 to appeal the decision of the zoning board of adjustment, as the challengers were directly affected by the proceedings pursuant to RSA 677:2. Thomas v. Town of Hooksett, 153 N.H. 717, 903 A.2d 963, 2006 N.H. LEXIS 99 (2006).

Where the legislature did not intend to grant standing to request a rehearing to all municipal boards that could initiate an appeal, a town conservation commission lacked standing to request a rehearing or to appeal a zoning board decision. Hooksett Conservation Comm'n v. Hooksett Zoning Bd. of Adjustment, 149 N.H. 63, 816 A.2d 948, 2003 N.H. LEXIS 5 (2003).

Aggrievement is found when the appellant shows a direct definite interest in the outcome of the proceedings; the existence of this interest, and the resultant standing to appeal, is a factual determination in each case. Caspersen v. Town of Lyme, 139 N.H. 637, 661 A.2d 759, 1995 N.H. LEXIS 70 (1995).

The plaintiffs did not have a sufficient interest in contesting the effect of a zoning ordinance on the availability of low- or moderate-income housing so as to be aggrieved by the alleged exclusionary effect of the ordinance where they admitted that they were not in the construction business and had no present or future intention to provide low- or moderate-income housing on their own land. Caspersen v. Town of Lyme, 139 N.H. 637, 661 A.2d 759, 1995 N.H. LEXIS 70 (1995).

The plaintiffs' properties were too remote from a proposed hospital addition, which was to house an exercise and rehabilitation center open to both patients and the public, to be sufficiently affected by the zoning board of appeal's decision so as to confer standing, as the only adverse impact that might be felt by the plaintiffs as a result of the decision was that of increased competition with their businesses. Nautilus of Exeter, Inc. v. Town of Exeter, 139 N.H. 450, 656 A.2d 407, 1995 N.H. LEXIS 28 (1995).

Persons entitled to protest by reason of ownership of property in, or adjoining, or across from, an area sought to be rezoned could be regarded as having a direct pecuniary interest in the change and, as such, to be entitled to review. Towle v. Nashua, 106 N.H. 394, 212 A.2d 204, 1965 N.H. LEXIS 177 (1965). (Decided under prior law.)

5. Prior law

Prior to the 1949 amendment, the provision for an appeal from the city government to the superior court was held to confer the same right of appeal as that granted from the board of adjustment (Scott v. Davis, 94 NH 35, 45 A2d 654, 1946 N.H. LEXIS 137 (1946)). The right of appeal was analogous to the award of a new trial by which the previous verdict is entirely set aside and the case heard anew (Scott v. Davis, 94 NH 35, 45 A2d 654, 1946 N.H. LEXIS 137 (1946); Vogel v. Board of Adjustment for City of Manchester, 92 NH 195, 27 A2d 105,

1942 N.H. LEXIS 55 (1942)) and the appellate court heard the case like an original action (Vogel v. Board of Adjustment for City of Manchester, 92 NH 195, 27 A2d 105, 1942 N.H. LEXIS 55 (1942)) and could substitute its judgment for that of either the city government or board of adjustment (Scott v. Davis, 94 NH 35, 45 A2d 654, 1946 N.H. LEXIS 137 (1946)).

6. Prerequisite for appeal

The filing of an application for rehearing on a decision of a zoning board of adjustment was a precondition of appeal to the court by an aggrieved person. Shaw v. City of Manchester, 118 N.H. 158, 384 A.2d 491, 1978 N.H. LEXIS 364 (1978). (Decided under prior law.)

Under the statutory scheme for zoning, an application for a variance was to be first directed to the zoning board of adjustment, and the superior court only had jurisdiction to hear appeals from decisions of the zoning board of adjustment. Town of Derry v. Simonsen, 117 N.H. 1010, 380 A.2d 1101, 1977 N.H. LEXIS 485 (1977). (Decided under prior law.)

The statutory scheme for zoning in this state was geared to the proposition that the board of adjustment was to have a first opportunity to correct any action it had taken, if correction was necessary, before an appeal to the court was filed; thus a party could not appeal the decision of a board of adjustment to the superior court without first applying for a rehearing before the board under former RSA 31:74 (now covered by RSA 677:2). Bourassa v. City of Keene, 108 N.H. 261, 234 A.2d 112, 1967 N.H. LEXIS 168 (1967). (Decided under prior law.)

The statutory scheme for zoning contemplated that the parties were to exhaust their administrative remedies prior to the court appeal. Bourassa v. City of Keene, 108 N.H. 261, 234 A.2d 112, 1967 N.H. LEXIS 168 (1967). (Decided under prior law.)

7. Filing of appeal

Where a zoning board of adjustment denied a realty company's request for a variance and special exception for construction on November 3, 1975, but later granted the variance and special exception on January 5, 1976, after the realty company had filed a timely motion for rehearing, and the plaintiff properly applied for a rehearing on January 12, 1976, but was notified by board on January 20, 1976, that the hearing of January 5, 1976, was a rehearing and that his next move was to appeal to the superior court, the plaintiff was an aggrieved party as a result of the January 5, 1976, order and the board's notification to him amounted to denial of a rehearing, at which time the limit on appeal began to run, so that his appeal to the superior court on February 10, 1976, was timely as being within 30 days from the day action complained of had been recorded. Shaw v. City of Manchester, 118 N.H. 158, 384 A.2d 491, 1978 N.H. LEXIS 364 (1978). (Decided under prior law.)

An appeal was untimely where it was not filed within thirty days after the action of the board of adjustment was recorded, and lack of written notice was no defense as such notice was not required by statute. Salmonsen v. Town of Rindge, 113 N.H. 46, 299 A.2d 926, 1973 N.H. LEXIS 196 (1973). (Decided under prior law.)

Under the statute, in order to transfer the cause to the superior court, an appellant was required to do no more than to seasonably file the appeal. Kelley v. Hopkinton Village Precinct, 108 N.H. 206, 231 A.2d 269, 1967 N.H. LEXIS 155 (1967). (Decided under prior law.)

8. Statement of grounds for appeal

The filing of a document entitled "Appeal from Board of Adjustment" did not alone constitute compliance with the statute for this so-called appeal failed to claim that the board of adjustment decision was illegal, unjust or unreasonable and failed to specify any grounds for an appeal. Town of Derry v. Diorio, 113 N.H. 375, 308 A.2d 523, 1973 N.H. LEXIS 279 (1973). (Decided under prior law.)

9. Notification of other parties of filing of appeal—Generally

This statute and former RSA 31:78 and 31:79 (now covered by RSA 677:6 and 677:7) imposed no requirement of notice to any party in advance of filing of an appeal. Kelley v. Hopkinton Village Precinct, 108 N.H. 206, 231 A.2d 269, 1967 N.H. LEXIS 155 (1967). (Decided under prior law.)

Upon the seasonable filing of an appeal under the statute, the superior court was vested with jurisdiction of the subject matter, and the fact that the order of notice first issued was erroneously directed to the wrong party did not operate to divest the court's jurisdiction, even though proper notice remained to be given. Kelley v. Hopkinton Village Precinct, 108 N.H. 206, 231 A.2d 269, 1967 N.H. LEXIS 155 (1967). (Decided under prior law.)

10. Continuance pending notification of appeal

The provisions of RSA 514:3, relating to continuances pending notification of a party of an action, applied to an appeal under this statute. Kelley v. Hopkinton Village Precinct, 108 N.H. 206, 231 A.2d 269, 1967 N.H. LEXIS 155 (1967). (Decided under prior law.)

Cited:

Cited in Narbonne v. Town of Rye, 130 N.H. 70, 534 A.2d 388, 1987 N.H. LEXIS 271 (1987); Margate Motel, Inc. v. Town of Gilford, 130 N.H. 91, 534 A.2d 717, 1987 N.H. LEXIS 272 (1987); New London Land Use Ass'n v. New London Zoning Bd. of Adjustment, 130 N.H. 510, 543 A.2d 1385, 1988 N.H. LEXIS 39 (1988); McGovern v. City of Manchester, 130 N.H. 628, 546 A.2d 1057, 1988 N.H. LEXIS 54 (1988); Jensen's, Inc. v. City of Dover, 130 N.H. 761, 547 A.2d 277, 1988 N.H. LEXIS 60 (1988); Crossley v. Pelham, 133 N.H. 215, 578 A.2d 319, 1990 N.H. LEXIS 64 (1990); Bow School Dist. v. Quentin W., 750 F. Supp. 546, 1990 U.S. Dist. LEXIS 15500 (D.N.H. 1990); Allen v. Wetlands Bd., 133 N.H. 379, 577 A.2d 92, 1990 N.H. LEXIS 71 (1990); Portsmouth Advocates, Inc. v. City of Portsmouth, 133 N.H. 876, 587 A.2d 600, 1991 N.H. LEXIS 13 (1991); Korpi v. Town of Peterborough, 135 N.H. 37, 599 A.2d 130, 1991 N.H. LEXIS 142 (1991); Quinlan v. City of Dover, 136 N.H. 226, 614 A.2d 1057, 1992 N.H. LEXIS 159 (1992); Grey Rocks Land Trust v. Town of Hebron, 136 N.H. 239, 614 A.2d 1048, 1992 N.H. LEXIS 162 (1992); Asselin v. Town of Conway, 137 N.H. 368, 628 A.2d 247, 1993 N.H. LEXIS 89 (1993); Nestor v. Town of Meredith Zoning Board of Adjustment, 138 N.H. 632, 644 A.2d 548, 1994 N.H. LEXIS 77 (1994); Carnie v. Town of Richmond, 139 N.H. 21, 648 A.2d 205, 1994 N.H. LEXIS 99 (1994); City of Portsmouth v. Schlesinger, 57 F.3d 12, 1995 U.S. App. LEXIS 14582 (1st. Cir. 1995); Husnander v. Town of Barnstead, 139 N.H. 476, 660 A.2d 477, 1995 N.H. LEXIS 36 (1995); Ray's Stateline Market, Inc. v. Town of Pelham, 140 N.H. 139, 665 A.2d 1068, 1995 N.H. LEXIS 111 (1995); Conforti v. City of Manchester, 141 N.H. 78, 677 A.2d 147, 1996 N.H. LEXIS 52 (1996); Bourne v. Town of Madison, 494 F. Supp. 2d 80, 2007 U.S. Dist. LEXIS 47625 (June 29, 2007).

RESEARCH REFERENCES

New Hampshire Practice.

15 N.H.P. Land Use Planning and Zoning §§ 7.15, 16.01, 21.16, 25.01–25.03, 26.03, 35.15, 36.10, 36.17, 37.04, 39.03.

New Hampshire Bar Journal.

For article, "Lex Loci: A Survey of New Hampshire Supreme Court Decisions," see N.H.B.J. 46 (Spring 2006).

677:5. Priority.

Any hearing by the superior court upon an appeal under RSA 677:4 shall be given priority on the court calendar.

Source.

1983, 447:1, eff. Jan. 1, 1984.

RESEARCH REFERENCES

New Hampshire Court Rules Annotated.

Docketing of cases for trial generally, see Rules 10 and 11, Rules of the Superior Court, New Hampshire Court Rules Annotated.

New Hampshire Practice.

15 N.H.P. Land Use Planning and Zoning § 25.07.

677:6. Burden of Proof.

In an appeal to the court, the burden of proof shall be upon the party seeking to set aside any order or decision of the zoning board of adjustment or any decision of the local legislative body to show that the order or decision is unlawful or unreasonable. All findings of the zoning board of adjustment or the local legislative body upon all questions of fact properly before the court shall be prima facie lawful and reasonable. The order or decision appealed from shall not be set aside or vacated, except for errors of law, unless the court is persuaded by the balance of probabilities, on the evidence before it, that said order or decision is unreasonable.

Source.
1983, 447:1, eff. Jan. 1, 1984.

Cross References.
Evidence considered on appeal, see RSA 677:10.

Hearing on appeal, see RSA 677:13.

NOTES TO DECISIONS

Analysis

1. Prior law
2. Nature of proceedings generally
3. Presumptions
4. Standard of review
5. Particular cases
6. Remand to zoning board of adjustment

1. Prior law

On an appeal from the decision of the city government in a zoning case, the burden of proof in the superior court remained upon the party who had the burden of proving a public need for the amendment of the zoning ordinance. Scott v. Davis, 94 N.H. 35, 45 A.2d 654, 1946 N.H. LEXIS 137 (1946). (Decided under prior law.)

2. Nature of proceedings generally

The decision of the board of adjustment was deemed on appeal to be prima facie lawful and reasonable upon all questions of fact before the board and could not be upset on appeal, except for errors of law, unless the court was persuaded by the balance of probabilities that the decision was unjust or unreasonable; although the court could receive additional evidence on the appeal, the decision of the board could not be overturned except for the foregoing reasons, and there was no trial de novo. Glidden v. Town of Nottingham, 109 N.H. 134, 244 A.2d 430, 1968 N.H. LEXIS 137 (1968). (Decided under prior law.)

There was no trial de novo before the court under the statute. Gelinas v. City of Portsmouth, 97 N.H. 248, 85 A.2d 896, 1952 N.H. LEXIS 3 (1952); Conery v. Nashua, 103 N.H.

16, 164 A.2d 247, 1960 N.H. LEXIS 3 (1960); HIK Corp. v. City of Manchester, 103 N.H. 378, 172 A.2d 368, 1961 N.H. LEXIS 55 (1961). (Decided under prior law.)

Under the statute additional evidence could be introduced in superior court, but there was no trial de novo. Beaudoin v. Rye Beach Village District, 116 N.H. 768, 369 A.2d 618, 1976 N.H. LEXIS 466 (1976), overruled on other grounds, Cook v. Sanbornton, 118 N.H. 668, 392 A.2d 1201, 1978 N.H. LEXIS 267 (1978), questioned by, Barry v. Amherst, 121 N.H. 335, 430 A.2d 132, 1981 N.H. LEXIS 314 (1981). (Decided under prior law.)

3. Presumptions

A statutory presumption exists that a zoning board's findings are prima facie lawful and reasonable, and they may be set aside only when a court is persuaded by the balance of probabilities, on the evidence before it, that said order or decision is unlawful or unreasonable. Korpi v. Town of Peterborough, 135 N.H. 37, 599 A.2d 130, 1991 N.H. LEXIS 142 (1991).

A presumption exists that zoning board's findings are prima facie lawful and reasonable, and they may be set aside only when a court is persuaded by the balance of probabilities, on the evidence before it, that said order or decision is unreasonable. Rowe v. Town of N. Hampton, 131 N.H. 424, 553 A.2d 1331, 1989 N.H. LEXIS 5 (1989).

All findings of a zoning board of adjustment, upon all questions of fact properly before it, were deemed to be prima facie lawful and reasonable, and the decision appealed from could not be set aside, except for errors of law, unless the court was persuaded, by a balance of probabilities, on the evidence before it, that the decision was unreasonable. Biggs v. Town of Sandwich, 124 N.H. 421, 470 A.2d 928, 1984 N.H. LEXIS 211 (1984). (Decided under prior law.)

The factual findings of a zoning board of adjustment were deemed prima facie lawful and reasonable on appeal. Richardson v. Town of Salisbury, 123 N.H. 93, 455 A.2d 1059, 1983 N.H. LEXIS 231 (1983). (Decided under prior law.)

All findings of the zoning board were deemed prima facie reasonable and lawful. Barrington East Cluster I Unit Owners' Association v. Town of Barrington, 121 N.H. 627, 433 A.2d 1266, 1981 N.H. LEXIS 385 (1981). (Decided under prior law.)

In a zoning appeal, there was a statutory presumption that all findings of a zoning board of adjustment were prima facie lawful and reasonable. Pappas v. City of Manchester Zoning Board, 117 N.H. 622, 376 A.2d 885, 1977 N.H. LEXIS 395 (1977). (Decided under prior law.)

Where a question presented on appeal was a question of law, the court was not bound by the conclusions of the zoning board. Gratton v. Pellegrino, 115 N.H. 619, 348 A.2d 349, 1975 N.H. LEXIS 379 (1975). (Decided under prior law.)

4. Standard of review

State supreme court affirmed the trial court's decision that affirmed the decision of the zoning board of appeals; the trial court had to treat the factual findings of the zoning board of appeals as prima facie lawful and reasonable, and, under that standard, the findings that the cost and liability decisions that the zoning board of appeals imposed on the property owner of record in order to obtain a requested variance were neither arbitrary nor unreasonable. Robinson v. Town of Hudson, 154 N.H. 563, 914 A.2d 239, 2006 N.H. LEXIS 200 (2006).

Regardless of whether the trial court correctly reviewed a planning board's decision denying site approval under RSA 677:15 or incorrectly reviewed it under RSA 677:6, the provision applicable to appeals from zoning board decisions, the standard of review was the same, and the trial court properly found no legal error and sufficient evidence supporting the planning board's determination that a proposed site plan for a neighborhood shopping center failed to comply with landscaping and buffer zone regulations; there was no denial of due process or equal protection to the owner and developer, because the denial was without prejudice to submission of complying plans, and because a statute regarding disqualification of board members did not preclude them from raising the issue before the board. Bayson Props. v. City of Lebanon, 150 N.H. 167, 834 A.2d 202, 2003 N.H. LEXIS 159 (2003).

Superior court was not to set aside or vacate the decision of a zoning board of adjustment except for errors of law, unless the court was persuaded by the balance of probabilities, on the evidence before it, that the order or decision was unreasonable; the evidence supported the grant of a variance to build a barn where the applicants showed an unnecessary hardship in that the zoning interfered with the reasonable use of the property, considering its unique setting in its environment. 8 Bonnita Rancourt v. City of Manchester, 149 N.H. 51, 816 A.2d 1011, 2003 N.H. LEXIS 2 (2003).

Construction of terms of a zoning ordinance is a question of law, upon which court is not bound by interpretations of zoning board. Sundberg v. Greenville Bd. of Adjustment, 144 N.H. 341, 740 A.2d 1068, 1999 N.H. LEXIS 119 (1999).

Trial court's decision is limited to determination of whether, on balance of probabilities, decision of board was unlawful or unreasonable. Bartlett v. Town of Kingston, 142 N.H. 702, 708 A.2d 60, 1998 N.H. LEXIS 21 (1998).

When construing zoning appeals, the superior court must treat all findings of the zoning board of appeals as prima facie lawful. Dube v. Town of Hudson, 140 N.H. 135, 663 A.2d 626, 1995 N.H. LEXIS 113 (1995).

When construing zoning appeals, the order or decision appealed from must not be set aside or vacated, except for errors of law, unless the court is persuaded by the balance of probabilities, on the evidence before it, that the order or decision is unreasonable. Dube v. Town of Hudson, 140 N.H. 135, 663 A.2d 626, 1995 N.H. LEXIS 113 (1995).

A zoning board's decision is subject to limited judicial review, and the appealing party must show that the decision is unlawful or unreasonable. Labrecque v. Town of Salem, 128 N.H. 455, 514 A.2d 829, 1986 N.H. LEXIS 314 (1986). (Decided under prior law.)

A zoning board's decision is subject to limited judicial review, and the appealing party must show that the decision is unlawful or unreasonable. Labrecque v. Town of Salem, 128 N.H. 455, 514 A.2d 829, 1986 N.H. LEXIS 314 (1986). (Decided under prior law.)

Whether an appeal could be sustained depended on whether the record before the board, together with such other evidence as might have been received by the court, persuaded the court that the order of the board was unjust or unreasonable. HIK Corp. v. City of Manchester, 103 N.H. 378, 172 A.2d 368, 1961 N.H. LEXIS 55 (1961). (Decided under prior law.)

A court could not substitute its judgment for that of zoning board of adjustment; on appeal from an order, the order could not be set aside or vacated except for errors of law, unless the court was persuaded by the balance of probabilities that the order or decision was unjust or unreasonable. Pappas v. City of Manchester Zoning Board, 117 N.H. 622, 376 A.2d 885, 1977 N.H. LEXIS 395 (1977). (Decided under prior law.)

The statute did not impose an absolute requirement that the board's decision be erroneous as a matter of law before a trial judge could change it; the court was required only to inquire whether there was such error when it was not persuaded by the balance of the probabilities, on the evidence before it, that said order or decision was unjust or unreasonable. Cook v. Sanbornton, 118 N.H. 668, 392 A.2d 1201, 1978 N.H. LEXIS 267 (1978). (Decided under prior law.) See also Ouimette v. City of Somersworth, 119 N.H. 292, 402 A.2d 159, 1979 N.H. LEXIS 300 (1979); Associated Home Utilities, Inc. v. Town of Bedford, 120 N.H. 812, 424 A.2d 186, 1980 N.H. LEXIS 395 (1980); Belanger v. City of Nashua, 121 N.H. 389, 430 A.2d 166, 1981 N.H. LEXIS 328 (1981); Colby v. Town of Rye, 122 N.H. 991, 453 A.2d 1270, 1982 N.H. LEXIS 507 (1982); Richardson v. Town of Salisbury, 123 N.H. 93, 455 A.2d 1059, 1983 N.H. LEXIS 231 (1983). (Decided under prior law.)

5. Particular cases

Where property owners applied to town planning board to further subdivide lots that were previously subdivided, the town's planning board and zoning board of adjustment erred in denying the applications on the basis that owners did not adhere to the density requirements of the town's zoning ordinance and because they were not consistent with the original intent of the cluster subdivision approvals because (1) RSA 672:14(I) provided that a resubdivision was included in the term "subdivision,"

and (2) because the specific density provisions of the local ordinance had been eliminated. Furthermore, inconsistency with the intent of the original subdivision was not a proper ground for denying the applications and the owners were entitled to have their new applications reviewed on their own merits under the applicable regulations, unconstrained by the prior subdivision approval. Feins v. Town of Wilmot, 154 N.H. 715, 919 A.2d 788, 2007 N.H. LEXIS 5 (2007).

In a zoning appeal wherein a trial court reversed a city's denial of an applicant's variance request to build a halfway house on the basis that it was a correctional facility that was not permitted within any of the city's zoning districts, the reviewing court reversed the trial court because no evidence existed in the record that demonstrated how the size and layout of the specific building proposed made the property particularly appropriate for the proposed use, no evidence demonstrated that the proposed site was unique, nor did the evidence reasonably support the trial court's conclusion that the applicant's property was burdened by the restriction in a manner that was distinct from similarly situated property. Thus, the applicant did not satisfy the first prong of the Simplex test to establish unnecessary hardship. Cmty. Res. for Justice, Inc. v. City of Manchester, 154 N.H. 748, 917 A.2d 707, 2007 N.H. LEXIS 11 (2007).

6. Remand to zoning board of adjustment

Nothing in the plain language of RSA 677:6, RSA 677:10, RSA 677:13 or RSA 677:11 or in the New Hampshire case law prevented a superior court from remanding a matter to a Zoning Board of Adjustment for clarification based on the preexisting record. However, the remand was not an opportunity for any party to enlarge the record or to introduce new evidence. Kalil v. Town of Dummer Zoning Bd. of Adjustment, 155 N.H. 307, 922 A.2d 672, 2007 N.H. LEXIS 57 (2007).

Cited:

Cited in Chester Rod & Gun Club, Inc. v. Town of Chester, 152 N.H. 577, 883 A.2d 1034, 2005 N.H. LEXIS 137 (2005); Nadeau v. Town of Durham, 129 N.H. 663, 531 A.2d 335, 1987 N.H. LEXIS 230 (1987); Saturley v. Town of Hollis, 129 N.H. 757, 533 A.2d 29, 1987 N.H. LEXIS 256 (1987); Narbonne v. Town of Rye, 130 N.H. 70, 534 A.2d 388, 1987 N.H. LEXIS 271 (1987); Margate Motel, Inc. v. Town of

Gilford, 130 N.H. 91, 534 A.2d 717, 1987 N.H. LEXIS 272 (1987); Goslin v. Town of Farmington, 132 N.H. 48, 561 A.2d 507, 1989 N.H. LEXIS 68 (1989); Peter Christian's Inc. v. Town of Hanover, 132 N.H. 677, 569 A.2d 758, 1990 N.H. LEXIS 7 (1990); Lake Sunapee Protective Ass'n v. New Hampshire Wetlands Board, 133 N.H. 98, 574 A.2d 1368, 1990 N.H. LEXIS 38 (1990); Crossley v. Pelham, 133 N.H. 215, 578 A.2d 319, 1990 N.H. LEXIS 64 (1990); Bow School Dist. v. Quentin W., 750 F. Supp. 546, 1990 U.S. Dist. LEXIS 15500 (D.N.H. 1990); Portsmouth Advocates, Inc. v. City of Portsmouth, 133 N.H. 876, 587 A.2d 600, 1991 N.H. LEXIS 13 (1991); Daniel v. B & J Realty, 134 N.H. 174, 589 A.2d 998, 1991 N.H. LEXIS 43 (1991); Quinlan v. City of Dover, 136 N.H. 226, 614 A.2d 1057, 1992 N.H. LEXIS 159 (1992); Grey Rocks Land Trust v. Town of Hebron, 136 N.H. 239, 614 A.2d 1048, 1992 N.H. LEXIS 162 (1992); Ray's Stateline Market, Inc. v. Town of Pelham, 140 N.H. 139, 665 A.2d 1068, 1995 N.H. LEXIS 111 (1995); Peabody v. Town of Windham, 142 N.H. 488, 703 A.2d 886, 1997 N.H. LEXIS 121 (1997); Gray v. Seidel, 143 N.H. 327, 726 A.2d 1283, 1999 N.H. LEXIS 5 (1999); Mountain Valley Mall Assocs. v. Municipality of Conway, 144 N.H. 642, 745 A.2d 481, 2000 N.H. LEXIS 1 (2000); Heron Cove Ass'n v. DVMD Holdings, Inc., 146 N.H 211, 769 A.2d 373, 2001 N.H. LEXIS 60 (2001); Cosseboom v. Town of Epsom, 146 N.H. 311, 771 A.2d 565, 2001 N.H. LEXIS 76 (2001); Hynes v. Hale, 146 N.H. 533, 776 A.2d 722, 2001 N.H. LEXIS 111 (2001); NBAC Corp. v. Town of Weare, 147 N.H. 328, 786 A.2d 867, 2001 N.H. LEXIS 219 (2001).

RESEARCH REFERENCES

New Hampshire Practice.
15 N.H.P. Land Use Planning and Zoning §§ 22.02, 25.10.

New Hampshire Trial Bar News.
For article, "Presumptions in New

Hampshire Law—A Guide Through the Impenetrable Jungle (Part 1)," see 10 N.H. Trial Bar News 55, 60 n.82 (Winter 1990).

677:7. Parties in Interest.

Any person whose rights may be directly affected by the outcome of the appeal may appear and become a party, or the court may order such persons to be joined as parties as justice may require.

Source.
1983, 447:1, eff. Jan. 1, 1984.

Cross References.
Right of appeal generally, see RSA 677:4.

NOTES TO DECISIONS

Parties to appeal
In an appeal from the decision of a zoning board of adjustment, the municipality, rather than its board of adjustment, was the proper party defendant. Kelley v. Hopkinton Village Precinct, 108 N.H. 206, 231 A.2d 269, 1967 N.H. LEXIS 155 (1967). (Decided under prior law.)

Members of the board of adjustment were not proper parties to an appeal from a decision of the board. Kearney v. Hazelton, 84 N.H. 228, 149 A. 78, 1930 N.H. LEXIS 68 (1930). (Decided under prior law.)

RESEARCH REFERENCES

New Hampshire Practice.
15 N.H.P. Land Use Planning and Zoning §§ 16.01, 25.05, 33.05.

ALR.
Standing of civic or property owners' association to challenge zoning board decision (as

aggrieved party). 8 A.L.R.4th 1087.

Standing of municipal corporation or other governmental body to attack zoning of land lying outside its borders. 49 A.L.R.3d 1126.

Standing of owner of property adjacent to zoned property, but not within territory of zoning authority, to attack zoning. 69 A.L.R.3d 805.

Standing of zoning board of appeals or similar body to appeal reversal of its decision. 13 A.L.R.4th 1130.

677:8. Filing Certified Record.

Upon the filing of an appeal, the clerk of court shall issue an order of notice requiring a certified copy of the record appealed from to be filed with the court.

Source.
1983, 447:1, eff. Jan. 1, 1984.

Cross References.
Evidence considered on appeal, see RSA 677:10.

Filing of appeal, see RSA 677:4.

Furnishing of record on appeal, see RSA 677:12.

Hearings on appeal, see RSA 667:13.

NOTES TO DECISIONS

Effect of failure to require certification of record

Where there was sufficient evidence presented at trial from which the court could reasonably and fully decide the issues before it, the trial court did not commit reversible error in not requiring the board of adjustment to certify a copy of its record to the court. Johnston v. Town of Exeter, 121 N.H. 938, 436 A.2d 1147, 1981 N.H. LEXIS 433 (1981). (Decided under prior law.)

RESEARCH REFERENCES

New Hampshire Practice.
15 N.H.P. Land Use Planning and Zoning § 25.06.

677:9. Restraining Order.

The filing of an appeal shall not stay any enforcement proceedings upon the decision appealed from, and shall not have the effect of suspending the decision of the zoning board of adjustment or local legislative body. However, the court, on application and notice, for good cause shown, may grant a restraining order.

Source.
1983, 447:1. 1995, 243:5, eff. Jan. 1, 1996.

Revision note.
Substituted "for" for "on" preceding "good cause".

Amendments
—**1995.** Rewrote the first sentence.

Cross References.
Filing of appeal, see RSA 677:4.

RESEARCH REFERENCES

New Hampshire Court Rules Annotated.
Granting of injunctions and restraining orders generally, see Rules 161–163, Rules of the Superior Court, New Hampshire Court Rules Annotated.

New Hampshire Practice.
15 N.H.P. Land Use Planning and Zoning § 25.08.

677:10. Evidence; How Considered.

All evidence transferred by the zoning board of adjustment or the local legislative body shall be, and all additional evidence received may be, considered by the court regardless of any technical rule which might have rendered the evidence inadmissible if originally offered in the trial of an action at law.

Source.
1983, 447:1, eff. Jan. 1, 1984.

Cross References.
Burden of proof on appeal generally, see RSA 677:6.

Furnishing of record on appeal, see RSA 677:8, 12.

Hearings on appeal, see RSA 677:13.

NOTES TO DECISIONS

Analysis

1. Generally
2. Purpose
3. Consideration of evidence not presented to board of adjustment
4. Admissibility of testimony of members of board of adjustment

1. Generally

Technical rules of evidence did not apply to the admission of evidence in appeals from zoning boards of adjustment. Levesque v. Town of Hudson, 106 N.H. 470, 214 A.2d 553, 1965 N.H. LEXIS 192 (1965), overruled on other grounds, Winslow v. Town of Holderness Planning Board, 125 N.H. 262, 480 A.2d 114, 1984 N.H. LEXIS 281 (1984). (Decided under prior law.)

2. Purpose

Purpose of this section is not to afford a trial de novo but rather to assist the court in evaluating the action of the board. Lake Sunapee Protective Ass'n v. New Hampshire Wetlands Board, 133 N.H. 98, 574 A.2d 1368, 1990 N.H. LEXIS 38 (1990).

The purpose of this statute was not to afford the appealing party a trial de novo, which was no longer available, but rather to assist the court in evaluating the action of the board where the record was incomplete, even though the evidence itself was not presented at the hearing before the board. Sweeney v. City of Dover, 108 N.H. 307, 234 A.2d 521, 1967 N.H. LEXIS 176 (1967), overruled on other grounds, Cook v. Sanbornton, 118 N.H. 668, 392 A.2d 1201, 1978 N.H. LEXIS 267 (1978), questioned by, Barry v. Amherst, 121 N.H. 335, 430 A.2d 132, 1981 N.H. LEXIS 314 (1981). (Decided under prior law.)

3. Consideration of evidence not presented to board of adjustment

Nothing in the plain language of RSA 677:6, RSA 677:10, RSA 677:13 or RSA 677:11 or in the New Hampshire case law prevented a superior court from remanding a matter to a Zoning Board of Adjustment for clarification based on the preexisting record. However, the remand was not an opportunity for any party to enlarge the record or to introduce new evidence. Kalil v. Town of Dummer Zoning Bd. of Adjustment, 155 N.H. 307, 922 A.2d 672, 2007 N.H. LEXIS 57 (2007).

Under this section, if the record of the evidence before the board is either incomplete or nonexistent, a party may present further evidence to the trial court; the additional evidence may be taken into consideration even though it was not before the board. Lake Sunapee Protective Ass'n v. New Hampshire Wetlands Board, 133 N.H. 98, 574 A.2d 1368, 1990 N.H. LEXIS 38 (1990).

To the extent the record of evidence before the zoning board of adjustment was incomplete or nonexistent, an aggrieved party could avail himself of this statute and former RSA 31:85 (now covered by RSA 677:13) and present evidence to the trial court; such additional evidence could be taken into consideration even though it was not before the board. Pappas v. City of Manchester Zoning Board, 117 N.H. 622, 376 A.2d 885, 1977 N.H. LEXIS 395 (1977). (Decided under prior law.)

In an appeal from a board of adjustment, the superior court was authorized under this statute and former RSA 31:85 (now covered by RSA 677:13) to receive evidence in addition to that presented before the board. Conery v. Nashua, 103 N.H. 16, 164 A.2d 247, 1960 N.H. LEXIS 3 (1960). (Decided under prior law.)

4. Admissibility of testimony of members of board of adjustment

The trial court did not abuse its discretion in allowing the chairman of a board of adjustment to testify as to matters not set forth in the minutes of the board meeting relating to the matter on appeal where the minutes were not contradicted, ambiguities were clarified and matters not shown by the bare minutes were brought to the court's attention. Alcorn v. Rochester Zoning Board of Adjustment, 114 N.H. 491, 322 A.2d 608, 1974 N.H. LEXIS 309 (1974). (Decided under prior law.)

It was discretionary with the superior court to admit testimony of members of the board of adjustment as experts. Plourde v. Zoning Board of Adjustment of City of Nashua, 93 N.H. 376, 42 A.2d 736, 1945 N.H. LEXIS 137 (1945); Gelinas v. City of Portsmouth, 97 N.H. 248, 85 A.2d 896, 1952 N.H. LEXIS 3 (1952). (Decided under prior law.)

Cited:

Cited in Peter Christian's Inc. v. Town of Hanover, 132 N.H. 677, 569 A.2d 758, 1990 N.H. LEXIS 7 (1990); Estabrooks v. Town of Jefferson, 134 N.H. 367, 592 A.2d 1154, 1991 N.H. LEXIS 67 (1991); Robinson v. Town of Hudson, 149 N.H. 255, 821 A.2d 959, 2003 N.H. LEXIS 33 (2003).

RESEARCH REFERENCES

New Hampshire Court Rules Annotated.

Admissibility of evidence generally, see Rules of Evidence, New Hampshire Court Rules Annotated.

New Hampshire Practice.

15 N.H.P. Land Use Planning and Zoning § 25.09.

677:11. Judgment.

The final judgment upon every appeal shall be a decree dismissing the appeal, or vacating the order or decision complained of in whole or in part, as the case may be; but, in case such order or decision is wholly or partly vacated, the court may also, in its discretion, remand the matter to the zoning board of adjustment or local legislative body for such further proceedings, not inconsistent with the decree, as justice may require.

Source.

1983, 447:1, eff. Jan. 1, 1984.

Cross References.

Allowance of costs of appeal, see RSA 677:14.

NOTES TO DECISIONS

Analysis

Modification of order of zoning board
Remand

Modification of order of zoning board

The authority of the superior court with respect to zoning appeals did not extend to modification of the order of the zoning board. Perron v. City of Concord, 102 N.H. 32, 150 A.2d 403, 1959 N.H. LEXIS 11 (1959). (Decided under prior law.)

Remand

Nothing in the plain language of RSA 677:6, RSA 677:10, RSA 677:13 or RSA 677:11 or in the New Hampshire case law prevented a superior court from remanding a matter to a Zoning Board of Adjustment for clarification based on the preexisting record. However, the remand was not an opportunity for any party to enlarge the record or to introduce new evidence. Kalil v. Town of Dummer Zoning Bd. of Adjustment, 155 N.H. 307, 922 A.2d 672, 2007 N.H. LEXIS 57 (2007).

New Hampshire Practice.
15 N.H.P. Land Use Planning and Zoning
§ 25.11.

677:12. Appeals to Court: Certifying Record.

An order of court to send up the record may be complied with by filing either the original papers or duly certified copies thereof, or of such portions thereof as the order may specify, together with a certified statement of such other facts as show the grounds of the action appealed from.

Source.
1983, 447:1, eff. Jan. 1, 1984.

Cross References.
Filing of appeal, see RSA 677:4.

Issuance of order of notice by clerk of court, see RSA 677:8.

New Hampshire Practice.
15 N.H.P. Land Use Planning and Zoning
§ 25.06.

677:13. Hearing.

The court may take evidence or appoint a referee to take such evidence as it may direct and report the same with the referee's findings of fact and conclusions of law.

Source.
1983, 447:1. 1995, 243:6, eff. Jan. 1, 1996.

Amendments
—**1995.** Substituted "the referee's" for "his" preceding "findings".

Cross References.
Burden of proof on appeal, see RSA 677:6.
Evidence considered on appeal, see RSA 677:10.

NOTES TO DECISIONS

Consideration of evidence not presented to board of adjustment

Nothing in the plain language of RSA 677:6, RSA 677:10, RSA 677:13 or RSA 677:11 or in the New Hampshire case law prevented a superior court from remanding a matter to a Zoning Board of Adjustment for clarification based on the preexisting record. However, the remand was not an opportunity for any party to enlarge the record or to introduce new evidence. Kalil v. Town of Dummer Zoning Bd. of Adjustment, 155 N.H. 307, 922 A.2d 672, 2007 N.H. LEXIS 57 (2007).

To the extent the record before the zoning board of adjustment was incomplete or nonexistent, an aggrieved party could avail himself of former RSA 31:82 (now covered by RSA 677:10) and this statute and present evidence to the trial court; such additional evidence could be taken into consideration even though it was not before the board. Pappas v. City of Manchester Zoning Board, 117 N.H. 622, 376 A.2d 885, 1977 N.H. LEXIS 395 (1977). (Decided under prior law.)

In an appeal from a board of adjustment, the superior court was authorized under former RSA 31:82 (now covered by RSA 677:10) and this statute to receive evidence in addition to that presented before the board. Conery v. Nashua, 103 N.H. 16, 164 A.2d 247, 1960 N.H. LEXIS 3 (1960). (Decided under prior law.)

Cited:
Cited in Rowe v. Town of N. Hampton, 131

N.H. 424, 553 A.2d 1331, 1989 N.H. LEXIS 5 (1989); Estabrooks v. Town of Jefferson, 134 N.H. 367, 592 A.2d 1154, 1991 N.H. LEXIS 67 (1991).

RESEARCH REFERENCES

New Hampshire Court Rules Annotated.
Appointment of and proceedings before referees, see Rules 81–85-A, Rules of the Superior Court, New Hampshire Court Rules Annotated.

677:14. Costs.

Costs shall not be allowed against the municipality unless it shall appear to the court that the zoning board of adjustment acted in bad faith or with malice or gross negligence in making the decision appealed from.

Source.
1983, 447:1, eff. Jan. 1, 1984.

Cross References.
Judgment on appeal generally, see RSA 677:11.

RESEARCH REFERENCES

New Hampshire Practice.
15 N.H.P. Land Use Planning and Zoning § 25.12.

Appeal and Court Review of Planning Board Decisions

Cross References.
Appeal and review of building code boards of appeals decisions, see RSA 677:16 et seq.

Appeal and review of decisions of local legislative bodies and boards of adjustment, see RSA 677:4 et seq.

Appeals of historic district commission decisions, see RSA 677:17 et seq.

Powers of planning boards generally, see RSA 674:1 et seq., 674:5 et seq., 674:9 et seq., 674:35 et seq., 674:43 et seq.

Procedure for consideration by planning boards of plats or applications for subdivisions, see RSA 676:4.

677:15. Court Review.

I. Any persons aggrieved by any decision of the planning board concerning a plat or subdivision may present to the superior court a petition, duly verified, setting forth that such decision is illegal or unreasonable in whole or in part and specifying the grounds upon which the same is claimed to be illegal or unreasonable. Such petition shall be presented to the court within 30 days after the date upon which the board voted to approve or disapprove the application; provided however, that if the petitioner shows that the minutes of the meeting at which such vote was taken, including the written decision, were not filed within 144 hours of the vote pursuant to RSA 676:3, II, the petitioner shall have the right to amend the petition within 30 days after the date on which the written decision was actually filed. This paragraph shall not apply to planning board decisions appealable to the board of adjustment pursuant to RSA 676:5, III. The 30-day time period shall be counted in calendar days beginning with the date following the date upon which the planning board voted to approve or disapprove the application, in accordance with RSA 21:35.

II. Upon presentation of such petition, the court may allow a certiorari order directed to the planning board to review such decision and shall prescribe therein the time within which return thereto shall be made and served upon the petitioner's attorney, which shall not be less than 10 days and may be extended by the court. The allowance of the order shall stay proceedings upon the decision appealed from. The planning board shall not be required to return the original papers acted upon by it; but it shall be sufficient to return certified or sworn copies thereof, or of such portions thereof as may be called for by such order. The return shall concisely set forth such other facts as may be pertinent and material to show the grounds of the decision appealed from and shall be verified.

III. If, upon the hearing, it shall appear to the court that testimony is necessary for the proper disposition of the matter, it may take evidence or appoint a referee to take such evidence as it may direct and report the same to the court with the referee's findings of fact and conclusion of law, which shall constitute a part of the proceedings upon which the determination of the court shall be made.

IV. The court shall give any hearing under this section priority on the court calendar.

V. The court may reverse or affirm, wholly or partly, or may modify the decision brought up for review when there is an error of law or when the court is persuaded by the balance of probabilities, on the evidence before it, that said decision is unreasonable. Costs shall not be allowed against the municipality unless it shall appear to the court that the planning board acted in bad faith or with malice in making the decision appealed from.

Source.
1983, 447:1. 1991, 231:14. 1995, 243:7, 8, eff. Jan. 1, 1996. 2000, 144:4, eff. Jan. 1, 2001. 2005, 105:2, eff. Aug. 14, 2005.

Amendments
—2005. Paragraph I: Added the last sentence.

—2000. Paragraph I: Rewrote the second sentence.

—1995. Paragraph I: Substituted "decision of the planning board has been filed and first becomes available for public inspection" for "filing of the decision" preceding "in the office" and added "or of its clerk or secretary" at the end of the second sentence.

Paragraph III: Substituted "the referee's" for "his" preceding "findings".

—1991. Paragraph I: Added the third sentence.

NOTES TO DECISIONS

Analysis

1. Construction
2. Application
3. Jurisdiction
4. Persons entitled to review
5. Decisions subject to review
6. Time limitation
7. Verification requirement
8. Evidence
9. Standard of review
10. Proceedings upon receipt of petition by court

1. Construction

Letter from town counsel, advising landowners of planning board's position on consolidation of lots, was not a "decision" of the planning board concerning subdivision, and appeal was therefore not required within thirty days. Blevens v. Town of Bow, 146 N.H. 67, 767 A.2d 446, 2001 N.H. LEXIS 32 (2001).

2. Application

Where property owners applied to town planning board to further subdivide lots that were previously subdivided, the town's planning board and zoning board of adjustment erred in denying the applications on the basis that owners did not adhere to the density requirements of the town's zoning ordinance and because they were not consistent with the original intent of the cluster subdivision approvals because (1) RSA 672:14(I) provided that a resubdivision was included in the term "subdivision," and (2) because the specific density provisions of the local ordinance had been eliminated. Furthermore, inconsistency with the intent of the original subdivision was not a proper ground for denying the applications and the owners were entitled to have their new applications reviewed on their own merits under the applicable regulations, unconstrained by the prior subdivision approval. Feins v. Town of Wilmot, 154 N.H. 715, 919 A.2d 788, 2007 N.H. LEXIS 5 (2007).

Trial court erred in finding, pursuant to RSA 677:15, that the decision of a town planning board to deny a developer's special use permit for failing to address the extent of impact in wetland buffer areas was unlawful and unreasonable. It was neither unlawful nor unreasonable for the board to require the developers to establish that the design and construc-

tion of the proposed subdivision road would minimize detrimental impact upon the wetlands buffer and that no feasible alternative design would have a less detrimental impact. Cherry v. Town of Hampton Falls, 150 N.H. 720, 846 A.2d 508, 2004 N.H. LEXIS 63 (2004).

City satisfied its constitutional burden of assisting a developer seeking site plan approval where the city provided rigorous review, input, hearings, opportunity for public comment, and the opportunity to file evidence on the final day of the hearings; therefore, a trial court erred in finding that the city's planning board incorrectly denied the developer's site plan application. Richmond Co. v. City of Concord, 149 N.H. 312, 821 A.2d 1059, 2003 N.H. LEXIS 43 (2003).

The plaintiffs' properties were too remote from a proposed hospital addition, which was to house an exercise and rehabilitation center open to both patients and the public, to be sufficiently affected by a zoning board of appeal's decision so as to confer standing. The only adverse impact that might be felt by the plaintiffs as a result of the decision was that of increased competition with their businesses. Nautilus of Exeter, Inc. v. Town of Exeter, 139 N.H. 450, 656 A.2d 407, 1995 N.H. LEXIS 28 (1995).

This section authorizes trial court review of planning board decisions and grants the court discretion to hear additional evidence, and to reverse, affirm, or modify unreasonable decisions. Dumont v. Town of Wolfeboro, 137 N.H. 1, 622 A.2d 1238, 1993 N.H. LEXIS 28 (1993).

Superior court erred in reversing planning board's decision approving subdivision lot with restrictions as to location of septic system and buildings, where board's decision replaced an earlier decision approving lot on contingency that study be conducted; board's review of its own decision pursuant to stipulation was analogous to review on rehearing or reconsideration, and board had opportunity to affirm, reject or modify its earlier decision. Deer Leap Assocs. v. Town of Windham, 136 N.H. 555, 618 A.2d 837, 1992 N.H. LEXIS 207 (1992).

3. Jurisdiction

Because an abutter filed its appeal five months after a planning board approved an application for site plan determination, its appeal was untimely under RSA 677:15(I) and, thus, the trial court did not err when it ruled that it lacked jurisdiction to decide the appeal. Prop. Portfolio Group, LLC v. Town of Derry, 154 N.H. 610, 913 A.2d 750, 2006 N.H. LEXIS 206 (Dec. 21, 2006).

Review of a planning board's refusal to accept an application was proper despite the fact that in the absence of an accepted application, it could not be approved or denied; the trial court could properly treat the appeal as a certiorari petition, and exercise jurisdiction in that way. DHB, Inc. v. Town of Pembroke, 152 N.H. 314, 876 A.2d 206, 2005 N.H. LEXIS 99 (2005).

Landowners were required to seek zoning adjustment board review of a planning board's decision to apply only an architectural design review to a parking lot application, and failure to seek board review resulted in the reviewing court's lacking jurisdiction to consider the landowners' appeals. Heartz v. City of Concord, 148 N.H. 325, 808 A.2d 76, 2002 N.H. LEXIS 131 (2002).

Superior court in zoning appeal correctly declined to address propriety of zoning board of adjustment's decision; since plaintiff filed its direct appeal under RSA 677:15, rather than RSA 677:4, superior court lacked jurisdiction beyond evaluating decision of planning board. Mountain Valley Mall Assocs. v. Municipality of Conway, 144 N.H. 642, 745 A.2d 481, 2000 N.H. LEXIS 1 (2000).

4. Persons entitled to review

Despite the fact that neither of two property owners challenging a decision of a planning board approving a subdivision owned property abutting it, where one of them owned property across a public highway from the proposed subdivision and the other owned a right of way across it, with which the approved plan would interfere, where both property owners alleged that increased traffic and noise would reduce their enjoyment of their respective properties, and where they had participated in the hearings before the planning board, they had standing to seek certiorari for review of the planning board decision. Price v. Planning Board, 120 N.H. 481, 417 A.2d 997, 1980 N.H. LEXIS 328 (1980). (Decided under prior law.)

Whether a party had a sufficient interest in the outcome of a planning board or zoning board proceeding to have standing was a factual determination in each case, and the trial court in making its determination could consider factors such as the proximity of plaintiff's property to the site for which approval was sought, the type of change proposed, the immediacy of injury claimed, and plaintiff's participation in the administrative hearings. Hancock v. Concord, 114 N.H. 404, 322 A.2d 605, 1974 N.H. LEXIS 287 (1974), overruled in part, Carter v. City of Nashua, 116 N.H. 466, 362 A.2d 191, 1976 N.H. LEXIS 382 (1976), and, Weeks Restaurant Corp. v. City of Dover, 119 N.H. 541, 404 A.2d 294, 1979 N.H. LEXIS 349 (1979). (Decided under prior law.)

Nonabutters could appeal from planning board decisions under the statute provided they had a definite interest in the outcome. Hancock v. Concord, 114 N.H. 404, 322 A.2d 605, 1974 N.H. LEXIS 287 (1974), overruled in part, Carter v. City of Nashua, 116 N.H. 466, 362 A.2d 191, 1976 N.H. LEXIS 382 (1976), and, Weeks Restaurant Corp. v. City of Dover, 119 N.H. 541, 404 A.2d 294, 1979 N.H. LEXIS 349 (1979). (Decided under prior law.)

5. Decisions subject to review

A decision of a town planning board denying a developer's request for a waiver of certain subdivision requirements, which was claimed to be unreasonable, was a decision of the planning board concerning a subdivision permit, and, therefore, the superior court could consider the developer's petition for review of the planning board's denial of the waiver pursuant to the criteria set forth in the statute. Town of Hinsdale v. Emerson, 122 N.H. 931, 453 A.2d 1249, 1982 N.H. LEXIS 494 (1982). (Decided under prior law.)

A town planning board's conditional approval of a preliminary layout of a subdivision was not a decision of the planning board subject to review where the conditional approval was not a final order, did not create any substantive rights, did not constitute approval of the final plat, did not require the board to give final approval and did not authorize any construction or development. Totty v. Grantham Planning Board, 120 N.H. 388, 415 A.2d 687, 1980 N.H. LEXIS 299 (1980). (Decided under prior law.)

6. Time limitation

Town planning board's decision with respect to a site plan determination was a final appealable decision for purposes of RSA 677:15 where, despite the fact that the applicant for site plan determination submitted the official planning board forms for the application after the fact, the record showed that the proposal submitted

before the hearing, which was sufficiently pub-
licized to abutters and the public, functioned as
an application and the proposal came in response to the town's request for proposals and
met the requirements of that request. Procedural defects shall result in the reversal of a
planning board's actions by judicial action only
when such defects create serious impairment of
opportunity for notice and participation; by
approving the application for site plan determination and, therefore, waiving site plan review,
the planning board followed the expedited procedure for site plan determination set forth in
the applicable regulations and, thus, the proposal was an application upon which a valid
final decision could be made and appealed.
Prop. Portfolio Group, LLC v. Town of Derry,
154 N.H. 610, 913 A.2d 750, 2006 N.H. LEXIS
206 (Dec. 21, 2006).

Town planning board's decision granting approval of applicant's site plan determination
with conditions constituted a final decision that
was appealable to the superior court under
RSA 677:15, I as the conditions were not conditions precedent, which contemplate additional
action on the part of the town and, thus, cannot
constitute final approval, but were actually
conditions subsequent, which do not delay approval; the "condition" for approval in this case
was not required to be fulfilled before any
renovation commenced, and, thus, was a condition subsequent, not a condition precedent.
Furthermore, within the context of the site
plan determination process, what the applicant
received from the planning board was an approval; had the planning board intended that
the applicant go through the rigors of site plan
review, it would have denied the application for
site plan determination. Prop. Portfolio Group,
LLC v. Town of Derry, 154 N.H. 610, 913 A.2d
750, 2006 N.H. LEXIS 206 (Dec. 21, 2006).

Although an applicant for site plan approval
had a right to expect the town to assist with the
application process, instead of failing to respond to the applicant's communications, the
issue was moot; the trial court had lacked
jurisdiction over the applicant's appeal from
the planning board's action application of its
site plan review rules, because of the applicant's failure to seek review within 30 days,
and it lacked jurisdiction over the applicant's
appeal from the planning board's application of
zoning regulations because, in the absence of a
ruling by the zoning board of adjustment, there
was nothing to appeal to the trial court. Route
12 Books & Video v. Town of Troy, 149 N.H. 569,
825 A.2d 493, 2003 N.H. LEXIS 79 (2003).

The triggering event for the start of the
appeal period is the filing of the signed notice of
action. K & J Assocs. v. City of Lebanon, 142
N.H. 331, 703 A.2d 253, 1997 N.H. LEXIS 99
(1997).

Because the plaintiffs failed to appeal the
planning board's decision within the 30-day
period prescribed by this section, subject matter jurisdiction was never conferred upon the
superior court, which remained powerless to
grant the plaintiffs' petition for certiorari. Der-
mody v. Town of Gilford Planning Bd., 137 N.H.
294, 627 A.2d 570, 1993 N.H. LEXIS 71 (1993).

J. E. D. Assocs. v. Atkinson, 121 N.H. 581,
432 A.2d 12, 1981 N.H. LEXIS 367 (1981) is
overruled to the extent it may be read to hold
unqualifiedly that a constitutional objection to
a property disposition required by planning
board regulation need not be litigated by appeal
brought within 30-day period provided by paragraph I of this section. Town of Auburn v.
McEvoy, 131 N.H. 383, 553 A.2d 317, 1988 N.H.
LEXIS 129 (1988).

On appeal of planning board decision approving a subdivision, claim concerning the board's
failure to appoint alternates was properly dismissed where it was not raised within the
30-day period after the filing of the decision in
the office of the planning board. Frisella v. Town
of Farmington, 131 N.H. 78, 550 A.2d 102, 1988
N.H. LEXIS 94 (1988).

7. Verification requirement

Verification requirement in statute governing review of planning board decisions was not
a jurisdictional prerequisite, and thus zoning
applicants' failure to verify petition did not
divest trial court of subject matter jurisdiction.
Simonsen v. Town of Derry, 145 N.H. 382, 765
A.2d 1033, 2000 N.H. LEXIS 73 (2000).

8. Evidence

There was no abuse of discretion in a trial
court's decision, on review of a planning board's
decision to limit the height of a flagpole it would
allow a dealership to erect at its site, not to
allow the dealership to offer an affidavit in
evidence that would supplement the evidence
already before the trial court; the dealership
simply failed to sustain its burden of showing
that concerns about factors such as noise and
lighting were unreasonable bases for the
board's decisions. Summa Humma Enters.,
LLC v. Town of Tilton, 151 N.H. 75, 849 A.2d

146, 2004 N.H. LEXIS 93 (2004).

Although paragraph III of this section refers to a hearing, it does not require the court to conduct one to determine if additional evidence is necessary. Webster v. Town of Candia, 146 N.H. 430, 778 A.2d 402, 2001 N.H. LEXIS 91 (2001); Sanderson v. Town of Candia, 146 N.H. 598, 787 A.2d 167, 2001 N.H. LEXIS 116 (2001).

Where trial court had before it the certified record of planning board proceedings and the pleadings in the instant case as well as those in plaintiff's related cases, it was not an abuse of discretion for the trial court not to admit additional evidence. Webster v. Town of Candia, 146 N.H. 430, 778 A.2d 402, 2001 N.H. LEXIS 91 (2001).

Where the trial court was presented with a voluminous certified record, including audiotapes, a multitude of pleadings and memoranda, and found that the record accurately reflected proposed testimony, it did not abuse its discretion when it precluded live testimony of an expert witness and failed to review videotapes of planning board proceedings. Star Vector Corp. v. Town of Windham, 146 N.H. 490, 776 A.2d 138, 2001 N.H. LEXIS 102 (2001).

Legislature's use of phrase "may take evidence" indicated that appellant was not entitled to a full evidentiary hearing in zoning appeal; rather, it was court's prerogative to determine whether admission of further evidence would advance justice or judicial economy. Mountain Valley Mall Assocs. v. Municipality of Conway, 144 N.H. 642, 745 A.2d 481, 2000 N.H. LEXIS 1 (2000).

The practical effect of the statute providing for court review of planning board decisions was to broaden the scope of review by way of certiorari by granting to the superior court discretion to receive and to consider additional evidence when it was deemed necessary. Price v. Planning Board, 120 N.H. 481, 417 A.2d 997, 1980 N.H. LEXIS 328 (1980). (Decided under prior law.)

The court did not abuse its discretion by not allowing a full evidentiary hearing on a petition for certiorari to review a planning board's decision approving a subdivision where the trial court had the record of proceedings before the board, as well as the arguments of counsel, before it and, given the nature of the issues involved, the court could well have concluded that receiving further evidence would not advance justice or judicial economy. Price v. Planning Board, 120 N.H. 481, 417 A.2d 997, 1980

N.H. LEXIS 328 (1980). (Decided under prior law.)

9. Standard of review

Regardless of whether the trial court correctly reviewed a planning board's decision denying site approval under RSA 677:15 or incorrectly reviewed it under RSA 677:6, the provision applicable to appeals from zoning board decisions, the standard of review was the same, and the trial court properly found no legal error and sufficient evidence supporting the planning board's determination that a proposed site plan for a neighborhood shopping center failed to comply with landscaping and buffer zone regulations; there was no denial of due process or equal protection to the owner and developer, because the denial was without prejudice to submission of complying plans, and because a statute regarding disqualification of board members did not preclude them from raising the issue before the board. Bayson Props. v. City of Lebanon, 150 N.H. 167, 834 A.2d 202, 2003 N.H. LEXIS 159 (2003).

When reviewing superior court's disposition of appeals from planning board, supreme court will uphold trial court unless its decision is not supported by evidence or is legally erroneous. Mountain Valley Mall Assocs. v. Municipality of Conway, 144 N.H. 642, 745 A.2d 481, 2000 N.H. LEXIS 1 (2000).

Superior court's decision on review of planning board action will not be overturned unless unsupported by evidence or legally erroneous. Deer Leap Assocs. v. Town of Windham, 136 N.H. 555, 618 A.2d 837, 1992 N.H. LEXIS 207 (1992).

A decision of a planning board could not be set aside by the superior court unless there was an error of law or unless the court was persuaded, by the balance of probabilities, on the evidence before it, that the decision was unreasonable. Durant v. Town of Dunbarton, 121 N.H. 352, 430 A.2d 140, 1981 N.H. LEXIS 318 (1981). (Decided under prior law.)

10. Proceedings upon receipt of petition by court

Under the statute, a justice of the superior court was required to review the petition to determine whether a certiorari order should issue. Price v. Planning Board, 120 N.H. 481, 417 A.2d 997, 1980 N.H. LEXIS 328 (1980). (Decided under prior law.)

It was for the trial court to determine from the petition, together with any other pleadings, whether a certiorari order should issue. Price v. Planning Board, 120 N.H. 481, 417 A.2d 997, 1980 N.H. LEXIS 328 (1980). (Decided under prior law.)

Under the statute, a certiorari order to a planning board directed the board to forward its record to the superior court. Price v. Planning Board, 120 N.H. 481, 417 A.2d 997, 1980 N.H. LEXIS 328 (1980). (Decided under prior law.)

Under the statute, the superior court was not provided with authority to order what amounted to a rehearing; the review mentioned was to be performed by the court subsequent to its decision that a certiorari order should issue. Price v. Planning Board, 120 N.H. 481, 417 A.2d 997, 1980 N.H. LEXIS 328 (1980). (Decided under prior law.)

An order of notice from the superior court to a planning board, directing the board to reconsider its opinion regarding intervenors' subdivision, was erroneous, since the statute required review by the court itself subsequent to its decision that a certiorari order should issue; because the board declined to review or reconsider its opinion, the error was harmless. Price v. Planning Board, 120 N.H. 481, 417 A.2d 997, 1980 N.H. LEXIS 328 (1980). (Decided under prior law.)

Cited:

Cited in Cutting v. Town of Wentworth, 126 N.H. 727, 497 A.2d 839, 1985 N.H. LEXIS 422 (1985); Rancourt v. Town of Barnstead, 129 N.H. 45, 523 A.2d 55, 1986 N.H. LEXIS 379 (1986); Nadeau v. Town of Durham, 129 N.H. 663, 531 A.2d 335, 1987 N.H. LEXIS 230 (1987); Victorian Realty Group v. City of Nashua, 130 N.H. 60, 534 A.2d 381, 1987 N.H. LEXIS 278 (1987); Bedford Residents Group v.

Town of Bedford, 130 N.H. 632, 547 A.2d 225, 1988 N.H. LEXIS 65 (1988); Morin v. City of Somersworth, 131 N.H. 253, 551 A.2d 527, 1988 N.H. LEXIS 109 (1988); Condos East Corp. v. Town of Conway, 132 N.H. 431, 566 A.2d 1136, 1989 N.H. LEXIS 121 (1989); Quality Discount Market Corp. v. Laconia Planning Board, 132 N.H. 734, 571 A.2d 271, 1990 N.H. LEXIS 18 (1990); K & P, Inc. v. Town of Plaistow, 133 N.H. 283, 575 A.2d 804, 1990 N.H. LEXIS 50 (1990); Bow School Dist. v. Quentin W., 750 F. Supp. 546, 1990 U.S. Dist. LEXIS 15500 (D.N.H. 1990); Ossipee Auto Parts, Inc. v. Ossipee Planning Bd., 134 N.H. 401, 593 A.2d 241, 1991 N.H. LEXIS 74 (1991); Zukis v. Town of Fitzwilliam, 135 N.H. 384, 604 A.2d 956, 1992 N.H. LEXIS 46 (1992); Batakis v. Town of Belmont, 135 N.H. 595, 607 A.2d 956, 1992 N.H. LEXIS 88 (1992); Lampert v. Town of Hudson, 136 N.H. 196, 612 A.2d 920, 1992 N.H. LEXIS 143 (1992); Smith v. Town of Wolfeboro, 136 N.H. 337, 615 A.2d 1252, 1992 N.H. LEXIS 176 (1992); State v. Roy, 138 N.H. 97, 635 A.2d 486, 1993 N.H. LEXIS 166 (1993); White v. Francoeur, 138 N.H. 307, 638 A.2d 1250, 1994 N.H. LEXIS 27 (1994); Blevens v. Town of Bow, 887 F. Supp. 38, 1994 U.S. Dist. LEXIS 14408 (D.N.H. 1994); K & J Assocs. v. City of Lebanon, 142 N.H. 331, 703 A.2d 253, 1997 N.H. LEXIS 99 (1997); Heron Cove Ass'n v. DVMD Holdings, Inc., 146 N.H 211, 769 A.2d 373, 2001 N.H. LEXIS 60 (2001); NBAC Corp. v. Town of Weare, 147 N.H. 328, 786 A.2d 867, 2001 N.H. LEXIS 219 (2001); AWL Power, Inc. v. City of Rochester, 148 N.H. 603, 813 A.2d 517, 2002 N.H. LEXIS 178 (2002); R.J. Moreau Cos. v. Town of Litchfield, 148 N.H. 773, 813 A.2d 527, 2002 N.H. LEXIS 213 (2002); Monahan-Fortin Props. v. Town of Hudson, 148 N.H. 769, 813 A.2d 523, 2002 N.H. LEXIS 214 (2002).

RESEARCH REFERENCES

New Hampshire Court Rules Annotated.

Appointment of and proceedings before referees, see Rules 81–85-A, Rules of the Superior Court, New Hampshire Court Rules Annotated.

Docketing of cases for trial generally, see Rules 10 and 11, Rules of the Superior Court, New Hampshire Court Rules Annotated.

New Hampshire Practice.

14 N.H.P. Local Government Law §§ 916, 972–974, 986.

15 N.H.P. Land Use Planning and Zoning §§ 2.08, 11.02, 16.01, 17.05, 19.03, 22.02, 26.03, 28.09, 32.16, 33.01–33.03, 33.06–33.08, 33.10, 33.11.

Appeal and Court Review of Building Code Board of Appeals Decisions

Cross References.

Administration and enforcement of building codes generally, see RSA 676:11 et seq.

Appeal and review of decisions of local legislative bodies and boards of adjustment, see RSA 677:4 et seq.

Appeal of historic district commission decisions, see RSA 677:17 et seq.

Building codes generally, se RSA 674:51 et seq.

Powers of building code boards of appeals generally, see RSA 674:34.

677:16. Court Review.

Any person aggrieved by a decision of the designated building code board of appeals may appeal the decision to the superior court for the county, and said court shall make such orders as justice may require.

Source.

1983, 447:1, eff. Jan. 1, 1984.

NOTES TO DECISIONS

Cited:

Cited in R.J. Moreau Cos. v. Town of Litch-

field, 148 N.H. 773, 813 A.2d 527, 2002 N.H. LEXIS 213 (2002).

Rehearing and Appeal of Historic District Commission Decisions

Cross References.

Administrative and enforcement powers of historic district commissions generally, see RSA 676:8 et seq.

Appeal and review of building code boards of appeals decisions, see RSA 677:16 et seq.

Appeals and review of decisions of local legislative bodies and boards of adjustment, see RSA 677:4 et seq.

Appeals from decisions of historic district commissions exercising powers of boards of adjustment, see RSA 676:10.

Historic districts and historic district commissions generally, see RSA 674:45 et seq.

677:17. Appeal When Zoning Ordinance Exists.

Any person or persons jointly or severally aggrieved by a decision of the historic district commission shall have the right to appeal that decision to the zoning board of adjustment in accordance with the provisions of RSA 676:5 and RSA 677:1–14.

Source.

1983, 447:1. 1987, 256:6, eff. July 17, 1987.

Amendments

—1987. Inserted "RSA 676:5 and" preceding "RSA 677:1–14".

RESEARCH REFERENCES

New Hampshire Practice.
15 N.H.P. Land Use Planning and Zoning
§ 19.03.

677:18. Appeal When No Zoning Ordinance Exists.

In municipalities which do not have a zoning board of adjustment, motions for rehearing and appeals from decisions of the historic district commission shall be governed by the applicable provisions of RSA 677:1–14.

Source.
1983, 447:1, eff. Jan. 1, 1984.

Cross References.
Rehearings and appeals from historic district
commission decisions generally, see RSA
676:10.

Invalid Ordinances

677:19. Subsequent Amendment.

Whenever an appeal to the superior court is initiated under this chapter and the court finds that the ordinance, or section thereof, upon which the board of adjustment, board of appeals, or local legislative body based its decision was invalid at the time such appeal was initiated, or that the application should have been approved but the ordinance was amended to prohibit the type of project applied for during the pendency of the appeal, notwithstanding the fact that the ordinance may have been amended to remove the invalidity subsequent to the initiation of the appeal or that the type of project applied for is no longer permitted, as the case may be, the court shall, upon request of the petitioner, issue an order approving the application, provided that the court finds the application complies with valid zoning and subdivision regulations existing at the time of the application.

Source.
1989, 381:2, eff. Aug. 4, 1989.

RESEARCH REFERENCES

New Hampshire Practice.
15 N.H.P. Land Use Planning and Zoning
§§ 16.04, 25.09.

APPENDIX OF RELATED LAWS

The statutes listed below relate to the performance of planning and land use regulation by municipalities in New Hampshire. Since they are employed by local officials less frequently than those statutes set out in the body of the pamphlet, they have been summarized rather than reproduced in full. The text of these statutes, accompanied by related notes and annotations, appears in LEXIS New Hampshire Revised Statutes Annotated.

RSA
CHAPTER

12-E   **Mining and Reclamation, 12-E:1–12-E:14**

This chapter provides for a procedure governing mining and prospecting permits; specifies operator duties during mining and reclamation; and provides emergency authority to halt such operations.

32   **Municipal Budget Law, 32:1–32:24**

This chapter authorizes the establishment of the local budget committee and describes their duties.

34   **Capital Reserve Funds for Cities, 34:1–34:5**

This chapter authorizes the establishment of reserve funds by cities for capital improvements.

35   **Capital Reserve Funds of Counties, Towns, Districts, and Water Departments, 35:1–35:18**

This chapter authorizes the establishment of reserve funds by municipalities for capital improvements.

35-B   **Public Recreation and Parks, 35-B:1–35-B:7**

This chapter allows municipalities to acquire and administer park land. It authorizes the appointment of a recreation or park commission and establishes their organizational procedures.

36-B   **Interstate Regional Planning Compact, 36-B:1–36-B:2**

This chapter provides that the Office of State Planning and/or a regional planning commission may negotiate with adjacent states for interstate regional planning services. Articles of a compact agreement are presented.

48-A   **Housing Standards, 48-A:1–48-A:15**

This chapter authorizes the governing body of any municipality to correct dwellings that are unfit for human habitation due to dilapidation, lack of maintenance, etc. Ordinances, codes and bylaws may be adopted to establish a three-member board to administer provisions and specific standards that qualify a structure as being habitable or unfit.

49-B   **Home Rule—Municipal Charters, 49-B:1–49-B:13**

This chapter authorizes municipalities to select one of five forms of local government and to legally establish, by charter, the selected governmental form.

49-C   **Local Option—City Charters, 49-C:1–49-C:34**

This chapter enables municipalities to draft city charters within the framework of part I, article 39 of the New Hampshire constitution.

49-D   Local Option—Town Charters, 49-D:1–49-D:5

This chapter provides for optional forms of town government that municipalities may adopt pursuant to part I, article 39 of the New Hampshire constitution and RSA 49-B.

52   Village Districts, 52:1–52:25

This chapter authorizes the establishment of village districts or precincts for the purposes listed in RSA 52:1. Administration procedures, powers and duties are also described.

79-A   Current Use Taxation, 79-A:1–79-A:26

This chapter establishes an administrative framework that allows managed open space land to be taxed at rates lower than those accorded to the lands highest and best use.

79-D   Discretionary Preservation Easements, 79-D:1–79-D:14

This chapter allows a property owner to convey a discretionary preservation easement of an historic agricultural structure which provides one or more demonstrated public benefits to the municipality in which the structure is located. The bill contains special taxation provisions for historic agricultural structures subject to a discretionary preservation easement.

147   Nuisances; Toilets; Drains; Expectoration; Rubbish and Waste, 147:1–147:22

These sections set forth the responsibilities and administrative procedures associated with municipal health officers.

149-J   New Hampshire-Vermont Interstate Sewage and Waste Disposal Facilities Compact, 149-J:1

This chapter authorizes cooperative agreements and sets procedures and conditions to govern intergovernmental agreements.

149-K   New Hampshire-Massachusetts Interstate Sewage and Waste Disposal Facilities Compact, 149-K:1

This chapter authorizes cooperative agreements and sets procedures and conditions to govern intergovernmental agreements.

149-M   Solid Waste Management, 149-M:1–149-M:42

This chapter is administered by the Division of Waste Management of the Department of Environmental Services. The Division is responsible for review of district plans; regulation of the storage, transfer, treatment, processing and disposal of solid waste, including administration of a permit system; investigations; hearings, and other activities contributing to orderly management. Rules may be written and adopted by the Division of Waste Management. Towns are required to participate in district planning.

155   Factories, Tenements, Schoolhouses, and Places of Public Accommodation, Resort or Assembly, 155:1–155:2

These sections provide that town and village districts may make bylaws for public structures to insure health and safety. The bylaws shall conform to the life safety code, as promulgated by the State Fire Marshal.

155-B   Hazardous and Dilapidated Buildings, 155-B:1–155-B:15

These sections provide municipalities with the administrative process for repair or removal of hazardous buildings.

155-D   Energy Conservation in New Building Construction, 155-D:1–155-D:10

This chapter establishes a statewide energy conservation code for all new buildings or structures/additions designed primarily for human occupancy. The "New Hampshire Code for Energy Conservation in New Building Construction" is administered by local building officials or by the Public Utilities Commission where no building official exists.

162-G   Acquisition, Development and Disposal of Industrial Land and Facilities, 162-G:1–162-G:17

This chapter authorizes cities to encourage industrial development by acquiring and marketing land, issuing bonds for project costs, establishing an Industrial Development Authority, and other activities which promote industrial development.

162-H   Energy Facility Evaluation, Siting, Construction and Operation, 162-H:1–162-H:20

This chapter establishes the Site Evaluation Committee and outlines procedures for the review, approval, monitoring and enforcement of compliance in the planning, siting, construction and operation of energy facilities.

162-K   Municipal Economic Development and Revitalization Districts, 162-K:1–162-K:15

Through adoption of this chapter. municipalities may establish one or more development districts to improve commercial development, employment, open space relief and other facilities which benefit their economy. Establishment procedures, financing options, and administrative requirements are described.

204-C   Housing Finance Authority, 204-C:1–204-C:55

These sections establish the Housing Finance Authority as a separate, nonprofit organization not associated with state government. A nine-member Housing Finance Board is established (appointed by the Governor) to appoint an Executive Director and oversee responsibilities. Authority and administrative guidelines are provided. RSA 204-A and 204-B are repealed.

205-A   Regulation of Manufactured Housing Parks, 205-A:1–205-A:31

This chapter establishes administrative rules concerning business relationships between the manufactured housing park owner/operator and the manufactured housing owner/lessee, rules governing health and safety conditions, and rules governing notification of tenants prior to sales of housing parks. A nine-member Board of Manufactured Housing is established to hear and determine matters involving manufactured housing park rules.

231-A   Municipal Trails, 231-A:1—231A:8

This chapter authorizes municipalities to reclassify Highways as municipal trails, designate public trail use restrictions, and acquire or discontinue trails.

310-A   Engineers, Architects, Land Surveyors, Natural Scientists, and Foresters, 310-A:1–310-A:74

License requirements are established for the practice of engineering, architectural design, surveying, and soil science in the state. Administration procedures for application, qualifications, fees, violations, hearings, renewals, and disciplinary actions are presented. A joint board is formed to meet quarterly for administrative purposes.

319-C   Electricians, 319-C:1–319-C:15

This chapter establishes a registration requirement for individuals performing electrical installation work. An Electricians' Board is formed to evaluate applicants, issue licenses to qualified practitioners, and conduct other administrative duties.

329-A   Plumbers and Plumbing, 329-A:1–329-A:18

This chapter provides for the licensing of qualified plumbers, and requires that the practice of plumbing be undertaken only by licensed plumbers. Administrative guidelines are described, such as establishing a board, examinations, licenses, renewal, rulemaking, and penalties.

356-A **Land Sales Full Disclosure Act, 356-A:1–356-A:22**

This chapter establishes a registration requirement for subdivisions of 16 lots or greater, administered by the Consumer Protection and Antitrust Bureau of the Division of Public Protection of the Department of Justice.

356-B **Condominium Act, 356-B:1–356-B:69**

This chapter is administered by the Consumer Protection and Antitrust Bureau of the Division of Public Protection of the Department of Justice. The statutes establish legal guidelines for the creation, sale and management of condominium property. RSA 356-B:5 provides the statutory framework within which municipalities may regulate condominium developments. Specific provisions for condominium conversion/development must be cited in local subdivision regulations for applicable review.

432 **Acquisition of Agricultural Land Development Rights, 432:18–432:31-a**

These sections authorize the establishment of an Agricultural Lands Preservation Committee to administer funds for the acquisition of development rights associated with land suitable for agricultural use.

477 **Solar Skyspace Easements, 477:49–477:51**

These sections authorize the establishment of and provide a form for the creation of a solar skyspace easement.

479-A **Unit Ownership of Real Property, 479-A:1–479-A:28**

This chapter sets forth the guidelines for single unit ownership within multiunit developments (condominiums). It enables the establishment of a Board of Directors to administer bylaws governing the various properties in the development.

482-A **Fill and Dredge in Wetlands, 482-A:1–482-A:15**

These sections establish the Wetlands Board to oversee fill and dredging activity in the states. The sections authorize the Wetlands Board to review, hold hearings, and approve or disapprove applications for filling or dredging activity. Three copies of the application must be sent to the town or city clerk who, in turn, distributes them to the Board of Selectmen/Mayor or City Manager, Planning Board, and Conservation Commission.

485-A **Dredging (Terrain Alteration), 485-A:17**

This section requires individuals proposing to dredge, excavate, place fill, mine, transport forest products or undertake construction in or on border of the surface waters of the state and individuals proposing to significantly alter the characteristic of the terrain to submit detailed plans of the activity to the Division of Water Supply and Pollution Control of the Department of Environmental Services.

Sewage Disposal Systems, 485-A:29–485-A:44

These sections require the submission to, and approval of plans by, the Division of Water Supply and Pollution Control of the Department of Environmental Services in order to protect water supplies, and to prevent pollution in the surface waters of the State. They also set forth procedures and penalties.

669 **Town Elections, 669:1–669:75**

This chapter establishes procedures for the election of local officials, including elected planning board and budget committee members.

670 **Village District Elections, 670:1–670:12**

This chapter establishes procedures for the election of village district officers.

User's Guide to the Index

This index contains treatment of the laws compiled in the *New Hampshire Planning and Land Use Regulation, 2007-2008 Edition.* Statutory provisions from the Lexis New Hampshire Revised Statutes Annotated are referred to in the index by section number (e.g., §424:6).

A few basic rules for using this index are:

(1) *Consult the most pertinent subject.* For example, if you were looking in an evidence book for information about depositions, you would start with DEPOSITIONS rather than broader headings like EVIDENCE, TESTIMONY or WITNESSES. The broader headings may also exist, but to find the material more quickly, look for the specific subject first.

(2) *Cross references.* Pay close attention to and make full use of the index cross references. An index cross reference directs the index user to go to another part of the index to find treatment. This serves to keep indexes to a manageable size by reducing repetition of treatment under different headings.

(3) *Use definitions to aid in your search.* Starting a search under the DEFINED TERMS heading exposes the index user to a diverse sampling of statutory terminology which could suggest to the user other headings to consult.

The index benefits from customer suggestions. Especially helpful are popular names or legal terms specific to your area of practice. We are grateful for your assistance in the ongoing improvement of the index.

To contact the indexers, you may use any of the following methods:
- Contact the indexers via a toll-free number, 1-800-897-7922, for assistance in locating material within the index, or to make comments or suggestions.
- Contact the indexers by e-mail to lng-cho-indexing@lexisnexis.com.

For issues not directly related to the Index, such as missing pages, ordering or other customer service information, you may contact Customer Service via a toll-free number, 1-800-833-9844, or by toll-free fax at 1-800-828-8341.

Index

A

575

INDEX

INDEX

INDEX

Notes

Notes

Notes

Notes

Notes

Notes

Notes

Notes

Notes

Notes

Notes

Notes

Notes

Notes

Notes

Notes

Notes

Notes

Notes

Notes